Penguin Books
Hope Abandoned

Nadezhda Mandelstam is the widow of the Russian poet
Osip Mandelstam, who suffered banishment, humiliation
and death after his denunciation of Stalin in the 1930s.
After his death, in 1938, she managed to survive by leading
an inconspicuous existence as a teacher of English in remote
provincial towns. In 1956 she was at last allowed to come
back and live in Moscow, where she at once began to write
a memoir of the ordeal she shared with her husband, *Hope
Against Hope* (Penguin, 1975).

Mrs Mandelstam, who is now 75, still lives in Moscow.

Hope Abandoned

A Memoir

Nadezhda
Mandelstam

Translated by
Max Hayward

Penguin Books

Penguin Books Ltd,
Harmondsworth, Middlesex, England
Penguin Books,
625 Madison Avenue, New York, New York 10022, U.S.A.
Penguin Books Australia Ltd,
Ringwood, Victoria, Australia
Penguin Books Canada Ltd,
41 Steelcase Road West, Markham, Ontario, Canada
Penguin Books (N.Z.) Ltd,
182–190 Wairau Road, Auckland 10, New Zealand

First published in the U.S.A. 1974
Published in Great Britain by Harvill Press 1974
Published in Penguin Books 1976

Made and printed in Great Britain by
Richard Clay (The Chaucer Press) Ltd,
Bungay, Suffolk
Set in Monotype Times

Translator's Foreword

In the first chapter of this book Mrs Mandelstam herself defines her purpose in writing it, but it may be helpful, particularly for readers unfamiliar with the first book,* *Hope Against Hope*, to say a little more about the relation between the two. The 'First Book' (as it was originally called by her) is essentially a narrative about the last four years in the life of her husband, Osip Mandelstam. Despite the avowedly discursive manner that frequently allows her to stray into other periods – as she says, her method is 'unchronological' – the first volume is basically contained within this limited time span. It begins abruptly with an account of the poet's first arrest in May 1934 and ends with a review of all the scraps of evidence about the circumstances of his death in a camp near Vladivostok in December 1938. Having decided there could be no compromise with a system that had reversed or traduced the cultural and ethical values he believed in, Mandelstam consciously chose martyrdom and death by denouncing Stalin as a murderer in a poem which he then read to a few people in private – with the inevitable consequence that the text was speedily relayed to the secret police by one of his listeners. He was saved from immediate execution thanks only to the pleas of Bukharin (who at that time still had a little influence), Pasternak, and others. Through this officially arranged 'miracle', he was given a few years respite, which he spent mainly in enforced residence in the provincial town of Voronezh. Here he wrote several brilliant cycles of poems (the 'Voronezh Notebooks') before returning, at the end of his term of exile, to Moscow in 1937 – just in time for the Great Purge. Though as a 'proscribed person' he could find no work and was not allowed to live within the city limits of Moscow itself, he was at first left

* For such readers the Chronology at the end of this book may be helpful, since it recapitulates a good deal of what is told in *Hope Against Hope*.

alone and for several months suffered nothing worse than the constant humiliation of literally having to beg for alms in order to keep himself and his wife alive. But Stalin had not forgotten him. Towards the end of 1937, the Union of Soviet Writers began to take an ostensibly benevolent interest in him, and in the spring of the following year arranged for him to go to one of its 'rest homes' in a remote place in the country called Samatikha. Here, during the night of 1 May 1938, he was arrested in the presence of his wife, who never saw him again. At first Mrs Mandelstam continued to live within easy travelling distance of Moscow in the hope of learning something about his fate and of getting food parcels to him. But, as for all the countless other women in her situation, the heartbreaking business of trudging from one Moscow jail to another (which had to be done on brief visits from small towns near by, because of the ban on residing in the capital) and waiting endlessly in lines was all in vain. It was not until the end of the year that she became virtually certain, after the return of one of her food parcels, that her husband was dead. This was officially confirmed in June 1940 by the issue of a death certificate that gave the date of his death as 27 December 1938. It was only gradually, however, that Mrs Mandelstam was able to obtain some details about his terrible end in a 'transit camp' near Vladivostok, where he was evidently awaiting transfer to a forced-labour camp in Kolyma or Magadan. *Hope Against Hope* concludes with a careful account of all she was able to glean from a few people who had been in that camp at the same time, or had heard more or less credible stories about Mandelstam's last days there.

This second book (called *Hope Abandoned* in translation at Mrs Mandelstam's request) is not a mere continuation of the first, or a sequel to it, but is complementary to it in at least two vital ways. The first is in filling some vast and conspicuous biographical gaps in *Hope Against Hope*, where larger perspectives on the life of Osip Mandelstam and his wife are sacrified – often tantalizingly – to the telling of his story during the four years in which he went to his doom. Thus, *Hope Abandoned* gives a fairly extensive account of their life together from their first meeting in Kiev in 1919 up to the time of Osip's arrest in May 1934 (there are only sporadic backward glances at this period in *Hope Against Hope*). The author's own life after her husband's death, from 1938 almost up to the present, is similarly described in much richer detail; she also adds considerably to her portrait gallery of contemporaries, bringing Mandelstam's lonely eminence into even sharper relief. One of these portraits, the extraordinarily candid one of Anna Akhmatova, whose presence in the first book is more episodic, gives the second book a wholly new dimension.

The second way in which *Hope Abandoned* complements the first volume is by providing much broader interpretative background to Mandelstam's unique act of defiance and self-immolation. To have done this in *Hope Against Hope* – though some of the issues are sketched out there too – would have slowed down the central narrative intolerably; but within the larger confines of this new work, the author has felt free to dwell on aspects of her husband's life and times that illuminate the sense of his ordeal and his poetry with insights only she can possess. In the years after his death, during all her painful wanderings from one dreary provincial town to another, her only aim in life was to be a living repository of his memory and his poetry, to preserve them from the total extinction to which they had been condemned. The publication of his work abroad (once attempts to have it published in the Soviet Union after Stalin's death had failed) and of the tale of what happened to him in *Hope Against Hope* are the fulfilment of Mrs Mandelstam's pledge to keep her husband's name alive and to perpetuate what he left behind. In *Hope Abandoned* she goes a stage further by endeavouring to complete on his behalf something he did not himself have time to do before his life was cut short, namely, to set forth a system of values and beliefs that run quite counter to the dominant ones of the age we live in, whether in the East or the West. Mandelstam was distinguished by his immunity to the beguilements of the times, both before and after the Revolution. By the end of the twenties – when most of his fellow intellectuals had succumbed to the overwhelming 'temptations' of the age – after a period of uncertainty and confusion, he achieved the 'inner freedom' which in Stalin's Russia could be purchased only by death. The arguments that led him – alone among his contemporaries – to make this choice are unfolded by his widow partly through interpretation of his poetry and essays, partly

through her intimate knowledge of his otherwise unrecorded
thoughts and reflections.

In a work of this complexity, containing many references to persons, events, and other things not necessarily familiar even to
Russian readers, it has been found essential (as in the case of the
first volume) to add a good deal of explanatory or supplementary
material in the form of footnotes, a chronology, and special
appendixes of biographical notes and notes on the various terms
relating to Russian literary movements and organizations that
frequently recur in the text. The biographical notes often include
information of direct relevance to a fuller appreciation of the text,
and where this is of particular importance, it has been indicated in
footnotes. A certain amount of cross-referencing to *Hope Against
Hope* has also been supplied. Otherwise, editorial intervention has
been kept to a minimum. Scarcely any cuts have been made, except
for one or two sentences that seemed obscure in meaning (the
Russian original very occasionally may be slightly garbled), and
several others that were plainly superfluous in translation. Two
chapters have been given different titles than in the original. In a
few instances I have felt justified in correcting or questioning statements that are clearly based on faulty or confused information.
There could be no more painstakingly truthful witness than Mrs
Mandelstam. She is ruthlessly honest about herself and her friends
(and more charitable, incidentally, than might appear at first sight
towards those who destroyed her husband and made her life into a
nightmare), but, apart from the fallibility of all human memory,
she has lived in circumstances of such unimaginable isolation, both
from the outside world and within her own country, that it is
scarcely surprising if she has not always been able to verify the
stories and rumours that naturally gain currency from time to time
in a community denied access to all normal channels of information. A case in point is the story on page 404 – reported as hearsay,
it should be noted – to the effect that 'some Oxford students' were
sent by Sir Isaiah Berlin to interview Akhmatova and Zoshchenko
on their reaction to the Party denunciation of them in 1946. This is
a legend (which probably arose from a quite pardonable misunderstanding on Akhmatova's part) and I have supplied a foot-

note summarizing the rather different facts – known to me from firsthand sources – on which it is based. Another case that should be mentioned here, but that readers can judge for themselves without benefit of special annotation, is the author's lengthy comment on T. S. Eliot's *Notes Towards the Definition of Culture*. As she says, Mrs Mandelstam read this in a Russian translation published in the West – perhaps she did so in some haste and rather cursorily, since such surreptitiously imported materials tend by their nature to be passed rapidly from hand to hand. Whatever the reason, however, several of her specific strictures on Eliot's views would evidently seem to derive from a faulty memory of the text, or from a misreading of certain passages. There further appears to be no foundation for Mrs Mandelstam's belief that the *Notes* originated from lectures given at Oxford. Since Eliot's essay serves mainly as a point of departure for her own arguments, most of what she had to say in this chapter is by no means invalidated by any wrong construction she may have placed on Eliot's meaning.

A major problem in translating *Hope Abandoned* (as also *Hope Against Hope*) is the large number of verse quotations, both from Mandelstam and Akhmatova. Apart from the usual difficulty of rendering verse extracts without utterly destroying the poetry, there is the additional one that knowledge is sometimes assumed of the context in which they occur. It would have been impractical, and a source of irritation for the general reader, to have attempted to supply elaborate references for these numerous verse (and prose) quotations, let alone to summarize their contexts. In some cases – perhaps rather haphazardly – some information of this kind has nevertheless been given in footnotes when it might be essential to a better understanding of the passages in question. Russian scholars, who will of course prefer to read the work in the original (published under the title *Vtoraya Kniga*, Paris: YMCA Press, 1972), can easily track down most verse quotations in the three-volume collection of Mandelstam's poetry and prose published in the United States by Gleb Struve and Boris Filippov (second revised and expanded edition, 1967–9). It should also be noted that since this collection was published a number of new Mandelstam and Akhmatova poems (some of them referred to in *Hope Abandoned*) have appeared in the tri-monthly journal of the Russian Student

Christian Movement (*Vestnik russkogo studencheskogo khristian-skogo dvizhenia*, Paris–New York). The general reader with no Russian is not at present well served with translations of Mandelstam's work, except for the autobiographical stories frequently referred to in *Hope Abandoned* (*The Prose of Osip Mandelstam*, translated, with a critical essay by Clarence Brown, Princeton: Princeton University Press, 1965). The first extensive selection of Mandelstam's poetry, translated by Clarence Brown and W. S. Merwin, is published by Atheneum Publishers (New York, 1974), and Oxford University Press (London, 1973).

Acknowledgements

I am deeply grateful to: Mrs Valerie Jensen, for devoted help in research for the notes; Miss Joan Clifton, for unflagging secretarial assistance; Mr Jacques Kayaloff of New York, for his invaluable expertise about various Caucasian matters; the Rockefeller Foundation and the Director of the Villa Serbelloni, Dr William C. Olson, and Mrs Olson, for generously providing refuge at a time when it was most needed.

I also wish to record my great indebtedness to Gleb Struve and Boris Filippov, the editors of Mandelstam's collected works. I have benefited from their scholarly notes and comments at many points in preparing this translation.

MAX HAYWARD
St Antony's College
Oxford
May 1973

Contents

14 *Contents*

1 The 'Self'

I am now faced with a new task, and am not quite sure how to go about it. Earlier it was all so simple: my job was to preserve M.'s verse and tell the story of what happened to us. The events concerned were outside our control. Like any other wife of a prisoner, like any other *stopiatnitsa** or exiled person, I thought only about the times I lived in, racking my brains over the question: How could *this* happen, how had we come to *such* a pass? Thinking about *this*, I forgot myself and what had happened to me personally, and even that I was writing about my own life, not somebody else's. The fact is that there was nothing exceptional about my case. There were untold numbers of women like myself roaming the country – mute, cowed creatures, some with children, some without, timidly trying to do their work as best they could and constantly 'improving their qualifications', which meant joining study groups to sweat year in, year out, over the 'Fourth Chapter',† including the story of how the ape turned into *Homo sapiens* by learning to distinguish left from right. (This development was aided to some extent by food rich in vitamins and protein – more than we could say of ours.) But at least we had our work, and we clung to it frantically, knowing that without it all was lost . . . One of my colleagues at the University of Central Asia,‡ a woman who seemed to me to be very well off indeed – she had a place of her own to live in – once confided to me as we were walking home one

---

* Literally: 'hundred-and-five', a person refused permission to live closer than 105 kilometres to any large city. See *Hope Against Hope*, page 412.

† The chapter on Dialectical Materialism written by Stalin in *The History of the C.P.S.U.* [Communist Party of the Soviet Union]: *Short Course* (1938).

‡ In Tashkent. The author taught here during the war.

night from our study group that every autumn she felt an overwhelming urge to reread the 'Short Course' and the 'Dialectic of
Nature'* because this gave her the strength to face the new
academic year. She was already fifty and terrified of being 'super-
annuated'. This was before Khrushchev, when pensions existed
only on paper, so the reasons for her 'keenness' were all too clear.
I faced the same prospect: the 'enthusiastic' study of philosophy as
retirement age approached – that is, if I was lucky and allowed to
carry on to the end, unflagging in my zeal to master the wisdom of
our rulers. The only difference between myself and this other
woman was that while I would eventually, before I died, have a
sealed bottle with a message to cast upon the waves, she had only
empty bottles† – and even these she was saving up for a rainy day.
At that time there was no hint of what was to come, and we had
nothing to hope for. We were only at the beginning of a reign
destined to last a thousand years, something infinitely greater than
the span of our own lives.

People like myself were the lucky ones who had not gone to
prison. Knowing what it was like to live in 'freedom', I was always
thinking of those who were behind barbed wire. This was why I
could not think about myself, but only about all the others – those
who had gone away and would never return, those who still
nourished hopes of coming back but would never live to see the
day. Every time I heard rumours of new arrests, it was like salt in
my own fresh wounds. In the midst of such general misery and
doom, the word 'I' lost its meaning, becoming shameful or taboo.
Who dared talk about his own fate or complain about it when it
was the same for everybody? I remember how once – it was
already in the 'new era' – I was listening to one of the forbidden
radio stations‡ when they happened to read an extract from a book
by someone who had been in a camp and was released, if I remember rightly, together with the Poles.§ His main theme, at least in

* By Friedrich Engels.

† The deposit returned on empty bottles is a source of income for the very
poor in the Soviet Union.

‡ Foreign stations broadcasting in Russian, such as The Voice of America,
the BBC, and Radio Liberty.

§ Many Poles deported to the Soviet Union after the Soviet occupation of this particular extract from his reminiscences, was: How had they dared to tear him, of all people, away from his hearth and home, his mother, the neatly laid table, and throw him into this dreadful camp where he had to sleep on a stinking bunk . . . In a fury I switched off the wretched thing: who did he think *he* was, whining like this! So he didn't want to go and do forced labour, eh? It is true that 'forced labour' is too mild a term for the camps of the twentieth century and that nobody in the world would actually want to go into a camp or gas chamber. But here was this man talking only about himself . . . In the 'West', as I noticed, they were making a great fuss of him.

Once I even had a row with Akhmatova about her use of the word 'I'. She had asked me to look up one of her poems in the first-line index, noting quite innocently that many of her things began with 'I'. I flew into a rage and started telling her that this concern with herself was the worst of her failings. For all her touchiness she made no attempt to defend herself on this occasion – she was evidently disarmed by my conviction that there was something disgraceful or taboo about the word 'I'. She had probably gone through the same revulsion against it herself. In any case, I soon thought better of my outburst; for one thing, she had no more poems beginning with 'I' than anybody else – what can be more personal than lyric poetry? – and, for another, it is not just the frequency with which 'I' occurs, but the general spirit of a person's work that shows to what extent he is afflicted by the besetting sin of 'egotism'. And anyway, wasn't it something of a feat to keep a grip on one's own personality and a true sense of identity in our era of wholesale slaughter and death camps on such a vast scale? Times such as these breed only individualism based on the principle 'every man for himself', not a true sense of one's own worth.

The loss of this sense is not something our age can be proud of, but a sign of its sickness. I know the symptoms from observing myself and those around me. People suffering from loss of identity are divided into two types: some, as I did, sink into a torpor and think only of how to 'shed the burden of time'. Deep inside them

eastern Poland in 1939 were allowed out to fight with the Western Allies in the army of General Anders in 1942.

they often cherish the mad hope of surviving to a future in which they will recover their lost selves – something that will be possible only when true values have come into their own again. Their whole life thus consists of waiting for the first glimpse of a promised land, like a radiant shoreline on the horizon. Even though no such thing has ever existed on our planet, and never will, they have no eyes for anything else. I used to try to get over this 'waiting sickness' by scornfully comparing myself with the retired servants of the bygone age. They too sit in their hideouts (rather comfortable ones by our standards), longing for the return of the twenties or – in most cases – of the thirties and forties, so they can 'restore order' and send off where they belong all the people who have learned to 'talk too much' during the last fifteen years. These worthies, of course, have more chance of seeing their dreams come true than I have; for them the idea of the individual personality has never meant anything, and they would soon put an end to mine when they restored order, once they learned of my existence from their spies. Though, who knows, I might survive – they would be interested in more recent history, and since I no longer go to work I do not stick out anywhere like a sore thumb.

The second type of lost identity is quite different. This afflicts people for whom the 'self' is just an accidental and fleeting windfall to be exploited for every drop of pleasure it can give: you must enjoy life while you can. For such people the 'self' is an amusing plaything, a delicious awareness of living matter, a craving for pleasure conferred on the flesh by a quirk of blind evolution. Hence it follows that the most important thing in life is self-preservation: everybody looks after himself, by whatever means he pleases. In a world that has arisen by chance, nobody is responsible for anything, and all your deeds will vanish into the abyss, together with you and the age you live in.

The loss of 'self' leads either to self-effacement (as in my case) or to blatant individualism with its extremes of egocentrism and self-assertiveness. The outward signs may differ, but it is the same sickness: the atrophy of true personality. And the cause is the same in both cases, namely, the severing of all social bonds. The question is: How did it happen? We saw it come about in front of our very eyes. All intermediate social links, such as the family, one's circle of

friends, class, society itself – each abruptly disappeared, leaving
every one of us to stand alone before the mysterious force embodied in the State, with its powers of life and death. In ordinary
parlance, this was summed up in the word 'Lubianka'.* If what we
have seen in this country is only a process taking place throughout
Europe, then it must be said that we have demonstrated the sickness of the age in a form so acute and unadulterated as to merit
special study in any search for the prevention and cure of it. In an
age when the main cry is 'Every man for himself', the personality is
doomed. Personality is dependent on the world at large, on one's
neighbours. It defines itself by reference to others and becomes
aware of its own uniqueness only when it sees the uniqueness of
everyone else. The individualist, emphasizing his own distinctiveness, marks himself off from those around him and fights for a
special place in society, or simply for his right to a special share or
ration – which could include even the hours and days of his life.
In every sphere your ration was supposed to depend strictly on the
services you rendered, and our individualists had to show great
ingenuity in boosting the goods they had to offer. However low the
quality of their performance, they always begged indulgence
beforehand, disclaiming responsibility for the system and saying
they were only bowing to circumstances. In fact, however, no
indulgence was needed: the concept of sin had been abolished as an
'idealistic' fallacy. Our individualists, concerned only with the
gratification of their deadened egos, formed the upper crust of
Soviet society and were thus the most conspicuous part of it. The
extraordinary thing was how the inert, torpid masses below –
among whom I counted myself – were entirely overshadowed by
this handful of individualists.

Having lost their 'selves', both types – the individualists and the
inert – forfeited everything that makes for a normal existence, for
what we call 'culture'. Who cared about traditions offering only
personal salvation – of which there was in any case no guarantee
whatsoever? What was the point of fussing over a concept of 'self'
now rejected and useless? . . . Stifled and crushed, it lingered on
here and there only in full knowledge of its worthless, outlawed
status. Like Solzhenitsyn, I sometimes got my unexpected skewer-

* Headquarters of the secret police, and political prison in Moscow.

ful of shashlik,* and prized it as something real, almost as though it were a ration, all the sweeter for being unearned. But in general I had no time for my own 'self', only for 'them' and 'us', and an inner pain greater than anything caused by the worst of heart attacks. If you lost your self, the sense of life vanished with it. As a boy M. had written the strange and clumsy words: 'If in this life there is no sense, then to talk of life makes no sense.' . . . There was no longer life or sense of life for me, any more than for all the others, but most of us were saved by the existence of someone else, by the thought of a 'you'. Instead of sense, my life had a concrete purpose: not to allow 'them' to stamp out all traces of the man I thought of as 'you', to save his poetry. I had an ally in my task: Akhmatova. For eighteen years – the length of a good camp sentence – we lived without a ray of light, without help from any quarter, not daring to speak aloud the cherished name, except when we were alone – and then only in a whisper – trembling over a handful of his poems. When at last the first signs of hope appeared, Akhmatova kept saying: 'Nadia, all's well with Osia.' By this she meant that he was being read again. It took me some time to appreciate the importance of *samizdat*,† and I was upset because M. wasn't printed, but Akhmatova had an answer to this as well: 'We live in the pre-Gutenberg age' and 'Osia has no need of a printing press' . . . I gradually saw how right she was: poetry is an elusive thing that can neither be hidden nor locked away. It was poetry that blazed the trail for prose along the mysterious byways leading to the new readers who suddenly sprang up from nowhere. These readers emerged quite unexpectedly, when there was no longer any hope of them. They learned to pick out what they needed, and the poetry that came into their hands transfigured them and set them on the right path.

It is now forty years since the last volume of M. appeared in print, and the total number of copies of his nine books cannot have

---

* Reference to *Cancer Ward*, Chapter 35, in which the autobiographical hero receives an unexpected gift of *shashlik* (pieces of meat grilled on a skewer) on a Tashkent street after leaving a hospital.

† Literally: 'self-publishing' (a pun on Gosizdat: 'State Publishing House'), that is, the circulation of literary and other works, generally in typescript, that has become widespread in the last ten years or so.

been more than thirty thousand altogether, but he lives and thrives in a more real sense than all the best-selling authors whose works are today a drug on the market. Akhmatova never ceased to be astonished at the resurrection of poetry once trampled underfoot, wiped out, it had seemed, once and for all. 'We never realized that poetry has such a long life', she was always saying, and 'poetry isn't what we thought it was when we were young'. Perhaps we really didn't understand what it was, but at least we must have had some inkling. In the years when we preserved M.'s verse, we scarcely dared hope, but we never ceased to believe in its rebirth. It was only this faith that kept us going. And what was it but faith in the abiding value of poetry and its sacramental nature? We must have understood instinctively that a poet's fate is decided only by time and that we must not die, therefore, without making sure his work was submitted to the judgement of the world as a whole. Now that this has come to pass, what happens in the future is out of our hands. All we can do is believe and hope. I never ceased to believe in M.'s and Akhmatova's poetry. In our depersonalized world where everything human was silenced, only the poet preserved his 'self' and a voice which can still be heard even now.

The main difference between the two forms of loss of the self – i.e., of the personality – was that the individualists renounced all values (of which the personality is a repository), while the others, those who had sunk into a torpor, although they totally suppressed their personalities, managed to keep a tiny spark of inner freedom and to cling at least to some of their values. The vast majority retained perhaps only a dim memory of them, but even this was enough to save them from many of the things to which they would otherwise have been driven by the hard facts of life.

It is impossible to tell how many copies of M. – and of much else besides–circulate nowadays in *samizdat*, but it seems likely that the number greatly exceeds that for volumes of verse by the younger generation. So much can be gauged by the fact that the only small book of M.'s reprinted in recent years, his 'Conversation About Dante',* was immediately sold out and disappeared from the bookstalls. We have seen the new readers come into being before our very eyes, but to understand how it happened is quite im-

* In an edition of 25,000 copies (Moscow, 1967).

possible. All one can say is that it came about against all the odds. The whole educational system was geared to *preventing* the appearance of such readers. The names of some poets were simply suppressed altogether, while others were denounced in the press and in Party decrees, and it had begun to seem unthinkable that any of them could ever survive such massive efforts to obliterate their memory. Then, quite suddenly, everything changed, and we had *samizdat*. Who started it, nobody knows, and the way it works is beyond our comprehension; the fact is, however, that it not only exists but also caters to its readers' actual wants.

I would love to know who these readers are. I have no great faith in their quality, since they were brought up on a rationalist pap which has impaired their capacity to think logically – every idea is mulled over for them in a thousand ways before it actually reaches them. Nowadays the average reader doesn't even look for new ideas – he is suspicious of them. For too long now he has been hoodwinked, palmed off with bogus ideas masquerading as genuine ones. Still unable to figure all this out, he is drawn to the other extreme, to anything beyond the bounds of his primitive reasoning process. He therefore welcomes things he doesn't understand, what he calls the 'irrational' or 'subjective', though the meaning he attaches to these words, given that all his mental categories have become somewhat warped, is not easy to fathom. His attitude has no connection with the ordinary notion of subject and object, though it is rooted in a naïve belief that these are tangible, three-dimensional concepts: an 'object' lies on a table and a 'subject' dissects it, rather as a 'man of the sixties'* cut up a frog. Moreover they imagine that, though a 'subject' may walk the 'objective' world, he must somehow get outside himself to understand it. The 'subject' is small, the 'object' is large, and all other properties of both flow from this fact ... Such an oversimplified way of looking at things comes from the kind of education, a hodgepodge of positivist fodder, that was the undoing of the older generation. They spoon-fed this stuff to their offspring, with disastrous results that can still be seen in the younger generation: the pabulum they were given as children has entered their blood-

* Radical intellectuals of the 1860's (like Bazarov in Turgenev's *Fathers and Sons*, 1862).

stream and works like a poison. Ruled by a primitive fear of reality, they are too overpowered by it to seek meaning or logical connections in it; most of all they are terrified of conclusions dictated by logic and try to avoid them. The great mass of people thus prefer to glide over the surface of reality, always shirking the effort of trying to understand it.

One of the most brilliant men in the history of mankind once said that as soon as thought dries up, it is replaced by words. A word is too easily transformed from a meaningful sign into a mere signal, and a group of words into an empty formula, bereft even of the sense such things have in magic. We begin to exchange set phrases, not noticing that all living meaning has gone from them. Poor, trembling creatures – we don't know what meaning is; it has vanished from a world in which there is no room any more for the Logos. It will return only if and when people come to their senses and recall that man must answer for everything, particularly for his own soul.

But with all this, whatever his quality, the reader is the final arbiter, and it is for him that I kept M.'s poetry and it is to him that I have handed it over. And now, in this long period we are presently living through, a curious process is taking place: people casually leaf through a volume of poetry and, scarcely aware of what is happening, gradually soak it in, until it stirs their numbed and dormant spirits, waking them up and itself coming to life again as it revivifies those it touches. It is a process of diffusion, of inter-penetration, by which at least some people are brought back to their senses and given the strength to shake off their accursed inertia. I do not know how it is elsewhere, but here, in this country, poetry is a healing, life-giving thing, and people have not lost the gift of being able to drink of its inner strength. People can be killed for poetry here – a sign of unparalleled respect – because they are still capable of living by it. If I am right about this, if the verse I have preserved is of some use to people, then my life has not been wasted and I have done what I had to do both for the man who was my other self and for all those people whose humane, that is, human instincts are roused by poetry. If this is so, it means that I probably had a preordained task to fulfil and that I have correctly understood it.

The fact that I have begun to ponder whether I had a task, and how well I have acquitted myself, is a sure sign that I have begun to recover my 'self'. In writing my first book, I excluded myself. This happened quite spontaneously, without any conscious intention: it was simply that I still did not exist. I came back to life only when my main task was at an end. It is clear that, crushed as it was, my 'self' had survived and needed only a short breathing space to come into its own again – it is particularly active in old age when a certain peace of mind has been achieved, but before the pain of past years has died away. Later, the pain too no doubt goes and gives way to senile complacency, but I have not reached this stage yet. Then it will be too late to write – pain acts like a leaven for both word and thought, quickening your sense of reality and the true logic of this world. Without pain you cannot distinguish the creative element that builds and sustains life from its opposite – the forces of death and destruction which are always for some reason very seductive, seeming at first sight to be logically plausible, and perhaps even irresistible. I feel my pain keenly now, and am going to write about myself alone, though in fact there will be much more to it than that. I am really concerned less with myself than with the scraps of experience I have stored up during my life. In going over them all now I feel I may come to a better understanding of certain things. If this life was given to us, it must have a meaning, although the very idea was dismissed out of hand by everybody, young and old, whom I have ever known in my lifetime. Seduced by the 'scientific' approach, they turned their backs on anything not capable of clear-cut proof. Their ideal was logic of a mathematical kind, though they only paid lip service to it, alas. Science is not responsible for all the pseudoscientific theories of charlatans, and why bother about the meaning of things if it always evades you?

When I was young the question of the meaning of life had been superseded by the search for an aim. People are so used to this that even now they fail to see the difference between the two. In those years it was the revolutionary young who raised the question of an aim in life, and they had only one: to bring happiness to mankind. We know where that landed us. The problem of meaning, as opposed to an aim, is appreciated by very few people when they are young, since it can be grasped only through personal experience, and overlaps with the question of one's own predestation. People are thus more inclined to think about it in their old age – and then only those who prepare for death and look back on their past life. Most people do not do this.

'Predestination' is perhaps too big a word to use of a person without very pronounced gifts. It is better to think in terms of having chosen the right path, by a conscious act of will, among all the millions of false turns and steps it is possible to make in life. Looking back on it, you may feel the path you have travelled was predetermined, but all along the way there were thousands of turnings and crossroads at which you could have chosen a completely different route. What we do with our lives is to some extent socially conditioned, since we all live at a particular moment in history, but the realm of inevitability is confined to our historical coordinates – beyond them everything depends on us. Freedom is boundless, and even the personality, one's own 'self', is not something 'given' once and for all; rather it takes shape in the course of one's life, depending to a large extent on the path one has chosen.

It is only especially gifted people – generally with a philosophical rather than a poetic bent – who ponder the meaning of life in their youth. M.'s words on the subject, quoted at the beginning of this chapter, appear only in a rough draft and were never incorporated in any final text. He accepted life as it was, intensely aware of all its richness. I believe this was because he saw right at the beginning that his poetic gift was a matter of predestination. Some of his early, only very recently published verse bears witness to this:

> His heart seems wrapped in cloud
> and his flesh pretends to be stone
> Until the Lord reveals his poet's destiny.
> Ready for song as for battle
> He awaits the secret sign
> and the simple joining of his words
> is like the sacrament of wedlock.

He never had any doubt of his predestination and accepted it just as simply as he did his subsequent fate – this indeed he brought on himself by the calm assurance with which he regarded his work as a poet. The professional writers, the high priests of Literature, were infuriated by it. M. would have fallen foul of them in any country, let alone here, where literature conceived as a personal and private matter is taboo, and any breach with the literary establishment always leads to the intervention of the State. They might just have been able to tolerate him if he had at least been full of his own importance and put on airs, like one of them – nothing so much impresses as a grand manner. But he was totally unconcerned about winning a place for himself in the world of letters. He was much too busy. What with books, people, conversation, the events of the day, and even the lowly business of running to the shop for bread or kerosene, his time was fully occupied . . . For all my light-headedness, even I was astonished at his improvidence. And the times were not propitious.

2   The Stampede

I am not proud of my early youth. The image that comes back to me is of a great herd of cattle stampeding over a field of ripe corn and trampling it underfoot in vast swaths. In those days I ran around as one of a small herd of painters. Some of them later became well known. We wielded rough house-painters' brushes, dipping them in buckets of colour wash to daub crude shapes on fantastic canvases which we stretched across the street for demonstrations to parade under. They were hung up at night. Together with the 'house manager'* (a type which sprang up after the coming of the 'Reds' – as they were then called – like mushrooms after rain), members of our group burst into people's apartments, flung open windows, and, exchanging curses with their helpers down below, firmly attached their decorative works of art to the balcony railings. We girls did not take part in these nocturnal frolics and only heard about them from the boys next morning – they told us laughingly how scared the unfortunate tenants were when the whole mob burst in on them in the middle of the night, led by the 'house manager'.

*The superintendent of an apartment block, similar to a concierge.

Mardzhanov put on a play by a Spanish classical author:* it was about a village revolting against their señor because he had infringed their ancient rights. At the end, after the victory of the people, the women raised their hands above their heads and came on rhythmically swaying their hips, and then, to howls of delight from the audience, the whole cast declaimed in chorus: 'All power to the Soviets!' As the crowning touch, one of the stage decorators, Isaac Rabinovich, had festooned the stage with a huge garland of artificial fruits, vegetables, fish, and birds, all suspiciously phallic in appearance. As the applause swelled, Isaac came out to take his bow, hand in hand with his two assistants – me and my friend Vitia, who had once worked for Alexandra Ekster. Vitia and I had painted the phallic fruits, refining the crude shapes made by the property man. We were showered with cheap Kiev roses and came out of the theatre carrying armfuls of them; as we walked home, the pale blossoms shed their petals, except, fortunately, those still in bud.

We were kept busy all the time making stage decorations or painting posters, and we had the feeling that life was a hectic round of pleasure. With their first cash advance the boys bought purses for themselves – until now they had never had money, let alone purses. We spent it in the coffee-houses and pastry shops which were being opened all over the place by ladies who had fled from the north – they did the baking and served the customers themselves. The money we got for our posters was worth mountains of pastries – this was the time when our new masters were flirting with 'left-wing art', and nothing could have been more 'left-wing' than the little herd to which I belonged. The boys adored Mayakovski's *Left March*,† and nobody had the slightest doubt that he really did have a drum where his heart should have been. Instead of just talking, we yelled at the top of our voices and were very proud when we sometimes got passes authorizing us to walk the streets after curfew. If we forgot to take them with us, the patrols had only to see our paintbrushes to wave us on our way through the empty streets. A paintbrush was every bit as good as a piece of paper issued by the commandant. The patrols were made up of boys just

* Lope de Vega. The play was *Fuente Ovejuna*. See page 349.
† Famous Revolutionary poem of 1918, addressed to the Red sailors.

like ours, though they were armed with guns and pistols. While they went around shooting, we painted . . .

Our comradely mob was gradually infiltrated by new arrivals from the north. One of the first was Ehrenburg. He seemed to view everything with great detachment – what else could he do after his *Prayer for Russia*?* – and took refuge in a kind of ironical know-ingness. He had already understood that irony is the only weapon of the defenceless. Left-wing young artists like us had the blessed advantage of not even realizing we were defenceless. Whenever there was shooting we ran and ducked into doorways. In 1919 there was scarcely any more sporadic shooting in the streets, but the town was shelled by five-inch guns as a prelude to its takeover by the Whites. We were already pretty used to it.

In the evenings we gathered in the Junk Shop, a night club for artists, writers, actors, and musicians. It was in a cellar of the city's main hotel, which was being used to accommodate some officials of the second or third rank from Kharkov. M. had managed to get a place on the train that brought them, and so he was also put up, by mistake, in a very nice room in the same hotel. On the first evening he came down to the Junk Shop, and we at once took up with each other as though it were the most natural thing in the world. We always dated our life together from 1 May 1919, though we were forced to live apart for a year and a half after this. We didn't actually feel all that much tied to each other at this period, but we already shared the two qualities which were to remain with us for the rest of our lives: light-headedness and a sense of doom.

On the floor below, in the same hotel, they had put Mstislavski. He always had children's socks hanging up to dry on his balcony, and I remember being astonished that people should have children during all this turmoil. Mstislavski came into everybody else's rooms to tell about the arrest of the Tsar. He always took pains to remind us of his own descent from Riurik, emphasizing that this was a more ancient lineage than the Romanovs. Such talk made M. wince.

The young do not bother their heads about anything, and we were quite unconcerned by the fears and worries of our elders. Our grim-faced parents went to their doom while we enjoyed life

* A poem attacking Lenin's seizure of power in October 1917.

hugely. The great wave of refugees from the north, already well acquainted with famine and havoc, ate themselves sick in the as yet undevastated Ukraine, trying to put on all the fat they could before they were swept on somewhere else. Our money was gradually falling in value, but people who had brought worthless wads of paper money from Moscow were overjoyed at the amount of good food they could still buy for it.

M., though just as light-hearted as everybody else of his age, was yet different in some way. Our sudden friendship annoyed everybody for some reason. The boys came and argued with me, telling me I should leave M. without more ado. Once Ehrenburg took me on a long walk through the streets and tried to persuade me that I could not rely on M.: if you – he used the familiar 'thou' – want to go to Koktebel,* then go down to Voloshin; he's reliable, and you won't come to any harm with him. (We all wanted to go south; it exercised a strange pull on us, drawing us farther and farther away from home.) I knew that Ehrenburg was dying to clear out himself and go to stay with Voloshin – he hoped to shelter behind him, as though he were a stone wall. I don't know how Voloshin had acquired such a reputation, but I imagine he had created it himself, with the help of all the women around him – such legends die hard. Ehrenburg and I had started saying 'thou' to each other simply in fun, when we happened to see the New Year in together in 1919. He called me Nadia, but I addressed him respectfully by his name and patronymic. Though we later went different ways, I kept on good terms with him – and particularly with his wife Liuba. He was always the odd man out among the Soviet writers, and the only one I maintained relations with all through the years. He was as helpless as everybody else, but at least he tried to do something for others. *People, Years, Life*† is in effect the only one of his books to have played a positive part in this country. His readers – mostly members of the minor technical intelligentsia – first learned dozens of names quite new to them from this book. Once they had read it, their further evolution proceeded rapidly, but with the usual ingratitude of people, they were quick to disown the man who had

* Resort town in the Crimea (now called Planiorskoye), noted for its mild climate and the artists and writers, such as Voloshin, who lived there.

† Memoirs published in the mid-sixties.

first opened their eyes. All the same, there was a great crowd at his funeral, and I noticed that the faces were decent and human ones. It was an antifascist crowd, and the police spies who had been sent to the funeral in force stood out very conspicuously. It was clear, in other words, that Ehrenburg had done his work well, difficult and thankless though it was. It may well have been he who first roused people into reading *samizdat*.

I did not of course take the advice Ehrenburg gave me in 1919 and later made fun of him to the others, mimicking the way he had tried to lecture me. Alas, apart from my good eccentric friends the Makkaveiski brothers, all my listeners took Ehrenburg's side. As to his remark about M., I already had a feeling that his brand of improvidence was quite different from the frivolity of my other friends. He sometimes came out with statements the like of which I had never heard from anyone else. The remarks that most stick in my mind are those he made about death. As though surprised by the idea himself, he said that death had something peculiarly triumphant about it – this he had realized when his mother died. At the time I probably failed to grasp the significance of a great deal of what he said on this subject, and later on, when I had begun to understand certain things myself, he never reverted to it. I had the impression that death for him was not the end, but a kind of justification for one's life. In those days, when people were being killed all over the place, I was inclined to think that death was simply an absurd matter of chance.

He also tried to explain to me the process by which we recognize things – a question that intrigued him more than any other at that time. He had heard that there is no explanation for it in psychology. He was interested in broader aspects – not just in the question of how we recognize something we have seen or knew before, but why we also recognize in a flash something previously hidden or un- known that comes to us just at the 'right' moment, as though predestined to. This is the way you recognize a word, seemingly 'made' for it, needed in a line of poetry; or the way someone you have never seen before comes into your life, after a kind of premonition that your paths were bound to cross. He always talked with me very cautiously, opening up a chink into his inner world, only to shut it again at once, as though protecting it from me, yet wanting me to have a glimpse at the same time. There was something chaste, in the true sense of the word, about this – I also sensed it in his poetry – but such a thing was beyond the wildest imagination of the people around us. Innocence of mind or body, or any other kind, if they had ever encountered it, would have seemed to them like a sprained limb or a broken bone. Yet there was nothing at all cynical about them – at least in the case of those who later became real artists, even though they may have repeated Nikulin's favourite dictum: 'None of us is a Dostoyevski, all we need is the money . . .'* Their principal sin was what I would call rather a peculiar kind of avant-garde tomfoolery. In its carnival time of 1919 Kiev loved the Mardzhanov play and any other display of 'leftism', whether it was in politics, public speeches, ideas, or love (in this most of all). In reality, however, there was no question either of ideas or of love, but only of mutilated travesties of them.

For my part, I told M. about how I had once posed for a young sculptor – he was still only a boy – by the name of Epstein. He lived high up on Lutheran Street in an aristocratic apartment abandoned by its owners. It was here, in his room, that I first saw real grinding poverty: an unmade bunk with tattered rags instead of a sheet, and a tin mug for tea on the table. I don't know what happened to Epstein, but I later saw the bust he made of me in the Kiev museum. It is unlikely to be there still: a portrait of a Jewish girl by a Jewish sculptor is bound to have been a little too much for the inter-nationalists of the Ukraine.

Once Epstein stopped work and called me over to the window. Over the waste lot outside some soldiers were leading a haggard man with a large white beard who stumbled as he went. Epstein told me that for this man, who had been the Kiev chief of police or something of the kind, they had devised a special torture: they took him out every day to be executed, but instead of shooting him, they then brought him back to the prison. This was their idea of retribu-tion for his cruelty to revolutionaries. He was not an old man, but his hair had gone grey from the ordeal . . . Epstein, a Jewish boy who would not have been allowed to come and study in Kiev if the man had still been in charge of the police, could not stomach the

* *Hope Against Hope*, page 333.

barbarity of this vengeance on him (I don't remember who was in power at the time – the Ukrainians or the Reds. Each side tried to outdo the other). Cruelty is anathema to any true artist. I could never understand how Mayakovski, who certainly was one, could say the brutal things he did. He probably keyed himself up to utter such words, believing it was the modern and manly thing to do. Weak by nature, he trained his delicate soul to keep up with the times, and paid dearly for it. I hope the blame will be put on those who corrupted him, rather than on him personally.

M., also a Jewish boy with a deep aversion to killings and torture, spoke with horror of the hecatombs of corpses with which 'they' had responded to the assassination of Uritski. All forms of terror were unacceptable to M. He had met Uritski's assassin, Kanegiesser, in the Stray Dog.* When I asked about him, M. said: 'Who set him in judgement?' As a youngster, under the influence of Boris Sinani, he had believed that 'glory is in the f.o.'† and had even asked to join the terrorists (for this purpose he travelled to Raivola, as he relates in *The Noise of Time*, but was rejected because he was under age). Later on, the attitude to terror changed completely. I remember a conversation with Ivanov-Razumnik in the middle twenties. Like us, he was also living in Detskoye Selo‡ at that time, and we once went to call on him. A few days previously a bomb had exploded in the Business Club in Leningrad. Ivanov-Razumnik was quite elated about it and very surprised that M. did not share his feelings. Eventually he asked outright why he was so indifferent to such an important event: 'Do you mean you are against terror?' . . . In any conversation about theoretical matters not directly connected with poetry or philosophy, M. always became rather listless. Quite baffled, Ivanov-Razumnik asked what view he took of terrorist exploits in the past – the assassination of Alexander II, for example – and was filled with something close to scorn when M. replied that he was against all terror, whoever the target. Strange as it may seem, in those years

---

* See Pronin, Appendix A.
† 'Fighting organization', i.e., the section of the Social Revolutionary (populist) Party responsible for acts of terror, etc.
‡ Soviet name for Tsarskoye Selo, the small town with the imperial summer residence, near Petersburg.

rejection of terror was regarded as tantamount to supporting the Bolsheviks, since they did not recognize terror as a means of revolutionary struggle. This is no doubt the conclusion Ivanov-Razumnik now drew about M.; unfortunately he did not take the trouble to find out M.'s view of terror as practised by the new regime, of which we had all had a taste by now. During this conversation I was silent and unhappy: we were always failing to see eye to eye with people. Why couldn't M. tone down his disagreements? It would have cost him nothing to evade an answer or to murmur something indistinguishable. Why did he always have to stress how much he differed, instead of meeting people halfway? When one is young, one longs so much for harmony in one's relations with others. M.'s intransigence wearied me and went against the grain of my still unsophisticated nature . . .

M. bought and looked through the publications of the Central Archives,* among which were many volumes of documents relating to the terrorists. He could not speak badly of the executed, but he was struck by how shallow and narrow-minded they were (I should have liked to think that Kibalchich was an exception, but the record of his case was apparently never published – at least we never saw it). M. abhorred terror in all its forms.

During our early days together, in the Kiev of 1919, M. was perhaps the only person I knew who pondered the meaning of events, as opposed to their immediate consequences – the only concern of the older generation – or the garish manifestations of the 'new', which was all the young thought about. Older people were worried by such crucial things as the collapse of legal standards and principles, the disintegration of the state and economy, while the younger generation revelled in what their elders called 'demagoguery', no matter where it came from, eagerly lapping up 'the latest' and taking good note of everything they might one day be able to use themselves. We sometimes glanced at the newspapers, but could not read them because the hectic process of 'educating' the people had begun and the peculiar idiom designed for this purpose was already being adopted in decrees, speeches, and the press.

* A series of publications of historical and literary archives, 1922-8. It included a number of volumes relating to political trials in tsarist times.

M. once remarked to me that 'they' were founding their party on authority, like a church, but that it was an 'inverted church', based on the deification of man. This conversation took place in the tiled bathroom of his hotel room with its two windows and white Dutch stove. He was wiping his hands when he suddenly noticed where he was: 'A strange place for a conversation like this.' The idea had come to him in the wrong place and at the wrong moment – we were in a hurry to have supper before going down to the Junk Shop.

One day just before the Bolsheviks left, when they were shooting hostages, we looked out of the window – by now M. had been thrown out of the hotel and was living with his brother in my father's study – and saw a cart piled with naked corpses. Some matting had been carelessly thrown on top of them, but limbs were sticking out in all directions. The Cheka was located in our neighbourhood, and dead bodies were carted like this through the centre of the town, presumably to some place outside. I heard they had made a special gutter for the blood to drain away. The methods were still primitive. Another time the soldiers drove past in a dray with a bearded man, his hands tied behind his back. He was on his knees, shouting at the top of his voice, imploring people to help and save him from being shot. In that year there were cases in which prisoners were rescued by the crowd, but there was nobody around now because of the curfew . . . We saw him struggling with the soldiers who were trying to force a gag in his mouth. We caught only a momentary glimpse of him, but I can still see the man even now. They were probably not taking him to be shot, however – executions were carried out in the Cheka headquarters up on the hill, but the dray was coming down the hill. I think they must have been transferring him to the Lukianov jail, or even to the hospital.

From another window which looked out on the building of the City Council we saw a crazed mob – this was just after the Whites had taken over – running down some red-haired women and literally tearing them limb from limb with a hue and cry about 'Rosa of the Cheka'.* Several women were killed like this as we

* Nickname of a red-haired Jewish woman who gained notoriety as a Cheka interrogator during the first Bolshevik occupation of Kiev.

watched. Later, after M. had managed to leave, the town was seized for several hours by the Reds. They got through to the prison and released all the inmates. Then the Reds were driven back again, and the town was given over to looting by the victorious Whites. The inhabitants barricaded themselves in their houses, banging on copper bowls and shrieking at the top of their voices as soon as any soldiers appeared. There was a terrific din all over town, and corpses were lying in the streets. The savagery of the Civil War had begun. The carnival was over, to be revived only on rare occasions later on in some of the flamboyant productions of the Moscow theatres. Who needed it? It was like a herd of cattle trampling a field.

If I failed to go down to the Crimea with M., it was not because of Ehrenburg's heart-to-heart chat with me. M. had left on the spur of the moment, taking advantage of a sudden opportunity – he went with some actors who were being evacuated to Kharkov in a special coach. Actors enjoyed the favour of all regimes, whether Red or White. M. had to leave Kiev, where he had no friends and was thus bound to attract, as always, the hostile attention of the mob and the authorities, whatever their colour. I had promised him I would come down to the Crimea with the Ehrenburgs, but with all the bloodshed in the streets outside I just couldn't bring myself to move. I had by now understood that the apparent levity of M.'s behaviour was simply a serene acceptance of life. Already then he knew that nothing could be evaded and that you have to accept things as they are. He tried to get me to adopt the same attitude, but it was not so easy; not everyone can live for the moment, as M. did. I couldn't, for one. 'The bosom of a broad-beamed deck,' it seemed to me, would have been a much more agreeable way of travelling than all our vain attempts to row without oars. I was not alone in my longing for a settled existence, but for half a century of our life it was a will-o'-the-wisp. Every time we made a home for ourselves, it collapsed almost at once. There was no such thing as stability in our times – as Akhmatova put it: 'Nowadays all you need is an ashtray and a spittoon.'

Kiev during the Civil War, with its brief moment of carnival, its corpse-laden carts, and its three days of pillage accompanied by the shrieking of fear-crazed citizens, is by no means the worst thing

I have been through in my life. It was only the overture. Much
worse was to come.

My separation from M. lasted a year and a half, during which we
scarcely had any news at all of each other. Communications
between the cities had broken down completely. People who had
got separated put each other out of mind, since it seemed inconceivable they would meet again. In our case chance willed otherwise. M. had got back to Moscow with the Ehrenburgs and then
travelled on to Petersburg, but before leaving them he asked Liuba
to try to find out where I was. In January Liuba was able to write
him that I was still in Kiev and gave him my new address there – by
this time we had been evicted from our house. In March he came
down to look for me – to this very day Liuba refers to herself as our
'matchmaker'. He found the apartment empty – my parents, it so
happened, had been evicted the day before for the second time. At
the moment of his arrival, a bevy of female prisoners burst in: they
had been brought under guard to scrub the floors, as the apartment
had been allotted to some high official or other. We paid not the
slightest attention to either the women or their guards and stayed
for two hours in this room which no longer belonged to me. The
women swore at us and the soldiers mouthed obscenities, but we
just stayed put. M. read me a lot of poems and said he would
certainly take me away from here. Eventually we went down to the
apartment below, where my parents had been given rooms. Two
or three weeks later we travelled together to the north. From then
on we never separated again until the night of 1 May 1938, when
he was taken away under guard. I believe the reason he never liked
us to part for any length of time was because he sensed how few our
days together were fated to be. They flew by in no time at all.

3 'We'

At the time of our first meeting in Kiev in 1919, M. had an almost
childish faith in people's friendship and good will. He liked the
Junk Shop almost as much as the Stray Dog – the clients were nice
and the coffee was good. It soon closed down, however, because

the man in charge decided it was not worth his while just to serve Turkish coffee and various cheap snacks, so we migrated to a Greek coffee-house on Sophia Street. In the window there was a poster saying: 'Our yoghurt is best and can't be beat.' The proprietor, astonished at such an influx of customers, ground coffee in a huge mill while his wife baked cakes and dispensed smiles all around. When the Whites came, the carnival was brought to a halt and the coffee-house lost its customers. The proprietor's wife ceased to smile and stood outside for days on end keeping watch for her former clients in the hope of waylaying one to hand over to the Whites. Everybody who had brought a moment's prosperity to her coffee shop with the yoghurt that couldn't be 'beat' she now hated bitterly, regarding us all as Bolsheviks. The first to be ambushed by her was Ehrenburg, but he managed to get away. He warned me not to go along Sophia Street, and once again I ignored his advice, with the result that I was the next to fall into her clutches. The lady who until not so long ago had been so ready with a smile now demanded to know the whereabouts of the person 'you were going around with'. She regarded him as the chief Bolshevik and would have loved to see him hounded to death then and there, just as the crowd had killed red-haired women in front of the City Council, suspecting that each one of them was 'Rosa of the Cheka'. Though unable to share M.'s faith in people's good will, I did believe that a smile was some indication of a person's disposition. Even the superficial politeness that required people of the older generation to smile had a restraining influence on behaviour, but it disappeared from our life after all the bitterness of the Civil War, and there is no chance of its returning to this wretched land of ours.

Once, during our days in Kiev, M. said to me cryptically: 'When I am writing poetry, nobody ever refuses me anything.' I thought how pampered he must be and asked the reason, but he couldn't explain: he didn't know; it just happened like that . . . I concluded he must live among people who liked poetry and were always happy to do a kindness to someone endowed with the gift of it. In any case, as I knew already, his needs were simple enough: a cup of coffee and a piece of cake. In Petersburg he may also have had to raise the odd ruble or so to go to the Stray Dog.

A few years later, in the wretched, rundown Moscow of the NEP period,* he was acutely aware of how everything had changed. There was no question of asking for favours – everybody kept his little bit of tea or coffee strictly to himself, and nobody would have shared a crust of stale bread even with a friend. The attitude to poetry had changed as well. People no longer had an ear for it, and one had to use special effects to penetrate their deafness. When M.'s *Second Book* appeared,† various people came to ask him to sign it and made comments on it, but none of the reviews, whether favourable or hostile, had anything of any significance to say. People could no longer be bothered to make any kind of 'needless' mental effort. In one of his articles, M. described how the reader had been perverted by the rapid turnover of poetic schools and generations: '. . . he is beginning to behave like a spectator in the theatre – he turns up his nose, pulls faces, and is very hard to please.' Then, in a poem, he wrote: 'And they curse me . . . / in the language of streetcar arguments, / of which no one can make head or tail.' The same streetcar language was used to praise him, and this was even worse. He used to report what he had heard about himself during the day ('Can they really mean it?' he would ask me), until at last it dawned on him: 'They simply don't care for poetry.' Were they in fact capable of caring for anything? The people who have survived from the generation active in the twenties, now enjoying an utterly disgraceful old age, are still trying to meddle in the life around them and are bent on stopping the slow and faltering process of our return to sanity (if, that is, this process really exists and is not just a figment of our imaginations, as frightening to them as it is welcome to me).

Was it true that the people who never refused the young Mandelstam anything really loved and understood poetry? It is more likely that most of them were just showing the kindheartedness usual in their circles and that their attitude to poetry was merely one of good-humoured sympathy. As long as people cluster in groups, villages, townships, or any other kind of community binding them together by common habits, customs, roots, and

---

* New Economic Policy, with a limited revival of private enterprise, 1921–8.
† Moscow, 1923. A slightly expanded version of his second verse collection, *Tristia* (Petersburg and Berlin, 1922).

traditions, they will be obliged to smile at each other, and this is surely important. Our writers used to do their utmost to expose the humbug, deceitfulness, fraudulence, and even the secret crimes of outwardly decent, genteel, and smiling people, but it is a lucky society in which despicable behaviour at least has to be disguised. Some conceal, others curb or even suppress altogether the nasty instincts we all have in good measure. Perhaps self-restraint is the most we are capable of, but it can be achieved only among and in the sight of people living in a community. It is much harder for the lone individual.

The roots binding us together were cut in the twenties, and henceforth the tacit rule was 'All is permitted,' the principle which Dostoyevski fought all his life. The peculiar feature of this society – after it had been gripped in an iron vice and reduced at breakneck speed to a state of what is called here 'unanimity' – was the fact that it proved to consist of individuals working for their own self-advancement either singly or in small groups. Groups sprang up whenever there was someone to lead them, and they fought among themselves to get a monopoly from the government. This happened in all fields, not only in literature. It was the system that gave birth to Marr, Lysenko, and hundreds of thousands of lesser cliques of the same kind, all of them responsible for much bloodshed. Such cliques are not proof of the existence of a sense of fellowship, since they consist of individualists who are out to achieve only their own aims. They refer to themselves as 'we', but in this context the pronoun indicates only a plurality devoid of any deeper sense or significance and always ready to fall apart the moment a more enticing aim catches the eye.

We witnessed the disintegration of a society which was as imperfect as any other, but which concealed and curbed its wickedness and harboured small groups of people who were truly entitled to refer to themselves as 'we'. I am quite convinced that without such a 'we', there can be no proper fulfilment of even the most ordinary 'I', that is, of the personality. To find its fulfilment, the 'I' needs at least two complementary dimensions: 'we' and – if it is fortunate – 'you'. I think M. was lucky to have had a moment in his life when he was linked by the pronoun 'we' with a group of others. His brief friendship with certain 'companions, co-seekers, co-discoverers' –

to quote a phrase from 'Conversation About Dante' – affected him for the rest of his life, helping to mould his personality. In 'Conversation About Dante' he also says that time is the stuff of history and that, conversely, 'the stuff of history is the joint tenure of time' by people bound together as 'we'. If a man is mindful of the fact that he lives in history, he knows that he bears responsibility for his deeds, which, in turn, are determined by his ideas. The members of the generation to which both M. and I belonged were always shouting from the rooftops that they lived in 'historical times', yet they completely abdicated responsibility for what was happening around them. All the crimes of the age – as well as their own – they put down to the predetermined nature of the historical process. This was a very convenient approach for those who collectivized and deported the peasants – though why did they have to go to so much trouble, if history is predetermined anyway? . . . But I have no wish to accuse everybody in M.'s generation – some people belonging to it paid dearly for their lack of faith in official dogma. Among my own contemporaries, however, I failed to see any of this kind. If there were any, they must have been very discreet and lain very low indeed.

But to return to M. and the people with whom he shared his 'tenure of time'. Zhirmunski has told me that at the Tenishev,* where they were classmates, M. immediately met with great kindness and attention. The death of Boris Sinani, his first friend, must have been a great blow. We occasionally ran into people who in their youth had visited the 'Rose Room' in the Sinanis' apartment, among them a woman who told M. the story of the death of Linde, the Provisional Government's commissar at the front. The story is told by Pasternak in *Zhivago* and by General Krasnov in his memoirs. I don't know whether Pasternak knew Linde (called Gints in the novel), but Krasnov's version is much closer to the account given us on the street by this woman who was an old friend of all three – Mandelstam, Linde, and Boris Sinani. M. always spoke with great respect and affection of Linde, as of everybody else who had been in any way connected with his friend Boris.

After Boris Sinani's death, M. spent two years abroad. It was a time of loneliness when he wrote verse about the anguish experi-

* The Tenishev Commercial School in Petersburg.

enced by any young man. He felt particularly lonely in Italy, where he spent several weeks as a tourist rather than as a student. He regretted ever after that because of his inner turmoil he had seen very little and not used his time to better purpose.

His feeling of solitude left him only when he returned to Petersburg. In Terioki,* where he often went for a holiday, he got to know Kablukov, who was, I believe, secretary of the Religious-Philosophical Society. Kablukov's diaries, in which he writes a great deal about M., have survived. He tried to talk M. out of his attraction to Catholicism and hoped to convert him to Orthodoxy. He coaxed him into taking his university examinations – the sort of thing M. was organically incapable of – and was very dismayed when a new note appeared in M.'s poetry after his affair with Marina Tsvetayeva. Kablukov, like many fathers (real or spiritual), had expected his foster child to retain all the earnestness of his youth. M. was drawn to Kablukov, and probably owed a lot to him. He used to explain to me in a confused way that every young man needed the support of someone older. I do not know how much older Kablukov was than M. himself, but M.'s father was still alive, and he couldn't bring himself to say outright that he simply needed a substitute one.

One day M. went quite unannounced to call on the Merezhkovskis. He was received by Zinaida Gippius, who told him that if he wrote good verse she would hear of it and would then be pleased to talk to him: until then it had no point, since nothing ever came of people nowadays. M. listened in silence and left. Soon Gippius read his verse and invited him a number of times, through other people, to come and see her, but he stubbornly refused to go. (Such is the story exactly as M. told it to me.) This did not prevent Gippius from promoting M. in every way. She wrote to Briusov and many others about him, and before long M. was being referred to in her circles as 'Zinaida's Jewboy'.

In those days Gippius was an influential grande dame of literature, and the fact that she stood up for a young poet of whom, from the first, the Symbolists – Briusov in particular – took a very poor view spoke extremely well, to my mind, of the literary manners of the time, and of Gippius herself. The joke about the Jewboy had a

* Resort town on the Gulf of Finland.

sequel in the memoirs of Makovski, who invented a grotesque yarn about M.'s mother being a vulgar shopkeeper's wife.* Once they had emigrated and lost contact with their milieu, people had no compunction about talking the most utter nonsense. There are many examples: Georgi Ivanov with his yellow-press reminiscences of the living and the dead; Makovski, whose story about M.'s mother coming to see him at *Apollon* reached us while M. was still alive and deeply offended him; Irina Odoyevtseva, who has preposterous things to say about Gumilev, as well as giving M. light-blue eyes and making him out to have been uncommonly stupid into the bargain. It is she who claims that Blok – or it may have been Andrei Bely – came up to her in the Summer Garden and started telling her intimate details about the private life of Liubov Dmitrievna. Who can believe this sort of rubbish, or what she says Gumilev supposedly told her about a proclamation (which nobody else has ever come across) and the piles of money kept in a drawer of his desk? One must have boundless faith in the iron curtain between the two worlds (or, as in the case of our home-grown memoirist, Nadezhda Pavlovich, between the two eras) to write such stuff. As long as there was a community whose members referred to each other as 'we', however superficial or nominal it may have been, nobody would have had the nerve to write bunkum of this kind.

If any community, even the most heterogeneous, is artificially divided, the consequences are ugly in the extreme. This became horrifyingly clear when we saw people in prison denouncing their relatives and friends, associates and colleagues, while others outside the prison walls disowned their fathers and husbands, brothers and sisters. They acted, it is true, 'under duress', but I am convinced that this was not the whole explanation. I recently heard about the suicide of a woman who was haunted for thirty years by the memory of how she had turned away from her father when they came to arrest him and refused to say good-bye to him. She was only eleven at the time. Later she wound up behind barbed wire herself and had her own share of suffering, but she never ceased to be troubled in her mind at not having said good-bye to her father, whom she never saw again. Another woman told me how distressed

* *Hope Against Hope*, page 210.

her father had been when they arrested his superior, under whom he had served for many years. His daughter, then an eighteen-year-old member of the Komsomol, thought his reaction both suspicious and discreditable, and she warned him: 'If they pick you up too, I shan't believe it's a mistake.' ... Family unity crumbled under such pressures. Both girls, who were only eleven and eighteen when this happened, behaved as they did under the influence of their education, and of a public opinion which vilified the doomed and sang the praises of the strong. Nowadays, the older a man is, the more he bears the marks of the past. The grey-bearded writer of funny stories Ardov, whose father was shot at the beginning of the Revolution, wrote a letter to the court hearing Lev Gumilev's civil action* to inform them of the fate of Lev's father, adding that Lev himself had spent many years in a camp ... on a political charge. I have no doubt that Ardov has so often felt it necessary to dissociate himself from his own father that his treachery towards both Gumilevs, father and son, was a comparatively insignificant milestone on his road to glory. In such an atmosphere, the family, friendship, comradeship – anything that bound people together as a community ('we') – dissolved and vanished under our very eyes.

A real community is unshakable, indubitable, and enduring. It cannot be broken up, pulled apart, or destroyed. It remains unaffected and whole even when the people united by it are already in their graves.

4   The Odd Man Out of Acmeism

It took M. some time to find the people he could refer to as 'we'. In adolescent years a sense of communion with others arises only in a generation deliberately setting out to carry on the work of its fathers, but the twentieth century is the age of discontinuity. M.'s first friendship was formed in the Sinanis' 'Rose Room', but he had already been immunized at the Tenishev school against the positivism of Sinani senior. Thanks to V. V. Gippius, he had

---

* A case involving the legacy of his mother, Akhmatova, after her death in 1966. See page 348.

already at school conceived a passionate love of Russian literature – poetry in particular. Without this, it would have been much harder for him to define his place, to find people of like mind, and, hence, to discover his own self as well. This is how one is initiated into the traditions of a living literature; in *The Noise of Time*, M. notes that the 'first literary encounter is irremediable', and also exclaims: 'Literary anger! Without you, how could I have eaten the earth's salt?' From Konevskoi and Dobroliubov, now almost forgotten poets of early Symbolism, whom he came to know in school thanks to V. V. Gippius, it was easy for M. to graduate to Annenski and choose him as his teacher. This was a less thorny path than the one that in those years usually required an apprenticeship with the acknowledged masters of Symbolism: Balmont, Briusov, or Viacheslav Ivanov, then at the height of their fame. (M. naturally paid them due tribute, but to a lesser degree than others did.) Great fishers of men, they surrounded themselves with disciples to whom they handed down their theories. M. probably met Ivanov already before he went abroad, through either his mother or the Vengerovs, but the whole temper of even M.'s early verse is free of the seductive influence of *Transparence* or *Cor ardens*, whatever Ivanov's later devotees may say on this score. M. never took to visiting Ivanov's 'Tower'* either. Perhaps the only thing he got from it was an aversion to the idea of the poet as an oracle, so typical of the older Symbolists. Can one say that Blok and Bely were entirely free of it?

Though lack of outside influence may be organic to a poet's work, it does not mean he may not occasionally borrow certain things. Before writing his poem about the wedding and the tortoise, M. had sat in my room glancing through a slender tome of Viacheslav Ivanov's translations of Alcaeus and Sappho in the handsome Sabashnikov edition (I always bought his editions of the classics). It was here that he got the words 'brightly coloured boot', and he indicates the source precisely: 'Sappho put on her brightly coloured boot.' It happened to fit very aptly, since for want of proper shoes, I was wearing a grotesque pair of Kazan boots which I had bought at the Kiev fair (known as the 'Contracts'). The day

---

* Ivanov's fifth-floor apartment in Petersburg, where he held a famous literary salon on Wednesdays.

before, we had 'married', that is, bought ourselves a couple of blue rings for a kopeck apiece near the Mikhailov monastery, but as our wedding was secret, we did not put them on our fingers. He carried his in his pocket, and I put mine on a chain and wore it hidden in my bosom.

All kinds of weird and wonderful things were sold in the grounds of the Mikhailov monastery. I particularly remember their monstrous round combs with the inscription: 'May God save you!' M. gave me the roundest and most monstrous of all as a 'wedding' present. Being young and brazen, I wore it when I walked around town and went to the Junk Shop. Who would then have thought that we would stay together until the end of his life?

As for the cicada forging a little wedding ring, the source of this is Derzhavin. I don't know what view the entomologists might take of this, but M. believed that grasshoppers are to be imagined literally* as tiny smiths working away with hammer and anvil, as their profession demands. (The foregoing is for the benefit of those American–Russian professors who think that M. borrowed even the word 'spring' from Viacheslav Ivanov – though M. himself said that he could learn from and talk with anyone.)

From what Akhmatova told me I know that the Poets' Guild,† which gave birth to the Acmeist group, was created in revolt against the Academy of Verse, where Viacheslav Ivanov was the leading light. The ringleader of the revolt was Gumilev, who had been more closely tied than the others to the Symbolists, and thus found it more painful to break with them and rid himself of their influence. As often happens in such cases, he carefully studied the articles and theories of the Symbolists, thinking he might still not have understood them properly. His emancipation came all of a sudden, but it must be said that he was more deeply marked by Russian symbolism than any of the others. I think his last book showed him to be freer of it, and if he had been granted a normal span of life, he would have shown his true mettle. But his life was cut short. M. and Akhmatova were infuriated at the way literary

*The Russian word for grasshopper, *kuznechik*, means, literally, 'little smith'.

†See Appendix B for this and other references to Russian literary organizations.

historians tended to lump anybody they fancied together with the Acmeists: Kuzmin on account of his 'clarism', Lozinski because of his friendship with them, and all the young poets who reckoned themselves to be Gumilev's disciples (of whom there were a great many, since Gumilev was evidently a born teacher). In reality, however, the Acmeists numbered only six – and one of these was something of an interloper. I shall begin my account of Acmeism with this 'odd man out'.

In 1921, M. and I travelled to Tiflis in a special train belonging to the organization for aid to refugees known as Centroevac. Apart from the coach intended for the 'top brass', there was a string of converted freight cars crammed with the rank-and-file officialdom whose job it would be to resettle and find work for the Armenian refugees from Turkey. I trust they were able to do something for the unfortunate Armenians, but the same could scarcely be hoped of the people we were travelling with in the coach. The group was headed by Lopatinski, the artist once connected with the 'World of Art'* – God alone knows why he had been entrusted with this extremely tricky job – and consisted of various friends of his who had been appointed to responsible positions by Centroevac. Lopatinski had once served under M. in the Commissariat of Education.† Neither of them did any work, and they were frightened of their Bolshevik lady secretary. She was indignant about these two idlers – who wanted, for some reason, to save a church choir, completely ignoring the class approach. At least they were not responsible for destroying the school system.

We had left Kiev in the hope of getting on a similar train going to Afghanistan – the man in charge of which was Raskolnikov. In Moscow we learned we were too late for this venture, and Larisa Reisner's mother told us that in any case Raskolnikov had stubbornly refused to countenance the idea of taking 'that wretched poet' with him, despite all his wife's pleas. Instead of M. he had taken Nikulin. I now realize that this was all to the good, but at the

---

* Avant-garde art movement (and journal) formed under the leadership of Alexander Benois in the early 1890s.

† The ministry, headed by Lunacharski in the first decade after the Revolution, that was a controlling body for education, the arts, etc. It employed many intellectuals in the early days of the regime.

time I was upset. M. wasn't in the least put out, although the journey would have given us a respite from the hardships of those unbelievable years of hunger. He said he must thank his lucky stars at not having got mixed up in Raskolnikov's Afghan machinations, and began to look out for a chance of getting down to the Caucasus. Quite by accident he ran into Lopatinski on the street and, learning about the Centroevac expedition, brought him back home. We were staying at my brother's and living off fritters made of flour we had brought with us from Kiev. We treated Lopatinski to some of them – he was a splendid fellow – and decided there and then to go with him. As far as Rostov we travelled in one of the freight cars, but there Lopatinski transferred us to the coach, which had a sign at the entrance saying: 'For mental cases.' This saved it from being invaded by people trying to get on at stopping places. In the freight car we had lived off the bread rations issued to us; for a crust of bread hungry peasants were willing to exchange anything – a piece of meat, chicken, or sour cream . . . The inmates of the coach 'for mental cases', including us, lived off the cash advances doled out by Lopatinski. The whole country was then existing on advances, the spending of which would subsequently be accounted for by presenting obviously bogus receipts from cab drivers.

The journey proved to be quite a joy ride in its way. For some reason we stopped for a whole week in Kislovodsk,* although nobody had ever set eyes on any Armenian refugees there. We made the most of it, enjoying life away from the cold and hunger of more notable cities. Everything went well for us, apart from the fact that Lopatinski's chief assistant – who was also, of course, his drinking companion – made a fuss because we were getting advances too: this was, he complained, directly at the expense of the others. But Lopatinski stuck to his guns, and although we got less than the others, it was enough to pay for our *lavash*† and rice.

This pleasant existence suddenly came to an end in Baku when several people in the coach, including Lopatinski, fell ill with cholera. Our coach was shunted into a siding; now immobilized, we went on living in it like a gang of railway men, while the stricken members of our party recuperated in the city. We went to the public

* Resort town in the north Caucasus.
† Type of unleavened Caucasian bread.

baths, where they stamped our identity cards (or rather, the slips of paper that now served as such) lest we take it into our heads to have a second bath. We also visited Viacheslav Ivanov, and M. went on his own to visit Gorodetski, whom I too met a little later. He was thus the third Acmeist I had encountered (in Kiev I had met Narbut).

Gorodetski paid us a return visit to our coach in the sidings. Two bottles of wine were sticking out of his pockets. Sitting down, he took out a corkscrew and three metal noggins. He stayed for a long time, never ceasing for one moment to act the goat – but in such a way that I took him for someone in the final stages of senile decay. We had never had any experience of this kind of imbecility, and it was only many years later that Akhmatova invented the term 'senile marasmus' – referring to some demented old man, she would say with a sigh: 'His marasmus is coming on.' No expression could have applied more aptly to Gorodetski, both when we first met him – he was then barely forty – and later in Moscow, where he soon moved.

When Gorodetski left, I asked M. in astonishment how they had come to get involved with him – he was obviously already suffering from sclerosis and softening of the brain, so what would he be like later? M. explained that Gumilev had enlisted him, as he was loath to take the field against the powerful Symbolists flanked only by a bunch of striplings. Gorodetski at least was a poet with a reputation. After *Yar* all the Symbolists began to make a great fuss of him and nicknamed him the 'Sun Boy'. 'Was he always like this?' I asked. M. said yes, but that now his clowning also had a purpose: he was scared stiff he might be made to answer for his book *The Meeting of the Tsar*, which he had published just before the Revolution ... With his hatred of violence, M. clearly felt sorry for Gorodetski, but I immediately had a hunch that he was not the type to come to any harm. His buffoonery was real enough, but it was not the sublime kind which in literature may serve as the voice of truth. He was just a common or garden buffoon, something out of a burlesque show. And he had a face to match: a huge Adam's apple, tiny, deep-set eyes, and a funny hooked nose that had been twisted out of true. The perfect face for a 'Sun Boy' in fact ...

We later met him several times in Moscow; once or twice he

came to see us or we went to see him. He behaved differently from that first meeting in the coach, when his flattery of M. had verged on the indecent (as I later realized, he had thought M. was now an influential Soviet grandee). Even M., who obstinately refused to think ill of people, particularly of former comrades and poets, was forced to agree with me: 'Perhaps you're right, but does it matter?' In Moscow Gorodetski had already recovered from his fright and come to an understanding with the new rulers – helped no doubt by the fact that he had once been the 'Sun Boy', the hope of Russian literature. M. had rightly observed that the Bolsheviks took the opinions of the Symbolists as gospel truth and issued rations in accordance with their scale of values: 'They have taken us over from the Symbolists lock, stock, and barrel.'

Gorodetski had taken up residence in an old house near Iverskaya,* and assured visitors that it had once belonged to Boris Godunov. The walls in his apartment were certainly of tremendous thickness. His wife cut crosses in her pastry and affected an old Russian style in her conversation. A stout, easygoing woman, she never forgot that, since her first name was Nympha, she was expected to play the *rusalka*. M. persisted in calling her Anna (her patronymic was Nikolayevna, I think), and every time Gorodetski corrected him just as stubbornly: 'Nympha' . . . M. complained that he was organically incapable of uttering such an idiotic name. Since we were scarcely eager visitors to Boris Godunov's chambers, the problem soon proved of minor importance.

At this stage Gorodetski was still bearable – it was only a question of showing off. He was the first of a very long series of similar braggarts. Even today there are old men who ought to be thinking of their souls, but strut around Moscow boasting instead. There is no end of them, and I think they must do it out of frustration – because their hopes have come to nothing and they have nothing to show for their lives. Gorodetski was the first to indulge in this kind of thing, when he was only forty, or a little over. It was a case of premature dotage. He boasted about the trust shown him by the authorities, who had asked him to rewrite the libretto of Glinka's opera;† about the brilliance of the new poems and fables which

---

* Street in the old quarter of Moscow.
† See Gorodetski, Appendix A.

poured from him in a never-ending stream; about his skill in frying tomatoes; about the quality of his shirts made of some material that let the air through; about the money he earned and the rations he got . . .

The last time I saw him was in Tashkent, when we were there as evacuees during the war. He lived in the same tumble-down slum house as Akhmatova; she had a tiny room on the second floor, while he occupied a reasonable apartment on the ground floor. He gave no sign of recognizing me – whether deliberately or not, I don't know – but this suited me very well, as I had no desire to talk with such a type; all these years he had done nothing but publicly disown his former associates after they had perished, shrilly declaring that he had really belonged to the 'Adamists',* who, he said, had nothing whatsoever to do with the Acmeists. Yet he intercepted people on the way up to see Akhmatova and asked them how his 'backward pupil' was coming along. We got reports of the remarks he made at his tea table about the counter-revolutionary activity of Akhmatova, Gumilev, and other, unspecified, Acmeists. His daughter, a nice, slow-witted woman who adored her father, used to drop in on Akhmatova. In the simplicity of her soul, she repeated to us everything her father said, and advised Akhmatova to mend her ways. We just said nothing, sorry for the poor ninny. Everything that Gorodetski said smacked of denunciation, but I don't know whether he went to the authorities with his tales or confined himself to his public attacks and to gossip in his own backyard. I think the Acmeists were lucky that, owing to the force of circumstances, Gorodetski dissociated himself from them. It would have been far worse if, instead of being hounded, they had flourished and Gorodetski had made himself their spokesman, mouthing such nasty humbug as might be demanded by the fashion of the day. Fortunately, the Acmeists were spared this, but the fact remains that Gumilev, with his gift for organization, had rashly introduced into his new group this poet recognized by the Symbolists, thus wishing on it a corrupt type, a buffoon, and congenital talebearer.

There are two points to be made here. An unsuccessful poet, tasting praise and a modicum of fame in his youth, turns in his later

*An early name for the Acmeists.

years into a creature soured by hatred and envy and becomes a disgrace to his fellow men. The second point – or rather, question – is: How could the Symbolists have been so mistaken about him? One always thought of them as cultivated people who were invariably guided in their judgements by purely literary criteria, never by considerations of literary politics. Yet all of them, including Blok and Viacheslav Ivanov, took Gorodetski to be the hope of Russian poetry. I have read somewhere that Khlebnikov used to carry *Yar* everywhere with him and presented a copy of one of his own books to Gorodetski with a dedication saying: 'With love and gratitude from Khlebnikov, who has carried *Yar* next to his heart for a whole summer.' I have looked at *Yar*. There is not one iota of real poetry in it, not a single genuine word. Those who praised it to the skies must have been seriously wanting somewhere to make such a judgement. What could it have been, this inner weakness afflicting those who lived in the period still known as the 'Silver Age' of Russian poetry? Which leads to a second question: Was it really such a great period for art, poetry in particular, second only to the age of Pushkin, Baratynski, and Tiutchev? In my own deep conviction it was no such thing.

In painting, the 'World of Art' and the 'Knave of Diamonds'* was a time of gathering strength, of apprenticeship with the West, during which many talented people were mastering the tricks of their illustrious trade, mixing in elements of primitive native tradition and a nationalist tendency of the kind that never predominates during a real efflorescence of art. Cézanne was not in the least concerned about endowing his work with a specifically French character. In the Russian icon and in Rublev we see the qualities of the grand European tradition, with Russia, the land and the people, showing through them. Nationalism is at a lower level of consciousness. When it comes to the forefront, crowding out fundamentals, it is a sign not of health but of sickness; not of depth but of shallowness.

In poetry the first ten years of the century are represented by the Symbolists. I will say nothing about their verse as such – it speaks for itself – nor about their undeniable role in educating public taste, but there was something in their mentality that prepared the

* Avant-garde movement started in Moscow in 1909.

way for the debacle to come, and their mistake over Gorodetski
was not accidental, which is why I am dwelling on it here. It was
characteristic of the basic trend of the age and its sickness. By the
end of his life Berdiayev, who was flesh of the flesh of the Symbolists, came to prefer the literature of the nineteenth century,
but he continued to regard the beginning of the present century
as a time of revival. Blok, who combined in himself the two distinct
traditions of the Russian intelligentsia – that of the lower (or in
Berdiayev's terminology, revolutionary) section and that of the
higher group, or elite – was acutely aware of the sickness of the age,
but believed he could heal it by an injection of the spirit of the
sixties.* This medicine was useless, since the lower stratum of the
intelligentsia, the revolutionary underground, already lived by the
ideas of the sixties, and at the same time was stricken with the same
sickness as the upper stratum, the elite. Both were going through a
similar illness and a common crisis. The elite was desperately
anxious to find a remedy for the crisis, for the weakness that was
debilitating it. All kinds of ideas were put forward, a particularly
popular one being that the present could be revitalized by paganism as embodied in the ancient Russian gods such as Perun.† It was
taken for granted that pagans were strong and handsome, exuding
power and health. An earlier attempt to bring back the Greek gods
had hardly been a success, yet the people who now dragged out the
ancient Russian ones were welcomed with open arms. In such an
atmosphere, Gorodetski, with his wife Nympha and his *Yar*, hit
the bull's eye. The first to give his blessing was Viacheslav Ivanov;
it was at the 'Tower' that Gorodetski met Khlebnikov. Many
others flirted with paganism, thus indulging a veiled cult of power
in their desperate search for a way to heal themselves.

Paganism and the ancient Russian gods were a nationalist
solution, a home-brewed remedy. The more westward-looking
took up various forms of theosophy, grafting their simplified conception of Asia on to Europe. Rozanov wrestled with himself in
solitude, seeking salvation in the family and the Judaic principles
of life. If he succumbed during the years of trial, it was because he

* i.e., the radicalism of the 1860s.
† The God of Thunder – mentioned with other Slavic deities in the early
Russian Chronicle.

had always been against freedom, which is the very essence of Christianity. In his defence, however, it can be said that he had no time for the cult of power and was not impressed by paganism.

The moral to be drawn from the story of the 'Adamist' Gorodetski: one must not lose one's nerve to such an extent that one becomes utterly heartless and ceases to be human. Everything in moderation. In our stirring times nobody could fail to be frightened, but it was always a matter of degree. It is as simple as that. If any brave young fellow with no experience of these things feels inclined to laugh at me, I invite him back into the age we lived through, and I guarantee that he will need to taste only a hundredth part of what we endured to wake up in the night in a cold sweat, ready to do anything to save his skin the next morning.

One final word about the 'Sun Boy': bogus poetry is a poison. Under any circumstances, even if our life had been a bed of roses, Gorodetski would have been consumed with envy and cursed his 'backward pupil'. Poets should not be murdered, but neither should they be overpraised . . .

5 The Three

Three poets – Akhmatova, Gumilev, and Mandelstam – referred to themselves as Acmeists to the very end of their lives. I have often asked what it was that united three such different poets, so unlike each other, each with a different understanding of poetry, and why the bond was so strong that none of them ever renounced the youthful alliance which had lasted so briefly. Mandelstam invariably dismissed the question with a joke. Akhmatova, though she was always talking about Acmeism – particularly in her old age – was never able to give me an answer: the reason for the link between the three of them seemed self-evident to her. She talked mostly about the circumstances of the break with the Symbolists (or rather, with Viacheslav Ivanov), the composition of the Poets' Guild (the first one), and the creation of the Acmeist group. I will give here the basic facts, as I remember them from her account (there are not all that many – like a lot of people, she tended to repeat herself in her old age).

Gumilev, who had been more deeply involved with the Symbolists than either Akhmatova or Mandelstam, gradually drifted apart from them because the work of his younger friends – including his wife's – began to bring home to him the inner emptiness of Viacheslav Ivanov's theories. Gumilev's 'Prodigal Son' ('Kolia's first Acmeist poem', as Akhmatova called it) was read in the Academy of Verse, where Viacheslav Ivanov, surrounded by respectful acolytes, reigned supreme. Ivanov made a devastating attack on the 'Prodigal Son', and his tone was so scathing and rude ('We had never heard anything like it', in Akhmatova's words) that Gumilev's friends left the Academy and set up the Poets' Guild in opposition to it. Blok was invited to preside over it, but he quit almost at once. Six members of the Guild formed themselves into the Acmeist group – including Gorodetski, the 'odd man out'. By way of manifestos, the new group published articles by Gumilev and Gorodetski. Mandelstam also offered a manifesto (his article 'The Morning of Acmeism'), but it was rejected by Gumilev and Gorodetski. Akhmatova told me she fully shared the views expressed in this article and regretted that, being so young and hare-brained, she had not stood up for its publication as a manifesto. This is really the gist of what she told me. The rest is just minor detail: where and when they gathered, who styled themselves 'syndics' of the Guild, and why Lozinski didn't join them.

The manuscript of 'Morning of Acmeism' remained by chance in the possession of Narbut, who during his time as a commissar managed to get hold of some paper and publish a little periodical with the grand title *Siren*. It came out in Voronezh. Here he published M.'s manuscript, but without a date. He told M. about it when they met in Kiev in the spring of 1919. M. muttered something, but he never saw a copy of it. Narbut hadn't one with him, and later on they both had other things to think about. When M. put the collection of his articles together,* he forgot about 'The Morning of Acmeism'. Later he saw it reproduced in a volume of

* *On Poetry* (Moscow, 1928).

literary manifestos,* and regretted not having included it in his own collection *On Poetry*. It might just have slipped through the censorship.

There is an old writer still living in Voronezh who tells a story about how he first met M. there 'in the editorial office of *Siren*'. What kind of an office could a little magazine like that have had? . . . If anybody ever goes into all these things, he should bear in mind that all the people who really knew and understood M. died without writing down anything about him. (The only exception: Akhmatova's *Pages from a Diary*.) Now that a demand has grown up for it, apart from the balderdash published abroad we also have the native variety to contend with. One must distinguish between the various kinds of lying: the pernicious (the conversations of the 'blue-eyed poet' as reported by Vsevolod Rozhdestvenski); the naïvely stupid (Mindlin and Borisov); the stupid and odious combined (Nikolai Chukovski); the LEF-minded (Shklovski); the editorial (Khardzhiev, who quotes me as his authority for whatever he likes – if he does this to me who am still alive it can be imagined what he does to M.); and the innocuous – such as the tale about a meeting in the 'editorial office' of *Siren*. A good criterion for judging the authenticity of such things is suggested by Lidia Yakovlevna Ginzburg in the introduction to her unpublished book where she notes the 'extraordinary similarity between the articles, the poetry, and the table talk – they all formed part of the same pattern of thought'. This is a very true observation. What is more, all M.'s articles, from 1922 on, echo the intonation of his living voice: he dictated them to me, as he did *The Noise of Time* (apart from the last four chapters) and *Fourth Prose*. This is an excellent aid to picking out the occasional grain of truth in the largely bogus writings of all these memoirists. Natasha Shtempel is accurate in her reminiscences: she at least has an excellent memory.

In the last years of her life Akhmatova, recalling her youth as an Acmeist, was worried in case literary historians should describe Acmeists as 'Symbolists of the younger generation', or try to detach Mandelstam from them and lump him together with Khlebnikov and Mayakovski. Such a tendency certainly exists. In

---

* *Literary Manifestos: From Symbolism to October*, collection of materials, edited by N. L. Brodski and others (Moscow, 1929).

his notes* Khardzhiev mentions Mayakovski, Khlebnikov, and even Lilia Yurievna Brik, but for some reason omits all reference to Akhmatova and Gumilev – which made her very indignant. She was also very upset that Mandelstam had once written somewhere of the 'womb of Symbolism' from which they had all been born . . . For my own part, I am indifferent to the chicanery of future historians of literature, as long as the work itself is not extinguished and a living appreciation of poetry continues to exist. On the other hand, the question of what bound these three poets together, apart from their early friendship, seems to me very important. If it is solved, all kinds of fanciful theories will collapse – they are so obviously ill-founded that only mental inertia keeps them alive.

At the same time as the Acmeists, another group also came out in opposition to the older generation of poets. Consisting of the Burliuks, Khlebnikov, Mayakovski, and later Brik, its members called themselves Futurists (after the Revolution they joined LEF). Nowadays we would call them the 'avant-garde'. They were received with open arms by the Symbolists, in an almost fatherly way. The usual view is that Futurism took the field against Symbolism and dealt it a crushing blow. It was considered a truly 'innovatory' movement (and one must remember that during the last half-century there has been no greater word of praise than 'innovatory'); the Acmeists, on the other hand, were viewed as a splinter group of Symbolism, a small branch of a big tree . . . It seems to me that the Symbolists showed discernment in regarding the Futurists as their direct descendants and heirs. The Futurists took what the Symbolists had begun to its logical conclusion and perhaps, thanks to Mayakovski, influenced the Western avant-garde to boot. For many years literary scholarship has concerned itself only with externals – the verbal texture, the vocabulary, or, at the most, the question of what group some particular poet (Pasternak, for instance) belonged to. The reason for this is the desire to appear scholarly at all costs. An alternative, of course, is to study literature as a social phenomenon, but this applies only

---

* i.e., to the still unpublished collection of Mandelstam, prepared by Khardzhiev for the Poet's Library. It has now been officially stated in Moscow that this edition is eventually to appear 'in the second quarter of 1973'. See *Hope Against Hope*, page 421.

to literature as opposed to poetry. As regards the class approach, the less said the better – we all know what *that* has achieved. Art and particularly poetry belong to the study of man in general, and cannot be 'approached' with any such pair of methodological tweezers.

There is now no poet left alive from that era. Their work is before us, and not another line will ever be added to it. The time has come to explore what each of them considered his main concern in life, and then to see how it is reflected in what he wrote. One should not allow oneself to be side-tracked by secondary features which are in any case always deducible from primary ones.

It is my considered opinion that the Acmeists were brought together as a group not just by their attitude to poetry, but by a common philosophy of life in general (indeed, this may always be so with the formation of such groups). Perhaps, incidentally, 'philosophy' is not a good word to use about poets; it is better to talk of their sense or understanding of life since even with the most intellectual of them, the emotional element predominates over the abstractly cerebral. The poet's mode of thought is the product of all sides of his personality: the intellectual, physiological, spiritual, and emotional, a synthesis of what he perceives through the senses, his instincts and desires, and the higher aspirations of his spirit. All these can be bound together only by some dominant idea which shapes the personality. If there is no such idea, one will have, at best, a clever craftsman, a 'translator of ready-made ideas', a mechanical nightingale. The unifying idea can be located at any level of the personality – in its deeper reaches or on the surface. Mayakovski, for example, in his best verse, is a poet of adolescent rage. He screams and throws tantrums because the toys he wants are not immediately put in his hands. Like a child, he only hopes that one day, when it is too late, everybody will feel sorry at what they have done to him – 'everybody' being the grown-ups who treat him so badly (and all women were grown-ups) . . . Mayakovski certainly had a lot to thank Brik for; without him he would not have found such compensation in the writing of propaganda verse. This postponed his end, giving him a purpose in life and the sense of power so essential to a person of his temperament. His example shows that even at this level poetry is possible. What he put his faith in has proved to be an infirmity rather than a source of strength and, seeing this, people tend to be unfair to him nowadays. His tragedy lay precisely in his own weakness, which made it impossible for him to identify himself with real strength. The best he could do was to throw in his lot with his age, which was as infirm as he was himself. Such poetry as his cannot, of course, lead to catharsis, to inner purification, but this would be too much to expect of it. As M. once observed, poetry owes nothing to anybody, and no demands can therefore be made on it . . . It is said that every nation gets the rulers it deserves. This is even truer of its poets. Poets 'deserved' only by the few are generally killed off or – even worse – taken in hand and browbeaten into 'mending their ways'. This is what happened to Zabolotski.

Whatever their failings or virtues, the three poets who revolted against Symbolism did not thus detach themselves from the main-stream out of pique at the harsh judgement delivered on the 'Prodigal Son' – this was only the immediate pretext – nor for reasons of a purely formal nature having to do with poetic tech-nique, but solely because they had come to recognize the basic difference between their understanding of life and that of their late mentors. I was recently given a photocopy of a note written by M. in 1923 to a young poet who considered himself close to the Acmeists because in his verse he was fighting against 'the ballast of dead words purporting to be "Acmeist".' He was probably one of the many imitators of Gumilev in those years. In his note M. said: 'Acmeism in 1923 is not the same as in 1913. Or rather, there is no such thing any more. Its only aim was to be the "conscience" of poetry. It sat in judgement on poetry, but was not in itself poetry . . .'

This was written after the articles in which, having lived through terrible times and preparing to face the worse ones to come, M. stressed the moral importance of poetry and defined Acmeism not only as a literary but as a social phenomenon. To emphasize the contrast with Symbolism, he quoted the lines of Briusov: 'I want my ship to sail in freedom everywhere / The Lord and the devil I glorify in equal share.' Briusov was an individualist who under-stood freedom as the right to serve God or the devil at will. The aims he set himself were typical for the times and for Symbolism.

The main one he had decided on as a young man already: to become the leader of the new literary movement, whose adherents were then called the Decadents. Not content merely to ignore Christianity, he rejected it out of hand as a 'religion poor in content' and took a certain pleasure in blasphemy – one has only to recall what he had to say about the 'road to Damascus'. He let slip his view of his own role in the lines: 'Singing hosannas to myself / I do but serve the Lord / I do not know what they portend / But I bring tidings to the world.' He certainly was a harbinger of the future, of the era of individualism which inevitably resulted in the decomposition of the personality. What god did he serve, ostentatiously building himself up as a Leader and invoking the 'coming Huns'? A point to note is that according to another pronouncement of Briusov's, poetry is nothing if not revelation.

The person who paid most dearly for his enchantment with Briusov was Gumilev. In his early youth, right after he left school, Mandelstam also looked up to him for a while. Briusov, it must be said, really had become a Leader (all my life there has been no getting away from Leaders!) and made himself head of the new movement (though it is still a puzzle to me how it could have happened). Vladimir Soloviev brilliantly held him up to ridicule, but for a long time nobody saw the point. How right he was is at last clear, especially now that all Briusov's papers have become available, revealing for all to see what we were so slow to detect in his verse.

The Symbolists, almost to a man, were under the influence of Schopenhauer and Nietzsche, and hence they either rejected Christianity or tried to refashion it, adding elements of classical antiquity, a dash of paganism, the ancient Russian deities, or other things of their own devising. Even Blok, infinitely profounder than his brash contemporaries and the living embodiment of the Russian intelligentsia's tragedy, was marked by the times he lived in. But the main tempters and seducers were Briusov and Viacheslav Ivanov with their cult of art and the artist. Blok noted down something Ivanov said in a lecture: 'You are free, Godhead – everything is permitted, only dare' . . . Dostoyevski had devoted his life to showing the implications of the principle 'all is permitted', but none of them paid any attention. Viacheslav Ivanov thought of Dostoyevski as the 'Dionysian spirit' incarnate and was himself determined to break all taboos . . .

The three Acmeists refused to countenance any revision of Christianity. Gumilev's and Akhmatova's Christianity was of a traditional Orthodox kind, while M. accepted it in its philosophical aspect rather than as a matter of everyday observance – it underlay his view of the world. He regarded poetry as something sacramental, though in reference to his own work he talked only of 'a simple song of earthen hurts'. He had no ambition to be a theurgist. This was not for him . . .

Viacheslav Ivanov proclaimed the idea of art as theurgy and, inviting us to follow him *a realibus ad realiora*, promised initiation, by means of symbols, into a 'world beyond'. Or, to quote Berdiayev, who was close to the Symbolists: 'The world beyond is revealed to art only in its symbolic projection.' For Berdiayev the symbol was a link between the two worlds, a bridge between them. For the Christian, the link between the empirical world and the higher one is ensured not by means of symbols, but through revelation, the sacraments, grace, and – most important of all – through the coming of Christ. Christ is not a 'symbol', though it may be said of the Cross on which He was crucified.

For the three Acmeists, the theories of their elders, who called themselves Symbolists, sounded like blasphemy. Both Gumilev and M. were at one in their refusal to probe the unknowable. Gumilev pointed out that the unknowable cannot by definition be known, and M., by declaring his faith in the law of identity, evidently meant to suggest that knowledge of what is hidden from us is possible only through revelation. He accused the Symbolists of being 'bad householders' who do not set store by this world, the 'God-given palace'. I do not believe, however, that he shared the whole of Schelling's theory of identity with its concept of the extension (or development) of the absolute in nature and in history. In what he says about the law of identity ($A=A$), M. was more concerned to remind us that any symbol must have a rigorously defined meaning and cannot be invented at will or ad hoc. As he wrote in one of his articles: 'Monsieur Jourdain discovered in his old age that he had been talking prose all his life. The Russian Symbolists have made a similar discovery: that words are images by their very nature.' In another article (published in Kharkov in 1922) he made a remark about Andrei Bely – in connection with his 'Magic of Words' – to the effect that having discovered that words are images, he was so taken aback that he could not think what to do about it. M. knew perfectly well that 'man is a symbolist animal' (who said this?), and objected only to mumbo-jumbo about metaphors and symbols, just as he abhorred the sickness of the age in general with its mania for innovation at any price. He was all for continuity and for the kind of image, metaphor, or symbol that has not simply been foisted on words, but is inherent in them, having been conferred on them by tradition. The mania for innovation always leads to speculative traffic in arbitrary notions; and reliance on pure inventiveness invariably brings with it the spurning of man's accumulated riches, with all the fateful consequences this entails.

In their ignorance the philologists have absurdly misinterpreted the following sentence of M.'s: 'The word is Psycheia. The living word does not denote an object, but as though taking up residence in it, freely chooses some objective meaning or other, a thing in all its concreteness, a nice body to inhabit.' This has been taken to mean a rejection of the idea that words have fixed meanings, and hence a declaration of faith bringing M. close to the Futurists. But in fact M. was talking here only about something well known to any linguist conversant with the rudiments of his subject – namely, about the inter-relationship between word and thing, and the changeable nature of a word's connotations. There are still eager young scholars studying the language of Kruchenykh and the verbal inventions of the Futurists in the belief that any artificially created combination of sounds (whose unpronounceability only enhances their value) enriches the language and broadens the semantic range of human speech. M. always looked at things from a historical point of view, which meant that he did not take kindly either to the invention of symbols or to the creation of neologisms in which word roots are combined with each other and with prefixes and suffixes to make fanciful new formations; still less could he have indulged in the purely phonetic games of the type played by some pitiful crackpots. Such things he dismissed as idle pastimes.

The Acmeists renounced the cult of the poet and the principle that 'all is permitted' to the man who 'dares', although both Gorodetski, and to some extent Gumilev, inherited the idea of the 'strong man' from the Symbolists. Gumilev thought of strength and daring in terms of military valour (the soldier and explorer). M. could understand courage only in terms of standing up for one's beliefs. It was significant that in his years of trial he suddenly remembered a quatrain excluded from *Stone* (1913) and printed it in his *Poems* (1928): 'Here I stand and can do no other.' In his article 'On the Nature of the Word' he wrote: 'Everything has become heavier and more massive, and therefore man must be the hardest thing in the world, standing in relation to it as diamond to glass. The hieratic, that is, sacred nature of poetry is due to the fact that man is harder than anything else on earth.' In 1922, when this was written, everybody around us was talking about the new regime being hard, but nobody paused to consider that we are each one of us responsible for what happens in the world. Everybody was happy to divest himself of responsibility even for his own actions. M.'s words would have struck the wrong note, even if anyone had heard them – but I am sure nobody paid any attention, except possibly Akhmatova, who was always mourning the dead, whether martyrs for the faith or soldiers.

The 'handsome, twenty-two-year-old'* Mayakovski and the beautiful demigods of Khlebnikov's poetic fantasies are much closer to the Symbolists' 'man who dares' than to the 'hard man' called for by M. In my young days I must have made fun of the idea and particularly of his line: 'Only in battle do we find our allotted part.' This was because the word 'battle' evoked the sort of image later exemplified in Eisenstein's films: doddering old knights brandishing cardboard swords. M. never had the faintest idea how to handle a rifle, hated firearms with all his being, and had never worn a military uniform. How was I to know that real battles with real bloodshed (as opposed to Eisenstein's sham ones) would be fought in such an unwarlike field as poetry, of all things?

Luckily M. did not take offence; nor did he expect flattery from his wife. The 'strong' men of our heroic age always demanded praise from their womenfolk. This was by way of compensation for all the indignities inflicted on them in their public life. M. had

* Mayakovski's description of himself in his 'Cloud in Trousers' (1914–15).

no need of this, for a reason that is quite clear to me. His youthful association with the Acmeists had given him a genuine sense of community, helping him to achieve a feeling of 'self' which was not merely individualistic and thus not in need of constant affirmation.

6 The Five

Tiny groups of young artists or writers, with their extravagant manifestos and ridiculous hullabaloo – which impress nobody but themselves – are probably the best, if not the only, way of setting out in new directions. In a world always hostile to fresh voices, one needs the encouragement of a friendly eye or ear, good-humoured banter, and lively debate. To see a far-off speck of light and walk towards it alone is far harder without companions and friends. The existence of a thousand minute groups is amply justified if in only one of them somebody finds himself and the words he needs. As for the hostility of the world at large, it can only be of benefit to an artist – this is how he learns to overcome resistance. Things are much worse if everybody loves you; it is far harder to withstand the allurements of general acclaim than it is to swim against the tide. I am, of course, speaking of a normal 'hostile world' which only berates the artist, or ignores him, not of one which uses its punitive apparatus to 're-educate' him. Fate was kind to Mandelstam in his early years: they gave him strength for the rest of his life. He was seasoned by his companionship with the Acmeists and the members of the first Poets' Guild.

In 1928, on the seventh anniversary of Gumilev's execution, Mandelstam wrote a letter to Akhmatova from the Crimea (it was preserved in a copy made by Luknitski and is quoted by Akhmatova in her *Pages from a Diary*) in which he said: 'My dialogue with Kolia [Gumilev] has never been broken off and never will be.' I can confirm that M. was always recalling what Gumilev had said about one or other of his poems, or wondering what he might have made of new ones he would never be able to read. In particular, he liked to repeat some words of praise that Gumilev had once spoken to him: 'This is a very good poem, Osip, but when it is finished, not a single one of the present words will remain.' Then, there was what he had said to M. about his friendship with Georgi Ivanov, before M. had understood certain peculiarities of him and the other 'playboys' (as Akhmatova called them): 'Osip, pack it in, it's not for you.'

It is probably difficult to judge Gumilev's understanding of poetry and his ear for it just from a reading of his articles, and M. always used to say that he was much more impressive in conversation than on paper. He talked differently to M. than he did to Akhmatova. All his remarks about M.'s verse, which were usually jocular in form, referred to minor details, such as an imprecise epithet or simile. With Akhmatova, on the other hand, he was out to exert influence, trying to win her over to his own view of poetry. I know this much from the stories she told me, one of which I will quote here.

Once she was sitting by her window, combing her hair and reading a volume of Annenski's that had just appeared, when she suddenly realized the sort of thing she wanted to do herself. At that moment Gumilev was in Abyssinia. By the time he returned, she had already produced a good deal of the verse that later went into *Evening*. Gumilev was astonished by it. Until then he had always been suggesting things for his wife to do: 'You ought to go in for ballet, Anichka – you have just the right figure . . .' He took her poetry seriously, but kept telling her she should write ballads – he thought the best way out of the dead end into which the Symbolists had led poetry was to write narrative verse. I believe he may have been influenced by Briusov in this view. It may also have been dictated, to some extent, by the desire to appeal to his readers – as was his reluctance to speak his mind properly in his articles, which always make due allowances for the reader's indifference and ignorance. This tendency to pander to the readers was itself part of the legacy of the Symbolists, those professional 'fishers of men'.

Poems like 'The Grey-eyed King' (and to some extent the 'novelistic' quality of Akhmatova's verse in general) must be seen as a concession to Gumilev's talk in favour of ballads, but he had more success with Odoyevtseva, who produced something about grave-diggers and a tomcat (M. said that Gumilev was very pleased with this ballad of hers, and that his relations with her, which she

has so adroitly written up in her memoirs, were based on it).
Gumilev was impelled by his didactic streak to surround himself
with disciples. Neither M. nor Akhmatova had any connection
with his second Guild, or with the third, which was called, if I
remember rightly, the Sounding Seashell. As both always emphasized: 'This was Gumilev's idea . . . we had nothing to do with it.'
In the last period of his life Gumilev took a lot of trouble over
Otsup, Rozhdestvenski, and Neldikhen. One of these, Vsevolod
Rozhdestvenski, later went to great lengths to dissociate himself
from Gumilev, saying he was in reality a disciple of Blok. I am told
that in his most recent book he refers to M. as his 'older colleague'.
This is just as false as his claim to have been Blok's disciple, or the
Acmeist pronouncements he attributes to M. in his memoirs.
Luckily M., unlike Gumilev, felt no need of disciples and could not
stomach imitators. He was not plagued by such riff-raff.

I have a feeling that Gumilev's break with the Symbolists was
prompted, in psychological terms, by his urge to have his own
'school'. As an associate of the Symbolists, he was himself in the
position of a disciple, yet all the while his popularity was growing,
his books sold out at once, his public appearances were invariably a
great success and – in Akhmatova's words – the girls hung around
his neck like garlands. I have no personal recollections of him in
those years, so my opinion is my own and I can quote no one in
support of it, but I did witness the growth of his popularity. It continued to increase during the twenties and by the thirties had
spread down to an even broader reading public. Even I had a
weakness for him, and could not at first understand why M. was
not moved by 'The Streetcar' (a ballad!) and even less by 'Word'.
(The quotation from this at the beginning of M.'s article 'On the
Nature of the Word' was put there by the editor. M. did, however,
like the line: 'Dead words smell badly' and often repeated it.)
There are some echoes of Gumilev in 'Octets'. He liked bits of
'Star Horror' ('What is this victim with his broken crown'), and
failed to recognize one of them as a paraphrase from the Bible:
'fear, the snare, and the pit'. As in reading any other poet, M.
looked out for things he thought came off well, such as 'On Venus,
oh, on Venus'. Arthur Lurye is probably going much too far when
he writes that M. could not hide his boredom when listening to

Gumilev. The fact is that listen he did: in one of M.'s last poems, there is an echo (in the phrase about 'Kiev-Viy') of Gumilev's 'From the city of Kiev, from the dragon's lair . . .'

Narbut and Zenkevich were completely under Gumilev's spell. His theories and ideas were like canon law for them, though I doubt whether they understood them. They both threw in their lot with Acmeism, imagining it to be a revolt against Symbolism's call to higher things, a rejection of the spirit in favour of the flesh. Both were the kind who put youth above everything, and in Acmeism they saw its bloom and vigour. They always beamed at the sight of M., and even now Zenkevich does nothing but talk about the years before the Revolution in Petersburg, dredging up amusing episodes and stories from the depths of his memory – the way M. laughed, for example, when they once went to see one of the members of the Guild, Georgi Ivanov, and found they had arrived at an awkward moment, during a scene between him and his patron. 'We Acmeists never went in for that sort of thing,' says Zenkevich – now eighty years old – when he tells this story, guffawing loudly at the memory. Poetry figures very little, perhaps not at all, in his pleasant, good-humoured tales, but he will never forget such details as the way Akhmatova stood at her fireplace, or the escapades of Georgi Ivanov and his peculiar methods of getting money to spend on high living and fancy clothes. Talking about the adventures of this worthy, Zenkevich always emphasizes that they had nothing in common, pointing out that Georgi Ivanov was only a member of the Poets' Guild, and no more. I once read a manuscript written by Zenkevich after the death of Gumilev. It is the very private story of his sad farewell to youth, and had, as I remember, a light-hearted romantic aura about it – but no facts. He had no need of facts. He now keeps his manuscript hidden away and never shows it to anyone. Zenkevich has always lived in the present, rigorously shutting himself off from his own past. The present is a constant source of menace, so he skilfully adapted to it and kept his dreams of the past to himself. His devotion to it finds its chief expression in his small collection of manuscripts by the dead.

For Zenkevich Acmeism also meant the West – which later made it easier for him to take up translation work, the only way a writer could earn his living if he was incapable of turning out stuff to

order for the regime. As long as Narbut continued to have an
official position, he kept Zenkevich on his payroll, treating him
abominably; but Zenkevich minded not at all, since he was only
too happy to have found a niche in this uncouth and alien new world
under the wing of someone from his own circle. He feared strangers
like the plague. After M.'s arrest in 1938, we happened to meet on
the street, and he took me to task for letting 'strangers' come to see
us. By this he meant the biologist Kuzin and his friends. (These
were also angry with me, thinking Kuzin had landed in trouble
through meeting suspect people like Zenkevich at our appartment.)
In a way, both Zenkevich and the biologists were right: in times
like ours, the only thing to do was to take Zoshchenko's advice,
make yourself a hideout in the forest, and sit there, howling like a
wild animal. But this expedient was foreseen by Kafka, who
showed that, alas, even the most industrious of moles can be
ferreted out of the burrow he has taken so much trouble to dig . . .
Kuzin, in fact, had been in the bad books of our beloved authorities
for long before he met us, having been constantly harassed for
refusing to serve as an informer. He is now enjoying a peaceful old
age and loves only Goethe. We all belonged to the same category
marked down for wholesale destruction. The astonishing thing is
not that so many went to concentration camps or died there, but
that some of us survived. Caution did not help. Only chance could
save you.

At any event, Zenkevich now spends his old age reminiscing,
telling stories and thus reliving the heady days of his youth in the
decade before the Revolution. In his own way he is still faithful to
his associates of that time. In the terrible years he kept his mouth
shut and went in for various agreeable pursuits to keep his mind
off things a little. In 1937–8, for instance, he conceived a passion
for riding and got permission to practise, for an hour twice a week,
in a riding school. Just before we left for Samatikha, where he was
to meet his doom, M. went with me to see Zenkevich. Misha was
just leaving for his riding school and ran off without even taking a
last look at M. – now he talks ruefully about how he could so easily
have skipped his riding lesson just that once, but it never crossed
his mind that he would never see M. again . . . if only he had
known! Misha was by nature utterly naïve and innocent, but we

never expected anything remotely resembling help from him. On that last visit, however, I remember that M. tried to persuade Zenkevich's wife to steal one of Misha's shirts for him, but she didn't dare: Misha kept too good a count of them and was fussy about his possessions. Once, in quite recent years, I had to call him to ask about something, and his wife picked up the telephone. She started complaining how Duvakin was coming to see them to write down Misha's tittle-tattle, but she thought it was too bad of him to visit decent homes when Siniavski, now in prison, had been a pupil of his. In the terrible years she had been much more courageous, but now, with age, she had turned into a real specimen of Soviet womanhood. I am surprised, though, that she dared to voice her complaints over the phone – this is never advisable here.

Zenkevich was the only Acmeist – apart from the 'odd man out' – to be spared by fate. I am glad he survived. As far as I know, he has never done any harm in the whole of his life, being quite incapable of wickedness. Stolid, kind, mild-mannered, and inconspicuous, he is convinced that people perished only through carelessness and fails to realize how imprudent he was himself at times, as he collected his autographs and sighed for his dead friends in the privacy of his room – walls have ears and could have heard his sighs. He was just lucky. In recent years he started coming to see Akhmatova, and even once brought her a flower. His stories gave her pleasure, and she kept telling me I should find out everything about the Guild and Acmeism from Misha, and write down all his confused stories in proper fashion. I would rather somebody else do it. I do not fancy myself as the historian of Acmeism. I think it can do without a history.

The pitiful fate of Narbut had nothing to do with his Acmeist connections. He perished together with untold numbers of Party members of all vintages who had for one reason or another departed from the general line; he first attracted attention to himself in the house of Bagritski's widow, who was his wife's sister. What could have seemed safer than this – to go nowhere except the salon kept by the widow of an eminent Soviet poet? But doom lurked everywhere, and in any case survival was almost impossible for a man in Narbut's position – unless, perhaps, he had dug himself a lair in the middle of a forest. But even in the wilds you could not escape the dragnet. One of the commonest stories told in the thirties and forties, which gives a good idea of the daydreams indulged in by honest Soviet citizens, was about an old man and his wife living in a mountain glen near Lake Baikal. It was so hidden and secluded, with forest and mountains all around, that for twenty or thirty years they had never seen a soul from the 'outside' world. The members of an expedition who stumbled across their hut by accident were astonished at their blissful ignorance; until that moment the couple had never heard of the war and the Revolution. I am doubtful myself whether this idyllic pair ever existed. Either the old man and his wife were just shamming, or they were invented by people longing for seclusion and security. This was what Pasternak's Dr Zhivago dreamed of as well – to live by the sweat of his brow somewhere off the beaten track, in peace and quiet. But such things happen only in fairy tales, or in the imagination of Soviet citizens. I also once had fantasies of this kind, but any isolated homesteaders were invariably tracked down by the tax inspector, the collectivizer, the Party organizer, the vigilante, and – last but not least – by the representatives of our great guardians of public security, who would swiftly deal with any would-be anchorite or stylite, leading him back to a normal way of life, on one side or other of the barbed wire . . . There would have been nowhere for Narbut to hide, though blind chance sometimes saved people more surely than any secret hideout in the mountains.

I liked Narbut. A born aristocrat, a *khokhol*,* a descendant of Cossack hetmans, and hence the effete scion of lusty and cruel ancestors, he has left a batch of poems written in Russian but steeped in the spirit of the Ukraine. By vocation he was a publisher – commercially minded, canny, tight-fisted. He loved to save a few kopecks on authors' fees, even though, when he was in charge of a publishing house in the twenties, they accounted for only a minute percentage of a book's cost. This was just his *khokhol* sense of humour, which was still tickled by the memory of his little tricks many years after his fall from grace. His ideal was no different from that of any American publisher of thrillers: mass editions of any old rubbish in gaudy, eye-catching covers . . . In our hypocritical conditions, his talents as a grasping businessman found no scope,

* Jocular or pejorative nickname for a Ukrainian.

and he even had to practise the self-denial of a Party ascetic: from his tumbledown house out in Maryina Roshcha,* he went to his office in overcrowded streetcars, clutching a strap with his only hand (the other was missing and had been replaced with an iron claw covered by a glove), working from morning to night and enjoying no privileges to which he was not strictly entitled by his position (I do not know whether 'packets'† already existed in those days; if they did, he would certainly not have turned his nose up at them). When he took over the publishing house ZIF (standing for 'Land and Factory'), it was on the rocks, but by the time he left, it was in a flourishing condition, with large assets in the bank. After his working day at ZIF, he would hurry off to the Central Committee, where he had some important post. He had no time at all for poetry in those years, since he was up to the ears in Party intrigues. Unlike Voronski, who supported the Fellow Travellers, Narbut promoted writers whose only common characteristic, in his own words, was that they all had moustaches. They were probably, in fact, members of the 'Smithy'‡ and RAPP, but Narbut couldn't have cared less, since he never read their books – this was done by his subordinates. He concerned himself solely with the political and commercial side of the business. The only person he really welcomed in his office was M., with whom he haggled over money just for form's sake, making all the corridors resound with his voice and putting the fear of God up his already terrified underlings and assorted editors of all kinds. They knew, if anybody did, that there was no point in trying to argue with the 'boss', yet since M. was not one of the writers 'with whiskers', they concluded he must be a special favourite. After the boss's fall, they eagerly took part in the hounding of M. Narbut's successor, Ionov, was only too ready to lead the pack and needed very little encouragement in this. A former veteran of Schlusselberg§ – it is said that he still kept his manacles hanging over his bed – he was noted for his vile temper. He was, in fact, not quite right in the head. As head of the State

* Suburb of Moscow.
† Secret remuneration, in addition to the regular salary, given to favoured officials, etc., in the Stalin era.
‡ Kuznitsa: a group of 'proletarian' poets founded in 1920.
§ Notorious political jail in tsarist times, on Lake Ladoga.

Publishing House in Leningrad, he had behaved outrageously: on one occasion, when he got angry with a subordinate, he ordered the man to be kept suspended between floors in the elevator for a couple of hours. I believe Ionov eventually met the same end as everyone else.

It was Voronski who cooked Narbut's goose, with the help of Gorki. From somewhere or other he managed to unearth a document signed by Narbut while he was in one of Denikin's jails – in Rostov, I think. To save his skin, Narbut had renounced Bolshevism and cited his aristocratic origins. Voronski could have got rid of him even without this document – he belonged to the 'victors' by right, while Narbut was simply a hanger-on of the sort who were only tolerated during the Civil War. The irony is that typically, both came to the same bad end.

After his 'fall', used by now to playing the role of a Party ascetic concerned only with furthering the cause of Soviet literature, Narbut was quite at a loss what to do. But he soon pulled himself together, moved out of his slum (which was thereupon pulled down) into a decent one-room apartment, found a job in a publishing house specializing in scholarly works where Shengeli was an editor, and started paying frequent visits to us, as well as to Bagritski; he was sometimes taken there by his wife.

My impression is that Narbut became an Acmeist for the same reason that he later joined the Party. Cossack freebooters liked to roam in bands – and always remained eternally loyal to the companions of their choice. Except during his brief times as a dignitary, Narbut's constant ambition was to revise Acmeism – in a very different form, needless to say. In 1922 he often came to see M., bringing manuscripts by Babel and Bagritski and trying every kind of blandishment on him: 'But they're real Acmeists, don't you see?' . . . Since poets are always harder to place, he was less insistent about Bagritski than about Babel, who he thought was a clear case: Babel had produced his splendid tale about Benia Krik, showing that he valued strength and power in a man more than anything. I am not certain that Benia Krik had been published by then, but at any event his fame had already spread by word of mouth. Babel had found a 'strong man' of the type everybody admired – a Jewish one . . . That he was an Odessan bandit mattered not at all.

Narbut was bent on having Babel in a neo-Acmeist group headed by M., but without Akhmatova. I think he made this proposal with the knowledge and consent of Babel, who was still rather unfledged, though when he met M. later, he never mentioned it. At the beginning of the twenties an alliance with Narbut, on whom the Odessan writers depended for their daily bread, might have struck Babel as being to his advantage. For his part M. was dead set against a new Acmeism in concert with the Odessans. Narbut kept repeating his suggestion and blinked in astonishment every time it was turned down. It was really beyond him why M. was being so 'stubborn'. I think he can scarcely have understood a single word in the article by M. which he had printed in his Voronezh *Siren*.

In the thirties, after his fall, Narbut started busily casting around for what he called 'scientific poetry', convinced that this was what Acmeism should develop into. In his view, Acmeism was entirely concerned with concrete detail, with specifics, and should bring a magnifying glass to bear on the tiniest particle, showing it in large relief. Narbut's argument in favour of his new-style Acmeism was that since the poet is an inventor he can invent anything – even a machine – and 'scientific poetry' would hence be the best training for him in this role . . . M. treated Narbut gently, like a sick child. It was hopeless trying to explain anything to him, but he admired him for his *khokhol* wit and love of a good joke.

Despite Narbut's deep attachment to M., I saw him only perhaps once or twice after May 1934. Akhmatova stayed with him and his wife on a visit to Moscow in the summer of 1934, and she tried to go there a second time, but they didn't want to see her any more. Such precautions were never, alas, of any avail, as Narbut was to learn.

Both Narbut and Zenkevich had become associated with Acmeism only by chance, just through being friends in their young days with three poets marked down by fate. Neither of them ever had the slightest inkling of such things as a philosophy of life or a basic idea that shapes the personality. In fact they were not really concerned with the personality – for them it was always a source of amusement, a plaything, as in the bright days of their youth. Both of them kept their love of Acmeism and their loyalty to it because it was the main thing that had happened to them in their early years – and neither of them ever grew up.

All the same, they formed part of M.'s intimate circle, though only while Gumilev was still alive. With his death, the group fell apart, and it was M.'s friendship with Akhmatova, renewed in the middle of the twenties, that kept the old association alive – and the memory of Gumilev, with whom M. inwardly communed.

Akhmatova often invited Zenkevich to come and see her in the last years of her life, enjoying his vivid and detailed memories of the past. He told her his tales, and she drank them in, reliving her old adventures and delighted to hear once more how Gumilev had praised her beauty, and how madly he loved her. In her old age it became very important to her, for some reason, to believe that Gumilev's love for her had been undying, and that he had never stayed long with any other woman because he could find no one else like her. Both M. and Zenkevich believed that Gumilev did indeed really love only Akhmatova. I doubt, however, whether she ever loved him. This, at least, is what all their contemporaries believed, and she made no attempt to hide the fact. Why, then, did she have this need, after his death, to maintain that he had always loved her? Her own explanation was that it was for the sake of Gumilev's reputation as a poet. A not very likely reason . . . She was, incidentally, quite happy with Zenkevich's interpretation of Acmeism – but, of course, only in the last years of her life. I didn't yield to her wishes and question him about the days 'before you were born', both because I am neither a historian nor a literary scholar, and also because I had no desire to see things through his innocent, child-like eyes. I was not party to the early Acmeist association of their youth, and my relations with her were on a different footing. My only regret is that I never saw the rather ungainly and overweight Misha on his docile horse at the riding school. In his equestrian guise, this plump, good-humoured editor, horseman, and collector of manuscripts written by friends who had perished so terribly was probably even more captivating than on his hard chair in the bleak and somewhat squalid offices of ZIF.

7 Return

The dual number has been lost in Russian, and this enabled Khardzhiev to say that the poem 'In Petersburg We Shall Meet Again' refers to Arbenina. In fact, the poems to Arbenina come after this one and should appear in the following order: 'I Am Sorry That Winter Is Here'; 'Take a Little Sun and Honey . . .'; 'Because I Could Not Keep Your Hands . . .'; 'Equally with Others I Want to Serve You'; and perhaps 'Into the Circle of Dancing Shadows . . .' As I never tire of pointing out, the order of the poems in *Tristia* is completely haphazard, and presumably Gleb Struve was guided by it in putting the poems about the end of the affair before the two idyllic ones.

'Take a Little Sun and Honey' is dated 'November 1920' (as in *Tristia*?), while 'In Petersburg We Shall Meet Again' is dated 24 and 25 November, 1920. The first point to note here is that we do not know whether these dates were Old or New Style – still often confused in those years. In the second place, after 25 November the month still had five more days to go, during which the first and second poems to Arbenina were written. M. always wrote poetry in spurts – every explosion was followed by a long pause. This whole batch of Leningrad poems was written in November 1920. The poems to Arbenina came at the end of November, and 'St Isaac's' in the following January. M. had arrived in Leningrad only at the end of October, and left again at the end of January. The correct order was restored in *Poems*. At the time this volume was being prepared for the press, incidentally, we still had a lot of the first drafts, many of them dated. It is in the fair copies that one most often gets mistakes in dating; when a poem is recopied for any of a number of fortuitous reasons – for submission to a publisher, for example – the date put at the end is often only approximate. Apart from anything else, however, M. always remembered very well the order in which his poems had been written. There is no excuse for getting it wrong, but no editor seems capable of understanding this.

In Moscow, in 1922, when M. was putting his *Second Book* together, he recalled 'In Petersburg We Shall Meet Again' (it was not passed by the censorship), and I asked whom it had been addressed to. His reply was in the form of a question: Didn't I think the poem was addressed to men, rather than women? This surprised me – when one is young the only 'blissful' word is love, and I was puzzled by the fact that in this poem M. also calls it 'bereft of sense'. It was unlike him to use such a word about love. He laughed at me – trust a woman to see love everywhere! On this same occasion, or a little later, he told me that the first lines had come to him in the train as he was travelling from Moscow to Petersburg. He finished the poem during the first snowfall of the winter – he had put it aside for a while, but then suddenly it came back to him and 'shaped up'. But even apart from what he told me – in case anybody should not want to take my word for it or might doubt the accuracy of my memory – a simple analysis of the sense of the poem confirms that it is not addressed to a woman. You can meet 'again' only with someone you have parted from. The only people who could 'meet again' in Petersburg were people dispersed by force of circumstances and parted from their beloved city ('it's as though we had buried the sun there'). He would not have said this to a woman like Olga Arbenina whom he had just met and who had never left Petersburg. If, what is more, one is talking about a man and woman, the Russian word *soitis* ('come together') has a very different connotation than when it is used of people meeting again after their travels. I can say, for example, that M. and I first 'came together' (*soshlis*) in May 1919, but after we had been separated by events we could talk only of returning to each other, not of 'coming together' again. When applied to a man and a woman, in fact, the word implies 'living together' or 'setting up home' together, and it would therefore be impossible to use it with 'again' in the case of a woman one had met only a few days before. If M. had any particular woman in mind here, it would rather be the one addressed in 'I Have Studied the Science of Parting'. I scarcely know anything about her, except that she had something to do with the ballet. M. met her in Moscow when he spent several days there on his way from Georgia to Petersburg. She was very homesick for her native Petersburg, and he went to the ballet with her once. But would you say to a woman: 'At a brazier we warm ourselves from boredom, / Centuries, perhaps, will pass by, / And the hands of others' happy wives / Will gather up the light ashes that remain'? This is addressed to fellow poets, not to a woman he loved, and Khardzhiev is right to compare these lines with Pushkin's 'and good wives will gather up the light ashes of their scapegrace men', though he fails to draw the relevant conclusion about M.'s meaning. Finally, I should add that the 'dear, dark eyes' of the final text cannot possibly apply to Arbenina, whose eyes were light-coloured. 'Dear shadow', 'dear dark eyes', are words that always crop up in connection with music, and for Mandelstam – as for Marina Tsvetayeva – this theme was associated with his mother. I know only one detail (which I heard from both him and her) about M.'s relations with Olga Arbenina: they too once went to the ballet together; afterwards M. took her home – this was when their quarrel took place – and despite the curfew, Arbenina left him late the same night. After this he wrote the poem about their parting: 'Because I Could Not Keep Your Hands.'

To appreciate M.'s poem about meeting again in Petersburg, one has to understand the situation that had arisen for people like us who belonged to the intelligentsia by birth and had grown up in an atmosphere of our own intimate small talk, bound together by common interests. Suddenly, without any transition we found ourselves in a new world, among utterly strange people who did not talk our language. I had the odd sensation of looking around and feeling I no longer knew anybody – the words, ideas, concepts, and emotions were quite different. Yet I was much younger than M. and had not in fact had the time to distinguish all that well between people of our own kind and outsiders. Many others have told me they experienced the same sensation – among them Zenkevich's wife, the 'Turkish bondsmaiden', who really did seem like a prisoner kept in thrall by the lumpish Misha. This was why I found her words about poor Duvakin and Siniavski so outrageous. She had 'adapted' to the world around her, and it is only in the last ten or twelve years that I have found other people – of a younger generation, needless to say – with whom I have again found a common language. Obviously, both they and their parents had survived only by lying low, never daring to utter a word. Young though he still was, M. was already set in his ways by the time of the Revolution, and the transition to the new world was thus harder for him than for me. Only bearing in mind this abrupt break of continuity between the two eras can one appreciate what he meant in the poem by 'blissful word bereft of sense'.

In love too there can be blissfully senseless words, but M. never spoke of them (except, perhaps, in letters to me). The 'blissful words' in 'Solominka' refer to the names of women loved by poets, and he simply enumerates them: 'Lenore, Solominka, Ligeia'. 'Blissful word bereft of sense' has to be read in the same way as 'blissful laughter' (in the line 'blissful laughter will break out') which returns only when someone again feels at one with the world around him. This is the bliss not of love but of communion with others, with a circle of kindred souls who understand each other instinctively. Going back after all his wanderings to Petersburg in 1920, M. still believed that everything was intact and that other wanderers scattered by the historical cataclysm would regather there, whereupon he would once more find himself among people he considered part of his circle. He had never ceased to feel nostalgic for this community of fellow spirits, one of whom – Akhmatova – was a woman. He had last seen her in Zachatyevski Street in Moscow, but in the winter of 1920–21, she was sitting things out in the Marble Palace with Shileiko, and M. did not once see her.

In 1922, in an article published in Kharkov, M. gave a more precise definition of what he meant by an intimate circle of friends, thereby, in fact, supplying a gloss on the poem we are discussing. Describing how Rozanov had fought the antiphilological spirit, which had 'issued forth from the very depths of history', he recalled the seminar he had attended at Petersburg University: 'Literature stands for public lectures, a crowd right off the street; philology is a seminar with five students who call each other by their first names, who sit and listen to their professor while branches from the familiar trees in the university garden reach in through the windows. Philology is a family – bound together, like any other family, by accents, allusions, and undertones in common use among its members. In every family even the most casually uttered word has its shade of meaning, and an endless, unique interplay of nuances is always at work' . . . If for Rozanov 'we' meant the family, for M.

it was half a dozen fellow students at a seminar, a few poets, and a handful of other friends. He recalls the seminar of the 'young professor' (as he describes him) Shishmarev, which was attended, among others, by both Gumilev and M. They read old French texts – for which M. never lost his love to the end of his days. I met Shishmarev when he was an old man. He affectionately remembered his student Osia Mandelstam as a gifted but lazy member of his seminar.

In M.'s eyes 'philology' was a profound concept of moral importance – the word, after all, is Logos, the embodiment of all meaning. A people – and this applies to the Russian people – exists only while it possesses the living word, the word untouched by necrosis: 'For Russia to forsake history, to secede from the realm of historical necessity and continuity, from freedom and a sense of purpose, would be to forsake her language. It would require only two or three generations to lose the power of speech for Russia's history to come to an end.' (In M.'s usage 'historical necessity' was allied with 'continuity', thus having nothing to do with the determinism of the Marxists.) His whole life was devoted to the defence of 'philology' in his sense – it was connected in his mind with inner freedom, but we lived in the realm of dead words shorn of meaning, good only as a means of doping the people. A living word – in the church, in the family, or in the company of the friends and fellow poets who formed his circle and upheld the same values – this was what M. hoped to find in Petersburg in 1920.

M. had a peculiar way of dividing humanity into 'men' and 'wives'. The 'men' bore all responsibility for worldly matters, while the duty of 'wives' was to weep for the dead, to consult the oracles and gather up 'the light ashes that remain' – though he never allowed me to play the second role, and it upset me to be barred as a 'wife' in this respect. Once, finding me with a fortune-teller, he chased her away and said: 'Why do you need a fortune-teller? You know everything as it is.' But what did I know then, if even now I know nothing? . . .

M. set the highest value on friendship among 'men' with its 'handshake at moments of danger', 'battle', competition for women, common language, and shared jokes. The idea of 'battle', as I have already said, struck me as comic, but he was preparing for it in earnest. In our life, civic courage is a much rarer thing than military valour. People distinguished by utter cowardice in public life could prove to be brave officers or soldiers. How was this possible? The reason is, no doubt, that at the front they were under discipline and simply carried out orders. This was not 'battle', but doing one's duty, which requires not courage, but only stamina and submission to discipline rather than to a moral imperative. Indeed, a man who has lost his personality often regains a sense of his worth as a soldier, during a war. In this country he remains under discipline in peacetime as well, continuing to obey orders even if they run counter to his ideas of honour and duty (how many people still know what these are?). Dreadful as it may seem, the Second World War brought inward relief to some people, because it put an end to the divided feelings so characteristic of peacetime. M. did not survive until the outbreak of war, and in his moment of danger there was not one 'man' ready to shake him by the hand. There was, however, a woman to mourn him: Akhmatova, the last person he thought of as a member of his circle. Her farewell kiss meant much more than anything the puny 'men' of our era would have been capable of.

In the Petersburg of 1920, M. found that the group he referred to as 'we' no longer existed. The circle of his friends had been decimated – though I suspect that it had always in any case been too embryonic to survive the first test it was put to. Gumilev was surrounded by new people with whom M. had nothing in common. After the Guild, the Sounding Seashell seemed like a caricature. The old men from the Religious-Philosophical Society were quietly dying off in their corners. A lot of writers had been put in the former Yeliseyev House,* where there were still cheerful goings-on that seemed ominous against the background of the subdued and dying city, now plunged into darkness. I know about it all from what M. told me, and if the carnival in Kiev appears in memory like a massive trampling of the fields in the still not entirely ruined Ukraine, the last flicker of gaiety in the dead Petersburg was a thousand times more macabre. We now know what kind of a junket it was. In order to give their last revelries the air of a carnival, the residents of the Yeliseyev House of Arts even held a fancy dress party, for

* See Yeliseyev, Appendix A.

which they managed to lay their hands on all kinds of cast-off theatrical costumes. M. dressed up as a Spanish grandee. When somebody asked a flunky left over from Yeliseyev's days where M. was, he replied: 'The gentleman is ironing his jabot',* and this was a source of jokes for many days to come. Everybody was equally delighted by the entry in the house register: 'Mandelstam, age 40, *pote.*'

The oil lamps flickered; heating was provided by makeshift iron stoves fuelled not with wood but with bookkeepers' ledgers – a bank had once occupied part of the building. It was a time of earnest activity in the field of popular education. Men of mature years sat on editorial boards and repertory committees, dead set to bring the whole of world literature to the masses and acquaint them with the best of human achievement from ancient Babylon to modern Paris. M. did not sit on committees and to the end of his days never became a man of mature years, but even he thought for one moment that 'culture, like the church, has been separated from the State . . . The State's present unusual attitude to culture is best characterized by the world "tolerance". At the same time we see the beginnings of an organic kind of new relationship linking State and culture in the way that the feudal princes were linked with the monasteries. The secular rulers turned to the monasteries for counsel. One need say no more.'

There was never any question of tolerance. It was simply that the State had not yet got around to dealing with literature – it was still too busy with famine and war. Leningrad was the centre of these pipe dreams. Gorki demanded that the intellectuals there be 'preserved' on the grounds that they knew *so much*. Such was the argument by which Gorki hoped to appeal to the new State: the *amount* of their knowledge. This is something that always impresses certain types of self-educated people – as do popular encyclopedias such as *Man and Woman* that tell you everything you need to know in one volume. This quantitative principle was now applied to publishing programmes, and later to school curriculums. As for 'tolerance' and the taking of 'counsel', selected members of the intelligentsia, together with their charming ladies, were assigned to

* There is an untranslatable pun here. The footman mistakes 'jabot' for the Russian word *zhaba* ('toad').

'cultural' duties and given translations to do, though some might still have been capable of independent thought and work. The intelligentsia was thus kept busy with so-called voluntary activity. M. would never for a moment have been taken in were it not for the presence of two people on all these committees and subcommittees: Blok and Gumilev. Who could resist, with 'counsellors' such as these?

M.'s own 'counsellor' until recently had been Florenski, and the news of his arrest and subsequent deportation came as a devastating blow.

At the beginning of the twenties one could keep alive only on the rations issued by various public bodies, and there was a constant scramble to get them. The militia proved to be a powerful patron of the arts – both Georgi Ivanov and Gumilev were fed by it. M. was also given a militia ration, either because there were no more 'academic' ones left or because he was thought unworthy of such favoured treatment. It was up to Gorki, the protector and patron in chief, to decide who got how much. He held all the keys to the modest, very relative comforts we enjoyed, and for this reason there was always a stream of people going to him to beg for things. When M. arrived after his endless wanderings and two stretches in White prisons, he found he was eligible for a little State charity. The Union of Poets applied to Gorki on his behalf for a pair of trousers and a sweater. Gorki agreed to the sweater, but the trousers he crossed out with his own hand: even then there was no nonsense about 'egalitarianism', and everybody got what the amount of his knowledge entitled him to – M.'s was not enough to earn him a pair of trousers. Gumilev let him have an extra pair of his. M. swore to me that walking around in Gumilev's trousers, he felt unusually strong and manly.

Akhmatova also turned to Gorki for help, asking him to find her work and get her a ration, however small. She too had been refused an 'academic' ration and lived with Shileiko on the salted herring that he got from the Academy. Gorki explained to Akhmatova that she would get only the most beggarly of rations for doing office work of some kind, and then took her to see his collection of carpets. They were no doubt magnificent – you could buy things for a song at that time. When M. and I were leaving Moscow in

1921, we sold somebody a Tekin carpet of fairly good quality (we delivered it in a baby carriage). But my carpet was a quite ordinary one, not the sort you want for a collection. Akhmatova looked at Gorki's carpets, said how nice they were, and went away empty-handed. As a result of this, I believe, she took a permanent dislike to carpets. They smelled too much of dust and a kind of prosperity strange in a city that was dying so catastrophically.

M. did not stay very long – three and a half months, no more – in Petersburg. In February he fled. Even if he had not got a letter from Liuba Ehrenburg telling him I was still in Kiev – though at a new address – he would not have stayed in any case; of this I am sure. His last impression was the thunder of guns from Kronstadt* and 'a touching rite owed to us all – a requiem mass at Isaac's'. Of M.'s friends – those of whom he said 'we' – none except Akhmatova was honoured with a requiem mass, and she not 'at Isaac's', now closed and sealed.

8   Disintegration

M. and I lingered in rich and happy-go-lucky Georgia for about six months. The moment we crossed the Georgian frontier† in our compartment for the 'mentally ill', we realized we had come to a different world. The train stopped and all the passengers, led by the engineer and the conductors, rushed to some peasant carts standing a little way off with barrels on them. When the train moved again, we were all happy and light-headed from wine – it was sold freely in Georgia, and a whole bottle cost no more than a hunk of *lavash*. The sun, this rollicking train-load of happy, tipsy people, was a very far cry from sullen, grimy Moscow, where a handful of flour from the Ukraine was like manna from heaven, and the street urchins sold loose 'ARA'‡ tobacco on the street – every cigarette

* The rising against the Bolshevik regime at the naval base of Kronstadt, opposite Petersburg, was crushed in March 1921.

† The independent Georgian government was overthrown and the country brought under Bolshevik rule in February 1921.

‡ American Relief Administration, led by Herbert Hoover, which administered aid to Russia in the famine after the Civil War (1921–3).

we smoked came from their frozen, red little mitts. We travelled through Georgia as free as birds, strange and incomprehensible people who had fled from a destitute country to a rich and indifferent one. It must have been just like this for the refugees from Soviet Russia in opulent Constantinople. I came to realize in those days how bitter is the stranger's bread. Occasionally Kandelaki, the Minister of Education – or rather the 'commissar', as he was called then – would write us out a slip for a small pittance we had earned by translations, but it was always vetoed by the ascetic Brekhnichev, the Russian delegate attached to the generous and easy-going Georgian. It was said that Brekhnichev was an unfrocked priest and that he did not get away with such stinginess towards people who were 'in' with the regime. All I have left of some comic verse written about them by M. in those days is the line, 'Brekhnichev serves him as a watchdog (*sobaki*)', and the word that rhymes with it at the end of the preceding line, Kandelaki.

M. was not downcast; we drank Teliani wine, had somewhere to live and various people to talk to. Once we tried to leave and actually got places in a nice clean freight car, which would have meant a journey of two to three weeks. Trains composed of converted freight cars were often held up for ages at the main junctions, and the station-master had to have his palm greased before he would provide a locomotive. The stations were great places for trade and barter, and we reckoned on being able to get enough to eat by exchanging our wretched possessions for food – but this would be possible only when we got over the frontier into Russia; Georgia was too well off for us to find takers there. The doors of the freight car had been slammed shut, and the train started to roll. At once the car was transformed: in no time at all a table was improvised from suitcases and covered with a rag in lieu of a tablecloth. Magnificent food and wine were produced. As the only woman, I was seated in the place of honour. The feast began, but at the first station the train moved off and left our car standing – we had not noticed as it was uncoupled. The Georgians rushed to the doors but could not open them. A moment later, the doors were flung wide and in came several armed men headed by a stocky, broad-shouldered civilian. He had the face of a eunuch and was wearing huge glasses which made me think he must also be blind. In a high, castrato voice he announced that he was a representative of the Extraordinary Commission for Combating Speculation and Counter-revolution.* The armed men carried out a search, but showed no interest in our wretched stuff. The Georgians, as we now learned, were dental mechanics; the suitcases they were taking to Moscow were filled with medical supplies and materials for making false teeth. They were also suspected of smuggling gold. While this was going on, our car suddenly began to move again – back to Tiflis. The Georgians were taken away under guard, and we were simply released. This was the first time I had ever witnessed an arrest; until then I had seen nothing more than endless searches. The hospitable Georgians, whose feast had been interrupted so brutally, were now deathly pale. I could only hope they would manage to bribe the grim-faced eunuch and be set free again . . . On several other occasions I was to see these patrols going through the trains, taking bundles from the women. This was what they called the fight against black marketeering.

So we again found ourselves stranded in Tiflis, making out as best we could, drinking Teliani and eating scalded cream, ewe's milk cheese, and *lavash*. Once, in the bazaar, we got caught up in an immense *shakhse-vakhse* procession. It was the last to take place – the next year it was forbidden for good. Half-naked people walked along to the monotonous beating of Eastern drums and rhythmically scourged themselves with leather thongs. They moved in regular square-shaped formations and were followed by others holding daggers and making rhythmical movements of a more complicated kind: keeping the same regular formation, with perfect timing, they raised first their right and then their left legs, striking themselves with their daggers, always in the same place. Had it not been for the blood trickling from their wounds one might have thought it was ballet. Then came camels, donkeys, and horses, all beautifully caparisoned, carrying women and children who represented the family of Mohammed's brother; the whole of this pageant was in memory of his murder. A large horse came by bearing a dove, and then another with its rider swaying in a curious manner. He had a dagger stuck in his back, and the fresh blood gleamed on his white robe. The crowds of onlookers kept drawing

* The full name of the Cheka.

back in horror – and we with them. I wanted to leave, but M. refused to budge, making me stay until the endless procession was over. All the participants kept shouting out two short words in chorus – they served to synchronize the whole intricate and gory ballet. It is said that in former years, any European who happened to get caught up in this Muslim crowd would immediately have been torn limb from limb. The procession was making for a hill outside the city where other rites of some kind were supposed to take place, but we decided not to venture any farther. The next day, all the shopkeepers in the bazaar had bandages. The man who kept the tea-room where we always drank wonderful Persian tea in small glasses was likewise covered in bandages. I don't know whether it is the Sunnites or the Shiites who go in for *shakhse-vakhse*, or what these two words mean (they are the ones shouted out during the procession – hence its name), but it did help me to understand why Armenia, 'with shame and pain', turned away 'from the bearded cities of the East' . . . Yet all the same, however vicious the self-laceration and bloodletting may have looked, nobody in the procession was any the worse, apart from a few scratches and superficial wounds which were then bandaged. This was all there was to it. Europeans have been known to make a more formidable showing . . .

For a while we got on close terms with the embassy of the RSFSR* in Georgia. The ambassador, Legran, was an old schoolmate of Gumilev's. He appointed M. to the embassy staff, which entitled us to two meals a day on the lines of those supplied by staff canteens in Moscow. We used to go to the embassy, chat with Legran, and then take away our meals in covered dishes, together with the newspapers from which M. was supposed to make cuttings as part of his official work. The embassy had no need of a press reader, and the whole thing was quite bogus – as was our entitlement to meals, and the embassy itself. The newspapers came from the north or from abroad with the speed of a

---

*The Russian Soviet Republic, to which the non-Russian areas like the Ukraine and Transcaucasia (later Georgia, Armenia, and Azerbaidzhan) were joined in the early twenties to form the Soviet Union in 1922. Diplomatic relations were maintained between Moscow and the nominally independent republics like Georgia.

tortoise, and Legran got his news not from them but from the Transcaucasian Central Committee, which was in touch with Moscow by telephone, or through myriads of couriers.

One day Legran, who was usually phlegmatic and restrained, rushed out of his office to meet us and took us to his private apartment. There he told us about the execution of Gumilev. He was really scared, though he managed to keep his diplomatic composure. Since this was the last time we ever saw him, I do not know whether he later moved up in the ranks to something better than Soviet ambassador to Georgia. His wife, to all appearances a pleasant and friendly woman, butted in to say she had never liked Gumilev, describing him as standoffish, rude, and impossible to make out. Legran's wife was thus something of a pioneer: in those early years, people had not yet learned to disown the victims so quickly, saying – in all sincerity – what bad characters they had been, and how wrong-headed. Later everybody behaved like this, with an enviable display of directness and honesty. The stories of 'honest Soviet citizens' about M. are an example of the same kind of behaviour; these fabrications still circulate, giving comfort to all those who simply looked on while he was done to death. What was so bad, they ask, about finishing off an absurd and conceited crackpot like him? Even the gullible, examining such legends, occasionally shake their heads and wonder how the quirks of character mentioned by his contemporaries can possibly be reconciled with the verse that flowed so freely from him. What today would be seen as inner freedom, profundity, independence of mind, and straightforwardness was then looked on – quite sincerely – as the petulance of a crank . . . Legran's wife meant every word she said. The effect on us of these remarks, the like of which we had never heard before, about a man who had just been executed was so strong that we had no heart to continue going to the embassy for our meals and newspapers. We left with our food on this occasion, but never went back. Soon a soldier appeared; he had been sent by the embassy to collect their dishes. We never saw the Legrans again.

'Now where can we go?' M. asked, adding that he would not return to Petersburg. The death of Gumilev – without benefit of a requiem at St Isaac's – had finally turned it into a city of the dead.

There is an allusion to this in one of M.'s late poems: 'Petersburg, I have addresses / at which I can find the voices of the dead.' Now that his native city had become impossible for him, he was utterly opposed to going back to the north. With the death of Gumilev, his circle of friends had fallen apart, the community to which he had belonged was finished.

Despite having nowhere to go, we nevertheless decided to leave, simply because there was no place we could stay in. On New Year's Eve, 1922, we boarded a steamer lying off Sukhumi. It was called the *Dmitri*, and we had been allowed on without tickets by a woman commissar, formerly the ship's nurse, a large, friendly type who coped magnificently with the rowdy horde of demobilized Red Army men on board. Very much the worse for drink, they demanded to know why she had hung a portrait of Lieutenant Schmidt in her cabin above Lenin's, and they were also very curious about us: who were these two people she had put on a mattress outside her door, and why was she hiding them from the ticket collectors? In actual fact she had made no effort at all to 'hide' us, but was simply shielding us behind her broad back, telling the ticket collectors to leave us in peace – which they did, since they were anyway utterly helpless in the face of the large numbers of other passengers travelling without tickets.

On the deck of the *Dmitri* I saw half-drunk, half-crazed soldiers writhing in convulsions due to bayonet wounds they had received during the Civil War. The war was still going on, and demobilization had so far affected only the sick and the wounded. Really serious cases, such as those who had lost limbs, were transported by train, and most of the men who had swarmed aboard the *Dmitri*, though unfit for further military service, were able to move around quite freely. They were the sort who, on arriving back home, became very active in their native villages and small towns: having been politically indoctrinated by their commissars and commanders, they now appeared as apostles of the new order 'at the local level'. The war invalid in Platonov's *Pit* is not a product of the author's idle imagination, but represents what was a major factor in the life of the provinces. Many of them came to an untimely end because they had got too used to settling all arguments with their fists. Others, when they had been elbowed aside from power at the local level by the influx of fresher forces, raised an outcry that was heard throughout the country: 'What did we fight for?'

The crowd on board our ship divided up into small groups, and at the centre of each stood a self-appointed agitator. Sometimes the group gathered around one of the soldiers who had fallen down, his body convulsed and his head twisted back, as he thrashed about on the wooden deck. In a raucous voice he re-enacted the moment when he had got his wound, shouting orders and slogans, hurling himself into the fray, cursing the 'White scum' and vowing not to spare even his own father if need be... Four of his comrades would hold him to stop him hitting his head on the deck, while a fifth would try – usually without success – to push a spoon into his mouth, because with so much cursing his tongue would keep lolling out and instead of words he could utter only hoarse moans. The re-enactment would end with a stream of filthy language – this was the moment when a 'sister' had run up to him in the middle of the battle, and he told her what he thought of her. The people standing around would now sigh with relief – once it had reached this point, the fit must be nearly over. And sure enough, the convulsions began to lessen, the man calmed down and started to fall asleep. They then left him alone, but meanwhile, at the other end of the ship another crazed invalid would already be lying on the deck, starting to writhe and wail in the same way. It was like what had happened to the whole country, exhausted by the bloodletting and frenzied invective of the Civil War. I believe nobody can win in this kind of conflict, because even the victor, driven out of his mind by all the fratricidal hatred, is also drained of blood and reduced to a state of epilepsy. How many times must this have been said already? Why does it always fall on deaf ears? With his large, boyish eyes – because he was the older of us I did not at that time realize just how young he was – M. saw and heard everything. Sometimes he said: 'Nadia, don't look ... Nadia, don't listen,' and at other times: 'Just look what they're doing ...' Once or twice he said: 'It will all pass', but more often he was less hopeful: 'They all talk exactly alike, whether they have fits or not: you can't tell one from the other.' It was only too true. They all talked like epileptics. I was to witness many worse things, first together with M. and through his eyes, and later without him, through my own eyes which he had taught to see and understand.

We disembarked at Novorossiisk to the wild howling of a north-easterly gale. We were nearly blown off our feet by it, and shivered with cold after the six months we had spent in the splendid climate of the south (where one moment we were overcome by heat, and the next, we might be splashing in our elegant wooden sandals through puddles covered by a thin film of ice). But we were not worried by the cold now that we had suddenly ceased to feel like émigrés.

I often have to listen to the complaints of former émigrés, who were so lucky never to be killed or hauled off at night to the incredible jails of the twentieth century, but I do not close my ears to them, because I know from my own experience how bitter the émigré's bread can be in foreign parts. I discovered this in Georgia. The people of my generation had a choice: either the bitter bread of the stranger or a repast with death at home. Neither of these alternatives was a 'lesser evil'. Evil is never greater or lesser – evil is always simply evil. But at least in Russia everybody speaks Russian, and this was a great blessing. It was no accident that in an article written on our way back to Moscow M. sang the praises of the Russian language. Once back in Russian-speaking territory again, he keenly felt the power of his mother tongue.

Unfortunately, we all came to experience the extreme mutual estrangement which results when speakers of the same language no longer form a real community. It can reach such a pitch that people entirely cease to understand each other. M. had lost those he referred to as 'we'. Even talking about the two of us, he no longer said 'we', but 'you and I': 'You and I will sit in the kitchen for a while,' or: 'How dreadful for you and me!' . . . The union of equals, the men and one woman who could say 'we' of themselves, had fallen apart with the death of Gumilev – all that was left was a never-ending, inner dialogue with him.

As we travelled north now, it was not to Petersburg but to Moscow.

9 En Route

In Novorossiisk we spent the night sleeping on desks in the offices of the local newspaper, and then moved on again. In those years, wherever we went, we had young friends who knew M. and were always ready to provide him with a night's lodging, train tickets, or a little money. He found he had friends of this kind on the newspaper in Novorossiisk. We next spent a month in Rostov, where M. published a couple of articles in the local newspaper. In February we got places in a special rail coach to Kharkov which had been put at the disposal of a surgeon, Professor Trinkler – he had been summoned to perform an operation on some important official – and we arrived there in no time at all. Special coaches were a sign of high status and were always the first to be coupled to the locomotive, unlike the wretched freight cars in which most people travelled. Kharkov was a transit point via which hordes of people from the south were trying to reach Moscow.

M. was met on our arrival by some poetry enthusiasts. They felt out of things in Kharkov and were heading for Moscow, where they were bent on staking their claims as writers. The Civil War had thrown up a special type of person who was impatient to tell you his experiences, or get them down on paper. None of them had time for considered opinions about events, the significance of which was thus lost on them. They were concerned only with specific incidents, picturesque or amusing details, surface phenomena, the pretty patterns in the froth. One of them, Valentin Katayev, who then cut a rakish and colourful figure, tried to make a bet with me: which of us would 'conquer' Moscow first. Not aspiring to conquer Moscow, nor harbouring any other ambition, except perhaps to paint a couple of still lifes, I refused the bet. Probably under M.'s influence, I was already quite indifferent to publicity and self-promotion. M. was clear in his mind that poetry is a purely personal affair – this was the secret of his strength. Communing with oneself alone, one says only things that really matter. If they also prove of value to others, so much the better, but this depends on the person who says them and how much there is to him. M. never paused to think about who he was and what he was worth. At the same time he felt no need to apologize for himself, his ideas, or such things as had been granted him in life. It is preposterous to suggest, as somebody does, that he was talking about himself in the line: 'Ashamed, strange fellow, of his poverty / Yevgeni breathes in petrol fumes and curses fate.' Nor was he referring to himself in the phrase: 'a pedestrian proud, yet modest withal' – he liked walking, and he admired the world of which automobiles were also a part. He was alluding here to Parnok, who was simultaneously self-assertive and shy, like a mountain goat. Even if M. had a tiny little bit of Parnok in him, it disappeared while he was very young. There might have been something of the kind immediately after he left school, while he was abroad, but only for a brief moment, to be remembered later with a smile. But never, for one second, could M. have thought of saying about himself that he 'cursed fate'. Together we went through all kinds of ordeals and endured terrible disasters. It sometimes happened that I cursed life and fate, and everything under the sun. But it was I who did so, not he. I never once heard him say such things. It was not in his nature. Whether he was in rags or well dressed, with money or without, indignant or happy, whether in moments of wild jealousy or complete harmony, whether boisterous or subdued, whether writing poetry or reduced to silence – he would never, in any circumstances, have cursed fate. He took life as it was, would have no truck with any kind of theodicy and was certainly not ashamed of his poverty, since he regarded himself as a rich man: 'Who has not warmth enough under his glove / to travel all of harlot Moscow's streets?' And then, we were forever having banquets: even something out of a tin, or a little buckwheat laid before us on a plank or suitcase – whatever served as a table – we considered a feast. The fate of St Alexis* really did seem more enviable to him than that of any banker, dignitary, or Soviet specialist† (particularly of the literary species) . . .

In Kharkov he made his first literary earnings – much more considerable ones than in Rostov, because here there was not only a

* *Hope Against Hope*, pages 287 and 302.
†The term is used in the sense of members of the former professional classes who were employed by the new regime.

newspaper but a publishing house, albeit as poverty-stricken as everything else in the country. It was the brainchild of Rakovski's sister, a thin, dark-haired woman, rather like a nun, whom for some reason I remember only in profile, as though she had no substance. When she started her publishing concern, M. wrote an article for her 'On the Nature of the Word', and his first piece of prose, a sketch called 'The Fur Coat', part of which appeared in the local paper. The copy of the paper which had this piece of prose has been lost, together with all of the archives belonging to Rakovski's sister. 'On the Nature of the Word' was published after we left Rostov, and we were sent an offprint. This, later found by the secret police in our trunk in May 1934, was confiscated, but some people have kept copies. The epigraph to the article was added by the Kharkov publishers. It wasn't there in the original. But it may as well stay – as a memento of the friendship of two poets.

When I saw Rakovski's sister, I felt quite astonished: how could such a woman be 'with them'? In those years of utter mental confusion, a woman like this could be with anybody and anywhere, and who knows what in fact she really was. You could not judge by appearances. I imagine it was the same in her case as with everybody else, and I may well have taken her for a nun because of my inexperience and ignorance of people. All the same, it would be nice to think that an ascetic profile is not without meaning. Perhaps, on the other hand, my memory is playing tricks; or it could be, as M. remarked at the time, that we were just not used to the Latin-Rumanian type – European features which contrasted oddly with those, say, of our wonderful broad-boned ship's nurse-turned-commissar. All I can say for sure is that in the demented crowds of those years one sometimes caught a glimpse of faces marked by this kind of asceticism – which suggests that among the crowd (though not among the leaders) there was some sense of inner conviction.

In Kharkov we were told about certain new developments already known to a lot of people: news of the theory of relativity and of Freud, delayed because of the war, had only now reached Russia. Everybody was talking about them, but actual information was vague and amorphous. The talk about writers who had already managed to stake their claims was rather more concrete. Pilniak was then all the rage – he was having his day. Everybody was excited by the new subject matter. In Georgia we had grown unaccustomed to conversation because we were outsiders there and talk was always between the initiated, among whom we could never hope to count ourselves. In Kharkov we were struck by the fact that nobody *conversed* any more. Conversation had come to an end – forever. On the other hand, there was no end of *talkers*, all vying with one another to tell their stories.

We were quite well off for clothes, such as they were. The Co-operative in Batumi, playing the part of patron, had rewarded M. for a lecture on Blok with enough material to make a suit and two dresses for me. In 1934 (at the end of April), M. recalled in a poem how we had 'a dress made by a poor seamstress, / in a balconied canyon above the lemon-coloured Kura'. In May this poem was confiscated together with other manuscripts and it is lost: we were not able to reconstitute it later because it had been too fresh. The fur coat which prompted the writing of his sketch was made of moulting raccoon and had been bought in the local bazaar.* There were cruel frosts that winter, and having come from the south, we suffered from the cold.

M. noticed that there was a new mood in the air: everybody now dreamed of a strong regime, so that they could rest and digest the experience of the years of chaos. This craving for an iron hand to rule them had affected everybody in the country. They were still hesitant to say outright that it was time to curb the population, but the thought was implicit in everything that was said. It slipped out in such phrases as: 'It's time for all the fools to go . . .' There was growing contempt and hatred for all forms of democracy and particularly for those who had 'cleared out'. The legend that Kerenski had fled disguised as a woman was especially popular. All the pre-requisites for a fully fledged dictatorship had already arisen – without even the pretence of an appeal to the masses. It was by now quite clear who the victors were; and, as always, people were bowing and scraping to them. The older generation, still democratically minded, provoked the scorn of the young. A year or two later, I was walking with M. over a bridge on the Neva when he pointed out an old man in rags who was barely able to shuffle along. It was

* On the ultimate fate of this coat see *Hope Against Hope*, page 232.

a well-known historian whose weighty tomes I had read as a schoolgirl. His historical ideas were naïve and distinguished for their moderation: such people were the first to perish. Nobody heard about his death – he must have died somewhere in a hospital or at home in an unheated room. He was an intellectual, and for thirty-year-olds clawing their way to the top, there was no greater term of contempt. We had already heard it used like this in Kharkov by all the live wires eager to stake their claims in Moscow . . .

From Kharkov we set out for Kiev, probably at the very beginning of March (there was still much confusion in dates between Old and New Style), but at any event it was still very cold. We travelled in a so-called staff coach, for which only people on very important official business could buy tickets. We had wangled them through the writers' organization, which was then only just getting on its feet but was already displaying unusual ingenuity. Our fellow passengers were either administrators or, perhaps, Party functionaries, but in any case clearly people of the new type. They wore good-quality boots and jackets made of real leather. They did not drink or sniff cocaine – which was extremely widespread in the first years of the Revolution – and talked hardly at all among themselves, or with us. The only thing they permitted themselves was to pull my leg a little. I was lying on the top bunk, and they looked to me like telegraphists – both the two on the lower bunks and the others who visited them from the next compartment. They took me for an upper-class young lady, and whenever M. left the compartment, they jumped up and said that girls like me should be grabbed by the hair and made to learn how to type. This was their idea of a joke. But I didn't find it funny and had an eerie feeling that a new and incomprehensible world was already closing in on us, right here in this 'staff coach'. They were starved of female company because of the war and had still not been given their own secretaries, which was why they paid all this attention to me. M. looked at them with curiosity. He noticed at once that they didn't talk among themselves, only occasionally quoting an article or a newspaper. 'They have nothing to talk about,' he said and wondered who they might be. Some of them could have been organizers of almost any branch of the economy or administration, including security, but what exactly each of them in particular was doing we just could not make out. They were all cut to the same pattern.

We later hardly ever had any contact with this class of people, so both of us never forgot our sole encounter with these specimens of the organizers of the new order. Their uncommunicativeness, deriving from a new kind of discipline, was ominous and frightening. Such people were the material for an *apparat* which had overcome or spurned human weakness and functioned like clockwork, according to instructions, whatever their nature. This *apparat* has stood the test of time and exists to the present day, even though the individual members of it have constantly been replaced by more efficient ones, like cogs in a machine, their predecessors being thrown out to moulder in concentration camps or in the provinces.

We used to think of arriving in a new town as a kind of game. We had passed through Moscow, Rostov, Baku, Batumi, and Tiflis, and now, going in the reverse direction, Novorossiisk, Rostov, and Kharkov. We seemed to spend all our lives coming to strange cities, and I went on doing it without M. – but then it was no longer a game. In those early years the trains sometimes came right into the stations, but more often than not they stopped somewhere outside. Then we had to heave our possessions on our shoulders and make our way towards the city along country lanes, or main roads and streets. The first street was always greeted with a sigh of relief. Sometimes you could find a horse cab or a cart, but that would be a rare stroke of luck. I can still remember our arrival at the station square in Kiev, but I have no recollection of how we got from there to my parents' home. Perhaps a few street-cars were running by then. I can only remember knocking on the door and seeing it open. My parents welcomed us as though we had come back from the dead. Going away meant disappearing into the void. They had not received a single letter or message from us, though letters occasionally got through from Moscow, where my brother lived (by this time, going to Moscow did not mean you were cut off from those you had left behind).

Kiev proved to be strangest of all to us, even more foreign than Georgia. To offset the fact that the Ukrainian and Russian languages are so close to each other, the Ukraine was trying to accentuate its distinctiveness with particular zeal. Later I found a sure way of telling Ukrainians from Russians: I would ask, 'Which is your capital, Kiev or Moscow?' Everywhere, all over the country, you can hear the southern Russian or Ukrainian accent, but only real dyed-in-the-wool Ukrainians will reply that Kiev is their capital and pronounce it with a broad *i* sound all their own, giving you a canny look of a peculiar kind as they do so. What to M.'s ear sounded like an echo of Ancient Russian was to them their native language, separate and quite distinct from Russian. It was always a puzzle to me how these strong-willed, energetic, and in many ways cruel people, with their love of liberty and music, their own peculiarities and sense of community, never created a state, while the easygoing, somewhat anti-social Russians, though scattered over enormous territories, devised an extraordinary and highly effective state system, which in essence has never changed – right from Muscovite Russia to the present day (its essential feature is the total gulf between rulers who do exactly what they want to do and the ruled who just put up with it, grumbling slightly). This cannot be explained simply by the Ukraine's geographical position – between Russia and Poland. I have always believed with Kliuchevski that the destruction of Kievan Russia by the Tartars, when it was developing as a brilliant European state – as witness Vladimir Monomakh, Yaroslav the Wise, the Cathedral of St Sophia, and the city itself on the steep bank of the Dnieper – was a calamitous turning point in Russian history. M. never gave a thought to all this. He liked the colourful and lively city on the Dnieper for its own sake, respected Kliuchevski, and had read the 'Testament', 'Russian Truth', and *Poltava** – but this last only once. Without him I never thought my ideas on this subject out any further, and it all remains a puzzle for me. All the same, I am glad that *my* capital is Moscow, not Kiev – my native language, after all, is Russian, and if the Jews are going to be slaughtered in both places, better it happen to me in Moscow. In Moscow there will

---

* 'Testament,' the 'Instruction' of Vladimir Monomakh (1153–1225), Grand Duke of Kiev, to his children, is one of the finest works of early Russian literature; 'Russian Truth', the early Russian legal code, was compiled mostly during the reign of Monomakh's predecessor, Yaroslav the Wise (978–1054); Pushkin's long poem *Poltava* (1828) is about Peter the Great's victory over the Swedes under Charles XII at Poltava, despite the support they received from the Ukrainian Hetman Mazepa (1644–1709).

always be some kindly old soul who will try to stop the mob with a few good-humoured oaths: 'Don't you touch this one,' she will say, 'you so-and-so sons of bitches!' It will be easier to die to the familiar sound of Russian swearing.

From Kiev we went on to Moscow. Before buying a ticket for a 'special' coach (not a 'staff' one this time), we had to pay a visit to the Register Office to obtain a marriage certificate. As soon as we arrived in Moscow we lost it. I am not even sure, in fact, that we got it on that particular occasion. It may have happened in preparation for a later journey to Moscow; the only reason for getting it was that the commandant of the train, whenever it was, had said he was tired of taking women who were 'wives' only during the journey: 'I won't take you without a certificate,' he had said. We otherwise attached no importance whatsoever to the registration of our marriage, since it was a totally meaningless formality. Come to think of it, it was spring when we went to the Register Office, but at the time of our departure from Kiev that year the weather was bitterly cold, and my father travelled with us to Moscow. I do, however, remember that Benedikt Livshitz went to the Register Office with us. The first time we got there too late; the young lady in charge was already picking up her things and putting her lipstick on, about to clear off home. With his usual asinine wit, which he privately imagined to be Rabelaisian, Benedikt tried to persuade the young lady to stay a moment longer and perform the marriage ceremony there and then 'because the young people cannot wait'. She took one look at us with her cold, experienced eye and said: 'So I see – but they can wait until tomorrow.' . . . We got our piece of paper for the train commandant only the next day. In the middle fifties I obtained a court order to say I was M.'s legal wife. People of my generation have no trouble getting the courts to issue these: we all either forgot to 'register' or have lost the piece of paper. It was quite simply of no importance . . .

By the end of March (what Style?) we were in Moscow. There was no question of returning to Petersburg. M. wouldn't go there even to see his father. He just hadn't the heart to return to the 'darkness of nonbeing'. So we settled in Moscow, which was a strange and alien city to him. (He had already earlier written the line: 'All is foreign to us in the unseemly capital' – by 'us' here, I think he meant people of Petersburg.) It was easier for him to begin a new life in Moscow than it would have been in his native, but now ravaged Petersburg. Even if Moscow too was ravaged – and very considerably – it was not in the same way as Petersburg. It was also much less noticeable: Moscow was constantly replenished by an influx of new people, and we could see it growing visibly, almost by the hour – though this growth was not expressed in new houses and buildings (nothing was being built at all; everything was crumbling and falling apart), only in the ever increasing numbers of people who flocked into Moscow from the four corners of the country. The city transport was already being patched up after a fashion, although the chief means of getting around the vast city was still on foot or by horse cab. Cabbies were outrageously expensive, and we had as yet no patron who could pay our fares for us.

The real Muscovites were swallowed up by hordes of newcomers and found themselves in a small minority in their own city. The gruff Moscow accent was scarcely heard any more. Once, going into a chandler's store to ask the way, we were delighted to receive the excellent advice to go out *na ploshchad*,* and then turn off in the direction we needed. The janitors still remembered the old way of speaking – but none of them ever spoke like Pasternak's janitor in *Dr Zhivago*. Such a language never existed, any more than that of his Siberian grocer's wife. Pasternak himself spoke a wonderful Russian, but it was something all of his own: he sang, mooed, boomed . . . He was a Muscovite born and bred, and as a child already spoke of going to collect *gryby*.† Jewish children who grew up in Moscow were particularly quick to pick up the city's accent, but Pasternak also had a born sense of music which gave his speech an orchestral quality. M. used to tell me that Akhmatova 'works only with her voice', that is, always paid very careful attention to the sound of her verse. The same was true of Pasternak, and partly of M. too, who heard his own voice, as well as the sounds reverberating in his mind.

---

*'Onto the square', as opposed to the standard 'into the street', for 'outside'.

† For normal *griby*.

We were not Muscovites, but strangers to the city, and we found it hard to get used to, hungry, rationed (as it still was), uncouth, and overrun by vast hordes of people all speaking with different voices. Yet even so, with the adaptability of youth, we managed to feel at home and gradually grew accustomed to the 'unseemly' and noisy capital ...

10 Some Contemporaries

Before I go on to the many grim and painful things ahead, I should like to say a few words in a lighter vein, not to be taken amiss, about some of the poets with whom M. had dealings at one time or another. He never once quoted in conversation anything said about poetry by Viacheslav Ivanov, Sologub, Voloshin, and other poets of the older generation. His attitude to them was even rather comic, being one of outward deference combined with inner disrespect. Living as they did in an atmosphere of real adulation, it was no wonder they were irritated by this stripling with his tongue in his cheek. The only poet M. looked up to as his teacher was Annenski, and he was very fond of his work. In fact, however, he conceived his apprenticeship in broader terms: 'I learn from everybody – even from Benedikt Livshitz,' he said once, after writing his poem about the woman singer with a low voice.* I have already mentioned that in reading over poets he always picked out the felicitous lines, ignoring the rest. He taught me that even people who had written only two or three real poems (such as Mei) were part of Russian poetry, occupying a legitimate and honourable place in it. The only two in whose work, with the best will in the world, he could finding nothing at all were Maikov and Briusov. In my presence he once leafed through some of Voloshin's verse and put it down with a sigh. He could not stand the cloying richness of it. Nor did he believe in Voloshin's hospitality – it was too much of a good thing. In Sologub he looked for lines with a lighter touch, the more ethereal ones ... But I don't want to talk about judgements and influences, only about a few personal encounters ...

* See *Hope Against Hope*, page 223.

M. was still a schoolboy when he went to see Annenski, who received him with great friendliness and attention, advising him to go in for translation as a way of acquiring technique. But nothing came of this. When he tried his hand at translating some Mallarmé, one of the lines came out as: 'A young mother who suckles on waking,'* and he used to tell this as a funny story against himself. He went to see Annenski on his bicycle, and for some reason that escapes me he felt this had been very naughty and churlish of him.

He used to tell me that Sologub always sold his verse for different prices, depending on the quality – he would sort it into three grades or so. The idea appealed to M. enormously, but whenever he sold his own verse, he always asked the highest rate for everything – not that he thought all his poems of equal worth, but he simply lacked the energy to sort them out, and also there were never enough of them. He once took me to see Sologub, who greeted us with the words: 'One can already see the toothmark of the times on you.' When he lived in Tsarskoye Selo in a little boarding-house with Akhmatova (this was in the early spring of 1925, from March on), Sologub often came to see her – he was vacationing near by with some friends. He always gave a nod of recognition to M., but once he shouted at me because the doorbell was out of order: I had rushed to help when I saw him pressing on the lifeless button, and he must have taken me for the maid. Maids were a splendid type of people, and I wasn't offended. The old man was very odd and grumpy.

M. told me several funny stories about Viacheslav Ivanov. In addition to those reproduced by Akhmatova, I can mention one more: Two people were travelling in a horse cab and reciting verse by Ivanov; the cabbie turned around and said: 'Poisonous prettiness.' I am sure it was an invention from beginning to end: the cabbie, his remark, the two passengers . . . On hearing this tale, I asked: 'And who paid the cabbie?' If he really said that, he deserved enough for a good measure of vodka.

The stories about Briusov were of a different kind: the venerable maestro himself figured as a prankster, not as the butt of jokes in-

---

* There is a *double entendre* in the Russian: *so sna* ('on waking') and *sosna* ('pine tree').

vented by the disrespectful young. Once – before my time – Briusov called M. into his office (it was at the very beginning of the Soviet era, and I don't know what the institution was) and went on for a long while praising M.'s verse, finding every possible good quality in it. The joke was that, reciting long passages to illustrate his points, Briusov quoted not a single line by M. – it was all from the work of an eccentric Kiev poet Makkaveiski, who always introduced chunks of Latin into his erudite verse . . . M. listened to Briusov in silence, thanked him warmly for his kind words, and left without showing the least sign of consternation or anger. I think he was in fact much more surprised than irritated: for the sake of his ten minutes' fun, Briusov must have learned by heart at least fifty difficult and not very memorable lines. It was a practical joke very much in the style of the pre-Revolutionary years, but was it really worth all that trouble?

We learned about another of Briusov's little tricks from someone who served with him on the committee for the allotment of academic rations.* After our return from Georgia, those two woebegone, kindhearted, old Marxist fuddy-duddies, Kogan and Fritsche, raised the question of giving M. an academic ration. This was just before the beginning of NEP, or during the very first days, when two or three fantastically expensive stores were opened. The first of them was called Estomac – what it sold I never found out, since we all still lived only on our rations. Hearing M. mentioned as a candidate for an academic ration, Briusov pricked up his ears and managed – not without difficulty – to get him put down for a second-category one. The interesting thing is the way he did it: he pretended to confuse M. with a lawyer of the same name who had once been an active member – I believe – of the Cadet party. (I later met the wife of this namesake when we both stood in line outside the Butyrka† jail in 1938 – he had been brought there from the hospital, where he was being treated for a serious heart ailment.) As a Bolshevik, Briusov said, he could not see his way to giving a first-category ration to someone who had once been active in a bourgeois political party. Briusov claimed, furthermore, that

---

* One of the committees set up by Maxim Gorki for aid to intellectuals after the Revolution. 'Academic' rations were of a high category.

† Main transit prison in Moscow.

Mandelstam was a rich man who had one of the best libraries in
Moscow (at that time, M. had only one book in the world to call his
own: *The Pillar and Foundation of Truth**). Most of the benighted
people on the committee believed Briusov, of course; the attempts
of two or three better-informed members of it to disabuse them
were to no avail. These same two or three urged M. to appeal
against the decision – without, however, mentioning Briusov's mis-
chievous role, lest they be accused of divulging the committee's
secrets. The new regime's call for complete openness in public
affairs – particularly in international relations – was followed by an
unparalleled mania for secrecy about absolutely everything, down
to the pettiest of details. At the present day – in 1970 – the little
differences between our government and the handful of intellectuals who as a result of them land up in forced labour camps really
spring from only one thing: we are forbidden to let out 'state
secrets', that is, to talk about the crimes committed against the
nation in the past, about the crimes being committed against it – on
a smaller scale – in the present, and about those which will be
committed against it in the future (on what scale remains to be
seen).

When I heard about the mean trick Briusov had played on us, I
gave way to youthful indignation at being robbed in this way of an
extra scrap of meat and a bag of buckwheat, but M. was merely
amused by Briusov's behaviour – what energy the man had! He told
me to hold my peace, saying that one should feel flattered to have
been the object of such a prank on the part of the renowned
maestro. Needless to say, he did not submit an appeal. He was, however, upset by the class criterion – the refusal of a ration to a former
advocate . . .

I saw Briusov only once – when he was standing in line for the
packages that A R A had sent for scholars, writers, and artists. In
the ragged crowd of those years – which were already less hungry –
he looked decently dressed, but had a rather old-fashioned and
markedly official air about him. In the whole of his clothing – his
hat, his tie, his gloves, and his polished shoes – there was a dandyish
touch as out of date as it was incongruous. His clothes apart,
Briusov would have looked little different from all the other old

* See Florenski, Appendix A.

fogies standing in the queue (he was then fifty or thereabouts), if it had not been for his gaunt features and fastidious expression. M. gave him a polite bow, whereupon Briusov shook his hand and said something. I think he asked what M. was doing in this queue, but he probably expressed it by a gesture, rather than in words. Briusov was let through out of turn, but when he was handed his package, there was a holdup because he refused to sign the standard slip acknowledging receipt and expressing thanks. Briusov evidently thought it an insult to the national honour – or perhaps to his own personal honour – to thank A R A for a jar of pale-white fat and a little bag of flour. People behind him in the queue expostulated mildly at the delay he was causing, remarking that A R A was not obliged to feed us, and that it cost nothing to say thank you.

For some reason M. was pleased by Briusov's obstinacy – though it struck me as ridiculous. M. liked people who made a fuss, and he followed the altercation with curiosity. I don't know how it ended, except that Briusov eventually left with his package. Perhaps, having made his point, he did in fact sign the slip, or the young lady handing out the packages may have scribbled something on it to spare the maestro's feelings. I used our A R A flour to make some fritters on our Primus stove. I am occasionally tempted to make them again even today, though it beats me how we managed to avoid ruining our guts with them. The whole of our younger years were spent over a spluttering frying-pan, heating soggy fritters made of flour, with a pinch of soda to make them 'rise' – God knows what we used for cooking-fat. As an alternative we made *perepechki* – the same kind of fritters, but griddled without fat over the iron ring on top of the small portable stoves we used for heating in those years. They were remarkably tasty – particularly in hungry times, when one's sense of taste becomes exceptionally keen.

I never saw M. together with Voloshin. After the winter spent in the Crimea under Wrangel's occupation, M. – like Ehrenburg – never again went to Koktebel while Voloshin was still alive. I once went there without him, and was invited by Voloshin into the large room – it was hard to say whether it was a study or a studio – which aroused such wild enthusiasm among his host of female admirers. With my sense of the absurd, I was not so easily won over by his charms. His watercolours seemed to me pretentious and far too amateurish – in other words, I thought they were simply hideous. Voloshin made all kinds of witty remarks – about how, for instance, delivery by mail deprives correspondence of the peculiar charm it has when you receive it from the hands of a courier, or a chance visitor. But, actually, I like a properly functioning postal system, and always get on very well with the splendid women who deliver our letters – it is scarcely their fault if letters are held up or disappear, because of the ham-handed way in which they are intercepted by the censorship. At that time,* it so happens, there was a very funny postman in Koktebel, who was also responsible for telegrams. He liked M.'s long cables with all their terms of endearment, and never handed them over without first reading them aloud and asking me questions, such as: was it worth getting married, how did I get on with my husband, did we have rows, and what was the way to avoid them? This kind of 'interception' did not worry me at all, and I was always glad to chat with him. I am not easily persuaded that one can do without the conveniences of life – I have always suffered rather too much from the lack of them.

Voloshin's main reason for inviting me was to tell me about his quarrel with the Ehrenburgs. In his memoirs, Ehrenburg says not a word about it, but I know that it was an extremely trivial affair involving saucepans. To give Voloshin his due, it must be said that a saucepan or frying-pan is a utensil of enormous importance – one can't boil potatoes or make kasha without it. In an emergency one can use a pot, but in the absence of the real thing a substitute is indispensable. The Ehrenburgs did not return to Koktebel and never mentioned the wretched business, quickly forgetting the reason for it. Voloshin assured me that the whole affair of the saucepan had been a 'legpull'. 'You must have heard how we like to pull people's legs', he explained. To this I said rudely that such things were beyond me and I failed to understand their attraction, though I did know how hard it was to cook cabbage soup without a saucepan. I can scarcely believe, in fact, that the Voloshins, who had lived a settled existence all their lives in Koktebel, had only one single saucepan . . .

Voloshin did not mention his contretemps with M., who was equally reluctant to talk about it. Mindlin refers to it in the ex-

* Evidently the winter of 1925–6.

tremely silly chapter he devotes to M. It arose, as Mindlin writes, because Voloshin suspected M. of going off with his deluxe illustrated edition of Dante. (M., being then homeless and constantly on the move, would have needed to hire a porter to carry such a sumptuous tome for him.) Voloshin wrote an angry letter to the port authorities at Feodosia requesting them not to let the culprit leave until he had made good the loss. On learning this, M. wrote Voloshin a letter breaking with him once and for all. Poor Mindlin tells how he advised M. not to send it, but he sent it nevertheless – it was probably destroyed by Voloshin. Mindlin venerates Voloshin and thus fails to comprehend that even for one of the luminaries of Koktebel it was improper to write a denunciation of this kind asking for the detention of someone already leading a very precarious existence in the demented cities of the Civil War years, with their murderous passions. The letter to the port authorities was a denunciation in every sense of the word. Whether or not M. in fact walked off with the deluxe edition of Dante is absolutely beside the point: in any scale of values a man's life cannot be set against a book, however valuable. But I do not in any case believe M. could have done such a thing. At that time he was not yet able to read Italian, and he mistrusted translations. He first read Dante, to my knowledge, in the thirties. Apart from anything else, however, nobody on the move would be tempted by a deluxe edition – he would obviously have use only for a portable, lightweight edition. And even supposing M. simply lost the book, how could anybody put a man's life in jeopardy on account of something missing from a library? It is a pity that M. made no copy of his letter to Voloshin, and that it was not preserved either among his papers or in our trunk, later to be plundered during the search of our apartment.

I do not like cult figures of Voloshin's type – all these bogus sages and prophets who so much appeal to hysterical women with a frustrated love life. Voloshin liked to walk about Koktebel in a garland and white robe (referred to as a tunic), surrounded by his female admirers. I used to run into him as I went out walking with two enormous dogs – they were savage, vicious, and faithful – which I took to ward off the pilots from the local gliding school when I did not want to chat with them, and I always politely declined his invitations to go and see his new watercolours. After M.'s death, Voloshin's widow sent me a message suggesting I come and live with her. This was touching, but unacceptable. One can live only with people one is close to – though better still is to live alone. I rapidly learned the art of doing this and discovered that the worst part is sitting down to eat by yourself. You never accustom yourself to that, but living with a person you are not close to is even harder.

Akhmatova accused Voloshin of telling endless scandalmongering stories about M., whom he made out to be dishonest and not quite right in the head. At the most charitable he described him as 'a modern Villon', and his behaviour as 'larking about'. Offensive stories put about by Voloshin's female admirers were constantly reaching us from Koktebel, and M. took them very much amiss. His letter to Fedorchenko, who went to Koktebel and heard all these stories on the spot, still exists. I am surprised that Tsvetayeva belonged to the coterie of Voloshin's admirers. Can she really have been impressed by all his talk about the postal system, the distinction between 'books' and 'notebooks', and the greatness of art? I am sure it can only have been because she was still at an age when we are all naïve and undiscriminating. For all my dislike of memoir writers of the type of Georgi Ivanov, I fear I have now sunk to the same level, at least in the present chapter, which is so full of ill will – though more towards Voloshin than the freakish Briusov. Well, there it is: 'No old woman without her folly', as the Russian saying has it.

I would like to dispel another legend, the one put about by Ehrenburg to the effect that it was Voloshin who saved M. from Wrangel's jail. What actually happened was the following: a rumour reached Koktebel about M.'s arrest just before he was about to leave Feodosia for Georgia (it was true – as a result he missed the first transport and had to go in some dreadful tub). Ehrenburg rushed to see Voloshin and with great difficulty persuaded him to go to M.'s rescue in Feodosia. In those years, I should point out – just as later – one had a very good chance of being put against a wall and shot after being picked up. Voloshin had enormous connections; he was something of an institution locally. He delayed things for several days, and by the time he got to Feodosia, M. had already been released. He owed this to Colonel Tsygalski, about whom there is a chapter in *The Noise of Time*. There are grandchildren of

Tsygalski's still alive somewhere, and I very much hope this comes to their ears. From what M. told me I know that Tsygalski was quite exceptionally kind – a quality M. taught me to value above all others. As regards Voloshin's part in the affair, I don't think he was guilty of deliberate misrepresentation – when he got back he simply told Ehrenburg that M. had been released, and Ehrenburg jumped to the conclusion that it was his doing. As the years went by, Voloshin, surrounded by a thousand adoring females, gradually came to believe he had saved everyone, including M. But it is unlikely that the thousand adoring females ever mentioned M.'s name, having no interest in such small fry; the misunderstanding more probably originated with Ehrenburg alone. Ehrenburg is also mistaken about the role of some Georgian poets in extricating M. from jail in the Georgian port of Batumi. The poets did indeed come to the police station where M. was being held together with his brother. They asked that M. be released immediately, and offered to vouch for him, but they refused to do the same for M.'s brother, Alexander, saying they were not to know who he was (in other words, they were unwilling to accept M.'s assurance on behalf of his own brother!). In these conditions M. refused their help, and the poets left Batumi without giving the matter another thought. M. was saved by chance: one of the guards, a man called Chagua, took M. for a Bolshevik. It is possible, admittedly, that the Georgian poets did play some slight part in the sense that the civil governor may have heard about M. thanks to them and thus let him go. There is now no way of knowing, since all concerned have perished – nothing was easier in the last half-century, since opportunity was never lacking. Rescuers, on the other hand, were always slow and half-hearted – which never prevented someone from later presenting them with unsolicited testimonials to their humanitarianism. This one should never do. There are still many ordeals ahead, and nobody should be allowed to forget that you have to put all of yourself into the battle for another man's life – as Frida Vigdorova's example showed.

I was recently told about Chukovski's sentimental account of Gorki's part in the efforts to save Gumilev. According to Chukovski, Gorki immediately rushed to Moscow to see Lenin, but when he got back to Leningrad with the order for Gumilev's release, he learned he had already been shot; Gorki was so upset that he began to cough up blood. This is supposed to have happened in the House of Arts on the Moika in the presence of many witnesses. Just in case Chukovski or his listeners have made a written record of this cock-and-bull story designed to whitewash Gorki, I should like to say here that – according to Akhmatova, Otsup, and many others who were in Petersburg at the time – Gorki, having been informed of Gumilev's arrest by Otsup, promised to act, but in fact did nothing. He did not go to Moscow. There was no order for the release of Gumilev. The touching detail about Gorki's coughing blood is new to me – there was no mention of it forty years ago during a conversation (at which I was present) between M. and Chukovski about the killing of Gumilev. At that time Chukovski subscribed to the general view that nobody had so much as lifted a finger to help, and that it was all over before anyone even managed to heave a sigh. People were then being killed so casually and on such a scale that nobody had time for tears or words of sympathy. From the beginning of the thirties, it became customary to vilify those who perished, so there was no longer any question of shedding a tear for them. How things will be in the future remains to be seen.

Ehrenburg and Chukovski imagined they were defending the good name of literature by describing how writers went to the rescue of their colleagues or at least – as in the case of Gorki coughing blood – demonstrated a certain minimum of concern. In this they were trying to keep alive the cult of literature and the writer. But literature had so thoroughly disgraced itself that such attempts to salvage its honour were of little use. This kind of cult is typical of our times. The cult of a recluse like Voloshin, living out his life at a fashionable resort, is only one particular example of the millions of such cults of which even the most minor figures may be the object in our country, whatever their field of activity. If worst comes to worst, a man's cult can be kept going by his wife's constant praise for everything he does. He may be humiliated and spat upon by the world at large, a total nonentity who never has the courage of his convictions – or avoids having any at all – a man without a family in the proper sense (even though possessed of wife and children), who always meekly votes yes, not knowing where to look for shame, who is incapable of praying for the gift of faith, since he no longer has the slightest notion of what faith is, but craves only for somebody's praise and the vindication of his every action. I believe this is not peculiar to us, being rather a malady of European civilization in general now that it has lost the central idea on which its life was based; with us the consequences are simply more glaring because the degradation of man has gone so much further. Far from becoming the 'hardest' of creatures, our 'men' serve in their appointed places, obeying the orders of their lords and masters, their masculine pride sustained only by the adulation of their womenfolk. I had good reason to laugh at M.'s faith in the friendship of 'men' whose parts are allotted 'only in battle'. We were on the threshold of a new era in which 'men' ceased to exist.

11   Khlebnikov

In 1922 Mandelstam met Khlebnikov on the street. Khlebnikov complained that he had nowhere to stay in Moscow, and had nothing to eat. At that moment he was going through a phase of intense hatred for Brik, and this is reflected in the notes of the artist Miturich, who looked after him during his last illness and buried him. It is not for me to judge whether he had serious grounds for his anger with Brik. It is possible that Khlebnikov, in his utter naïvety, may have thought Brik was omnipotent and demanded miracles from him. The only question is whether Khlebnikov could ever have demanded anything – I just can't imagine his voice taking on the required intonation. The little he said about Brik did not really amount to very much: that he had not wanted, for instance, to publish two or three volumes of Khlebnikov's verse, and that in general he would do nothing for him . . . A man of few words, Khlebnikov told us nothing further by way of explanation, and we did not try to draw him out. He was very quick to take offence – it would have been enough, for instance, if Brik had not bowed in the right way on meeting him in the street. After his death, some champion of his posthumous reputation started alleging that Mayakovski had stolen everything he wrote from Khlebnikov. The man went the rounds of Moscow, shouting incoherently about plagiarism. M. tried to reason with him, but he got nowhere and simply had to throw him out. It brought home to us that madness is contagious – one madman just hands over to the next, as in a relay race. The nature of the mania may change, but the torch of lunacy has been passed on and continues to burn.

Be this as it may, Khlebnikov was hungry, and with our second-category rations we felt like millionaires by comparison. Once a month we were issued with buckwheat, flour, sugar, a chunk of butter, and a revolting pig's head. We handed all this over to the old janitress in Herzen House,* where we had just been given a room. She made galantine out of the pig's head for us, and we ate it with kasha, trying not to think what it was made of. The butter didn't go very far, of course, and we bought sour cream on the side to put in the kasha. The old woman lived in the basement of the building. She was kind and friendly, and after M. had taken Khlebnikov to see her, he came every day and sat down with all three of us to eat this delectable fare. In those days kasha and sour cream, not to mention the extras, seemed the height of luxury, particularly to the old woman; poor as we were, we had occasionally managed to get hold of a little beefsteak, but she, honest soul that she was, had never known how to forage for herself and had forgotten the taste of normal food during the long years of hunger.

She greeted Khlebnikov not just affably, but even with joy, treating him as a wandering 'man of God' – this pleased him and brought a smile to his face. M. lavished much more attention on him than he did on me and the janitress – in general he tended to adopt a rather bluff and jocular tone with women. In the fashion of the times, or out of my own foolishness, I was quite capable of being very rude to anyone, but with Khlebnikov I had to watch my tongue because of M. and the old woman: they would both have jumped down my throat. Khlebnikov had his meal, rested for half an hour, and went away to return the following day – which we all three, M., the old woman, and I, carefully reminded him to do each time. To our astonishment, he was punctual and never once came late. From this I concluded that he somehow managed to keep an eye on the time. He did not of course have a wrist watch, a luxury

* Building that housed the writers' organizations in the twenties.

found only among top officials and 'former people'.* We lived for a quarter of a century without wrist watches – they came in only after World War II. By 1922 I think they had already put up big electric clocks on the streets, or perhaps Khlebnikov had inherited an old pocket watch from his father. Such things were not unknown.

Conversation with Khlebnikov was out of the question – he was completely withdrawn. He sat silently on one of the old woman's straight-backed chairs – he was himself very tall and erect – and moved his lips without pause. Self-absorbed to the extent that he never heard a question, he reacted only to something quite specific and to the point at a given moment; if asked to 'have a little more' or drink some tea, he just nodded his head. I remember that he never said good-bye as he left. Despite the motion of his lips, his face was absolutely expressionless, and his whole head seemed immobile on a neck that was equally rigid. He never bent down to his plate, but brought the spoon right up to his mouth – which was a long way considering how tall he was. I don't know what he had been like earlier, but it soon occurred to me that he could only have been reduced to this state of immobility by approaching death. I was later to see schizophrenics in frozen postures, but this was quite unlike Khlebnikov's condition. There is always something unnatural and grotesque in the poses adopted by schizophrenics, but such was not at all the case with Khlebnikov: he was obviously quite at ease in his immobility and self-aborption. Incidentally, he did not walk but strode, as though measuring out each pace, and almost without bending his knees: this seemed quite natural in view of the shape of his hips and legs, which could easily be made out through the outrageously tattered clothing which he, like the rest of us, wore. I should mention that there could have been no greater contrast between him and M., who was full of energy, wiry, high-spirited, and talkative, reacting to the slightest thing, while Khlebnikov was all bottled up and silent, only nodding occasionally and constantly mulling over the rhythmic lines running through in his head. I do not think there can be any real reader of verse capable of liking both these poets. The mechanical kind of reader who revels only in rhythm and the external form of words,

*i.e., who had been well-to-do before the Revolution.

bludgeoning his mind with them, might find no incompatibility, but anyone sensitive to deeper poetic meaning will live either in the world of Khlebnikov or in the world of Mandelstam. If there were anybody who could live in both worlds, I would define this, in M.'s use of the term, as 'omnivorousness'. M. could not stand 'omnivorousness' in anything, and he regarded a capacity to select and define the components of one's own inner world as the most important thing about a person.

M. has discussed his own attitude to Khlebnikov in articles, but I suspect that, in addition, like the old janitress he also looked upon him as a 'man of God'. He never showed as much care and concern for anyone else as he did for Khlebnikov. As regards Khlebnikov's verse, he liked bits and pieces of it, but no single item as a whole. In Samatikha* in the spring of 1938, we had two volumes of Khlebnikov with us. M. was going through them and looking for bits he liked. When I said that some poem as a whole was shapeless, he laughed at me: 'What do you expect? Isn't this bit enough for you? What's shapeless about that?' He was probably right.

Not long before he went away, Khlebnikov complained that he didn't want to leave, but was forced to for lack of a roof over his head. The government had put Herzen House (where, I believe, Herzen never lived) at the disposal of the writers' organizations. Some smart operators had managed to sell the best part of the left side of the building to a group of Danish concessionaires;† one remaining apartment on this side, and the damp and squalid right-hand wing, had been used to house homeless writers. We were among the first to move in, while both wings were still unoccupied. As soon as Khlebnikov mentioned his problem, M., whose reactions were very quick, at once took him over to the writers' bookshop in Nikita Street so he could have a word with Berdiayev, then chairman of the Union of Writers.‡ Berdiayev was often to be

* The sanatorium at which Mandelstam was arrested.

† During NEP, commercial 'concessions' were granted for the exploitation of certain resources by foreign capital.

‡ Like its pre-revolutionary predecessor, this was still largely a genuine professional organization, not an instrument of State control like the Union of *Soviet* Writers founded in 1932. Berdiayev was expelled from the Soviet Union in 1922.

found in the shop, which was a source of income for him. It was still allowed at that time to find private ways of earning one's daily bread. It may seem a small thing, but a private income apparently makes for a certain freedom of thought. If you receive every morsel of your daily bread from the hands of the powers-that-be, then you are wise, if you want to be sure of getting a little extra, to give up thinking altogether. The writers were quite happy to do this – at first for a pittance, and later for much more handsome emoluments. Looking back, I find it very hard to say what we should have done: if M. had meekly agreed to receive his benefits like the rest, he would have remained alive. We would have lived a long and comfortable life together, and he would never have known the horror of waiting for death and his atrocious end in the concentration camp. My heart aches so much when I think of his last days that I involuntarily begin to wonder how it would have been if we had agreed to the sort of compromise always regarded as 'reasonable'. I invariably advise my friends to do so. Unfortunately, 'compromise' in this country means something different from elsewhere – namely, selling yourself body and soul. What is one to do?

They found Berdiayev in the shop, and M. tackled him with all the vehemence of his Jewish temperament, demanding a room for Khlebnikov. I wasn't actually present at this scene, but I had more than once borne the brunt of M.'s fury (sometimes for good cause, sometimes unjustly), and I can imagine how it must have frightened the unsuspecting Berdiayev. M. told me himself that he had never seen Berdiayev have such a bad attack of his tic as during this conversation. M. based his demand on the claim that Khlebnikov was the greatest poet in the world, before whom all others were as nothing, and that he therefore deserved a room of at least six cubic metres. He pointed out that in our apartment, the only one in this wing not taken over by the Danes, there were a few cubbyholes of about this size at the back of the kitchen. Hearing such praise of himself, Khlebnikov suddenly began to beam and express assent – in M.'s words, stamping one foot on the ground and moving his head back and forth.

Berdiayev, caught off guard by this pair of insolent braggarts he had never seen before, brayed with embarrassment and tried to explain that all the rooms had already been promised to such important writers as Dmitri Dmitrievich Blagoi . . . It was quite clear that he was absolutely helpless in practical matters and did not know what was going on – he had left everything in the hands of crooks who just used his name. He had not even been inside the building where rooms were being allotted, failing to understand what a mean trick it had been to sell one wing to the Danes in order to make money for the Union. Soon after this, a few more cubbyholes were created in the course of minor alterations, and Blagoi was given a large bright room. Some of the cubbyholes had windows and others had no light at all, but Khlebnikov would have settled for any dark corner. Nobody, however, lifted a finger to help him – Berdiayev did not go to check whether there was any possibility of fixing one up for him, as M. had asked, and he was forced to leave. He was thus virtually thrown out of Moscow and given no choice but to set off on his last wanderings.

A little later we heard the news of his death somewhere in the wilds, without the benefit of proper medical help. Could he have been saved by the Moscow specialists? Who knows . . . his illness had probably been very neglected. In the place where he died there would of course have been a country doctor and a *feldsher** – experienced people with an old tradition of care and kindness for their patients. I had known some doctors like this in my childhood. Always wearing top boots, they used to come and visit my parents, because they had once been students together in Petersburg. My mother was a doctor and had been one of the first to graduate from the medical courses for women. Older doctors and professors have often seen the likeness between me and the young girl who was once their student. One of them has shown me a photograph of one of his classes taken on graduation day, and among all the other solemn and learned young ladies, I could make out my mother, still just a girl. My father was a graduate of the mathematics faculty. The doctors who came to see my parents were intellectuals in the true sense of the word, as one could tell from the conversation at table and the books they took away with them to their homes deep in the

* Semi-qualified medical attendant, once particularly common in Russian country districts.

country. I hope that Khlebnikov got into a local hospital with humanitarian doctors of this kind, and I am not entirely convinced of the story that he received no medical aid. But the fact remains that the writers' organization – this was while it was still headed by Berdiayev and before it had become an official institution – did nothing at all to help him.

The virtual expulsion of Khlebnikov from Moscow was actually only one of the first exploits of organized literature, and it was not ordered from above, but undertaken spontaneously. This shows that our literature became what it is today through no accident, and that from the very outset it revealed the qualities that have now borne such rich fruit. Beginning with the cases of Gumilev and Khlebnikov the writers have continued on the same glorious path right up to the present. One cannot put *all* the blame on the men at the top – from their lofty eminence they cannot be expected to see everything the pigmies down below get up to. They deal directly only with the informers, denouncers, petitioners, delegates, and advisers who come to them by virtue of what is called 'popular initiative'. This is how contact is maintained between the higher and the lower levels. Expelling someone from the Union of Writers, sending him to a camp, to prison, or to the firing squad, our kindhearted writers try to make out that it is none of their doing: they are merely carrying out orders, much as it goes against the grain. But if you think about it, a society is no better than its rulers. It would be well for people to remember this, instead of putting on a resigned air or an innocent smile – nothing strikes me as more indecent.

It is a matter of great good fortune if the ruling circles or their representatives go no further than reducing the category of your ration, striking out a pair of trousers from a list of needed items, or boasting about a collection of carpets. It is worse if they get the right to send their opponents to death camps or gas chambers. For Briusov, the category of the ration he gave one was in the nature of a value judgement, or a dirty trick like one of Voloshin's 'leg-pulls'. Crossing out a pair of trousers, Gorki felt he was doing what was only right and proper. It was no accident that he was the one who failed to make a phone call or a train journey to Moscow in time to save Gumilev's life – a fine beginning to the era in which I have lived my life. The only good thing is that Gorki was succeeded by petty officials who can barely put pen to paper. In this I see a certain ray of light.

As regards Berdiayev, he was only doing his honest best in protecting the nice young Blagoi from that brazen pair, M. and Khlebnikov. I am not suggesting that rooms should be taken from the Blagois and given to the Khlebnikovs, but I would plead for careful attention even to the most minor matters, however humdrum or fatuous, to the needs and hardships of any man – even if he is a poet. Unless you respect life in its lowliest and least interesting aspects, you are bound to involve yourself in contradictions. I remember the way Lenin's sister insisted that M. could not be given another room in the slummy right-hand wing of Herzen House (this was at the beginning of the thirties) and assigned it instead to a certain Ruderman. Her reason, which she gave with the fervour of the underground worker she had once been, was: 'It is bad if one writer has two rooms and another has none.' The poor woman was out of touch with reality and quite in the dark about who had how many rooms. On the other hand, she had her principles. In accordance with these she had forgotten to add up the number of her own rooms, thereby helping to prepare the ground for the decision to 'combat egalitarianism'.* Under the new order, you see, everybody 'receives according to his merits'. At the moment, through a lucky chance, I happen to have a one-room apartment which I have not 'merited'. I dream of living to the end of my days in it, with the use of the toilet and bathroom, though whether I shall succeed in this I do not know. I very much hope so . . . The majority of my compatriots do not enjoy such luxury even now, because they have not 'merited' it . . . If I had my way, people would get such things irrespective of their merits. M. and Khlebnikov, as I know only too well, received according to their 'merits', and the mere thought of it fills me with pain even now. Who decides on a man's 'merits'?

The people M. referred to as 'we' were those he continued to converse with all his life, even when they were no longer here. There

* 'Egalitarianism' – giving people equal wages, etc. – was denounced by Stalin in 1931 as a 'left-wing' deviation.

were three of them – but apart from these three, there was also the whole of world poetry, which knew no bounds of time and space. It does not matter what place a poet has in it, however small it may be. The very smallest place – just a couple of successful lines, one good poem, a single well-said word – entitles him to enter the fellowship of poets, to be one of 'us', to partake of the feast. I am quite sure that no poet ever aspired to become 'President of the Earth' – the very title was only a joke of one of the most naïve of them, the homeless wanderer befriended by the old janitress at Herzen House. The pass to poetry is granted only by faith in its sacramental character and a sense of responsibility for everything that happens in the world. Khlebnikov, seemingly oblivious to everything except the invitation to come and eat the same time next day, wrote a story about the shooting of a hare by a man with a gun; the hare, believing this to be his first sight of a real man, had not run away. Khlebnikov also wrote a poem about the Cheka and a poor fool who boasted of the brave deeds he had performed and all the people he had killed, but then it was discovered that the gore covering his sabre was only red paint. Unworldly as he seemed, Khlebnikov had seen the crimes of the age and turned away from them in horror. Who can say he was not entitled to his pass to poetry?

A poet is always grateful to other poets who played a part in the growth of his own verse, when he was only beginning to find his voice. This kind of gratitude also serves as a pass to poetry. I am always sceptical about the young rebels who repudiated Pushkin. They were simply putting on a show of bravado because they were ashamed of their love for our first poet. May their youthful arrogance be forgiven – they must certainly have paid for it.

Another thing that distinguishes a poet is a sense of his own sinfulness – particularly important in the twentieth century, now that the very concept of sin has been abolished. Pushkin set an example by repeating a prayer which 'sustains the sinner with a strength unknown'. Akhmatova spoke about her 'sins and infirmities'; M. thought his only merit was not to have 'shed hot blood'; Khlebnikov, the creator of legends, who dreamed of 'maidens' surrounding a demigod, was sure he would 'wake up trampled in the earth, my dusty skull grieving yet'. I believe their sins will be forgiven and people will remember them at a moment of need for at least a single line or word which they found and gave utterance to. The mortal pity I feel for each of them gives me the strength to live.

12 'The Murk of Nonbeing'

If we spoke of 'staying' in Moscow, of 'going' there, or 'living' there, we could speak only of 'returning' to Petersburg. This was M.'s native city: beloved, utterly familiar, but a place he could only flee from. The 'city-love, city-passion, city-hate' he mentions in 'Conversation About Dante' are feelings he knew from his own experience. Petersburg is a constant theme with him – both *Noise of Time* and *Egyptian Stamp* are about it, as well as much of the verse in *Stone*, nearly the whole of *Tristia*, and a few poems of the thirties. In the lines 'the pencil cases of canals are even blacker under ice' one senses an aching nostalgia. He even bequeathed his shadow to Petersburg: 'Thus my shadow gnaws with its eyes that black-grained granite, seeing by night the rows of hulks that in daylight it took for houses.' M. fled from Petersburg to the south, and then returned – only to flee again. Petersburg was M.'s pain, his poetry, and the cause of his dumbness. Who invented the story that I did not like Petersburg and was always hankering after Moscow because my beloved brother lived there? This gives an all too sentimental picture of our life: I never had the slightest influence on M., and he would have thrown me over rather than his city. In actual fact he had left it long before we met, and was to leave it many times again afterwards. As he explained himself: 'Living in Petersburg is the same as lying in a coffin.' I would like to know what my brother (to whom I have indeed always been close) has to do with this.

M. quite liked to live in 'Buddhist' Moscow, in the 'unseemly capital', and even came to see a certain charm in it – because of its sprawling, scattered character, its Buddhist inertness, its air of having been outside history for a thousand years, even the fact that it was always full of hidden menace for him. It is easier to live with a pistol pointed at your head than in a necropolis with an immigrant, constantly shifting, always lifeless population, its citizens walking the streets like automatons, their already dead eyes glazed by the worst terror in the country. In Petersburg, M. would not have survived until 1938. The only thing that saved him in the early days was his flight to 'the Nereids of the Black Sea' – though it must be said that the Nereids of the Black Sea gave no more protection than those of the Baltic. Only chance, in fact, could save you.

M. had early forebodings of the end of Petersburg and the whole Petersburg period of Russian history. During the 'July demonstration'* he was serving in the Union of Cities and went out on to a balcony with his colleagues. He said something about the end of culture, and spoke of the nature of the party which had organized the demonstration (describing it as an 'inverted church', or something very similar). He noticed that his 'colleagues' seemed to bridle at his words: only later did he learn that two of them were members of the Bolshevik Central Committee who were just sitting pretty for the time being in the Union of Cities, waiting for their hour to strike. He told me their names; one of them, I believe, was Zinoviev, and the other Kamenev. This intimate exchange of views on the balcony predetermined the later attitude of these 'colleagues' – particularly Zinoviev's – towards M., as we were keenly aware when he lived in Leningrad in the middle twenties. The constant spying on him and the early (1923) ban on publication of his work were a natural consequence of M.'s general situation, but in Leningrad it was all done more blatantly than in Moscow. I was under the impression that Moscow had more pressing concerns, while Leningrad, no longer at the centre of affairs, had all the time in the world to pry into the lives of those marked down for destruction. It is a moot point whether M. would have survived if he had been in Leningrad at the moment of the wave of terror after the Kronstadt rising – this was a full-scale affair, with Moscow urging the Leningrad authorities to step it up even more, accusing them of not allowing the local working class to give full vent to its anger.

*The first Bolshevik show of strength against Kerenski's Provisional Government, in July 1917, in Petrograd. The Union of the Cities was one of the so-called 'voluntary organizations' started in 1914 to help the war effort. Though dominated by the Liberals (Cadets), it was infiltrated by left-wing organizations.

It was during this particular orgy of terror that Gumilev met his death. I should say a word or two about the 'young man from a naval family' who came to see him in 1921. He had been sent by Admiral Nemits to invite Gumilev to go down to the Crimea so he could rest and eat proper food for a while. Khodasevich naïvely imagined that he had been put up to it on purpose, but the ability to identify specially assigned provocateurs is a peculiar Soviet art which Khodasevich left the country too early to master, and he preferred to see spies everywhere. This is certainly the Soviet habit, but it only wears people out instead of keeping them on their guard. There is no need of any special techniques of entrapment – during a wave of terror no motive is required for the destruction of this or that particular individual. Nothing is simpler than to 'make a case', and it is time people understood this. A poet is always surrounded by minor riff-raff ready to have 'evidence' wrung out of them if need be, and nobody would have bothered to spend money on sending a special agent from Moscow. The name of the young man was Pavlov. I cannot say any good of him. Under pressure he would have signed anything to save his own skin. (He was also arrested, but then let off scot free.) There is also a purely technical flaw in Khodasevich's supposition – Admiral Nemits had taken in Pavlov on his own initiative, thinking to save a young man 'of good family'. He could have been used to spy on his patron, Admiral Nemits, but this would have been an assignment of major importance, and it is quite out of the question that such a valuable agent would have been entrusted with the further task of helping in the liquidation of Gumilev. Such a dual role was inconceivable. The various departments of the security services used their agents according to their qualifications, not just at random. To destroy a poet they would have employed some wretched little hack writer, not a military person. Otsup, who knew all about the Gumilev case – it was he who went to see Gorki and learned such details as reached us – never suspected Pavlov of anything; nor did he break off relations with him before he left the country, but stayed with him the last time he was in Moscow (this is where we went to say good-bye to him).

Otsup took the death of his teacher as a personal tragedy, and I cannot believe he would have kept up relations with a man he considered responsible for what had happened. Among the legends which have been made up about Gumilev's death, there are various things attributed to Gorki and invented by Lord knows who. One of them is to the effect that Pavlov's evidence formed the basis for the sentence. I am quite prepared to believe this may have been so, though I am by no means convinced. Even if true, it would still not mean that Pavlov had been specially sent to Gumilev, only that he served an incidental purpose in the mounting of the case. M.'s involvement in the whole affair was quite minor: he learned that Pavlov was being sent up to Leningrad by Nemits with an invitation to travel to the Crimea and asked whether it would be possible to get him a ticket in the 'staff coach' as well. Pavlov did as he was asked, and M. went to Petersburg to say good-bye to his father before setting off on his Caucasian 'expedition'. Khodasevich was a man of the old school who believed that provocation was essential to the business of destroying a chosen victim, and furthermore, he had succumbed to the new fashion of seeing a spy in everyone who came along. One remembers how Zenkevich suspected the man who suspected *him* of informing, while at the same time neither of them noticed the real informers so obvious to M. and me. It is hideous to see this disease afflicting vast numbers of people, including the informers themselves – indeed they suffer from it most acutely of all, and you can tell them by their eyes, despairing and full of frozen horror. In Petersburg this disease, the mania of seeing a police spy in everybody, reached its highest peak. Even today it is the bane of people's lives. Petersburg has a curse on it: 'This place shall be empty . . .' *

Akhmatova called Petersburg a 'city in mourning'. It is the living who mourn the dead, but the only time I ever saw *living* faces in Petersburg-Leningrad was among the many thousands of people who came to Akhmatova's funeral, crowding around the church of Nikola of the Sea in a dense throng. The old women for whom church is home could not get inside and were rightly indignant at

* This curse was pronounced by Peter the Great's Russian wife, Avdotia, whom he abandoned for a German mistress, Anna Mons. It symbolizes the view of Petersburg as an 'alien' city, more foreign than Russian.

all these non-churchgoers now filling every nook and cranny during the service for Akhmatova. It was a young crowd: students had abandoned their classes that day to come and pay their last respects to the last poet. Here and there one glimpsed women of Akhmatova's generation who had put on the remnants of their coquettish Petersburg dresses for the occasion. The water of the Neva is kind to the skin, and the old women had delicate, pellucid complexions. The Muscovites stood out as a group apart, stolid and ungainly. The young people did not know how to behave in church, and there was some jostling as they pushed their way through to the coffin. I stood next to Lev Gumilev, who had not seen his mother for several years. He had tried to see her in the hospital, but had been stopped by Ardov's wife, Nina Olshevskaya. I was present on one occasion when she came to the hospital to prepare Akhmatova for the latest 'non-meeting' with her son. Nina told Akhmatova that if she saw him it might kill her. Akhmatova was indignant, but there was nothing she could do. Everything possible was done to 'protect' her from her son.

When I came home from the hospital, I found Lev at my door. He was at his wits' end, weeping tears of anger. He told me in detail how Olshevskaya, the idiot woman, had given him precise instructions about what he could and could not say to his mother. She told him in no uncertain terms that he would not get in the hospital without her permission (or in her absence) and threatened to take all necessary measures to this end. He was told to go back to Leningrad and wait until he was summoned – which of course never happened. From me Akhmatova was protected by Punin's grand-daughter, an angelic-looking creature with a wicked little face. Once she overheard Akhmatova talking to me about her will – a conversation she did not like at all. Coming down to Moscow, she telephoned and told me sweetly but firmly not to go to the hospital for fear of 'tiring Akuma'.* From time to time Akhmatova made a fuss, and then I was urgently called to her bedside, but they always tried to make sure one of them was present during my visit. Akhmatova, old and helpless, was besieged by these claimants to the fabulous heritage she would leave. Fortunately, it went to her son – she managed to outwit the small-minded, grasping fe-

---

* Akhmatova's nickname in the Punin family. See page 408.

males who were after it by destroying a will in favour of Irina Punina which had once been extracted from her while Lev was in a concentration camp and had no legal rights.

Among the crowd at Akhmatova's funeral there was one other mourner who also felt orphaned in a real sense: Joseph Brodski. Of all the younger friends who made life easier to bear in her last years, he was the most serious, honest, and selfless in his relations with her. I think Akhmatova overestimated him as a poet – she was terribly anxious that the thread of the tradition she represented should not be broken, and imagining she was again surrounded by poets, as in her youth, she thought she could detect a ferment in the air like that of those early years. She even believed the young poets were all in love with her – the same foible she suffered from in her youth. In their old age, as I have seen with my own eyes, people really do revert to features that distinguished them in their young years (is it due to a weakening of self-control? I don't think it has happened to me yet). All the same, it was providential, the existence of these young men who sincerely loved the mad, passionate, and brilliant old woman. Having spent the best years of her life monstrously alone among a breed of men utterly alien, in her old age she now had this circle of friends, of whom the best was Brodski.

I have heard Brodski read his verse. An active part in the process is played by his nose. I have never known anything like it before in all my life: his nostrils expand and contract and do all kinds of funny things, givng a nasal twang to each vowel and consonant. It is like a wind orchestra. He is, nevertheless, a remarkable young man who will come to a bad end, I fear. Whether a good poet or not, the fact is that he is one, and this cannot be denied him. In our times it is hard luck to be a poet – and a Jew into the bargain.

Where have so many Jews come from, after all the pogroms and the gas chambers? In the crowd at Akhmatova's funeral their numbers were disproportionately large. I never saw anything like this in my youth. Then there were many brilliant Russian intellectuals as well, but now you can almost count them on the fingers of one hand . . . People say they have all been destroyed, but since all ethnic groups were equally affected by the various waves of wholesale destruction, I do not find this explanation convincing. The fact is that the resurgent intelligentsia of the present consists of Jews and half-Jews – though they often come from grimly positivist families in which the parents still go on mouthing the same old ossified balderdash. Many of the younger ones have also become Christians, or think on religious lines. I once said to Akhmatova that we are going through the times of early Christianity all over again, which was why so many Jews were becoming converts. She nodded her head in agreement, but I am no longer happy with this theory of mine. More and more I incline to the belief that the end is approaching, finally and irrevocably, though I am not sure how to explain this feeling: whether by my own approaching death or by the shadow of the future over a world until recent times still Christian. But whatever the future holds, I only hope I do not live to see it with these mortal eyes.

In these days the sense of approaching doom has spread down to the great mass of the people. This is not only because of the brilliant way in which science has demonstrated its capabilities. I sometimes even feel that science only provides a rationale for people's natural sense of dread at the work of their own hands – as witness the sterile upsurge of philosophical pessimism which overcame the West after the Second World War. They say it is now on the wane there, but here – having been artificially held back – it is sapping the morale of people already hagridden enough without it. But pessimism, even though I have called it sterile, is still better than the monstrous faith, blind and malignant, in various 'saviours' of mankind, from whom we are eventually saved only by the mysterious law through which evil tends to destroy itself. This accursed faith in nothingness still has a deep hold on immature minds, as one can judge from the portraits hanging in certain hapless Western universities. The miserable wretches cannot wait to let themselves go: murdering a couple of thousand of ordinary people would give them the feeling of strength so much coveted by the poor in spirit. They know that an executioner always feels superior to his victim, gloating at the sight of his fear-crazed eyes and the trousers slipping down because his belt has been taken away. The well-fed brute also likes to starve his prisoner – nothing lowers the will to resist better than hunger. But when, in accordance with the law by which evil destroys itself, the executioners begin to murder their own kind – who, until recently, have interrogated, tormented, and killed 'alien elements' (or sanctioned their killing 'for the good of the cause') – then yesterday's 'good comrades' suddenly disintegrate and, with cries of dismay, rush to try to prove themselves purer than the driven snow.

Everywhere we have these portraits, and a feeling that the end is not far off. People sense it with all their pores and fibres, in body and soul. A certain philosopher* noted for his inordinately brilliant insights once publicly declared that an eschatological mood is the hallmark of dying classes. The same philosopher showed that the class approach is the most scientific and infallible one. The question then arises: Who constitutes the dying class in this country, now prey to such intense feelings of anguish and forebodings of doom?

13   The Young Levite

M.'s first spell of eschatological presentiments began during the time when *Tristia* was in the making. The theme unfolded gradually. I see its genesis in the poem of 1916 in which he says: 'In translucent Petropolis we shall die . . . / With every sigh we drink the deadly air, / And every hour is our dying day.' This is about his own death, and that of all those he referred to as 'we'. Petersburg was thus seen as a city of doom, where life consisted of waiting for the end. In November 1917 he wrote the poem (dedicated to Kartashev) about the young Levite who foretold the destruction of Jerusalem; and in the early spring of 1918 he composed his mournful lament on the end of Petersburg: 'Translucent star, wandering flame, your brother Petropolis is dying . . .'

His poem about the young Levite is one of the not numerous – but always deeply significant – ones in which he touched on a Jewish theme. Dying Petersburg, the end of the Petersburg era of Russian history, brought to mind the fall of Jerusalem. The fall of both cities is equated: the modern city is destroyed for the same sin as the ancient one. Petersburg is not Babylon, the great Whore foretold by the prophets, but Jerusalem. Babylon, a pagan city, was sunk in

* Probably Lenin.

fleshpots and iniquity. But Jerusalem, like Petersburg, had to answer for another sin, a more cardinal one – this is implicit in the whole system of the poem's imagery. M.'s prose, as always, provides a gloss on his verse, revealing the thoughts and state of mind behind a particular poem. In this instance I am referring to the paper on the death of Scriabin which M. read in the Religious-Philosophical Society, where he sometimes used to meet Kartashev.

M. gave the text of this paper to Kablukov. When he returned from his second visit to Georgia (the one on which I accompanied him), he learned that Kablukov had died and that his archives had been handed over to the Public Library – it appeared that Kablukov had no heirs. Several times M. went to the library to inquire about his paper on Scriabin, but it had disappeared. The loss upset him very much. 'I have no luck,' he said, 'this is my most important article.' In 1923 M.'s father fell ill. While he lay in the hospital, we took his things to his younger son, Yevgeni Emilievich, since the old man would not be able to live by himself any more. I was against taking him to live with this son, who was unfeeling and hard-hearted, and the future was to show that I had been quite right – he behaved abominably towards the old man. But at the time he insisted, and it was the easiest solution. All we had to do was transfer his belongings there.

I went through the old man's trunks. Among all the piles of rubbish – worthless banknotes from the time of Kerenski and the Tsar, mouldy crusts of bread, rusty knives, old lace curtains and strips of dusty velveteen tablecloths – I came across a bundle of papers covered with writing in a familiar hand. It contained verse of M.'s early period, probably written down at the time when he was putting *Stone* together, various other odds and ends, and some pages from the lecture on Scriabin. M. was overjoyed, looked through all the pages, found it was about half of what he had given to Kablukov, and instructed me to keep it. He never came back to it again, since publication would have been absolutely out of the question. I still have the manuscript, though someone (alas, I know not who) has walked off with the first page. There were two first pages, completely identical except for the title. On one the title was:

'Pushkin and Scriabin,' and on the other: 'Scriabin and Christianity.' It is the first which has disappeared. But it will turn up after my death – this was only the work of a collector . . .

A word or two about the old man's trunks. Widowers without daughters all ended up homeless like this, with exactly the same kind of junk. When the hard times came, it was suddenly clear how important women had been in the ordering of a man's daily life. Whatever fancy airs they may have given themselves, they were the builders and mainstay of the home. In this there was no difference between a rich woman and the humblest peasant's wife. In fact the richer they were, the more energetically they fulfilled their role, though it must be said that the better off people had been in the past, the weaker they proved to be in the face of hunger and the breakdown of everyday life. Even so, the women were always stronger than the men, as everybody sees well enough today. 'Who will wash his clothes for him if he's left all alone?' is now the watchword at all levels of society.

I did not do a very thorough job of searching the trunks, and after the death of the old man another bundle of papers turned up, thus falling into the hands of M.'s brother – the one to whom M. wrote letters forbidding him to refer to himself as such (knowing that Yevgeni Emilievich would destroy the originals, M. kept copies of these letters). Now that it is no longer dangerous to mention M.'s name, Yevgeni Emilievich has discovered that some scientists, on the strength of his being 'the brother of Mandelstam', are glad to give him expert advice in connection with his popular science films, and he has started a special 'album' for 'family papers'. I hope these family papers will eventually find their way into the archives. There is not much – only a few oddments touchingly salvaged by the old man from the writings of his prodigal son.

The lecture on the death of Scriabin, despite the fragmentary form in which it has survived, is in every sense a companion piece to the *Tristia* volume, from 'Phaedra' at the beginning right through to the last poem about the granaries in which 'the grain of faith, profound and full' is stored. The most important passage is where M. says what he understands the chief sin of the epoch to be, the one for which we would all have to pay: the whole of modern history, he writes, 'has turned away from Christianity to Buddhism and theosophy'. Petersburg, in which M. spent his childhood and youth, had run through the gamut of the various forms of apostasy from Christianity, giving them expression in all the fashionable trends of the decade before the Revolution; what is more, the city had shown by its very history that it would be the first to bear the brunt of the reckoning. The lecture also gives a precise idea of what M. understood by Christian art. In his view it is neither sacrifice nor atonement – the Atonement has already taken place – but joyful communion with God, a game that the children play with their Father. Perhaps this way of looking at things explains the blithe good spirits which never deserted Mandelstam. Though this is not really true: in inhuman conditions nobody can remain the same, or keep his spirits up – a poet in particular, with his openness to external impressions, is far too vulnerable. I have heard that the only people to withstand their ordeals were priests and sectarians of deeply religious faith – they welcomed a martyr's death, because they were ready for it.

M., a man of extremely deep feeling, was always acutely aware of death, which seemed ever present to his mind. This is indeed not surprising: poetry, even more than philosophy, is a preparation for death. Death encompasses all the fullness of life, its essence, its real pith and substance. Death is the apex of life. Nearing the end of my days, I have also come to understand that death, as M. once explained to me, is a triumph. Earlier I had always looked upon it only as a liberation. But may no physical suffering blur the meaning of our last act on earth? I ask this question about myself, but a thousand times more frequently I ask it about M. – we have learned by experience that conditions can be created in which people cease to be human. A victim being burned at the stake during the Inquisition had a good chance that someone in the crowd who had come to admire the leaping flames and watch the spectacle of his terrible agony would at least hear the curses he hurled at his tormentors. Indeed, burning at the stake at last came to an end when the screams of the victims began to reach the ears of bystanders willing to listen. But among the vast hordes of brutalized camp prisoners, as they were slowly worked to death and made to yield up the last ounce of their 'social utility', there was no question of anyone's seeing or hearing his neighbour. When everybody is dying slowly, people lose all capacity for human contact and withdraw into themselves. It is no wonder that out of all the millions who went through the camps, only a tiny handful have been able to describe the experience – and one of these served his sentence only after the war, and did not, hence, know the camps as they were at the end of the thirties,* while one of the female survivors† was able to keep her memory of it all because – according to what everybody says – she was in a women's camp where, terrible as it may have been, things were nevertheless easier than in the camps for men. How do people die in those places? Is there anything in such a death apart from the pain of a crushed animal and, perhaps, the joy of liberation?

The camps in which 'the last ounce of utility' was squeezed out of the doomed inmates must have been a ruinous drain on the country's resources. To turn a man into an executioner, a prison guard, a torturer, a camp commandant, or a security officer, you must gorge him with the good things of life until he is utterly stupified, and then build up the whole system of intimidation that reduces everybody to a state of cretinism. All this costs a great deal, not to mention the fact that productivity inevitably gets lower and lower, both in the camps and outside them too. What sort of work could be done by those poor broken souls? I am least of all concerned with productivity – something the organizers of our life have been prating about for the last half-century – or about the economic side of forced labour in general, but even here our rulers have hopelessly miscalculated.

There are few people left in the world capable of understanding the idea of death as a triumph. People are so terrified of the end that they lose their capacity to enjoy life, putting their faith only in medicine and gerontology, seeking one nostrum after another as they prepare to enter the world beyond – in which they have long ago ceased to believe. I am all for looking after the old, as is now the fashion after the long period in which useless members of society were speeded on their way, but I do not myself particularly

* Solzhenitsyn.
† Yevgenia Ginzburg.

want to be artificially kept alive, any more than I want to be destroyed. All I ask for is to remain human at the moment of final suffering.

I think it can only have been his intense concern with death that led M. to attach such significance to Scriabin's premature and rather fortuitous end, attributing a universal meaning to it, and making so much of the supposed attitude of the ordinary people towards it. He would scarcely have bracketed Scriabin with Pushkin if he had been in a less exalted mood. Pushkin's death, after all, made an impact on people, but Phaedra-Russia would never have thought of bestowing her love on Scriabin for the simple reason that she has never bestowed her love, either sinful or pure, on any of her sons – or rather, stepsons; good stepmother that she is, she has done nothing but ill-treat and destroy them. Our people loves its rulers, and the rulers love only themselves. The highest honour they can confer on a writer is to steal his body – as happened with Pushkin – or throw him in a mass grave. A nation which has chopped up icons to light its stoves has given proof of an incredible failure of love. Yet it *did* love its great art of icon painting, and has never ceased to love it, even now. A long-suffering nation of stepsons, each kindly and forgiving by nature, continually seethes with hatred and rancour, loving nobody and bestirring itself only at the call of its stepmother to tear one of its elect limb from limb. Where on earth do they come from, these elect, and why do they continue to appear, bearing the distinctive marks of their age, ineffably pure and innocent to the point of holiness? But I can never forget something else: the peasants living in the vicinity of concentration camps who used to catch escaping prisoners for a bounty consisting of part of a sack of flour per head. Flour is a fine thing.

The article on Scriabin's death explains the opening poem in M.'s second volume of verse (*Tristia*, or *The Second Book*). Phaedra is both mother and motherland – and also a stepmother consumed by illicit passion for her stepson. The artist is an eternal stepson. Despite the emotions always roused in him by death, in this instance Scriabin's, M. was not blind to his guilt in regard to the age he lived in: his apostasy from Christianity. Scriabin was a tempter who combined the Dionysian principle with the dementia of those Russian sectarians who burned themselves to death in coffins. M.

describes him as a frenzied Hellene who seduced people by 'the siren call of the piano', though the real foundation of music as an organized form is to be found in the voice, the choir. (Here he is certainly arguing against Viacheslav Ivanov – Nietzsche with his Dionysian interpretation of art.) In M.'s eyes, the voice and the choir to some extent embodied the element of *sobornost* * in music: 'All partake, play and *sing* together'; then there were his words about 'the crystal of high notes', and his boundless joy at hearing plainsong in Armenia. He also told me of the overwhelming impression once made on him by the plainchant of a Catholic choir, though I don't know where he could have heard it; it must have been abroad, and very likely an amateur performance, since I do not think plainsong was very highly regarded in the first years of the century. Perhaps it is used, if only occasionally, in Catholic church services? As regards 'the siren call of the piano', this was somehow associated in M.'s mind with Chopin, in whom he sensed an acutely individualistic element, calling him 'the passionate Pole, / zealot of the pianoforte' . . . Much later on, in our Voronezh days, I was present during a conversation about Scriabin between M. and a well-known, but not very intellectual, violinist. M. said he could not take Scriabin's symphonies, but he spoke more indulgently of the piano pieces. In the twenties Iza Khantsyn, the wife of Margulis, often played Scriabin to him, and this had convinced him that the destructive, frenzied element was much less evident – or even nonexistent – in the piano pieces.

The poem about Phaedra is the first in which M. speaks of the 'black sun', the sun of guilt and doom. In the article on Scriabin he says that the nocturnal sun, or black sun, is 'an image in the last tragedy written by Euripides, a vision of the hapless Phaedra'. I do not remember whether in fact the nocturnal or black sun of Greek mythology (the *nyctelios* of the Orphics) really does occur in Euripides, and I have no intention of going to a library to find out – others can do that for me – but I do recall that the black sun is mentioned, as a vision seen by Phaedra, in one of Annenski's articles, and M. may very well have taken his teacher's word for it. Rozanov, incidentally, also talked about the 'black sun'. At times when an

---

* The sense of spiritual fellowship in the Russian Orthodox Church. See page 459.

era is ending, the sun turns black: 'Roused by its games, / the mob buries the nocturnal sun . . .'

In the third volume of M.'s collected works* I found among the notes a list of all references to the 'black sun' both in M. and in world literature. It is done with loving care, but the compiler should at the outset have distinguished between the black sun of guilt and doom, and the words about 'the poet's body like the sun' (referring to Pushkin) in the article on Scriabin, and also the line: 'On a black bier they carry yesterday's sun.' These two instances echo Gogol's words about how Pushkin, yesterday still a sun, drawing people to himself by his force of gravitation, now lay dead in his coffin. Akhmatova, jumping to conclusions, had decided that 'sun', as used here, always referred only to Pushkin. But for M. any man was a 'sun', a centre of gravity, as long as he lived, turning into a dead sun – 'yesterday's sun' – as soon as he died. Therefore, 'yesterday's sun', in the line above, is not Pushkin but any man, and it is the bier which is black – for mourning – not the sun.

The nocturnal sun, the sun of Erebus, the sun of guilt and doom, belongs to a different set of images relating to sin, crime, and retribution. Nerval has a black sun of melancholia – deriving, I believe, from Dürer. Akhmatova was very fond of Nerval and often mentioned him, but I do not remember M.'s having any particular feelings about him one way or the other. Since he was also not in the least prone to melancholia, Ivask and Lurye are wrong to derive M.'s black sun, which created such a stir in the years just before the Revolution, from Nerval. The list gives other sources far closer to M. than Nerval. These are *The Lay of Igor's Raid* and Avvakum's *Life*, a book he was always reading. But how can one overlook here that cardinal image of the darkness which came over the land at the sixth hour 'and lasted unto the ninth hour', when 'the sun was darkened'?† This was the sun under which, as a Jewish boy, M. was born: 'I awoke in the cradle, lit by a black sun.' For M., the fate of Jewry after the beginning of the era was life under this black sun. I would also suggest a study of the word 'black' in M.'s poetry. He probably used it in a quite traditional way, always indicating

---

* i.e., the three-volume edition published in the United States.
† Matthew 27:45 and Luke 23:45.

darkness, gloom, death, nonbeing, as in 'flakes of black roses' (about his mother's death), 'black sail', the 'black velvet' of universal emptiness, the 'black ice' of a Stygian recollection, the 'black Neva' and the 'black snowdrifts' of Revolutionary Petersburg. The sun is light, life, man, courage (following Plato). When the sun is combined with blackness (as in the line about the mob burying the nocturnal sun), or when the sun is not visible ('The sun cannot be seen and the earth floats on'), it means that life is ebbing, nearing its end, sinking into twilight as freedom is extinguished . . .

M. had a fairly large 'key-board of references', to borrow the expression he uses in 'Conversation About Dante', but it makes me laugh when he is presented at one moment as an expert on the chthonic deities and, at the next, as a poor fool who even had to borrow the word 'spring' from Viacheslav Ivanov. With all its short-comings, Russian education at the beginning of the century was quite respectable. When M. read me his lines about 'the rounded maiden's brow', even I recognized his allusion to the passage in Plato's *Ion* where the poet is compared to a bee gathering honey: the cornbins of memory had stored up what is said here about 'milk and honey' drawn straight from the rivers, and about the honey gathered by poets – 'the blind lyre players'. Why does the expert on Viacheslav Ivanov, discussing M.'s references to bees, fail to notice that there is nothing about Homer the 'blind lyre player' in Viacheslav Ivanov's translations of Alcaeus and Sappho, but that he is the subject of Plato's *Ion*? The same expert on Viacheslav Ivanov advises us to read all the things that M. read. This is good advice, but one should not suppose that M. read nothing except such leading lights of the pre-Revolutionary years as Viacheslav Ivanov. One would have to go through all the poets, particularly the Russian ones, bearing in mind the line: 'What good fortune, golden grasshopper, that you forge in the forest alone' (M. was convinced that the grasshopper – as its Russian name implies – is a minute blacksmith hammering on an anvil), and collecting at least some minimum of information about the likely scope of a young man's reading in the pre-Revolutionary decade, as well as about the early life of M. in particular. This same scholar wrote to another one in Moscow, asking him for information about when M.'s wedding took place. I am sorry to say that nothing of the kind ever took place at all – apart from the blessing conferred on us in a Greek coffee shop by my comic friend Makkaveiski. Since he came from a priest's family we thought this was quite good enough. It was the same Makkaveiski, as we were recovering from the revels of the previous evening, who suggested the word 'wheel' used by M. in the poem he wrote on the occasion. Terapiano's mention of this is the only bit of truth in the memoir by him quoted in the notes to the first volume. The rest is fiction – especially M.'s supposed speech about how he wrote verse. As regards the phrase about 'creaking labour that darkens the sky', nothing could have been more in M.'s style – my efforts at daubing canvases with imitation folk designs in the Kiev Merchants' Garden seemed to him like forced labour of an intolerable kind, though in fact it was nothing more than an amusing game played by the 'little herd' of artists I belonged to. Anyway, this is how our marriage – or life in sin – began, and neither of us could have imagined it would last for the rest of our lives. Those were the days of our youth, unclouded by thoughts of the 'black sun', but they had barely ended when M. was again assailed by eschatological forebodings.

In the poem about the young Levite, doom is foretold only for the city. I believe that by the 'young Levite' M. meant himself, not Kartashev, the man who was to organize the last Church Council in Russia. I have a vague recollection that in conversation with Kablukov, Kartashev actually referred to M. as a 'young Levite', but I cannot vouch for this. The elders whom the young Levite calls upon to flee the doomed city regarded the ominous colours black and yellow as those of their ritual: 'Lo, the black and yellow; Lo, the joy of Judea.' As some commentators have rightly pointed out, M. saw the same colours in doomed Petersburg, even as late as 1930, in the poem with the line: 'yellow yoke mixed into ominous tar'. The frightened editors who bid fair to spend another hundred years mulling over their niggardly volume with its garbled versions of M.'s poetry* asked Amusin, the Bible scholar and expert on the Dead Sea Scrolls, to explain to them who or what exactly is being 'wound in linen clothes', why it happens on the bank of a stream,

* The still-unpublished Soviet edition. See page 56.

and what the poet means by the other mysterious Jewish goings on mentioned in these lines. They did not know that houses of prayer were generally built on the banks of rivers; they had no idea who was 'wound in linen clothes' and where these clothes were later found; they had never heard of Him who was called 'our Passover', nor read the words: 'For that Sabbath day was an high day.' They are unaware of all the memories, traditions, and ideas which form the basis of European culture. It is to such as them that the words of another poem are addressed: 'Bethlehem is strange and foreign to you / and you have never seen the manger' (this poem was thought to be lost, but it has turned up in Rostov, written in a copy of *Poems*, where the person who preserved it, Lenia Landsberg, probably perished). This kind of ignorance is the real abomination of desolation and 'murk of nonbeing' – when people know less about their past than even the animals, who at least retain full possession of their instincts, the body's memory. We are, however, still walking on two legs, and able to keep our balance when we stand upright. While people still live and have their being, all is not lost: they can talk to each other, read books, and learn where it is written: 'The sun and the moon shall be turned into darkness . . .'*

What is the point of guessing about where M. got his 'black sun' from? It crops up even in the *Eddas* – so Meletinski tells me – and is universally associated with the end of the world.

After his verse and article about the doomed city, M. went on to his completely escahatological words about an earth without people. These came to him in Petersburg in 1922, in his article 'The Word and Culture'. M. here calls Petersburg the most advanced city because it was the first to exhibit symptoms of the end: 'The grass growing in the streets of Petersburg is the first sign of the virgin forest which will cover the ground on which our cities stand . . . Our blood, our music, our body politic – all will have an aftermath in the gentle abode of a new nature . . .' How could Ivask, in the simplicity of his soul, take these words as referring to a utopian vision of future brotherhood – a brotherhood of stones, trees, and earth? In the very same article, after all, M. speaks of an earth *without people*. He saw the future as a kingdom of the spirit

* Acts 2:20.

devoid of mankind. 'Word and Culture' is by and large a sequel to the article on Scriabin. The article on Scriabin identifies the sin of the epoch, while the second article speaks of the inevitable consequence, namely, the destruction of the human race.

Having realized the inevitability of the end, M. speaks of the futility of all efforts to avert it: 'Stop it? Who can stop the sun as it wheels like a sparrow to its father's house, overwhelmed by a longing to return?' The sun is here compared to the whole of mankind (one is reminded of Blok's line in which the sun-son returns to its mother), and M. suggests singing a dithyramb to it, rather than 'begging favours' from it. By 1921 it was clear to him that mankind, having renounced the gift of life, was returning (as foreordained?) to the nonbeing from which it had once been summoned forth.

After his first bout of eschatological forebodings, which initially involved only Petersburg and the Petersburg period of Russian history (the poem on the Levite), M. left for Moscow, where he wrote his poem about the ship of history: 'Even in Lethe's coldness we shall remember / That the earth cost us ten heavens.' The realization that a clumsy hand on the tiller had already cost us the earth as well as the heavens came to him two years later, when he was back in Petersburg again, and it never left him to the end of his life, occasionally coming out in his verse, especially in the last years.

It has now become clear that the destruction of mankind will be brought about by its own hand – that is, it will be suicide, not the end foreordained: rather than wait for this, the species will probably dispatch itself of its own accord. Our only hope is the caution of our fat and pampered rulers, who have no wish to go under with everybody else. Nothing else can defer the moment of suicide. Ordinary people are powerless to affect the course of events, and – as we know only too well – nobody listens to poets, seers, and Cassandras. The elders of Jerusalem paid not the slightest attention to the young Levite.

14 Living Space in the Superstructure

I had never before seen M. so preoccupied, sombre, and with-drawn as he was in those years (the beginning of the twenties) after we had settled in Moscow, living in Herzen House, that 'vile mansion' with its view of 'twelve lighted Judas's windows'. The change in his poetry had come about in Tiflis already. I could hear the new intonation in the poem 'I Washed at Night in the Court-yard'. Moscow was the period in which he took vows: the vow of poverty – though it was more a question of spiritual discipline than of poverty as such – is taken in 'St Alexis' and elaborated on in 'Aliscans'. Neither of these is a mere translation, and they should both be included in the corpus of his original work, like 'The Sons of Aymon'.* In these poems M. was talking about himself and his thoughts concerning the future. He wanted to publish all three in one of the books he brought out in 1923 (in *Stone*, as republished by the State Publishing House, or the *Second Book*), but the editor objected, or it may have been the censorship – which is the same thing. It is not the censors who emasculate books here – they only round the process off after the editors have had their way with them, savaging them like dogs. There have been a few tiny changes in recent years, but they are of no great importance . . . In 'The Sons of Aymon', the personal element is in the mother's lament: 'Children, you are reduced to beggary and rags', and in 'Aliscans' it is the pain at the sight of the crowd of prisoners, an aching feeling of the kind I have known continuously for half a century now – though neither I nor any of 'our ladies' (as we are referred to in the poem) ever demanded anything but caution from their menfolk. I certainly never did, since there was just no point in offering advice to M.: he did not listen.

In the translations from Barbier, too, there is more than meets the eye. They are an attempt to comment on the present by refer-ence to the past: the poems about the bridled mare, drunkenness, and in particular the one about the sharing of their loot by the victors and bone thrown at the feet of the hungry bitch. This last, for some reason, was not included in the three-volume collected

* Translation of the chanson de geste *Quatre Fils d'Aymon*.

works, though the editors have been careful to print all kinds of rubbish done only to save us from starving, and even some of the laboured translations turned out by a namesake, *Isai* Mandelstam. One day people will collect all of Akhmatova's translations too, but only about ten lines of them are actually her own unaided work, the rest having been done in collaboration with others. Whenever she was commissioned to do such things – which for the likes of us was tantamount to receiving a prize or a handout – she farmed them out to other people and shared the fees fifty-fifty. She managed it very shrewdly and saved needy people by getting them paid handsomely for their drudgery – she was entitled to the highest rates of payment for such work. It was silly of her to destroy all the drafts, from which it would have been possible to determine who exactly was responsible for them. Many people – including Lev, who did a great deal for his mother – are aware of the way in which she produced these translations, but nobody is likely to mention it, with the result that all this translated stuff will duly appear in her collected works. One must protect poets from this kind of thing: it is terrible when they are forced to do hack translation work, and there is no earthly reason why it should all be reproduced in their books. The only serious translations done by M. were *Gogotur and Apshina** and Barbier. Belatedly taking Annenski's advice, he found he had something to learn from doing them. The choice of texts from Barbier was a calculated one, particularly in the case of the 'Pack of Hounds'.† Here M. expresses his view of the people's Revolution and his disgust at the spectacle of the victors battening on the fruits of the people's victory. For us this remains a burning issue.

I am still upset by the relish with which M. pours scorn on women in some of these translations. There is the 'proud and jealous bitch' waiting for her mate as he hurries home with his share of the loot; and then there is the passage where Gogotur says to his wife:

> How thou dost babble, silly woman,
> without wit or understanding . . .
> Do not meddle, who art so ill-begotten,

---

* Epic by the Georgian poet Vazha Pshavela. See note, Appendix A.
† See *Hope Against Hope*, page 211.

> In matters of honour to be settled by steel,
> Thy place is at the spinning wheel,
> Making yarn and weaving hosiery.

We almost had a row over 'ill-begotten' and 'bitch' – the language of the translation had a vivid and highly personal note about it. Admittedly he did this kind of thing only in translations. In his own lines on a similar theme about the poor Europa who longs to escape from her 'oarless rower' to the bottom of the sea, if need be ('And she would have liked to slip from those rough steep flanks'), there is pity for the poor child-woman, and he understands how much she would prefer 'the creak of oarlocks, a deck broad as a bosom, a flock of sheep', in other words, a peaceful existence with an ordinary kind of home-loving husband – a breadwinner, rather than a feckless vagabond who drags her with him from place to place, like the bull who abducts Europa. M. said I even looked a little like the Europa of Serov's feeble painting: presumably on account of her long face and expression of sheer horror.

There was of course something in me both of the young Europa and, potentially, of the 'proud bitch', and M. spared no effort to curb my craving for a proper home and my dream of living like everybody else. To tell the truth, he kept a very tight rein on me, and indeed I was rather frightened of him, but I did not show it and kept trying not so much to escape as to slip away for an hour or so. But it did not work even for a single minute. He understood me too well and could read my thoughts like an open book – not that there was very much to them: what sort of thoughts does a foolish slip of a girl have at twenty?

I remember the wretched things I hankered after, in common with all the women of my generation: a little place to call my own or, rather, a room in a communal apartment; a wad of rubles, at least enough to last the week through; a pair of shoes and some nice stockings. All of us, whether housewives or secretaries, were obsessed about stockings. Made out of real, but slightly spoiled silk, they never lasted for more than a day and, swallowing our tears, we all learned to mend ladders. And there was not one of us who did not weep real tears when the high heel – a legacy from a very different life – broke on her beloved only pair of those foolish shoes which had once been designed for stepping from one's gracious residence into a waiting carriage, and no farther. Actually, none of us would have had any gracious residences or carriages in the well-ordered life of earlier years either. Marriage to a banker would have been too high a price to pay for such luxurious existence – and bankers would have wanted something better for their money than silly girls like us. Still, with our one pair of shoes, and our one pair of stockings, we got ourselves up as best we could . . .

It was not very clever of Bulgakov* to make fun of the poor women in the days of NEP rushing to get new clothes because they were tired of going around in old castoffs, or in outlandish dresses made out of a pair of father's trousers. Of course they were sick to death of poverty, and of all the trouble it took even to have a wash in a city where bathrooms had been abolished. We used to wash balancing on one leg while putting the other under a cold-water tap. If we ever happened to lay our hands on some tattered piece of material, the imagination ran riot as we at once tried to think of something nice to make that could be worn on any occasion. With the money he got for his *Second Book*, M. bought me a blue fox fur, and all my girl friends nearly died of envy, but then it turned out to be not a real pelt, but tufts of fur which had been cleverly sewed on to fustian. Poverty was universal, and only the victors' daughters and their 'proud bitches' took systematic steps to shake it off. Their numbers grew from year to year, and I was only too conscious of the fact that we belonged to different classes.

M. was moved to smile at the Moscow working girls who, not to spoil their hard-earned shoes, took them off and splashed barefoot through the puddles. He talked about them in his short prose piece 'A Cold Summer' with feelings of sympathy that made me jealous. 'Ladies', on the other hand, filled him with horror and disgust. A few still flourished in Moscow and Leningrad, sometimes keeping salons. They had mysteriously managed to adapt to the new circumstances and were not to be trusted. Whenever we happened to run into one of them, M. always put on a stony expression, while I trembled in case he blew up and told them exactly what he thought of them. Some of the wives and sisters of the victors were patrons of 'culture'. Smart operators like Efros danced attendance on

* In *The Master and Margarita*, Chapter 12.

them, fixing things on their own and their friends' behalf. M. and I
never had anything to do with people of this type, and there has
now been a falling off in the cretinous legends to the effect that at
this period he enjoyed a rich way of life which had been denied him
in his youth – just as one no longer hears things suggesting the
opposite, for instance that he once wolfed down all the pastry or all
the caviar at Kameneva's* . . . If you want an idea of the unsavoury
implications of a comfortable existence in those years, I can recommend the recollections of the woman painter Khodasevich. She
also tells an absurd story about how Babel supposedly got her
husband released by the Cheka – there is as much truth in this as in
her yarn about someone pointing M. out to her as he stood among
other 'modernists' in a Moscow salon frequented by the Symbolists – at the time in question he was still going to school in
Petersburg, satchel in hand, and never went anywhere near
Moscow.

The austere person I now found myself living with in Herzen
House was completely different from the carefree one I had met
during the Kiev carnival. Eating our émigré bread together in
Georgia, we had grown used to each other, even if we had still not
become really close. In Moscow, before I had time to look around
me, he lassoed and bridled me, and at first I tried to kick over the
traces. I was eager to meet people and join in what was left of the
carnival: there was still a slight backwash from it here and there. I
was invited out by a woman I knew, the mistress of a noisy one-
room apartment frequented by none other than Agranov – and his
future victims. M. would sometimes agree to go there for a minute
or two during the daytime, but nothing would have induced him to
set foot in the place in the evening. Nor would he let me go anywhere by myself, so I never got to know the Moscow salons in those
early days of the new imperial epoch then beginning. People came
to invite me out to a basement night club – on the lines of Pronin's
Stray Dog – but M. would not hear of it. 'But you used to go to the
Dog,' I protested, to which he replied: 'I'm very sorry,' or 'Times
are different now' . . . From the window of our apartment we could
see the windows light up in the opposite wing of Herzen House
whenever there was a meeting of the Union of Writers, or the

* This allegation appears in Georgi Ivanov's memoirs.

Union of Poets; in those days these were separate organizations, though they shared the same premises. When we first arrived in Moscow, M. attended some meetings or other there, but after that he never went again. People were always coming up to our window on their way to the offices of the writers' organizations, and M. would exchange a few polite words with them, but he never got personally involved with any of them. He had thus already managed to isolate himself before his official ostracism had yet begun. Knowing there were no longer people he could refer to as 'we', he avoided casual meetings and contacts. Indeed, who was there for him to hobnob with? With Aseyev? With Narbut's moustachioed crew? With the Fellow Travellers? Lopatinski used to come and see us, and Yakulov, a caustic, witty man of easy disposition, looked in from time to time, as did the clever, irritable Aksionov. Yakulov once took us to see Krasnushkin, where we drank ourselves silly, but this was the last time anybody ever managed to tempt M. with free vodka. Yakulov told us that the Russian Revolution was not cruel, because all the cruelty had been 'sucked out' by the Cheka. He was later to learn by bitter experience what sort of a bird the Cheka was. Lunacharski forked out a great deal of money for his funeral, much to M.'s indignation: while he was alive they had let him starve and deprived him of his wife (she was put in prison), but now that he was dead expense was no object . . . Our apartment was near to the Kamerny theatre, to which we were always being invited by the set designers, and we also often went to new productions by Meyerhold; they were all incredibly different, sometimes arousing our interest and sometimes our disgust. We never really took to the theatre: underneath it was empty and frightening, despite all the surface glitter. The shibboleth of the day was 'biomechanics', which sounded both grand and stylish.

In 1922 there was still some demand for M. Apart from Narbut's call for a new Acmeism (without Akhmatova but with Babel and Bagritski), there were dozens of other proposals to create literary alliances of a practical nature. Once M. was summoned by Abram Efros – I went with him – to hear a proposal for an alliance of 'neoclassicists', or something of the sort. All the people claiming to be 'neoclassicists' had gathered there: Lipskerov, Sofia Parnok,

Sergei Soloviev, and two or three more whose names I don't remember. Efros trilled away like a nightingale, impressing upon us that, as things now were, we should survive only if we stuck together. A great operator, he frankly tried to tempt M. with the prospect of being able to do well for himself if he would agree to the creation of a literary group ('We need you') . . . There was talk of the Arts Theatre and other potential sponsors somewhere in the background. M. refused outright. He told those present – each in turn – why he could not go along with them, sparing only the silent Sergei Soloviev ('because of his uncle', as he explained to me later). Even at the time I could see full well how utterly preposterous such a coalition would have been, but M. had a knack for making enemies by a blunt outspokenness which was quite needless in situations of this kind. Efros never forgot that gathering, and in later years his resentment quite plainly backfired on us in a thousand and one nasty ways, some serious and some just petty. The others, who were all harmless enough, simply never forgot the insult.

A similar thing happened in Leningrad during our first visit there when he had to go and see Anna Radlova; this was because M. was related to her by marriage, and we had arrived just after the death of her sister, the wife of his brother Yevgeni. Radlova's mother, Maria Nikolayevna Darmolatova, had stayed on in the household of her hated son-in-law in order to be with her now motherless grand-daughter Tatka. It was for her sake that we paid our 'family visit' to Radlova. We found Kuzmin and Yurkun there – and also Olga Arbenina, I believe – as well as the artist Lebedev, who was married to Radlova's second sister, Sarra Darmolatova (later to make a name for herself as Sarra Lebedeva, the sculptress), and a few other people. Now again there was an attempt to lure M. into an alliance or coalition – this time intended to bring together all the arts: poetry, the theatre, painting . . . Sergei Radlov, the producer, told M. quite unabashedly that the cream of all the arts was at that moment gathered around his tea table – the best poets, painters and producers . . . Whether there was also a composer present I do not recall, but Yurkun represented prose. The material side would be taken care of by the theatre, guaranteeing support for M. and the other members of the group. M.'s name was essential to enhance the group's artistic standing, and in return he could count on their support in all things . . . Kuzmin sat in silence with a sly look and ate catfish, the best tinned food then obtainable. Yurkun did the talking for him – rather too forcefully, in fact. 'A low type,' as Akhmatova said of him (and also: 'A real disgrace').

On this occasion M. behaved much more politely than at Efros's: he just mumbled and pretended not to understand. Finally both Radlov and his wife tried to pin him down with a direct question: was he prepared to forget all about Acmeism – now so ludicrously behind the times – and throw in his lot with active exponents of modern art such as themselves in order to work together in a co-ordinated fashion? M. said he still thought of himself as an Acmeist. . . . Everybody started attacking the Acmeists for all he was worth, with only Kuzmin continuing to keep his own counsel, except that from time to time he put in a word of praise for Radlova's poetry. I got the impression that in fact he was behind the whole thing, though he was laughing up his sleeve at all of them – Radlova in particular. In all likelihood he had nothing but contempt for it all, but was managing to turn his friendly connection with Sergei Radlov to advantage – which meant that he had to praise Radlova. Yurkun was the loudest of them all, and for the first time I heard someone vilifying Akhmatova.

Later on I met the trio at Benedikt Livshitz's, and Olga Arbenina asked me which of the two Annas I was for: for Akhmatova or for Radlova. We were on opposite sides, and in Radlova's house – the meeting place for the 'cream of all the arts' – it was the thing to denounce Akhmatova. This was how it had been from the beginning, and Akhmatova's friends had good reason to stop going there. M. broke the old agreement on this one solitary occasion and got away only by the skin of his teeth. I sometimes met Radlova at her mother's, and as soon as she saw me she always said something nasty about Akhmatova, but for the most part it was comment on a purely feminine level: she neglected her appearance, didn't know how to dress or do her hair – in other words, she was a real slut. It was the sort of demented hatred of which only human beings are capable. Sometimes – because of my loyalty to Akhmatova – she went for me as well, but always in a roundabout

way (somebody, I think it was Miklashevski, had married a
woman from Odessa, and all his friends, so Radlova informed me,
didn't know where to look every time she opened her mouth.
'And you're from Kiev, aren't you? Isn't the accent there the same
as in Odessa?'). At other times she would try to use me to make
approaches to M., suggesting for instance that we should make a
habit of going out walking together in the mornings: 'You could
come back and have lunch with us, and then M. would pick you up
afterwards . . .' All this soon came to an end. In 1922 literary
associations and literary life of a sort still seemed possible. The
last group to be formed was the so-called Oberiu.* The surviving
remnants of the Serapions† and OPOYAZ‡ still love to recall the
twenties as a time during which there was a thriving and colourful
literary life. In fact, however, there was only the pitiful aftermath
of the pre-Revolutionary years – as in the case of Efros or the
Radlovs – or an association of the doomed, like the Oberiuty, who
clustered around Marshak and made their living by writing nursery
rhymes for children. The isolation chosen by Akhmatova and M.
was the only possible course. It was the beginning of an age during
which a few lone figures held out against a vast, organized mass.
We are still living in the same age – except that now there are no
longer even any lone figures.

In 1923 – whether as the result of a high-level conference, a
decree, or Lord knows what – there was an abrupt change in M.'s
position: he was simply put under a ban. His name was removed
from the lists of contributors to all the journals, and everywhere
people began to write that he had given up poetry and taken to
translations – all of which was unquestioningly reproduced abroad
in 'well-informed' newspapers such as *Nakanune*.§ In short, we
now saw the beginning of the official ostracism that still continues
to the present day. 'Society' immediately shied away from him,
and nobody invited him to join literary associations any more. The

* See Kharms, Appendix A.
† See Appendix B.
‡ Acronym for 'Society for the Study of Poetic Language', founded in
1916 by young literary scholars and linguists, including Shklovski, Brik, and
Jakobson. It was the forerunner of the Formalist school of literary criticism.
§ *On the Eve*, published in Berlin, 1922–4, was pro-Soviet and Moscow-
financed.

new ruling ideology was gathering strength. While the Civil War had still been on, the State smiled on everybody who offered to collaborate with it – hence the brief flirtation with 'left-wing art'. By the end of the war, supply exceeded demand, and the 'leftists' were speedily ousted. Averbakh moved into the ascendant, and the future, as it turned out, belonged to him. To the extent that literature still continues on the lines laid down by him, he was the victor. Nowadays he is never remembered or given his due for the simple reason that he happened to get shot. They were always shooting friend and foe indiscriminately.

In order to earn money for the support of his 'Europa', M. was forced to make the rounds of editorial offices. They all fell over themselves trying to get him to see the light, and not be so monstrously out of touch with reality. Once he told me the latest titbit he had been given for his enlightenment: 'It turns out that we live in the superstructure!' Somebody had thought he should know about the relationship between basis and superstructure.* We could both see that life in the 'superstructure' was revoltingly squalid and ignominious, and that all human relations were disintegrating. The first thing to disappear was the art of conversation. Suddenly people began to spin yarns instead, since any normal exchange of views was by now out of the question. How would you have dared tell anybody that the idea of the basis and superstructure was an absurd piece of dogmatism? The amazing thing was how long people went on parroting it. Even decent people – not scoundrels or careerists – could be heard discussing with a straight face the process by which 'the classical heritage is transferred from one superstructure to another'. 'In suitcases,' I once suggested to a man I trusted completely. What do children who have been brought up on this sort of stuff have to go through before they learn to talk and think properly? These people who substituted storytelling for conversation – they are often inordinately boastful as well – still rule the roost. The older generation keeps *The Twelve Chairs*,† Olesha, and Bagritski in suitcases under their beds just in case they have to transfer to a new superstructure.

* In Marxist terminology, the basis is the economic order of a society, while the superstructure consists of its legal, political, and cultural institutions.

† See Petrov, Appendix A.

In the twenties humour disappeared altogether, except insofar as it was made to serve, during the next fifty years, as a well-paid propaganda technique; but this kind of humour was the special province of LEF circles, and it originated with Petia Verkhovenski,* the first Russian Futurist. It was designed to startle and throw one off balance – the sort of thing Petia did to his poor sensitive papa. *LEF* and *On Guard* were the two leading literary journals at the beginning of the new era, but if you leaf through them now, you almost choke. Though seeming to be on opposite sides, they in fact were twins. The humour of Mylnikov Street†was harmless enough while it existed only as folklore in the mouth of Katayev. Once it had been ideologically processed by Ilf and Petrov, it came close to the ideal of Verkhovenski.

In the Moscow of the twenties there was nobody to exchange jokes with. The jokes of Petia and the Odessans stuck in one's gullet. The only healthy kind of humour we had was anecdotes. They came in right at the beginning and have never dried up for a moment. The anecdote is a unique form of comment on the life around us. Who makes them up? At one time they were attributed to Radek, but we were not at all convinced he was the author – and sure enough, the anecdotes went on after he perished. Our rulers have done their utmost to suppress this illicit genre. At the beginning of the twenties they deported a man who had collected all the anecdotes and tried to classify them. He disappeared forever. After him there were others, all caught in the act of passing on the latest anecdote (only to their friends of course). Despite such measures, however, there was no way of stamping them out – it is an elusive and invincible form. Anecdotes can originate in the big cities, in the provinces, in small towns, or in the villages, and they spread around the whole country even more quickly than *samizdat*. I noticed that in the Khrushchev era there were anecdotes not only congenial to 'us' (here understood in the very broadest sense to include all types of intellectuals, technocrats, schoolboys, and even our very human taxi drivers), but others of an opposite type as well. Akhmatova and I were both struck by this. Not outwardly different from the ordinary kind, they were virulently anti-Khrushchev, and

* Character in Dostoyevski's *The Possessed*, the chief of the nihilists.
† The Bohemian quarter of Odessa.

often anti-Semitic, being a staple of the crowds standing in queues for beer, as well as of the convivial groups noisily clacking their dominoes in the courtyards of apartment buildings. At the same time, 'our' kind of anecdote has widened its range and still goes from strength to strength. In recent years its concern for human values has become more pronounced than ever – not to mention its ruthless treatment of those who condone murder 'for the good of the cause', as a matter of principle . . .

Somebody has started a legend that M. was a pastmaster at making up anecdotes. But there is no truth in this. He liked anecdotes, laughed at them, and was always curious about where they came from, but his brand of humour was of an utterly different kind from the anecdote, the epigrammatic story with a biting satirical sting in its tail. M.'s humour, based on the absurd, was a kind of mischief or teasing for domestic consumption, only very seldom with a political slant, and directed mainly at his friends – Margulis, me, or Akhmatova. It took the form of impromptu verses made up for the occasion, or the sort of spoof he liked to perpetrate together with my brother – for instance, their mock memorandum to the Communist Academy,* pointing out that 'life is a thing of joy'. In M.'s humour there was always an element of what he called 'the blissful word bereft of sense'.

Kuzin and Yakhontov often joined in M.'s jokes. Kuzin went in for a kind of student whimsy foreign to M. – he loved bouts-rimés, for instance, something quite out of keeping with M.'s free-ranging and spontaneous type of joke. Yakhontov never took part in the making up of these things, but he was very good at faithfully reproducing them. M.'s friendship with Yakhontov was subject to ups and downs. It began at the end of the twenties, at a time when there was no question of M.'s composing any kind of verse, humorous or not. In the thirties, however, their periods of friendship coincided with the production by M. of a great deal of humorous verse, often in the form of dialogue, such as:

> Oh, how she loved Siberian furs, old Karanovich,
> Which is why she let her Petrovka flat
> To such a lean and hungry chap.

* Founded in 1918. Merged with the Academy of Sciences in 1936.

'Grandma,' shouts her grandson, out of breath,
'That coat will have to wait,
Mandelstam just snaps his fingers at the rich.'

This referred to our two months' stay in a room on the Petrovka.
We rented it from a woman who had gone away to Siberia, and
then we couldn't pay for it. Since M. was now totally ostracized, I
had become the mainstay of the household, but my health broke
down under the strain and I had to go into the Botkin hospital.

I earned our keep by working in the offices of the newspaper
For a Communist Education. I had been talked into this by
Margulis: 'Old man Margulis behind my back / Induced my wife to
tread the beaten track / And go to work for a certain horrid paper /
What little return for shame so black / May God forgive him for
this caper.' The best of these 'margulets' have been lost. The rule
of the game was that they had to begin with the words 'Old man
Margulis' and meet with the approval of the 'old man' himself.
Here is another one relating to the newspaper: 'Old man Margulis
has eyes / To haunt a man's imagination / I read in them with wild
surmise / The words: "For a Communist Education."' Margulis
was barely prevailed upon to approve this one: 'Last night I had a
dream – the devil sent it – / That old Margulis had made a dinner
jacket / For Bubnov, but then the two changed places: / Margulis
wore it with poor Bubnov's braces.' But Margulis was very fond of
the little ditty about how he and M. strolled down the boulevard
whistling Beethoven – I can't remember the words now . . . Somebody called Osipov has put a preposterous construction on what
was just innocent fun, but to hell with him: 'Old man Margulis
from Narkompros* / Is no natural scientist or geographer / But to
the sources of Tigris and Efros / He is a famous voyager.' 'Tigris
and Efros' was a dig at Abram Efros, the great fixer who had
condescended to arrange a little translating work for Margulis.

We almost never copied down this kind of humorous verse. In
Voronezh I was presented with some wonderful, strong Japanese
paper, and I used it to copy out everything I could still remember.
It later disappeared with the other things handed over to Rudakov.†

*The People's Commissariat of Education. See note, page 46.
† See *Hope Against Hope*, pages 325–9.

A small number of humorous poems have survived in the archives;
some were written down by my brother, and others by M. himself
in Voronezh. I don't know whether such frivolous stuff is of any
worth – Shklovski and Khardzhiev despise it, though it gave us
nothing but pleasure. One or two of the comic poems have been
included in the main body of his work ('What Street Is This? This
Is Mandelstam Street,' 'Our Sainted Youth,' and others). There is
no house on which it would be possible to put up a plaque saying
'Mandelstam lived here', there is no grave on which to put a cross,
and in this country we call our own they have for many years been
trying to stamp out all he did. So it has been, and so it will be. It is
thus a good thing that he had the foresight to name a street in his
own honour: 'And that is why this street, / Or rather, row of slums /
Is called by such a funny name / – Osip Mandelstam's.'

Margulis died in a camp almost at the same time as M. Yakhontov
threw himself out of a window in a fit of panic that he was about to
be arrested. How could we go on living and laughing, knowing all
the time what end awaited us?

15 On the Threshold

When we were living in Herzen House on Tverskoi Boulevard, we
once had to pay a visit to the militia – probably to get our residence
permits. This is something we have always had to put up with, but
in the twenties it was a fairly straightforward procedure and did not
scare us out of our wits. There is always a queue at the militia. To
while away the time I got into a conversation with a peasant
woman of about my own age who had a fine little baby in her arms.
'What did you marry such an old 'un for?' she asked, looking M.
up and down. 'Did they marry you off to him or something? I
picked my man myself . . .' At the time M. was thirty-one or thirty-
two, and the peasant girl's husband was a mere stripling by comparison, looking about five years her junior. Marriages like this
are fairly common in the villages. A youngster is snapped up by
an enterprising girl who drags him off to the city where he can make
money for her. This one was very pert, and she can have ended up

in only one of two ways: either she was denounced as a 'kulak' and deported or she did the same to her neighbours.

This absurd conversation has stuck in my mind only because I already felt that not only in appearance – he had always looked older than his years – but in his very being too M. had attained a state of maturity none the less real for having come before its time. I believe that his basic ideas and conceptions – the foundation on which the personality rests – had taken shape in him very early, already before he was twenty. This is borne out by his early articles, particularly 'On the Reader', which he wrote at the age of twenty-one. It seems to me comic that Lurye should refer to him as a 'divine child', while Nikita Struve speaks of the 'divine babbling' of his letters. In the few letters not written to me there is no 'babbling' at all, and those which are addressed to me (they have become known only because I copied them out for Akhmatova and she passed them to other people without telling me) are deeply personal, showing his feelings towards me when I was very young, extremely immature – and ill into the bargain. In his eyes I was always the younger one who had to be soothed, protected, and, if need be, taken in hand to stop me from doing silly things. Even in the letters from Voronezh,* by which time we both knew very well what was coming and I had long ceased to be a silly girl, he would break off in the middle of a despairing sentence ('Who knows what will come next . . . ,' 'If we're still alive . . . ,' 'I have no hopes of anything good . . .') and suddenly change his tone, saying that we were not weaklings and it was 'shameful to lose heart'. He 'babbled' to me in his letters to make me smile and shake off the despair it was almost impossible to stave off. But why do I say 'almost'? It was not 'almost', but completely impossible.

Nikita Struve thinks that M. did not understand the 'tragic reverse side of the gospel', that he was sustained by the dream of a golden age and was prone to a peculiar kind of chiliasm. Is this really so? Chiliasts believe in a kingdom of harmony on earth, but M. combined his cheerfulness of spirit with full awareness of the tragic way in which both history and his own fate were unfolding. In his last days he rejoiced in the 'magnificence of the plains', won-

---

* During the Voronezh exile, the author was allowed to visit Moscow, and received letters from M. there.

dering at the same time whether 'he of whom we shriek in our
sleep, / the Judas of nations yet to be' might not already be 'slowly
slithering' across them. M.'s strength was in his consciousness of
freedom, in his free acceptance of his lot and boundless gratitude
for all he had been granted. The sky, the air, the grass, breathing,
love – these were the treasures in his possession. He never set himself aims or cherished illusions of happiness and good fortune, but
he valued his 'living allotment of air' more than wealth, fame, or
the praise and affection of people. These were not the attributes of a
child – a child is ignorant of life and full of desires, depending
entirely on those around him and demanding their attention. Only
a really mature person can have inner freedom. M.'s more sober-
minded contemporaries spoke of his frivolity – and I had more
than enough conventional wisdom myself to feel the same way.
They were astonished at his love of life, and so was I, considering
how hard it is to love life in our times. Everybody who has written
about him makes him out to be almost a simpleton – always
laughing, incapable of earning money (Georgi Ivanov mentions
this, but it would have been more accurate to say he was incapable
of *making* money); in other words, not a serious man at all . . . The
various ways of making money, both in our times and before, are
simple enough and M. was aware of them, but he refused to use
them. Neither would he agree to sell me – even to a newspaper . . .

The main thing about M. was that he did not fight for his place
in life because he did not *wish* to. Nor did he try to establish a hold
over other people: he was not a 'fisher of men', like so many other
poets and writers (especially in the years before the Revolution).
M. quite consciously refrained from such things and was content to
live in any conditions – as long as I did not totally despair. I was
his only property, and he put a great deal of effort into the business
of adapting me to himself – however slightly – and of getting me to
see things his way to some tiny extent. Only because I was able to
assimilate a little of his point of view do I understand the source of
his good spirits and grateful acceptance of the world, puzzling as
these were to all the petty lovers of life who were forever betting
on some horse or other – always a different one – and gnashing their
teeth when it failed to romp home.

Even Akhmatova did not completely understand him. At the

best period of her life she had a marked tendency to asceticism and self-renunciation. Not finding the same trait in M., she was at a loss to know what to think – everybody tends to judge others by analogy with himself, and this was particularly true of a woman as feminine as Akhmatova. She tried to judge me and my relations with M. in the same way – with the result that she got a lot of things wrong, if not everything. Nobody was closer to us than Akhmatova, and if she failed to grasp the forces that shaped M., then there is no point in expecting others to. I believe that time will reveal him in his essence. He has not even been properly read yet: the three-volume edition has not been out for long and is available only to a few. For me it is an enormous joy. I had never dared hope I would one day see M. published, that I would hold his books in my hands, make notes in the margins, correct mistakes in the texts, and feel the joy of knowing that the work of my life is done: the books are there, and though some things are lost, the bulk is preserved and exists. Who could ever have hoped for so much?

M. stubbornly insisted that, in living with him, I should fully share his sense of concern about the world. This was less intense at the end of his life, when everything was all too clear, than in the twenties (up to the time when he wrote *Fourth Prose*, in the winter of 1929), because then we could see the future looming ahead only in dim outline, and he still alternated between hope and despair that people might come to their senses, stop their fratricidal bloodletting, and start to build a proper life for themselves. Sometimes he even doubted his own powers of vision: was he himself at fault, perhaps, for not seeing everything in the same way as enormous numbers of other people? But most of the time – as appears in his poetry – he was convinced that only rivers of blood would heal the world, that somebody would have to 'join with their blood the vertebrae of two centuries . . .' 'At the threshold of new days' he felt himself to be a 'hanger-on', living in fear and unable to come to terms with reality.

Being so cut off from the outside world, we had no idea that similar processes were taking place in other countries, though in a different form. In our own country it was all so flagrant that we had no eyes for what might be going on elsewhere. To all intents and purposes life seemed to be on the mend, and to many it even seemed to be booming, but every day brought something new to fill us with horror and destroy any hope of recovery. The future must already have been casting its shadow over this most idyllic period of our life. The revolutionary terror had ended, there was no more shooting on the streets, the streetcars were running, the shops and markets were open. Once there were rumours of widespread arrests among the intelligentsia, but then Kuzmin-Karavayev (one of the members of the first Poets' Guild – I think it was he) came to bid us farewell, saying they had all been released the next day and were being sent abroad. He was a Catholic and had decided to go to Rome – to kiss the Pope's slipper. Several people did not want to leave and managed to get out of it. There was nothing at all cruel about this measure: ostracism is the mildest sanction against dissidents. Most people maintained that there had been a turning point and that the era of shootings was over; true, there were a few cases of banishment to Solovki,* but the young, still vulnerable State – so it was argued – had to protect itself unless there was to be a relapse into anarchy. We were told to drop our 'intellectual whining'.

We heard that in Solovki the exiles were living very well, working, mending their ways, bringing out their own newspaper . . . We were even shown some literature on the subject which had been presented to certain people by a visitor from the institution in charge of these things. His hosts were very proud at having been honoured by such a visit and passed on the 'confidential' information he had given them over a cup of tea. Whenever I mentioned anything of this kind to M., he commented that he had never once *seen* any exile who had returned from Solovki, and that until he did, he would put no credence in officially inspired rumours. In the whole of my life I have never met a single person who went to Solovki and came back to tell the tale. How does one explain that?

People were dispatched to Solovki on the quiet, directly from the Lubianka. Before being sent off, some of them were occasionally allowed to go home for a day or two to put their affairs in order. This gave them a chance to tell us about the conditions in the inner prison of the Lubianka, about the methods of questioning and

* Former monastery on an island in the White Sea, notorious as a place of detention for political prisoners in the early Soviet period.

other techniques of the interrogators, who were already gathering strength for the great days to come. These people would come to see us for ten minutes and then dash off to deal with all their urgent business. I remember one tall, blue-eyed man who had known M. from the days when he frequented the Sinani household. By an irony of fate he had found himself sharing a cell with a white-bearded old man who had once been a well-known Okhrana* official (could it have been Dubrovin, I wonder?). He had been in jail since the very first days of the October Revolution, for the most part in solitary confinement. He was given a 'cell mate' only when the prison became too overcrowded, and he was glad of the chance to talk thus granted him. Though he had been condemned to death, he was being used as a consultant. He was only too pleased to pass on his expertise to the Cheka – it was all for the good of the country!

During our journey from the Caucasus we had seen – not for the last time – refugees from the Volga region at the stations and other stopping places: emaciated mothers clutching tiny skeletons in their arms. I once saw a child with meningitis, and this was just how these children from the Volga looked. I have been haunted down the years by this kind of sight: a mother dying from hunger with a child still alive, or a mother just barely still alive with a dying child; famine in the Volga region, famine in the Ukraine, the famine caused by collectivization, and the famine caused by war – all compounded by chronic malnutrition. One of these women I remember with blinding clarity. I was walking along Zhukovski Street in Tashkent to the university. This was shortly after the war. On the way there was a square, laid out in response to a whim of Kaufman's as an imitation of the Paris Étoile. In a small garden on the square there was a Russian peasant woman sitting on the ground with her back resting against the trunk of a high tree; her face was blue and puffed up, her legs were monstrously swollen, and her thin arms hung helplessly at her sides like sticks. Next to her a sickly child, a year old or a little more, was crawling about and crooning happily to himself. It is hard to tell the age of such children – their growth is slowed down, and a three-year-old can easily look two years younger. I noticed that the eyes of the mother were glazing over. She was still alive, but had lost consciousness or

* The tsarist secret police.

was dying. The child was scooping up pebbles with his little hands and laughing. Well-fed people came walking past – the local population had recovered and were living tolerably well, and the wartime evacuees had returned home already. Somebody called a militiaman and an ambulance. They undid her kerchief and found her papers there. She had signed on for a job somewhere and either run away from it already or collapsed on her way there. The Uzbeks are good to children: they took in war orphans of all races, who then grew up in peasant homes with the little Uzbek children, becoming just like them, despite fair hair and blue eyes. This particular child may well have been saved, unlike the children in the Volga region after the country had been exhausted by the Civil War: then they died wholesale by the roadside and even more commonly at home, next to their mothers on the stove.* There was nowhere to go, and every crust of bread was beyond price.

There were rumours about the famine on the Volga, and a letter about it from Patriarch Tikhon, who wanted to organize aid for the victims, was passed from hand to hand. The Muscovites flippantly dismissed it as a joke, saying that the new State did not need any help from priests. In Bogoslovski Street, not far from where we were living, there was a little church. I remember how once, stopping at the sight of a small crowd gathered outside, we were told that all church property was being confiscated. I do not know whether it was the same everywhere else, but here it was being done quite openly. No one tried to bar our way as we went inside. An elderly, dishevelled priest was trembling all over, large tears rolling down his cheeks, as the icons were stripped of their coverings† and flung to the ground. The people doing all this were simultaneously carrying on loud anti-religious propaganda while old women wept, and the crowd jeered, hugely enjoying the spectacle. The church, as we all know, belongs to the 'superstructure', and it was now being destroyed together with the old 'basis'.

We are always hearing it said that old Russian painting, previously hidden under the icon coverings, was exposed to view for

---

* The large stove in a Russian peasant house was traditionally designed for sleeping on.

† These could be of gold or silver and were sometimes studded with precious stones.

the first time after the Revolution, but nobody mentions the way in which it was done. We also prefer to gloss over the fact that untold numbers of icons were destroyed and chopped to pieces, and that many churches in Moscow and all over the country were razed to the ground. The best was if a church was converted into a warehouse – it then had some chance of survival. In Pskov I was once standing near one of the marvellous churches there – they are small and remarkably well proportioned – when a passer-by who looked like a worker stopped and asked if I knew that the churches here had been used to house prisoners. They had been crammed in like sardines when there was no more room in the huge old jail. This conversation took place at the beginning of the sixties. This man still remembered it, but otherwise it will soon be forgotten. Witnesses are dying off . . . My method being quite unchronological, I can also mention here an old woman whom Frida Vigdorova and I visited when we were collecting material for *Pages from Tarusa*.* She lived in a filthy hovel with a leaking roof, everything mildewed, bits and pieces of broken crockery, a wretched bunk covered with rags. The old woman was nevertheless always produced for the benefit of visiting journalists because she was a model member of her *kolkhoz* who always did everything asked of her and also had the gift of the gab. She started spinning a tale to us, when Frida suddenly asked her: 'But do you have any icons?' 'I don't believe in icons,' she said. 'I believe in Soviet power.' We had a car waiting for us and got out as fast as we could. Frida said to me: 'A fat lot of good Soviet power has done her. Did you see how she lives?' The old woman was then around seventy, and three years later she would have been given a pension – if she lived that long. Out of the kindness of his heart Khrushchev introduced pensions, first for old people in the towns, and then for those in the villages. The faith of the old woman would now be rewarded by an income of thirty rubles a month. In her time she no doubt jubilated with the rest as the church in her native village was pulled down: she was angry with God because he had not filled her pockets with gold.

I do not know whether the priest with tears running down his cheeks survived: he looked as though he would have a stroke any

*A literary miscellany published in Kaluga in 1961. (See Vigdorova, Appendix A.)

moment. I remember the appalled look on M.'s face as we returned home after watching the 'confiscation' for a while. He said it was not a question of the valuables as such. It had happened before in Russian history that the bells had been removed from the churches and melted down to make cannon, or that all their gold had been given up to help save the country (from my childhood I remembered the lines: 'We will pawn our wives and children'). The church, he went on, really would have helped the starving, but Tikhon's proposal had been turned down, and now they were shrieking that the church people had no pity for the starving and were hoarding their treasures. In this way they were killing two birds with one stone: while vilifying the church, they were also grabbing its gold. He also doubted that the funds thus obtained would be spent on the needs of the starving rather than on 'World Revolution'. Recently, one of our journals, the most 'progressive', published the memoirs of a woman who had seen the effects of the 'confiscation' of church property from another angle: she was one of those who were sent to distribute aid in the famine areas. They were not able to give the peasants food, only seed grain, and somehow keeping alive by eating weeds, nearly dropping from hunger, the people did manage to sow their crops. The woman in question is a real follower of Lenin, and her humane heart bled from pity. It did not occur to her to ask why all the wealth of the church, stored up during the ages, had not sufficed to feed the hungry even in that relatively small and under-populated region – if she had given it any thought she would no doubt have blamed the 'grasping church people'. Who now remembers the hungry crowds in the cities and the peasants silently dying on their cold, crumbling stoves? In Russia people die in silence.

We had gone into that church quite by chance and heard the jeering of the mob and the wailing of the old women. Similar disconnected scenes from daily life appeared kaleidoscopically like this before our eyes, never forming into a complete picture. Everything we learned was a chance detail, the result of a momentary glimpse. Conflicting rumours provided a commentary on events from different points of view. The twenties are still looked back upon as a period of the rule of law and general prosperity. The Meyerhold Theatre flourished, the cinema was coming into its own,

Mayakovski was thundering away, the Fellow Travellers were perking up. I am often accused of subjectivism, because I keep harping not only on 1937 but also on earlier phases of the suppression of 'alien elements': the church, the Freemasons, idealist philosophers, peasants, engineers, ordinary people held in prison cells until they yielded up their gold, collectors of anecdotes, and suspect intellectuals. I remember the crowds of beggars who flooded the cities both during and after collectivization. I looked at it all through the eyes of M. and hence saw things that others did not see. Brik was right to call him an 'alien element': he gave a wide berth to the salons kept by ladies close to the government and never made the acquaintance of Agranov. The city bustled noisily about us, and it seemed that real life was about to begin in earnest. We were already standing on the threshold of it. We were indeed. People got what they wanted and had helped to bring about, fostering it with their own blindness, cruelty, and ignorance.

16 First Quarrels

There was nothing at all of the ascetic about M., and no end to the things he was fond of, or would have liked to have. He was always hankering after the south; he loved large rooms with plenty of light, a bottle of dry wine for dinner, a well-made suit (and not some monstrosity produced by the Moscow Tailoring Combine); and most of all, he loved well-baked bread rolls, something we always particularly longed for after our first experience of hunger. He liked order and would always put things back in their proper place after I had scattered them around the room. Some men, as I have noticed, are possessed by a mania for order, but M. simply had a normal approach to the problem of keeping a room tidy, unlike me with my Bohemian attitude. But I did do the dusting – even on top of the cupboard . . .

At the beginning of the twenties, we were still 'feeling our way' with each other, as it were, and this was no simple matter. We had our first blazing row after I had once slipped off to an airfield where I was taken up in a training plane – quite illicitly – and learned what it was like to 'loop the loop'. I came home bursting with impressions, but he gave me no chance to talk about them. In 'Journey to Armenia' there are a few words about looping the loop; this information, however, he got not from me but from Boris Lapin, who had been taken up by the same man (soon to be killed when his plane crashed somewhere in the Caucasus). There was something odd about the man in question, and he was too well connected; M. was indignant that I had let him into the house. I used to let everybody in, understanding nothing about either people or the times we lived in.

Looping the loop, of which I never hear anything nowadays, was then a new fad, and I was unable to resist it. M. simply could not understand how I could develop a taste for something if he did not share it. He wanted me to look to him and only to him, in the way that Alexis's wife-to-be waited for her betrothed, and he found I was lacking in the 'dignified wifely charm' – as he put it – which he later noted in the Armenian peasant women. But neither meekness nor forbearance was in my character, and we were constantly colliding head on, quarrelling loudly like all young couples, and then making up again. He always intercepted me whenever I tried to get away – not for good, of course, only for a while – and kept trying to din it into my head that we had sown our wild oats and the time for idle pleasures had gone by. I did not believe him: everywhere young wives of my age were always trying to make off and have a good time, and their boy-husbands kicked up a great fuss until the moment they too found some way of keeping themselves happy. I did not understand the difference between a husband and a lover, and I must confess that I still don't. I only know that M. had a hard core, a deep bedrock of principles, which set him apart from anyone of his own or later generations. He believed in the concept of a 'wife', and maintained that a man should have only one. My generation, which destroyed the institution of marriage (something I still regard as an achievement), did not recognize any vows of fidelity. We were ready at any moment to break off a marriage (regarded anyway only as a protracted love affair) and get a divorce – or rather separate, because in fact there was no real marriage to begin with. It is amazing that such markedly casual relationships often resulted in lasting unions which were very much more stable than the marriages, founded on lies and pretence, of earlier generations. Coming together without a thought for the future, we sometimes found that we neither could nor wanted to part. A good thing about being so terribly poor was that we were completely uncalculating in money matters, which therefore played no part in the ups and downs of our love life. No young man thought twice about spending money on a bread roll for his girl friend.

This was how things were with M. and me. In Kiev, as I have already mentioned, we took up with each other unthinkingly the day we met, and I kept telling him we would be through in two weeks, hopefully without any 'fuss' . . . When he brought me to Moscow – before our trip to Georgia – I was stung to the quick by a remark Ekster made to Tairov: 'You remember my pupil? She's married Mandelstam.' I took this as gossip and interference in my private affairs: what business was it of anybody's whom I chose to live with? But I soon found that despite all my equivocations everybody thought of me as M.'s wife, and gradually I got used to the idea. M. laughed at my foolishness, reproved me for 'nihilism', and slowly but surely began to take me in hand.

Despite the firm principles I have mentioned, M. was also a man of his generation, and they were fancifully combined with a good deal of silly humbug from the past. If he was indignant at my easygoing feelings about marriage, I had no time for all the old Petersburg mannerisms which smacked too much for my liking of the Stray Dog and the dandies who frequented it. Although he influenced me greatly and moulded me in his own image, I also affected him in certain ways with my impatience and readiness to pack up and leave at any moment.

Once he asked me to start saying 'thou' to him. In our first years together, like most of the girls of my age, I had always said 'you' for ordinary daytime purposes. I would probably have gone over to 'thou' of my own accord, but M. was impatient and told me so in the way required by the rules of conduct he had learned at the Stray Dog. 'I have no end of girl friends who say "you" to me, but you are the only one I want to call me "thou".' I now believe he got his ideas partly through Florenski, whom I had not yet read, but at the time I was struck only by the Stray Dog manner of telling me this. I replied that I was quite happy to continue as before, and that if he wanted to take up with someone else (of which there was not in fact the slightest question), he was welcome to leave me, and I would go off with one of the boys . . . He was genuinely astonished: all his Petersburg friends had girl friends, but this did not prevent them from also having faithful wives – though he was aware that the most seemingly virtuous of wives 'to their bedchambers, if they saw fit, admitted scoundrels now and then'. He didn't want anything like this to happen to him, and he never took his eyes off me. He was always telling me that the literature of all countries was concerned only with the faithlessness of women, never attaching any importance to that of men. This I translated into female logic: what a man does away from the home, a woman does in it, but since we had no home, I promised that if ever I got involved in anything, I would do so 'away from the home . . .'

Our squabbles were about nothing at all, and it was some time before we realized from our own experience that betrayal on either side was not just fun, a carefree fluttering of butterflies, but a real disaster. Nevertheless, during the whole of our life together, he was always trying to get me to make a scene, to fight for him with a great display of emotion. By the unwritten laws of my generation (as opposed to his), we were not supposed to do this kind of thing, and the only time I broke a plate and uttered the sacramental 'It's either she or I!' he was beside himself with joy: 'Now you've become a real woman at last!' . . . This happened much later, though on the whole these problems passed us by, not fundamentally affecting our lives, or at least never going beyond a passing fancy – either on his part or on mine – for someone else. If it had not been for his Stray Dog code of behaviour, even these momentary aberrations need not have happened. It is fashion, custom, or the general mood that dictates such things, but fashion or no fashion, we were clearly too frightened of losing each other and decided that the dance of the carefree butterflies was not for us.

Today all my ideas are out of date. The stock of women has fallen, and we see them struggling desperately to keep their homes together, clinging to their fickle, recalcitrant husbands with might and main. In some cases they frantically try to assert themselves and enhance their value by complaining to their bored husbands about the way they are pestered in the street and at work. The most horrible thing is to see how they throw themselves around a man's neck, desperately working on the poor devil with cajolery, threats of suicide, and a thousand other cheap tricks. This had already begun in my youth and has now blossomed out on a grand scale. I have been told about an old man who walked out on his wife after forty years with her. He left a note saying the past had been one big mistake. I am all for divorce while one is still young, rather than allowing mistakes to drag on forever.

For my generation the 'cult of the fair sex' seemed hopelessly outmoded: all the passions aroused by chance encounters, the 'first glance of the beloved', and those ambiguous relationships cultivated by women ten years senior to me against the background of a crumbling marriage based on mutual deceit (the celebrated 'loneliness together') . . . Quite frankly, I do not believe in love without sex, and I more than once shocked Akhmatova by asking her: 'But did he ask you to sleep with him?' Another criterion which always causes indignation when inquired about is: 'How much has he spent on you?' I have known this to infuriate both the 'ladies' of a bygone day (if this is how I may refer to the bedraggled old trollops) and the pushing wenches of later generations. In other words, by asking this I touched them on the sorest spot of all . . .

For M. and me things were quite different. When a man was isolated – at first by his own wish and later thanks to the official disfavour still in force today – it was natural that he should look for someone to whom he could say 'thou', and M. stubbornly tried to make a wife out of me, a wretched girl he had found quite by chance. The role of 'wife' did not suit me, and the times were not favourable to the very concept. A wife makes sense if one has a home and a stable way of life, but such things did not exist – and perhaps they never will again. We all lived on a volcano – and still do. Love and passion apart, a wife is there to build a home and organize a domestic routine. In our times a girl friend was handier than a wife. A girl friend shares a man's life, but has no rights. I did not need any 'rights' – in love they are not much help. There was no question of a home, since the ground was always opening up beneath us. This was why I baulked so much at the absurd, old-fashioned role of 'wife' and tried to insist on being instead a happy-go-lucky girl friends with no rights. I felt M. himself only stood to gain from this – one can also say 'thou' to a girl friend, after all . . .

Meanwhile, the people on the opposite side of the fence from us, the killers who ruled us, were busily restoring conventional family life and reverting to the middle-class ways of a previous age, believing, evidently, that they were already secure and firmly in the saddle; but in reality they were just as liable to be destroyed as we were. I have always been curious about what goes on in the mind of a woman who lives with a murderer. Most likely she doesn't think about it at all, but merely glows with pride at having such a good family man for a husband.

I had occasion to come across the ideas about marriage of our pre-Revolutionary generation in a somewhat different context. In those early years in Moscow we caught a brief glimpse of both Georgi Ivanov and Khodasevich, who turned up one after the other to arrange their departure abroad. At the beginning we – and the Fascists – were happy to let people go, but later every would-be émigré came to be regarded as a person capable of betraying state secrets, since he knew that the actual state of affairs in his country was quite different from what was written about it. This is why we were subsequently made to stay where we were, any conversation with a foreigner being treated as espionage. People were allowed out only after the most careful scrutiny, and the same applied to those who were let in – such as Aragon and his wife,* for instance. Making a career out of 'love' for us, this pair also carried on excellent propaganda in their own country. It is said that Aragon has now fallen out with his cannibal friends and even signs various protests. But how can he forget that he used to live on the scraps thrown to him from their table? Only let him not pretend that he suspected nothing. He knew everything from all the cannibal talk he heard in the houses of his wife's relatives. The only people who knew nothing were those who did not want to know – and that's no excuse.

I think that at the beginning our rulers still believed in the rightness of their cause – hence their willingness to let out some of those who wanted to go. The first to come and see us on his way out was

* See Brik, Appendix A.

Georgi Ivanov. He left his suitcase with us, ran off to settle his affairs, returned in the evening, and then rushed straight to the station. On me he made the impression of a minor variety show entertainer, or a hairdresser, and I was astonished that anybody should ever have taken him seriously. This time M. could not put the blame on Gumilev, as in the case of Gorodetski. From his mumbled explanations I gathered that what appealed to him about Georgi Ivanov was his love of humorous verse, and of poetry in general. In Odoyevtseva's memoirs I read that I was supposedly wearing M.'s suit when Ivanov came and that I gave him an excellent dinner. I do not know which of them is responsible for this fiction, but my recollection is that Ivanov caught me in pyjamas. They were dark blue with a white stripe. Pyjamas had not yet reach Petersburg, and several times I was asked by people there: 'Is that how you people in Moscow dress nowadays?' Both of them – Ivanov and Odoyevtseva – are shameless embroiderers of the truth. What a vile invention – his story about the last meeting with Gumilev, or hers about Andrei Bely unburdening himself to her when they happened to meet in the Summer Garden. There is no limit, however, to what people in the West are prepared to swallow.

Khodasevich stayed several days in Moscow and came to see us once or twice. An evening was arranged for him at the Union of Poets, and it attracted what for that period was a huge crowd. He was popular then and still is at the present time. Today's young people know both his verse and his bilious prose writings, though none of it has circulated in *samizdat*. Copies of his books, on the other hand, are sold for high prices.* Many people find him congenial because he was such a lost, tormented soul, but his poetry brings no illumination. Inspired mainly by negativism and non-acceptance of life, there is a bitter infirmity of spirit about it. Catharsis comes only from a true sense of tragedy, based on an understanding of the nature of evil.

Khodasevich was in a cheerful, talkative mood, and very pleased at the prospect of getting away. He told us he was leaving together with Berberova and begged us not to pass this on to anybody, in

* i.e., editions published in the West and smuggled back into the Soviet Union, where they are sold on the black market.

case it should get back to his wife, Anna Ivanovna Khodasevich, the sister of Chulkov: 'There'll be hell to pay if it does!' There was something slightly put on and affected about his fears on this score. I was amazed he was going away without telling the woman he had lived with during all his years of hardship and called his wife. M. was also a little put out by this, but it was not his habit to think badly of a poet – there must be a good reason, he decided, telling me that Khodasevich was a sick man whom Anna Ivanovna had looked after like a child. Life had been very difficult for them, and according to M., Khodasevich would not have survived without his wife: she went out to hunt for food, chopped the firewood, lit the stove, did the washing and cooking, and bathed her sick husband, never allowing him to do any heavy work. A little while later I met her. She twittered away like a bird, saying how sorry she was for her poor Vladek and explaining what their relations had been ('Vladek is so ill – everything is bad for him'). Though upset that he had left without a word, she showed everybody his new verse sent to her from abroad, never saying anything bad about him and insisting that she loved only him. At a difficult moment in my life she started urging me to leave M. When he heard this he was furious and forbade me ever to go near her again. She said she feared M. would throw me over just as Vladek had abandoned her . . . Looking for all the world like an Italian boy, she had nothing but trouble with the men she loved. Pasternak tried to save one young man, almost the last of them, but he was unsuccessful and Anna Ivanova wept inconsolably. Many years later, when I happened to meet her in a streetcar, she showed me a little note-book with some of Khodasevich's poetry. A poor, scatterbrained, infinitely devoted creature . . .

Independently of each other, both Khodasevich and Georgi Ivanov told M. that I was quite unsuited to be his wife – I was, they said, too young and feckless. I suppose they thought M. was also a 'child of God' in need of constant care. In his younger days M. had often heard his 'dandy' friends saying they were on the lookout for rich wives. But with the onset of general poverty, the ideal changed: now it was the energetic wife who could manage things for her enfeebled husband. M. innocently blurted out what his worldly-wise friends had been telling him on these lines. I was stag-gered by the total contrast between the previous ideal of a meekly submissive wife and the new preference for a high-powered, pro-tective one. Fortunately, I had noticed by then that M. could not stand the type. If I had been at all like this, he would have dropped me and run off with the first damsel in distress to come his way. Both mentally and physically he was the sort of person who would not brook any attempt to domineer him, and he regarded women as by their nature subordinate, even rather inferior beings who needed care and attention – frightened, wide-eyed, shrinking creatures given to telling fibs and – even more to his liking – a little brainless . . . He believed a man should always win his bride by taking her away from home – ideally by abducting her – and that she must be the younger partner, entirely dependent on his will. In his very early youth, not yet sure of his own preferences, he had been briefly attracted by the cult of 'beauty' in a woman, so assiduously fostered by Akhmatova. The great beauties of the day must all have managed to get away after the Revolution – at least I have seen only the leftovers, all of whom struck me as funny in a somewhat excruciating way. I remember one who used to come and visit Akhmatova in Tashkent. Since it was dangerous to walk home after dark, she sometimes stayed overnight. Undressing to go to bed, she would stroke her legs – yellow as old parchment they were – and say: 'My body . . .' Akhmatova talked with her about the past and often spoke in praise of her daughter, a nice, modest girl who was scarcely to blame for the ancient Greek name her mother had given her out of a whimsical desire to perpetuate a cult of yesteryear among the younger generation.

As is clear already from *The Egyptian Stamp*, the fashionable worship of beautiful women was only a passing phase with M., and as the years went by, the attitudes which reflected his basic nature came to predominate ever more conspicuously. He always, for instance, cut short any attempt on my part to fend for myself, or do work of my own; least of all would he countenance my earning money. He was angered by the least display of independence, and would have given anything to make me less irreverently mocking and unruly. At the same time he was always making fun of me and teasing me in a way that only I would have put up with, having been inured to such treatment by two elder brothers who had broken me in according to the classical rules of *haute école* . . .

In the years of our Voronezh exile he willy-nilly allowed me to do various chores for him, but it made him very unhappy: he could not stand the idea of being dependent on his wife in the slightest degree. Yet I have no regrets that our whole life together went by as it did, and if he were still here I would ask nothing more than to sit quietly at his side, never saying a word out of place or interrupting when he talked to people. I would have been content with this. All my activities without him, all the things I have done independently of him, have been a matter of necessity; otherwise I should long ago have stumbled and fallen by the wayside, failing in my mission to preserve his writings. Once, when Susanna Mar came to see us, I brought up in M.'s presence the bright ideas he had been hearing from Ivanov and Khodasevich about the need for energetic wives who help their husbands. Susanna Mar, a member of the Nichevoki* group, was a woman with a great love of mischief, a head of classical beauty, and legs rather on the short side, as one finds in Armenians. She always prattled away without pausing for breath and said the most outrageous things, but in some mysterious way it had the effect of bringing her listeners closer together, rather than causing bad blood between them. On this occasion, for instance, she poked fun at me because M. kept me locked up at home and never let me go anywhere, but at the same time – by what quirk of logic I cannot imagine – she said I ought to listen to what my elders said and not be so obstreperous. When I told her about Georgi Ivanov and his ideal of womanhood, she burst out laughing and sang a little ditty, to the great amusement of us both: 'He lives with a milkmaid, oh, what luck, / Milk to drink and a girl to . . . !' Reduced to such a 'milkmaid' level, the ideal of the energetic wife collapsed, and we never gave another thought to the wily Georgi Ivanov until he began to peddle his memoirs about his former acquaintances – by then so completely muzzled that they couldn't even swear in reply.

Susanna herself married a husband who was poor as a church

* From *Nichevo* ('nothing'), a short-lived group of poets started in Rostov-on-Don in 1920. It proclaimed its affinity to Dadaism.

mouse, the clever, irritable Ivan Alexandrovich Aksionov, a great expert on Cubism and Shakespeare. Through no fault of hers they lived in a room where the ceiling was propped up with planks to prevent its falling down on their heads. Vivacious and talkative, Susanna was one of the rare women who were indifferent to making a home and doing well for themselves. For a long time we lost touch with her – until we suddenly ran into her again during our wanderings around Moscow in 1937. She looked at me and said: 'Nadia can hardly stand any more . . . well, what can you do? There's no rest for Antigone.'

I always envy Antigone – not so much when she acts as a guide for her blind father as when she gives her life in return for the right to bury her brother. The right to pay one's last respects to the dead, the right to say good-bye and lay them in the grave, is enshrined in the customs of all tribes and peoples. This was the right Antigone fought for, rising up in defence of it against the bad ruler of her small country. It is good to live in a small country where one can loudly assert one's right and lay claim to a proscribed body, instead of wandering in Pushkin's footsteps, as M., Akhmatova, and I did, over the island of Golodai and through various strange woods near Petersburg where, according to rumour, Gumilev might have been buried after his execution.

In the mighty states of the twentieth century, celebrated by some poets and numerous orators as the only hope of mankind, rulers and tsars dwelled at such dizzy heights and in such isolation that no human voices ever reached their ears. Millions of would-be Antigones cowered unseen, filled out forms, and trudged to their daily work, not daring even to weep for their dead, let alone to bury them. A weeping woman would have lost her job and died of hunger. It is far harder to die of slow starvation than to be executed. Even if we had work, we starved, and I will leave it to the Aragons of this world to describe what it was like without . . .

I have nothing but respect for statistics and would dearly love to know how many women were not able to bury their fathers, brothers, and husbands. Wartime widows received official notification, but those whose husbands died in prisons or camps – and then by no means in all cases, only if they had been arrested not earlier than 1937 – were handed notices of posthumous rehabilitation on which the date of death was given quite haphazardly. In the vast majority of cases the dates given are those of wartime years. This was not, however, because they had actually died during the war, but rather because it was hoped in this manner to jumble up together the two categories of victims of mass extermination – those who died in camps and prisons, and those killed in the war. Somebody was concerned to make proper statistics impossible by creating deliberate confusion. What is more, nobody will ever know where those near or dear to him are buried. The mass graves into which the bodies with tags on their legs were thrown are inaccessible. One day, perhaps, they will dig up all the bones and burn them, or throw them into the ocean. To try to destroy all traces of the past, they will summon the old 'professionals '– or their loyal sons – and give them the money they need for the job. But the past cannot be hidden, even if there are no statistics. Every dead man will still tell his tale.

As a widow who was unable to bury her husband, I pay my respects to a body with a tag on its leg, remembering and mourning without tears, because we belong to a tearless generation. At any moment I expect them to come and take away these notes of mine. I will not give them up of my own free will. They can take them away only together with me. If that happens, I shall no longer envy Antigone.

17 Meeting in an Editorial Office

Thanks to my unchronological method I can now, having mentioned Susanna Mar, tell of our last meeting, which took place just before the Twentieth Congress, when officials at the highest levels already knew of the forthcoming speech* and everybody's head was spinning – in some cases from joy, and in others from fright. Some discreet rehabilitations were already under way, and at Akhmatova's urging I went to see Surkov. About my conversations with him and what they led to I shall speak later; here I shall

* Khrushchev's speech denouncing Stalin's crimes, at the Twentieth Party Congress, February 1956.

talk only about a scene in the reception room of a certain Kotov, the director of the State Publishing House for Literature, to whom I was referred by Surkov.

I had come to Kotov to ask for work. For many years I had not been allowed to present my dissertation, which would have given me some little return for all the donkey work I was made to do in the teacher's training courses where, as the suspect wife of a suspect husband, I was allowed to teach side by side with real Soviet citizens only on sufferance. My dissertation was sponsored by Zhirmunski in the Institute of Linguistics, which was headed by V. V. Vinogradov. Vinogradov only frowned and looked the other way, and the dissertation was actually blocked by two lady 'Candidates of Science',* Akhmanova and Liubarskaya, who were very active in implementing the anti-Semitic policy at the end of the forties and the beginning of the fifties. As Zhirmunski said of them: 'They "write" all the time . . .'† By now they are probably working in the department to which they used to 'write', combining this with their labours in the academic field. Akhmanova's line was that I could not be allowed to present the dissertation because I had been 'married to a scoundrel'. Zhirmunski was supported by a whole cohort of Doctors of Science (Steblin-Kamenski, Admoni, and others) and by academician Shishmarev, but Akhmanova and Liubarskaya had infinitely more influence and got their way at all stages. Without my degree, I was forced to work for a pittance and was always being kicked out of jobs in the name of 'vigilance'. For this reason I had jumped at the suggestion that I should do some translating work. In my presence Surkov had talked about it to Kotov on the phone. Kotov had responded with enthusiasm and given me an appointment to see him.

My arrival was announced, and Kotov came bounding out of his office with a smile. I was not used to being smiled at: people always looked at me as though I were a snake or a pariah, and indeed I was a pariah – of a kind they have never seen in India. He asked me to wait until the end of a meeting they were just having about a complete edition of the works of Dostoyevski; this he told me with an air of triumph. I gasped: if they were talking of a complete

* Degree lower than a doctorate.
† i.e. denounce people. See *Hope Against Hope*, page 42.

Dostoyevski, it really must be the beginning of a new era. He had been under a ban for more years than I could remember. An exception was made for *Crime and Punishment*, but *The Possessed* provoked gnashing of teeth. I often recall the complaint Dostoyevski made in a letter to his wife on the eve of his Pushkin speech: 'They have come to instruct me . . .' The progressive young people of the day had come to set him on the path of truth, but for some reason he did not listen, and has been paying the price ever since – until that day I came to see Kotov.

I liked Kotov. He did not hide how pleased he was that a new age had dawned – as shown by the meeting going on in his office and the fact that I had come to see him. I had heard stories about an attempt to get rid of him by involving him in the notorious Alexandrov case, when a number of leading functionaries were accused of debauchery and visits to brothels. They were mostly high-ranking officials in charge of philosophy and culture. Very little or nothing at all got into the press, but rumours of it were passed around in gleeful whispers. I have no doubt that the whole thing was a court intrigue, and that admission to brothels was regulated according to rank, with no nonsense about egalitarianism. A thing of this kind would not have been left to private initiative. At the beginning of the thirties a friend of mine told me that Fadeyev had once taken him to such a place. The chauffeur (who was also Fadeyev's friend and informant), on being told to take them 'you know where', had driven to a comfortable dacha in which complete service was provided behind a high fence. It must be said, however, that in repeating stories of this kind one might be guilty of unwitting slander against these worthy men – it is, after all, well nigh inconceivable that the official philosophers of our glorious epoch should have retained their normal human appetites.

Kotov's waiting-room gradually began to fill up with other people, and there was already a shortage of chairs. I was standing by the wall to the right of the door. Preparing for this interview, I had wondered for a long time how best to distract attention from my ragged clothes. As a result I had on my head the sort of hat which the Ukrainians, God bless their hearts, would call a *shlychka*, and around my neck I was wearing a muffler. I was acutely aware of how outrageous they must have looked. Poverty trying to look its best is comic. When you are well over fifty it is time to wear a skirt and woollen sweater, but on my salary such a luxury was unthinkable. In China, where I had worked the previous two years, there were queues for bread, soap had to be brought from Moscow, and in the market they sold horse and camel meat. In the basement cafeteria of the college they allowed me to take little bags of sugar – on the sly, so as not to upset the students – in exchange for fifty vouchers worth a hundred glasses of tea. All my money went on food and train fares to Moscow. There was nothing left over for clothes, which were sold on the street at fantastic prices. A few years later, when I was at last allowed to defend my dissertation, I did not bother to disguise the wretched state of my clothes and hence felt completely at ease, but in Kotov's waiting-room I looked like one of those ladies in Leningrad who keep trunks of clothes from the old days and appear in coquettish items of apparel smelling faintly of mothballs. The other people hanging around the waiting-room were not exactly the picture of well-fed prosperity, but at least they had normal complexions, without the bluish-green hue I was used to seeing in my colleagues.

Suddenly the tiny wizened figure of Shaginian appeared in the doorway. At the sight of me she almost swooned, though how she recognized me after twenty years I really cannot say. She was then no older than I am now, but passionate love for the powers-that-be and concern for the People had left their mark on her face and whole appearance. Somebody gave up his chair for her. She sat down facing me and asked in a loud voice: 'And what are you doing here? Hoping to publish Mandelstam or something?' All heads turned in my direction, and not a single face showed any sympathy – only wariness and puzzlement. Shaginian went on insistently inquiring about my reason for being here. I plucked up my courage and said I was there on my own business at the moment, but that Mandelstam would certainly be published – of which she need have no doubt. Her whole face was suddenly contorted: 'Why are you so confident?'

It must be terrible to realize all of a sudden that the world in which you were what is called 'a somebody' has lost its stability. Sonia Vishnevetskaya, the widow of Vishnevski – now dead herself – met me on the staircase of the writers' apartment block on Lavrushenski Street in the days when a collection of M.'s work had just been scheduled to appear in the Poet's Library series. She was very well disposed to me, but her legs literally gave way and she nearly collapsed when I showed her the prospectus of the Library's forthcoming publications. Only Fedin kept his head. I met him on the same staircase the day after a meeting at the Union of Writers had approved the proposal to publish M. – even some well-known scoundrels had supported it. I was on my way down the stairs, and ahead of me I saw an old man looking like a toadstool. Suddenly he turned around and I heard him say: 'Hello, Nadezhda Yakovlevna.' From his eyes, colourless as a fish's, I recognized Fedin. For a quarter of a century until this moment he had never once greeted me, though we had often got into the same elevator, and once he had stopped Akhmatova for a long conversation when we were both walking in a side street leading to Lavrushenski. To spare him embarrassment, Akhmatova had not named me, and I had moved away a little to wait until they finished their talk. At the time I thought he had simply not recognized me – this was still in Stalin's day, just after the war. But now, when I had changed beyond recognition, he knew who I was at a glance: occupying such a high post, he had learned the art of diplomacy and was less put out when the ground trembled under him than the excitable Shaginian, who made such a fuss on seeing me in Kotov's waiting-room.

I stood there by the wall in my preposterous hat and muffler, conscious of them all staring at me, these Soviet writers, critics, literary scholars, and translators who had come to their very own publishing house on their normal literary business – one about a small matter of editing, another to talk about a preface to some book, and yet another to propose a complete edition of his esteemed works. Among these people of flesh and blood, I was a mere shadow, a ghost, a dim echo of something that had long since mouldered away and been consigned to total oblivion. 'There was a poet of that name . . . ,' as I was once told by a woman inspector who had been sent from Moscow to Ulianovsk with the special task of looking into all the suspicious people in my faculty, and had been given some preliminary information by the relevant comrades. In briefing her, they had even told her about the 'poet of that name', though it is quite possible that the poor wretch did not even know that 'poets' write verse. The people in Kotov's waiting-room needed no particular briefing because everyone of them was familiar with the Zhdanov Decree, that basic literary document of our times. Shaginian had made a special study of it and came to Tashkent (while I was working at the university there) to explain it. In the very early days of our epoch she had a nasty habit of kissing Akhmatova's hand whenever she met her. This always put Akhmatova in a frenzy, and at the mere sight of Shaginian, she fled or dived into the nearest doorway. Having switched from adulation to contempt for the 'decadent poetess', Shaginian was naturally anxious at the thought of having to turn yet another somersault and start being nice to the Acmeists again. This was why she now questioned me with such insistence. I was getting quite desperate when suddenly help came from an unexpected quarter.

A new visitor had appeared in the waiting room, and I heard the cheerful, brassy voice of Susanna, the former *nichevok*: 'Don't you worry about them, Nadia . . . Osip will be published all right – maybe not straightaway, but sooner or later – he's there and he always will be . . . he won't disappear into thin air, and you'll be able to read him one of these days, Marietta Sergeyevna . . . I don't suppose you remember him very well, but I do . . . Don't let them get you down, Nadia . . .'

This was my last meeting with Susanna Mar, that wild and frivolous woman, who never became 'a somebody' in Soviet literature and was not worried by such 'disruptive' acts as the publication of Mandelstam. She was not all that old when she died, and they say she wrote some authentic verse of real quality. I never had a chance of telling her how sweet it was to hear a human voice and kind words in that waiting-room dominated by ideology, where a portrait of the late monster was still hanging. (Lord, are they really human, people like those I saw there? I suppose it's a mortal sin to turn one's back on them, as I do, refusing to believe, even for one moment, that they are human too.)

The waiting-room continued to be a scene of lively activity. The meeting on Dostoyevski ended, and exercising the right of precedence conferred by her venerable age, Shaginian was the first to enter Kotov's office. A few minutes later, Kotov came running out and embraced me. Shaginian appeared behind him and stood in the doorway. Kotov explained in a loud voice: 'Marietta Sergeyevna also thinks you ought to be given some work. She says you are a most cultured person, the widow of Osip Emilievich Mandelstam.' 'A most cultured person . . . a most cultured person,' Marietta repeated after him like an echo, still standing in the doorway. And Susanna chimed in again: 'Marietta Sergeyevna, did you think Nadia had changed her name and nobody knew she's Osip's widow? Everybody knows it, and they all remember him.' Kotov confirmed in a loud and cheerful voice that everybody indeed remembered Mandelstam, and that I had come here under my own name, not hiding that I was his widow. He took me into his office and sat me in an armchair, and for the next hour I listened in as he haggled with Shaginian. He did it with gusto, and I had the impression that he was deliberately trying to make her suffer for her nasty backhanded compliment to me (such a great thing to be 'cultured'!). She got more and more furious: how could anyone be so cruel to an old woman, trying to beat her down by such a huge amount? My sympathies were all with the handsome, high-spirited Kotov – particularly since Shaginian, formerly a member of the intelligentsia, had once applied her mind to combining Lenin with the Christian spirit and the lofty ideas of Goethe. But at the moment she was making play not with Goethe, but with the fact that she never needed to make more than one phone call to be received in the Central Committee – and they would force Kotov to pay her the top rate or even more for her 'hundred tomes of Party books'.* She enumerated all the things to her credit – oddly enough, omitting to mention how she had toured the country to explain the famous Decree. At that time she was as old as I am now, but she still had boundless energy, and she ran out of Kotov's room to go to seek justice on Staraya Square.† I have no doubt that all the time he was haggling with her, Kotov knew perfectly well

* Line from Mayakovski's 'At the Top of My Voice'.
† The address of the Party Central Committee in Moscow.

that she would get her way in the end. He simply wanted to take her down a peg or two – rather a dirty trick perhaps, but I found it amusing all the same . . .

With great difficulty Kotov managed to get some translating work for me. The members of the department concerned resisted for all they were worth, not wanting to give such a lucrative job to an upstart like me. By the time I handed in the finished translation, Kotov was no longer alive. People who had lived through our great era and yet retained some human qualities were now dying off wholesale from strokes and heart attacks. Having thus lost my protector, I was asked to hand over half my fee to the woman who would edit the translation. I refused to give what amounted to a bribe and informed the new director of this attempted extortion. It was the end of my employment as a translator.

Shaginian proved to be right, and M. was not printed. Her reaction to my appearance in Kotov's waiting-room is the best possible explanation of why it is still out of the question to publish him in this country.

Even now Shaginian has not ceased her fruitful labours. Attending meetings at which 'protest signers'* are called to account, she thrusts her ear trumpet right in their faces, not to miss a single word. For all I care, she can live to be a hundred years, together with Fedin and his tribe. Kotov and Susanna Mar, on the other hand, I remember with gratitude and affection. They were like first swallows who had no sooner spread their wings than they were stricken by the cold of the grave. For Susanna, Ivan Aksionov, and Kotov 'I will pray in the Soviet night.' Nobody has given me the right to judge my fellow creatures, but I can find no words to pray for those others who killed all the human qualities in themselves. That is my sin, I know . . .

* People who sign letters protesting against the persecution of dissidents, etc. This has become a widespread movement since the trial of Siniavski and Daniel in 1966. Such protesters may be arraigned at meetings of their colleagues.

18 Memory

I have read in Sergei Trubetskoi that miracles convince only those who believe already. A man wanting in faith will not acquire it on the strength of seeing a miracle. I am not sure what to say of myself. Belonging to an age of emptiness, I sometimes have faith and sometimes lose it. I have seen miracles, Lord knows, but to see them one needs eyes, and my sight is poor; the light often comes to me dimly. But perhaps I feel no need of miracles for another reason: what is the point of one particular instance of a miracle – say, a healing – when everything around me is in itself a miracle that passeth all understanding: the world and all living things, but most of all man and the human mind. I think there is no greater miracle than time and the phenomenon derived from it: memory. These have been given to us, and we should ask not from whom, but *why* we have received this mysterious gift. It is memory that converts irreversible time into our inner world. By bringing things back to mind, we can relive them, even if we are unable to make changes in the immutable course of past events. How lucky this is so. The strength of youth is in its blindness. How the pattern of past events would be distorted if in middle or old age we could modify all we did in our youth . . . This is what some poets try to do by 'correcting' their early verse: with the benefit of later attitudes, in the light of other feelings and a different vision, they chop and change what they wrote in their young years, and the result is verse no longer all of a piece, but a hybrid, a curious patchwork of ill-assorted elements. Pasternak went in for this procedure in his old age, and other poets have been known to do it at an even earlier stage in their careers. M. used to tell how he once came across Blok engaged in the absurd business of changing one of his best poems ('Acts of valour, exploits, fame / All in this sad world went out of mind / When your face in its simple frame / Shone there before me on the tabletop').

With poetry it hardly matters: a future editor, unless a complete idiot – which is sometimes the case – is free to restore the earlier version. But what would it be like if we had the power to bring back events and transform them at will? I am horrified at the mere thought: what a shambles I would make of my early years if, armed with the relentless logic of my middle years or the clear vision of old age, I were again to find myself face to face with M. during our ludicrous squabbles and stormy confrontations! How fortunate that memory brings back the past not for us to refashion, but for us to peruse, lament, and understand. We answer for everything – for every deed and every word – and memory invites us to consider why we have lived, what we have done with our lives, whether we had a preordained purpose, and if so, whether we have fulfilled it; whether our life had a unifying thread of meaning, or whether it consisted only of random and absurd happenings.

We answer for everything, but there are many ways of trying not to. The first is by deliberately not recalling something (as opposed to passively 'remembering' it): 'Between remembering and recalling, my friends, / the distance is as great as from Luga / To the land of the satin loup.'* In her two poems 'Basement of Memory' and 'Three Epochs of Recollection', however, where she set out to talk about memory, Akhmatova was more concerned with forgetting. In another poem she had said:

> To the past the way has long been barred
> And what do I need the past for now?
> What is there? Bloodied flagstones
> Or a bricked-up door,
> Or an echo that still cannot
> Die away, however much I beg . . .

This is a plea that memory be blotted out – something always prevented by the insistent echo of the past. The second of the poems mentioned above tells how a certain recollection is growing dim, and its purpose is hence to analyse the process of forgetting. The 'echo that still cannot die away' refers to her memory of the cruel and bloody events we have lived through and from which, in her old age, she had hoped to gain a little respite. If a recollection is really fading away, it must relate to something that was very short-lived, a chance event which invaded one's life for no particular reason. Translated into the familiar language of love, one might say that oblivion swallows up only the sort of thing we call an

* A line from Akhmatova's *Poem Without a Hero*. Luga: a small town south-west of Leningrad. 'The land of the satin loup': Venice.

'affair', but is powerless to affect the principal strands running through our life – these never just disappear into the void. 'It is always the same with an affair,' Akhmatova said on one occasion. 'While it is actually going on, you think you cannot live without it, but later it leaves no trace – only dust . . .' Such dust is best left alone, but people love to poke around in it, hoping to find a glittering trinket here and there: this is a much more agreeable occupation than trying to unravel the main skein of life's experience; here you are less likely to chance on alluring bagatelles wrapped in flashing tinsel, pretty souvenirs to gladden the heart. Such things create a mirage, obscuring the reality and pain of life, thus sparing one the need of having – God forbid! – to confront the truth. As I review my own life, I shall try to dispense with tinsel trappings, believing that 'purer weft than truth's fresh canvas is scarcely to be found'. I wish to speak the truth and nothing but the truth – but the *whole* truth I shall not tell. The ultimate truth I shall keep to myself; nobody else but me needs it. I doubt whether anybody reveals the whole truth about himself, even in confession.

If the first way of evading responsibility is not to recollect at all, the second and most widespread way of silencing the voice of memory is to embellish and streamline one's recollections – in other words, to deceive oneself and indulge in wishful thinking – which is, of course, much simpler with reference to the past than to the present. This is a most typical human weakness. How easy to console oneself by touching up the past to make it look as though it was a bed of roses! The operation can be performed on an individual life history, or on the past of a whole nation. As we know only too well, history is constantly being falsified right in front of our eyes, and the older generation, exploiting the indifference of the young, cleverly hoodwinks them. One and the same event can look quite different when treated from varying points of view. As an example I could mention my memory of how a church was pillaged during the confiscation of ecclesiastical property, as compared with an account of the same events published in one of our literary monthlies. The woman responsible for this other version was an actual participant in the events, while I was only a chance observer. We could have stood side by side in the same church and still seen things in a quite different light. As an interested party, she prefers not to think about what happened to all the money raised by looting the churches, and the word 'sacrilege', needless to say, has absolutely no meaning for her. She does not wish to see the past – any more than Shaginian, after all her lectures on the Zhdanov Decree, wanted to see me in Kotov's waiting-room. From two 'activists' such as these one can expect nothing more, but many of our well-meaning 'liberals' were upset by what I said in my first book about the twenties and early thirties. In their view, to be objective, I should have mentioned Papanin, Meyerhold, football matches, gymnasts in coloured jerseys, the massed pageants, the great forward march of literature (for some this means Sholokhov, for others Olesha or Marshak), and Lord knows what else besides: 'workers' faculties',* higher education, and the spectacle of a happy people engaged in the most democratic of sports. It is hard to look truth in the eye, whether you were an active participant in events or just a well-disposed onlooker receiving your share of crumbs from the master's table. I have learned to beware, in particular, of those who affect love of art and culture: these are great disseminators of falsehood, unless they have a sharp eye for the ideas on which art and culture are based, making their judgements accordingly. People of our generation have seen 'art' and 'culture' in the kind of avant-gardism that glories in the strutting gymnast, the mailed fist, the 'bloom' of youth, power, speed, mobs shrieking at a signal from their leader, rows of heads held high, the beating drum (whether standing for the human heart or the humble toy of the Young Pioneer), the class or national interest, mighty Italy, Germany, or the Motherland with its love of mushrooms and quaint folk customs. What this leads to we know well enough. But people nonetheless go on slowly, stubbornly, embroidering the facts, inventing one detail after another, weaving them together to re-create the fabric of 'history'. Fifty years hence nobody will ever be able to clean up this gigantic mess.

Sometimes the falsification is deliberate; sometimes it results from applying a different standard. Here is a tiny example. Some people were once telling me about all the sterling qualities of Lebedev-Polianski, who was censor-in-chief during the twenties. I

---

* Day or evening schools to prepare workers and peasants for university entrance. Abolished at the end of the thirties.

thereupon described how M. and I had visited him in an attempt to have a banned poem released for publication (there were so many, I don't remember which one it was). We couldn't get him to change his mind, though it still involved only the *Second Book* or the State Publishing House edition of *Stone*. The conversation was very unpleasant, and as we were leaving, Lebedev-Polianski added a few threatening words behind our backs. He pretended to address them to an official sitting at the next desk, but they were clearly spoken for M.'s benefit. I do not remember the exact form of what he said, but the sense is etched in my memory: this fellow (that is, M.) is alien and suspect, his behaviour is provocative, and we must check up on him. This was how one was 'warned', in other words intimidated, in those idyllic years. The people I told this to were indignant and assured me that I was quite mistaken: Lebedev-Polianski had been a person of utmost tact and refinement, a connoisseur of literature and art, an admirer of all things beautiful and 'cultured', who could never have done such a thing. For these people the twenties had been halcyon days. The woman – it was a man and wife – is a daughter of the 'victorious' class and will never forget the sweet taste of having belonged to it. In 1937 the circles in which she moved were wiped out, and this brought something home to her. Her husband had made a career for himself in films and journalism, and even 1937 made no impact on him. He came to his senses only during the campaign against the cosmopolitans,* when he had his nose tweaked slightly. For both of them Lebedev-Polianski was not a censor engaged in the destruction of what remained of literature and civic courage, but a 'wonderful human being'. Their angle of vision is quite different from mine in regard to both him and the whole of our past history. At the moment they have adopted what is known here as a 'liberal' position, but in their conversation you can still detect deposits belonging to much earlier geological strata – especially from the twenties, when weaklings and doubters were always so promptly put in their place. They have not yet found time to scrutinize their past, but meanwhile memory obligingly smooths away the rough edges and tinges every recollection with the right emotional colouring.

* 'Homeless cosmopolitan' was a frequent term of abuse in the thinly disguised anti-Semitic persecutions of Stalin's later years (1949–53).

I was once visited by an old man who had spent a good twenty years in camps and exile, but had throughout kept his loyalty to the victors, his party card being engraved on his heart (the actual document was taken from him during his arrest). It was the time of the Siniavski affair, and I asked him his view of it. The old man began to seethe with unfeigned indignation: Siniavski had 'hidden behind a pseudonym'. 'Not like us Bolsheviks,' he continued. 'We went right up on the platform and said exactly what we thought'. I laughed at him: 'And you never lied, by any chance? I always did, you know – not that I ever went up on a platform, of course, but I lied and hid my real thoughts every day and every hour: in the classroom, in the lecture hall, at home, in the kitchen . . . How could I do otherwise? One truthful word, and I would have got ten years' forced labour, right there and then.' But the old man really hadn't lied: in denouncing 'enemies of the people' from the platform and disowning his arrested friends he had been completely sincere. He had really hated all these hapless wretches, and when he himself was cast down among them, he consoled himself by thinking it was a mistake. His arrest, he felt, had been part of the 'overhead on production', as it were. He acted in all sincerity, and paid the price. He was not simply an idiot, but a product of the times. The basic ideas which went into his makeup (one cannot use the word 'personality') have warped his mind, and his memory holds up a distorting mirror to past events and actions.

I happen to have read the memoirs, written down in all honesty, of a certain person who was politically active in the twenties. For a brief moment, he supported the 'left deviation',* and even though he later recanted, he went through camps and exile just the same. 'Always remember that you are a Leningrad Komsomol', were his wife's parting words, and he never indeed forgot it. I would publish his book in a million copies – it would bring home the essence of our times even to the mentally deficient. The only complaint of the 'Leningrad Komsomol' is that the kindred spirits in the secret police, instead of having a heart-to-heart talk with him, had used certain little tricks normally applied to 'enemies', not 'friends'. In the place to which he was afterwards deported, he gave hell to fellow exiles unwilling to admit the error of their ways and recant.

*i.e. Trotski.

A specialist in 'education', he easily mastered an unfamiliar branch of engineering in one night (he had previously attended a short course at the Polytechnic specially designed for Komsomols), and the next day was already in charge of engineers and workers, stunning them with his knowledge. Deported peasant girls were only too happy to serve under one who was so clearly born to lead and command. Thanks to him, an ancient boiler did not blow up, and the best of the girls catered to his physical needs while he was separated from his beloved wife. (The beloved wife later, without reading it, signed some document which resulted in his transfer to the harsher conditions of a forced labour camp, but for this he loved and respected her even more: she had put her signature to the paper only after being given to understand that it was needed by the Party.) Now rehabilitated, the man lives in Moscow, writing these memoirs and proclaiming his faith in the high ideals of the twenties. At that time he read Zharov, Kirsanov, and Mayakovski, and conceived a great respect for culture and the new life in general. When I hear the rattle of dominoes in the courtyard, I know he is down there playing with his friends, telling them the story of his life and going on about how faithful he had always been to his wife, his ideals, and the Party line . . .

It also happens that I have read the 'clandestine' work of a certain very clever woman who tries to show, with the tedious reasoning characteristic of her, that any scoundrel, while actually engaged in doing something despicable, always thinks he is acting correctly, in accordance with the highest principles: such a man remembers with deep satisfaction how he once denounced people and sighs for the good old days. The future historian will have a vast amount of material from which to try to re-create an 'objective picture' of the times, but his selection of facts and treatment of them will be decisively influenced by the particular standpoint he adopts. I anticipate, for instance, that there will be studies about the importance of events in this country for the development of the workers' movements in France, Italy, and other progressive countries such as Paraguay, Uruguay, or the Republic of Chad . . . I was claiming a little earlier that I never butted into masculine conversation. This is true, but once I did: it was such a rare occurrence that I have a very clear recollection of it. Early one autumn, shortly after we had gone to live in Leningrad, Pasternak turned up at our apartment on Morskaya. Standing by the window in the small room, he talked with M. while I sat near by on a sofa. This was the time when he was writing *Spektorski* (part of which he sent to M. soon afterwards), after the success of *Lofty Illness* (what a beginning this has!), after *1905*, perhaps even after *Lieutenant Schmidt*. Wrapping up his ideas, as usual, in illustrations and images, he was holding forth about simple but crucial matters: what had come was there to stay, the People were with it, we were right in the thick of it all – and there was no other way because every worker . . . At this point I looked up and interrupted: 'This is the only country in the world to get the upper hand of its workers' movement.' How this idea had come to me and why in this particular form I just cannot say, but it simply flashed through my head the moment I heard Pasternak talking about 'the workers'. He started at my remark – which quite appalled him, I thought – and asked M.: 'What does she say?' I clearly remember the way he referred to me in the third person. M. just chuckled, quite good-humouredly, and replied: 'She talks like a real Menshevik.' I was not a Menshevik, had never had anything to do with them, didn't read the newspapers, and would have been at a loss to back up my words. All I now remember is the expression on Pasternak's face and his use of the third person, and I believe that the wary and distant attitude he always subsequently displayed towards me went back to that moment, although I never again made any such remark in his or anybody else's presence.

The capacity of memory, both collective and individual, to gloss over, improve on, or distort the facts is particularly evident at periods when the foundations of a society are collapsing. Those disorders to which memory is prey – the tendency to embellish or suppress 'awkward' detail, the need to vindicate oneself – show how dangerous it is to rely on one's own conviction of being right; since this is all too often based on a false criterion, our main task is to find a true one. There is also the problem that, while distorting our recollections and thus hindering a proper appreciation of individual or historical experience, memory is yet the one feature that distinguishes us as human beings. How can we resolve this contradiction and arrive at the unadulterated truth, so that we stop deceiving ourselves and others and draw the right conclusions from our bitter experience? We have all played our part in the work of destruction, and heaven help us if it is taken to its logical conclusion.

I too joined in the process of destroying the foundations on which our life was based, making my contribution to its disintegration and the present alarming state of affairs. Small as my part has been, I must nevertheless bear full responsibility for it – to a greater extent, perhaps, than those who aided the work of destruction unconsciously and therefore at least never tried to find ways of justifying themselves. To illustrate what I mean: repelled by the hypocrisy and tedium of conventional family life, I helped to undermine it, if only by seeking my own solution in a free union based on love, not marriage. It so happens that in my particular case it succeeded – though it was very much always touch and go. Perhaps it worked out with us simply because the time span was so brief – only twenty years or so. But an even more likely explanation is that though he systematically wrecked all attempts to achieve any form of settled domestic existence, consciously preferring poverty and death, M. was nevertheless determined to preserve his union with me and never allowed it to break up. He was stronger than I and always got his way, but even so it was surely chance that held us together and kept us from the act of mutual destruction that a parting would have brought. I now know what sort of 'chance' this was and how it fits in with the boundless freedom granted to human kind. But while we were together, we never had a second to stop and ponder our actions, or the possible consequences of our imbecility. We are all the children of our era and bear its mark on ourselves. This whole experience of the age of nihilism is highly significant, and it is most important that we fully understand it, as something eventually destroying life altogether. It has manifested itself in every individual, as well as in whole nations. We did away with institutions which had grown up over the centuries, creating a bond among people, but failed to put anything in their place. Our only merit is to have shown by experiment how tawdry and blighted our grand innovations are, if we have lost our memory and forgotten the torch 'bequeathed by our forbears'.

To lose one's memory – provided it was an honest one – is to lose touch with reality. The present becomes meaningless when facts are 'processed', and you serve them up to yourself and others in whatever guise happens to suit the moment – like the 'truth' my Bolshevik friend says he always spoke from the platform. The centuries of enlightenment made great inroads on faith, and hence on man's sense of responsibility for his actions. As long as the institution of the confession existed and every man answered in this way to the Supreme Judge for all his deeds, he never dared forget what had happened the day, the week, or the year before. Confession stirred the memory and forced a man to review his actions 'in the light of conscience', as Marina Tsvetayeva would have said. To be able to do this one needs a conscience to begin with, of course, but the vast majority kept some vestige of it even in the worst of times, however muffled by the 'roar of events' it may have been, and bound though it was to exist in a shrunken, pitiful form when no man trusted his neighbour, shunning him like the plague. Conscience and a sense of sin weaken when a man lives in isolation. Not everybody had the strength to say, with Pushkin: 'And reading with abhorrence my life's tale, / I quake and curse, / Complaining bitterly and shedding bitter tears, / But the sad lines I'll not wash away.' For their own peace of mind my contemporaries will certainly 'wash away' or embellish their 'sad lines' – though they will most likely not even realize just how sad they are.

What I say above applies only to the average person, to such as my sinful and abominable self, not to the corrupters and sowers of iniquity, or to those who in the name of 'science' and 'for the good of the cause' will countenance any behaviour or actions needed to achieve the aim of the moment, thereby, as we know so well, laying the country waste and turning people into shadows of themselves. The corrupters live by special laws of their own devising, and only people like myself, that is, we who have been corrupted by them, are in need of self-justification because, try as we might to still the voice of memory, our consciences have not entirely deserted us. How many real people are there among us, capable of repentance? How many are capable of naming the real sin of the age, of telling good from evil by the only true criterion, of forcing memory to speak out loud, of calling themselves and others to repentance?

Weak and shamefaced creatures, we cringe in our corners, mumbling under our breath.

Loss of memory must be overcome even at the price of death; otherwise human life will turn into something like the dance of fire-flies which once so intrigued M. in Sukhumi – though what insects would destroy their own kind in the name of 'science'?

Going over your own past, you commune with yourself, as though preparing for confession. It is hard to make sense of your own experience, to find its meaning, to see where you went astray. The experience of others is scarcely any help in setting you on the right path: 'and like a swallow before the storm, each single soul will fly its separate and incomparable way'. What about literature, one might ask, which is supposed to reflect the writer's experience, his search for truth, or the road to it? But, unfortunately, books which really do this are few and far between, and most of the turbid trash that pours from the presses is counterfeit, churned out expressly to please the rulers or pander to the tastes of the masses. Genuine books are always marked with the author's character and convey the cherished theories, however outlandish, from which he has drawn sustenance himself. It clearly pays to read as M. did: turning only to the best and passing over the bad and the bogus. Nothing need be said here about Soviet literature ('sold', in M.'s phrase, 'to the pockmarked devil for three generations to come') or about the way writing in general, as it has evolved in Europe and Russia, beckons either to the edge of the abyss or to the cesspit. Only poetry is pure – until it is invaded by 'literature'* and begins to shout out the same messages of hate and self-glorification.

What horror that history too, when people write books about it, thereby comes into contact with literature and is exposed to the same diseases; even more distressing is the fact that this embodiment of mankind's collective memory never serves as a warning to posterity, as a deterrent, but only puts a 'modern' gloss on the mistakes and crimes of previous generations, decking them out in glittering new rationalizations. One might think it was only a case of learning to read history and of knowing how to draw the right

---

* Here and elsewhere, the author uses the word somewhat pejoratively particularly when speaking of the Soviet literary 'establishment' and its output. See also page 232.

conclusions, but there is no simple key to its mysteries, not to mention the problem of distortion, whether deliberate or unwitting. Nevertheless, history does contain what is called a sign, and if we had eyes we should see it. Isn't it time we paused to wonder why the nineteenth century, with its glorification of humanism, freedom, and the rights of man, led straight to the twentieth, which has not only surpassed all previous ages in its crimes against humanity but has managed, into the bargain, to prepare the means for total destruction of life on earth? In our century the ardent champions and defenders of reason have proved to be the merchants of mass hypnosis, and in all their activities reason has played the least part of all. Those who once advocated realism and called on us to fight prejudice were quite remarkably quick to lose all sense of reality, and none are now so mortally afraid of facts. In this country people were killed because they happened to know a couple of trivial facts, or refused to give up their sense of reality.

In shedding all this blood, we declared it was done for the sake of people's happiness. Even Pasternak, in his innocence, believed in 'happiness' for a while, but unable completely to lose sight of reality, he insisted that happiness must be for each individual, as well as for the millions. One master mind has informed us that 'Man is made for happiness as a bird is made for flight'. The stupefied masses parroted the word 'happiness' at every end and turn, but they have still to recover from the untold miseries inflicted on them in its name. Those great days are over, and at present even the most lightweight prattlers with higher degrees and salaries to match are embarrassed to use the word 'happiness' – they prefer to talk more modestly about the pursuit of 'pleasure'. In our benighted existence there is always a queue for any little drop of whatever promises oblivion, and everywhere else in the world there is a constant hunt for 'pleasure'; sated by the most trivial forms of it, people are aggrieved when death suddenly approaches before they have had time to cast a backward glance at their life or the fate of their generation.

Few people are willing to scan their own life story; even fewer are ready to turn their thoughts to the particular period of time in which they were most actively engaged in the pursuit of pleasure.

The majority just shrug their shoulders, silently connive at the crimes of the age, while others eagerly justify the past. Already somebody has informed the world in verse that his generation has duly lamented its mistakes and paid for them in full. This magazine poet thus absolves both himself and those with blood on their hands, although the thought of repentance has never entered the murderers' heads, and the accounts have not even been presented for payment, every measure having been taken to prevent anyone from doing so; there is plenty of room in the camps for people who talk too much. I follow the fate of the one man who has dared to speak up.* He has not yet been murdered, or even run over by a car. It has clearly become harder to deal with those who misbehave – it used to be such child's play, when these things were done in dead secret, with the tacit approval of the masses. When they destroyed M., there was not so much as a squeak from any brave little Aragon, and people who journeyed abroad from Moscow at that time had no compunction in proclaiming from public platforms that just before they left they had talked with Ivan, Peter, Abram, or whoever it might be – though they knew perfectly well that he had already been done to death in some secret dungeon in one of the capital city's jails. Now, however, it appears that people have at least come to question the right of the strong to destroy the defenceless – the only hopeful sign I have seen. The value of human life has risen slightly. Much that was hidden has become known, even though most people close their eyes to it. What counts, however, is that memory has not been totally erased: a few among millions have recovered their wits and started asking what actually happened and how we could have permitted such a bloodbath. It may be that a new day has dawned, but who knows how long it will last?

M. could not have put it more exactly: 'We live, dead to the land beneath us.'† It is still the same today. Isolated, sick, exhausted, we remain utter strangers to one another . . . Among us there are still those who would like to go back to the past: murderers, self-seekers, advocates of a 'strong regime' ready to destroy anything standing in its way. Then there are still the vast, sullen, and inert

* Solzhenitsyn.
† Line from his poem denouncing Stalin (1933).

masses; who can tell what goes on in *their* minds? What do they remember? What do they know? In what directions can they be pushed? Will they come to their senses in time as well, or will they sink into utter torpor and look on passively at the destruction of all the tender new growths that have sprouted in the last few years?

A country in which people have been engaged in mutual destruction for half a century does not like to recall the past. What can we expect to happen in a country with a disordered memory? What is a man worth if he has lost his memory?

19   Fear

Who are we, one might ask, that anybody should call *us* to account? We are mere chips of wood swept along by the raging torrent of history, fortunate if we are washed into a quiet backwater, or out into the mainstream, away from the whirlpools. Where the current is taking us, the devil only knows, but this is scarcely our fault: we didn't jump in of our own free will, did we?

This is only a half-truth. In some mysterious way even the most ordinary of human wood chips, as he floats willingly in the mainstream, or uncomplainingly allows himself to be tossed in a whirlpool, has the power to affect the direction of the current. Everyone of us, to some degree or another, had a share in what happened, and there is no point in trying to disclaim responsibility. We may have felt utterly powerless, but at the same time, uncertain of what we had to defend, we were always only too quick to surrender. The fateful years were the twenties: it was then that people not only became convinced of their helplessness but even exalted it, learning to ridicule as old-fashioned, as a mark of backwardness, the very idea of intellectual, moral, or spiritual resistance. One could not, it was argued, hold out against the inevitable: the historical process was predetermined, as was the state of society. Every member of society was a mere particle, a chip, a tiny drop among an infinite number of similar ones. All these individual particles, it was further believed, then generate the 'collective' consciousness, that great discovery of the twentieth century which supposedly causes a society's myriad cells, each having a peculiar direction finder insensitive to good and evil, to swim with the current in the wake of a victorious leader. Victory went to those who had managed, supposedly, to discover the general trend of history and turn the knowledge to their advantage. As we all know, our rulers were able to foretell the future not by reading tea leaves, but with the aid of 'scientific principles', and also influenced its course by that most efficient means of intimidation which consists in persecuting not the guilty or the recalcitrant, but anybody who happens to come to hand – just as a lesson to the rest. For this the mob had to be trained to follow along meekly after the victor in the belief that he knows where the tide of history is flowing and has learned to control it. The mob learned its lesson, swarmed behind in droves, and woe betide anybody who dragged his feet: he was accused of anarchism, abject individualism, and blindness to the laws of historical development. We denizens of the 'superstructure' were required to tread lightly lest we hold up the development of the 'basis', which the best of us were called on to serve as propagandists.

The generation which had grown up before the First World War and the Civil War had been psychologically prepared to view history as a purposeful flow of human masses under the guidance of those who know what the goal is. The 'basis' as such interested them very little, only insofar as there was a permanent shortage of food and items of daily use – beds, saucepans, material for clothes, and other manufactured goods. By comparing the historical process to a river in which human beings are swept along like so much floating debris, I am emphasizing the feeling of helplessness – as though in the face of the elements – which overwhelmed every individual drawn into events: in times of upheaval it is very difficult, if not impossible, to avoid becoming involved in them. But people with military experience used a different analogy for the peacetime life of the twenties and thirties – they talked instead of a *controlled* movement which reminded them of the army, but an army on manoeuvres rather than at war, since no enemy was shooting at them and 'action' consisted of ridding their own ranks, on personal initiative or orders from the high command, of anybody who got out of step or broke discipline. They had no doubt as to the value of this operation. Only at the end of the thirties did a few of them come to feel that the number of victims might be excessive; but hardly any confided such doubts even to their wives, let alone to their children, who as a rule were kept in total ignorance. Scared out of their wits, they injected even greater fervour into their newspaper articles and statements vilifying the victims, only to perish themselves later on. It is terrible now to reread these things in which, before going to their own doom, people heaped abuse on those already put to death. It was the height of satanic refinement to give the victims of terror every opportunity, before their arrest, to dishonour themselves by extolling it.

By accepting the validity of this analogy with an army, the active members of our generation renounced the 'wood chip's' mysterious power to influence the direction of the torrent sweeping it along. The whole of European culture was based on awareness of this power, whose source is the Christian teaching on the intrinsic worth of each individual personality. A man in military formation is not a personality but a cipher. The thoughts of such a cipher are insignificant and his views of no interest to anyone – who is concerned to read the mind of a unit of 'cannon fodder'? You can stand out in the ranks only by the smartness of your drill. M. and I once noticed a militiaman on Red Square directing the traffic with his little baton. The way he flung out his arm, swivelling around now in one direction and then in another, made it look as though he were dancing the solo part in some kind of mechanized ballet. 'He's not right in the head,' M. said, as we stood watching him for a few moments, horrified by the inspired precision of his movements: here was a cipher who, allowed to leave the ranks for the performance of this solitary duty, had decided to demonstrate the brilliance of his movements, their unbearable perfection.

In every sphere attention was switched from ideas to style and technique. One day somebody may count up how many articles have been written about the 'style' of leadership, not to mention style in literature: the techniques and language of writers, whose great ambition was to learn Dahl's dictionary by heart, and also, incidentally, to promote the publication of all kinds of special reference books on every branch of knowledge, treasure troves of information they could draw on to show off the smartness of their literary drill. In literature and painting there was occasional bleating about the right to experiment, but nobody ever said a word about the need for *ideas*. This voluntary renunciation of ideas goes back to the twenties, though actually there was precious little worth clinging to by then. When it came to ideas, we had already run into a blind alley in the pre-Revolutionary years. With their forebodings of catastrophe our distraught thinkers sought a way out in a hundred and one worthless panaceas, from the cult of the 'beautiful woman' to the cult of the family – not to mention the people with a university education who proclaimed themselves pagans, Buddhists, or theosophists, or dressed up as fauns with gilded horns.* With such poverty of thought there could be no question of a revival until after the sickness had passed; but it has not yet even been diagnosed, and its nature can be determined only after a careful study of the last fifty years – clearly a task of prime importance. If this is accomplished and life on earth survives, there is some hope that we may see a rebirth of ideas. Until we have made sense of the past, there is no point in cherishing any hopes: they will be disappointed. As 1937 was approaching, M. wrote a poem containing the lines: 'One fancies the battlements of a wall not yet begun, / with soldiers of captious sultans tumbling down / from foaming stairways to fall apart and separate in spray below, / while frigid eunuchs serve up poison all around.' The image of 'a wall not yet begun' shows how well he understood the insubstantial nature of all our grand ambitions. At the very beginning of the thirties he said on one occasion: 'Why should we get so excited about Five-Year plans? If somebody we knew suddenly went mad and stopped eating in order to decorate his apartment and buy typewriters and toilet bowls in bulk we should say: "To hell with him."' There is always something suspicious about a whole people existing only to fulfil plans; the greater the success of the plans, the worse everybody lived – you could 'fancy battlements' all right, but of the wall there was no sign. The reference to 'soldiers' in these lines shows how much the quasi-military analogies and all the talk about discipline had sunk in during those years. One glance at our newspapers and official

* See Glebova-Sudeikina, Appendix A.

decrees is enough to see how saturated they are with this kind of terminology. M.'s attention is focused on the victims of the 'captious sultans', on the unbearable way in which they are reduced to isolated atoms: he likens them to the surf into which a wave is smashed; they 'fall apart and separate in spray . . .'

Drops of spray, wood chips, soldiers, or ciphers lined up in formation, we were all too painfully aware of our isolation, of being kept apart from each other. All permitted groupings of people were purely mechanical in nature: tenants of communal apartments,* queues, trade unions (whose sole function was additional surveillance and indoctrination), the personnel of institutions. In Tashkent I had a friend, a linguist who was just as nauseated by Marr and Meshchaninov as the biologists were by Lysenko. (There are some blockheads who would like to resurrect Marr – they should first have a look at the appeal he made as early as 1918 to scholars and scientists, urging them to switch their allegiance to the only true science based on genuine materialism.) He was a thoroughly decent man who was even inclined to think for himself a little. After spending the war years in Tashkent, he decided to return home and reached an agreement with another university concerning jobs for both himself and his wife. His family left, but he was not allowed to go with them until a replacement could be found of exactly equivalent rank, to avoid any change in the establishment as laid down. In this country, as in any militarized society, nothing is more important than rank or title. Our wretched teachers, exhausted by inhuman work schedules, are constantly being pressed not only to broaden their meagre knowledge by further study, but without fail to go on earning higher degrees.

My linguist friend was trying to get his release from the Dean, a bitch of a woman about fifty. Women can be even more horrible than men in such administrative posts. She refused to release him the whole of the first semester, and at the end of December, already quite beside himself, he warned her that he would not stay on for the second semester and named several people willing to take over

* A standard type of apartment in the Soviet Union: tenants live in rooms off a long corridor, sharing a bathroom and kitchen situated at either end.

his courses. 'What are you telling me about *people* for? I need a replacement of the proper grade,' she replied indignantly.

He told us about this imbecility on New Year's Eve, 1946; we were spending it with our mutual friend Alisa Usova, a great connoisseur of the Moscow vernacular, who said exactly what she thought of the Dean and what she could do with herself. Afterward I was haunted for a long time by the thought that if I had paid a little more attention, I might have guessed what was in his mind and been able to stop him; alas, we always reproach ourselves when the irrevocable has happened.

We all went home in the early hours. Later in the day people knocked on our colleague's door several times, but there was no reply. Finally, the room was broken into and he was found hanging from a hook. On the table there was a note in which he said he did not want to be a mere cog. When his wife came for the burial, his note had disappeared, and the Dean or the Party secretary informed the sobbing woman that during her absence he had gone around with other women and contracted syphilis. At first she broke into a howl of rage at her dead husband, but it soon dawned on her that she had been told the usual kind of official lie to cover up for a suicide. Anyone who killed himself was treated as a deserter – we could not possibly admit there might be cases of desertion in the beautiful army of the builders of socialism. Syphilis is a 'survival of capitalism', and deserters could neatly be written off as its victims. Otherwise it might be thought that a man had been driven to suicide by mistakes in the 'style' of leadership. For such a thought – that is, 'slander' – one could wind up in a camp.

This linguist was the only 'cog' I ever remember to have revolted. 'He comes from the peasantry,' Usova said. 'Peasants can't take it.' It is fantastic to think that only a little over a century ago they were still serfs.

Knowing, as I now do, that half a century passes in a flash, like a terribly protracted moment, it is clear to me that not enough time elapsed between Emancipation and the Revolution for the peasant to gather his strength and develop the powers of endurance he needed. Yet I believe Pushkin was right to say that even under serfdom the peasant kept a sense of his own worth and his personality.

It was probably the domestic serfs* who became corrupted – one should not confuse the two forms of serfdom. I would like to think that all today's scoundrels, murderers, and bureaucrats are descended from domestic serfs, not from real peasants. But this is just a fancy of mine: there were too few domestic serfs to account for *all* the rabble we have now.

Cogs did not revolt; they just went right on functioning. I always consoled myself with the thought that I could kill myself if I was finally discarded even as a cog and reduced to begging for my daily bread. The fear of being thrown out of work haunts people even of the most impeccable background, let alone those 'with something in their past'. I was recently visited by a former colleague, the widow of the unfortunate violinist† who avoided being rearrested by travelling from one small town to another, keeping clear as far as possible of the large centres. Just before his death, at the beginning of the new era, he received a nice clean identity card. A militiaman came to him at his home and handed over the precious document with a word of congratulation to the lucky man. 'It's too late,' said the violinist, who was already dying. His widow has had her troubles almost from birth. She is the daughter of a priest and even now still has an icon case in her room, though all the icons have been removed long ago. Her father was lucky – he died in his own bed of cancer, without, I believe, either leaving the priesthood or joining the 'Living Church'.‡ His children scattered all over the country, each trying to get as far away from home as possible so nobody should know their family background. Her first husband, a minor journalist, was arrested right after their marriage, and she had to leave Leningrad, returning to her native town, where she still lives, now that her second husband, the violinist, is dead.

She bears the name of her first husband because she was afraid to register her marriage to the second one – who formally adopted

* Until the Emancipation Acts of 1861, serfs were virtually the property of the landowners and could be bought or sold. Most worked the land, but others were employed as domestic servants.

† See *Hope Against Hope*, pages 354–6.

‡ An officially encouraged breakaway movement from the Russian Orthodox Church in the early years of the Soviet regime. Priests who joined it were looked on as collaborators of the Bolsheviks.

their young son before his death. All her life, right up to the present moment, this woman has never ceased to tremble – and with very good reason, I must say. If I myself no longer constantly quake in my shoes, it is because I have no son to worry about, and after the publication of M.'s poetry I was able to say to myself: 'Enough – no more trembling!' Nowadays of course there are a million less grounds for it than during the reign of the great friend of little children and the peoples of the world, or even during that of the author of the speech on the 'cult of personality'. But even at the present time any normal person still has plenty of reason for apprehension: things may not look too bad today, but what about tomorrow? This trembling middle-aged mother of a young son – she was well past forty when he was born, and he is still going to school – never has a moment's respite from her worries about him: he too is a violinist, and she has taken it into her head that all violinists are liable to be persecuted, like her second husband. Someone told her that her name might do her son no good, since her first husband had not been rehabilitated, so rather than stir up the past, she hesitated for a long time to put in for his formal rehabilitation, getting around to it only after the fall of Khrushchev – by which time such applications were no longer of interest to anyone. She eventually received a piece of paper to the effect that the prosecutor's office could find no grounds for rehabilitation. Her first husband had gone to prison at the end of the twenties, and nobody will ever look into cases of wrongful arrest so far back. I got a similar piece of paper at the time of the Hungarian events. A kindhearted woman prosecutor had advised me, after going through the very thin dossier on M.'s arrest in 1938, to apply for a review of the 1934 case. 'He committed no crime,' she had told me. 'It was only verse, after all, and he never even read it in public. Mention that in your application.' Times must indeed have changed, I thought, and did exactly as she suggested. But before two months had gone by, the poem had already become 'criminal' again, together with any kind of independent thinking. I am guarding that piece of paper religiously – as a permanent reminder of how everything, at any moment, can so easily swing around again by any number of degrees. Unfortunately, I do not remember the name of the woman prosecutor: I wonder what she would say now.

To inquiries from Soviet publishing houses,* the prosecutor's office coyly replied that it was all one case in effect, and that there was no need for two rehabilitation notices. What their answer would be at the moment I do not know. The whole game of 'posthumous rehabilitation' is now over, and nobody wants to publish M. in any case – so what does it matter? My concern is with a man long since dead, who for more than thirty years has been lying somewhere in a mass grave – though he still manages, without the aid of Gutenberg, to be a thorn in the side of all 'true Soviet writers'. My former colleague, on the other hand, has to worry about a young son with his whole life still ahead of him, and she is terrified that some harm may come to him because of this refusal to rehabilitate her first husband. She also fears she could be summoned and asked why all these years she has made a false entry whenever she filled out a form by describing herself not as a 'widow', but as 'divorced'. 'Who is going to bother about that,' I asked her, 'now that you're retired and drawing your pension?' 'But they have a personnel department in the Social Security office as well,' she replied. She is frightened of everything and everybody – the manager of her apartment block, personnel departments, her former colleagues, her neighbours, all the teachers and administrative staff of her son's school, militiamen, people in general, but most of all she fears the place where you can be taken at night and plied with myriad questions. 'If anybody asks why you lied in your forms, say you were afraid to lose your job,' I suggested, reminding her of a woman who had worked as a laboratory assistant in our college. She had arrived from Moscow with her four children and complained to all and sundry that her husband had gone off with another woman and deserted her. Her wages were miserably low, and both she and her children went hungry. People advised her to apply for alimony and denounce this scoundrel to whom she had borne so many children. To this she replied proudly: 'We will never take a penny from him.' It was a remarkably close-knit family, but the children were shy of strangers, and they all kept

---

*i.e. in 1955–6, when there was some hope that Mandelstam might be published in the Soviet Union, which was only possible after a dead author had been formally 'rehabilitated', in other words, cleared of the trumped-up charges brought against him in the Stalin years.

very much to themselves. One day the husband suddenly turned up, and a rumour went around the college that to get his residence permit he had produced a document issued to him by the administration of a labour camp. It thus came out that he had been in prison all the time, and his wife had just been putting on an act to keep her job . . . Only, as the violinist's widow reminded me, he had been arrested not under article 58,* but simply for dishonesty at his place of work – he would not have come back otherwise. All the wives of people sentenced under article 58 knew they belonged to the most abject category of citizens, infinitely worse off than the fortunate spouses of embezzlers and thieves. My former colleague had often agonized over what she should say if summoned and asked to explain why she had lied over the years. She would not have dared to admit, as I advised her, that it was from fear: 'A college teacher, a person entrusted with the education of youth – how can you be so cowardly?' they would have said. The woman still goes in fear and trembling, and I can only vouch for the fact that she has had every reason; nor is there any guarantee that we won't all one day have good cause to shake like aspen leaves again. Actually, this particular woman has been extremely lucky: her father and one of her husbands died at home, and her son has not been denounced as a 'parasite'† or signer of protest letters . . .

Fear and trembling is the natural state of anyone who has reached retirement age, or is approaching it. People of thirty may feel a little scared, but they don't positively shake with fear. Only very few 'cogs' overcome their terror altogether; such people are even rarer than pensioners who do not tremble, or repent at having written denunciations. I have never actually met any repentant informers, and know of only one, but I'll be talking about him later. I do, however, know a few people who have ceased to tremble, and I marvel at their peace of mind. Many more have stopped trembling only for the time being, but they remain wary, never dropping their guard for a single moment. All our lives we

---

* The article of the Criminal Code in the Stalin years covering 'political' crimes.

† Under Khrushchev, laws were passed making it possible for the authorities to deport as 'parasites' persons considered to be antisocial on political or other grounds. (See Brodski, Appendix A.)

have been exhorted to exercise vigilance – little wonder if we continue to do so . . .

People rarely change their outlook on life: it takes shape in their young days and stays with them to the end. I asked the violinist's widow: 'Did your father teach you to believe in God?' She didn't know what to reply. The family's livelihood had once depended on the church, and as a child she had been taken to see all the main services, but later on, having to learn dialectical materialism, she had been told that religion is the opium of the people – although all she knows about opium is that it is used in certain painkillers. The only thing that really stuck in her mind is that religion is a sign of backwardness, so she threw away her icons without giving it a thought, and henceforth her life was dominated by only two things: intense pity for her husband and fear for her son. Love and pity are her only faith, and she has never harmed a soul in her life. Somewhere among her priestly ancestors there must surely have been one, pure in mind and spirit, from whom this woman, having lost her faith through no fault of her own, has inherited her capacity for love, pity, and sorrow, as well as a marvellous purity of mind and the gift of music. She is beginning to go blind and has no idea where her son will be sent,* or whether she will be able to go with him. Will he too have to move from town to town, always wandering on somewhere, so that she never catches up with him? He has grown up to be a terribly shy and withdrawn young man, constantly afraid, like his mother. Though fear is normally an acquired characteristic, we have seen that it can be passed on from generation to generation.

I also know what it means to be a widow, but at least I have been spared the terror one feels on behalf of a son – I realized in time that one must not have children. And I had the great consolation of poetry. In full consciousness of being a slave, I repeated to myself: 'For free is the slave who has overcome fear.' I could not really, of course, overcome fear, but verse gave inner freedom, showed that man was capable of higher and better things: love, pity, a feeling for music and poetry, ideas, grief, sorrow, and pain – and also the mysterious joy which sometimes comes over us at

* After finishing their studies, Soviet graduates are 'directed' to jobs, often in very remote places. See page 390.

moments of silence and sadness. Is it not time to pause for thought about who we are, what we have done with ourselves, where and how we are living?

It is good if a man can cling to his inner freedom. This was hardest not in the worst period of the terror, but earlier: in the years between the end of the Civil War and collectivization, when fond hopes were still entertained of returning to a normal human existence. This was the period when people were quite extraordinarily deaf and insensitive. I am judging not by myself – I was then as silly and light-headed as anyone of my age and sex – but by what I saw around me: the universal poverty of thought and feeling. People of strong character, like M. and Akhmatova, were reduced to silence. Many good ones, such as Tynianov, frittered away their talents trying to prove how ingenious they were. Pasternak was busy writing his long narrative poems. Everybody, in short, was bent on promoting himself or simply played a role of his own devising. Their inner voices, however, had been stilled by the victory of the 'new', and there was a deep crisis of the spirit. You cannot imagine what such a crisis is like unless you bear in mind that the few who regained their inner freedom did so only because of the healing effects of *fear*. This, at least, is what happened in the case of weak people like me. M. was to recover for a different reason. Although he could be momentarily frightened or taken aback (as, for instance, by the sudden appearance at my parents' home of a man in a *papakha** inquiring about the 'strange type' who had come to live with them, by a nasty look from some son of a bitch, by contact with anything cheap or vile, and by various other things which were not in themselves a cause for fear), he was immune to terror in the proper sense. He could, in other words, be alarmed by the shadow of evil when it fell across him without ever knowing real fear. Hard as it is to explain, I saw with my own eyes how he lived his life unafraid. He therefore recovered his inner freedom, not under the impact of terror, but with the return of his essential gaiety of spirit; this he had lost for a time, but it came back to him at the beginning of the thirties after the effects of earlier illusions had worn off. This way of recovery was unique, something

* A high fur hat often worn by military people, giving them a fierce appearance.

peculiar to him. For me and other people of my generation it happened in a different manner.

The fact is that in ages such as the one we have lived through (and which is still so much with us), fear can have a positive function. Akhmatova and I once confessed to each other that the most powerful sensation we had ever known – stronger than love, jealousy, or any other human feeling – was terror and what goes with it: the horrible and shameful awareness of utter helplessness, of being tied hand and foot. There are different kinds of fear. As long as it is accompanied by a sense of shame, one is still a human being, not an abject slave. It is the sense of shame that gives fear its healing power and offers hope for regaining inner freedom. While M. was still alive I feared only for him and had no other feelings. After his death all my sleepless nights, all my days and hours, were filled with bitterness and shame – a healing sense of our disgrace.

Slaves never have this sense of their own dishonour, firmly believing that – barring a 'mistake', of course – nobody will touch such devoted and willing servants as themselves. In the era now gone by, these were a comparatively small minority. They sat in their luxurious hothouses and had no contact with ordinary mortals. Knowing no doubts, they would only sigh if the man next to them was hauled off at dead of night: even their little corner of heaven could be infiltrated by traitors. Most city dwellers with a respectable status – those who lived on a salary, a 'packet', or author's royalties – exorcized their fear by closing their eyes, telling themselves that if only they were sensible they would come to no harm. The fear experienced by such as these made pitiful cowards of them and had a corrupting effect that will last for several generations. The survivors among these morally depraved specimens, who believed they could exorcize their fear, are still active and continue to talk ecstatically about the marvels of the twenties, when there was supposedly such a boom in all the arts.

To protect their children, these 'exorcists' generally brought them up in a state of total ignorance. Thus spared, the children grew up not knowing what fear was. If their parents went to prison, it was all too easy afterwards to recruit the poor little wretches as informers; or one of them – the most 'unfrightened' of all – would be picked up as well, and in all innocence, or being threatened for the first time in his life, he would pour out anything the interrogators wanted by way of 'evidence' against his own parents, his friends, or even strangers he had never met. Akhmatova and I invented a saying about them: 'Better scared than spared.' If such a family was lucky and the parents did not land in jail, you could bet that one of its 'unfrightened' younger members would be the sort who wrote indiscreet letters, kept a diary, and went the rounds of people's houses freely speaking his thoughts – a kind of imbecility for which others had to pay dearly. Such 'unfrightened' young men were far worse than professional informers; these you could outsmart, but there was no coping with some young innocent who prattled on and on, looking at you all the time with utterly guileless bright blue eyes.

There was also a nasty game of pretending to be innocent. Once we missed the last train back to Kalinin,* or at least had some reason to spend the night in Moscow. Looking for a place to stay, we went to Adelina Adalis. I still find it hard to forgive M. for having praised her verse somewhere. In my view this was an unpardonable lapse, an act of blindness. When I worked on the Komsomol newspaper, Adalis was always coming to try to wheedle an advance out of me, or a commission to write an article. Everywhere she went she dragged her cross-eyed son with her and showed how good she was at bringing up children by continually shouting at him. She had another child, an unwanted one which she had put in an orphanage. When her husband, or it may have been her lover, was arrested, she disowned him so vehemently to the interrogator in charge of the case that even he was embarrassed. M. must really have believed she was a poet if he thought fit to go and ask her to let us stay the night. She wanted to know why we didn't go home to our own apartment. When we explained that Kostyrev,† our former lodger, now in sole possession, would call in the militia the moment he saw us, Adalis began to shout that she

*Town (formerly Tver) on the railway line to Leningrad, about 100 kilometres north-west of Moscow, where Mandelstam lived for a time after his return from exile in Veronezh in 1937. See *Hope Against Hope*, pages 335 ff. As a returned exile, he was not allowed to reside in the capital but, under the regulations, could spend the night there.

†See *Hope Against Hope*, page 156.

would go with us and talk to the militia if they came: 'I won't let them touch you.' A sort of lesser Shaginian, she had a diabolical way of affecting faith in the law and the power of words. Before the war someone once asked her what she knew of my fate. She went for the man, shouting at him and asking why, if he had reason to think I was reduced to earning my living somewhere, he had not arranged for me to go to the best sanatorium for treatment. Adalis had learned some of her tricks from Briusov, with whom she got on close terms after arriving from Odessa. Her cross-eyed son had grown up to be worthy of his mother. It is said that in the section of the Union of Writers where he works as a translator, he makes no secret of his double role. Not only 'unfrightened', but also doubtless a man of high principle, he takes after his mother in being able to convince the authorities of anything he likes . . .

At the present happy time there is no end to the number of pure, 'unfrightened' innocents who could always, at a moment's notice, be made to say absolutely anything required of them. There are also quite a few others who have conquered fear, and are now trying to think for themselves and speak their minds. But until people have recovered their memory, these voices will not be heard. If most people are still asleep it is because they have been artificially deprived of memory. They have to learn what happened to us – to the generation of their fathers and grandfathers – otherwise, innocent and 'unfrightened', they may well drift into a new round of disasters, proving utterly helpless in the face of them. The whole thing could start all over again. Among the younger members of the ruling class there are now those who have never experienced terror and would be quite happy to 'get tough', not knowing that 'captious sultans' are liable to be destroyed as surely as their soldiers. Not only memory, but a sense of fear too, is sometimes important.

From the very first days, when we were still so courageous, fear began to stifle everything in us that makes life what it is. In 1938 we learned that 'they' had gone over to a method of 'simplified interrogation'; in other words, prisoners were being beaten and tortured. For a short while this made us think that if they were no longer using 'psychology' (by 'psychology' we meant anything that left no actual marks on the body), then there was nothing to be afraid of any more. 'Now it's all very simple,' Akhmatova had said. 'They just stick a hat with ear flaps on your head and whisk you off behind barbed wire.' We very soon had second thoughts: how could one say there was nothing to be afraid of? It was essential to be afraid; otherwise they would break you down and make you say exactly what they wanted, and no end of people would then be picked up from the lists you gave them. This happened all the time to the most ordinary kind of people. We were only human after all – how could anyone know how he would behave in conditions that were inhuman? So we kept saying to ourselves: Help me, Lord, I cannot answer for myself. Nobody can be sure of anything. Even now I worry, if only because I might be injected with some beastly stuff that robs one of both will and reason. How can I stop being afraid? As long as we feel our helplessness and the common shame we shall not lose our sense of fear. Fear can be a constructive thing, helping one to keep in touch with reality. Not every slave is capable of feeling the kind of fear which gives one strength and endurance: for this one must master fear and never give way to cowardice. He who has mastered fear knows all the terrors the world holds and can look them in the eye.

I can only repeat the words of M.: with such fear you have nothing to fear. This does not mean that there is anything sinful about the sort of debilitating fear to which the violinist's wife is prey. The real danger comes more from those in high places who are 'unfrightened' than from anybody 'below' – and also from all who have lost their memory. It is from their ranks that the cowards and 'captious sultans' are recruited.

A man possessed of inner freedom, memory, and a sense of fear is the blade of grass or wood chip that can alter the course of the swift-flowing stream. It was cowardice that led to the horror we have lived through, and cowardice could easily plunge us back into it. I shall not live to see the future, but I am haunted by the fear that it may be only a slightly modified version of the past. Then people will fall asleep never to awake again. If they were not properly awake now, how can they possibly survive if they fall into yet another deep slumber? It frightens me, and I have every reason to fear – not for my own sake, of course, but for humanity's. The legacy of the twenties is almost impossible to overcome. We have to get over our loss of memory. This is the first task. We have to settle the accounts presented by the past – otherwise there will be no way ahead.

20   Stray Recollections

'Reality,' M. once noted, 'is a continuum, and prose is a disjunct expression of it.' Recollections are equally 'disjunct' – you cannot string them together to form an unbroken line. This remark of his showed M.'s unwillingness to join in the pursuit of comprehensiveness which so affected everybody in the first half of our century. I believe that this urge to give expression to the continuum, to reproduce processes in the unbroken flow of their development in time, was the result of a peculiar craving – almost physiological in character – to feel everything in all its tangibility, to finger the flow of reality: time, life, movement, events. This yearning, so overwhelming in literature, probably also made itself felt in every branch of philosophy, art, and science. The arrested moment, slow motion in movie films, the breaking down of matter into its minutest particles – all these related phenomena were dictated by the wish to relive the past, to reanimate bygone events, to drag out each second to such an unheard-of extent that it lasts indefinitely.

The more the pace of life quickened, the more value people attached to the passing moment. The kaleidoscopic rapidity with which things moved made one reel, and the Futurists, with their cult of speed, clutched at split seconds. Though M. never made any attempt to re-create life as an unbroken continuum, he was fond of retarded motion: a lumbering ox, the slow movement of Armenian women, the long and sticky flow of honey from the rim of a jar – all this was out of the same need to savour the passage of time. ('But only once a year nature is suffused all through / By lingering time as in the metre of Homeric lines.') For M., dwelling on the passage of time was not an end in itself but rather, perhaps, an aspect of his quest for the Spirit, of his thirst for grace. ('Here is that immovable land, and with it / I drink the cold mountain air of Christianity . . . And from those Christian heights, through space caught unawares,

/ Grace flows down like a madrigal by Palestrina.') Sometimes it was by way of trying to get a sense of eternity, with the Eucharist seen as the only moment that lasts eternally: 'Like an eternal noon-tide, the Eucharist goes on for ever,' allowing all who share in the Mystery to partake of eternity: 'so that outside time we sigh with all our breath / for the meadowland where time stands still.' The sense of the moment as eternity, the dream of this 'meadowland', is blotted out by the 'noise of time', by the 'clamour of fevered human strife'.

M. was acutely aware that a man's life or personality is all of a piece, and he never therefore tried to re-create isolated moments from the past. With his love of life he lived each fleeting moment to the full and never sought to repeat it. The line 'All things gone by will come to pass again' is intended to mean not that actual moments in life will be repeated, but rather that all people experience life in the same way. What is more, M. always spoke of the sensation of time everlasting not with reference to his own personal experience, but always drawing on something objective, outside himself. By focusing attention on a reality existing apart from himself, he showed how futile it was, in his view, to try to recapture or relish moments from the past. It was thus the simple truth when he said that his memory was hostile to everything personal. In her *Pages from a Diary* (there was, by the way, no actual diary), Akhmatova correctly pointed out that M. did not like to reminisce. To this I may add that his recollections were always fragmentary and never personal in character. Sometimes – though rather seldom – he talked about things he had seen or encountered, but it was always by way of illustrating something in the present. He once recalled, for instance, how he had run into a group of Mensheviks in a corridor of the Metropole hotel just after they had been expelled from the Soviet. As they came towards him, they were loud in their indignation at the words used by the speakers who had demanded their expulsion. M. stood aside to let them pass and heard one of them say: 'What do they mean – "lackeys"?' He mentioned this episode only because the recollection of it was stirred by an observation he had just made about the present, namely: 'They have always, from the very first, used not words but marked cards.'

I believe that M. was able to live out his life so fully because he was blessed with the gift of play and joy. I have never known his equal in this. When he went out of my life, I would have died too but for the joy breathed by his verse and his absolute injunction against suicide. It was his very capacity to live filled 'full of space and time' that made it unnecessary for him ever to retrace his steps. His life was divided into distinct periods, but life and work were so indissolubly linked that the different stages in his biography overlap entirely with the phases of his growth as a poet. His verse always reflects the events of his life at the time of writing. Prose, on the other hand, always lags behind: the stuff of prose needs time to sink in and mature; this cannot be done in a hurry. While always remaining himself and preserving his personality intact, M. went through a series of phases – though it was always a question of growth rather than change. External events had their impact on his inner life, but they were not the source of it – better to say, indeed, that they were to some extent determined by it. The catastrophic nature of most of what happened to us in our times certainly had no part in shaping the personality, tending only, if anything, to deform it. One needed enormous powers of endurance to maintain a capacity for growth despite the crushing pressures and stifling atmosphere. It was possible only for people whose personality was based on a formative idea of such strength that instead of the growth of their personality being affected by events it was rather the other way round: the events of their lives were influenced by their attitude towards them. In all the legacy of the twentieth century – its science, scholarship, humanism, and analytical spirit (not to mention its ideas of 'progress' and 'culture', its various abstract forms of deism, theosophy, rationalism, and positivism) – there is absolutely nothing that ever helped anyone to preserve himself intact. All it did was assist the process of decay and disintegration. We saw this process taking place and turned our heads away in shame. The greatest pitfall for M. was humanism (in the Russian sense of the word); it was the source of both his faith in the search for social justice and his horror at the spectacle of ever-mounting brutality and fraudulence. I never cease to marvel at M.'s strength and the richness of the inner resources that enabled him to live a full life and approach the end whole and uncrushed – at least right up to the very last moment I was with him, during the night of 1 May 1938. This was in fact the end of the road – what happened later in the Lubianka and behind the barbed wire was worse by far than the gas chambers.

I find it difficult to name what precisely had shaped M.'s personality because his basic idea cannot be put into simple words. It was really a question of his view of poetry as a gift from above, as a vocation, and also his belief in its sacramental nature ('children at play with their Father'). I never encountered anyone else who was able to spend his days under fire and yet not lose his capacity for intellectual and spiritual growth. Nobody could endure under fire. Some people retained their human qualities by managing to lie low, but then they could scarcely be expected to go on growing and achieving greater maturity – and in any case those able to do so belonged mostly to the older generation which had been wiped out almost at the very beginning. I have recently read that Florenski was arrested in the 1930s, but I believe that before this – in the middle of the twenties – he had already spent some time in exile. In our incredible isolation it is all too easy to get things wrong, but I do remember that M. was in despair over Florenski's wretched fate already in the twenties. (In the thirties we never heard anything more about him.) The people of M.'s and Akhmatova's generation either surrendered without a struggle or lived in total seclusion. Those who refused to give up, people of firm religious convictions, died the death of martyrs.

Akhmatova drew her strength from standing firm. Her poetry is not easily divided into distinct periods, and even so they only mark off periods in her biography rather than the stages of her spiritual growth. Whenever she was left in peace, she always reverted to the pure and placid manner of her early work. The seclusion of her existence helped her to survive, but, as we know, the blows fell on her all the same. Fortunately she had a quiet old age: ten years of almost peaceful, even if still unsettled existence. To her great good fortune she also kept her capacity for work in the last years of her life. It was astonishing, though, that any breathing space always brought out not her mature traits of asceticism and self-renunciation, but a youthful egoism, a passion for success, and a certain gay abandon. I pulled her leg about it – though in fact I was glad she could feel like this in her old age. She sometimes took my remarks amiss, but before long she would be laughing with me at her own expense.

Looking back on my own life from my present vantage point, I can see quite clearly both its unity and its sharp division into very clearly defined periods, but with me they were determined exclusively by external circumstances. My childhood was important only as a preparatory stage and in no other way. In general I fail to understand people's excessive interest in their own childhood; I believe it must have something to do with the desire to treat reality as an unbroken whole and to relive past experience. This is a feature of the age, connected no doubt with an increasing individualism – which hinders the attainment of maturity and the growth of the personality, and was much aided in our country by all the insuperable obstacles put in the way of really growing up, by the furtiveness of frightened people labouring under a feeling of their own inadequacy. The desire to take refuge in one's childhood is invariably a symptom of some such feeling of inadequacy. Oddly enough – and though I do not like him – I can forgive only Nabokov's somnambulist excursion into his childhood. Separated from his native country, no longer immersed in its language and history – and having lost his father in the way he did – Nabokov re-creates the idyll of his childhood as his only link with the country of his forbears. Living the life of an expatriate, he was deprived of the chance of coming to maturity.

A person grows up only in the period when he begins to have a feeling of responsibility for everything that happens in the world, but in this country no such thing was possible, and in adulthood we developed instead a hypertrophied instinct for self-preservation. This stands in the way of any kind of proper growing up: hence the tendency we have to go into raptures over our childhood when we were not expected to answer for anything and could simply enjoy life for its own sake. Later we turned into a flock of sheep, happy enough to be shepherded as long as our lives were spared – of which, alas, there was no guarantee: sheep may be slaughtered as well as shorn.

My life really began when I met M., and the first period was our life together. The second period I call my life in the tomb – which is exactly what it felt like, though it was not life everlasting but an unbelievable charnel-house existence which dragged on for fifteen years (1938–53); altogether I spent twenty years just waiting (1938–1958). For me there was nothing at all in these years except my ceaseless vigil, even though various events took place and I travelled enormous distances, always doing something or hurrying off somewhere. I never for one moment paid the slightest attention to what befell me personally. Those twenty years – particularly the first fifteen – remain in my mind as a solid lump, a dead, inert mass through which time did not flow but only seeped away. I was constantly tormented by the sense of total divorce between the first and second periods of my life, their unrelatedness to each other: one had been full of meaning and events, while the second was empty of everything, even of the awareness of passing time. Not only I had this feeling – all my contemporaries shared the same acute sensation of time getting madly out of hand and slipping away, leaving no traces in the mind. Of course, there are recollections of moving from one place to another, of work and teaching, and of endless, grisly occurrences, but these are mere disjointed images, devoid of the content an experience must have to be significant. The chief feelings were anguish, a sense that life was sundered in two and that everything going on around us was inexplicable. Someone who spent several years in a camp under Khrushchev told me that he had met there a demented Polish Jew who had been given some incredibly long sentence and did not qualify for rehabilitation. 'In Russia,' he used to say, 'there is no space, only kilometres'. I suppose I felt like this mad Jew – living without space or time. Another thing that conveys how I felt in those years was a hallucination I had in 1934 after falling ill with typhus and being taken to an infirmary, a converted barracks set up to deal with such cases. As I was brought in and saw shaven heads rising from their pillows at the sight of me I imagined, in my fever, that they were putting me in the men's wing. I was in this kind of bemused state throughout all those years, eternally uncertain where I was and what was happening to me. The only real thing during the whole time was my meetings with Akhmatova – and then only if we were alone.

The third period was from the end of the fifties when I regained the right to speak my name, to say who I was and what I thought.

Almost at once two parts of my life – the first and the third – came together, crushing the one in the middle and flattening it like a pancake (made not of flour, I need scarcely say, but of something infinitely nastier). My life thus became a single whole again, particularly after I had written my first book describing what happened to us. In the period of waiting, when life consisted of lying low and concealing my identity, I had two aims: to preserve the poetry and to leave something in the nature of a letter telling of our fate. The first book is in fact precisely that – a rather detailed letter. I could not have hoped for such luck: where could I have hidden the manuscript at a time when they were always coming into my room while I was out and going through all my stuff? Perhaps I will also be able to preserve the second book, this one I am writing now, but I don't even trouble my head with such trifling questions any more. The main thing has been done.

What about the disjointed recollections I have mentioned? They remain in my mind much as the whole of that period of time which raced past me, out of my control, the way time evidently always does if stripped of proper content and meaning. This segment of my life simply vanished into an abyss, leaving no traces and not affecting me permanently at all. The stray images of the period, never linked together by inner meaning, have dimmed and faded. They stick in my mind only as a witness to the barrenness of those years. In these later years I have managed to summon up both strength and fury; others – the vast majority – simply wasted away without saying anything. It must be said, however, that I had an easier time of it: I knew what I was waiting for, while they spent themselves trying to save their children, helping their families, driving themselves to utter exhaustion in the process. I too was always ready to drop from weariness, but because I simply did not dare, I managed to preserve my strength. I have all the staying power of the Russians – it developed during my years of waiting. For half a century it was all that kept people going here and has become a weakness with them. Only if it serves some purpose is it justified. Otherwise, kept up too long and undirected, it turns into mere inertia.

I said earlier that one should search for a meaning in life rather than set oneself aims, but now I seem to be justifying my existence by talking about the aim for which I have lived. The contradiction is more apparent than real. My aim was to justify M.'s existence by preserving the things that gave it meaning. My own life was mutilated and robbed of meaning – apart from the aim which had been forced upon me. Instead of living my life, all I did was wait until its two severed parts could be joined together again. In such periods of waiting an aim in life is all that matters: while hardly enriching, it at least keeps some flicker of the soul alive . . . I could do no more than this, and did not expect to: everything went into carrying out my task. I was lucky; it could have been much worse: I could also have ended in a mass grave with a tag on my leg, and then all my papers would have mouldered away or been burned. I thank God it did not happen. I see His hand in this and quietly whisper words of love and gratitude.

21 A Honeymoon; a Tale of Two Cooks

People of my generation firmly believed that poets scraped along writing verse only until they were ready to launch into prose, at which point they automatically rose in the world. The prime examples quoted were no mean ones: Pushkin ending with prose, and Gogol switching to it after his early attempt at poetry. This was something constantly being pointed out in conversation by Tynianov, Eikhenbaum, and Shklovski, and perhaps they wrote about it too. They themselves probably began with verse – what feeble stuff it must have been! – and concluded from their own experience that poetry is only the prelude to prose. Like Pasternak, they all secretly dreamed of writing a novel: it meant fame and money, and even the chance of winding up as a classic. As regards achieving the status of a classic, I have been taught by M. to scorn the very idea, but when it comes to money I have some sympathy for them. I believe people should be paid for their work, however ordinary. But what was the point of all these theories about the relationship of prose to poetry? Listening to the scholarly arguments of our best literary specialists, M. used to sigh and say: 'They simply don't like verse.' This was a period when it was all too often a case of sheer prejudice. People were against poetry, just as they were against easel painting. At the same time they loved everything new and showy, particularly original theories of any kind. Even people who were secretly fond of verse became tongue-tied and evasive the moment they began to discuss it (for example, Tynianov in his article entitled 'The Interval'). I have noticed that scholars, like everybody else, choke on their words when they have nothing but the dross of rationalism to operate with (and rationalism, by its very nature, produces only dross). Those I have mentioned, if one adds Gukovski and Tomashevski, were the very best in the field of literary theory, though they had scarcely reached their peak when they rapidly went into decline. (This, I hasten to make clear, was not their fault but that of the times they lived in and the regime.) They were all infected by the shallowness of the age, its rationalist, pseudoscientific delusions and passion for innovation at any price, and were then muzzled before they had time to grow out of it. The only thing left was to write touching accounts of their own or other people's childhood.

I am absolutely convinced myself that prose and poetry spring from different sources and have different functions. Verse comes from much deeper down and – as M. would have put it – crystallizes only under high pressure. The production of either is very taxing, and as I saw in M.'s case, it is hard to go in for both simultaneously. When he was writing prose, verse came to him only if it was a matter of what he called 'floating lines', that is, things that had already taken shape in his head and were merely waiting to be put down on paper. If the mind is wholly occupied by a piece of prose about to be written, there can be no room in it for a new poem. During the year and a half which, with one gap, he spent writing *Noise of Time*, he did admittedly manage some poetry as well, but the chapters written after the gap (the one about the 'aristocratic fur coat' and the parts relating to Feodosia) were made up of other, already existing material and were literally just tacked on to the main part about his childhood (which, thank goodness, is free of the maudlin self-adulation usual in this kind of thing).

My impression is that *The Egyptian Stamp* is of a composite nature. It was written in a period of deep poetic silence, but material of poetic origin somehow intruded into it, intermingling with elements from a purely prosaic source. This is probably just the reason why I do not like it very much. Apart from its being a hybrid, I feel that its skeleton of a plot is a sign of inner weakness, a concession to the general enthusiasm for 'major works' – wearisomely intricate novels or long stories. But what most rouses my suspicions about *The Egyptian Stamp* is that the impulse to write it came from M.'s desire to project back into the pre-Revolutionary years the mental confusion that overtook him in the twenties – a sure sign that he had temporarily lost his bearings and his judgement. (I am not trying here to defend the pre-Revolutionary years. The fact that they are referred to as the Silver Age makes me laugh; it was mainly a time of anxiety and forebodings of doom. The roots of all the subsequent evils, however, are to be found neither in those years nor in the twenties, but go much deeper.)

At the beginning of the twenties M. gloomily described himself as 'the drying crust of a loaf long since taken out', though he never forgot for a single moment that the 'loaves' of his bakery image had once been of proper weight, and that in any case there had never been any question of his being able to fit in with the new realities of life. His verse of that period is always steeped in his feeling for the tragic nature of the age; in his articles he spoke of how we had lost the 'torch handed down by our forbears' and called for the injection of a little reason ('the elementary principles, the general concepts of the eighteenth century may again prove to be of use . . . now is not the time to fear rationalism. The irrationalism underlying the coming era is already casting its shadow on us. In such times the reason of the Encyclopedists is the sacred fire of Prometheus'); he was horrified by the 'social engineering' calculated to crush and destroy the personality. At the beginning of the twenties he still harboured the illusion that it would be possible to exercise a civilizing influence, or – as we put it jokingly – to 'give the Bolsheviks some good advice' and get them to stop the trend towards utter brutalization. By the second half of the twenties things seemed to have settled down: produce appeared in the shops, people began to eat properly and their skin no longer had the bluish hue of previous years; streetcars and trains began to run again. More than anything else in the world people now longed for peace, with the result that they were stricken with the incurable blindness that always goes with moral sclerosis. They all paid a terrible price for their self-induced complacency, particularly the really decent people like Zoshchenko, who suffered far more than the scoundrels. To the end of his days Zoshchenko believed in the possibility of giving 'good advice', and, acutely sensitive to the horror of what was going on, even when there was nothing one could do except howl like a wild animal, he still went on trying to be a restraining influence, warning us, drawing our attention in his stories to the way people behaved: a militiaman in white gloves, saluting politely, torments the life out of a much abused and harassed peasant; a woman lugs along a heavy suitcase, and passers-by, taking her for a domestic servant, are indignant at the man sauntering behind her with his hands in his pockets, but when they learn she is only his mother, they apologize – the family is sacrosanct, and you have every right to turn your mother into a beast of burden. Poor innocent Zoshchenko: people took him for a writer of funny stories and laughed themselves silly at this kind of thing . . . Everybody paid a price, and *The Egyptian Stamp* was still only a small one, but that is nevertheless how it must be regarded, despite one or two magnificent passages (the lynching scene, for instance, or the death of Bosio – it was not advisable to be a singer in this country!). It is significant that with M. prose usually prepared the way for verse, but *The Egyptian Stamp* did not fulfil this function; it failed to induce the composure of mind and spirit he needed for the writing of poetry.

At the very beginning of the thirties M. once said to me while we were waiting for a streetcar: 'We always think everything is all right just because the streetcars are running.' Now again intensely aware of the horrors of our times, in a state of deep inner distress, he had torn away what he referred to as the 'veil thrown over the abyss' – not that it any longer served to conceal what lay below. He had, in other words, by now rid himself of any lingering dependence on the generally accepted point of view and thereby become a free man. This defiance was to end in his death, but how could anybody have been content to live in a dacha at Peredelkino* in our criminal times?

* Writers' colony near Moscow, where members of the Union of Writers live in considerable State-subsidized ease and comfort.

The rest of his prose consisted of essays and articles which he always wrote in a few hours for a newspaper or journal (except, of course, 'Conversation About Dante'); they were invariably based on some idea which he had already worked out in his head. He wrote his first story in Kharkov in 1922; entitled 'The Fur Coat', it was printed in the local newspaper. Later he sold it in an expanded version to Rakovski's sister. It has been lost, together with the copy of the newspaper in which the first version appeared. It is a good thing that at least his essay 'On the Nature of the Word' has been preserved – though the odds against it were very great. It should always be borne in mind by our friends in distant parts that this was true of everyone of us, and of every scrap of paper we managed to save. The survival of each single article or manuscript is the result of a miracle. I am very conscious of the fact that in certain conditions it is more painful to live on in order to preserve such things than it is to die, but, as is well known, we are not hedonists, and were not created merely for our own happiness or pleasure . . .

No trace is left, either, of M.'s second attempt at writing prose work, the fruit of a pleasant and peaceful little adventure. One day, walking through the Smolensk market in Moscow (we were always very fond of markets as centres of bustling city life at its most authentic), we got into conversation with some eastern carpet sellers. M. was very good at talking with ordinary people – with anyone, in fact, except officials, writers, and lackeys. The dusky carpet sellers took us to a hovel in the slums behind the Kiev railway station.* In a squalid upstairs room we were shown something quite extraordinary and marvellous: an enormous tapestry with a hunting scene. The central figure was a youth holding a bow and arrows, and round about were tiny horsemen, hounds, and all kinds of wild animals, foxes, and birds. It was a treasure beyond price, but with the collapse of the normal scale of values such things could be had almost for a song at that time. Our swarthy friends made us a tempting offer, saying we could pay in instalments, and we were very attracted by the idea, though we could not be sure that the carpet had not been stolen from some museum or palace. We went away, leaving our address, and the carpet sellers

* One of the main stations in Moscow.

started coming to see us on Tverskoi Boulevard. Once they even brought the tapestry to us, and the whole of our wretched room was filled with its gorgeous colours.

M. fell in love with it, just as though it had been a woman. What a rational little idiot I was, never feeling jealous, not even of this tapestry, thus denying myself so much in life by way of anguish, despair, sleepless nights, tears, and reconciliations. To him, I felt, it must have seemed like a beautiful slave girl he must deliver from the hands of her abductors, but he tried to cajole me into having it by suggesting we should get on even better with each other under the eye of the young prince. For me it would have meant serving as the prince's handmaiden – and a youth like this I had certainly never seen before. But M. was the first to come to his senses: he ordered the carpet to be rolled up, lifted it from the floor, and after wheezing and shaking himself like a dog, took a deep breath and said: 'It's not for us . . .' It was so large that we should both have choked to death beating and shaking it out in the courtyard. It stayed with us a few more days, but M. kept telling me that there was no room in our life for such a huge museum piece, and I tearfully agreed to let the carpet sellers take it back to their slum. We never saw it again, and M., missing it, began to write a story about this tapestry found in a Moscow hovel. But he soon gave it up; the pages went into our trunk and disappeared when the hour came for them to do so. There is a faint echo of the incident in the few lines about a Persian miniature in 'Journey to Armenia', though the detail about the frightened, squinting eye refers to me, not the young prince.

The third batch of prose pieces were those he published in *Ogoniok*:* 'Sukharevka' and 'Cold Summer'. In 'Sukharevka' a few words were cut out of the following sentence for 'moral' reasons: 'Only on the parched soil of a continent's heartland which is so well trodden, which people trample *as they would their own mother*, which is like nothing else, could you have this fierce, surging market covering the earth with its foul oaths.' 'Soviet people,' M. was admonished, 'respect their mothers. Just think of Gorki's "Mother"' . . . M. never used bad language, but now he came out with a foul oath himself. He was given this explanation only after

* Leading illustrated journal.

the piece had already been printed without the offending phrase . . .
The summer described in the other story really was cold, and before
the onset of the even colder winter that year we had to think of
how to keep warm. M.'s horror of the cold and his craving for
warmth and sun were a consequence of the years of hunger and
chronic malnutrition. In relatively good years, when we had
enough food, he did not mind the cold at all, so that by the end he
was quite reconciled to it – only to undergo, before his death, cold
and hunger more than sufficient for a whole lifetime. I know
myself how cold you feel when you are hungry – though I experienced it not in the camps but only as a 'free' Soviet citizen. The
hunger suffered in a camp is unimaginable – all the sons of bitches
who still block up their ears and close their eyes should know
this.

Quite unexpectedly we learned of a new way of getting to the
south: through the CEKUBU* rest homes. Despite everything,
we still at that time belonged to a privileged group, even though in
a second-class category. We were given free vouchers for the
Gaspra† rest home, and the money earned by the pieces for
Ogoniok paid for our tickets (which were obtained for us by
CEKUBU). Vacationers who had been given places in rest homes
were always transported in whole groups, and we found ourselves
in a compartment of a 'hard' coach‡ together with Vyshinski –
who could not have been more amiable – his wife, and daughter;
each such compartment had six bunks, two of them being placed
crosswise. Vyshinski was wearing a Russian-style shirt of the kind
once favoured by Social Revolutionaries,§ and he looked as
though it were the most natural thing in the world for him to travel
'hard' like this. I would like to suggest that right from the moment
when their star begins to rise – as soon as the first ray shines forth –
all such future great men should be given private parlour cars to
travel in: they should not have to rub shoulders with ordinary

* Acronym for 'Commission for the Improvement in the Living Conditions
of Scholars'; set up by Maxim Gorki in 1921.
  † Small resort near Yalta, in the Crimea.
  ‡ To avoid the use of the word 'class', Soviet rail coaches are graded as
'soft' (first class) and 'hard', in which the seats are not upholstered.
  § The populist party banned and liquidated by the Bolsheviks in 1922.

mortals. At that time Vyshinski was head of Glavnauka,* and I do not remember whether he had yet conducted his first case, the trial of the Social Revolutionaries, in which the legal procedures invented by him were already demonstrated in practice. M. read the accounts of all the trials. However thoroughly they were edited, there were always slips which made it possible for us (who could read between the lines) to reconstruct what the case was really about. It is now almost fifty years ago, but I still remember him pointing out to me something said by a defendant in reply to a question from Vyshinski about the preparations for the Yaroslav uprising: 'But you know more about it than I do ...' This uprising was the first ray in Vyshinski's career; he plotted it and then betrayed it at the right moment. The trial was a turning point for him – neither he nor his wife and daughter ever again had to travel 'hard'.† The professors at Gaspra behaved respectfully towards him as their superior: such is the ingrained Russian habit. It was he who later travelled from one end of Siberia to the other and reported that he had not seen a single camp watch-tower. He was speaking the literal truth: one can't see them from the window of a train compartment ...

But to have done with him, I will tell a story I heard from the director of the Pskov Teachers' Training College. The director's elder brother, a Komsomol in his first year at college, had been arrested, but managed to escape and get to Moscow, where he went with his younger brother (the one who told me the story) to see Vyshinski. He was ushered in straightaway, and Vyshinski listened very attentively, making notes as the boy described how he had been beaten and forced to make statements. The two brothers believed that everything would be all right, but suddenly the door opened, some uniformed men came in, and the Komsomol in search of justice was taken away, never to be seen again. His younger brother, who was still a schoolboy – and also had a different surname – hid for a very long time until he was certain that he was not being sought. The director knew it was all right to

* Department of the People's Commissariat (Ministry) of Education concerned with museums, and artistic and academic institutions (from 1930 it was known as the 'Science Sector').

† See Vyshinski, Appendix A.

tell me this story, but as he did so the door of his office suddenly opened and in came the Secretary of the Party organization at the College – a man with a higher degree who had been excused all other duties. I have noticed that certain 'Candidates of Science' somewhat resemble the immortal Smerdiakov* – they like strong coffee and culture and wiggle the toes of their well-polished shoes. The only difference is that they do not hang themselves; Smerdiakov still had something in the nature of a Christian conscience – which cannot be said of his latter-day imitators. I saw a look of mortal fear come over the face of the director, and his words stuck in his throat. There was nothing to do but say good-bye and leave. This was my last place of work. At the beginning of the conversation the director had been trying to persuade me to stay on in the faculty of general linguistics and give one of the courses laid down in the new curriculum. I replied that I was sick of lying to the students. It was this that prompted him to tell me his story. As a sop to his conscience, the poor devil managed to underpay me – not by very much, a couple of hundred or so. If he is still alive, he must be retired by now, and my story will not do him any harm. I suppose that in his office Vyshinski had a button he could press and that this was how he summoned the men who took the trusting searcher for justice away to his death.

In front of the rest home in Gaspra there was always an old man sitting in a deckchair. They told us he was a former member of the Menshevik Central Committee, a favourite of Lenin, on whose orders he had been spared. The old man spoke with nobody and looked as miserable as sin. At the table we were put next to Kablukov, the scientist. He was the soul of kindness; he always carried around in his pocket a little tin of fruit drops, and whenever he saw a child he would offer it one with old-fashioned courtesy: 'Would you care to help yourself?' As I was still little more than a girl myself, I came in for quite a large share of Kablukov's sweets. He sometimes came to our room to see us, or rather me, and I basked in the warmth of his quite extraordinary loving kindness. Why is it that everybody who has written about him mentions only the 'Spoonerisms' in his speech, never saying a word about the light of saintly kindness that he radiated? He used to go about

* Character in Dostoyevski's *Brothers Karamazov*.

Moscow with a rucksack for carrying his rations; he was always losing or forgetting things, and had a smile for everybody.

Another person at our table was Chulkov, the former mystical anarchist. Once he noticed that I was writing the address on an envelope in the old orthography* – without 'hard signs'. Saying this was a betrayal of Russian culture, he made a scene and immediately went to sit at another table. There is a photograph showing M., Akhmatova, Chulkov, and Petrovykh all together. It was taken in our apartment in Furmanov Street. At Akhmatova's request this was a 'literary' photograph, but a second one included our family group as well: me, M.'s father, and his brother Alexander. Chulkov came to our apartment only to see Akhmatova. He lived out his life in peace and got on remarkably well with the authorities. He used to regale Akhmatova with stories about Liubov Dmitrievna Blok. Everything he said about her was taken, with slight modifications, from her diary.

There were constant arguments among the people staying at Gaspra as to whether the system of issuing vouchers for the rest home was a good one or not. Many were indignant that they were given to 'outsiders', that is, to people like us. (I even had to explain to one of them that M. was a member of CEKUBU and got a ration from it.) All this was by virtue of traditional jealousies about precedence and privilege, and these arguments flared up with particular violence when it was a question of 'disreputable' people such as M. There were also disgusting scenes over the allotment of rooms in the rest home, with everybody shrieking about the learned qualifications that entitled him to a bigger and better one. One wonders whether it wasn't people like this who prepared the ground for the famous decree against 'egalitarianism'.† We were very put out by this state of affairs and to avoid recriminations rented a room in a Tartar house away from all the uproar in the rest home.

*In 1917 the Provisional Government decreed a reform of the Russian alphabet. Letters of no phonetic significance were dropped, including the mute 'hard' sign at the end of words. Some émigrés still do not accept the changes.

†A resolution adopted by the Seventeenth Party Conference in January–February 1932 specifically condemned the concept of equal pay as 'egalitarianism'.

The uproar bothered M. more than it did me. I even rather liked it. The people staying in Gaspra were twice or even three times my age, the only younger ones being two junior members of families of the new ruling class: 'How quickly they become like grand dukes or the sons of millionaires,' said M. As behoves princes, they kept very much to themselves. The only real prince M. ever saw was the young Palei – he wrote verse and used to go and see Gumilev. Isn't he the one who was killed by being thrown down a well? They say he was a charming and touching youth. Akhmatova and I read the memoirs of his sister and were surprised to see that ruin overtook families such as his in much the same way as it did ours. People did not speak very well of the sister, but did they ever of anybody in this country?

I spent my time with the older men, playing chess with Chaplygin and Goldenweiser. (With Goldenweiser I also played tennis, and he got very angry with me for serving badly and often muffing my stroke.) On the terrace of the main building, onto which Kustodiev, already a very sick man, was wheeled out every day in a chair, I suddenly realized that love was not just a kind of joy or pleasure limited only by the drabness, not to say poverty, of our daily existence, but something incomparably greater. Kustodiev was there with his wife, who looked young, but very tired. She cared for him in a quiet and devoted way, without giving any sign that she was making a sacrifice for him, or losing patience with him when he was irritable. I told M. of my discovery, which was a great surprise to me, and he gasped at how ignorant I still was ... Kustodiev made some paintings of me: they were pretty watercolours showing me looking very girlish in a silly blouse with gaudy colours. He was surprised that I didn't ask him to let me have them, but I belonged to the avant-garde, believing in Futurism, the 'Knave of Diamonds', and turning my nose up at the rest ...

M. would go off to bathe and leave me on the terrace to wait for him. He generally went walking by himself so as not to tire me. I was the thinnest person in the whole place – nobody had ever seen anything like it. In rest homes and sanatoriums one is always weighed, and I got used to the expression of amazement as my weight was noted down. M. made me drink milk and eat grapes, and insisted that I lie down during the rest hour prescribed by the doctors. If he left me by myself, however, I always escaped – and for this he gave me hell.

I have a vivid memory of one occasion when I was sitting in front of the building with two of my 'old men' ('your staff officers,' as M. called them), an ex-sailor and an artist. The sailor was now a professor, of what subject I don't remember, but he liked to talk about the past. He had got hold of some coffee and made a point of preparing it in what he said was the Malayan or some such fashion: he put the coffee in an earthenware pitcher, poured water on top, and kept it buried in the ground for three days. A lot of the coffee was wasted, and the result was only so-so, but I was flattered by the way in which he went through these antics for my sake. I asked both him and the artist why they made such a fuss of me, and the artist replied for both of them: 'Because you're the youngest here.' All I remember about him is that he had an Italian name and was the first person ever to explain to me that anarchists are not advocates of chaos and violence, but members of a serious movement with a firmly anticentralist programme.

On this particular day I remember so well, I was sitting with my 'old men' when M. came out of the building and summoned me in an angry voice. 'He treats you like a puppy,' the artist said indignantly. I was pleased that he should take my part like this, but I told him I was used to such treatment and had no intention of putting on ladylike airs about it. I then jumped up and ran off in response to M.'s call – he had not even stopped to wait for me, the wretch. For some reason I can still see myself in my mind's eye running along after him over the sunlit grounds in front of the building and then at his side up a steep lane leading to the Tartar house. I was wearing high-heeled shoes with the soles almost worn through – I had stitched pieces of silk from an old dress under them. M. was walking quickly with great strides, and I had to run, skipping along beside him to keep up; in town he disapproved of this, but he didn't mind in the country . . .

On the veranda of the Tartar house (where we slept on a mattress laid on the floor) he went on at me a long time about how he had spent a whole hour trying to find me, about how hard I was making it for him to do his work – I had got quite out of hand and would never learn any sense. I stood up for myself like an angry cat: nonsense, I said, you took only five minutes to find me, and you must stop treating me like a puppy – it's making us into a laughingstock . . . What's more, I went on, I was already a grownup, and why had he got so spoiled that he wouldn't work without me any longer? . . .

He was then dictating *Noise of Time* to me on the veranda – or rather what was to become *Noise of Time*. We got down roughly a chapter at a time. Before each session he often went out walking, for an hour, or even two. When he returned he was tense and bad-tempered, ordering me to sharpen my pencils and start work at once. The first few phrases he dictated so quickly, as though he remembered them by heart, that I could scarcely keep up with him. Later the pace slowed down, but I often got confused by the long sentences. He just failed to understand why I couldn't get them down at one go, but at the same time I sometimes found him leaving out one or even several words, as though he thought I would hear them without his actually having to utter them. 'Can't you see that it doesn't hang together without that?' he would ask impatiently. 'Do you think,' I snapped back at him, 'that I'm sitting in your head and reading your thoughts? . . . Fool, fool, fool!' He got really angry at the word 'fool' and called me an idiot in return. I shrieked with rage, and he defended himself by saying that 'idiot' was a beautiful Ancient Greek word. So I was an Ancient Greek fool into the bargain . . .

When a certain number of pages had piled up, he asked me to read them out loud – 'only without any elocution'. He made me read like a ten-year-old schoolgirl – before teacher has started getting her to modulate her voice and put some 'feeling' into it. He wanted to hear how each sentence actually sounded. What he really needed was a Dictaphone, not a secretary, but from a Dictaphone he wouldn't have been able to insist on the understanding he could demand from his wife. If he didn't like something on hearing me read it back to him, he wanted to know how I could possibly have written down such rubbish without a murmur; if, on the other hand, I protested and jibbed at something or other, he hissed at me: 'Sh! Don't interrupt . . . You don't understand, so keep quiet.'

Later on, when he was dictating 'Conversation About Dante' to me, I protested at the point where he talks about Dante's needing to lean on authority, and refused to write this down. I thought for a moment he meant the authority of rulers, and was condoning Dante's acceptance of their favours. The word had no other meaning for us, and being heartily sick of such authorities, I wanted no others of any kind: 'Haven't you had enough of authorities?' I yelled at him, sitting in front of a blank, grey-coloured sheet of paper, my hands defiantly on my knees. 'Do you still want more?'

M. was furious with me for getting above myself and interfering in something that was none of my business. I advised him to go and find another wife: 'Find another fool for yourself, or hire a short-hand typist, as any decent person would – she'll write it all down without batting an eyelid.'

It was a stormy scene, and M. had great trouble trying to get me to see that there are two kinds of authority: false and true. I calmed down when he explained the danger of false authorities, and I identified them in my mind with graven images. But I am still worried by the question of authority. M. taught me to beware of any kind of authoritarianism, and I hate a metallic note of command in anybody's voice, much preferring reasoned argument, or even the passionate appeal of genuine conviction.

This was the only time I ever intervened with such vehemence. Usually I did no more than laugh and ask him whether he wasn't making something up, or going a little too far – a pity really, because otherwise, if I had had more sense, I might have refused to write down all that Acmeist drivel about 'biological' methods in poetry. Whenever I did make any remark, M. said I reminded him of Balaam's ass (this I deserved, idiot that I was, for having suggested the analogy myself), or of Yelena Ivanovna, a member of the Baptists, who had worked for us as cook in Detskoye Selo. She was no ordinary cook, but a real professional of some renown, who was really in fact having a winter vacation at our expense. All day long she sat in an armchair reading her Bible. It took her only half an hour to prepare a three-course meal for us, including *piroshki*.* The house was kept in perfect order. She always went through her accounts with us after buying food in the market and took only the 10 per cent traditionally allowed. We had never lived so cheaply.

* Small pies, generally eaten with soup.

Once a week we were expected to get out of the house while Yelena Ivanovna had visitors – an elderly carpenter and two or three married couples, all Baptists like herself.

Our troubles with her began because of the carpenter. He put it into her head that it was dangerous to work for us because M. wrote poetry, and that people were saying he was really none other than the godless blasphemer, Demian Bedny. She blurted all this out one morning at breakfast and said, almost in tears, that she would have to leave us. M., urging her not to do anything rash, gave her all his books and asked her to judge for herself. She put her Bible aside, read every line of his verse, and after consulting her friends, told us everything was all right: the rumour about Demian Bedny was false and she would stay. The book she liked most was *Tristia*. M. was very pleased.

For a year we lived in clover. Yelena Ivanovna occasionally told us we must not spend our time in idleness or we would have no money. We only once had a row. This was when she wouldn't let Kostia Vaginov into the house because the 'gentleman' was asleep. We met Kostia in the park when we went out later for a walk and learned that he had been turned away from our door. M. tried to reason with her, saying that he was not a 'gentleman' and that it was quite all right to disturb him if anybody came. She would not accept this: she had once worked for Count Kochubei, and nobody had ever been allowed to disturb *him*. Another thing was that she hated any guests to appear without warning: she 'lost face' if she wasn't able to come up with some nice new dish in their honour. She and M., both being artists in their own ways, understood each other, and he was flattered when an Armenian poet (it may have been Akopyan, the 'Red Monk', as we called him), who had arrived on the scene to get himself translated, took Yelena Ivanovna for M.'s wife and showered her with compliments for a whole hour while we were out walking. When we got back he was covered with confusion and made no attempt to be nice with me. Yelena Ivanovna left us in order to work in a private boarding-house where she could earn more money and help her community. We had spent only one winter under her loving care, and now, comparing my interruptions with what she had said about his poetry, M. said that she understood everything very much better because she knew where she stood – whereas I was 'remarkably short of ideas' and reminded him of a 'map with terra incognita all over it'. Perhaps he was right.

The final stage of our work on a piece of prose was to spread out all the pages on the floor – or table if it was big enough. It was always a dreadful mess, because my habit was to number the pages anew at the beginning of each session, and then everything got mixed up, so I never knew which particular page six it was that followed page five – there was always quite a lot of both. I was lucky that M. was not the sort of writer to whom it was all-important how *many* pages he was able to turn out. If he had been like the rest of them I should never have been able to sort out my page numbers. He always wondered up to what number I could count, but never found out. He checked the order of the chapters as I read everything back to him, and sometimes he would cut out pieces with scissors and put them somewhere else or throw them away. He was greatly upset at having to fuss with this kind of nonsense and failed to see why I was incapable of doing such a simple job for him. He could hardly bear the sight of these great heaps of paper covered with writing and kept wanting to get out into the fresh air – 'What do we need all this for? Let's go for a walk . . .' – and off we went, laying a large stone on each pile of papers so they wouldn't blow away. I was not exactly devoted to the work and would probably have been an even greater nuisance to him if it had been possible . . .

Tired, tear-stained, and at the end of my tether, I would doze off on his shoulder, and then, at night, I would wake up to see him standing by the table, crossing out and making changes. Seeing me awake, he would show me a new bit he had just written, cheer me up, and make me laugh before we both fell asleep again. I had begun to understand his attitude to me during our first trip to Georgia. We had arrived in Batumi and were spending our first night there on the terrace of the apartment of an engineer (I have forgotten his name and remember only that he had belonged to the Poets' Guild, either the first or the second one). He was not in town himself, and his wife, as she showed us to the terrace, warned us about the mosquitoes. The whole of that night, whenever I woke up, I saw M. sitting on a chair next to the bed and waving a piece of paper to chase the mosquitoes away from me. How well we got on – if only we had been allowed to live out our lives together . . .

Towards the end of our time in Gaspra – we stayed there about two months – Abram Efros (an active member of the Union of Writers) turned up. 'We have voted to reprimand you,' he briskly informed M., who asked what he meant and how anybody could be reprimanded without first being summoned and asked to explain himself: 'I thought it was a public organization.' Efros replied that the reprimand was of no importance and had resulted from a complaint by Svirski that M. had been 'rude' to his wife, telling her not to make a noise in the kitchen. As later turned out, Svirski had never made any such complaint, and the whole thing was an invention of Efros's – he was a celebrated schemer of a type common in the Union of Writers. (At a later date he was behind the publication of the Zaslavski feuilleton* which was handed in while Efros was on night duty in the editorial offices.)

Our room on Tverskoi Boulevard was next to the communal kitchen, in which there was a constant din going on; it was made by two or three women under the command of a former general's wife who was the last survivor of the house's previous inhabitants. She now worked as a cook for a war invalid who eventually married her. This fact led to her recognition as a 'working-class element' and saved her from being evicted from her apartment. The good-hearted lady baked pies and buns for us all, particularly for Yevgeni Emilievich; during his spell in prison† we took them to him there. She was always saying that nobody could 'braise meat like me', and she tried to teach me to make a roast in the Ukrainian way, keeping all the fat in, and also pies of puff pastry with a filling of cabbage or eggs: 'Look how I do it, or you'll never learn.' The Svirskis, who were just as kind-hearted as the general's widow, enjoyed their food after all the hungry years. M. often went out into the kitchen and asked the women to make less noise, but it never made any difference for more than twenty minutes.

M.'s first brush with the writers' organization was thus culinary in origin. He told Efros that he would give up the room allotted to

---

* See Zaslavski, Appendix A.

† *Hope Against Hope*, pages 137–8.

him by the Union of Writers, since it had shown itself capable of reprimanding a member behind his back without first asking for an explanation and hearing both sides. Efros thought this was a pettifogging attitude and advised M. not to give up the room – there was a housing crisis! But we sent a letter from Gaspra giving up the apartment, and on our return to Moscow we were homeless.

We were glad to have given up our Writers' Union hovel, but nobody has ever yet managed to wriggle out of the clutches of this organization. Its treatment of M. was only a try-out, which took place well before it had really got into its stride. Gradually gathering strength, it soon became the most powerful body of its kind in the world. One can't live without it, but neither can one live with it. It holds everything and everybody in its grasp, and is in direct contact with the most powerful authorities of all. Nobody should imagine that it became the opposite of what it was originally supposed to be simply because of orders from above. From the very first its inner structure incorporated the features that are now so striking – and they originated not in Soviet but in Russian literature.

I may be accused of blasphemy here: when people mention Russian literature, they generally have in mind a number of holy names, the pride and honour of the country. But literature is never limited to them. Not only Pushkin, but Grech and Bulgarin too would today be members of the Writers' Union. Which of these would feel most at home in the leadership of the Writers' Union, demanding the expulsion of Zoshchenko, Akhmatova, Solzhenitsyn, Pasternak, or giving their written assent to the destruction of Kluyev, Klychkov, M., and many others? The Greches and Bulgarins have always been there from the very beginning, and they are still with us today – sitting in the presidium of the Writers' Union. They get their support from the kind who in the old days came to 'instruct' Dostoyevski – the same ones who propagated nihilism, the Pisarev doctrine, the notion of art as defined in that famous dissertation in which a living woman is compared with her representation in a picture, not to mention sundry other such delusions. It is well to remember the words of a certain philosopher* whose hundredth anniversary we have yet to celebrate: 'Let us

* Stalin. See *Hope Against Hope*, page 407.

drink to science – to the science we need, not to the science we do not need.' This toast was proposed in the last year of M.'s life, and he liked to repeat the wondrous formula by way of attuning his mind to the thought that doom was inevitable . . .

Russian literature – 'the one we need' – was always a corrupting thing. The same is probably true of any literary establishment, but the Russian one has proved to be the most powerful of its kind ever to exist. It is appropriate that these reflections about it were prompted by my recollection of an incident involving a kitchen: everything that goes on in our literature smacks of something concocted in a monstrous kitchen. M. made a distinction between 'literature' and 'poetry', regarding them as incompatible concepts. A poet is a private person who works 'for himself' and has nothing whatsoever to do with literature as such. In the Union of Writers the poet is always a foreign body, subject to expulsion like Pasternak or Solzhenitsyn. There is no point in making a great fuss when this happens, and I have little faith in the well-meaning youngsters who do: they also eat their oats from the feed racks of the Writers' Union.

22 Interlude

We spent the winter of 1923–4 in a rented room on the Yakimanka.* Old Moscow houses can look cosy and charming enough on the outside, but we now saw how poor and dilapidated they are inside, in every room a whole family presided over by some old woman – worn out but still tough as nails – who constantly scrubbed, cleaned, and scoured everything, trying to keep the place spick and span in country fashion as it fell more and more into decay. We lived in a large square room which had once been a sitting room; it had a Dutch stove no longer in use and was heated by a small iron one which was always cold by the morning. Firewood was sold on the near-by embankment; there were no more rations, but we managed somehow, spending enormous sums on horse cabs. In those days the Yakimanka was at the end of the world, and in

* An old quarter of Moscow.

the streetcars people hung from the straps in clusters, like bunches of cherries.

We celebrated the New Year of 1924 in Kiev with my parents, and it was then that M. wrote his poem about not being anyone's contemporary. He could well have added that nobody regarded him as a contemporary, but it was still too early for him to know that time was on his side, not on theirs. This was the year in which ideology was born, triumphing in all spheres, and in which our rulers began the task of peaceful reconstruction – though peasant resistance had still not been completely stamped out in the central regions (when we travelled to Kiev every carriage of our train was guarded by three machine-gunners). It was a sure sign of a return to normal peacetime conditions, on the other hand, that our train was made up of ordinary carriages, not of converted freight cars – those delightful dachas on wheels in which demobilized soldiers or other people travelling on official warrants always had such a riotous time. But with us peace was always accompanied by unspeakable outbreaks of self-destructiveness. I would be glad if someone would tell a certain Italian writer (who, I trust, will not be reading this book) that when a 'hundred flowers' are torn up by the roots, the earth is soaked in blood and nothing ever grows on it again. How many Peking ducks must you eat to go into raptures over wonderful new methods of 'fighting bureaucracy'? Beware of literature. Its most innocent form is the detective story.

That winter we first heard the expression 'literary front', and somebody was already standing *On Guard*.* The critics launched a rumour that Mandelstam had thrown over poetry, and the *Change of Landmarks* newspaper † picked up this exquisite tale. A man can throw over his wife or mistress – and, in my day, women abandoned their husbands and lovers – but can anybody tell us how you 'throw over' poetry? What is the technique? This is something that only adepts at 'changing the landmarks' can appreciate: you pull up

---

* *Na postu*: journal of the 'proletarian writers'. It existed from 1923 to 1925 and, under the new name *On Literary Guard*, became the mouthpiece of RAPP after its foundation in 1925.

† i.e., *Nakanune* (see note on p. 145). *Change of Landmarks* was the manifesto of a group of White émigrés who adopted a pro-Soviet attitude after the introduction of NEP in 1921.

one set and put in new ones, and the caravans start moving in a different direction.

Bukharin had revealed to M. that he would not be allowed to print his verse – only translations. We now first came to know the taste of real isolation (as opposed to voluntary seclusion): not one of our 'contemporaries' ever came to see us on the Yakimanka. They were all too busy with important matters of absolutely no concern to M.: there was a battle royal going on as to who should be in charge of literature. While some fought for power, others attached themselves to the various contenders in the capacity of hangers-on. LEF still thought it would win, the 'moustachioed ones' and the Fellow Travellers had taken up entrenched positions, and Averbakh, the young desperado who was destined to come out on top, was still sitting in his tiny editorial office on Nikita Boulevard, just at the approaches to Herzen House.

We had got to know Averbakh while we were still living on Tverskoi Boulevard. It had happened through an urchin who used to come to our room to sell cigarettes. The boy had impressed M. by his thorough-going urbanism: he despised Moscow with its lack of motor traffic and used to tell us how in America there were so many cars that they followed each other bumper to bumper – traffic even got slowed down as a result. M. sent the young urbanist to Averbakh, who took him on as an errand boy. On the principle that one good turn deserves another, Averbakh commissioned M. to translate a poem by some Hungarian revolutionary. When M. handed in the translation, Averbakh ran his eyes over it, shook his hand, and said: 'Congratulations, Mandelstam, you have done great work.' M. responded abruptly with a few heart-felt words about the various ways of destroying literature and poetry, and Averbakh smiled at him like a general. The young urbanist did not last long: he stole Pasternak's gloves and was thrown out in disgrace. I gave Pasternak hell for having been so mean about his gloves, but he was so repentant that M. told me to shut up. He went to Averbakh and tried to reason with him, saying that the Komsomol should not sack people but reform them. The reply to this was that at a time of intensified class warfare, there was no point in wasting time on persons unworthy of the name 'proletarian'.

Averbakh had learned the right patter in the cradle, and M. realized that he would go a long way.

In our isolation on the Yakimanka the only sign we noticed of an intensification of class warfare was our growing difficulty in earning money – that is, in getting translation work. M. did not yet quite understand that we had already entered an era in which not only literature but even thought was subject to regimentation. That summer, while we were staying at a dacha belonging to the State Publishing House in Aprelevka, he was to complain that 'they' would let him publish only translations. 'They' in this sense, then adopted by him for the first time, is used by everybody. Nikita Khrushchev is supposed to have complained that 'they' would not let him do what he wanted and were making his life a misery because of *Ivan Denisovich*.* There is a kind of endless ladder on which those standing higher up are regarded as 'they' by people lower down, who in their turn are looked up to as 'they' by those below – and so on ad infinitum. When the 'Boss'† was still alive the top rung was occupied by a man whose name was spoken with the appropriate expression on one's face – anyone who failed to utter it with a pious tremor in his voice could expect to be denounced in writing (vaguer suspicions were always reported by word of mouth to the personnel department or to one's immediate superior). 'They' still exist and always will, but as regards denunciations, things are not quite the same. It is said that they are falling off in volume. A study of the number of denunciations by periods and by the age of their authors would have enormous importance. The question of their quality and style would also repay investigation. But, alas, sociological studies are not well regarded in this country.

· Living now in retirement, I am no longer interested in 'the clamour of fevered human strife', but at that time, when we lived on the Yakimanka, we followed all the new trends with astonishment – and doubt as to their permanence. We had still not learned to keep our ears to the ground and figure out the real alignment of

---

* The publication of Solzhenitsyn's novel is supposed to have been sanctioned by Khrushchev personally in 1962.

† Standard nickname for Stalin.

forces from all the little incidental signs. Everything that happens at the top is shrouded in mystery, and in our innocence we failed to notice the star already gleaming balefully on the horizon. The first time a portrait of the 'Boss' appeared on the cover of *Ogoniok*, it was in the very same number which contained M.'s first published prose, and also had the excellent photograph of him in a sweater. This wonderful photograph, which is a very good likeness of him, thus appeared in the most terrible issue of the vile and hideous magazine.

But in fact there is nothing to choose between one magazine and another: every issue of every magazine is disgusting, and there is always something that makes you want to run to the end of the earth – if only you could. M. came out so well because press photographers always know their business, and if it hadn't been for that horrible magazine I should not have had this one first-rate photograph. The same man photographed me as well – M. refused to have his taken without me – and these pictures are much more alive than the ones made about three years later by the famous Nappelbaum, a portrait photographer who specialized in the Leaders. In Nappelbaum's photographs I am very prim and proper with a frozen expression on my face (which I never had), while M. appears as a young man wearing a look of refinement totally out of character. He always came out very well on snapshots taken by street photographers – much better, anyway, than in Nappelbaum's studies, which are as mawkish as Ehrenburg's pen portrait of him (the puny, delicate Jew with the powerful voice).* It is much easier to do a photograph of a leader than it is of a poet. A leader has to have his portrait embellished, whereas a poet must be shown as he is. The age of socialist realism has disaccustomed people to looking at the representation of any object with a fresh and unbiased eye. What makes poets awkward is that they themselves do just this. Everybody else is a slave to his preconceptions and, like Nappelbaum, 'improves' on his subject.

That winter on the Yakimanka was an exceptionally dismal period in my life. Either the walls exuded some deadening spirit or we had lost our capacity to enjoy life, but I cannot remember our even having indulged in the kind of frivolous things which every-

* *Hope Against Hope*, page 367.

where else always cheered us up a little. On the other hand, I do remember how late one night, as we were returning home from Narbut's in an empty streetcar (they were empty only very late at night), we suddenly saw the driver stop the car and jump down into the roadway. He came back carrying a newspaper: it was a special edition announcing the death of Lenin. There were terrible frosts just then, but the next few days and nights the enormous queues to get into the Hall of Columns stretched for miles. One night we walked past one of these queues which reached to the Volkhonka, and then for many hours we stood in it – together with Pasternak – somewhere near the Bolshoi Theatre. The queue was not moving, and we also feared we might be asked to leave it – at this point on the route there was some delegation or other. The rest of the crowd, straggling out in a narrow line, consisted of the usual drab and sullen citizenry. 'They've come to complain to Lenin about the Bolsheviks,' M. commented, 'but it's a vain hope: it won't do any good.'

Bonfires were burning in the streets, and we went over to one to get warm. I was wearing only a cloth overcoat, the best I ever had in my life, with which I made do all year round. M. was already saying he would take me home before I turned into an icicle, when suddenly there was an unexpected incident: Kalinin came walking across the square. Our leaders had still not lost the habit of going on foot. Some Komsomols rushed over to him, asking to be allowed in as soon as possible. ('They're demanding privileges,' said one of my companions.) Kalinin sent them packing with a good old-fashioned obscenity. We were not surprised by Kalinin's reaction – at that time we still looked upon our leaders as ordinary men, capable of using ordinary words. What was to astonish us was the speed with which they soon began to lose their human qualities.

Kalinin had several people with him. One of them noticed us – we were only a few paces away – and called us over. With this 'protection' we were able to jump the queue and go through with Kalinin straight into the line of people filing past the coffin. As we went home on foot, M. marvelled at the spectacle: this was the Moscow of ancient days burying one of her tsars. The funeral of Lenin was the last flicker of the Revolution as a genuine popular movement, and I could see that the veneration for him was inspired not by terror, like the later adulation and deification of Stalin, but by the hopes which the people placed in him. This was the only occasion in my lifetime on which the population of Moscow came out into the streets and formed queues of its own free will. People stood patiently, in grim silence. There was no crush, not the slightest hint of a Khodynka.* The Komsomols, who had got such short shrift from Kalinin, were standing in a queue reserved for delegations. Not satisfied with this, they had wanted special privileges. The 'new life' was now beginning, and it was probably just such organized groups as this which were responsible for the disaster at Stalin's funeral when everybody wanted to get ahead of his neighbour, if only by half a nostril. This I did not witness, since I was far from Moscow at that time.

At the period we lived on the Yakimanka we had to make several trips to Leningrad because M.'s father was ill. I had already met him during his visits to Moscow in connection with his leather business, while we were still living on Tverskoi Boulevard – we travelled up to Leningrad only after the death of the wife of M.'s brother Yevgeni. At that time the main centre for translating had shifted to Leningrad, and the big man in charge of it all was Gorlin, whose headquarters were in Book House, opposite the Kazan Cathedral. In Moscow we were coming to the end of our earnings on Barbusse (whose dreary stories literally poisoned our existence), and also on Barbier. In Leningrad, empty and desolate, the housing shortage was less acute than in Moscow, where every room was occupied by a whole family, with visiting relatives being put up in whatever corner they could be squeezed into. We hence began to prepare to move to Leningrad, alien as the city now was to M. – all he cared for there was the architecture, the white nights, and the bridges. On one of our visits during spring he took me on a tour of the embankments by night and rejoiced in the 'pure, ship-like lines of the city'. We looked at fantastic apartments on the Neva with windows mirroring the grey water below. Their owners had aban-

---

* Field near Moscow on which about two thousand people were crushed to death in a stampede to get souvenirs at the celebration of the coronation of Nicholas II in 1896. The term is also applied to the similar disaster in central Moscow at the time of Stalin's funeral. (See page 436.)

doned them when they fled the country. Nobody wanted them because it cost a fortune to repair and heat them. All M. and I could do was lick our lips, but Akhmatova lived for a whole year in one of them, fitting beautifully into the background; however, she couldn't keep it up for long and had to leave. Instead of one of these marvels on the Neva, we contented ourselves with two charming rooms – once a bachelor's apartment perhaps – on Morskaya, moved our furniture from Moscow (a rosewood side-board, a dressing table, a mahogany bureau), bought a few new things in Leningrad, which was choked with bric-à-brac, and took up residence amid mahogany, Karelian birch, old faïence, and blue glassware; all this junk I found in the Apraksin market, quickly spotting 'bargains' with an eagle eye . . .

The only trouble about our new apartment was that it had no door: either the rooms had once been separated from the lobby by a thick curtain or the door had been chopped up for firewood during the hungry years and burned in the stove. We hired one carpenter after another to put a new one in but they just spent our money on drink and disappeared; eventually some odd bird made us one out of unpainted planks which was so unbelievably crude that it somehow toned down the incongruous elegance of the place. The workmen of Petersburg had forgotten their skills and despised the new type of client.

Such was the beginning of our Petersburg idyll, with visits to Gorlin and occasionally to Benedikt Livshitz – where Kuzmin, who despised us all and did not bother to conceal it, led a thriving existence. He was always flanked by Yurkun and Arbenina, who was quite pleasant, though affected in an old-fashioned way. She told me the details, on the quiet, of her fleeting romance with M., and I was convinced she was speaking the truth, implausible as it was. At New Years, the Livshitzes came to our apartment to cele-brate, bringing some old friends of M.'s from the days when he had frequented the Sinani household, and who just happened to have arrived from Moscow. In general, however, we kept very much to ourselves, and M. was glad that at last I had a nice place to live in and a pair of grey boots to wear on my visits to the Gostiny Dvor.*

* The shopping area of Leningrad, near the Apraksin Market mentioned earlier.

The poetry he wrote held no hint of coming disaster, and a new January was under way – when, suddenly, our life was turned upside down.

23 A Case of Touch and Go

In the middle of January 1925, M. brought home a young woman called Olga Vaksel whom he had run into on the street. He had known her in Koktebel when she was just a little girl and had once, at her mother's request, been to see her at the women's college where she was studying. She now started coming to see us every day. She complained a lot about her mother and was always kissing me in a frantic way (a mannerism she had picked up at her college, I assumed) – all the while vamping M. under my very nose. Soon I noticed he had stopped looking at me or coming close to me, and no longer talked to me about anything but practical matters. He went on writing poetry but did not show it to me any more. At first I just didn't know what to think, and was so spoiled that I refused to believe my eyes. This is the mistake a woman always makes: only yesterday he couldn't live without me, so what can it possibly mean? . . . Olga's behaviour could scarcely have been more calculated to open my eyes and arouse me to fury. In my presence she made scenes, sobbing loudly and demanding various things, accusing M. of indecision and cowardice, insisting he make his mind up: it was high time, she kept on saying, how long could things go on like this? All this began more or less at once. M.'s head had really been turned, and he was blind to everything else around him. This was his only affair during the whole of our life together, but it was enough for me to learn what it was like to have a marriage break up. This was what Olga was trying to bring about, and everything hung by a thread.

She had her charms, as even I, the injured party, was bound to admit: she was just a girl still, beautiful, helpless, defenceless, and lost in the city's terrible wilderness. Her husband had left her, and she and her son were totally dependent on her mother and stepfather – who was evidently not happy with the situation. I never saw him, and Olga scarcely mentioned him at all. The mother, a domineering and energetic woman, was in complete charge of everything and also ran her daughter's affairs. She summoned M. to go and see her and also came to see us in order to 'have things out', clarifying her daughter's wishes in front of me. She insisted that M. 'save Olga' – which necessitated his taking her away to the Crimea: 'She will get used to you there and everything will be all right.' All this too was said in my presence, and in reply M. vowed he would do everything Olga wanted. He was expecting a large payment from the State Publishing House and had been intending to send me down to the Crimea that spring. Olga had learned about this on her very first visit to us and said she wanted to go to the south as well – whereupon I had at once suggested we all go together. Once, when her mother started talking about 'saving Olga', I butted in and said I was going to Yalta in the spring and suggested Olga come with me. (Her mother called her Daisy, after the homely yellow flower.) At this Olga's mother really put me in my place. Eyeing me crossly, she said I was a complete outsider as far as she was concerned and that she was here to talk family business with her old friend Mandelstam. It was a cold-blooded piece of insolence in real Petersburg style, spat out through the teeth. I had no idea that society ladies (she had been a lady-in-waiting at court) arranged their daughters' affairs so openly. After the catastrophic end of the world in which she had lived, she probably thought that M. was as good a prospect as any for her daughter – if only for the time being. At the sight of our rather fancy apartment, she must have imagined that M. was a better provider than was in fact the case. Olga just couldn't wait to go south with M., and I was holding things up. The only reason she and her mother discussed their plans in my presence was in the hope of precipitating my departure. I still cannot understand why I didn't get up and leave there and then. Even now I regret not having done it – though nothing would have suited the former lady-in-waiting better. But then I remembered that it was my apartment and that she was sitting drinking tea at my table. I could not bear to make scenes, but I will never forget that moment. I looked at M. He had a strange, faraway expression, as though he hadn't heard a word – though generally he was very quick to notice any slight to me. When

Olga's mother had left, I reproached him for allowing her to treat me like that. He made no response at all. This meeting with the mother had taken place in the afternoon. That same evening Olga came, asked how we had 'got on with Mummy', laughed loudly, and then went out with M. As they were going, she kissed me and, for some reason, began to snivel.

I realized that I must seek refuge somewhere. I never saw Olga's mother again; whenever she phoned to say she was coming I simply went out. Occasionally I had quite a high fever, and every time I took my temperature I put the thermometer back in its holder without shaking it, hoping that M., who always worried terribly about me, might look and see what it said. But he never did. Sometimes I had to stay in bed. My tuberculosis had suddenly got so bad again that I could scarcely stand up. Leaving with Olga, M. would tell me to be sure to take my temperature and not get up on any account. Once M.'s father came to see me. He looked approvingly at Olga, and when they had gone (she and M. now always left together), I heard him say: 'That's a good thing – if Nadia dies, Osip will have Daisy.' I didn't want to say anything to hurt the old man, but I couldn't help suddenly remembering that M.'s mother had died on learning that her husband had a mistress. I was horrified at the thought that M. had something of his father in him. Similar feelings of horror always came over me whenever I saw M.'s brother Yevgeni. But I know I was being unfair to my Osip: he was a completely different type, and if he had inherited any such traits, he had managed to suppress them. At any event, it is difficult to imagine two people more different than M. and his brother.

In those years divorce or separation was complicated by thousands of practical problems because of the acute housing shortage. People who were divorced, or had changed wives or husbands, often had to live for years in some wretched room. I had no intention of letting this happen to me, and I got in touch with a man who I knew was willing to take me in. He would never have deliberately set out to take me away from M., but he could see what the situation was just as well as I could. Coming to see me, this man (I will refer to him as T.) several times saw M. leave with Olga and noted the look of triumph on her face. It was clear, as they said in the language of those days, that M. had 'taken up with a girl'. More experienced and observant than I, T. immediately saw that Olga belonged to the type of women who boost their own egos by humiliating a rival. He kept urging me to leave at once and was eager to have it all out with M., but I couldn't make up my mind and sat by our fireplace watching the dying embers and wondering whether it wouldn't be best to leave this life for good rather than go away with T. and try to start all over again. Thoughts of death came easily to me. I looked on it as liberation. It was not love for M. that stirred such thoughts. At that time I still didn't know how to love anyone. T. was close to me in some ways, but my feelings for him bore no relation to love. At that moment what I wanted most of all was to be on my own, and it would have been a long time before I chose a new husband . . .

Once M. told Olga over the telephone in my presence that he would be coming to see her after a visit to the State Publishing House. Insisting that he hand the receiver to me, she told me: 'Osip and I will come and see you this evening.' A nasty detail was that M. then asked me whether his clothes had come back from the laundry and, angry to learn that they hadn't, he sent our charwoman to fetch his underwear, changed, and went out. This was the last straw. I rang T. to ask him to come for me, packed my suitcase – fortunately the charwoman had brought my clothes too – and got ready to leave. My farewell note, saying that I was going to T. and 'will never come back to you', was lying on the table.

I sat by the fireplace, as I always did, and waited for T., but quite by chance M. suddenly came back again – either he had forgotten to take his money or Gorlin had given him a lot of books to look at and he didn't want to lug them around with him. Whatever the reason, his sudden return was a completely unforeseen intervention in our fate. M. immediately saw the suitcase and flew into a rage. When T. came, he at once showed him out with the words: 'Nadia is staying with me.' I told T. I had still not made up my mind and asked him to leave for the time being. He went away sadly, and I heard him complaining to M. in the lobby that here he was, already forty years old and still without a wife. The poor devil treated his wives so badly that they always left him. I knew this, but I had just wanted to clear out anywhere as fast as I could.

M. picked up my note, read it, and threw it in the fireplace. Next he ordered me to get Olga on the phone for him: he wanted to break with her in my hearing, so I should have no doubt of it – though I would have believed him without any such crude demonstration. He said good-bye to Olga very brusquely: 'I'm not coming, I'm staying with Nadia, you and I shall never see each other again – never.' And then he used a dreadful phrase which has stuck in my mind ever since: 'I don't like the way you treat people.' I have no idea what these words were in reply to; I snatched the receiver from him and heard Olga weeping at the other end of the line, but he put his finger on the rest and we were disconnected. I still find it odd that it needed my words of explanation for my packed suitcase – T. did not appear until about a quarter of an hour later – to bring home to M. what a humiliation the whole thing had been for me: all these visits of Olga's, her kisses and tears, the scenes and reproaches to M. in my presence. 'I am tired of being insulted by Olga,' I told him, and then, when he seized my note, I repeated what I had written in it: 'I'm going away and not coming back' . . . This whole business with Olga taught me something new: what blind and terrible power love could have over a man – it was more than mere infatuation with Olga. Many years later he told me he had only twice in his life been passionately in love: with me and with her.

Just as a few hours previously M. had been quite oblivious to me, he was now totally unmoved by Olga and her tears. He ran around to the hotel – it was almost next door to us – where the day before he had been with Olga (and from where she had announced her intention of coming and seeing me that evening). He had left his identity papers there and now needed them because he had decided to take me away at once. When he came back, he stuffed all the clothes brought from the laundry into his suitcase, grabbed mine – already packed for a quite different purpose – and whisked me off to Tsarskoye Selo. I am still surprised even now at the ruthless way he chose between us and at the decisiveness with which he acted. People had a free and easy attitude to divorce in those days – it was easier to separate than to stay together. What made him break off with Olga so abruptly? Could it be that jealousy at the sight of T. – he was always terribly jealous – got the better of his love for her? Another factor, probably, was that it was Olga, not I, who played the part of the demanding, reproachful, weeping woman – something that generally falls to the wife rather than the mistress. It was as though Olga and I had changed roles, though I was perhaps the silent party only because I realized the futility of talking. M. simply no longer listened to me, and any reproaches I made would have fallen on deaf ears. The only thing I still suspect is that if none of his poetry had yet been written, he might well have decided to let me leave him for T. at that moment when he came back and found me waiting with my suitcase packed. This is one of the questions I never got around to asking him. On the other hand, he told me that right at the beginning he had thought of a harebrained scheme to get me back if I had gone off in a huff and refused to live with him any more: he was going to get a pistol and shoot himself, but only through a piece of skin on his side which he would have bunched up with his fingers, making it look as though he were badly wounded. In fact, though bleeding profusely, he would have been in no danger, but I would have felt sorry for him and come back to him at once. (He was probably mistaken on this score.) Even I could scarcely have expected him to think of anything so imbecile, and I still laughed at the earnest way in which he revealed this plan to me. The ideas people get!

Several years later Olga did manage to go south – not, however, with M. but with his brother Yevgeni. Evidently women had already fallen very much in price by then if it took such a beauty as her so long to find a replacement. After this trip she suddenly came to see us again – it was while we were living at Tsarskoye Selo in the Lycée.* Again she wept, reproached M., and asked him to come with her. As before, it all happened in front of me. I was sitting in an armchair by the table, and when she suddenly walked in I moved the chair away from the table with such force that it spun into the middle of the room, and I found myself sitting opposite the door through which, out of the blue and unbidden, she had made her entry. It was a quite ridiculous position. At the sight of her, M., who had been pacing the floor, stood stock-still by my chair. He listened to what she had to say in silence, and I noticed the tense and frozen expression on his face. It was the same expression I had

* School founded by Alexander I and attended by Pushkin; partly converted into apartments in the early twenties.

often seen during our drama, or melodrama, on Morskaya. It went right through me like a knife. Pointing at me, Olga asked him: 'Have you tied yourself to her forever? What do you want with her?' I got up hastily to leave the room. M. put his hands on my shoulders and forced me to sit down again. He was strong and always fiendishly exploited the fact that I weighed almost nothing. His face resumed a normal expression, and he said coldly: 'My place is with Nadia.' He held out his hand and said good-bye to her. She had no choice but to go – this was the first time she had gone away from us alone . . . After she had left I made M. a scene according to all the rules of this feminine art, though he had behaved impeccably and done nothing to deserve my hysterics. I suppose it was by way of making up for my silence on Morskaya. I just couldn't help it, and M., unused to such things, was too taken aback to do anything. We very soon made up, however.

It was all the easier to make up because they had not seen each other since his break with her – as I understood from Olga's words. While I howled and raged, throwing everything within reach at him, M. tried to point this out: 'You didn't believe me – now you've heard for yourself . . .' I really hadn't believed him. He had lived alone in Petersburg for quite a time while I was sick in Yalta (most of his letters to me were written while I was there). How could he possibly have left it at that brutal telephone conversation with her, I had wondered, and never seen her again? Indifferent as I was to T., I had at least gone out of my way to see him later and say a few consoling words. We had both acted out these affairs according to our own different ideas: M. took the romantic view that one should make a clean break, while I was in favour of softening the blow. A few years later M. astonished me even more by his outrageous treatment of M.P., who for a brief moment came between us because of Akhmatova (M. even asked me not to quarrel with Anna Andreyevna over this – which I had no intention of doing anyway). For two or three weeks, losing his head completely, he kept telling Akhmatova that if he weren't married to me he would go away and live only for his new love . . . After Akhmatova had left, M.P. continued to come and see us, and once M. spent the evening with her in his room, saying they had to 'talk about literature'. A couple of times he went out to meet her, and to

this I responded in traditional fashion – by smashing a plate and
telling him: 'It's either she or I!' He was overjoyed in a comic way:
'Now at last you've become a real woman!' He rang M.P. – I had
earlier invited her to dinner that evening – and told her not to
come, using the same phrase he had used before to Olga: 'I don't
like the way you treat people' . . . The next morning M.P. paid us
a visit. (Akhmatova writes* that M. was 'passionately and hopelessly in love with her'. Everything M. did was passionate, while
M.P. was the sort who chased men and, like all women, went about
it with considerable energy.) M. could think of nothing better than
to bring her into the room where I had slept in his bed after making
up with him . . . We all three had an absurd conversation together,
and when M.P. had left, I pitched into M. for behaving so atrociously (I had no grounds for being angry with M.P. – she was just a
silly girl trying out her powers on another woman's husband, and
at least she didn't weep on my shoulder). He was very pleased with
himself for having made it so clear to her where he stood. I have
never ceased to marvel at the strangeness of male psychology when
it comes to the awesome business of love and sex, and M. was so
wildly spontaneous and unpredictable in his behaviour that even
now I am still amazed by it all: his love for me, his infatuation with
Olga, and the slight spell of light-headedness over M.P. (He wrote
two poems to M.P., one of which has been lost, and according to
her she destroyed his letters. I am sorry about these – they were
probably superb.) Our life together was too short for us to have had
many reasons for finding fault with each other. If M. had been rich,
or at least comfortably off, there might have been many more
temptations, and, wanting to enjoy himself in his old age, he could
well have walked out on me, leaving a note on the table to say it had
all been a mistake. What wouldn't I give if this had been the worst
to happen in our life! I can just imagine how bitterly I would now
complain, listing all my sacrifices and recounting how they had
been forgotten or scorned. Struck by the number of old men who
leave their wives, I once asked Akhmatova whether she thought
Osip would have done the same. 'Of course,' she said emphatically.
'Zhenia Pasternak also thought she was irreplaceable, but Boris

* In her memoir on Mandelstam, where she identifies 'M.P.' as Maria
Petrovykh.

threw her over.' It was Akhmatova's belief that after seven years with any woman a man was bound to lose interest and leave her. I am not sure this law of hers always holds good, but I find it hard that a woman's prime is over (and with it her capacity to change husbands) much earlier than her male partner's. I suppose it pays to have children – not to be alone in your old age – though I have noticed that children are not always eager to waste time on their boring old mothers. I sometimes think that my generation was wrong to undermine the idea of marriage, but I still feel that I would rather live by myself than in the false atmosphere of the traditional family. The only thing I am quite sure of is that people should not live together if the inner link between them is broken, and also that nothing is more terrible than to tear people apart and send them to die slowly in concentration camps or to be exterminated in gas chambers. Everything else is no more than the normal misfortunes of the imperfect creatures known as human beings. I am told that a crazy woman once came to see Ehrenburg and, standing in the doorway, shouted, 'Give me back my family life!' He found it very hard to get rid of her. I feel very much the same way as this old woman, but I put it in different words, using only the name of the man who was dear to me.

Olga Vaksel committed suicide in Oslo. She had married a Norwegian she met while working as a waitress at the Astoria,* after failing to make a career in the movies (she studied under Kozintsev at FEKS†). In the verse written in memory of her, M. refers to her 'Stockholm grave' – he was misinformed about the place of her death by a strange man, a Petersburg eccentric, whom Olga often referred to as her admirer. He told this to M. on the street when we both happened to run into him one day. Before her death Olga dictated some wild, erotic reminiscences to her husband, who knew Russian. The page devoted to our joint drama is full of hatred for me and M. The tone in which this part is written calls to mind the voice of her mother rather than that of the girl who came to weep on my shoulder and take M. away from me. In her memoirs she is concerned above all to get her own back, and

---

* Hotel in Leningrad.

† 'Factory of the Eccentric Actor', a theatrical group in Leningrad. (See Kozintsev, Appendix A.)

she quotes only one phrase of M.'s ('the cabbie is the friend of man') to show that she had retained some impression or memory of the funny man who once complained in a poem: 'Life has forked down like summer lightning, an eyelash false to the very root falling into a glass of water.' She accuses M. of mendacity, but this is quite unjust. It is true that he deceived both me and her during those days, but that is in the nature of such situations. I do not understand why Olga is so spiteful about me as well. I think I should not have hated her if she had gone off with M. for good. How could I have blamed her? I could well have had hard feelings with regard to M. for ceasing to love me, but how can anyone stand in judgement over such things? All the same, I will never forget those dreadful weeks when M. ignored my existence and, unable to dissemble and lie, fled the house with Olga and begged all our friends not to tell me about his affair with her and the poems he was writing to her. Talking with outsiders like this was, of course, a stupid, rotten thing to do, but who is not guilty of it in such situations? Even now I feel the wound left by the vacant glances and empty words we exchanged. It was then that I first came to know that love is not merely a source of joy or a game, but part of the ceaseless tragedy of life, both its eternal curse and the overwhelming force that gives it meaning.

In her memoirs Olga says nothing about the person she went to the south with. She evidently didn't get on with Yevgeni Emilievich, M.'s brother, to whom she transferred her affections. Here she has nothing but my sympathy. I do, however, take strong objection to the fact that she calls M. not a poet but a translator. In her thirst for revenge, the wretched girl followed the lead of the Soviet literary establishment in reducing him to this status . . .

I am still curious to know what it was that bound M. and me together. Perhaps it was destiny rather than love. But how could it have been destiny when everything might so easily have fallen apart through blind chance? If I had gone off to live with T., Olga would certainly have moved into our apartment, M. would not have got a revolver and put a bullet through a bunched-up piece of skin on his side, and I would on no account have returned to him. It all turned out differently only by pure chance, because M. returned home when I was least expecting him to, or rather when I was expecting someone else. Our original meeting was also quite by chance, yet the bond between us proved to be so unbreakable that it was almost frightening. In the days when we left Kiev together, I could never have foreseen what was to become of us, and all the time I imagined it would end sooner or later, simply because love always has a beginning and an end. When he was taken away from me I understood that there would be no end, but even then I did not yet realize that from the time of our first meeting a whole half-century would pass by without the bond between us being broken – precarious as it was for one brief instant. I have painfully come to believe that there never will be an end, even though I am afraid to believe it and try not to – but my faith still remains. I am living out my days with it, and I shall never know whether my hopes and faith are justified – here it is not given to us to know, so one can only believe, but *there*, when all will become clear, things will be utterly different, not like here . . .

There is one question to which I still have no answer: Why did M. choose me at that moment and not Olga, who was incomparably better than I? As I told him, I had only my two hands, whereas she had everything. We had both until that moment forgotten his line 'gentle hands of Europa – take everything', and he asked me how I knew about my hands, adding of course that he really could not live without them. Yet all the time I could see he was getting on perfectly well without me, hands or no hands.

I have one explanation, not an entirely flattering one, as to why his choice fell on me. Man is free and shapes not only his own fate but himself as well – and it is a question of *shaping* one's fate rather than choosing it. M. was very active in this sense, and I never stood in the way or prevented him from being himself. In shaping himself, he shaped me as well – the two things went together, and for this reason he came to need not so much me and my hands as the work of his own hands. It is a good thing that the problems raised by Ibsen already seemed trivial and ridiculous by then, otherwise I should have taken offence at this lack of respect for my personality and left M. like some provincial Nora (the play about whom, incidentally, I have never got around to reading). It is interesting to see how a woman puffs herself up and puts on airs if she suddenly feels people ought to respect her. I have never suffered from such pride, and very glad I am too: this is not what people live by. They live by something very different – on that I would stake my head, as long as it stays on my shoulders.

24 The Beggar

In March 1925, having been taken by main force from my charming but now defiled apartment, I found myself in a small boarding-house in Tsarskoye Selo. The Petersburgers, M. explained to me, had always gone to Finland to have things out with their women, but now they were forced to make do with Tsarskoye. The first night I was very restive and begged to be given my freedom. 'What do you need me for?' I asked. 'Why are you keeping me? What's the point of living in a cage like this? Let me go . . .' It was not the first time I had implored him to let me go, but I was particularly insistent that night. By running away to T., I would not only have got my freedom but also, perhaps, been able to return to painting, though I understood that I would never be more than a dabbler in it (most people who take up painting or poetry are really only out to amuse themselves and belong to the category of dabblers). What was more, I felt that my failure in life entitled me to kill myself. I was convinced of my right to depart this life if it did not go well for me, but M. absolutely refused to recognize such a right. Someone in Moscow had let on that I had managed to acquire a small bottle of morphine which I kept in case everything went wrong. He had taken it away by force, though I fought and scratched like a cat, and he made me promise not to get another one. If I had still had my little phial on Morskaya I would have used it then instead of just sitting by the fireplace. You have to live your whole life to realize that it does not belong to you.

All the same, I still wonder whether suicide may not be justified as a way of avoiding not only the horrors of our camps and prisons, but also the kind of torture under which people betray all and sundry. I began to toy with the idea of suicide again after M.'s death, but since there was no escaping my responsibility for what M. had left behind, this was no more than a way of trying to relieve my mind. I think that if I had died first M. would not have lived on very long after me. There was something about him of the wild animal which so much rebels against captivity that it dies by throwing itself against the bars of its cage. I feel ashamed at having proved to be so long-lived. Does he understand that I have lived only for him? To become so determined to live I first had to travel to the end of the road with him and see how they did him to death, my poor wild animal. But in 1925 I did not yet feel so close to him or so determined to live for his sake; all I wanted was my freedom, while he pleaded with me: Do not destroy our life . . .

In my eagerness to escape I used the idea of painting only as a pretext. M. had by then managed to get it into my head that if you were not already at work, then you had nothing to say: idle prattlers always make practical difficulties an excuse for doing nothing. He was the first person who ever told me that one must have 'something to say', and not just talk for the sake of talking, like everybody else. I knew he was right, but I tried to close my ears to this. Behind everything he demanded of me there was always a deep meaning, a serious inner motive; nothing could have been further from the outlook of my generation with its desire for an easy life and freedom without responsibility. In our squabbles and arguments, though I never openly gave in, I could not but feel how right he was. Once I was sitting outside our house on Tverskoi Boulevard, crying at the latest injury to my feelings. Klima Redko, one of the artists from my Kiev days, sat there with me. He was now living with a rich patroness, and he suddenly suggested a way in which I could escape from M. 'Let's go,' he said. 'I'll make her take you in as well.' 'She'll only throw me out,' I objected, 'and you as well.' But Klima was nothing if not sure of himself: 'She won't dare! Come on . . .' 'But Osip's right, you know,' I said all of a sudden, and leaving the flabbergasted Klima in the middle of the street, I went back to the lion's den where a furious M. was waiting for me. We had been arguing about some such thing as whether he should say 'you' or 'thou' to me. Now, however, in Tsarskoye Selo, it was I who was in the right. M. admitted that he was entirely to blame for everything and just kept repeating that our life together was much too precious and important to be thrown away because of any past follies and mistakes: 'This you must understand,' he implored me. 'How could you let Olga come and humiliate me?' I countered. 'What next will you do to me?... Let me go.'

The following morning Marietta Shaginian came into our room – the first event to make us laugh again. It turned out that she was our neighbour, living in the next room behind a flimsy partition. If she had not been as deaf as a doornail she would willy-nilly have heard a great many things which I would not dream of revealing even in these candid notes. It was a great stroke of luck that the next room was occupied by none other than this deaf old bore with her thoughts on Lenin and Goethe, and her discovery of a direct relationship between a miner's hammer, the useful activities of Faust, and the famous plan for the electrification of our young Socialist motherland. Deaf as she was, Marietta nevertheless sensed there was something wrong and began to overwhelm us with advice – her main recommendation being that we should not take baths, since modern medicine was against it. Her second piece of advice was to consult a friend of hers, a remarkable doctor, and have an affair with him. At this point, incidentally, she asked me whether I knew her husband – Armenian women are jealous. An hour later she brought the doctor to us. He looked as solemn as a funeral attendant and mouthed such portentous words that I began to snicker, at which M. gave me a clip on the ear and we both burst out laughing. Marietta soon went away with her funereal friend, and we cheered up completely.

That same day we ran into Punin, who had come to find a place for Akhmatova: her tuberculosis had got worse with the approach of spring. He was very glad at meeting us and promised to bring Akhmatova around to see us the next day. But M. did not believe she would come – she had a knack of avoiding her friends. I know this well enough from my own experience. It might seem that we could hardly live without each other and she could not bear to be parted from me, but then I would hear not a word from her, nothing ... Many years previously she had suddenly told M. to stop visiting her so often, and he had been furious because it just seemed to make no sense. She herself explained that it was a matter

of decorum ('What will people say?'), and also that she was concerned for one still so young ('What if he falls in love with me?').
M. put this kind of thing down to Akhmatova's 'quirkiness' and
laughed at her obsession about everybody being in love with her.
For me it was not so much quirkiness as what I thought of as old-
fashioned Petersburg hocus-pocus. I found the same thing in M.
too. Right at the beginning, when we first got to know each other,
after he had spent the whole day with me in view of every passer-by,
both friends and strangers, he would come up to me in the Junk
Shop the same evening and greet me formally. This had been the
custom at the Stray Dog, but to my free and easy generation it
seemed comic and silly. What had we to hide? I might have wanted
to spare my parents, but they were happy to turn a blind eye to
everything as long as I did not leave them. Our little secret was soon
out in any case.

In the upshot Akhmatova did come to see us after all, and in
some mysterious way her arrival put an end to our squabbling. She
immediately got all the information she needed; both M. and I had
already told her some of it, of course, and so had T., who little
suspected that he had been dragged into the whole business only
because of the housing shortage. She expressed her sympathy for
everyone concerned, heaved a sigh or two, but gave no advice.
She was far too sensible for that. I think very highly of her last
word on such matters: 'Let everyone straighten out his own
troubles.'

Before this meeting in Tsarskoye, I had seen very little of Akhmatova. M. had taken me to see her a couple of times – as I shall tell
later – and she had once come to see us on Morskaya, in the autumn
of 1924 when we had only just moved there from Moscow. She
found me alone. M. had returned to Moscow to collect our furniture. I was wearing those same striped pyjamas which Georgi
Ivanov has taken for a man's suit. I suddenly realized we had run
out of cigarettes, but not wanting to change in order to go out and
get some, I sent her instead: 'You go, Anna Andreyevna, while I
make the tea.' She never forgot this incident; years later, in Tashkent, she was still telling people how I had spoken to her: 'And I
trotted out as meekly as a little calf.' Though she had tired of the
simpering adulation of all the women admirers who danced atten-

dance on her, she was so used to it by then that she could never forget how I sent her out for cigarettes. It was a good thing I did this to her and not to Radlova – she would have made a great to-do about all these brazen hussies from Odessa who had been brought to the sacred city by failed poets.

My real friendship with Akhmatova began on the verandah of the boarding-house as we lay there swaddled in fur coats breathing the salubrious air of Tsarskoye Selo – it really must have had healing properties, given that we both survived. The man who owned the boarding-house – he also did the cooking – was called Zaitsev; every day he went into Leningrad to see the tax inspector, trying to save his small private establishment from bankruptcy, and we had to wait hours and hours for him to come back and feed us. The 'private sector' was now being destroyed in the catering business, just as in literature, and in both cases the state-provided substitute causes indigestion. In 1926 when we returned to spend the winter in Tsarskoye, Zaitsev's boarding-house no longer existed – the tax inspector had gobbled it up. The boarding-house to survive longest was one run by relatives of Uritski (this was the one where the Baptist woman who cooked for us got a job). To keep a tiny private boarding-house one needed contacts in government circles. In 1937 it too came to an end: Uritski's relatives were all arrested, like everybody else. One of them, the wife of the poet Spasski, was accused of having wanted to blow up a monument to her uncle, though no such monument even existed. The police interrogators – with higher permission, needless to say – amused themselves with gruesome jokes of this kind, particularly in Leningrad. Spasski himself also 'went away' as a member of a 'terrorist group' headed by none other than Fadeyev and Alexei Tolstoi – or it may have been Tikhonov.* If any Soviet woman follows the train of her associations, as I have done here, it always leads back to the same theme!

On returning from his trips to the tax inspector, Zaitsev prepared our dinner on tiny frying pans, producing extraordinary rissoles, pancakes, and veal cutlets, and delighting us with his skill in the art of cooking. We shall never see the like of it again. They say that cooking has gone down all over the world, but nowhere did it

* *Hope Against Hope*, page 379.

happen with such rapidity as here. The same is true of poetry, but such poets as were left at least held on to the very last.

The verandah still had great piles of slightly melting snow heaped up around it, but the sun shone feebly through the dirty window panes which had not been washed since 1917. Akhmatova and I constantly took our temperatures and cheerfully looked forward to dying. In those years Akhmatova had no fear of death at all – it overcame her only in the last ten years (otherwise so peaceful!) of her life. I am free of it even now and don't believe I shall ever succumb – though I wonder whether it gets us all sooner or later? As we lay on the verandah in Tsarskoye Selo there was very little life in either of us. We were both so weak that we could barely move our lightweight day beds around to keep out of the sun (we had been told to lie only in the shade, avoiding even the March sun). There was nothing that wasn't forbidden to us two young, weak, and madcap creatures. M. and Punin drank wine, joked, and constantly teased us. We gave as good as we got. 'They're all fine while they're still courting you,' Akhmatova once said later, remembering that time and playing the hard-bitten female. Her affair with Punin was in full swing. Her things were still in Shileiko's rooms in the Marble Palace – he had himself moved to Moscow. Punin was going to put her stuff in his apartment on the Fontanka, where his wife and daughter lived. Akhmatova was in something of a state about it all. Once, as she was going to her own room in the boarding-house, she alarmed M. by stopping him and saying: 'Don't go away – it's easier with you here.' He told me this with amazement (we were always amazing each other): 'Why is she being so silly? Everything's going all right with Punin, but she's behaving like a wounded bird.' He always thought everything was all right, when in actual fact nothing about our lives was ever in the least bit all right.

One day a beggar came up to our verandah. He was on his last legs and had the greatest difficulty making his way through the slightly melting snow. This must have happened during the very first weeks or even days of our stay in Tsarskoye Selo, because later on, our day beds were put outside in the asphalted yard at the front of the house. We turned out our handbags and gave everything we had to the beggar, ashamed at the smallness of our offering, but he went away scarcely crediting such generosity. This incident marked the beginning of our real friendship (as opposed to our calendar one!).* I told her how my heart sank every time I saw a beggar, since I always wondered how long it would be before my father and mother, my brothers, and my sister would also have to start going around with outstretched hands. She responded at once to these words: her mother and sister were at death's door somewhere in the south, and her two brothers, Andrei and Victor, had disappeared.† I do not remember whether she had already by then received word of Andrei's suicide, but we often talked about him. I had once stayed with my father in Sebastopol and remembered how her brother Andrei had frequently come to see us and told me – I was still only a girl in my teens – about his sister, her marriage to Gumilev, and her divorce. I knew from him that the family had regarded the marriage as doomed to failure, and for that reason none of them had come to the church for her wedding. Akhmatova confirmed this and told me she had been very offended by her family's attitude . . . She had heard that her second brother, Victor, had been shot in Yalta. The story was that his body had been thrown with others into the sea from a jetty and that the next day the water had been so calm and clear that they could all be seen lying on the bottom. There were many such stories, and who could tell whether they were true? All I know is that by the twenties I had seen so many corpses and killings that I could hardly bear to look at God's world.

You have to have lived our kind of existence to know that when the streets and highways are littered with corpses, then life is still bearable. The most terrible thing is when you no longer see the corpses. While 'someone's wife – whose I do not know – seeks her husband in the streets of Kiev-Viy',‡ there is still a human

* Allusion to a line in Akhmatova's *Poem Without a Hero*: 'And over the legendary embankment / the real, not the calendar / Twentieth Century drew near.'

† Both brothers emigrated. Andrei committed suicide in Greece.

‡ Line from one of Mandelstam's last poems (dated May 1937) with a premonition of his wife's fate after his disappearance. 'Viy' is a nightmare monster in Ukrainian folklore and the subject of a story by Gogol.

element, but when 'someone's wife' just puts on her lipstick and goes out to work, life is scarcely livable any more.

By the time of this incident with the beggar we had both gone through a great deal: the loss of people dear to us, terror, utter impoverishment, and the first real hunger. Akhmatova had spent the famine years in Petersburg, standing endless hours in queues for Shileiko's ration, while I had been on the move, wandering from place to place. M. wrote of himself in a poem: 'I have a ragged convict's look, my trouser leg is torn.' This was true of all who were forced to leave their homes during the Civil War – and then of all the refugees in the Second World War, not to mention the people sent to the camps. No wonder the language acquired a new word: *dokhodiaga,** for people who die on the move. The starving peasants who died on their unheated stoves were not *dokhodiagi* in the strict sense, but their brothers, all those who were deported or fled from the villages at the end of the twenties, certainly came under this heading. We all witnessed this and must answer for it. Didn't we eat the bread taken away from them?

The line 'Children, you are poor and dressed in rags' will be understood by all the mothers and all the waifs of our era. Fortunately, M.'s mother died before the catastrophe, but his father lived on until 1938; completely abandoned by his youngest son, he waited in the hospital for his oldest son to come to his rescue, unaware that he was already in the Lubianka, preparing for death himself. At the time of my meeting with Akhmatova, I was in a constant state of anguish at the thought of my parents, now left all alone, my missing brother – where and how he had perished we did not know – and my sister, who lived in mortal terror. Her own destitution and helplessness apart (she would hardly otherwise have agreed to move in with the Punins), Akhmatova was sorely distressed by the desperate plight of her mother and sister, her separation from her son, the tragic fate of the country, of her brothers, and of people in general. The thoughts aroused in me by the sight of the beggar were scarcely very original, but my feelings were by no means common to everybody in our ravaged anthill. People in our circle (if one could still talk of such a thing, which I

* Camp slang for a person already dying, a 'goner' (plural form: *dokhodiagi*).

doubt) now tried to put past ordeals out of their minds and persuade themselves that the worst was over. A remarkable thing
about most people is that they always believe the worst has disappeared into the bottomless pit of time and the future is sure to
be a bed of roses. This is what keeps them going. Those few who
sense the shape of things to come often lose their capacity to live
in the present, so terrible is their vision of what lies in store.
Akhmatova – or Cassandra, as M. called her – was horrified not
only by what she saw when she looked back, but also by her
presentiments of future ordeals and woes, relatively quiet as things
were in 1925. M. and I were also full of anxiety, though he retained
his capacity (not shared by me) to enjoy the present. Our anxiety
lessened somewhat in the years we spent in Leningrad and
Tsarskoye (1924–7). M. was slightly affected by high-level propaganda to the effect that we had seen the last shootings and hardships, and such things would never be repeated. In the same way
the Civil War was supposed to be the war to end all wars . . .

Isn't it this kind of mentality that gives birth to all the other
mirages: chiliasm, the cult of Sophia,* theories of 'progress', and
other such optimistic notions? How many times we have been
taken in, and even now, in the ominous calm of 1970, people are
suppressing their qualms and putting great hopes in the future. But
what does it hold, this future that I, thank God, shall not live to
see? Faith in the future reached its highest point in the middle of
the twenties. Everybody, including the peasants, was obsessed by a
single thought: how to make up for lost time and get on his feet
again. The peasants who managed to do this in the twenties were
denounced as 'kulaks' and wiped out at the end of the decade. This
happened only to those who had come up during NEP – the 'rich
peasants' of former times had been disposed of before NEP began.
The towns ignored the existence of the countryside, though from
time to time they were flooded by hordes of hungry people from it –
no longer peasants, but beggars. The townspeople were interested
only in getting their bread and butter, and for an incredibly long
time were utterly complacent about everything else. Members of
the top layer of the new intelligentsia, as they turned into 'cadres',
had only one aim: to assure themselves of a permanent ration from

* See Vladimir Soloviev, Appendix A.

the State and a place behind the high wall which shielded the elect, allowing them always to eat well (perhaps even better than before) and keeping out everybody else. Once ensconced behind their high wall, they ceased to give a thought to those who were taken away from their homes at dead of night. The hungry years had taught people to attach the greatest importance to a full belly and, even more, to a life of plenty. From the very first the new regime began to feed people on a differential scale, in accordance with their value to the State. All those touching tales about members of the government living like workers were sentimental humbug. During the Civil War they lived modestly, but a difference in levels was always maintained. As time went on, this difference grew until in the middle thirties the way the rulers lived was surrounded by secrecy. They had by now turned into real grandees, but did not like it to be known. During NEP, engineers and technicians were picked out to become a favoured group, and writers began to move heaven and earth to be recognized as 'engineers of human souls', thus making certain of a share in the cake. What they had to do to achieve this is all too clear to everyone, and they did it with the greatest zeal, fully deserving their title of 'engineers' – as witness their great piles of books and their dachas in the country around Moscow.

Everybody goes the way he wants. We had chosen to live in poverty of our own free will. As I gradually changed from a timid 'girl-Europa' into a 'beggar's helpmate', my relations with Akhmatova grew closer – renunciation of earthly goods, of everything that arouses people's greed, had always been part of her character, from her very young days. M. had noted this quality already before the Revolution: 'In Akhmatova's recent verse there has been a turn toward hieratic stateliness, a religious simplicity and solemnity. I would say that she is now no ordinary woman; of her it can truly be said that she is "dressed poorly, but of grand mien". The voice of renunciation grows stronger all the time in her verse, and at the moment her poetry bids fair to become a symbol of Russia's grandeur.'

How have people managed to overlook the main and best strand in Akhmatova's poetry, failing to notice that she is a poet of renunciation, not of love? They drool over her line about the right-hand glove put on the left hand (or the other way around – just try it!)* but miss what really matters:

> In this life I have seen so little yet.
> All I've done was sing and wait,
> Never hating a brother, I know,
> Nor betraying a sister.
> So why has God punished me,
> Every day and every hour?
> Or was it an Angel showing me
> A light unseen to us all?

These lines she wrote at the age of twenty, and they give the measure by which her poetry must be judged.

This was the main path she followed in life. By comparison everything else was only minor detail or a concession to human weakness. We are all only human after all. I am very glad I sent Akhmatova out for cigarettes. This simplified our relations and opened the way for our friendship. One should always do this sort of thing to people one loves and respects. With those you don't – better not smoke or drink at all.

But as regards M., I doubt whether I did the right thing. I should have left him – how could he have dared to love anyone but me? I was a fool who did not really know how to be jealous or make a scene. What joys I denied myself.

25 Our Alliance

It was in Tsarskoye Selo, on the veranda of that small private boarding-house, that we concluded our triple alliance. It was done without words or explanations and has never once been broken ever since – though I cannot claim that it was always unclouded. It would be better to say that, however troubled it may have been at times, all three of us remained loyal to it. We lived out our lives together: at first there were three of us; then, after M.'s death only two, and now I am the only one left. 'Why do you need me?' I used

---

* Detail from an early Akhmatova poem.

to ask M. 'I feel free with you,' was one reply, and another: 'Because you believe in me.' Many years after his death, sitting on a bench in the churchyard on the Ordynka* where Akhmatova and I always went to talk about things we feared to discuss in the Ardovs' apartment, I heard the same words from her: 'You, Nadia, have always believed in me.' Both of them, fully aware of their purpose in life from the earliest years, needed the friendship of a woman whom they themselves had taught to appreciate poetry on first hearing. Even if a poet is surrounded by people, his loneliness is such that he has much greater need of one close and utterly devoted person than of any number of admirers. Akhmatova never lacked admirers (or detractors too, for that matter), but one real reader, or rather listener, was more precious to her than all of them put together.

How was it possible for three such incredibly light-minded people to keep up this unbreakable friendship and alliance throughout their lives, and even beyond, for all times. Many people imagine that Akhmatova's main concern in life was love, but all her affairs collapsed like houses of cards (jealousy came more easily to her than love), while her very wrought-up and intense relations with M. survived every test. M. very easily got on friendly terms with both men and women, but he just as quickly lost interest in them. It even frightened me, the way he visibly cooled towards people whom he had only recently been talking with, seeing a great deal, or looking forward to meeting again. He admitted that his attitude to people was predatory: he took what he could and then dropped them (just as in the case of his only affair – the one with Olga Vaksel, which was all over in about two months). At one time he liked to gossip with Emma Gerstein, but suddenly I heard him say: 'What an old hen she's become all at once, Emma.' With her it was not an affair; they were just friends. He listened to everything she had to say on the subject of Marxism, which took her about a month, and then he began to avoid conversation with her. The same thing happened with Kuzin, although he lasted something like a year before coming to the end of his conversational treasures. The most durable friendships were the playful ones – as with Margulis – which involved banter rather than serious conversation,

* Street in Moscow.

or the longstanding but completely empty relationships of the type he maintained with Narbut and Zenkevich.

All I can say in M.'s defence is that people did not converse but only told stories – which soon petered out anyway. Nobody wanted to think. In both my generation and M.'s, capacity for thought had been exhausted too early. Punin used to say: 'I cannot keep pace with Mandelstam.' He was a clever man, but at a certain point he had suddenly ground to a halt. Shklovski, Tynianov, Eikhenbaum, and Gukovski were the cream of literary scholarship in the twenties, but what could you talk about with them? They simply repeated what they had written in their books, but did not really respond to living conversation. Most of the people we met were frantically trying to promote themselves – in other words, they did nothing but brag. I cannot imagine that any other generation has ever gone in for such unbridled bragging. Those of them who have survived still go on doing it to the present day – unhappy old men who never did very much with their lives puff themselves up like turkey cocks as they talk about their successes and achievements. . . . Recently I heard that Bobrov, who was a clever man, became very depressed at the end of his life when he realized how little he had done. This is so much more dignified than constantly indulging in self-deception, as everybody else does. In their youth they aspired to be geniuses, but spent themselves prematurely. Humiliated, tormented, confused, intellectually sterile, they went on producing their 'discoveries' and sticking out their chests, not to see their own inner emptiness. The leftovers of rationalism on which they fed, the passion for innovation and pyrotechnics during the twenties (and to a considerable extent in the pre-Revolutionary years as well), were not exactly conducive to original thinking. The poor Rudakov, when we met him in Voronezh, kept telling us he was writing a book about poetry which would at last open people's eyes, but everything he said was utter nonsense. When I asked M. what he thought the book would be like he said: 'Let him amuse himself; don't hurt his feelings.'

M. at first listened eagerly to all these storytellers and braggarts and then, recoiling from them, passed them over to me. He was always hopeful of hearing something really new, but it was a lost cause. It is just possible that we were simply unlucky not to find what may have been lurking out of sight, but I saw no people of original ideas around Akhmatova either. She mentioned Engelhardt and respected Tomashevski. I did not know them, though when I read Engelhardt's article on Dostoyevski, I thought there was something in it. Many people certainly concealed their thoughts, of course, while others simply languished for lack of air.

M. had to make the best he could of easy-going friendships with undemanding people, but what mattered most to him in all circumstances was to preserve his relations with me and his friendship with Akhmatova. With her he talked, joked, laughed, drank wine; most important of all, they were travelling the same road, taking the same view of essential things, supporting each other in work and misfortune. They were allies in the literal sense of the word: two people standing up for the same thing. You have only to glance at everything written during the last half-century to see the gulf that separates them from all the other forces active in their day. They both liked Pasternak and had a lot in common with him, but at that time he was clearly drawn to other people and did not seek M.'s friendship – the occasional dialogues between them were short-lived and their paths were too different: each was going his own way. From time to time a friendship sprang up between Pasternak and Akhmatova, but this too never lasted because he always failed to keep it up. It is possible that Pasternak did not want relations with equals, never indeed suspecting that anybody could be his equal. He always felt he stood quite apart. Moreover, he set great store by external success. Oddly enough, the paths of all three did eventually converge, though Pasternak was unaware of it. M. and Akhmatova always knew that their path lay close to Pasternak's, that they were heading in the same general direction – even at the time of *Second Birth*, although *My Sister Life* meant much more to them. Of the later verse Akhmatova particularly liked 'Hospital'. For me this poem has rather too programmatic a ring.

Among the people who were close to us I must also mention Natasha Shtempel, a woman of rare spiritual grace. She came late into our life, but will always be part of it. About Vasilisa Shklovski I have already written.* Deep as these relationships were, they were not the same as the bond with Akhmatova because they were with

* *Hope Against Hope*, pages 415–21.

people travelling different roads. When all was said and done, there were three of us, and only three. After M.'s death Akhmatova said to me: 'Now you are all that remains of Osip.' His death brought a new element into our friendship: henceforth I was her only living link with M. She often said that by my appearance on the scene I had helped bring about the renewal of her friendship with him. It may well have been so. He was then at a crossroads, uncertain of his bearings, and might easily not have found his one natural ally. Nowhere else, I believe, were people so much deafened as they were here by the din of life, the furious drumfire of the demands and aspirations of the moment. The noise was such that it drowned out everything else in the world. One after another poets fell silent because they could no longer hear their own voices. The noise drowned out thought and, in the case of millions, conscience as well. Petia Verkhovenski has a lot to say for himself, and the mad logic of his words seduces people, poisoning their minds.

I remember a chance conversation I once had with a fellow evacuee as we were travelling on a boat along the Amu-Darya.* 'You have a strange way of talking about your family,' I said to the man. 'Don't they mean anything to you? Don't you love them?' He was a Pole who had only just been released from a camp. He laughed and replied: 'I haven't lost only my family, I've lost myself as well. If I find myself again, I shall know what I think of my family.' This had happened to him after two unhinging years in the camps. In the delirium of our existence we had lost ourselves, no longer hearing our own voices or seeing the road ahead. You were very fortunate if you managed to pull yourself together in time, but it was the hardest thing in the world. To add to our confusion, we were always starting out on different tacks, never pausing to think of their implications. Led astray by a false sense of freedom, we recklessly did as we pleased, oblivious to the fact that every action always has to be paid for. Akhmatova had once nearly forfeited M.'s friendship when she told him to stop seeing her for the sake of appearances (or rather, for the sake of two of her women friends who imagined a new lover was worshipping at her feet), and he, childishly resentful, almost broke with his devoted ally as a result.

* The Oxus. This journey was during the war, when the author was on her way to Tashkent.

It was to Akhmatova's credit, I hasten to add, that for a long time she was able to keep a firm hand on herself and not think of all her relationships in terms of people being in love with her. In her mature years she got out of the habit altogether. In M.'s defence I can point out that he gave up all other alliances and remained true to his youthful friendship and the first people he thought of as 'we' – the Acmeists.

He and I also nearly lost each other because of his infatuation with Olga and my heartless 'principles'. He pulled himself up just in time, but out of pique, feminine pride, and an illusory belief in freedom of action, I almost threw away both our lives. If my life had any meaning at all, it was only because I shared all the tribulations of Akhmatova and M. and eventually found myself, my own true self, through my closeness to them. While he was still alive, incidentally, I had no thought of 'finding myself'. We lived too intensively and intimately to think of 'searching' for ourselves. There is a curious poem of M.'s which he wrote in the Crimea, while he was thinking about me. He did not tell me at the time what the meaning of the poem was – at that tender age I should have been up in arms if I had known the fate he had in mind for me. The poem is about a woman who will be named Leah, not Helen, 'because to Ilium's sun / you preferred a yellow twilight'. Our relationship must have aroused in him a keen awareness of his Jewish roots, a tribal feeling, a sense of kinship with his people – I was the only Jewess in his life. He thought of the Jews as being one family, hence the theme of incest in the poem: 'Go, no one shall touch you, / let the incestuous daughter / lay her head at dead of night / on her father's breast.' The daughter, having fallen in love with a Jew, was destined to renounce herself and be dissolved in him: 'No, you will love a Jew / and disappear in him, and God be with you.'

This was a strange and cruel poem for M. to write while thinking about the woman from whom he was cut off by the Civil War, but he could always foresee what shape his relations with women – including me – would eventually assume. Actually he not only foresaw what they would be like, but worked to make them that way, always taking what he thought fit from any relationship, with men or women. From me he wanted only one thing: that I should give up my life to him, renounce my own self, and become a part of him. This was why he so stubbornly dinned his own ideas into my head, getting me to see things his way. Once, while he was telling me that I not only belonged to him but was a part of his own being, I remembered the poem about Leah. The biblical Leah is an unloved wife, and I said: 'Now I understand who that poem is about.' It appeared, however, that Leah was the name he had given to a daughter of Lot. He now told me that when he wrote the poem he had not at first realized whom it referred to. One night, thinking about me, he had suddenly seen that I would come to him, as Lot's daughters had to their father. The sense of a poem, its latent meaning, is not always immediately apparent to the person who has composed it. I often heard both M. and Akhmatova say that they had now at last understood whom some poem or other was about – originally the poem had just 'come' to them, without their knowing what or who had prompted it. Then, after a time, this would all suddenly become clear. I find it astonishing that there have been poets who wrote 'outlines' of future poems in prose beforehand, not to mention those who 'put into verse' ideas suggested to them by others. This kind of thing, it seems to me, can be possible only during the years of apprenticeship (the middle part of M.'s *Stone*, for example – the verses about sport, *The Egyptian*, and other such things), when the first steps are being taken by the poet towards his mastery of word and thought; later the two become inseparable, the word only precipitating the thought. In the work of any poet I can always very clearly distinguish between verse that wells by itself up from the depths of the mind and that which sets forth a preconceived idea. Akhmatova told me how she had heard Pasternak talk about being taken to the hospital and what he thought at the time. The poem he later wrote thus merely embodied his already existing account of the experience. Some of Akhmatova's poems are also written in this premeditated fashion. Such verse, though lacking the miraculous quality of spontaneous creation, always appeals to the unschooled reader because it 'tells a story' or conveys a ready-made idea. I can do without this kind of verse. It's a matter of taste.

The poem about Leah's love for a Jew came from the very depths of the consciousness, taking M. himself by surprise – it would appear that all he had wanted from me at first was affection, and he was loath to recognize that the poem foreshadowed a very different future for me in his life. Even in the smallest things he was always to expect the same from me as from himself, and he could make no distinction between my life and his own: if I am given a permit to live in Moscow, then so will you be; what happens to me will happen to you; you will read this book, if I read it ... He firmly believed that I should die when he did – or that if by any chance I died earlier, he would follow me very soon afterwards. He was upset if I knew something in which he was not interested, or if I was lazy about reading the Italians and the Spaniards together with him. In the last years I read a lot of Shakespeare, and he was jealous; in the end he wrote and asked me to teach him how to read my 'Englishman'. He had immediately taken over my love of painting – since it could not be eliminated – and decided on the same policy with regard to Shakespeare. Loving different things was the same as separating, and he just could not bear the thought. He behaved in exactly the same way with my friends: he either adopted them himself or – which was more often the case – 'eliminated' them. If he was awake, he expected me to be awake too, going to sleep only when he did. My brother used to say to him: 'Nadia doesn't exist – she is just your echo.' 'That's how we like it,' he replied gleefully. At the same time, he believed I could read his thoughts and hear the same words going through his head that he did. Both he and Akhmatova had an uncanny way of replying to a question just as it crossed your mind, before you have spoken it. 'It's witchcraft,' I used to say to Akhmatova, astonished that she had intercepted some thought before it had barely had time to form in my mind. M. literally read my thoughts and was astonished if I didn't know what he had been thinking at a given moment. Perhaps I just didn't take enough trouble to penetrate his thoughts and gave him good reason to get angry with me for not 'sitting in his head'.

Occasionally, withdrawing into himself, or into his friendship with someone, he would let me be for a while. I liked these breathing spaces (particularly if it was friendship with a man, or with Akhmatova – that is, with a woman he addressed as 'you', not 'thou'!), and quickly tried to escape from my captivity. But it never worked: he always noticed my bid for freedom and abruptly pulled me back to him. Leah did not, and could not have a separate existence. Living with him was hard and easy at the same time. It was hard because of the incredible intensity with which he lived; I was always having to run to keep up with him – as that time when we were crossing the sun-lit square in front of the rest home in Gaspra. I tried not to show how hard it was for me to keep pace with him and his thoughts. I didn't want him to stop in his tracks for my sake, but I was upset when he failed to see that I was out of breath. What made life with him easy, on the other hand, was that I was never bored – and also, perhaps, the fact that I loved him. I can't say exactly.

I now understand that I could have had no better fate and quite see how it was that some of the dimwits who hung around us did not appreciate his brilliance. Emma Gerstein, for instance, looked on our apartment as a place where she met 'interesting people' and unsuccessfully pursued her amorous designs on Lev Gumilev, Narbut, and whoever else happened to be there, but she paid little attention to M. and never understood his poetry. Needless to say, these were not favourable times for M. – his ideas, the brilliance of his conversation, his humour, could not be appreciated without equipment of a different order than anything produced in the first half of the century. We were surrounded by swarms of people who saw everything in another light from M., and they were always trying to turn me against him, tempting me with the thought of a more ordered and sensible existence, and the good things that would go with it: common sense, Marxism, innovation, an easy life, theatres and bars, a proper home, and all the latest trends. I hate to remember my brief and feverish bouts of vainglory which, fortunately, I never took to their logical conclusion. All the artists with Russian and Italian names, all the Marxists with the brains of a Petia Verkhovenski, all the avant-gardists and young men with Marxist or, come to that, anti-Marxist views in various branches of learning, all the cynics and all the lovers of life, all the melancholics and outsiders who have ever crossed my path held my attention for no more than a minute as they looped the loop over Moscow – without exception they proved to be duds, windbags, and braggarts. If I had ever taken up with any of them, or branched off on my own to become a painter – as I had wanted in my youth – or if I had never been anything but the language teacher I was forced to become in my later years, then my life would certainly have been frittered away in vain, and I would indeed have turned into a mere cog, replaceable at will, in some vile institute or other. In all probability, however, I should at least not have strutted around in the manner we have come to expect from women active in academic life or the arts, but would soon have revolted like my Tashkent friend whose suicide note so much astonished his superiors.

Akhmatova was my ally because her attitude to M. was the same as mine. She listened with pleasure to the horde of worshippers who coupled her with Pushkin, for whom her love and veneration were boundless, but she knew beyond doubt that her place was with M. What she feared most of all was that some avant-gardists might try to dissociate them by making him posthumously into a Futurist, a fellow spirit of Khlebnikov, or even, perish the thought, a member of LEF. She went wild with fury if anyone dared suggest that M. was a pupil not of Annenski, but of the august mentor celebrated for his 'poisonous prettiness'. People who connect M. with the Futurists fail to understand both him and them. Akhmatova didn't know what it was that made her so close to M. 'We shouldn't be viewed as twins,' she used to say, 'but neither can we be separated: we go together.' For his part, M., who was quite unconcerned about where he was placed, used to tease me by saying: 'Nadia, don't get above yourself – we are recognized only by two women: Anna Andreyevna and Vera Yakovlevna.' Vera Yakovlevna was my mother, whom M. once dubbed his 'illegal mother-in-law' at the time when we had to go out and meet her on the street because she was afraid to come up to our apartment.* They were always making fun of each other. Whenever she made something not very good for dinner, he would say: 'Vera Yakovlevna, you know much more about poetry.' She gave as good as she got . . .

Nobody should imagine that we thought of nothing but work and poetry. It was all quite different: we lived intense, boisterous lives, making merry, playing games, having fun, drinking wine and vodka, going on a spree, seeing friends, quarrelling, jeering at each

* *Hope Against Hope*, page 350.

other, gloating over each other's follies, many times trying to run in opposite directions, but never managing, for some reason, to part even for a single day. I cannot explain why myself.

It really is a mystery how a spoiled and silly girl such as I had been in the heedless days of my youth could see the 'light unseen to us' and calmly accept such a terrible destiny. In the days when Olga Vaksel came to cry on my shoulder, we had one conversation during which I said that I liked money. She was incensed at my vulgarity and carried on so charmingly about the crassness of the rich, saying how much she preferred poverty to wealth, that the lovesick M. beamed all over at the contrast between such high-mindedness and the bad taste displayed by me. Even now I like money, comfort, the smell of success – and M. too liked all the pleasures that money can give. We were not ascetics by nature, and neither of us practised self-denial for its own sake; we were simply forced into it by circumstances, because the price demanded in return for an increase in one's rations was just too high. But we did not *want* to be poor, any more than M. wanted to die in a camp. (To this very day I am still mortally afraid that in my old age I might be packed off to a madhouse or camp.)

We wanted to live, not to die, but everybody saw right from the start that we would come to a bad end. Even people with whom we had nothing in common saw this, if they still had a spark of ordinary sensibility. There were not many like this, but by no means everybody had become unfeeling, even among the intelligentsia. In 1932 we stayed in Bolshevo, in one of the CEKUBU rest homes. Among all the frenetic young academics and bland professorial types who read Selvinski and Kirsanov, with a bit of Bagritski in between, there was a tall, thin Ossetian woman who rather resembled Akhmatova in her middle years: she had the same gaunt, ascetic look, light step, and meekness of spirit. She was from a peasant family, but her sons had come up in the world and had been able to send her on a vacation to this rest home for scholars and writers. We became good friends and went out walking with her along the snow-covered paths of the grounds in order to get away from the arguments between the young Marxist rabble and the crafty professors. She had no idea what all this literary wrangling of the early thirties was about, but she sensed how precarious M.'s position was, how out of place he felt in this academic milieu where he was always being buttonholed by philosophers and students of literature expressing an interest in his work. 'Osia,' she said to him once (she found his name funny, because in Ossetian it meant something quite incongruous, such as 'girl' or 'woman'), 'Osia, you don't want to join their *kolkhoz*, I can see that . . . But you must, or you'll come to a bad end – honest to God you will . . .'

I have heard the plainchant laments sung at Ossetian funerals. People who can sing such songs are more adept at foreseeing a man's fate than any visitors to academic rest homes organized by Gorki – let alone all the scum who produced the literary monuments to our era.

In literary circles people kept asking about M.: 'Does he really not understand even now?' This was how it was put by the 'activists' who shared, or were helping to set up, the new 'platforms'. Others were just surprised: 'If we can, why can't he?' These were all the artful dodgers who had deliberately remodelled themselves and changed their colours and were now busy carrying out orders. They took the death of M. and millions of others as a matter of course. The thirties and forties were the years when ideology triumphed over everything else, and the extermination of anyone who refused to accept its propositions or – even more important – its phraseology was regarded as a normal security measure. Subsequently many people referred to such measures as the destruction of the 'fifth column'. At the time the mob howled its approval, happy at being allowed to pick up the scraps from the masters' table. The poorer people are, the easier it is to rule them. Nothing creates such perfect 'unanimity' as hunger.

We rejected the ideology and its jargon and turned our backs on the feast, the bones and scraps tossed down from the table. We did not join the *kolkhoz*. The Ossetian woman understood our position very well and took pity on us already then. I would like to know what *Osia* means in Ossetian – it belongs to the Indo-European group of languages, something I used to specialize in. What a good thing I didn't find my own feet when I was young and go in for a decent professional career which would have given me independence. As it was, I was to have more than my fill of 'independence' and loneliness for more than thirty years. I am sick to death of it, and of scraps from the masters' table. I will gladly die in a prison or camp for the right to turn my back on this life and say what I think of it.

26   Veiled Admissions

In the crowd of braggarts M. stood out like the proverbial white raven, and he always watched me very carefully in case I tried to put on airs. If ever I dared say a boastful word, he made fun of me so openly in the presence of other people that I learned to hold my tongue, for fear of bringing disgrace on him. But he took a lenient view of other boasters: 'Why should you worry?' he would say of someone. 'Let him boast, if it makes life easier for him.' He was himself incapable of boasting because he was quite convinced that everyone else was better, and he would genuinely have liked to be as others: they managed to get along so well and knew when silence was the best policy – all except him. Or he would say things like: 'See how beautifully he chops wood – it's a joy to watch.' If I happened to blurt out some word of praise to him (which was against our rules), he was sincerely taken aback, and I often heard him use the phrase: 'I'm worse than everybody, I think.'

It was a completely sincere admission, there can be no doubt of it, but I was amused to see that, feeling this way about himself, he showed no desire whatsoever to change or to try to improve himself. He knew he was worse than everybody else, but it didn't worry him in the slightest: that's how he was, and it couldn't be helped. There was just one time when he promised me to 'mend his ways', but that was on the last night of our life together – half an hour, perhaps, before they came to take him away forever, when we had just made up after an argument. It still pains me to think how I nagged him that night over something quite unimportant and absurd – over his lack of caution, in fact. As though caution could have saved him . . .

The only thing I can say in defence of myself is that I very rarely nagged him. I certainly did not think of him as worse than every-body else, and I meekly put up with his smoking, his despotism (he was always snatching cigarettes out of my mouth), his mischievous-ness, his love of 'banquets' improvised out of canned foodstuffs, and his weird capacity to enjoy life at times when I could have died from fear. As the years went by, this love of life grew stronger and he could take delight in any unconsidered trifle – a stream of cold water from the tap, a clean sheet, a book, a rough towel. When death was already close at hand, while we were staying in Savelovo in 1937, he used to take me to the tea-room called the Invalids' Echo to drink tea, look at the people, read the newspaper, and chat with the man who ran the place. He had a rare ability to see the world before his eyes, and consumed by curiosity, he drank in every detail. Irina Semenko has noted that in M.'s translations of Petrarch there is a peculiar shift of focus compared with the original: attention is transferred from subjective experience to the object of it. This is very characteristic of him. Even in everyday life he rarely spoke of himself, or of his feelings and sensations, prefer-ring to talk of what aroused them. His field of vision at any given moment was dominated not by the personal element, but by the events and objects of the external world. This was even reflected in the way he spoke about the smallest of practical matters: not, 'This mattress is so bad that it makes my back ache,' but 'I think a spring has gone; it ought to be repaired.'

Both in his private, everyday life and in his work he always spoke about himself with the greatest caution, veiling any personal disclosures in an outwardly objective form. I see a peculiar contra-diction here: on the one hand he was an extraordinarily straight-forward and open person, incapable of any kind of dissimulation, but on the other, a certain inner diffidence prevented him from making direct statements about himself. As I wrote down 'Con-versation About Dante' at his dictation, I noticed a number of times that he was working a lot of personal things into the essay. 'You're settling your own scores here,' I would say to him. 'That's the way it should be. Don't interrupt,' he replied. He concealed such personal admissions in the most unexpected places where they are likely to escape the attention of the casual reader. They are mostly to be found scattered here and there in his prose writings.

In verse self-revelation is of the kind that comes up of its own accord from the depths of the poet's consciousness, but what I have in mind here are deliberate disclosures about the opinions, outlook on life, tastes, and leanings which offer a key to the poet's biography – as opposed to the confession of faith contained in his verse.

In Voronezh we worked together on the script for a broadcast about the young Goethe, using Goethe's own autobiographical tale as our main source. All the connecting passages and other technical parts written by me have been left out of M.'s text as published. I noticed that he chose those episodes in Goethe's life which he thought typical for the development of any poet – insofar, that is, as he himself had experienced something similar. The young Goethe, for example, once got involved with some crooks and barely managed to extricate himself – and then only with the help of a girl. 'Did this happen to you too?' I asked M. 'There was Georgi Ivanov,' he replied, and to some extent Voloshin as well – a spiritual corrupter, a windbag, a preacher of insidious nonsense . . . Goethe went through a phase of youthful neurasthenia which he got over by visiting an anatomical theatre and climbing to the top of Cologne Cathedral (I think this part of our script has been lost). M. also suffered from youthful depression and neurasthenia during the two years he spent studying in Paris and Heidelberg, and particularly during his visit to Italy when he went as a tourist rather than as a student. He was never able to go to Italy again, and he regretted that he saw so little on this one visit (and on a previous outing of a day or two – to Turin, I think – from Switzerland). When Goethe talks about his meeting with Klopstock he describes how the young people who came to see the maestro were respectful and irreverent at the same time. This was exactly the attitude of M. and Akhmatova towards their elders. Only Bely provoked a different reaction in M. – he was so tragic that he aroused compassion and respect. By the time he met Bely, however, M. was no longer all that young himself.

There is one passage in the script that has no counterpart in anything written by Goethe, and although M. is talking about him, it clearly refers to himself: 'Only it should be borne in mind that his friendships with women, for all the depth of feeling and passion involved, provided the firm bridges over which he passed from one phase to another.' His work on the young Goethe took more than two months – from the end of April (when we moved from the house of the 'disappointed landlord' with his Russian leather boots to the centre of town)* until the end of June. We borrowed several German lives of Goethe from the university library, and glancing at the portraits of the women in them, M. observed that they all looked a little like Olga Vaksel – though she had Lithuanian rather than German blood. It was this that probably prompted his group of poems about her and her death – not for nothing is there a direct reference to Goethe in them ('the lap of nature that lured young Goethe') as well as more oblique allusions ('wheels of watermills', 'the postilion's bugle', and a mention of Schubert associated with Goethe through his setting of *The Erlking*). I recently remembered the lines: 'Let the little Italian girl, while snow crunches on the ground, fly along after Schubert in her narrow sleigh.' Here the reference is to Bosio, a dark-haired girl who used to sing Schubert when M. was still young (before he met me), and I believe that the theme of Italy ('laughing, becoming Italian, Russian') and Schubert ('And Schubert's talisman froze in its shuba') crops up in the poems about Olga Vaksel because he associated her with Goethe's Mignon. Olga's mother was a pianist, and Olga herself sang and played as a ten-year-old school-girl. Hard as it is for me to admit it, there was music in her (though not in her memoirs).

At the end of that May our friend Roginski, the anthropologist, came to Voronezh. He had just been released from the Lubianka: all the anthropologists were being rooted out on the suspicion that their very subject had ideological links with fascism. Unable to find work in Moscow at the end of the academic year, he had eagerly accepted an invitation from Voronezh University to come there and give a few lectures and seminars. (In the biological faculty at Voronezh there was a very good man, called, I think, Kozo-Polianski, who tried to give work to decent people. I did not know him, but heard about him from many biologists.) I took advantage of Roginski's arrival to make a trip to Moscow – I knew that M. would not feel so lonely with him around. (The young Rudakov

* *Hope Against Hope*, Chapter 30.

was not company enough, and I couldn't rely on the young rascal either.) It was during my brief absence that M. wrote the poems to the memory of Olga Vaksel. He no longer found it possible to write verse to another woman if I was with him, as he had done in 1925 (the verse to Petrovykh was written during a few days while I was in the hospital having tests – how is that for a dirty trick?). The thought of unfaithfulness always troubled him deeply, and he went through agonies when such 'faithless poems', as he called them, came to him. He even put his poems to Natasha Shtempel in this category. He decided to destroy the poems to Olga's memory before I returned, but I already knew about them from Roginski, who arrived back in Moscow before I left. Together with Rudakov I persuaded M. to dictate them to me – which was easier after we discovered one page which he had torn up and thrown into our refuse bucket: he hadn't been able to think of a better place!

While he was still alive he refused to publish his 'faithless' poems: 'We are not troubadours,' he explained. In 1931, when there was a plan for a two-volume edition of his work, I urged him to end the section after *Tristia* with another poem to Olga Vaksel which I knew existed ('When You Made Your Son Drink Tea') but he wouldn't hear of it. I saw this poem only in Voronezh, though I knew about its existence from the very beginning when he dictated it to Akhmatova 'in strict confidence', and then gave it to Livshits for safekeeping. I think the actual fact of unfaithfulness bothered him much less than the resulting poems. At the same time, however, he defended his right to them: 'I have only my poetry. Keep it all. Forget about these.' Their existence pains me, but respecting M.'s right to a part of him that he kept hidden from me, I have preserved them together with all his other verse. I would rather he had done it himself – but for that he would have had to stay alive.

His feeling of being 'faithless' was no less acute when he read non-Russian poets: 'And in punishment for pride, incorrigible lover of sounds, / you will receive a sponge with vinegar, for your faithless lips.' For one of M.'s anti-individualist temperament, pride was a mortal sin, and he saw a manifestation of it in the enjoyment of foreign speech which he indulged by rolling around his tongue 'delicious double clusters of confederate sounds'. Reading Ariosto and Tasso, as well as the German Romantics ('To the German Tongue'), seemed like an act of betrayal to him, but he felt quite differently about Dante. In reading the 'Great European' (I have found a similar attitude to Dante in T. S. Eliot), he was not gratifying his love of sounds, enjoying their 'delicious double clusters', but entering the inner sanctum of European culture and poetry. He thought of all European poetry as no more than 'Dante's liberated bondmaid', and reading *The Divine Comedy* was an act of homage and communion, not faithless indulgence in the sweetness of alien sounds. This explains his revolt against Tasso and Ariosto which breaks through in the lines: 'What if Ariosto, Tasso who so enchanted us / are monsters with blue brains and scales of misty eyes' (Italy, with its maritime climate, gives birth to a poet-mermaid!) and his note about the sad fate of Batiushkov, who 'was ruined because he tasted the delights of Tasso before being made immune to them by Dante.' Pushkin, as we read in the same notes, was the only Russian poet who 'came close to a really mature understanding of Dante because he did not content himself with the phonetic, physiological joys of poetry and was fearful of succumbing to them, lest he share the melancholy fate of Tasso.'

M. always talks of poetry as though it were love, distinguishing between the nakedly sensual side and the other aspect that both love and poetry have in common. This other aspect defies definition, though I believe it was understood, or sensed, by Vladimir Soloviev. M.'s opinion of poetry should not be seen merely as a veiled statement about his attitude to love but rather as the clue to his understanding of the dual nature of both love and poetry, one aspect of it being directly linked with sex and hence purely physiological, and the other rooted in those qualities of man that mark him off from the animal world. In Schönberg's remarkable opera Moses and Aaron are contrasted with each other as the two poles of sensual and suprasensual consciousness. (What a pity that M. never heard Schönberg: we were cut off from the whole world.) In his notes M. is warning (himself, I think) against the enjoyment of physiological pleasures for their own sake. The sentences quoted above are to be found in his rough draft of 'Conversation About

Dante', but were not included in the final version because M. was chary of revealing these private thoughts.

Poetry, like all art (and, it seems to me, any cognitive activity – i.e. science – as well), is closely linked with man's sensual nature, with his physiology in general, but nowhere, neither in painting nor in music, is there such a close connection with love in all its manifestations as in poetry. The one thing I cannot conceive of and have never observed in any form is 'sublimation'. What gloomy German brooding in his study ever thought of this one! The actual work of producing poetry does indeed disturb the humdrum rhythm of love's physiological expression, but, then, it upsets the pattern of everything else as well – eating, drinking, sleeping, movement and rest – subordinating them all to the inner music, thereby heightening and magnifying the need for them. What does this have to do with sublimation, that is, the conversion of the sexual urge into spiritual activity? Dry-as-dust scholars with their roots in the nineteenth century, terribly deficient in sensuality (not only in love), invented this explanation of their own lack of passion and inability to find an outlet in anything but graphomania. The work of a poet, on the other hand, sharpens all his senses and brings the powers of his mind and body to their highest pitch of intensity. How this intensity manifests itself is another matter: some poems speak of self-denial and others of the total fulfilment of all the passions – the ecstasy of asceticism alternates with ecstasy of a very different kind. Some poetry is so permeated with sex that words fail one in talking of it – it is poetry of the night. In both the gestation and the birth of poetry, the carnal element plays a part – all the way from the asceticism probably characteristic of early youth ('And flesh pretends it has turned to stone,' as I have read in one of M.'s early poems) to the frenzy of utter abandon.

Love poetry is only a special case of the interfusing of the poetic with the sexual urge, and, strangely enough, it almost always belongs to the ascetic variety. The Lauras and the Beatrices, the beautiful damsels of the troubadours, remote and beyond reach, Blok's 'Unknown Ones' passing before the poet's eyes, were not just the fashionable conventions of the time, but something very much deeper, something springing from the very nature of poetry.

The most common type of love poem is born of longing for a woman, but if passion is fulfilled, the longing quickly ebbs away, as does the poetic impulse. A famous example of this – Pushkin's 'I Remember a Wonderful Moment' and his letter on the same theme – makes it absolutely clear to me. The poem resulted from the poet's amorous impulse, but after it was satisfied he could speak only in the language of his time and circle – that is, in a constrained and conventional manner, or so it seems to me from the letter. In an age when women are no longer inaccessible – as has been true in ours – the poet himself creates an aura of inaccessibility in order to maintain the impulse as long as possible. Neither Akhmatova nor Pasternak wrote poems to those they were living with until the relationship was breaking up. The mention of a woman in a poem does not necessarily mean that it is a love poem, since the impulse to write it may have come from an entirely different source.

Love poetry as such occupied a limited place in M.'s work, and for the most part the interplay between poetry and sex is of the more complicated kind with him – in particular, the kind which results from the fulfilment of *all* the emotions. He was aware of this himself and even spoke to me about it. This is perhaps why he was able to write verse to me as well. After writing out the poem 'Your Eye in Its Heavenly Pod', he said to me, with an air of surprise, that he and Baratynski were the only poets who wrote verse to their wives. In his personal life M. was the complete opposite of Blok. I would even say that he was by nature anti-Blok, since the highest aspect of love was not, for him, service to the 'Beautiful Lady', but something quite different which he summed up in the words 'my you'. His anti-Blok nature was also reflected in his choice of a wife – not a 'beautiful lady', not in fact even a 'lady' at all, but a mere slip of a girl, someone belonging to a lower order of womanhood with whom everything was simple, funny, and frivolous, but with whom he gradually attained to relations of such supreme closeness that he could say: 'I feel free with you.' At our first meeting already we both felt so free with each other that we took it to be a portent of fate. It is true that we both tried to rebel against fate – who has not? But our rebellion was always very

short-lived – a week, or a couple of months – and did not destroy
the bond between us. It always upset me that a large part in the
indestructibility of this bond was played by the element of purely
physical attraction, and I bewailed the fact to M., but for him this
was no reflection on our love, rather the contrary. He laughed at
me, and I didn't realize that, hearing the mysterious call of freedom
and fate at the very outset, he had made of me exactly what he
needed. Being an imbecile, I said nothing, but he talked openly
about it.

At his first meeting with people, especially with women, M. knew
just what their place in his life would be. How odd, for instance,
that immediately after his first encounter with me, he wrote a poem
in which he already spoke of our wedding, though the circumstances of the moment could not have been more inauspicious. In
the verse to Olga Vaksel he introduced the conceit of a 'land
beyond the eyelashes' in which she would be his wife, and showed
a painful awareness of how false his position now was: life had
become 'false to the very root'. He could not stand a double life,
duality, discordancy, or attempts to reconcile the incompatible,
and invariably felt himself 'to blame', as he puts it in one of the
poems to Olga's memory. He always remembered Olga, though
when he heard of her death he quoted the line: 'From indifferent
lips I heard the news of death / and indifferently I listened.' The lips
from which he heard the news were in reality far from indifferent,
and his at first indifferent reception of it I can put down only to the
fact that he was caught unawares, and also to the noise and bustle
in the street around. In the poem 'All Is Twaddle, Sherry-Brandy,
Angel Mine', I believe – though we never discussed it – that I am
'Angel Mary' (a woman picked up casually, just for fun!), while
Olga is 'Helen made off with by the Greeks'. The poem was
written at a party; I was gaily drinking vinegary Caucasian wine
with a crowd of friends while he paced up and down, muttering to
himself and throwing an occasional sidelong glance at us. Though I
never questioned him about it (why did I spare him? It must have
been out of instinct rather than consciously), I believe that his
Petrarch translations were also somehow connected with Olga.
Possibly, however, it could be the other way around – his work on

Petrarch stirred memories of Olga. This second theory is the more likely, since M. never gave me 'faithless' poems ('That's not for you, don't look at it,' he would say), but he often asked me to recopy the Petrarch translations and let me see all the variants. At any event, like 'Aliscans' and 'St Alexis', they should be printed not together with the other translations, but in the main body of his original verse. (The same thing applies, it goes without saying, to 'The Sons of Aymon' which was printed already in the third edition of *Stone*.) This is how M. himself wanted it, but I shall not live to see his work published in Russian, any more than he did.

His poem to Salomé Andronikova was a youthful homage to beauty, the usual calf love of a very young man for an older woman he scarcely knows. Even when they are the same age, a married woman is always 'older' than an unmarried youth. With Marina Tsvetayeva it was something quite different again, stemming from the finest impulse of her noble woman's soul ('In you I hallow a godlike boy of ten" she wrote of him). From everything that Marina has said about herself it is clear that she was incomparably generous and selfless – but at the same time wilful and impulsive to an overriding degree. She was the sort of Russian woman who longs to do something heroic and self-sacrificing, to wash the wounds of Don Quixote – though for some reason it always so happens that when Don Quixote is actually bleeding to death such women are always otherwise occupied and fail to notice anything amiss. No wonder M. sensed that 'to stay with such a mist-wreathed nun means to court disaster'. All his poems to Marina (except the first one in which she 'makes a gift of Moscow' to him) are suffused with presentiments of disaster: 'his bound wrists / and body dreadfully numbed, / the Prince is taken off, / and they light the yellow straw.' My poor Prince! He once recollected that his own blood was tainted 'by the legacy of shepherds, patriarchs, and kings'. In many of his poems at that time he had premonitions of being taken away by force and dying a terrible death, but nowhere did he yet speak of it as coming in the shape of mass deportation in crammed freightcars intended for the transport of animals, not people.

His poems to Akhmatova – there are five, all written in 1917 –

cannot be regarded as love poems. They are concerned with friendship of an exalted kind, and with misfortune, conveying his sense of
doom and his feelings about the common lot. The tone is set in
'Cassandra' and even in the comparatively serene 'The Marvel of
Your Speech' he says that death is more 'winged' than love, and
that 'our lips are flying to it'. I can understand why M. was so upset
when, after he had written verse like this, Akhmatova suddenly
brought their relations down to earth, telling him to keep away for
his own sake, on the grounds, as she put it to others, that she was
'very sorry for the boy'. As a friend Akhmatova was quite beyond
compare, and there was a real greatness about her, but when she
was surrounded by the women she referred to as her 'beauties', she
was affected by their blandishments and put on 'feminine' airs. In
her very last years she began to lament that M. had written too few
love poems – in effect saying it was my fault. It was clear enough to
me that all these 'beauties' of hers valued love poetry for its own
sake, and could not have cared a tinker's cuss about M. himself.
There was not much room left for love in our terrible life, and the
Akhmatova I knew was a fierce and passionate friend who stood
by M. with unshakable loyalty, his ally against the savage world in
which we spent our lives, a stern, unyielding abbess ready to go to
the stake for her faith. The 'feminine airs' were all put on. If they
also came out in her verse (as, of course, they often did), it was
only in the weakest of the poems, and as far as I am concerned, her
'beauties' are quite welcome to this side of her. I will keep the
other side – that of self-renunciation and wrath.

The group of poems to Arbenina are all about the rivalry of the
other 'men of Achaea' and the jealousy natural in such a situation.
Arbenina found her rightful place – she was looking for it already
at the time of her friendship with Gumilev – at the side of Kuzmin:
this meant admirers, porcelain, the height of refinement* . . . Once,
in Moscow, M. pointed out to me a woman mincing across Red
Square: 'Look how fancily she's dressed' . . . Everything she had
on was starched and somehow pleated in the style of the Petersburg
women who could not afford an expensive dressmaker. Olenka
Arbenina was of this type. Olga Vaksel, on the other hand, went

---

* Kuzmin and his entourage were homosexual. For the author's feelings
about porcelain see page 508.

around in a grotesque shuba which she herself called a 'greatcoat' – and blossomed out in it with a beauty I could not help envying.

The beautiful poems to Natasha Shtempel have a place all to themselves in M.'s love lyrics. He always linked love with the thought of death, but in his verse to Natasha there is also a serene and lofty sense of a future life. He asks Natasha to mourn him when he is dead and greet him when he comes back to life. But even in these poems to Natasha there is a slight hint of guilt: as they walked in a park the young greenery seemed to M. to be 'breaking its vows'. But in all honesty it must be said that there were no vows between us: who made vows in our generation, and who would have believed them? M. had a deep feeling of his poetic 'rightness', but in everyday life he was always ready to believe himself guilty. Though Akhmatova had much less sense of it in her poetry, in her private life, particularly when it came to unfaithfulness and divorce, she always insisted on her 'incomparable rightness'. The 'proofs' poured forth in a redoubtable torrent that swept all before it, but I could never understand why she always needed to show that she was so much in the right. She very likely *was* right – at least in the affair with Punin, which I witnessed from beginning to end. But is this really the point? As we all know, love – and physical attraction in particular – is not ruled by right and wrong. There are no criteria to judge what happens between people involved in a love affair or the breakup of one – even when somebody dies because of it. Akhmatova's rightness, like M.'s, was of a higher order, and all her femine arguments about who had betrayed whom were beside the point. They both had the rightness of inwardly free people who stood up for what they had to. This was the essence of their achievement in life. For the rest they were just like everybody else – which in no way detracts from their achievement or casts a shadow on the remarkable lives they led. They paid very dearly for their freedom – he with his death in a camp, and she with many years of ostracism and loneliness impossible to imagine. Though I know very well what it was like: the same thing was meted out to me, not, admittedly, for any inner freedom of my own, but for my 'senseless life' at the side of one who possessed it. It is painful to have to pay for other people's sins, but that is the usual way in this country . . .

As I have mentioned earlier, Akhmatova had a respite at the end of her life. There was no such respite for M., who was saved only by death. Such deliverance by death is a hundred times more exalted than anything we strive for in life. I await it myself as a good friend. Everything has been done, and I am ready.

27 Stages

When I say 'stages', I am struck by the coincidence – the word used in Russian for the transit points (each one called a 'stage') by which prisoners are taken to the camps is just the same as in the expression 'stages of poetic development'. We are bedevilled by camp associations (unlike the Freudian kind, which also never fail to take us back to the same thing, ours stem from real life). M., a poet whose work divides into very distinct stages, died at a 'stage' on his way to the camp. Speaking of stages in the one sense, one cannot forget about the use of the word in the other: they are interconnected. A certain friend of mine from across the ocean once said to me: 'Any poet of ours would be glad to change places with any one of yours.' 'With all the consequences?' I asked. 'Yes,' he replied. 'Poetry's a serious business with you.' In my opinion he underestimated the consequences.

In the years of the 'breathing space', during which this conversation took place, even Akhmatova had begun to forget about the consequences and what they are really like. At this period, astonished how people abroad – in particular Russian émigrés – utterly misunderstand our life, Akhmatova often repeated a phrase which infuriated me: 'They are envious of our suffering.' Such failure to understand has nothing to do with envy – it comes from the impossibility of imagining our experience and also from the deluge of lies by which reality has been twisted out of all recognition. To this one must also add complete unwillingness to think things out. I find it impossible to credit such lazy and indifferent people with the power to feel ordinary sympathy or even a drop of pity, never mind envy. They just didn't give a damn and looked the other way. But the main thing is that there was nothing to envy. There was absolutely nothing at all uplifting about our suffering.

It is pointless to look for some redeeming feature; there was nothing to it except animal fear and pain. I do not envy a dog that has been run over by a truck or a cat thrown from the tenth floor of a building by a hooligan. I do not envy people, like myself, who suspected a traitor, provocateur, or informer in everyone and did not dare utter their thoughts even to themselves for fear of shouting them out in their sleep and giving themselves away to the neighbours on the other side of the thin walls that divide our apartments. There was, I can tell you, nothing to envy. What reason was there to envy Akhmatova, who did not dare utter a word in the privacy of her own room and used to point to the hole in the ceiling from which a little pile of plaster had fallen on the floor? Whether or not there was actually a listening device is beside the point; the fact is that her finger pointed at the ceiling and she was afraid to open her mouth. To talk of envy here is preposterous.

M. had knocked out of me the idea that I had a right to be happy, but I cannot advise anybody to court suffering or to take pride in it. The next step from here is the notion of 'joy-suffering' and 'the pain of wounds unknown'. How you must love yourself to search for nonexistent wounds on your own body or to grieve at no longer being the curly-headed boy your mummy once dandled on her knee! Such self-love is a hangover from the pre-Revolutionary years, an instinctive expectation of special treatment for the so-called elite who felt that a dog's death, or even old age, was beneath them. We were not equal to the sufferings inflicted on us and had no answer to them except our belief that people should not be killed and tortured. This belief was our only asset – at least it made us feel better off than those who thought that killing was all right as long as they themselves were spared . . . Only a very small handful of artists and poets (and perhaps some scholars as well, but I have no personal knowledge of them) fought for their right to go on with their work. Among them was Akhmatova, and her strength was in her tenacity, not in suffering. Nobody was enriched by our sufferings. Far from making people more human, they only stripped them of all human qualities. In a sense the whole country came to consist of 'goners' – from the bureaucrat with his official chauffeur-driven car down to the last dying camp prisoner. The first is terrified of words and ideas, while the second can think only of his ration. I am told that in the camps those who held out best were the so-called *religiozniki* – those imprisoned for their faith – but it was by no means true of them all. It is impossible to endure the unendurable, the inconceivable, the unimaginable. Can a nation ever recover after it has ground into dust and destroyed whole generations, thereby stifling the intellect and condemning itself to collective loss of memory for further generations to come? Platonov, who was remarkable both as a man and as a writer, has a story about a people dying of hunger. By the time they were given food, they had ceased to be a people. Yet hunger is not the worst ordeal – as I have good reason to know.

At one time I used to think the West was suffering from a chronic, and we from an acute, form of the same illness, and I therefore had some hope that we might be the first to make a complete recovery. Now I know that our acute form of the disease has become chronic with deep-seated complications, so there are no grounds whatsoever for an optimistic prognosis. For a brief moment I had a flicker of hope, but hopes are always disappointed. During this brief moment Akhmatova, also taken in, urged me to 'forget about politics'. The things that preoccupy me, however, have nothing to do with politics.

It is easy enough to grasp the fact that we have been deprived of memory, the capacity to think, the gift of words, but I shall try to explain how we have been robbed of *time* as well. If you live in a state of constant terror, always listening for the sound of cars drawing up outside and the doorbell ringing, you begin to have a special awareness of each minute, of each second. Time drags on, acquiring weight and pressing down on the breast like lead. This is not so much a state of mind as a physical sensation which becomes particularly oppressive at night. But while the minutes stretch out, the years fly by at a monstrous pace, leaving nothing in their wake but a gaping emptiness. The twenty years from M.'s death in 1938 to the end of the fifties seem to me in retrospect to have been a shapeless mass devoid of meaning in which time did not flow but simply clotted – later to dissolve into nothingness. Again I ask: What is there to envy here?

Akhmatova first spoke of envy during the war, which for many of us was a breathing space of a sort: for a time we were forgotten or, rather, left in peace. Another thing was that during the war people knew what they were dying for. I hate war, but I see sense in the defence of one's country – whatever it may be like – from an enemy invasion. I even tried to join up as a nurse, but was rejected – they were mistrustful of me. When after the war the camps began to fill up with the country's defenders, people closed their eyes, hoping thus to prolong the breathing space. At the end of the forties Akhmatova and I were talking in the street (I remember it was Pushkin Street, formerly Bolshaya Dmitrovka) when she said: 'To think that the best years of our life were during the war when so many people were being killed, when we were starving and my son was doing forced labour' . . . During this breathing space of the war (imagine what our lives were like if war brought us a little peace of mind!) Akhmatova wrote her poem 'This Cruel Age Has Deflected Me', in which she mentions all the things she was robbed of because her life was forced to flow in a different channel: '. . . How many friends / I never had the chance to meet . . . how many foreign skylines I can dream, / not to be witnessed through my tears.' From the vantage point of this glimpse of a life that never was she looks with envy at the life she actually lived ('But if I could step outside myself / and contemplate the person that I am, / I should know at last what envy is'). She wrote at least three poems on this theme, and in all of them the woman she might have been is presented as a person of little worth – in one case as a 'business-like Parisian'. But what I find more to the point is the way time shrank to nothing in our lives – all the ideas never taken to their conclusion, all the poems never written. As Akhmatova herself admits: 'Their secret chorus stalks me, / close behind. One day, perhaps, / they'll strangle me.' All the work not finished – or produced in a mangled form – can never be offset by the rather vague things on the positive side which Akhmatova says our epoch gave her: a knowledge of 'beginnings and ends', of 'life after the end', and something else of which she is reluctant to speak. She evidently thought that the acceptance of unhappiness and misfortune flowed from a Christian attitude to life. I believe that only a deliberate act of self-sacrifice for the sake of the faith, readiness for everything in defence of your convictions, death with Christ's name on your lips – this and this alone constitutes the thing she hints at. But we were not the stuff martyrs are made of. A pitiful generation who had lost everything handed down to us by our forbears, bloated from hunger and scarcely able to drag our weary feet along, we cursed our blighted lives. We can claim credit only for endurance, not for heroism. I also know what 'life after the end' is like, and I wouldn't wish it on anybody.

What would have become of M. if he had not been forced into a 'different channel'? Being stronger than either me or Akhmatova, he would have accepted any channel, but suffering did not enrich him. It only destroyed him. He was hounded and stifled in every possible way, and the camp was merely the logical culmination of all he had been made to endure through the years. In effect, he was cut off before he had come to maturity – he was a slow developer – and he was still in the process of reaching it. His voice came through not because he was being hounded and smothered, but in spite of it. If it had not been for the 'different channel' he would most likely have become a poet in the philosophical mould. Once he had freed himself for a moment from themes which imposed themselves (and here I would include the 'Kremlin Mountaineer'),* he wrote his 'Octets'. I believe these show us the poet he was not allowed to become. He himself talked to me only once, already during our 'carnival time' in Kiev, about how he envisaged his poetic development. He had no doubt that he would always be remembered as a poet, but he was less sure whether he would survive in people's minds as a person (with our kind of memoirists that is indeed by no means a foregone conclusion!), that is, whether his poetry and life would be seen to merge into one whole. Considering the dynamic force with which he was endowed, he had no need of prison, exile, and the camp as the main element of his biography. It could have been much richer in content than the one in fact granted him – and also perfectly untroubled, at least outwardly. He generally got on well with people – unless they were lackeys, hangers-on, or the sort of writers who, as he put it, produce 'things solved in advance' and 'help the judges to visit punishment on the doomed'. People such as these are found everywhere, but here they have been given the

---

*The poem on Stalin that led to Mandelstam's arrest in May 1934. See *Hope Against Hope*, page 13.

right to dispense the air we breathe and the bread we eat. Unless you are prepared to bow down to the person in charge of your particular field, you'll be a dead duck in no time at all – in other words there is just no avoiding contact with the killers who rule over us. M. was consequently doomed from the start.

He got on very easily with ordinary people and mentioned the fact several times in his poetry: he needed to 'linger still with people and play with them', and he spoke of his constant readiness 'to be drawn tenderly without cause to strangers'. This suggests that as a general rule he was attracted rather than repelled by people – unlike Tsvetayeva, for example, who always came into conflict with those around her, wherever she was. It was simply in her nature. M., on the other hand, was unimaginable without people, and his relations with them were made easier by the fact that he had no urge to preach to anyone, always considering himself inferior to others. Agonizing over religious, ethical, and historiosophical questions, searching for social justice, trying to make sense of the humanist tradition, taking stock of his cultural heritage – such things might, perhaps, have provided a better foundation for his biography than a brutal confrontation with State and society; even in the best of circumstances this takes the form of a specially trained pack hunting a fear-crazed hare.

Tsvetayeva prophesied in verse that M. would perish 'through a woman'. In my view such an end was out of the question. He would have used women as 'firm bridges' and no more. I used to ask Akhmatova why Georgi Ivanov went on about M.'s always being in love. She said this was because he had never known M. as a married man. In fact, however, I doubt whether he was in a constant state of amorous excitement, even as a very young man – it was not like him. His attraction to people, his keen interest in them, whether men or women, his curiosity about anybody he happened to meet – all this could easily strike the vulgarian Ivanov as a permanent state of being in love, rather like the 'permanent wave' which was popular when I was a girl. What Akhmatova has to say is also not completely reliable, given her cult of love. M.'s line 'I secretly envy everyone / and with everyone I am secretly in love' speaks not of a tendency to fall in love all the time or of harbouring envious feelings, but simply of the delight he took in people. He said himself that he was often entranced by women, but that as a young man he had been really in love with only two: Salomé Andronikova and Zelmanova. In both cases, according to his own words, it was the kind of feeling that stirred him to poetry but was otherwise harmless – he was not overwhelmed by the desire to possess them. I am deeply convinced that intellectual crises, the conflict between unbelief and faith, the doubts which he called 'poison' (following Florenski?), were a greater potential threat to M. than any romantic involvements. There could have been tragedy for him in his search for communion with others (his 'we'), in his endeavours to deepen his relations with people, to find his other self (his 'you') and persons who could share his sense of play and joy; the fact that people are everywhere indifferent to these could have led to tragedy, but someone capable, as he was, of forgoing the 'purely phonetic, physiological charms of poetry' would not have come to grief because of a woman. Everybody knows from his letters that he loved me, but he was infinitely exacting (yet indulgent at the same time) towards his 'you', and if I had not agreed to become his shadow, ready to partake in his sense of joy, he would have had no difficulty in giving me up as well. There was something about him that I have never seen in anybody else, and it is time to say that what distinguished him from all the people around us (the Fedins and Fadeyevs of this world) was not irresponsibility, but this infinite sense of joy. It was utterly disinterested, and because it was always with him he never needed anything. Everybody else was always after something – but not he. He just lived his life and revelled in it. This was true until the very last day we spent together. Only prison and the camp were able to crush him, destroying both joy and life itself.

All M.'s inner conflicts, his transition from one phase to another, and his whole evolution are linked with the gradual deepening and maturing of his ideas. The growth of his poetry also went hand in hand with inner changes. These changes were caused by direct contact with reality – which included everything: relations with people, conversations, books, journeys, and events in the world outside. He lived a strenuous, almost hectic life. As I see it, the root of this process of constant ferment and growth was in his habit of judging all external events from the standpoint of the leading idea on which his inner world was based. He lived at such a pitch of intensity that he had almost no time for fear. Of everybody I knew, M. was the least susceptible in this respect – though he could on occasion lose his nerve in a ridiculous way (the incident with the man in the *papakha*, for example) because he could not bear direct contact with killers. You were in fact much less likely to perish through a chance encounter with one of them than as the result of organized mass terror, but M. did not think in statistical terms: he was unable to overcome his purely physical revulsion for killers and other prac-titioners of violence. But we lived in an age when it was almost impossible to avoid direct contact with them and their apologists – a fact which hindered rather than helped the process of M.'s growth. The air we breathed, the air of the twentieth century as a whole, inhibited people's growth and stunted the intellect. What could M. possibly gain from his arguments with Marxists? He debated with them for his amusement, and it was only for this reason that he remained untainted by such encounters. He was saved by his capacity for play; otherwise he would have shared the fate of all those who wore themselves out proving that a robin redbreast could not lay a cuckoo's egg because it would be too big for it.

I have deliberately used the word 'growth' rather than 'develop-ment'. M. got furious when he heard the word 'development' ('a boring development with a beard', as he said in 'Journey to Armenia', thereby incurring the wrath of the authorities). Develop-ment, it seems, means the passage from lower to higher forms and is a concept of the same order as 'progress'. M. knew only too well that any gain is always invariably accompanied by loss, and he told me that when he first heard the word 'progress' as a boy of five he burst into tears and wept bitterly, sensing something unholy in it. The idea of 'quantity becoming quality' also gives me the willies. It must be something very questionable to produce 'leaps' both of our kind and of the Chinese variety. Instead of 'development', so abhorrent to him, M. spoke of 'growth' as the process by which a man, even while changing, maintains the unity of his personality, passing from one stage (or age) to another, but always travelling the same road. The stages of M.'s work as a poet are thus indicative of his inner growth, not of his 'development'. His attitude to any question, even to that of death, changes at the various stages of his life, but at the same time it has an inner unity and consistency throughout. As a boy he could not believe that he was 'real and that death will really come', but at the same time he understood that 'without death I should not know I live'. As a young man, about to reach his early maturity, he realized that the death of an artist is his last creative act. As a fully grown man, already inured to the idea of death, he nevertheless 'fights shy of dying' and prepares for it by saying a prayer for the dying over himself. When he already felt death was at hand and his 'simple song of earthen hurts' would be violently interrupted, he summed up his life in one poem ('And when I die, my service done, / a friend in life to all who lived') and expressed his pity for me in another ('Someone's wife – whose I do not know, / seeks her husband in the streets of Kiev-Viy / and on her waxen cheeks, / not a single teardrop falls'), and then, in his poems to Natasha Shtempel, he makes ready for the future life. Throughout there is a single understanding of life as a temporary gift ('gift' is the word) followed by eternity after the end of one's earthly span.

I am now seventy years, and I know that only empty people fear old age and indulge in the absurd cult of youth. Each age of man has its own unique content, and it fills me with anguish to think how M.'s life was artificially compressed so that he was unable to experience the last stage: the gradual approach to the end. On the other hand it is hard to imagine anything being done gradually by a man who with such 'impatience lived and changed his skin'. M. talked about the future just as rarely as he talked about the past, but in 1937–8 when it became quite clear that our days were numbered (not only his, but mine as well – I survived only by a miracle or an oversight, which was the same thing), M. suddenly began to speak of old age. Every time I heard him talk in this vein I got into a cold sweat. After his death I regretted giving way to such unconcealed fear and trembling. I always felt it was all my fault and that he would have survived if I had shown more faith in the possibility of survival. Even now I have not quite overcome this feeling, but the question is: Was it necessary for him to go on living? In the long run, after all, he too would have succumbed to fear, catching it from me and all the others around him until he turned into a shadow like everybody else. For someone like him death was the only salvation: he was incapable of becoming the sort of trembling creature who fears not God but his fellow men. I believe that his talk about his future poetry (this was what he mentioned in connection with the subject of old age) helped him to ward off fear and the decline of his powers. Stubbornly, despite everything, he thought only of life, not of the violent end that awaited him. If it was so fated, he would die like that, but he had no desire to prepare for such an end beforehand.

He used to say in those days that his growth as a poet had been very slow and that he was only gradually feeling his way towards freedom. It was this that led him to believe he would still be writing in his old age – only then would he achieve complete freedom. At this stage, he said, he would never allow his verse to control him (he also wrote me a letter about this – it was a frequent theme towards the end) and would not allow any topics to impose themselves on him. This was around the time when his lines on the death penalty had burst from him; these, as he told me, had to some extent been forced on him by outside circumstances, since they were prompted by the decree abolishing the death penalty except for high treason and something else of the same kind. We had read this decree standing on a platform at Savelovo waiting for our train. M.'s comment was: How many people they must be shooting if they publish a decree like this . . . His poem about the death penalty was dictated by the terrible times and inhuman conditions we lived in. In this sense the subject had 'forced' itself on him. On the other hand, as he himself said: 'It concerns people, and we cannot isolate ourselves from people'. This poem was heard by only two persons: Natasha Shtempel and myself.

He thought that in his old age he would breathe a different air – an air which wasn't poisoned, in which 'enforced' themes would be a thing of the past. Furthermore, he hoped to bring the flow of his verse under control and learn to direct it at will. Seeing my petrified look when he began to talk about the future, M. would laugh and try to raise my spirits: 'Don't race ahead. What happens will happen. We're still alive – don't lose heart. Breathe while you still have air to breathe. You have never been inside yet. There really is no air in a prison cell. But you still have some. You must be grateful for what you have.' Here I have lumped together things he said to me at various times, on different occasions – it was never in the form of a speech or a sermon.

During the final stage, after Voronezh, he wrote about ten poems. They were confiscated during the last search. I was in such a state that I was unable to memorize them, or recall them subsequently. This means that they are lost forever – for which I am to blame. I am sorry about them, and even more about all the poems he did not write because he no longer had air to breathe.

28   Stages in My Life

I am even now constantly tormented by the thought of those years of life we were not allowed to live. I am always wondering what they would have been like if we had not been cheated of them. They would not have been a tidy, straightforward continuation of our previous years, if only because there was never anything mechanical about our life. It reflected the same stages which can be seen so clearly in M.'s poetry and in his own growth. We were just on the verge of a new stage when he was taken away, so we never knew what it held in store for us. On the very night it happened, he tried to explain to me that something was becoming clearer to him, that he could see something he had not understood before: 'You know, I think I've understood something – perhaps it's nonsense, but you and I . . .', he began. The conversation was never finished, because I fell asleep and had a terrible nightmare. I began to scream and woke up, so we were not asleep when the knock on the door came. I was so horror-struck that we did not even say good-bye properly. I moved around the room and got his things together, but when her husband is taken away, a woman turns to stone, into an automaton, into I don't know what; the frozen expression I must have had during those last minutes I have seen only on the faces of other women whose husbands had been arrested. This was the end of everything, and I never learned how M. saw the new stage in our life that was about to begin, as we paused to look ahead for that one brief moment.

When you live day in, day out, with someone, just taking it for granted, you often fail to notice any change in your relations, but there was something so distinctive about M. that even this everyday familiarity could not obscure the changes in him as he grew and matured. Despite our helter-skelter existence I saw and marvelled at them.

Although we were together only for such a short while, the relations between us changed at least three times – that is, we went through at least three stages. Perhaps this is why we did not tire of each other. Someone – it may have been I – once compared M. with the phoenix which burns in the flames only to come back to life the next morning and start singing again. He was a phoenix in the fullest sense: after undergoing a crisis, he would come to life once more and speak with a voice that had gained new strength. The bond between us was renewed and strengthened at the same time – though always changing its nature somewhat in the process. According to Akhmatova, the unmarried M. was a very different person from what he became with me. I knew the unmarried M. only when he was already slightly tied to me during the 'carnival' in Kiev. He combined the neurasthenia of youth with unbridled high spirits. I found it funny that he never wrote at a table like everybody else, but always put his paper on a chair and squatted in front of it on his haunches. He loved coffee-houses and was extraordinarily nimble and restless. We went out on the Dnieper in a boat which he rowed effortlessly, with great skill, but asking all the time: 'Where is the Old Man?' This was the name of a whirlpool in which swimmers were often drowned.

One felt that M., like any other immature young man, would be capable of all kinds of mischief, but the peculiar thing about him was that this quality became more, rather than less, evident as the years went by: 'Other dreams and other eyries, but always a brigand one must be' . . . He had an inner spirit of devilment about him which was intellectual in nature, but it affected the whole of his behaviour, coming out in his every word and deed. I do not count those few carnival months as the beginning of our life together. They were simply the prelude to our marriage – if it can be called a marriage – which we dated from 1 May 1919. The curfew had by then been abolished, and a whole crowd of us went to Vladimir

Hill* ('your hill', as it was later referred to) to celebrate. We had gathered the previous day as we left the Merchants' Garden, where the 'herd' I belonged to had been working on an exhibition of folk art; for some reason we camped out there at nights, making fires and baking potatoes in the embers. M. remembered Vladimir Hill because it was here that he explained to me how our meeting was no mere chance. I still had no inkling of this and laughed out loud at his words. Our journey to another country, to Georgia, brought about no change in our relations – or rather, perhaps I failed to see it: a new note could be heard in his verse, and this was always significant. I can make out this new voice in the poem 'I Washed at Night in the Courtyard'.

In Moscow, in our room on Tverskoi Boulevard, I found myself living with the withdrawn and austere person he became during the first half of the twenties, when he was trying to find his place in the world. At that time he treated me like a piece of booty he had seized and brought back by force to his lair. All his efforts were directed to isolating me from other people, making me his own, breaking me in and adapting me to himself. These were the years in which he stubbornly trained me not to read but to *listen* to poetry, learning to appreciate it by ear. He never let me hold a book in my hand but went through it with me, pointing out the successes and failures in the poets writing at the beginning of the century. I felt like a horse in the hands of a trainer, which indeed was what it was like, though he hardly thought of himself in such a role. He was lucky in that I was a willing learner and very easy to manage – I meekly nibbled the hay out of his hand. The only thing I jibbed at was his refusal to see people; this he imposed on me too by simply not letting me out of the house. At that time he was not yet admitting me to his own inner world either, so I could only guess what was going on in his head. Things became a little easier on the Yakimanka when we lived in such isolation that he no longer worried about my making off while he was out – to a tavern or an airfield or to go visiting a girl friend for a gossip.

The second period began after our crisis in Leningrad when he threw over Olga Vaksel and took me away to Tsarskoye Selo. Rozanov has written somewhere that unfaithfulness mends a

* In Kiev.

broken family, and this was certainly true in our case – though we scarcely constituted a family and our tie was of a different kind. This makes me sad when I think of it, as does another peculiar feature of our life together: with most couples the process of adaptation is mutual, but M. had no desire to adapt to anything, and he needed me rather than any other woman because, having already spent so much effort on adapting me to himself, he did not want to start all over again with someone else, without even the certainty that it would work out. I told him this to his face in Tsarskoye. He was very angry, but I think it played a large part in his attachment to me from then on.

The noteworthy thing about this second period was that he ceased to treat me as a prize he had carried off, a Europa abducted by Zeus, a little girl who had to be watched all the time. We now became a real couple. Perhaps this was because we talked about our relationship for the first time and somehow realized what it was all about. From then on, our dialogue never ceased and I always knew what was in his mind. He also became less jealous than before – but still more than enough for a dozen women to put up with. At the same time I found he was now more attentive than before. Previously he had been a 'nursemaid' to me, but henceforth, evidently because of the fright I had given him, he behaved much more like a protector and friend than as an overseer and trainer. He now appeared willing to do anything just to keep me – even to work like a slave so that I could go away on my own for a while, something he had never agreed to before. (What was the point of having a wife and living alone? He had never actually said this, but it was all too obvious what he felt.) From Tsarskoye Selo we went to stay for a while in Luga and after that he sent me down to Yalta; the majority of his letters to me date from this time. To live in a boarding-house cost 150 roubles for one and 250 roubles for two. To make out he had to translate about eight pages a day (the rate was thirty roubles per 'printer's sheet' – equivalent to sixteen pages). These were Grub Street rates, and as we had discovered from Narbut, they played a negligible part in the calculation of a book's cost. The stuff M. translated was absolute rubbish – not to mention that any enforced translation is poison to a poet. I was naturally upset, and in every letter I begged him to let me go to my parents' home in

Kiev. He was entirely occupied by this hack work and he had no time to breathe. Yet even so he had to fight tooth and nail to get the work in the first place. In his letters, which give the best picture of the situation, he lied brazenly about how well everything was going, with money simply pouring in from all sides. He was just trying to set my mind at rest and keep me in Yalta. Already then translation work was being used as a most remarkably efficient weapon in the destruction of literature. Hack translation, whether of prose or of poetry, stifles original thought and blunts one's feeling for language. After all the drudgery of translation how can anybody have enough strength left to speak, or even think his own thoughts? I cannot understand how M. ever managed to write letters. They came almost every day – as well as whole sheaves of telegrams in which he implored me to go on living in Yalta (so good for tuberculosis!), to put on weight, obey doctors' orders, and wait for him to arrive – which he eventually did.

In the late spring we left together for Kiev (where we revisited Vladimir Hill) and then returned to Tsarskoye Selo, staying there for the next two years. In the winter of 1927–8 M. wrote his *Egyptian Stamp*. I learned how to do various editing jobs on his behalf for ZIF,* and this gave him some respite. Leningrad no longer supplied us with work. There has never been any stability at all about life here. As in the Krylov fable,† people are eternally being shuffled around and things reorganized. Later on, working in various higher educational establishments, I saw how year after year we had to reach a provisional curriculum on the promise that a permanent one was about to be introduced – but this too would last only a year before being changed. It was exactly the same with publishing houses: they were constantly being reorganized, and writers were forced to go from one place to another in search of free-lance literary earnings. Then as now there was a permanent paper shortage and books were always being scrapped for this reason (though these days it is hardly the main problem – things you really might want to read only rarely get printed in any case).

Translations were a major, if only technical, cause of M.'s

* The 'Land and Factory' Publishing House, headed by Narbut.
† 'The Quartet' (1811) – whose members kept changing places. The fable was a satire on a reshuffling in the Council of State in 1810.

'silence'. People started to write that he had dropped poetry for translation even before anything of the kind had happened – but later they got their way and really were able to muzzle him. It was only after the Uhlenspiegel affair that M. gave up translating for good (i.e., 'literature' as opposed to poetry) and liberated himself from his bondage.

The third and final stage in our relations began with his journey to Armenia and return to writing verse. By now he had come out of the hypnotic trance in which the whole country was sunk, and had ceased to regard the new order as the beginning of the millennium. At the same time he began to write verse again – this happened in Tiflis on the way back from Armenia. At last, after many years, he had once more become conscious of the past and renewed his links with it. A 'drying crust of a loaf long since taken out' is so inhibited by its dependence on the past that it usually feels quite unentitled to claim any connection with 'modernity' (wasn't it Mayakovski, the poor devil, who cast doubters 'overboard from the steamship of modernity'?*). Once liberated from this constraint, M. began to live in the present, certain it belonged to him rather than to those who brandished their title deed to it and then proceeded to foretell the future with such aplomb. From the beginning of the thirties M. paid no more attention to these prophets: he had recovered complete inner freedom.

Just before we set off for the Caucasus a curious incident took place. Feeling in poor shape, M. went to the polyclinic for a check-up, but the doctors immediately passed him on to a psychiatrist. When I returned from Kiev (where I had gone for my father's funeral), M. asked me to go and have a word with the psychiatrist, who proved to be a very crude and cocksure type. His diagnosis was that M. had the illusion of being a poet and of writing verse, though in fact he was only a minor employee who did not even hold a post of any responsibility and harboured all kinds of grudges, speaking badly, for instance, about the writers' organizations. This was a well-known psychosis: persecution mania based on an exaggerated idea of one's own importance. The clinics were full of people who imagined they were Napoleon (the doctor did not dare

---

* In *A Slap in the Face of Public Taste* (1911), the Futurist manifesto signed by Mayakovski, Khlebnikov, and others.

say 'members of the Politburo'). M.'s case, he went on, was completely uninteresting, since his delusion took a dull and tedious form. Some cases were more interesting than others, and the general level of a person's development was reflected in the quality of his delusion. M.'s delusion was, moreover, a very deep one: it was impossible to convince him that he was not a poet. The psychiatrist advised me not to succumb myself to this psychosis (I had tried to explain that M. had some grounds for speaking of his poetry) and in the future to cut short all my husband's talk about writing verse. I went home in a rage – what an idiot, just like an official in the police or any other institution! But quite un-expectedly M. disagreed and said the doctor was not all that stupid. 'I wrote you, didn't I, that I shouldn't make such a great point of being the poet Mandelstam? I noticed the swine when the other doctors took me to task and was even indignant about it. This is always happening: why do I think I'm better than others?' This is not the sort of conclusion I would have drawn from his visit to the doctor. I believe the reason he was so light-hearted about it was because his *Fourth Prose* was already written.

In this third period M. made me a complete partner in his life. He had regained his sense of 'we' – and henceforth it included me. I believe that the bond between us was now unbreakable. Such a bond between two people is not a mirage, as Akhmatova thought. I recently learned that there is even a prayer to be said by two people together – this being the basic unit of human existence. I am quite prepared to admit that if he had survived to an old age of affluence and ease M. might well have allowed himself to be lured away from his wife, when she grew old, but this does not alter the truth of what I am saying. The bond between us existed and always will, and nothing can break it – not even the fact that he was taken away before I had a chance to learn what shape our relations would have assumed in the fourth stage, which we were just about to enter. I believe, in fact, that nothing would have changed between us and that the new period would have been different only in respect to his poetry.

In the third and last period of our life together we were closer than ever before. Talking with each other, we did not even worry about hurting each other by what we said, unable to believe that in a union as close as ours 'there is a hidden line you may not over-step'.* Possibly such a line exists when two people living together look in different directions, as to some extent everybody does, but with us the degree of divergence in our angles of vision was the smallest possible.

This, then, was how we lived. He used to tease me – I was no 'Beautiful Lady'† – and felt tremendously free and joyous to the very last day. As he grew, and even as he began to get old, he became younger. He had always looked older than his years, but as time went by, the more light-hearted, cheerful, and outgoing he became. In the thirties he rid himself completely of his earlier ten-dency to be withdrawn and reserved, and it never returned. It then began to seem to me that I was the older of the two, as he immersed himself in his work, becoming younger as he advanced in years (though, in fact, how can one talk of his beginning to grow old when he was not even allowed to reach his forty-eighth year?), while I turned to stone and aged from fear. I feel much younger now than I did in all those accursed years. It is impossible to forget them, despite the fact that even Akhmatova urged me to. How can I forget when our life together was cut short literally in mid-sentence? The words never said are like a lump in my throat, and the thought of them torments me. How can anybody be envious of our suffering? It was the suffering of the mute condemned to a meaningless death. It was nothing but dumbness and death and words cut short before they could be spoken. If it were not for my faith in a future meeting I should never have been able to live through all these many years of loneliness. I laugh at myself and do not dare believe, but my faith never leaves me. We shall meet, and there is no parting. Thus it was promised, and this is my faith.

* Line from an Akhmatova poem.
† Allusion to Alexander Blok's half-mystical vision of a feminine ideal in 'Verses about the Beautiful Lady' (1904).

29 Digression

I: 'PERNICIOUS FREEDOM'

Freedom of choice presupposes two paths, one leading to some distant beacon that makes existence meaningful, and the other into the 'night and murk of nonbeing'. Pushkin called the second path 'the madness of pernicious freedom'. After Dostoyevski we use the word 'licence'* to describe a person's choice of the second path. Pushkin's 'pernicious freedom' is little more than youthful frivolity, the sowing of wild oats wistfully recalled in mature years. Dostoyevski, on the other hand, shows us those extremes of licence that lead to death and decay. The essence is the same, much as we may all have some sneaking sympathy for the frivolity and folly of youth. 'Pernicious freedom' could not destroy Pushkin simply because he was Pushkin To a certain extent it even stood him in good stead, giving rise to his powerful verses of repentance (with Pushkin there is no doubt at all that his verse always fully mirrored his actual state of mind – he never posed, or invented non-existent situations). This was the way of a great poet: as he goes through life his experiences serve to temper him, deepening the emotions and intellect. He shares the sins of the world but is capable of remorse. Self-justification or indulgence for his own failings is out of the question for him. A sense of guilt is man's greatest asset. Sin is always concrete, and repentance commands unique and powerful words, an unequivocal language of its own. It may be the language of a specific moment of time, but it lasts forever.

The one thing a poet – or indeed any man – must not do is give up his freedom, become like everybody else, merge with his

---

*This key concept in Dostoyevski (*svoevolie*), sometimes misleadingly translated into English as 'self-will', is the abuse of freedom implied by absolute surrender to one's own desires. It is exemplified in such characters as Svidrigaïlov in *Crime and Punishment* and Stavrogin and Kirillov in *The Possessed*. In Dostoyevski's view it logically led to suicide as the culminating gesture of a man determined to demonstrate his freedom from all restraint.

surroundings, and speak in the current language of the day. He then becomes a corrupter, though his main victim is himself, since once he begins to speak in the language of the moment, a poet loses his power 'to burn the hearts of people with his words'.* The language and opinions of current fashion last no more than a day and appeal only to those who actively create them; these are always the real corrupters, and they do not hesitate to use poets in their work of seducing the mob (I say 'mob', not 'people', advisedly). But the mob has a short memory – it howls approval and then quickly forgets. That is the end of it, and the poet is left to pay the price – which, as always for a poet, is very high. The poet always pays a very high price for everything. 'Dire retribution awaits' him for every misdeed, for every ill-considered act, for every imprudence – and this, it seems to me, is his vindication. I once read somewhere how an American journalist asked his father, a learned rabbi: 'What is a Jew?' His father replied: 'Just a human being,' but then he thought a moment and added, 'only perhaps a little more of a human being than other people.' The same thing, I believe, is true of poets: hence their sense of guilt, the need for repentance, the payment of 'dire retribution'. Isn't this the reason that 'in our most Christian world the poets are the Jews'?†

The 'licence' explored by Dostoyevski not only destroys its adepts, but also spreads corruption all around, scorches the very earth, and lays everything waste. We have all read Dostoyevski and know the anguish with which he shows up licence for what it is, trying to warn people of its consequences. We who have lived through the great era of licence are well aware that his words fell on deaf ears. It is a feature of those who choose the path of licence that they are completely deaf and hear nothing. As they corrupt and lead others astray, neither they nor their victims heed anyone who tries to warn them. Dostoyevski knew this very well. His bitterest recognition of the fact comes out not in any direct statement, but in something he puts into the mouth of one of his characters, Hippolite, the puny youth with a pimply face.‡ Hip-

* From Pushkin's poem 'The Prophet'.
† Quoted from Marina Tsvetayeva.
‡ In *The Idiot*.

polite dreams of opening his window and talking to the people for twenty minutes. There is, of course, nothing he can tell the people, and in the same way, Dostoyevski achieved nothing but a tragic and passionate 'twenty minutes' by an open window. Hippolite sums up the result on behalf of Dostoyevski: the people stood and listened and then went home as though nothing had happened. Dostoyevski, I believe, deliberately chose this image of the 'open window' to describe his attempts to communicate with the people. It was quite within his power to fling his own window wide open, but he was not able to get others to open theirs and listen to his words. He was well aware of it. The people, just like any individual, is a monad, but a monad without a 'window'* – such is Dostoyevski's pessimistic conclusion. It has no ears and does not listen.

Dostoyevski is right, of course. To continue with the image of the 'open window', I too have stood among the crowd and listened – to Dostoyevski himself, of course, not to Hippolite. I took to heart what he said about licence leading to no good, and how absolutely wrong it is to tell oneself that 'all is permitted'.† However, since I had no intention of murdering an old woman,‡ I decided none of this applied to me and, far from condemning my own petty form of licence, I went right on cultivating it. True, like many others of my generation, I substituted the inconsequential 'this is what I want' for the more far-reaching 'all is permitted', but in fact it amounts to the same thing. The only restraining influence on me came not from Dostoyevski, but from M. It was he who stopped me from drifting with the current and aping the latest fashion of our cruel and tawdry age. In my case it affected only my private, not my public, life. Akhmatova was also not free in private life of licence, notwithstanding her perfect awareness of the fact that 'the convict of Omsk / had understood it all and shown it up for what it was.'§ We reread Dostoyevski together in Tash-

---

* Allusion to the philosophy of Leibnitz.

† Ivan's phrase in the *The Brothers Karamazov*.

‡ Raskolnikov murders an old woman pawnbroker in *Crime and Punishment*.

§ From Akhmatova's poem 'Prehistory' (1945), in which she evokes the Russia of Dostoyevski ('the convict of Omsk').

kent and were struck both by his prophetic insights and by his incredible lapses as a publicist: his hatred of Catholicism, his cheap nationalism, and his 'moujik Marei'.* 'Both of them are heresiarchs,' Akhmatova used to say about Dostoyevski and Tolstoi. She compared the two greatest Russian writers to twin towers of the same building. Both of them sought salvation from imminent catastrophe, the nature of which was understood by Dostoyevski, though not by Tolstoi. In their actual proposals for salvation both of them exhibited licence in the highest degree. In fact, however, not even the best of proposals would have been able to halt a process of decomposition already so far advanced.

Dostoyevski the artist is incomparably more profound than Dostoyevski the publicist. In the preparatory notes for his novels one sees the publicist's mind at work. While he was thinking about *The Possessed*, as is evident from his notebooks, he was planning to explain Stavrogin's behaviour by reference to his social background (how well we know this approach!) – a wealthy member of the upper classes, no longer having any roots among his own people, loses his religious faith. In this preliminary outline Stavrogin is thus a mere illustration to Dostoyevski's idea that loss of the 'national' religion leads to loss of national identity as well. The only thing remaining of this original plan in the text of the novel is a passing reference to the conversations Stavrogin had abroad with Kirillov and Shatov, and he is actually made into the centre of the whole satanic bacchanalia, the calm 'eye' of the storm, from which everything proceeds. Shatov, on the other hand, becomes one of the 'possessed'. Sergei Bulgakov has noted that there is something of Dostoyevski himself in Shatov, and I believe this is true: the devils by which the characters of the novel are possessed stand for the very temptations with which Dostoyevski constantly wrestled in his own torment of soul. He was possessed by them all, as was the nation as a whole, and each section of it.

The greatest danger to Dostoyevski was the 'devil' represented by Shatov, that is, the idea of healing the 'split' between people and

---

*From *Diary of a Writer*, February 1876. A somewhat sentimental description of a boyhood encounter with one of his father's serfs that, recollected in his days as a convict in Siberia, convinced Dostoyevski of the innate goodness of the ordinary Russian people.

intelligentsia, and the appeal for a return to the 'national' religion. Sergei Trubetskoi, a thinker of the highest integrity who could not himself have been less troubled by devils, wonders how this firm belief in a 'split' arose in the first place, pointing out that any nation always throws up an intelligentsia separate from itself: this is a normal division of functions in a complex organism. The intelligentsia is flesh of the flesh of the nation, exhibiting all its essential features, and it is not a case of the intelligentsia 'passing on' its devils to the people, since the people, exposed to exactly the same temptations and suffering from the same sickness, is already possessed by them.

To 'educate' the moujik Marei, as proposed by the Westernizers, or to learn from him, as Dostoyevski urged, was equally mad. It is impossible to say what we could learn from Marei, even though he is sometimes amazingly kind and – even more frequently – downright affectionate. As long as Marei does not lose control of himself he is distinguished by an excruciating capacity for endurance (it sometimes seems to me that in our confusion we have identified faith with patience and long-suffering – and what people has suffered more for so long?). After the war I was horrified at the speech – obligatory reading for all the citizens of our happy country – in which the notorious patience of the Russian people was duly acclaimed.* I thought I detected a note of satanic mockery in these words. The speaker, invested with a power never known before and declared to be a genius, was skilled in the art of exploiting this accursed patience for his own purposes. That same day I received a slight consolation as I stood in line to draw my salary from the university cashier. We politely invited the few 'Doctors of Science' among us to go to the head of the queue, as they were entitled to under a special regulation (many years previously we had gone to draw our rations in a store with a notice saying: 'Members of the People's Will† served first' – the highest token of esteem and recognition in our country). The

* 'I propose a toast to the health of the Russian people not only because it is the leading people, but also because it possesses a clear mind, a staunch character, and patience' – Stalin, at a reception in honour of Red Army Commanders in the Kremlin, May 1945.

† Veterans of the old populist revolutionary organization of the 1880s.

Doctors of Science graciously declined our offer and insisted on waiting their turn in proper democratic fashion. Just as graciously we continued to urge them forward, and this display of chivalry would have gone on indefinitely if the whole lot of us had not suddenly been swept out of the way by a mob of cleaning women and workmen employed by the university. They descended on us with their mops, buckets, hatchets, and other items of equipment and unceremoniously pushed us all aside from the cashier's window. 'What are they pushing for?' we wailed indignantly, only to hear voices shout back at us from the brazen mob: 'You're the patient ones – you can wait. We have no time!' This crowd of working folk went on swearing and cursing about 'patience' – they were sick to death of it and had not taken kindly to being praised for it. They too had sensed the mockery behind this part of the speech. They were tired of getting a miserable pittance for their work and then being expected to thank the authorities for all the care lavished on them. Their patience was exhausted, but I was the only one to rejoice. Headed by the Doctors of Science, the whole patient crowd of us went to the Dean to demand (such things we could even *demand*) that in future the workmen should be paid at a different counter, since they refused to wait their turn patiently and elbowed their way to the head of the queue, ignoring the rules of precedence and the corporate rights of the professors and lecturers. Because 'egalitarianism' was abominated, this request of ours was granted. In a workers' state one is not allowed to lose patience. It is a patience, moreover, born not of religious faith but of the traditional treatment of the ordinary people as a race apart.

A Russian empress once wrote to her German mother that in the fantastic country where fate had willed her to sit on the throne, the authorities treated their people as conquerors treat the vanquished. Which side – rulers or ruled – is more prone to licence here? I should like to know. All one can learn from the moujik Marei is not faith, but patience – the patience with which he responds to every imaginable kind of ill-treatment until the moment when, at the end of his tether, he goes on the rampage. But his rampages never last, and when he drops writhing to the ground it is easy enough to tie him up again.

If one is to talk of a split or a gulf, it is not so much between the ordinary people and the intelligentsia as between ordinary people and the ruling elite. Those at the top never hear what is being said at the bottom, even informers being geared to receive and pass on signals only of a certain kind, namely, disrespectful remarks about the powers-that-be. 'Top' and 'bottom' – these are the two sundered parts of what should be a single whole. It is only the rulers who constitute an elite in an ivory tower – something which came about not just in this century but has always existed here. Between the two, as an intermediate link, we have the *oprichnina** recruited from all sections of the population.

'Back-to-the-people' movements have always been sterile. The appeal to national peculiarities was inevitably taken up by the *oprichniks* and the exponents of licence, like any other cheap idea leading to the creation of barriers between people and an ever deeper sense of estrangement. Nationalism makes a ready appeal, and the masses are easily captivated by it. We have experienced total separation from the outside world, and we know very well where it leads; what is more, we shall probably have to go through it again in the future. In a closed world there is always hatred for any new idea, and the level of education falls catastrophically. Separation from the outside means a heyday for semiliteracy, fear, and 'patience'. It never led to any good, as one can see from the example of the Pharisees: they also fought for national independence and sovereignty. In their case there was a certain excuse, since the country was under Roman domination, but even so they proved to be utterly bankrupt. Seeking salvation in nationalism, Dostoyevski must have been aware of the role of the Pharisees in ancient Judea, but it had no effect on his own attitudes. His hatred for Catholicism was too overwhelming, and he looked with cold eyes at the 'sacred stones' of western Europe, only bored by them. He sought to separate Russia from the rest of Christendom, shielding her from temptation behind a high wall. Were we to expect salvation from the sister of Captain Lebiadkin?†

Nationalism, like the ideas of Leo Tolstoi, is an attempt to stop the course of history. Everything leading to separation is the result

---

*Ivan the Terrible's elite corps, similar in concept to the Ottoman Janissaries.

† Character in *The Possessed*.

of licence: it smashes what is whole, breaks and pulverizes it into tiny fragments that can never be joined together again. The truth of this has become completely apparent in our century. We have been witness to the process of distintegration. What has it brought us, apart from material and spiritual impoverishment? Even Dostoyevski, the great seer, the highest point of the nineteenth century, could not ward off the devils that prompted him to abandon the ecumenical idea in favour of national exclusiveness. Our experience has shown that the moujik Marei – unless he became an *apparatchik* – readily understands the intellectual who has been exiled to his village. I have had occasion to drink tea or share a bottle of vodka with him while we talked in whispers for fear of being overheard by informers. I also got on well enough with the ordinary working women whose husbands had been sent away along the same road as M. – they are now lying together in the same burial pit with identical tags on their legs. Nobody shied away from me because I was Jewish. Anti-Semitism is propagated from above and brews in the caldron known as the *apparat*. Between these ordinary people and myself there was not the slightest misunderstanding or breach. If there ever had been anything to separate us, we were now joined together by a common fate and mortal terror of the authorities: all the *oprichniks*, *apparatchiks*, bosses, informers, toadies, and various other kinds of hangers-on. My friend Polia, who lives in Tarusa,* has never had anyone close to her arrested, but she once pointed out to me with disgust a woman nicknamed 'Fatty' whose legs were so thick and swollen that she could scarcely move around. 'Fatty' had played an active part during collectivization and the liquidation of the kulaks, and as a girl squealed with joy at the sight of members of the old ruling classes being thrown from bridges into the water. 'Fatty's' daughter has been given a job as a shop assistant – by way of rewarding the mother for her past exploits. The daughter brings home whatever she fancies from the shop to give to her mother, who sits watching television recalling her days of glory. 'Fatty' receives no pension because she was always too busy with 'social activities' to work. Not daring to tell her neighbours about her past, she pretends to be just a poor *kolkhoz* member brought

* Small town south of Moscow. See Vigdorova, Appendix A.

to live in town by this daughter who has done so well for herself. The daughter is universally admired because she knows how to get hold of goods in short supply. 'Fatty's' grandchildren despise her.

It was Chaadayev's view that Russia exists only for the purpose of teaching the world a lesson. I believe this lesson has already been given to the world by 'Fatty' and her like. Her way is a profoundly national and distinctive one. The unfortunate thing is that people turn a blind eye to the lessons of history and are quite capable of travelling the same path all over again, if they so wish. Moujik Marei is no longer with us. Only the womenfolk are left in the villages, with a good sprinkling of 'Fatties' among them.

II: FREEDOM AND LICENCE

If it were not for a chance conversation with Akhmatova which put everything in a new perspective for me, I should not know what to set against licence. I had brought her a volume of Éluard from Liuba Ehrenburg. Liuba hoped that Akhmatova might be enticed into translating him. The Ehrenburgs were friends with Éluard, and his widow was always lamenting the fact that he had not been translated into Russian – and where else should he be translated if not in this country? Akhmatova leafed through it, pausing to read here and there, and then put it aside with a look of irritation: 'This is not freedom, but licence.' For me this contrasting use of freedom and licence was something new – I did not know then that it had been a commonplace in the years before the Revolution. Later I found it in the works of Sergei Bulgakov and Berdiayev. (We have been cut off not only from the outside, but also from our own past, from books, ideas, and everything else; as a result, when things eased a little, we all started discovering America, marvelling at the simplest things which had long been known to everybody in the rest of the world. At the moment we see people 'discovering' the elementary truths of Christianity, which had been forgotten after being buried away for half a century.)

Gradually it dawned on me that man has a choice between the way of freedom and the way of licence. The language of concepts is poor, and we use the word 'freedom' in two senses – in the full meaning and as in the expression 'freedom of choice'. There is an obvious difference between these two usages. Speaking of 'freedom of choice' we mean an act of the will. Man really is the master of his fate, as are individual nations and humanity as a whole: it too has freedom of choice. The concept of 'freedom' in the full sense is something quite different again, since it refers to values. A man chooses the way of freedom or, better, finds freedom, if he succeeds in overcoming the baser promptings of his own ego and of the times in which he lives. Having conquered them, he receives freedom from himself and his epoch in the sense in which in England one can receive the 'freedom of the city' and cease to pay taxes. This by no means brings freedom from sin, though such a feeling is no doubt familiar to anyone who has wholeheartedly partaken of the Eucharist, when 'all commune, rejoice, and sing'. For the religious-minded, freedom of the spirit means rejoicing and grace. Suffering in a state of grace is very different from the grim and terrible kind we endure – though at some levels this is still worthier than abject indifference (of the type which says: everything that exists is rational and justified by the needs of the times – as long as it does not impinge on my own precious self). Thanks to my life with M., I gradually came to feel that I would rather be run over by a truck than kill people at the wheel of a car.

As I have said, people who find freedom are not thereby cleansed of sin. Each one of us is sinful and shares in the sins of the world. But the labour of the poet is a gift of freedom, bringing illumination, even if not deliverance from sin – and, indeed, the man who has not lost his sense of his own sinfulness must count himself fortunate. (Perhaps this awareness of sin even fosters the freedom without which work of real value is impossible – at least in the realm of the intellect and in the arts.) The artist, being human, or even a little more human than other people, is human in his sins as well. There are, however, sins greater than the ordinary ones common to everyone, and it is these which can have a calamitous effect on an artist's gift and reduce it to nothing. The dangerous things for an artist are pride, self-promotion, leading people astray, complicity in the crimes of the age: all these, like drugs, are very hard to abjure. All of us, not only artists, are subject to such temptations, and I am tormented by the knowledge of where I have myself overstepped – and continue to overstep – the boundary line. The way of freedom is hard, particularly in times like ours, but if everybody had always chosen the other path, the path of licence, mankind would long ago have ceased to exist. That it still exists is due to the fact that the creative urge has remained stronger than the destructive one. Whether this will be so in the future is not for me to say. It is a dreadful thought that mankind may well have reached the crossroads at which it has to choose between Mangodhood – that is, the way of Kirillov, which leads to suicide – or the way of freedom and a return to the 'torch bequeathed by our forbears.'

Is it right to talk of only two tendencies, the creative and the destructive? Perhaps there is a third, a passive or conservative one, indifferent to good and evil, always hostile to anything new, whether it be to the Cross (which is eternally new) or the voice of a poet. Representatives of this trend stand guard over the familiar, indifferent to whether it spells life or death. All movement contains within it the force of inertia, and guardians of the status quo live by inertia alone. They are particularly in evidence when a country is going through a severe crisis. A crude example is the simple-minded old men who have spent half their lives in concentration camps, yet continue to operate with the same worn-out words and concepts in the name of which it all happened to them. The only word they have added to their vocabulary is 'mistake', but they are absolutely convinced that they and their kind were the *only* victims of the said 'mistake'. They do not want to be reminded of the sin of Cain, since they themselves, in the heyday of their activities, defended their right to destroy anyone who stood in the way of their grand design. After all, had they not promised in chorus – and they were nothing but choristers led by an accomplished choirmaster – to bestow happiness on the whole of mankind? For the sake of such an aim they thought it made perfect sense to abandon the ancient commandments (which in any case they regarded as the prejudices of a bygone age) and to do away with anyone who upheld them. They were unaware that crime has its own momentum, and when their turn came, they started to wail about a 'mistake'. Unfortunately it was not merely a mistake, or even a million mistakes, but the natural course of things, a chain reaction which can be prevented in future only by tackling the root cause. This, alas, nobody is prepared to do, since the defenders of the status quo constitute a vast, inert force unable to distinguish freedom from licence.

What, then, is the distinction? Freedom is based on a moral law; licence results from freely indulging one's desires. Freedom says: 'This is what ought to be done, so I may do it.' Licence says: 'I want to do it, so I may do it.' (But when egging others on to act, the believer in licence generally uses the first formula to get his way.) Licence frequently dons the mask of 'science': 'I know exactly what has to be done, so I am allowed to do what I see fit and will make everybody else do it as well.' Science, however misplaced its findings may be, is not to blame for this. It was not Nietzsche who created the Superman; he only gave expression to an idea that was already in the air, to the trend in European thinking which misunderstood the nature of the personality and set people on the road to individualism – and thence straight on to Man-godhood. In our age we have not only science but pseudoscience, and almost the whole of our philosophy, perhaps, has taken the same false path – not to mention all the mere dabblers in philosophy. Pseudoscience is all-pervading, particularly in fields relating to human society. The nineteenth century made a fetish of science, and pseudoscientific theories have ever since been very appealing. Pseudoscience is a characteristic disease of our times.

Freedom seeks meaning while licence sets aims. Freedom is the triumph of the personality, but licence is the product of individualism. The deification of the People and nationalism are also a kind of individualism, a special case of the cult of the individual. Leontiev, with all his claptrap about each nation having its own special roots and a foliage unlike that of any other, is a clearly defined preacher of licence. Oblivious to Christian teaching and the fact that mankind is an indivisible whole, he called for separation. When I speak of an indivisible whole, I am far from advocating that there should be a single, standardized culture throughout the world, a hybrid made up of all the different cultures. The house in which a man lives has grown out of his native soil and merges with the landscape: it is made of the timber and the clay produced by that particular soil and no other. Even when replaced by modern architecture, a man's home retains its link with the landscape, which in its turn will have been considerably modified by the people who live in it. The home is the beginning of culture, its first visible token, though it is not the main thing, and I have mentioned it here only as an illustration of the nature of cultural distinctiveness.

No man has ever existed in isolation from some form of religious consciousness or religious attitude to the world – the culture of his tribe, nation, or horde grows out of it. People are brought together by religion, and their culture springs from the bond it creates among them. A culture is never completely separated or totally isolated from the rest of mankind; every culture belongs to some larger group of other cultures rooted in the same religion. What Bergson calls a 'closed society' is always connected with other 'closed societies' by some fundamental creative idea which, in the final resort, drives it back into line with 'open' societies. A culture that regards itself as part of a larger whole gradually changes together with others of the same kind and may thereby maintain itself in a flourishing state, since change, or growth, is inherent to the historical process. Self-isolation means trying to put a stop to history and leads to atrophy – accompanied, as we have seen, by the pulling up of one's very roots. Self-isolation, like egomania, is destructive not only of the individual but of the nation as a whole. It is significant that total absorption in one's own self is a sure sign of mental illness – something to which whole nations may succumb just as well as individual members of them. Egomania is closely linked with licence, loss of memory, and the withering away of one's roots.

I am well aware that there are associations of people not based on a religious idea. The most obvious example is that of the criminal fraternity who look up to their *pakhan** and gather together for 'parleys', at which they draw up a temporary code of

---

*Slang word for a gang leader in the Soviet criminal underworld (in Solzhenitsyn's *First Circle* it is used as an epithet for Stalin). The Soviet underworld has an elaborate structure and code, not unlike the mafia. At their 'parleys' (*tolkovishcha*) the *pakhans* 'lay down the law', that is, decide policy, alterations in the 'code', etc.

'laws' and instructions, and pronounce sentences on individual members of the criminal underworld. All decisions are announced by the *pakhan*, but democracy is observed through the convening of the 'parleys'. This is the only example of a really closed society – and one, needless to say, with no religious idea as its foundation. Its way of life is completely parasitical and fatally afflicted by egomania, consisting, as it does, entirely of individual egomaniacs. Criminals, it is said, are incapable of love, only of lust, and they kill a girl friend for not tickling the soles of their feet properly. Shalamov says that they have a cult of the mothers they abandon at the very outset of their criminal careers. It is always easier to love someone faraway: this is the foundation of any false and sentimental view of life.

The criminals recognize each other by the way they walk – it is one of the mannerisms they adopt to distinguish themselves from the common herd, to stand out from the society in which they live (though 'live' is hardly the word for people whose whole existence is a pose). Criminals are very similar to bogus poets, artists and pseudoscientists – all are equally symptomatic of a morbid condition in society, a cancerous growth of cells that have become deformed and lost their structure. United only outwardly, criminals stick together because they have set themselves against their fellowmen and the society on which they batten parasitically. The bond between them is in fact always very tenuous – quarrels flare up at the slightest provocation, and then they go for each other with knives: it is one egomaniac against another. The *pakhan* has the power of life and death, but otherwise everything is in a state of constant disintegration. The links between criminals are hardly any more binding than those between mentally ill people confined in the same institution: afflicted with deep-seated love of self, both groups are dominated by extreme licence. The consequences of licence are horrifyingly destructive for the individual and for whatever social groups may be created by those who practise it. But one can scarcely call this tragedy. It is a simian grimace, a distorting mirror, an abomination of desolation, corruption, and decay.

Only freedom can be truly tragic. A free man is always wrestling with moral dilemmas – whether or not he is right to go his own way, in defiance of the general opinion, whether or not he is guilty of pride in his actions. The fact is that he often has to go against society, which is always in some degree prey to licence. The tragic nature of the free man is particularly evident in eras such as ours when whole nations are stricken by the disease. The free man must have knowledge, foresight, and understanding if he is not to lose his way; he must forever be on his guard and never lose contact with reality – even though it may seem to the common run of guardians of the established order that he has his head in the clouds. To preserve his freedom he must suppress his instinct for survival. Freedom does not just fall into your lap; you have to pay for it. There is a great truth in the Lives of the saints who always had to struggle with temptation. In our times there are no more saints, but temptations abound. A free man's task is clear: it is not to set aims, but to seek meaning. The search for meaning is made difficult by all the mirages constantly forming round about, and they are very slow to dissolve. The free man sticks to what he thinks is right because he cannot renounce the truth, but mirages too are always presenting an outward appearance of truth. I would not, for this reason, say that Khlebnikov was a free man: he was too wrapped up in the closed world of his own imagination. Reality only rarely broke through into his inner world, giving rise to isolated passages of great brilliance in his poetry whenever it did. I would not call Akhmatova a free woman, because she was too often carried away by certain generalizations – as, for instance, in her treatment of our sufferings, which she tried to equate with martyrdom. These general notions in her poetry are make-believe, figments of the imagination, evidence not of freedom, but of the fact that she too came from the same social group as the guardians of that status quo, and also that she was not immune to the blandishments of licence. M. always sought a free solution and kept his sense of reality, but even he was not a completely free man: the 'noise of time' and of life at times drowned out his inner voice, making him forget the idea on which his personality was founded, so that he lost faith in himself and his views because they went against the grain of the general trend. Drawn to people as he was, this tormented him and stirred up a multitude of doubts: 'I cannot be right if everybody else thinks differently.' Freedom does not come of its own accord; it can be won only in inner struggle, by overcoming both oneself and the world at large, by constant vigilance and self-torment. Yet even a small measure of freedom sharply distinguishes its possessor from the crowd. He walks upright and has a deep awareness of his own sinfulness – something almost entirely lost by the crowd nowadays. A free man does not go to a *pakhan* and is not taken in by what goes on at the 'parleys'. Instead of playing a role, he lives. It may be hard for him to live, but he is at least free.

The misfortune of the man who lives by licence (or of the whole society that lives by it) is that there is always a gulf between what he would like to do and what he can do. As we have seen, when he cannot achieve his aim, he goes berserk. The aim of his desires may vary – a woman, wealth, the reordering of society in accordance with a preconceived design, or anything you like. A woman may say no (though this is now a very rare event), wealth is not all that easy to come by, and the reordering of society is a very tough proposition indeed – as something that has grown up historically, it has a tendency to live by its own laws and to resist forcible reorganization. At the very beginning of our era, as M. noted, there took place a 'huge, ungainly, creaking turn of the rudder', but this 'turn of the rudder' was achieved at a moment of great exhilaration, at a time of popular revolutionary upheaval when the masses really did have faith in the man at the helm and helped him as best they could. Even though it creaked, the rudder did indeed turn the great hulk of the ship, setting it on the uncharted course it has ever since continued to sail by inertia. Where is it taking us, this course? Who knows . . . In any event, it is by no means a matter only of economic reorganization, although this is and always has been the most 'creaking' part of the business. Much more basic, in my opinion, are the changed relations among people inside the country, and the relationship of the country as a whole to the outside world, of which it was once a part and with which it has travelled its entire journey through history. Having become isolated, it has lost its link with the past and now moves towards an unknown future, constantly drifting further and further away from the aim originally set by people who believed themselves capable of foreseeing the future. Have the social sciences reached a point at which they are able to make good this claim? Is such a thing conceivable in principle? Is science aware of the consequence of self-isolation, the rejection of the past, and the destruction of values? Is there any science capable of estimating the damage caused by the undermining – or rather the eradication – of the ability to distinguish between good and evil among millions of people? At the very beginning of this voyage, M. suspected that 'the earth has cost us ten heavens'. Did he realize that we should lose not only ten heavens, but the earth as well? Perhaps he had an inkling of it, to judge by the line: 'Who has a heart must hear, time, as your ship goes under.'

The man who is rebuffed by a woman may put a bullet through his head; a man thwarted in his desire for wealth may stake everything on one last desperate throw at the gaming house or on the stock exchange. (Sometimes he becomes a criminal and robs a bank, going to jail for his pains.) The man governed by licence is prepared to destroy everything and everybody that stands in his way – himself first and foremost. Destruction and self-destruction are the inevitable consequences of licence. The suicide of Hitler and his holocaust is the supreme example of self-destruction as the final stage of licence. Hitler believed that the whole of Germany would gather around the fire he had lighted. I have read that he spent his last days issuing a constant stream of orders to armies that no longer existed or had disintegrated. He was indignant at these vanished armies for failing to carry out his instructions. His behaviour is an excellent illustration of Sergei Bulgakov's observation that licence always leads to loss of touch with reality. Bulgakov understood this at a time when licence had still not taken on the extreme forms we have seen in our days.

A man or a society governed by licence not only has no wish to take account of reality, but actually fails to see it. Or they try to remake it in their own image and are unable to believe it could be any different. I remember the curious shift that took place in the meaning of the word 'opportunism', a word the newspapers were full of in the thirties. 'Opportunism', it appeared, meant a tendency to point out not only our successes, but also our setbacks; 'opportunists' were people who said we were going through difficult times and it would be wise to stop and take thought. Most of them had started off as allies of all the other devotees of licence and were simply engaged in a struggle for power with them, trading on the fact that they were less out of touch with reality. There is an enormous difference between a free man's refusal to keep silent ('Here I stand and can do no other') and that of a man of licence who stubbornly insists on trying to change the world according to his own blueprint, rather than someone else's. The so-called opportunists were also bent on reforming the world, but they had a different recipe. Miscalculating badly, they were packed off to concentration camps, where they soon perished.

By that time ordinary people had learned to keep their mouths shut, and the only ones who still made any fuss were old women standing in queues. There were so many of them that it was evidently decided just to let them die out. They were succeeded by new contingents of old women of the kind who in their younger days had taken part in the liquidation of the kulaks or the confiscation of valuables belonging to the church. It became dangerous to stand in queues in the second half of the forties and the beginning of the fifties because of all these 'new' old women cursing the shop assistants and bystanders for their ideological shortcomings. I once fell foul of one of them because I had wrapped something in a newspaper with a photograph of the Boss (there were no paper-bags in the shops, and every newspaper had his picture in it). She raised a great hue and cry and snatched the newspaper from me. The things I had wrapped in it – apples or carrots, I don't remember which – were scattered all over the pavement. I didn't wait to pick them up and was glad to get away with my skin. It was a difficult time, with new purges taking place, and the guardians of order were everywhere active at the prompting of the practitioners of licence. Scenes like this were happening all over – in the street, in queues, on buses . . .

The history of the first half of the twentieth century, seen as an orgy of licence which had abandoned, as one expects it to, all the accumulated values of mankind, is a direct consequence of humanism deprived of a religious foundation. This process had lasted centuries and reached its logical conclusion in ours. The devotees of licence proclaimed the cult of man and ended by trampling him underfoot. They eagerly seized on the concept of Man-godhead, against which Dostoyevski warned us, and we have seen what the Man-god (alias Superman) is like in action. I would very much like to know why M. was so chary of Dostoyevski. There are allusions to him in his poetry and prose writings, but otherwise he never wrote or spoke about him. Was he alarmed by his conclusions, or was he put off by the theories of Dostoyevski the publicist? I believe he sensed in Dostoyevski a kind of repository of all the fiends and that in his search for a more serene relationship with his fellowmen he closed his eyes to the prophetic insights of the great convict. People of our generation were divided into supporters of Dostoyevski or Tolstoi, and M. tended to lean towards Tolstoi; but in a general sense he was immune to both, since he suspected that the one was just as much a heresiarch as the other.

I believe that all individuals, as well as all societies, have elements of freedom and licence within them. It is simply a question of the proportions. If the historical experience of our times does not help people to put an end to unbridled licence, then there remains only the last logical step: self-destruction. For a long time I could not understand why Kirillov had to end by killing himself. I had always thought that a man who had achieved full awareness of himself as a man is ready to enjoy the fruits of life rather than to do away with himself. It is difficult to understand this when one is young. Only a mature mind sees the difference between one who attains self-awareness because he has discovered himself in the image of God and one who magnifies himself and his own will, rejecting the divine principle and even erasing it from his soul. The second is doomed to self-destruction, as we have seen with our own eyes, and when he sets about the final annihilation of the world he will get every support from all the brutish forces determined to keep things as they are – forces which are presently standing guard over the monstrous superstructure erected by licence.

Man is a symbolic being. Isn't the age we have lived through a symbol, a kind of final warning perhaps, which we are too lazy to try to understand? The consequences of Man-godhead and licence have been made manifest, but we close our eyes rather than distress ourselves with the conclusion we would be bound to draw. For the sake of their well-being, people cultivate a healthy optimism: it is both harmful and unpleasant to upset oneself.

I think it possible that M. felt Dostoyevski was alien to him because, having nothing at all in common with the guardians of the status quo, he was full of eschatological forebodings and calmly awaited the end.*

III : PEASANTS

Kirillov is the most dangerous of all Dostoyevski's 'possessed', and not for nothing does he go to live in the same house as Shatov.† One day the two could form an alliance – and then it will be the end of everything. Sergei Bulgakov too was evidently more alarmed by Kirillov than by anyone else: his chief conclusions about licence result from his analysis of Kirillov's suicide.

Bulgakov's article was written at the beginning of the century when the stability of everyday life still prevented one from seeing that the intelligentsia, the ruling elite, and the revolutionary underground – as well as the neutral, in-between group that could gravitate to either pole – were all equally infected by licence, which was hence bound eventually to gush forth and sweep everything before it. Berdiayev failed to realize how much more dangerous a form licence had taken in the revolutionary underground. In his autobiography, one of his last books, he writes that the intelligentsia fought for the people in a spirit of self-sacrifice, only to be destroyed by the people in their hour of victory. This is nothing more than a cliché – Berdiayev did not take the trouble to cast a downward glance at what was happening in reality. The members of the intelligentsia who headed the revolutionary camp made use

---

* The difference between M. and Dostoyevski appears to be that the latter was to some extent on the side of the guardians of the status quo, and did not await the end calmly.

† Character in *The Possessed* who reflects something of Dostoyevski's own religious nationalism, and is also, like Dostoyevski himself, a revolutionary turned guardian of the status quo.

of the people to achieve victory, but once they had seized power, they immediately put the people in their place again. The people were just an instrument and, as always and everywhere, gained nothing at all. They fought and went on the rampage and fired into the air (and at live targets), but the real business of destruction began after all the shouting was over – and then it was done not by the people, but by case-hardened personnel specially trained for the job under the guidance of the victors. The licence of the people amounts to no more than shooting in the air. Real death-dealing licence takes other forms.

Sergei Bulgakov calls licence 'the devil' and writes: 'It is incompatible with the world; it can want the world only as an object, a plaything, and mankind only as slaves to do with as it pleases.' This sums up the fate of the people – of all sections of the people, including the intelligentsia – during the period when licence was at its most unbridled. Licence is the complete fulfilment of one's own will and, consequently, the overriding of everybody else's will. It goes hand in hand with the will to power and the desire to impose one's own ideas and opinions on everybody else. The man governed by licence always sets himself aims, and this only intensifies his lust for power: in order to achieve one's aim, one has to force everybody to act in concert and march in the same direction. Military formation can be highly recommended for this purpose. Whether in the bosom of his family, among his friends, or in politics, the man who lives by licence always wants to lord it over everybody. At the very beginning of the Revolution the same desire infected the vast masses of people who followed in the wake of their leaders and won victory for them. Every house, apartment, and village, not to mention every town and province, had its little tyrant (at first there would be several, until a single one took over), who gave orders and instructions, threatening always to 'make mincemeat' of anyone who resisted. In the early years I remember him as the 'house manager' who would burst into your apartment demanding that someone be evicted or moved in with you, that you carry out repairs, or goodness knows what else. His demands were invariably backed up by a stream of abuse and threats, with ominous remarks to the effect that it was time to wring the bourgeoisie's neck. Everywhere there were blustering bullies carrying on like this, and some of them fetched up in high places. They were prized for the useful information they were able to provide: where officers were hiding out, where peasants were hoarding their grain, who was keeping gold, where 'something fishy' was going on.

Once, in Kiev, searches were carried out all over town in the course of a single night for the purpose of 'confiscating surplus property', and when a group of people headed by a Chekist burst into our apartment I was able to see a clear distinction between the bullies and ordinary people. Among them was a loud-mouthed 'house manager' who knew exactly the layout of the rooms and was dying to uncover our secret hiding places. There were also several soldiers, grim-faced and knowing their drill, ready at a moment's notice to tear the place apart, and two workmen who had been brought along as 'experts' – they were supposed to decide what was 'surplus' and subject to confiscation. In my mother's bedroom there was a huge wardrobe where, as a child, I used to be locked up by my brothers until I squealed like a piglet and begged to be let out. The 'house manager' now tried to force the door, but one of the workers stopped him: why break it open when the key was there in the lock? Inside were hanging the sort of clothes all too common at that time, made by dressmakers whose imaginations had run riot. The 'house manager' was very much taken by a blouse decorated with shiny glass beads which seemed to him the height of bourgeois luxury. The worker took the blouse from him, hung it back in its place, and closed the wardrobe. I was the only member of the family in the bedroom – the others were sitting drinking tea under the eyes of a soldier in the dining room, trying to look as though nothing particular was happening. 'Our wives don't need your cast-offs,' the worker said to me, and he told the others to call off the search. The two workers had been 'mobilized' to take part in this large-scale operation, and they were just as disgusted by it as we. The Chekist was 'doing his job' – both he and the soldiers were mere instruments of destruction acting on orders. The only person who was actually enjoying himself was the 'house manager'. This was how things looked at the very beginning – at least as far as matters of no great importance went, in the humdrum perpective, as it were, of daily life.

Officious little bullies of the 'house manager' type and other petty practitioners of licence lasted until the beginning of the thirties. They were used to carrying out collectivization, but as power became more centralized, there was less and less need for them. The sort of people now wanted down below, 'at the local level', were efficient robots who automatically obeyed orders, not petty tyrants in their own right. These had had their day. Licence practised on a small scale was now swallowed up by licence writ large at the centre of things, in the sight of which all men were slaves. The concentration of power in the hands of a few, or of one man, is the inevitable result of licence in action: the strong are bound to subjugate the weak, manoeuvring for position and concluding alliances – only temporarily, of course – first with one and then with another, before turning on all former allies and destroying them. The first to be slapped down were the minor bullies of the 'house manager' type. By the middle of the twenties they were no longer in evidence in the cities – apart from the occasional jack-in-office who still contrived to take it out of his subordinates or some cowering citizen who had come to beg a favour. The same process went on in the countryside, only more slowly.

In the summer of 1935 M. was able to travel around Voronezh province; a local newspaper had commissioned some articles from him and had got permission from the police for his journey. We spent about two weeks in the Vorobyovo district, hitchhiking from village to village. Towards the end of the trip we happened to meet in the space of a single day both an old-style petty tyrant, of the kind who had flourished until recently – he still ruled over his *kolkhoz* in rough and ready patriarchal fashion – and a man of the new style, the director of a *sovkhoz* who was a real robot, carrying out with indifference all the orders and instructions, written on the thinnest of paper, that rained down on him incessantly from above. It must have been ruinous for the eyesight, the business of deciphering these scarcely legible instructions.

The small bully who had once tried single-handedly to remake the whole world – that is, his native village – was called Dorokhov. His story was simple and typical. He had returned home after fighting in the World War and then in the Civil War, and had at once got down to the task of building a new and happy life in his native village. (He was not of the type who suffered convulsions as a result of his wounds, but rather one of those who held down other comrades as they thrashed about in a fit.) His career had started in the Committee for the Poor,* on whose behalf he had pillaged the barns of kulaks, confiscating grain for the cities. Next, as a member of his district soviet, he had organized the first commune in the neighbourhood. It had later been disbanded, like all such voluntary associations for joint cultivation of the land. (They were, after all, *true* collectives in a sense, whose purpose was not only to serve the State but to feed their members' children.) With the launching of collectivization Dorokhov became chairman of a small *kolkhoz*, which was later amalgamated with others to form a larger unit. Believing he knew exactly where the road to happiness lay, he was hungry for power. Once he had become the first man in his village, his activity knew no bounds. Not long before we met him, however, he had been removed from his post as *kolkhoz* chairman for exceeding his authority: he had juggled the figures for his compulsory deliveries to the State, whose interests had thus suffered through his fault. Nobody cared about his behaviour in the village and what he had done to the people who lived there – in his treatment of *them* he was not held to have exceeded his authority. Stripped of his power, Dorokhov did not lose his head, and he managed to retain his prestige. He took a bag and went begging from door to door. In every izba he told the story of his great days and his fall from power, and people were glad to give him alms. By the time we arrived on the scene he had been reinstated in his post at the request of his fellow villagers. At that time it was still possible for them to kick up a little fuss in minor matters. In their appeal to the authorities they had enumerated Dorokhov's past services, the main one being that he had done a very thorough job of liquidating the kulaks in the shortest possible time without asking for any assistance from the city.

Dorokhov had set up his own jail in the village, and anybody who disobeyed was thrown into it, irrespective of his class origins, whether he was a poor peasant or a kulak. This had not turned his

* Set up on Lenin's instructions in June 1918 as an instrument of class warfare in the villages, and a requisitioning authority to supply grain for the city workers and the Red Army. Having quickly fulfilled their immediate tasks, they were merged with the rural soviets in November 1918.

fellow villagers against him. They respected him for taking the law into his own hands and for the fact that he never sent anyone to Siberia – except 'real kulaks'. The houses of these 'real kulaks' he had decided to convert into day nurseries, a recreation room, a reading room, and suchlike socialist institutions, but in the meanwhile, the dozen or so houses concerned stood empty and boarded up, awaiting the necessary books, staff, and equipment. Dorokhov was a great enthusiast for education. The only ones to feel any resentment against him were the Komsomols – as the 'new generation', they were also anxious to get their share of power. They tried to undermine Dorokhov's position by scribbling denunciations and sending them to the town. Anything could be used as an excuse for a denunciation. The Komsomols concentrated their fire on the fact that Dorokhov had put some former kulak associates to guard an orchard confiscated from a kulak who had been deported. Fearing for their skins, they did the job very conscientiously and even kept all the fallen apples to feed to the pigs. (People who are scared always lean over backwards to please the authorities.) Dorokhov seethed with indignation as he denounced the Komsomols: 'All they want is to eat the apples themselves – apple thieves, not Komsomols, I call 'em.' He had a flowery way of talking. Lapping up 'culture' for all he was worth, he had brought back many prize expressions from the army. 'Don't go out in the evenings,' he warned me. 'There are malarial vapours in this *climature*.'

Three days before we met him Dorokhov had issued an order that every house in the village must display two pots of flowers on the windowsill. He issued orders like this in a constant stream, and they were all couched in the language of the first years of the Revolution. He went around to a dozen houses with us to check whether his instructions had been complied with. He set enormous store by this measure, since he believed that flowers imbibe the moisture and thus help 'against the rheumatism'. The village women explained to him that they had nothing against flowers, but that one couldn't get pots for love or money, and that in any case three days was not enough time to grow burdock or nettles, never mind flowers. Dorokhov was furious, and only our presence restrained him from meting out punishment on the spot. We were told that he treated the villagers as a father treats his children and went for them with his fists, hitting them right between the eyes. He had it in particularly for those who denounced him to the town authorities instead of to his face. The villagers loved him because he was one of their own kind, and if he insulted you or told you off it was always possible to answer back. While he was in charge the women sat at home to cook meals and look after their children, and since the women had always ruled the roost in Russia, they got their own way with their menfolk, who still obeyed them in those days, however much they muttered under their breath. But things became much tougher for the women, and they were driven out to work in the fields when Dorokhov, as we heard, was once more kicked out of his job – this time for good – and had to go begging again. He thus failed to achieve happiness either for himself or for his village – yet it had seemed almost within his grasp . . .

Dorokhov was already an anachronism in the thirties, and so he was destroyed – like all the rest who had taken part in the popular uprising and returned to their native villages and small towns to educate the people and give them culture. He had yielded his last drop of utility, in war, revolution, and the liquidation of the kulaks, only at last to be liquidated himself. In the second half of the thirties his house stood boarded up, like those of all the people he had packed off to Siberia. Yet wasn't it this same Dorokhov, according to Berdiayev's scheme of things, who had done away with the self-sacrificing intelligentsia? I can testify that in the period when Dorokhov enjoyed his illusory power, the 'self-sacrificing intelligentisa', having sent the remnants of the liquidated political parties to do forced labour, was still enjoying the fruits of victory. Its own turn came only at the end of the thirties, nearly ten years after the total collectivization carried out with its approval.

M. drank a bottle of vodka with Dorokhov and listened sympathetically to what he had to say, realizing he was a doomed man. He made a mental calculation of the number of people Dorokhov must have deported from his village. I do not remember the figure, but it was about the average, that is, something quite incredible. What to us seems quite ordinary is unbelievable and monstrous to a normal person. Our self-sacrificing intelligentsia did not bat an eyelid at such things, any more than the foreign red-plumaged birds reared here in test tubes, later to be sent to their native countries with the task of literally putting the same things into practice at home; they just went on cleaning their feathers with their beaks and looked the other way. At the same time writers came from abroad to admire our experiment and to buy fur coats à la Triolet* in our commission shops,† after which they returned home to advocate the introduction of our methods of implanting culture in the countryside and ensuring a just distribution of wealth there. They should have been kept for a year or two on the rations which the village women got after collectivization. Dorokhov, in his fatherly way, at least cheated on his compulsory deliveries to the State so that the women and children in his *kolkhoz* should not go around with legs and bellies swollen from hunger.

The representative of the new style of administration (I have already spoken elsewhere about the way we were fascinated by these questions of style), the director of a local *sovkhoz*,‡ drove us around his domain in a small truck to visit the 'field camps'. At every stop he asked to be given a taste of the cabbage soup and kvass. 'We must look after the people's welfare,' he explained to M., as a representative of the press, and he sometimes told the cook off for the quality of the soup – that is, the water with bits of cabbage floating in it. The next question the director asked, in accordance with his latest instructions, was about the newspapers: had the reading of newspapers been properly organized (reading *aloud*, of course – otherwise people might just look at them without really taking things in) during breaks? Then he wanted to know exactly who was reading them, since the instructions said it should be done in a literate fashion with plenty of expression. Occasionally the director gave vent to his pleasure as a farm manager by

* See Brik, Appendix A.

† In effect, State pawn shops, once much patronized by visiting foreigners because of the antiques, jewelry, Fabergé, and other valuable objects, often sold off by 'former persons', that could be had relatively cheaply.

‡ The *sovkhoz* (unlike the *kolkhoz*, which is in theory cooperative) is State managed and the workers are paid cash wages as in a factory (in the *kolkhozes* they were paid mostly in kind). They often cover a large area, hence the need for the 'field camps' described.

dashing up to piles of freshly harvested grain waiting to be thrashed, and plunging his arms and legs into it, as though wading into the sea of peasant wealth it represented. M. looked at the still-unharvested fields as we drove by and remarked to me that in the director's place he would stop swigging kvass and start worrying a little: the fields were choked with weeds which stood higher than the stunted wheat. The director had failed to notice this because so far he had received no instructions from above ordering him to fight weeds. He only fought things specified in the instructions. There was no shortage of things he was supposed to fight . . .

Towards evening we arrived at a meadow on which, barely visible, there was a *zemlianka*, a peasant hut sunk into the ground with a roof over it. For the first time that day the director really leaped into action. Together with the driver and three farmworkers who were accompanying us in the truck, he jumped down, raced over to the hut, climbed on the roof, and started to dance a jig on it. While the director and his driver stamped on the roof, the workers set about demolishing the hut with crowbars. Even in a small job of manual labour like this, due hierarchical precedence had to be observed. The boss and his flunky – the driver – could not stoop to breaking up the hut side by side with ordinary workers. They had to work separately on their own section – in this case, the roof of the *zemlianka*. Nobody knows how many different grades of officials we have, but they themselves have a very keen sense of all the nuances, and none of them would dream of wielding a crowbar if it were not appropriate to his station. Chauffeurs stand outside the class hierarchy – they are symbols of power together with the vehicles they drive, and anybody, of whatever rank, may sit beside them. For this reason the driver did not take up a crowbar either, but joined the director in dancing a jig on the roof. It is interesting to note that these fine hierarchical gradations were introduced into the army later than in the civil bureaucracy. In 1938 I was teaching German in a barracks (I was allowed to do this by virtue of an instruction relating to wives whom it was not felt necessary to exile together with their husbands – this in the same town where a little while previously they had been looking for me with a warrant for my arrest!). My pupils were lieutenants, and I overheard them talking with some bewilderment about a new order forbidding them to play chess or checkers with their men, to carry heavy parcels in the streets (who was supposed to do it for them, their mothers or their wives?), or to consort with the waitresses in the officers' mess. If they wished to marry, their brides had henceforth to be approved by their superior officers to prevent their taking up with floozies unsuitable to their rank. In the universities and colleges there was similarly a constant preoccupation with degrees and ranks, and what a student was allowed or not allowed to do: whether it was all right, for instance, for him to stand at a stall in the market and sell the ham or honey he had brought back from his parents in the village. In Chita, the woman secretary (a high rank in a college) complained to me that some of our students, village girls by origin, were going out with ordinary soldiers instead of lieutenants. I pointed out that the girls had grown up with these boys at home, but the secretary, though she was from the country herself, shook her head disapprovingly: how could they behave like this . . .

The wretched peasant hut was now being taken apart by these five hefty men of the people in strict accordance with the rules of precedence. The first part to give way was the roof, and as it did so with a crash some people carrying their possessions began to file out of the hut. One woman was holding a spinning wheel, and another a sewing machine. M. was astonished at the number of people who had managed to squeeze into the tiny *zemlianka* – could it have some underground passages? he wondered. We had not yet read Kafka, but we knew that while a mole always has a spare exit, people invariably have to come out of their burrows straight into the arms of their persecutors. 'How clean they are,' said M. The last to emerge (they were all old people, women, and children), a woman wearing a dazzlingly white *sarafan* – a long embroidered dress – like all the others, was carrying a starveling child in her arms: it was a tiny living corpse, hairless, wrinkled, with greenish stumps instead of arms. I will never forget it. It seemed like a symbol of something. Of what? Perhaps of the realities of our life, and of our cruelty, including my own.

The women had nothing to lose, and they started cursing the director in a south Russian accent, using the foulest words they knew. (I like this kind of language: together with the anecdote, it is an expression of real life.) But the director went on undeterred until he had destroyed their pitiful burrow and filled in the hole where it had stood. So much for the fate of people who, following Zoshchenko's advice, had made themselves a burrow in the ground and lived like animals. The whole of the land – the fields, forests, and meadows – is accounted for; none of it is ownerless. When he had finished his work, the director came back, sat next to us in the truck, and launched into an explanation. The husbands of these women, he said, either had been deported or had wandered off to the cities in search of work, and their womenfolk were 'squatting' on *sovkhoz* land. The *sovkhoz* was a state enterprise, and as the director, he could not tolerate the class enemy, kulak dregs, on the territory for which he was responsible. There were constant visits of inspection, and if a nest of kulaks like this were suddenly to come to light during one of them, then he might well be accused of harbouring them. It was his opinion that the liquidation of the kulaks had still not been completed, and he felt that, frankly, not enough attention was paid to the views of provincial officials like himself. They would be unanimous in their recommendation that all these women be sent to Siberia to join their husbands; otherwise there was just no coping with them. It didn't have to be to the camps; the 'special settlements'* would do. The job really needed to be finished off. The law was the law, and orders were orders. As director of the *sovkhoz* he always acted according to the law and the instructions he received. He would have to answer for it if he didn't . . .

We were silent. There was no point in objecting: he knew what he was doing. Even if we had allowed ourselves to be drawn into an argument with this stickler for the law it would have been not only futile but dangerous. The director of a *sovkhoz* is part of the apparatus of power, and works hand in glove with the local representative of the very highest authority, part of whose daily job is to make sure that the laws are carried out. No warrants had been issued for the old men and women who had taken refuge in

---

* For deported people who, though not held behind barbed wire as in the forced labour camps, were made to work in the region to which they had been sent.

the *zemlianka* – probably because the plan for deportation had already been fulfilled or, as was often the case, overfulfilled. They had been allowed to wander off by themselves, the main thing being that they should clear out of their native villages with the 'houses of culture' created at the expense of their life's blood. These women in clean *sarafans* with their spinning wheels could actually count themselves very lucky, as I could after M.'s second arrest. With their skilled hands (more than I had!) they would find work in the cities and at construction sites as cleaning women or casual labourers. In this country, they would always be able to find some sort of job, just as I did later on. Without our husbands we women can always buckle down to work of some kind. A few years later, when I would no longer have M., we were to hear the great words that the son does not answer for the sins of the father.*
If that starving baby survived, he will have become a soldier, a factory worker, or even a party official. They will certainly have found a place for him, as they did for me.

The director invited us to have dinner with him, but we packed our things and got a lift on a passing truck to the district centre. Here we called on the district party secretary to say good-bye ('The district centre of Vorobyovo / I shall never forget'). It was obvious from his appearance that he had come down in the world, having been sent to this small town in the backwoods from some more important place. We decided we could raise the question of the *zemlianka* with him and asked whether there was anything to be done. He just shrugged his shoulders and, without giving us a direct answer, inquired whether there were still many beggars wandering the streets of Voronezh. There were fewer than when we had first arrived in 1934, and the convoys taking kulaks into exile had apparently stopped coming through the city the previous year already. 'So the numbers are going down,' the party secretary said, adding that beggars, people who had taken to the roads, or those living in *zemliankas* had got off lightly: 'You can't make an omelette without breaking eggs.' Coming from someone in his position, these words were incredibly foolhardy. In the presence of strangers he had uttered a phrase for which he could

---

*The 'Stalin Constitution' of 1936 lifted restrictions on rights due to class origins.

have got ten years. He himself, of course, had had a hand in the 'great agrarian revolution from above,' but we had a feeling that he had shown little stomach for it – though I admit we might well have been crediting him with our own kind of sentiments, just because he had the face of an intellectual. The *sovkhoz* director had the face of a real lout – he looked like an animal as he danced on the roof of the hut. We said good-bye to the secretary and drove off in a truck in which he had arranged a ride for us.

This may all be past history, but what about the effect the crimes of the fathers and grandfathers have on the generations that come after them? We were disgusted by the swine of a kvass-swigging *sovkhoz* director and cheered up a little by the party secretary who let fall those few chance, but nonetheless subversive, words in our hearing. In fact, however, there was nothing to choose between us: we had all washed our hands. Only the *sovkhoz* director made some attempt to find excuses: after he had finished his dance on the roof, the little worm into which his conscience had turned began to wriggle inside him. I do not even make excuses for myself; I saw these things and just swallowed them. I was to see much worse, but only when they took M. away did I begin to scream and howl – even then never within earshot of other people. The *sovkhoz* director with his pig's face, as it now appears in retrospect, did better than any of us. For half a century the most unspeakable things have been perpetrated without the slightest attempt at self-justification, and the people who witnessed them are still silent. It is a wonder we have not lost the use of our tongues through silence! But actually there has been no sign of such a thing happening even to those who, far from being silent, have gone out of their way to praise all the crimes that have been committed. We have the prospect of living through another half-century of silence or shameless panegyrics, since to speak out is not only dangerous but futile: 'Ten steps away no one hears our speeches.' By the time a hundred years of this have gone by, our tongues no doubt really will have withered away. We have learned to be silent, so we can learn to do without our tongues. The only people needed and valued here are 'slaves who know how to keep their peace'.

How did it all begin, the silence and the frenzied lying? It happened exactly for the reasons given by Sergei Bulgakov when he wrote that the person who lives by licence, losing his sense of reality, constantly eggs himself on with the thought that he can do anything. The tasks we set ourselves were certainly quite something: to transform the natural world, society, the mental and physical makeup of mankind, to conquer death and thus be in a position to reward the deserving with long life (while punishing the 'opportunists', that is, the doubters, with a bullet in the back of the head). For aims such as these it was perfectly in order to sacrifice the starving baby in the arms of that woman wearing the snow-white *sarafan*, not to mention M. and me. The only thing left to the victims was to let fly with a good Russian swear-word at the last moment. That's why I like such language.

We all held our tongues because of our cravenness and the terror that gripped us. The only slight consolation I have is that not only we but 'they' too were cowards and also sweated with dread. In 1930, while we were staying in a hotel (if it could be called that) in some wretched little town in the Caucasus, I went out on the veranda looking for a toilet and tried to open a door that was locked on the inside. Suddenly the key turned in the lock, the door was flung open, and a man in uniform rushed out at me, bellowing like a wild animal. He was an official of the security organs who had recently arrived in the town, and while looking for an apartment, he was living temporarily behind the locked door of this hotel room. Terrified at the thought of assassination, he raved and ranted, threatening to arrest me. Everybody in the hotel came running, and after much shouting and waving of arms, they managed somehow to calm him down and rescue me. As they explained to me, he was frightened too: 'Everybody's afraid, as you know yourself . . .'

The people who were least afraid were those being trained as philosophers in preparation for the work of urging others on to the fulfilment of the great tasks ahead. I once met a tiny woman philosopher for whom a chair was already waiting in a provincial institute. Her role would be to exercise vigilance and act as adviser to the local Party and Soviet organizations. We sat at the same table with her in the CEKUBU sanatorium in Bolshevo. Everybody grumbled about the weak tea, which was the colour of baby's urine. The budding professor of philosophy piped up to say that tea was an imported product which had to be bought with foreign exchange, and that it was time to start cultivating it ourselves in the *kolkhozes*, now that collectivization was a hundred per cent completed (this was in 1932). A honey-tongued old botanist pointed out that the tea shrub requires special conditions of climate and soil, and that in the Caucasus we had only small areas of the right kind of soil with iron in it. The lady professor had a ready answer to this: 'He who is born to crawl cannot fly,'* and she went on about 'bourgeois lack of faith in man and science.' Did she later advise her local Party authorities to graft tea plants onto cold-resistant shrubs? She would have been quite capable of it.†

The only way in which licence could respond to any failure was by the persecution of scapegoats. Every spring and autumn, as a kind of seasonal rite, there were always mass arrests of people – whether or not they had a direct connection with agriculture. The nineteenth century saw intensive efforts to rehabilitate Cain. Someone even explained that Cain, as a man with new ideas about husbandry, had no option but to kill the backward shepherd Abel. For our part, we simply ignored the two brothers in the Bible, and for the education of our children we invented a peculiar amalgam of the two: Pavlik Morozov. He ran away from home in order to kill his father (that is, to cause his death by denouncing him), and was later killed himself, like Abel. Children in the lower classes at school had to learn the edifying story of Pavlik by heart so they too would always be ready to denounce their own fathers. Our best educators followed in the footsteps of Cain. I knew a specialist in Spinoza who wore on his chest a medal he had been awarded for his services during collectivization. The director of the Chita Teachers' Training College distinguished himself during the deportation of the Crimean Tartars.‡ He was a splendid fellow who used to go off to the movies in the afternoons, telling the secretaries, as he left

* Phrase from Maxim Gorki's poem in prose 'The Song of the Falcon' (1895), much quoted in Soviet times for its contrast between the soaring bird of prey and the earthbound snake.

† The kind of hybrid Lysenko and his followers were always claiming to have produced.

‡ Together with several small nations in the Caucasus, these were deported to central Asia in 1944.

with his briefcase under his arm, that he was going to the Party Committee. What can be done to stop splendid fellows like this from carrying out criminal assignments? The past is irreversible, but what can be done to see that such lovers of the motion picture, who have never even heard of Cain, should not plunge us into new tragedies?

30 Poetry and People

I: THE READER

M. never made any advances whatsoever to his readers. He needed a confidant, a first listener (there were always several of them), but not readers. Unlike the Symbolists, he did not concern himself with the reader's education, nor did he try to attract readers – as the Futurists and their successors in LEF did. I believe that he respected his potential readers, and if you respect someone, you have no wish to make a special effort to educate or attract him. M. spoke to his readers as equals, or even as his betters, and all he expected from them was a 'sympathetic hearing'. In fact he never used the word 'reader'.* His *cri de cœur* of 1937 – 'A reader, a counsellor, a doctor' – was prompted by the ostracism to which he was then condemned, when he was unable not only to get his work published, but even to read it to an acquaintance met on the street (by this time most people affected not to know us). In more normal circumstances (I have put the word 'normal' in the comparative degree because this was the only way it ever applied to us) he never talked of readers, but quite simply of 'people': 'People will keep it.' 'If people need it, they will find it – they always find what they need.' Once, not long before his arrest in 1934, he said he would like to 'do something for people', since he had now lived so long without really giving thought to this. He seemed to feel the need to

* Mandelstam's word for 'reader' (except in the quotation that follows) is always *sobesednik*, literally a collocutor, a person one converses or communes with.

explore the misery of the human condition ('the things that cause them pain') and to search for a remedy, for whatever it was that was needed 'by their living hearts'. We had this conversation at a time when he had already realized that although everybody 'takes the pulse of the crowd and believes in it', contact with it, with people, by no means meant that you should pander to them. In the noise of the crowd, the 'noise of time', there are many different strains – superficial or profound, ephemeral and adventitious, or eternal and immutable – and you have to attune yourself first before you can learn to distinguish among them. To make matters more complicated still, even the ephemeral may contain some small element of abiding importance – if you can pick it out and interpret it. What an artist is able to make of it depends on his qualities of mind and character, and the basic idea underlying his personality. It is no contradiction on M.'s part that, while promising to take 'the pulse of the crowd', he also declares his determination to work 'listening to no one, alone with one other'. I believe that these two statements refer to different levels of the 'noise of the crowd'. The loneliness of the artist and his 'freedom of the city' do not preclude contact with the outside world – without which he cannot fulfil himself – but such duality often produces conflict. An artist always lives in his time, lost among the crowd of his day and merging with it; but being also a powerful detector of the 'noise of the crowd', he is nevertheless detached from it and is not, in effect, a contemporary of anybody.

The crowd easily loses touch with the past and does not see the future, but the artist by his nature is anachronous in the literal sense: he lives not only in the present but also in the future, at the same time retaining close links with the past through his sense of continuity with the poets who came before him – he communes with them as friends and teachers. These are, in fact, his true contemporaries, and this is what makes any purely 'Futurist' movement so questionable: it is bound to be nihilistic by its very nature. The basic idea of an artist (if he is a genuine one, of course) is formed in what Bergson called the 'open society', but it feeds on the 'noise of the crowd', the same sources drawn on by the 'closed' society whose language he speaks, as it rises to the surface. If one thinks about it, society, the crowd, is never completely 'closed'. Even half a century of isolation could not entirely efface all the ideas and concepts which, in however distorted, mangled, or perverted a form, nevertheless survived as the living traces of what once formed the bedrock of our culture and belongs to the heritage of the 'open' society. The crowd has a short memory, but something human always survives in it; hence the distress it feels whenever it is egged on to wanton violence by its leaders. The frenzied mobs at the beginning of our era were terrifying, but they were not as hideous as the submissive crowds who later, at public meetings, voted the death penalty for fellow citizens. (In 1938, while I was working at a factory near Moscow, I was comforted by the sight of women workers running away from meetings which they had been forced to attend: I saw them chasing out through the factory gates, knocking over officials who tried to stop them. But these were simple women of the people, not stooges of the *apparat* like 'Fatty'.)

A mob assembled in a public square or hall and welded into one compact whole is not the same as the crowds of human beings scattered around – on city streets and country roads, in houses and apartments. It is the dispersed crowds who really constitute 'society', but in this country there is nothing to bind them together, since all the forms of association that arose historically have been destroyed; at the same time the compact, howling mobs, the 'masses', have no pulse or words of their own – they are completely under the sway of their 'leaders' (or 'demagogues', as they used to be called). The roar of such mobs and fear of them are what drove many intellectuals to fall for the 'Change of Landmarks'. Brought up to respect the idea of popular rule, they mistook the howling of the mob for the *vox populi* and failed to take into account the role of the rabble-rousers behind it. A spontaneous popular movement is never durable, unless it is orchestrated by such ringleaders.

M.'s remark that he wanted to work 'listening to no one, alone with one other' could have been made in any age: it was dictated by the ambivalent situation of the artist who is always inwardly free, yet at the same time bound to the crowd. In our days the problem of relations between the artist and the crowd was resolved in the crudest possible way: literature (as part of the 'superstructure') undertook to serve the 'basis', that is, to obey the order of officials specially assigned to rule over it. At the beginning all the arts and sciences were spoken of in terms of 'class', but this word fairly quickly faded away to be replaced by the concept of 'art that serves the people'. When this was explained to us, it turned out to be synonymous with 'art that serves the Party'. Such ideological conjuring tricks were carried out quite blatantly, without any qualms whatsoever, and there was absolutely no point in challenging them. Nobody even tried to, though M. found it hard to curb his polemical fervour. I am not sure that he was really a polemicist by temperament, but I believe he became one simply because he lived in a lunatic era during which an attempt was made to destroy root and branch the basis of our social life, the very foundation of European and, consequently, Russian culture: to wit, the Christian understanding of time, history, and the personality.

There is certainly no hint of polemics in M.'s early articles published in *Apollon** where he defines his position vis-à-vis the Symbolists, dissociating himself from them without any contentiousness. (It was only in this negative sense that Viacheslav Ivanov had any effect on the Acmeists: like Andrei Bely, he was a theoretician of Symbolism, and the Acmeists defined their position by drawing the line between themselves and the Symbolists, chiefly Viacheslav Ivanov.)

Three articles appeared in *Apollon*: one on the reader, one on Chaadayev, and another on Villon. In the first M. says that the poet speaks not to a near but to a distant reader. The distant reader can neither be educated nor be treated cavalierly. M. here rejects the didactic, high-priestly role assumed by the Symbolists, with their view of themselves as an elite living in a 'Silver Age'. The article on Chaadayev dealt with a theme no less relevant to the day: a Russian thinker, greatly influenced by Western ideas, nevertheless returns to his native soil and in doing so finds inner freedom – 'the greatest gift Russia can bestow'. (It is indeed the case that Russian thinkers enjoyed an inner freedom that no despotic power was ever able to deny them. This does not, of course, apply to those nihilist spirits who were both slaves of the crowd and simultaneously its leaders.) Having understood the importance of inner freedom in his youth, M. was unable to give it up, as all the Fellow Travellers were to

* See Makovski, Appendix A.

do with such ease. M.'s early attainment of intellectual maturity made it impossible for him to live at peace with the new ideology. But at the time it was written, before the Revolution, what gave the article its topical relevance was something else: as a movement, Symbolism was a radical departure from the Russian poetic and intellectual tradition. Despite the use by some poets of Old Slavonic words and themes from the Russia of pagan times, it was a form of extreme Westernism. The left-wing movements too, for all their nationalist (rather than merely national) component, were almost totally identified with Western 'avant-gardism'. Such was the situation in poetry and painting (and perhaps in music as well?).

The third article, on Villon, also gives expression to M.'s anti-Symbolist attitude. Contrary to the Symbolists, he believed that the artist shares in the sins of the world – that he is not a privileged visitor to whom all is permitted, but a sinner like everybody else. Russian prose literature had always been didactic by tradition (is there anything it did not try to teach us?). 'Didactism is the main-spring of prose,' M. wrote in his article, 'and therefore a prose writer requires a rostrum.' It is quite different in poetry: a poet is not obliged to be superior to the age he lives in, to his society. In these three articles M. accuses the Symbolists of self-love and, in discussing his own affinity to Villon, he suddenly makes a few revealing remarks about himself: 'He [Villon] loved the city and a life of idle pursuits'; he 'lived in Paris in a constant whirl – like a squirrel on a treadmill, never still for a moment. He fancied himself as a lean and ravening little animal, proud of his crumpled fur.' M. thought of himself in just the same way: as a lean and dishevelled little animal – and this in fact is what he looked like to an extraordinary degree. It was indeed just what I loved about him – the restless, animal quality – and I never tired of watching him darting about tirelessly, like a 'squirrel on a treadmill'.

The article further contains references to Villon's working methods – close to M.'s and quite contrary to those of the Symbolists – and to other things they had in common: 'The moon and other such indifferent objects are rigorously excluded from his poetic stock in trade. But he immediately livens up when he talks about roast duck done in sauce, or eternal bliss – which he never quite lost hope of wangling for himself at the end.' There could be no question of roast duck in our day, and the equivalent for M., in periods of comparative plenty, was beefsteak; at all other times an omelette garnished with something out of a can would serve as the basis for a royal feast.

M. does not speak of eternal bliss in his poetry, only of his yearning for that 'meadowland where time stands still'. But he too never quite ceased to hope for it, and even worried in a peculiar way about whether his sense of his own infallibility as a poet – the greatest boon he derived from his self-awareness as an earthly being – would survive with him into the afterlife. He was quite certain there would be music there – on this point he trusted Dante. In his article on Villon, M. also outlines one of his fundamental notions about poetry and time – that is, the question of the relationship between the passing moment, as it is recorded in a poem, and future time, both here on earth and in eternity. 'The passing moment,' he writes, 'has all the pressure of the ages bearing down on it and yet remains precisely what it is.' In a sense this applied to eternity as well, since he understood it as an everlasting 'present moment', like the Eucharist, or as harmony ('harmony is crystallized eternity'). He did not share the view of the mystics who believe that eternity is outside time; for him the eternal passing moment existed *in* time. It must be as a result of M.'s influence that I believe such harmony as one may create on earth is a manifestation of the spirit living in eternity. In other words, even if poetry and music are destroyed in this world, neither can ever be lost because they are embodied for all eternity in anyone who serves as a vessel of harmony. 'Play and gaiety of spirit' – these are what nourish the artist, provided he has 'spilled no hot blood' – and even if he is nothing more than a lean and hungry little animal.

M.'s remarks about the present moment are directed against the Symbolists who sought to escape the confines of time in order to savour eternity here on earth. For M. the passing moment, the 'here and now', was a great gift which it never occurred to him to spurn – particularly since it was through the 'here and now' that he knew the joy of eternity. This was no doubt the reason for his exceptional capacity to live for the moment, to take boundless delight in the present, without any heed for the fleeting cares of this world or fear for his own long-suffering skin. If it had not been for this ability to live in the present, he would not have been able to write verse in 1937, when he knew perfectly well that his end was very close. We were able to go on treating ourselves to the feast of life only because he infected me with his own joy, not allowing the imminent catastrophe to cast a shadow on the beautiful moments of the present. Some people got the idea that M. must have been much better off in 1937 than ever before if he was able to write such serene poetry at that time. It was, on the contrary, sheer, unimaginable horror, and I should have fallen into the pit if it had not been for this extraordinary creature living at my side; blessed with gaiety of spirit and harmony in full measure, he knew that 'the fabric of our world is renewed by death' and so had no fear of his own approaching doom, seeing the 'activity of the spirit in art as a free gesture of self-assertion within the all-embracing element of the Atonement'. Such self-assertion has nothing in common with individualism – it is indeed the individualists who are most liable to be paralysed by fear.

In his early articles M. does not insist on his right to inner freedom – for the simple reason that he already possessed it. He did not polemicize with the dominant movement of the day, Symbolism, but merely dissociated himself from it. His main purpose in writing these articles was to set forth the basic ideas which he never subsequently abandoned. The amazing thing is that he wrote them between the ages of twenty-two and twenty-four. Where did he get such maturity?

For M. the subject of literature always overlapped with historiosophy and ideas about the world in general. The three themes were inseparable. He thought of poetry as a plough which turns over the deeper layers of time and thus vanquishes it. Its sacramental character means that the poet has a special responsibility to other people – his potential readers – for every word he utters. The poet cannot expect people to make any allowances for him, and there are certain things he must not do. He may play with people; in this he will be as sinful as anyone else, but it is not a mortal sin. What he must not do on any account is to seduce people. The poet is only human, like his fellow men, and thus he cannot know more than others. For this reason, if he sets himself up as an authority or preaches, he is a seducer. You cannot presume to lead people if you yourself are wandering in a world where you do not know the way: 'I thumb my meaningless life like a mullah his Koran.' The poet himself feels the need for authority, looks to it for shelter and warmth. Poetry may be sacred, but the poet himself is a poor sinner. Poetry can never be equivalent to revelation – as M. never forgot for a moment. What did he need a reader for? He only needed someone to try out his verse on, someone he could then drink a bottle of wine or go out for a walk with. In one's 'meaningless life' it is nice to have some friends . . .

Poetic trends had philosophical as well as literary significance for M. He was amazed at the intellectual poverty of the Futurists, and at the grand but hollow pretensions of the Symbolists with their 'bridges to eternity'. He understood the importance of 'schools' in painting and music, but was sceptical of them in poetry. He regarded any poetic voice, like a man's personality, as something unique and inimitable. He was particularly severe on any verse written 'in the Acmeist manner' – and of this there was a great deal in the twenties. He made some slight allowances for Gumilev's love of surrounding himself with disciples – largely out of his friendly feelings towards him – but he had no time for the disciples as such. The question of 'style' did not exist for him, because he believed that style, being a functional aspect of a poet's work, was wholly derivative of its general character. The words 'style' and 'form' had no place in his vocabulary. Neither did the word 'creative'. I never heard him use them. I must say that I too find it very hard to get my tongue around them.

This attitude of M.'s towards poetry was in itself a source of complete disagreement with his contemporaries. The era had given us a ready-made philosophy, and all it demanded of writers was formal excellence and richness of language and style. The Formalists studied formal 'devices', the stylistic aspects of language, and the interplay of literary schools – for instance the conflict between traditionalists and innovators. In other words, the Formalists thought on the same lines as the representatives of official literature. The only difference was in the degree of sophistication, rather than in substance – the people promoting the officially recognized line were simply barbarians. Poetry may, of course, be studied by any means at all, provided it yields points of substantive interest, but mechanically picking it over with a pair of forceps can only produce specious results. It is no accident that the Formalists spent so much time on Senkovski and Benediktov. The most attractive of their favourite writers was Kiukhelbeker, Pushkin's friend and the subject of an enthusiastic study by Tynianov.

It was only after 1922 that M.'s articles took on a highly polemical character and conversation with him tended to end in violent argument. Willy-nilly he found himself at cross purposes with his times and his contemporaries – whom, in common with everybody else throughout the world, he had at first taken to be men of a new era. He talks of his opposition quite explicitly in his verse: 'Against the world's grain we sing, / tuning our lyre, as if hastening / to grow a shaggy fleece' . . . Perhaps the reason M. liked Zoshchenko so much was because in one of his stories he describes a man who grows fur, digs himself a burrow in the forest, and howls like a wild animal – he had just not found it possible to live a simple human existence (let alone to try to write poetry!).

The twenties and thirties were the heyday of the 'new', the time when it found most sympathy and support. It was also the time when M. was looked on as a total anachronism, and when hosts of well-wishers, out of genuine friendship for him, wanted to help him 'reform' (as in China nowadays), to get over his backwardness and become a real human being like everybody else. This was done by well-educated young men who imagined that the future belonged to Marxism – people connected with LEF such as Shklovski, Bobrov (who was quite amazed at his own sneaking fancy for such 'bunkum' as the poetry of M.'s *Second Book*), Kirsanov (known by his pet name 'Sioma'), Eikhenbaum, and even Tynianov, not to mention hundreds of youngsters involved with the 'proletarian' literary groups, as well as personal friends like Yakhontov and his wife Lilia Popova. Their unsolicited advice took two different forms: some (Kirsanov, Lilia Popova, and the crowds of young-sters) urged him to pick themes 'in harmony with the age', while others bade him speak in a language comprehensible to the reader.

M.'s whole life was spent listening to this kind of thing. In the twenties it upset him because he believed the 'new' had come to stay for a long while and that there might be something in it. In the thirties, on the other hand, he blithely spoke up in a language 'forgotten of their own free will' by everybody around him, and countered all their suggestions with a joke. Only very rarely, and for brief moments, did he now allow himself to be lulled by the opiates they proffered him, wondering whether he must be blind to go against everybody else and not see what they saw.

I can count on my fingers the people who kept their heads and thought the same as M. The main ones were Stenich, Margulis, and Oleinikov – a man with a complicated life history who was the first to understand what sort of a world we now found ourselves in. It was not by chance that in his own work he followed in the footsteps of Captain Lebiadkin.* All three perished – two in the dungeons, and one in a labour camp. Akhmatova, it goes without saying, belonged with them, as M.'s ally and friend. There were of course many more readers than advisers, and M.'s books were always sold out immediately, but how many understood what they read and did not prefer Bagritski, seeing in him a stronger version of Mandelstam, who was blind to the life around him and had failed to 'reform'? Nowadays M.'s younger contemporaries love to talk about his small stature (thanks to a vulgar piece of journalism perpetrated by Ehrenburg), his arrogance, touchiness, and comic behaviour. What else can one expect them to remember if all they got in return for the good advice they used to give him was a scintillating – and sometimes mortifying – quip? There could be no common language between them because M. lived by ideas which had been erased from the minds of his contemporaries and denounced as outmoded obscurantism. Like the builders of the Tower of Babel, they had begun to speak in different tongues. M. had no hand in the building of the tower, and little wonder, therefore, that its builders found him incomprehensible.

The builders of the tower, whether knowingly or not, played a part in all the crimes of the age. To carry out crimes on this scale, those responsible had to feel confident of unwavering and sympathetic support in the rear. Some of the builders of the tower (though they were few and far between, and I knew none of them) had second thoughts, and many perished in 1937. It was among

* Character in Dostoyevski's *The Possessed*.

throngs of original builders of the tower that M. met his death, together with others who had never built anything and had known nothing but persecution. At the time, M.'s death was seen as something perfectly natural, and it made not the slightest impression either in the world of art and literature or among the reading public. What right had an anachronism like him to exist in such times? For the right to live one had to pay due tribute to ideology and the prevailing style. Alarmed only when those who did so were killed, people were quite indifferent about M. Those who failed to pay their dues were not admitted to the 'superstructure'. All they could hope for was a bunk in a labour camp – though in our camps, as in the German ones, there were not even bunks, only bare boards.

I would have gone to a labour camp rather than lived in a writers' villa, but for M. I would have preferred anything to those accursed barracks at the far end of the earth with their suffocating stench, filth, and typhus, lice, hunger and degradation, terror, armed guards, watchtowers and barbed wire . . . After this, to lie in a mass burial pit with a tag on your leg meant deliverance and peace. How is it possible to live when these thoughts are always with me?

II: INCOMPATIBILITY

M.'s articles preserve his living intonation, but in his conversation he was always making jokes, and his witticisms could be very caustic. I know about his public appearances only from people who attended them. He never allowed me or Akhmatova to go to his poetry readings or lectures. Our presence would have embarrassed him. He spoke in public only very rarely – the heavy pall of conformism on such occasions was scarcely conducive to the free expression of one's thoughts. He only once in my presence got involved in an argument at a gathering of writers in the State Publishing House for Literature. This meeting, which I have already mentioned, was concerned with 'scientific poetry'. M. spoke very scathingly about it, questioning the validity of the concept. Narbut was as pleased as Punch: this was his idea of real literary debate. But Sannikov, the other champion of this form of poetry, glowered angrily. He belonged to Andrei Bely's circle and was shocked by what was referred to among its members as 'Mandelstam's total lack of sensitivity'. By now, in fact, everybody without exception, whatever circle he belonged to, disapproved of any blunt expression of opinion. The Bazarov-like plain-spokenness of the twenties had given way to a preference for 'refinement', a simpering kind of smoothness. Marshak found just the right manner when he crooned breathlessly about love of art, about Poetry with a capital letter. Everybody was now easily taken in by this kind of thing. It was thought improper to call a spade a spade, and the height of tactlessness was to scrutinize anything in the harsh light of logic.

I was frightened by M.'s contribution to this meeting – there was a great deal in it to infuriate the authorities. There were of course informers sitting among the audience, but they would be too ignorant to give a proper report of M.'s words. I was more worried about the shorthand record of the proceedings, but fortunately, our stenographers had lost the art of taking down what people said, and all that came out on this occasion was utter gibberish. M. was upset and wanted to make his own record of what he had said. I was barely able to dissuade him. It was quite enough to be surrounded by police spies taking notes on everything we said. Luckily, however, they were so illiterate that one's words lost all meaning as rendered by them. They were utter yahoos, the whole lot of them.

Even now we do not have stenographers who can really take down what is said. They have clearly understood that in this country the facts are not important in any case. It so happens that I appeared as a witness in the suit brought by Lev Gumilev against Irina Punina, who stole Akhmatova's papers and was subsequently allowed by the court to keep them. My testimony was taken down in such a garbled form that it was not possible to enter it in the record. It would not in any case have had any effect on the outcome, which was decisively influenced by a letter from Ardov calling the court's attention to the fact that Gumilev's father had been shot for his intransigence and that the son had been sent to a camp for the same reason. He further recommended that Irina Punina should be recognized as Akhmatova's daughter, since she was a loyal Soviet citizen, unlike her former camp inmate of a son. This document will be a priceless piece of material for Akhmatova's biography. It illustrates the line: 'They have thrown around us the unseen fence of their well-crafted surveillance.' We were careful to watch what we said in Ardov's apartment: he knew only too well how to copy down what was wanted. It was dangerous to open your mouth anywhere, and after M.'s speech about 'scientific poetry', I was unable to sleep for several nights . . .

I only once ever heard M. read his verse in public. This was back in Kiev, in 1919, during the very first days after we met. Some bright sparks had decided to arrange an evening of poetry reading in the same theatre that put on *Fuente Ovejuna*, and for the very same audience which had been so enthralled by the producer's crude effects. Poets were now learning to become stage performers or variety artists. I am not referring to the ordinary kind of poetry reading, but to shows like those mounted in the years just before the Revolution, mainly by the Futurists, who were always so eager to attract an audience, and by Severianin, also a peculiar kind of Futurist in his own eyes. In the twenties the stage was dominated by Mayakovski, and if he failed to draw enough spectators on tour in the provinces, then his impresario, Lavut, would fill the theatre with the men of the local fire brigade, minus their helmets. The crowds also flocked to hear Yesenin. In the middle of the twenties, permission was once given for a public appearance by Akhmatova; the militia was barely able to hold back the crowds trying to storm the auditorium. This was the supreme token of popularity.

The idea of an evening of poetry – particularly in Kiev – was still unfamiliar in 1919. The only people to come were a few regular customers from the Junk Shop – of the kind who went there just out of curiosity, to see what artists and writers looked like. Visitors to the Actors' Club on the same street, with its excellent restaurant, were a rather more serious class of people, and none of these came to the evening. The theatre was filled, however, by a large number of Red Army men who had been sent along for educational and propaganda reasons. One after the other, the poets came out on stage – where had they all sprung from? – and read verse suitable for the occasion: loud, brash, peppered with slogans, and altogether in the spirit of a variety show. It is hard to imagine how they had already managed to produce so much claptrap, but the fact is that most of them came out with what was evidently the whole of their repertoires, though some just showed off their paces in a single turn. It soon appeared that the only important thing was to slip in some catchword from the new vocabulary. Then the poet would be acclaimed as a kindred spirit, like the peasants fighting for Soviet power in Lope de Vega's play. The whole place went wild with excitement when Valia Stenich recited a poem about a session of the Sovnarkom (Council of People's Commissars). Stenich had very soon understood the new state of affairs, and the poem was actually a trenchant comment on the underlying sense of the historical moment we were living through. But the crowd had no ears for this: they reacted only to the sound of individual words, such as 'Sovnarkom', which had the inflammatory effect of a red flag. People had already been trained to make the right responses. Such things can be inculcated with remarkable speed.

Up to now, whenever I had been to the theatre, it was generally to the workshop where the sets and stage props were made ; I was used to seeing the stage from the vantage point of the gridiron where I went with other members of my 'herd' of artists to help fix the scenery. From up there, at a height of four or five storeys, one had an excellent view of the actors concealed behind the wings as they waited for their cues and then, first crossing themselves, leaped jauntily right out to the front of the stage and immediately took up the postures required of them. From this bird's eye view, when the human figure is reduced to the crown of a wig and a projecting foot, all the trappings of the threatre are a pleasure to see: the anxious movements of the prompter's head (now, it seems, a thing of the past, alas), the stage itself, and the quivering of the wings – which have also gone for good. But we took the poetry evening very seriously and went to sit in seats in the first or second circle, from which I had a good view of M. when he suddenly came out to recite.

He was alarmingly untheatrical, quite out of place on the broad stage across which he sauntered all alone, as though walking down the street. He did so at an even pace, holding himself very erect, and all he needed was a walking stick to flourish slightly as he went.

Right in front of the footlights, without straining his voice, but so distinctly that not a single word was lost – it was clear that he was used to public appearances – he read a short poem from *Stone*: '"Lord," I said, not meaning to, / It was only a slip of the tongue. / God's name, like a large bird, / flew out of my breast.' The audience listened and even applauded – not very much, of course, but politely enough – and I was very struck at how ill-suited he was to this stage, and how incompatible his poem was with the prevailing mood.

Immediately after he had recited, I went backstage by a side entrance – as we had agreed beforehand – and, having collected our money on the spot in the good old way from the kindhearted manager, we made for the street as fast as we could go. Our favourite saying – I have forgotten when it first came to us – was: 'It's always better on the street.' It was indeed always better on the street, and once we were there I asked M. why he had chosen that particular poem. He replied that it was a good poem which he liked and had no intention of disavowing. This was all he would say, and we went off to the Junk Shop to spend his earnings on a meal. Rates of pay were laid down by Moscow, but Ukrainian prices were still such that we no doubt had a good meal for our money. I had still not experienced real hunger, even after my family suddenly became penniless (I remember the sharp stab of astonishment when my father happened to tell me that all our money had come to an end – it had just melted away, vanished into a hole in the ground), but M. had already known what it was to go hungry in the starving Moscow of 1918. He had been helped to get away to the Ukraine by a Bolshevik official called Malkin. (This Malkin perished in 1937, and Povolotskaya, Shklovski's neighbour, a fat police spy whose father had been a tsarist general – this type was particularly loathsome, though I know they did it out of fear – was summoned to the prosecutor's office after the Twentieth Congress and invited to take back her 'testimony' against him. Ehrenburg defended Povolotskaya to me – apparently someone he knew was friends with her – and asked how I knew she was an informer. It is true that I saw no documents, since we were never shown such things, but I remember how the woman, who was a complete idiot, went running to Vasilisa Shklovski to complain about what they were doing to her. Soon afterwards she was stricken by paralysis. We knew our informers – 'the country must know its heroes' – although we were never able to see any documentary evidence.)* Malkin had got M. a voucher so that he could order a made-to-measure suit for himself. These vouchers were already very difficult to come by, and later became altogether unobtainable, since such suits were reserved for the elite and for diplomats. He also gave M. a pile of paper money whose value was very much higher in the Ukraine. By the time M. got to Kiev, however, there was not much of this wealth left, since he had spent most of it in Kharkov on the way. I reproached him for spending it like this when he should have known I was waiting for him in Kiev. But even the remains of his paper gold were enough to keep us for a long time in veal chops and cherry pie. We were young and managed very well on what he had. After a month in Kiev, M. had fully recovered from his days of near-starvation in Moscow. The first time one starves it is hard to bear, but no irreparable harm is done. Akhmatova used to say she had 'starved in the clinical sense' three times. The third time was in Tashkent during the war – food was plentiful, but prices were very high and you could not live on a Moscow salary. She omitted to mention a fourth period of intermittent starvation in Leningrad right after the war. For me it is difficult to say exactly how many times I have been hungry or undernourished. The provinces began to get a little more to eat only during the Khrushchev period. Until then the shops had practically nothing in stock except coffee made of barley; whatever else 'came in' from time to time had to be queued for. These queues were so vicious that I never even tried to join them. It may not be such a bad thing to go without food sometimes – undernourishment delays the onset of arteriosclerosis.

But to return to the verse recited by M. in the theatre. It struck the wrong note altogether, and if the audience did not turn ugly it was only because most of them consisted of Red Army men who were there under orders and had not yet been properly indoctrinated. They were all peasant youths whose grandmothers lit the lamps under the icons as before and spoke God's name continually. There were not enough political commissars to cope, and these

* *Hope Against Hope*, page 55.

simple boys from the villages still remembered their grandmothers. That is why there was no outcry. But the word 'God' had already by then become an object of mockery. All who still honoured it were taunted and humiliated with a fervour shown only by people sincerely convinced that they have discovered a great new truth. After another six months of Civil War those same soldiers who clapped at M.'s poem because their indoctrination was not yet complete would have known the proper reaction to what was called 'religious propaganda', 'obscurantism', or 'opium of the people'. Their political commissars would by then have left them in no shadow of doubt that there is no God and never will be, and they would already have come to believe their commissars instead of their grandmothers. Even as it was, in those days when the new, completely scientific age was just dawning, if the audience had been just a little bit smarter, M. would have been hooted and whistled off the stage. The 'smart' public will always fall for propaganda and likes to keep a step or two ahead of progress. It was an age of innovation and the reaction to any 'mumbo jumbo' from the past was violent. Not only God, but poetry, ideas, love, pity, and compassion were hastily thrown overboard. We were to begin a new life 'without any nonsense'. True, we were not the only ones, and the new era was not our invention, but we had a receptive public and good political commissars who knew how to take advantage of the historical moment and the general mood.

M. behaved as though there was no such thing as a public or political commissar. For him there were just people, and he himself was simply one of them, a human being like anybody else. He refused to accept the idea of a 'public' before which one 'performed'. He lived and acted quite independently, wrote the things that poured out of him spontaneously (if they were not spontaneous, he did not write them down), said what he thought, and 'fashioned words, listening to no one, alone with one other'. He never tried to see himself as others saw him. He was absolutely indifferent to appearances. If ever I nagged him about his behaviour he just brushed me aside, impervious alike to my doggedness and claims to feminine infallibility, and said: 'Take me or leave me.' It was a good thing I was by nature different from most women, who spend all their time trying to put their husbands right; this was the only reason I did not pitch into him more often. No woman, political commissar, or anybody else under the sun could possibly influence him against his will. He always thought things out for himself before committing himself. His face had a quite special expression when he was thinking – rather as in the photograph of him in a sweater. Whenever he spoke of something that was an article of faith with him, as in his conversation with Ivanov-Razumnik about terror, his face took on an oddly abstracted and severe look. In the first half of the twenties this was the expression he wore most of the time: he was continuously making up his mind about matters of principle or reacting against something. At that time I did not yet know how his mind worked, but I often heard him give utterance to his conclusions, which tended to slip out in conversations with supporters of the 'new', provoking their derision – they felt that M. suffered from negativism or pathological backwardness. Occasionally I used to think there might indeed have been a touch of negativism about him: how could one be against *everything*, from the Lubianka to the NEP establishment opened by Pronin, the former owner of the Stray Dog?

I failed to see the connection between the literary salons of the NEP period, Agranov, and the Lubianka. I wanted to frequent them, though at the same time I closed my eyes to the horror of the life around us, saying how unbearable it was and just hoping it would end as soon as possible. In other words, I was the one who sought consolation in negativism, while M. allowed himself no such luxury – he probably had no need to try to console himself in any way. He used to ask why we should behave like ostriches. Life was what it was, and we had to take it as it came. We had no choice in the matter. There are echoes of such talk in his poetry, but I did not notice them at the time; when you are young you react to the rhythm, to the poem as a whole, not to the ideas behind it. In the poem in which M. declares he is 'nobody's contemporary', he has the two lines: 'Well, then, if we cannot forge another / Let's manage with the age we have.' However much he may have been tempted to seek refuge in negativism, he was able to overcome it, never turning his back on life, despite everything.

He thus managed 'with the age we have', not even consoling

himself with negativism, which, like all poses, can make things easier to bear. M. was the only person I knew who was absolutely devoid of all pretensions or affectations, always remaining utterly true to his own natural self. Once – this was in the thirties – he said to me with some embarrassment that women are never quite themselves, or, to put it bluntly, are always posturing and attitudinizing. 'Even you and Anna Andreyevna . . .' I could only gasp – at long last he had seen through us! In my case it went without saying: I was always putting on airs, while for Akhmatova negativism was not only second nature, it was also something she deliberately cultivated, like the methods taught her by Nedobrovo for the conscious improvement of one's speech, bearing, and manners – all modelled on the behaviour of his own wife, a 'real lady'. The only thing that saved Akhmatova was the vehemence of her gestures (which upset Nedobrovo but also amused him) and her natural untamability. Without these qualities she would never have become a poet. Poets are always vehement and untamable. Otherwise there can be no poetry.

The very idea of consciously adopting some 'attitude' or other was quite foreign to M.; his words and deeds always accorded with his feelings and thoughts at any given moment – hence his spontaneity, his sharp reaction to anything false or stupid, particularly to the kind of vile behaviour we encountered at every end and turn. I sometimes sympathized with him in his outbursts, but often I wished I could have taught him to be little more artful, to be mealy-mouthed like Marshak, to play the role of an amiable teddy bear, always determined to charm whomever he was talking with.

A complete absence of affectation, a stupefying naturalness, firmness in standing one's ground in the things that matter (a moral rather than a social attitude) – these qualities are a handicap, leaving a man defenceless and making his life far more difficult than it need be. In a way it is a defect, like the habit of always blurting out what you think. Rich and independent people can afford to – as long, of course, as they are not too much influenced by their milieu. Only the Russian gentry, I imagine, was able to throw up a Pierre Bezukhov, who could simply retire to his village and totally ignore his peers. But in our times of poverty, complete dependence on the whims of petty officials, general degradation and servitude (at first voluntary and then enforced), such qualities were fatal. At the beginning of the twenties – one has to bear in mind the sort of circles we moved in at that time – M. did protect himself with an old-fashioned politeness peculiar to Petersburg, and this served as a kind of camouflage. But he abandoned it as soon as he became fully mature. The line in which he apostrophizes his own verse: 'Now is the time, slipshod old man, to clump around in boots,' is also addressed to himself. This was written during the days when we had managed to trade in my father's insurance policy for a hundred roubles to spend at Torgsin* and M. had been able to have an excellent suit made for himself by a first-rate Moscow tailor. In such a suit it was easier to 'clump around in boots', since it in no way impeded one's movement. Also, since the pockets never bulged, one could cram them full of all kinds of trash. Are there any tailors left like that in the world? M. deliberately put on this same suit when he was taken to the Lubianka in 1934, but nothing helped there – not even the uniform topcoat of a Soviet diplomat.†

After he had left Kiev for the Crimea with the Ehrenburgs (I did not go with them, as we had agreed), I remembered him from time to time – always as I had seen him on the stage of the theatre, facing that mysterious and outlandish crowd. At the time I had thought they might tear him limb from limb, but the danger did not, in fact, come from them. As it was to turn out, there was infinitely less to fear from that kind of crowd than from the submissive 'masses' in the highly organized existence to come.

---

* Acronym for 'All-Union Association for Trade with Foreigners': a network of stores created in the thirties mainly for the benefit of foreigners who could buy scarce goods in them for currency or gold. Russians with any 'hard' assets were also allowed to use them.

† Allusion to Solzhenitsyn's *First Circle*, in which the arrested Soviet diplomat is stripped of his uniform in the Lubianka.

III: POLES APART

M. once mentioned the profession he considered the antithesis of his own. This was in Yalta. We had gone to Oreanda for a walk when we happened to meet a chance acquaintance from Moscow, a certain R. He was a Bolshevik from a family of priests, and he was rumoured to make his living by writing articles against religion, but we did not know whether there was any truth in it. He was a passionate collector of all kinds of bric-à-brac, and something of a Bluebeard. He liked to talk in riddles and was continually changing wives. Meeting M. and me, he insisted on taking us to see the latest one, who, I believe, was also to be his last. At some difficult juncture she threw him out of his own house with a great to-do and grabbed the whole of his collection. After this he disappeared. A specialist on India, she was firmly convinced that Ghandi had betrayed the working class there. She used to visit us occasionally – to report on us, I believe. She could only have got rid of someone like R. by blackmailing him: he loved his collection of antique knick-knacks far too much to part with them of his own free will, not to mention his 'living space'. Obviously this secretive man who always spoke in riddles had not been able to contain himself at some moment of despondency and let slip to his beloved wife that he did not believe what he read in the newspapers. Even in the most 'vegetarian' times – to use Akhmatova's expression – this would have been enough to spell a man's ruin. R.'s expulsion from his own home took place at the beginning of the thirties. I do not know what happened to him subsequently. He could have survived only by a miracle. An intellectual and a wit (who cleverly kept a curb on his tongue, however), he belonged to the first generation of revolutionary activists and was bound to have perished in the years just before the war when the old guard was removed *in toto*.

On the day of our meeting in Oreanda we had only the vaguest of forebodings about the future and hoped (just as people do today, in 1970) that the peak of cruelty and vileness had been reached and that henceforth things simply had to ease up. Fools always go on hoping like this, but R. probably had no illusions. He knew better than anyone what sort of people we were dealing with, and like many others, he took refuge in gentle irony. We were all four standing in front of his house, on the parched earth of Oreanda. It reminded M. of the real Crimea, the east coast which had no cypresses or other such commonplace southern embellishments. With great relish – he had a taste for such nasty stories – R. told us the reason why no luxuriant grounds had ever been laid out in Oreanda: it was all due to some monkey business involving grand dukes, insurance companies, arson, and premiums. Whether it was true or not doesn't concern me; it was a perfectly innocuous conversation to have even in the presence of his wife, the specialist on India, who wiggled her hips and smiled with pleasure at these revelations about the murky doings of the ruling elite in pre-revolutionary Russia. While I admired the uninhibited manner in which she wiggled her hips, M. listened indifferently to R.'s chatter, but suddenly we heard him say something that at once made us both prick up our ears: he said he had spent the previous evening in Yalta with someone whose speciality was the opposite of M.'s. As usual with him, M. just nodded and did not ask any questions. On our way home, I asked him what he thought this specialty could be. 'The theatre, probably,' M. replied. My conjecture was that R. had perhaps been thinking rather of a Chekist, but M. considered it hardly likely that R. would have had in mind such a crude antithesis between a jailer and his potential victim. But whatever R. may have been thinking of does not matter – the important thing for me here is that M.'s own idea of his antipode was an actor.

I believe that in contrasting the work of the actor and the poet, M. was thinking mainly of the total difference in their attitude to words, to verse, to poetry in general. He once referred to an actor's reading of verse as 'declamatory hogwash'. When we got to know Yakhontov (who, as it turned out, was our neighbour on the other side of the wall when we lived in the Lycée at Tsarskoye Selo), M. immediately set to work getting him to eradicate the theatrical inflections from his readings, particularly of verse. Mayakovski he managed fairly well because he had attended performances by the poet himself, but he read Pushkin in the style of the Maly or the Arts Theatre. M. liked Yakhontov's rendering of Gogol and Dostoyevski, and thought of him as a 'family retainer of literature'

rather than as an actor – he had made himself so familiar with
Akaki Akakievich and Makar Devushkin* that he was their living
reincarnation in the modern world. M.'s friendship with him dated
from their first meeting, and from then on he never ceased to work
with him on his poetry readings. While M. was alive, Yakhontov
did in fact give up declaiming verse in theatrical style, but later he
began to dream of winning the Lenin prize (or was it already then
the Stalin prize?), and to keep on the right side of the powers-that-
be, he began to imitate the manner of Kachalov. But even so he
failed to get the prize – one more proof that such efforts are always
wasted.

The Kachalov manner of reading was deeply repugnant to M.
We once happened to go to one of his recitals. How this happened
I do not remember, but it was probably because we had been
invited; otherwise we should never have gone to something so
uncongenial. As soon as Kachalov began to read poetry, M. got up
and left, waving his hand at the poor man as he went out of the
auditorium. It was a small hall, with few people, and M.'s gesture
was very noticeable. I remember the hurt and surprised look on
Kachalov's face as he watched us go. I reproached M. for his rudeness in not at least waiting for the intermission. But, as usual, he
completely ignored what I said. ('How clever she is, our Nadia:
she knows everything,' or 'Clever little Nadia, always giving
advice' – these were the customary words of mockery with which
he put me in my place.) But what's the point of having a wife if you
are unwilling to listen to the voice of feminine commonsense? This
time he suggested I send a telegram to Shanghai: 'Very clever stop
can give advice Chinese stop willing travel China stop . . .' I did my
best to explain to him that Kachalov had been offended, and I told
him Akhmatova's story of how, shattered by the death of Yesenin,
Kachalov had come to her and sat the whole evening reading
Yesenin's poetry very beautifully, without any histrionics. But this
only made M. even more scornful – this time at Akhmatova's
expense: how clever she was, agreeing to listen to Kachalov so as
not to spoil her relations with the Arts Theatre . . . The only thing
that was really pretty mean about this was that in fact I never did

* Heroes of Gogol's *The Greatcoat* (1842) and Dostoyevski's *Poor People*
(1846).

give him advice and only rarely nagged him – chiefly when he hurt the feelings of such nice people as Kachalov, our Prince of Denmark. What is more, I instinctively knew he was on the right track whenever he did something that would never have occurred to me – such as abandoning a recently arranged source of earnings in order to go to the Crimea, or spending our last penny on a nice new dress for me, a book on architecture, or five bottles of wine. He just did not live by the laws of female commonsense, and I did not try to argue – this way life was more fun. Sometimes, as a special treat, he even took me out to the theatre.

Although we went so rarely, I would not say that M. did not like the theatre. Impressionable as he was, he was easily captivated by the visual elements, by the stage effects. He loved the long table and final 'dumb' scene in Meyerhold's *The Inspector General* and the deck of the barge tilted over slightly awry towards the audience, as though it were riding the waves, in Shostakovich's opera *Lady Macbeth*. I can easily count up the number of visits we made to the theatre. We went most frequently of all in Voronezh, at times when people had come to see us from Moscow. We even went to see *Cricket on the Hearth** there, something we should never have plucked up courage to do in Moscow. We had first seen Mikhoels, by whom M. was really very taken, in Kiev while he was on tour there, and then later in Leningrad. We went to several of his performances together with Akhmatova, who prided herself on being able to follow the words† and was full of praise for him – but even so, she insisted on making the point that he was still not a patch on Mikhail Chekhov. Perhaps it was this which first drove M. to ask: 'How can we wean Akhmatova away from the Arts Theatre?' She went to the theatre just as seldom as we did and for the most part got excited only about people she knew personally. I agreed with her in the case of Ranevskaya, who really was very good, but I was irritated by the praise she lavished on Batalov, the film actor. She talked, incidentally, less about his quality as an actor than about the fact that he was the most famous one in the world. I doubt this,

---

*Adaptation of the Dickens novel, first produced in 1914 by Boris Shushkevich at the First Studio of the Moscow Arts Theatre, when Mikhail Chekhov performed in it. The play was revived after the Revolution.

† Mikhoels acted in Yiddish.

but even if he was, why should we care whether someone is famous or not? Public success impresses me about as much as last year's snow, and it upset me that in her old age even Akhmatova showed a weakness for this kind of thing. I was also amused by her exaggerated praise of Raikin, whom she had never seen on the stage (except perhaps on television). She had picked up this cult of Batalov and Raikin from the Ardov household (Batalov was Ardov's stepson, and he worshipped Raikin); one of Akhmatova's finest qualities, her capacity for passionate devotion, was in this case sadly misapplied.

None of us found the theatre congenial, and it is thus not for us to judge it. It meant very little to us, except insofar as it was a part of city life; as a 'city dweller and friend of city dwellers', M. even wrote several articles on the theatre, including something on Mikhoels. This enthusiasm for Mikhoels – he really was a remarkable actor, quite unlike anybody else – may have been due in part to M.'s interest in all things Jewish, and also to the fact that when an actor performs in a language you do not understand, you are unlikely to catch the theatrical inflections. Whether Mikhoels went in for these, I do not know. I rather think not . . .

I believe that poets and actors are at opposite poles not only in their completely different attitude to words, but in other respects as well. A poet lives by words, by seeking and finding the words he needs, and if he loses this gift he is finished – word and thought are indivisible for him. For an actor, on the other hand, words as such are less vital than the part he has to play. His part consists of a verbal text, but the actual words have only an ancillary function for him. The very intonation of the actor and that of the poet are as different as the sound of their voices. But this, I believe, is still not the whole story. There is nothing at all about the poet, whether of major or secondary importance, that resembles any specific feature of the actor's work. In one of his poems Pasternak compared himself with an actor,* and Akhmatova uses the following image about the poet: 'The footlights bristle at his feet, the spotlight's cold flame brands his forehead.' M., however, had a far keener sense of the absolute difference between actor and poet; I explain it by the fact that he thought of himself as speaking to

* In 'Hamlet', the first of the Zhivago poems.

listeners remote from him in space and time, not to people in close proximity. For this reason he could have no awareness of footlights at his feet, let alone of being picked out by a spotlight. The only close listeners a poet has – his 'first listeners' – are his friends. He may learn how many copies his books have sold, but this is the most he can gauge about the extent of his contact with the public. He certainly cannot draw any conclusion about his readership from what the reviewers say or, for that matter, from the mail sent him by compulsive letter writers. Akhmatova's image of herself as a floodlit figure in the middle of a dark hall full of people I can only put down to a sudden striving for superficial effect, rather than to any actual experience of this kind. Even at an evening of poetry reading, there is no sharp contrast between the poet and his listeners, as between actor and audience. The lighting both for the reader and for his audience is the same, and they remain on an equal footing with each other. It is like a conversation, except that one party to it consists of many people instead of just one. The actor has no sense of addressing a large number of people as individuals – they all merge together in the darkened auditorium to form an undifferentiated whole: 'the public'.

I do not know much about the theatre, but certain differences between the actor and the poet are immediately apparent, particularly as regards their relations with the audience, in the case of the actor, and with the reader, in the case of the poet. The actor plays to the public sitting in the auditorium. He has to carry it with him, getting across his own feelings, or rather the feelings of the character he is playing. Mikhail Bulgakov says the actor must 'provoke' the feelings of his audience, but the poet, as M. wrote in a letter to his father, works 'for himself', leaving the reader free to accept or reject the result. A poet who works for his reader is what M. called a 'magazine poet', that is, he is really writing prose dressed up in poetic form. The poet is of course linked with his contemporaries, like anybody else, but it is a different kind of link from the one between the actor and the public he tries to sway. The poet, far from trying to carry his contemporaries along with him, is always aware that he is only their reflection. This is well put by Akhmatova: 'I am your voice, the warmth of your breath, *I am the reflection of your face.*' The poet is dependent on his contemporaries to a far greater degree than the actor: instead of 'provoking' feelings, he is himself affected by other people's feelings and opinions, sometimes resisting them and at other times giving way to them. In the theatre it is the playwright, not the actor, whose relations with his contemporaries are of this kind – though his desire to please his public exposes him to greater temptations than the poet. The freedom of the poet is in his ability to appraise the feelings, opinions, and conduct of his contemporaries in the light of the leading idea on which his own personality is based, in this way deciding what to accept and what to reject. What the actor's freedom consists of, I do not know.

The work of the poet is a process of achieving greater self-knowledge; he is engaged in a constant search for 'the key to life's riddle'. I hesitate to stray into the thickets of philosophy, but I believe that at some point the work of the poet and the philosopher overlap. Both of them are trying to fathom the mystery of the 'self' in the world of things, and this is possible only by a process of interpenetration between subject and object. What the poet experiences through his senses is transmuted into a particle of his spirit, and, changing or renewing something in the makeup of his personality, it then becomes the stuff of poetry. I believe that an opposite sequence is also possible: experience, in becoming the stuff of poetry, brings about a change in the makeup of the personality. But in either case what it amounts to is that, as it comes into being and takes shape in words, a poem opens up to the poet the deeper meaning of his experience. Finally, there are cases in which the poet prepares for a future experience and, by thus anticipating it, grasps its essence. This happens, for example, when he 'practises at death', that is: 'dies' by arresting the flow of time and then, after dwelling in the protracted moment wrested from it, returns to life. (Is this how M. came to think of eternity as a moment perpetuated forever?) In a short poem which he wrote in connection with his translations of four Petrarch sonnets M. said:

> A thousand times a day, marvelling at myself,
> I have to die an actual death
> and in the same preternatural way
> come back to life again.

M. never used words lightly, or spoke of things he had not actually experienced. I believe, therefore, that his unshakable faith in resurrection, in a future life, was based on a real experience of death and resurrection. I share his faith, even though I have no similar experience but only a life which was real and joyful in love, devoid of meaning during the years of fear and waiting, and beautiful now that my life's work is done and I can look forward to the end.

In the work of any poet the process of attaining self-knowledge may take place on various levels, ranging from visionary insight to mere play. The word 'revelation' is used in talking about knowledge of God, but to a certain extent, all knowledge attained by man, whether through the physical senses ('the eye is a tool of the mind'), by intuition, or by means of intellectual or poetic cognition, must be regarded as a gift and revelation peculiar to human kind. Poetic cognition, it should be added, reaches to greater depths than philosophical or scientific cognition; the fact is that certain areas are closed to pure reason. By 'certain areas' I mean neither the other world nor the 'thing-in-itself', but much simpler things. Pure reason is abstract and thus incapable of taking in the experience of everyday life; but the poet keeps his sense of existence as an integrated physical and spiritual whole, converting his outward experience, in all its tangible particulars, into an inner, spiritual experience. In science, too, it may be that there is an element of play, but by no means to such a degree as in poetry, which, as M. remarks, is *essentially* play ('children at play with their Father') and gaiety of spirit. It is this which makes it possible for the poet to perceive things whole, to achieve unity between outward and inner experience, the merging of the passing moment with eternity. Play gives rise to a kind of joy which could be described as 'light-mindedness' or 'levity', but without an admixture of levity, poetry is impossible. For this reason poets always incur the displeasure of our heavy-handed guardians of order, particularly those who feel called upon to protect the honour of literature – these are the fiercest enemies of poetry. Whether in exploring hidden depths or in play, the poet is distinguished by spontaneity and self-sufficiency. This is what makes him a threat to public order: he cannot be forced to utter 'things known to be permitted', and what he might say of his own accord is unpredictable. This again is something that distinguishes him from the actor. The 'spontaneity' of the actor is severely limited by the role he has to play and the preordained lines on which the performance must unfold. The actor's personal contribution can be made only jointly, as it were, with the character he plays and whose words he speaks. Having to represent someone else, he becomes a dual personality who does not play in his own right, any more than he answers for the words he learns by heart: they have been put into his mouth on behalf of the character whose identity he assumes on the stage. But the poet answers for everything. He speaks solely for himself and on his own behalf. Even in types of poetry involving 'externalized' subject matter, such as the narrative poem or the ballad, which thus have a large 'literary' component in them, the poet still keeps his own voice and features. In this connection M. makes a curious remark in his essay on Villon: 'By his very nature, a lyric poet is a bisexual creature, capable of an infinite number of fissions in the name of his inner dialogue.' M. detected this feature, which he called 'lyrical hermaphroditism', in Villon, though it was not something he possessed himself – he spoke with only one voice. But Pasternak, for example, in 'The Childhood of Luvers', was quite clearly able to identify himself with his adolescent heroine and to feel with her through all the experiences typical of this period in a girl's life. This power of self-indication goes much deeper in the early story than in his novel, where the dialogues between Lara and Zhivago are simply variations on Pasternak's own words (which is precisely what I like about the novel: I appreciate this kind of thing much better than those neatly constructed novels in which the author manipulates his characters like so many marionettes). In his best things Pasternak is a poet of inner feeling and sensation, but he seems to have had a strong urge to get outside himself, to 'externalize' himself, and also to split himself up fissiparously, multiplying himself in as many different aspects as possible. It was this that drew him to experiment with poetry of the kind in which the poet attempts an objective projection of himself. If there is more than one voice in pure lyrics, it is generally due to a split in the poet's personality – which is seeking to become whole again.

The actor has a different way of trying to mend the split between his own personality and the character he plays. He has to efface himself, so to speak, in favour of his role, since he can put only very few of his own features into it. Mikhoels used to insist that makeup should emphasize the actor's own features instead of disguising them, and he thus avoided wearing an obvious mask or *persona* – yet mask it was, even though preserving his own features. An actor cannot exist without masks; otherwise he could never accommodate all the parts he has to play during his career on the stage. One young actor recently wrote in a newspaper that his task was not to identify with whatever part he was given, but to find himself in it, since he always played *himself*. This is an interesting way of looking at the problem of combining the two personalities involved in a role, but in fact, in any actual stage performance, the dichotomy is never resolved: the actor's self has to assume the features of someone else; in order to play the part, he must coexist in it, to some degree or another, with the other person represented by it.

Of course, the actor's work differs from that of other kinds of performing artists (the musician or the *diseur*) insofar as the theatre, with its own conventions of space and time, creates an illusion of real life; this is precisely what arouses the spectator's emotions. There is a wonderful book which describes the self-deception of the theatre audience:

the theatre has become my favourite place of entertainment, and its allurements an imagined need of my heart and soul. What does it mean, this love of being present at a theatrical representation of sad or tragic events which one would not like to go through oneself? Yet at the same time the spectator indulges in a feeling that he himself is sharing in all this sorrow and, what is more, finds pleasure in it . . . But how, I ask you, can one feel compassion in respect to events that are purely imaginary and take place only on the stage?

The author then has this to say about a friend who is carried away by the collective emotions of the audience in a theatre: 'He became unlike himself, unlike what he had been before he entered this place; he merged with the crowd, becoming just one of many spectators . . . looking, applauding, shouting, or going wild together with all the others.' This description of the effect of the theatre at the dawn of our new era somehow reminds me of the crowds during the upheaval of the Revolution: in them, too, the individual was swallowed up, until he later lost his identity among the depersonalized 'masses' at public meetings, where everyone did exactly what he was told. The theatre thus demonstrated the art of depersonalizing people, turning them into 'the public', even before the advent of producers able to stage-manage whole nations.

Poetry is preparation for death. The actor who dies on the stage does not come back to life, but merely turns back into himself, discarding his mask and the alien *persona* it represented. To a certain extent the actor is comparable with the writer of prose fiction, the man of letters, whose works also undermine the personality by leading it into an illusory world of the imagination. Nobody holds an actor responsible for the characters he plays, but a poet is rightly made to answer for every word he utters; for this reason, poetry is always 'the song of destiny'. In our mad times, however, anything is possible. Ehrenburg told me a story of Khrushchev's about how Stalin was once watching Buchma – at least, as I remember the story, it was about this remarkable Ukrainian actor – playing the part of a traitor. Stalin commented that a traitor could be played so well only by someone who actually *was* a traitor, and he demanded that the appropriate measures be taken. He gave this order to both Khrushchev and Malenkov, and quite independently of each other – it was always dangerous to concert one's actions – they managed to fool Stalin by saying they were having Buchma followed with a view to capturing all the other traitors connected with him. They did not have to keep this up for very long, because Buchma was saved either by his own death or by Stalin's – I do not know who died first, but at any rate Buchma survived to die a natural death. That's the sort of luck that only actors have. I am glad for his sake. It was possible only because Stalin's younger henchmen used to go to the theatre, where they unobtrusively joined the crowd in its acclaim of the cast. They would not have tried to save a poet. Poetry did not agree with them at all. Poetry brings out the reader's personality, deepens it, and makes him an accomplice in the poet's cause – something quite impossible for men who control the destinies of whole peoples. The two things are mutually exclusive.

IV: LITERARY THEORY

Comparing the poet with the actor, I had my sights on a more distant target, namely a theory once current (and still popular) among students of literature, to the effect that the poet and the actor are akin to each other in some of their characteristics. This theory has a great attraction for people engaged in the scholarly study of poetry, since it enables them to ignore the poet himself, the growth of his ideas and feelings, his inner doubts and inclinations. The theory arose during the twenties, when confusion reigned in people's minds and the process of diminishing or destroying the personality was well under way. It was Tynianov who thought up this idea and blithely launched it on its flourishing career. The gist is that the poet speaks not in his own voice, but through an intermediary, creating a kind of mouthpiece between himself and the reader. This intermediary was called the 'literary *persona*', and it was claimed that the poet could change his *persona* at will: one day he might be an innovator, the next a traditionalist (these then turned out to be the greatest innovators of all, except that they were rooted in their native soil, as it were, instead of looking to the West), and the day after that something else again – all depending on the literary school in vogue, the demand of readers, and the general climate of opinion. The chief reason for the poet's change of *persona*, according to the theory, was his transition from one school to another. (The members of OPOYAZ were always very fond of explaining to M. that he had long since had one foot in Futurism. Where on earth did they get this idea? They must have read the manifestos of all the Futurists, from Marinetti to the Burliuks and the Briks. What did all this Futurist literature have in common with the poetry and articles of M., which they must also have read?)

Tynianov attached enormous importance to literary schools, and in constructing his theory of literary 'development' he decided that the main cause of change was to be found in the passing of old trends and their replacement by new ones. Though he probably did not link the concept of 'development' with the idea of 'progress', the theory of successive schools, as Tynianov himself described it, was terribly all-embracing and left no room for such things as the stages in the growth of the poet's own personality, the process by which he acquires experience and comes to maturity. The link between a poet and his literary contemporaries is beyond doubt, but it is different both in degree and in kind from what Tynianov would have us believe.

Tynianov backs up his theory by reference to Pushkin, noting that after Pushkin had abandoned the 'lyrical *persona*' of his youthful Lycée years, he joined the camp of the innovators (the Karamzin circle, Arzamas*) only to go over later to the side of the traditionalists (Katenin, Kiukhelbeker) – who were, in fact, the true innovators. Apropos of this second change of direction, Tynianov tells the story of how Pushkin came to Katenin, handed him his stick, and asked him to beat him – just to teach him a lesson . . . A poet, of course, learns from all his contemporaries as well as from the poets of the past, but he scarcely needs to learn his lesson from any of them with the aid of stick, which would in any case be a poor way of maintaining his connection with them. The OPOYAZ people were a little overfond of anecdotes and took them too much on trust.

According to Tynianov, in changing his 'literary *persona*', the poet may give his biography a new direction. He came to this conclusion through studying the lives of the Romantics and the Classicists. He believed a Romantic equipped himself with a biography quite different from that of a Classicist; consequently, a Classicist who went over to the Romantics had to refurbish his biography. Tynianov also thought that a poet switching from one 'school' to another was like an actor taking on a new part. It is no accident that words from the vocabulary of the theatre crept into Tynianov's articles. He talks, for instance, about the 'makeup' Pushkin wore during his Lycée years and which he 'wiped off' when he joined the Arzamas. Once, in conversation with me, Tynianov quite seriously proposed that certain events in M.'s life should be accepted as 'facts of his literary biography', while others should be disregarded.

The theory of the 'literary *persona*' clearly owed much to the

* Literary circle formed in 1815 to promote the use of a contemporary literary idiom, instead of the archaic style advocated by the traditionalists.

spirit of the twenties with its mass changes of allegiance and capitulation to the victor; by putting oneself at his mercy it was hoped at least to gain a little by way of material advantages. At this time people deliberately refashioned their biographies and tried to live their life anew before fate, *moira*, intervened with a death warrant and cut it short. To be talented now meant that one was skilled at cheating fate. Tynianov himself, it so happens, was not as good as others at adapting himself and was constantly hounded until he switched to writing novels which found favour. He was first attacked by the 'vulgar sociologists'* for allegedly trying to suggest that literature had its own laws of development, unconnected with the class struggle. In fact, it would have been more to the point if he had been denounced for lifting the curtain just slightly on the real nature of human relations in our epoch by talking in terms of the 'mask' or *persona*. True, it was only a case of putting on, not of taking off, the mask, which in the preceding age had been unnecessary. What need was there for a mask when there was such a thing as private life and when society did not have the means to stifle dissidents as long as they refrained from open struggle against it? The masks that people put on in the twenties had the astonishing quality of sticking to their faces forever. Even today many writers of the older generation are still wearing them: it is now the only face they have.

Having adopted his theory of 'literary *personae*' and masks, Tynianov carefully devised one for himself, one that suited his own tastes and inclinations. We once met him in the street, when he was still able to get about, and M. whispered to me: 'He fancies himself as Griboyedov.' He had decided not to become a Kiukhelbeker – that would have been too dangerous. It is not much fun being a Griboyedov either, but at least Griboyedov got a brief respite and died at the hands of foreigners, not of his own people – which is always a little easier to bear. Tynianov himself died of a terrible disease; it was like a biblical scourge and quite incurable. He did not deserve such punishment. Of all our contemporaries he was one of the best and most pure. I shall never forget our last meeting

* Marxist critics who in the twenties applied purely 'sociological' criteria to literature; their theories were denounced as 'vulgar' in the early thirties.

with him. He sat in an armchair looking wizened and shrunken, his head as large and intelligent as ever, and talked spiritedly about Russian poetry, viewing it in grand perspective and proposing an extraordinary theory about the different strands in its heredity: the melodic one deriving from Zhukovski and the thematic from Pushkin. When he got up to see us to the door I noticed his legs were as thin as matchsticks. He could hardly walk at all even with his stick, and in the long corridor of the old Petersburg apartment in which he lived, he fell down. Hearing the noise, his wife, who struck me as a real witch, rushed out to help him to his feet, cursing as she did so. He wanted to say good-bye to us, but helpless and unable to resist, he was dragged away by the witch. The latter-day Griboyedov was done to death not by a frenzied Oriental mob in a foreign city, but by his own wife and a wasting disease.

Although Tynianov was persecuted and accused, like so many others, of being behind the times in his literary theories, they were in fact incomparably more pertinent to the age we lived in than anybody else's. The notion of the mask and biography changed at will are only details in his general theory of the *persona*. At the heart of it lay his deep certainty that nobody has lasting convictions or beliefs, or is really capable of sticking to them and deepening them as he grows to maturity. This was the conclusion Tynianov drew from the life he saw around him. Such a theory could arise only at a time when the personality was disintegrating, when it was very much easier to note the flaws and seams in a person's life history than to believe in the possibility that he might maintain an unbroken unity of outlook throughout his career. Tynianov compares the life history of a writer with a graph whose irregular curve is 'dictated by the literary events of the time'. The breaks in the line, according to Tynianov, correspond to shifts of literary allegiance, the transitions from one 'school' to another. He saw such breaks in the literary biographies which were taking shape before his eyes, but he was wrong about the reasons for them. I do not know whether he ever admitted even to himself that both he and his friends changed direction only out of the most primitive instinct of self-preservation. They themselves found it easier to the extent that, at the time of the catastrophe, they were still too young for their views of the world to have set in any particular mould. Most of them had grown up in families of vaguely humanist outlook. They had never been obliged to seek their own solutions, or stick up for what they believed – the times were hardly conducive to this.

For Tynianov the poet is not a personality in his own right; he is interested only in his place in what he calls the 'evolutionary sequence'. In Tynianov's writings on poetry and literature the word 'evolution' occurs frequently. Evolution, progress, development – these are all notions of the same order. What is one to make of them in the history of poetry, literature, or society as a whole?

Tynianov was the product of a rationalist age with its belief that everything could be remodelled for the better by a conscious process – historical circumstances, the social order, literature, one's own biography. He was one of the few people who quite frankly studied the life histories of Kiukhelbeker, Griboyedov, Pushkin – the heroes of his novels – with the aim of finding the same features as he had noted in his own contemporaries. He believed his theories were incontrovertible because, in accordance with the Marxist criterion, they were borne out by practice. Characteristically, the most important aspect of a writer in his eyes was not his view of the world, but his style and the techniques he employed.

I can only regret that I did not take Tynianov's advice in time and force M. (what a hope!) to adopt a mask, change his biography and his 'literary *persona*'. Even better: he should have put on a mask, bought a last, and become a cobbler. That would have meant work for him and shoes for me. I have heard that after the decree condemning him and Akhmatova, Zoshchenko wanted to make a similar 'break' in his career and become a cobbler. Soviet citizens sometimes have identical dreams, but the facts of life are stubbornly against their coming true. The commonest break in our biographies was to be turned into a convict doing hard labour, that is, into a camp inmate. M. and I tried to become beggars,* but this led to no change either in him or in his poetry; in any case

* *Hope Against Hope*, pages 364 ff.

there was never any question of his life's taking a different turn because he had switched his *persona* – M. never had one to begin with.

The theory of the 'literary *persona*' has proved to be tenacious and for a long time was highly regarded in a surreptitious way because it was the only rival to the 'class approach' urged in many a strident article. Sometimes it was even possible for a writer to 'cover up' and escape reprisals by pretending that some risky sentiment expressed not his own views but only those of a 'literary *persona*'. Like actors, everybody lived a double life – with the difference that for an actor his duality, the wearing of a mask, is essential to his art, whereas for Tynianov's contemporaries it was more in the nature of a protective device. The poet's equivalent of a 'role' would be a 'lyrical *persona*', but it would make no sense, because poet and actor are poles apart. Similarly it is no good for an actor to try to be like a poet. These are quite different types of activity: one in a mask and the other without.

V: POETIC RECOGNITION

In this world there are too many things – including poetry – which defy definition. People may cudgel their brains as much as they like, but they will never find a definition for poetry. Nor are there any criteria for distinguishing true poetry from false, or synthetic, poetry. Poetry lovers are rather like racegoers, backing now one, now another horse – except that poetry lovers never know which of their favourites has passed the winning post. People always say that 'time will show', but time is often wrong, merely perpetuating contemporary prejudices and misconceptions. Then there is no way of telling what span of time must go by before dispassionate judgement prevails. At the moment four poets are in the lead: Akhmatova, Pasternak, Tsvetayeva, and Mandelstam. But will it always be so? Nobody knows. At the moment scarcely anybody reads Pushkin, and one cannot help wondering what impact the work of these four poets who are at present always named in the same breath can have on the minds of people so out of touch with poetry that they no longer read Pushkin. The suspicion naturally arises that perhaps nobody reads anything any more, and that the four names now looming so large represent only four vague legends which may, if they are lucky, solidify into permanent shapes, but which might equally well gradually dissolve and fade away. Nothing can be predicted with certainty: people could even forget how to read altogether and books moulder away to dust. We might even stop talking with each other and communicate only by emitting call signs or blood-curdling war cries. Sometimes I think this is what we are coming to. We did, after all, learn to speak in a lying code language designed to conceal our real thoughts. One's descendants pay for such things by losing the power of articulate speech altogether, caterwauling instead like fans at a football game. But they may not even have the strength to do this – people are becoming more and more effete.

One of Akhmatova's great virtues was that she attached no importance to her early success in the pre-Revolutionary years and in the twenties. 'Such things happen,' she used to say, 'but it still doesn't mean anything' . . . M. never gave a thought to his post-humous reputation; he simply got on with his work. This, I believe, is as it should be. Tsvetayeva was apparently the same. Since there are no objective criteria, this seems to be the best attitude. Pasternak did make a vague attempt to 'grade' his con-temporaries – he once said to me that Akhmatova and M. had 'expressed themselves' better than he had. This was while M. was still alive, and I reported these words to him. He laughed and said that Pasternak had said this not because he believed it, but just to please . . . Akhmatova reacted with her favourite phrase: 'Very nice, I must say' . . . The subject was never mentioned again.

Pasternak once gave a delightful definition of poetry, though it by no means amounts to a criterion for gauging comparative merit:

> It is full-throated whistle,
> it is the crunch of jostling ice floes,
> it is the dew frosting a leaf,
> it is two nightingales duelling.

And he even suggests what the aim of poetry is: '. . . to carry to your creel / a star in wet and trembling hands.' This is pure

Pasternak, lost in wonderment at the faint gleam of the sky on his wet hand after a night-time swim. His views about who is best able to express himself in poetry have to be taken in conjunction with another line, which to my ear sounds a little like something from an official report: 'The aim of creating is the giving of oneself.' With us, I remember, the word 'create' in this sense was taboo. What would you think of an artist who at the end of his day's work said to you: 'I have created a lot today,' or 'It is good to have a rest after creating.' 'Giving oneself' – in other words, expressing oneself – cannot be made into an end in itself without indulging in a secret desire to assert and promote oneself. Though why secret? It is absolutely blatant! Isn't it better to give up once and for all such attempts to establish criteria, aims, definitions, and particularly anything that leads to the inflation of the self? Wonderment at living in this world and being endowed with the mysterious gift of speech, man's finest possession, this surely is the seed from which poetry springs, its very foundation. It is this that makes *My Sister Life** so remarkable: it is a book of knowledge about the world, of thanksgiving and joy . . .

None of the great poets was able to name the distinctive feature of poetry. Goethe's concept of the 'little extra' is very suggestive, but in the end it is just as elusive as poetry itself. In the last resort it is entirely a matter of having faith, both in poetry itself and in this, that, or the other poet. I myself have never lost such faith, although I know that women, especially poets' wives, err more frequently than anyone – except, that is, for the professional judges of literature, who are wrong not only even more frequently but with much more harmful results. The number of false reputations, within my memory alone, that have been created out of nothing by public opinion and the 'experts'! For all the sound and fury, nothing remains now but dust and ashes. Compared to the experts, what harm in some poor woman who believes in the gift of a husband, friend, or lover?

Instead of worrying what posterity would think of them, M. and Akhmatova, not wishing to remain in a vacuum, sought out other people who they felt came close to poetry in their verse, however remotely. M., easily carried away by enthusiasm, was constantly

* Pasternak's first major volume of poetry (1922).

'discovering' poets – as long as they did not try to imitate the Acmeists or employ 'pseudo-Acmeist words'. He and Akhmatova even invented a game: each of them had a certain number of tokens to be expended on the recognition of poets – but while she was tight-fisted and hung on to her tokens for all she was worth, he spent his last one on old Zvenigorodski, and then had to beg her to 'lend' him one, or even half of one . . . Having hoarded them up so jealously, in her old age Akhmatova began to hand out her tokens indiscriminately, right, left, and centre. I fear that many she awarded them to in her last years were phonies. She was too generous with them for it to be otherwise. It is up to other people to sort out who deserved them and who did not. I am past caring, and I wonder, indeed, whether any of these 'tokens' had any meaning . . .

Of one thing, however, I am quite certain: the last 'token' given by M. to Zvenigorodski was not wasted, since it quite possibly saved the old man's life. He came to us at the very beginning of the thirties and read some charming, old-fashioned, and very pure verse. M. sensed that he was having a very hard time making ends meet, and he lavished praise on him. Next M. ran around to people who might be able to help the poor fellow – whether they actually could or not – and started badgering the authorities to give him a pension; meanwhile he got him a pass to the writers' cafeteria, where he could eat reasonable meals (by our wretched standards) at officially subsidized prices. It was a hungry time, and everybody who could ate in such cafeterias. The old man started drawing his pension when we were already in Voronezh. (I believe it was finally pushed through by Pasternak, a man totally without resources or influence. It was only such people who helped each other, often quite effectively.)

In one way or another Zvenigorodski got on his feet and was even invited to join some committee (on Pushkin, I think) of the Writers' Union, a fact of which he was inordinately proud. With his blue blood he could scarcely have hoped for such a happy outcome. He really did have blue blood; as he explained to us, the Zvenigorodskis were a very much older family than the Romanovs, so ancient in fact that he, its last scion, had his heart on the right instead of the left side. From chronic hunger his skin was so translucent that the blue actually showed through, even after he had got his pension and pass to the cafeteria.

Zvenigorodski or, to give him his title, Prince Andrei (though it appears that some bully of a Tsar had stripped his branch of the family of its princely rank, and later, of course, all titles had been abolished anyway) sometimes used to visit us together with his grand-nephew, a good-looking gypsy boy. He did not bear the family name of Zvenigorodski, since he was descended from the feminine line, being the grandson of the Prince's sister (with whom he shared an apartment). But the gypsy boy had an excellent heart, and it was where it should be. Zvenigorodski cared not at all that his blood had mingled with that of the gypsies – worse things had happened to his princely stock over the last four centuries or so! – but he was upset by the fact that the boy's gypsy mother had gone away and left the family at this low ebb in its fortunes, and that his father had been arrested after a search of the apartment lasting many hours. Prince Andrei kept the boy alive by bringing him half of the meals he got in the writers' cafeteria. He trembled – as he did constantly – while he told us all the details of the search, how they had pried up the floorboards and smashed the stove looking for weapons, which, as always, they failed to find. If his grand-nephew had been a criminal, he would have had a chance of survival, but they eventually came from the Lubianka to pick him up, and after that I don't know what happened to him. Prince Andrei himself lived to a ripe old age and, when his sister died, even married a lady 'from a good family' – this he told me after the war when he came once to see me while I was staying at the Shklovskis (I always stayed with them on my visits to Moscow from the various god-forsaken parts of the country in which fate and the Ministry of Education forced me to live). We gave him some fruit to eat because by now he could eat nothing else. He had come specially to hand over to me before he died an early version of M.'s poem 'To the German Tongue', which he had written out in his own hand. M. had once dictated this version to him and said: 'Only Andrei Vladimirovich shall have this' – as though he sensed that Zvenigo-rodski would survive him. The old man had hung on to it, even though most people, in those cruel times, burned their papers or, if they had no stove, flushed them down the toilet. I was glad to see that he was enjoying such a long life, and that M.'s last 'token' had been expended to such good purpose. Zvenigorodski was able to feed not only himself on his pension, but also his wife 'from a good family' – old women of this kind were usually condemned to the most grinding poverty.

Though the award of 'tokens' was just a game, I discovered that M. really believed in something which amounted to much the same. He disliked a certain fairly well-known poet of a younger generation and completely different background, even though he was described as a 'Romantic' and – on the most dubious grounds – as a product of the Acmeist tradition. I believe I may have been partly responsible for M.'s dislike of him. I had repeated to him a story told by a female relative of the poet in question which had delighted the circles in which they moved but had infuriated me. Once, while the 'Romantic' was still living in his native province, he was visited by an old lady, the widow of a general who had lost her husband, as anybody of her doomed class was bound to – just as she herself, for the same reason, was now condemned to utter poverty. She brought along some trinket or other of the kind the general might have worn on his watch chain and asked the Romantic whether he would like to buy it. For a long time he played with it in his hand, all the time asking the old lady questions about her family, the general, and all their misfortunes and hardships. He sighed sympathetically, and the general's widow, not used to sympathy, forgot her fears for a moment and opened up in this friendly atmosphere. She was quite sure that the kind-hearted poet would have pity on her and buy her wretched knick-knack – he had even bargained with her a little and she had agreed to a lower price. Since it was their last hope, people in her position always asked far too much for their poor trash. All of a sudden the poet changed his tone completely and told her to leave. But what about the trinket? she asked. He gave it back to her – it was a miniature figure of a bear – and advised her: 'Stick it up your backside and let it bellow there.' The friends and relatives of the poet thought this was the height of wit and sophistication and recounted the story with the greatest relish to everyone they knew. For cynics like them, nothing could have been funnier. After I had told him the story, M. could not stand even to hear the name of the 'Romantic' and absolutely refused to regard him as a poet. But he gave as his reason not the business of the bear-shaped trinket, or even the quality of the poet's verse and the disgraceful nature of its subject matter (whether a genuine poet or not, he had churned out a great deal of revolting drivel which had earned him comparative material comfort and official recognition), but the fact that he was not recognized by any poet of the older generation: 'Neither I nor Akhmatova have recognized him – he has no right to call himself a poet.'

There were hordes of poets. Some used the vocabulary of Acmeism and others not, but M. was indifferent to how they styled themselves, and he certainly would not hear of the bear-trinket man being called a poet. 'But who recognized *you*?' I asked. 'Gumilev recognized me,' he answered. So in fact, as youngsters, they had all recognized one another. How did this differ from the later game of awarding 'tokens'? 'And who recognized Gumilev?' I persisted. 'Gumilev was recognized by Briusov,' he replied without batting an eyelid. Knowing what he thought of Briusov (he had once failed to find a single suitable poem by him for an anthology he was editing), I scoffed at this way of handing on the succession and compared it with the ordination of priests by the laying on of hands, or the kind of initiation into the knighthood of which we had read in historical novels as children. He stood his ground, however, and I was struck by the naïve and adolescent streak one finds in grown men. Is this how they manage to keep their 'freshness of feeling and sharpness of sight', and are thus able to do so much more in life – seeing and hearing a great deal more as well – than we women who become adult as girls already, and learn to look at the world with such nasty-minded matter-of-factness?

M. himself clearly lacked the blessing of the Symbolists, who, as Akhmatova has written and I saw with my own eyes, not only never recognized him but were actually extremely hostile to him (with the sole exception of Blok, who hesitated for a moment, but then wrote the entry in his diary about him).* Nor was he recognized by the avant-garde. To the end of his life Aseyev cursed

* In his *Diary*, under 22 October 1920, Blok describes a poetry reading he went to the previous evening: 'The *clou* of the evening was O. Mandelstam, who has just arrived [in Petrograd] after a stretch in one of Wrangel's prisons . . . He has grown considerably . . . One can see the artist . . .'

anybody who dared so much as mention M.'s name in his presence. In 1932, an evening reading of M.'s poetry was arranged in the editorial offices of *Literary Gazette*, and afterwards the newspaper printed a selection of his poems which had circulated the most widely in manuscript (*samizdat* existed already then, though it was restricted to much narrower circles than nowadays). At this reading Shklovski wavered for a moment in his attitude to M., but was immediately called to order by Kirsanov, who reminded him of the discipline and unity of views expected of members of their group,* and Shklovski at once fell into line. The group whose purity was so zealously guarded by Kirsanov also included Roman Jakobson and the Aragon family.† They too seem to be wavering a little nowadays, but this is all jiggery-pokery, a matter of tactics. I would happily see them return to their normal state of hostility to M.

Towards the end of his life, M. could contain himself no longer and accorded himself recognition in a letter to Tynianov: 'For a quarter of a century now mixing the serious with the trivial, I have been steadily encroaching on Russian poetry; but soon my verse will merge with it, affecting something in its structure and composition.' I do not know whether this letter has survived among Tynianov's papers. Most likely not. If he did not do so himself out of sheer fright, then his wife or daughter must have destroyed this humble scrap of paper on which M. recorded his recognition of himself. Natasha Shtempel made a copy before mailing it for M., and in this form it still survives among my papers. Tynianov never replied to it, but one cannot hold this against him: it was a terrible time and nobody replied to letters. Mandelstam's editors‡ find it astonishing that almost all his letters are addressed to me. It was only natural that he should want to communicate with me – by letter when there was no other way – but in normal conditions of life he would not have written to me alone. Even if they have some inkling, people cannot really imagine what our life was like. Even the Germans can have no idea – perhaps only the Jews who lived

* LEF (see Appendix B).
† See Brik, Appendix A.
‡ i.e. Struve and Filippov.

under German occupation. What M. and I lived through was the common lot of everybody in this vast and fear-crazed country.

In M.'s letter to Tynianov there is a distinct note of what he himself called 'poetic rightness', a feeling of which he became aware while he was still a very young man. Someone endowed with it has no need of recognition or initiation into the knighthood: poetry is a simple everyday thing that comes naturally to him. Such a person writes 'for himself', not imposing his work on his fellow men and leaving the final judgement to them: 'If people need it, they will preserve it.'

For a real poet recognition or the lack of it is of no importance, since he needs only the appreciation of his 'first listeners'. Anyone who writes verse always has these. Poets do not argue about their place; they leave this to their readers.

31 Major Forms

I: TRAGEDY

In the twenties M. made an attempt to live by literary work. All his articles, as well as *Noise of Time*, were written to order, having been commissioned beforehand (which, however, was in itself no guarantee that something would be printed). There was a fearful to-do over *The Noise of Time*. It had been commissioned by Lezhnev for his magazine *Rossia*, but on reading it he was deeply disappointed. He had been expecting a story of childhood rather like his own, or Chagall's, and this tale about growing up in Petersburg struck him as very tame stuff. After this M. took it to Tikhonov (a friend of Gorki's who ran 'World Literature'* and put out some private magazine or other) and to Efros. They

---

* An ambitious scheme, launched by Gorki in 1918, to present the whole of world literature in Russian translation. It came to an end in 1924. A. N. Tikhonov, who was in charge of it, should not be confused with the poet Nikolai Tikhonov.

returned the manuscript to M. with a comment to the effect that they had expected better of him. It is fortunate we didn't lose it – something we were quite capable of. In those days it had not even occurred to us that people keep their papers and that M. should do likewise. We did not, for example, keep copies of any of his articles: the hand-written originals were sent to the printers and the rough drafts we simply threw in the stove. Editors mutilated them at will (though in those days it was a question of cutting the text rather than altering it), and we had no drafts by which to check. In the case of *Noise of Time* we were lucky. I happened to have a large envelope into which I put the manuscript, and it stayed there for several years. The fair copy went the rounds of various publishers who all rejected it, devoid as it was of plot, story, class consciousness, or any kind of social significance. The only person to show interest was Georgi Blok, the cousin of the poet, who worked for a private publishing firm already on its last legs. By this time, M. had given up hope and was past caring. The book did now come out, but the manuscript was lost – presumably it was confiscated with the rest of Blok's papers when he was arrested. (He was picked up because he had been educated at the Lycée.) People and manuscripts were equally doomed to destruction. It is amazing that anything survived at all – and by a quirk of fate it could happen, as in this case, that something disappeared after surviving for a time by sheer chance.

With every year that went by it became harder for M. to place his articles. In the mid-twenties, since he had not 'reformed' (it was we, not the Chinese, who started this, and we should not give them credit for our own invention), he was banned from print in Moscow and Petersburg. In a 'reformed' world a man who not only cannot but – *horribile dictu* – does not even *want* to follow suit finds himself, like the fisherman in the fairy tale, left with only a broken crock (though we didn't even have the luxury of a broken crock, never having caught a golden fish in the first place). The 'unreformed' were divided into two groups: those who could be 'helped' to see the light and those it only remained to throw overboard as incorrigible. In the twenties M. was still counted among the poor simpletons who heeded 'help', but in the thirties he was downgraded into the category of those to be destroyed. He was indeed regarded as a prime specimen of such madmen. The maddest of all, the religious believers (or *religiozniki*, as they were termed), did not count and were marked down for annihilation from the very first. The borderline between the two categories was not entirely hard and fast, being laid down no doubt by special advisers, some of whom drew salaries and privileged rations, while others, even more numerous, worked for nothing. The borderline shifted in accordance with the general political climate, and the screws, as we saw, were gradually tightened as far as they would go. The man who devised them* would have screwed them pretty tight himself, though he might have hesitated to go as far as his successors. But even if the pressure had been a thousand times less, the result would have been the same: resignation, silence, and decay . . .

Clear as the eventual outcome was, M. went on being his chirpy, free and easy self, closing his eyes to the future. In Kiev he found a rather dim-witted newspaper editor who during the Civil War had once served as some kind of aide in the train of the Boss (this was before he had become the Boss) and was later given a whole newspaper to himself by way of reward. Some of his younger colleagues pulled the wool over his eyes and he printed a few articles by M. Since he remembered them ever after, he must have got into some trouble as a result. I happened to meet him many years later, after Stalin's death, when he was living in a room in the Shklovskis' apartment. The room had been lent to him by Arkadi Vasiliev. When Shklovski left his family he kept one room in the apartment for himself and put it at the disposal of Arkadi Vasiliev, who was chairman of the housing cooperative that owned the building. Vasiliev, a former Chekist who then found a niche in literature, is the very same who appeared at the trial of Siniavski as 'public accuser'. The former newspaper editor from Kiev, who had some connection with the cooperative, was living in this room on a temporary basis when I met him in the apartment. He started making fun of me for still remembering 'that Mandelstam fellow'. I gave him such hell – the times of the Boss were over and we were enjoying a breathing space – that he fled back into his own room and never opened his mouth again. When he left to move into a cooperative hen coop run by the Writers' Union he presented

* Lenin.

Vasilisa Shklovski with a large blue cup as a souvenir. Vasilisa quite happily drank her tea out of it, but I couldn't stand the thought and smashed it. Now Vasilisa drinks out of a blue cup given her by me.

I should not have got so angry at the poor fool. People of this type made life a little easier after all. If he hadn't been the idiot he was, M. would not have got those articles published; indeed they would never have been written – which would have been a pity, considering how splendid they are. Real idiots in the clinical sense are a godsend. Brainy fellows like Shcherbakov, Fadeyev, or Surkov – even though their heads were no less stuffed with nonsense than that of the man from Kiev – would never have permitted anything by M. to appear in the pages of a Soviet publication. The clever ones barred the pages of their magazines to him completely. In the thirties M. finally understood that there could be no question of making a regular income out of his work, and we had to learn to scrape a living as best we could, sometimes surviving on bottles, for instance.* But it did not come to this all at once. Such an existence takes some getting used to, and one may flounder about for a long time before giving up and bowing to fate.

Among other writers to be proscribed – as usual in this country, it was done not openly, of course, but on the quiet – was also Shklovski. He took refuge in a film studio, rather as a Jew in occupied Hungary might have hidden in a Catholic monastery. He strongly recommended M. to seek salvation in the same way, and urged him to write something for films. There was of course no hope, he explained, that their scripts would be passed for publication, but the point was that film studios always paid for everything they commissioned, even if it was only a few pages long. Shklovski gave the same advice to everybody he thought well of, suggesting they write a script together. Coming from him, a proposal of this kind was tantamount to a declaration of love or friendship. In fact, however, he never gave away the real secret of how he made money out of the film studios. It was rather different, as I now know: they simply kept people alive there by commissioning 'internal reviews', that is, reports on the scripts and scenarios which flowed in from all sides. This was a gravy train to which only the favoured

* See note, page 16.

had access, and the film people were partial to members of LEF. M. would never have been let anywhere near it. In Kiev once upon a time some employees of the local film studio had tried to sneak M. in as a consultant or editor, but it proved to be an impregnable fortress. There were no idiots in the film industry – only clever people who knew their business. To tempt M., Shklovski had even thought up a subject for a script; it was to be about a former court flunkey and his daughter, who goes off to do her bit for the Revolution while the father works as an attendant in the Catherine Palace,* now converted into a museum. 'You live in Tsarskoye,' said Shklovski, 'so you can get the atmosphere: go to the museum and let your imagination work on it . . .' He was as seductive as a siren.

A subject of this kind was called 'historical', though there was no history about it at all. It was easier to handle than a 'topical' theme about the machinations of conspirators and saboteurs against the revolutionary workers. Such stuff was paid at an incomparably higher rate, but it was 'history' which provided salvation for members of the intelligentsia, thus playing the same role as a Catholic monastery (though not even a Catholic monastery would have been any help to M. and me, two inseparable creatures of opposite sexes). The general background 'effects' were always the same: tsarist gendarmes, a prison, and then jubilant crowds with banners. The main question, in the case of Shklovski's proposal, was what to do with the father. Either he could curse his daughter and then end his days in bitter repentance, or he could immediately go over to the Revolution, like her, and perform a number of services for the future victors – in this case his reward would be to appear at the end, together with his transfigured daughter, among a crowd of joyous demonstrators. Another possibility would have been: the father angrily sets about demolishing the palace – the masonry, beams, and other architectural appurtenances of a set built for the purpose – but then they are all put together again and the palace is transfigured (instead of the daughter) into a 'historical monument' or museum, henceforth under the protection of the State. All this offered an excuse for showing the glories of the Tsarskoye Selo palaces and parks on the screen.

* Built in the eighteenth century. Famous for its gallery by Cameron.

We took Shklovski's advice and went off, first of all, to look at the former palace. When we got home M. said he could write the script in three days, and he dashed off the first two or three pages there and then. It appeared that so far he had hit upon only one idea: at the entrance visitors were given slippers made of string so they would not damage the precious parquet floor with their clumsy footwear. This would have made some fabulous shots. M. had noted various specimens of wretched footwear and torn trousers, and he was going to construct the beginning around the contrast between string shoes, parquet floor, and the ragged garb of the visitors. His mind was clearly working in quite the wrong direction – nobody had the slightest desire to make our poverty into a point of pride. In Shpikovski's film *Shpigun*, on which M. wrote a review, whole sequences had to be redone because the Red Army men in the Civil War were at first shown exactly as they had been: in rags. At the insistence of the ideologists they were spruced up and made to look almost smart. After reading through the few pages of the script he had dictated to me, M. sighed; it was clear we would not get rich that way. I suggested a modified approach: throw out the shabby footwear and concentrate on the parquet floor and the string shoes, but M. had had enough. 'We are ruined,' he said, and gave up all thought of films. But what was wrong with my idea? It would have given a neat play of contrast, and our film producers were very fond of such detail – a slight ripple of the surface of water, grass or ears of wheat stirring in the breeze, a bird ruffling its feathers, fishing nets, and so forth. For those few of my ageing contemporaries who still survive, the motion pictures of the twenties – like the theatre – remain the chief symbol of a flourishing cultural life in those days. On the subject of literature and painting they are a little more restrained, but the cinema means the famous Odessa steps with the child's baby carriage, drought and sheep with their thirst-parched tongues hanging out, apples falling into the mouth of a smiling Ukrainian, the inglorious end of St Petersburg, maggots wriggling in a piece of rotten meat . . . Future generations will marvel at the wealth of detail and the poverty of ideas in these films. Perhaps ideas are not needed in films, but these, as propaganda productions, had pretensions to them – which only brings out even more their underlying cruelty. I particularly remember that sadistic baby carriage teetering down the steps, and the elegant church procession during the drought.

One would have thought that a historical subject demanded historical insight, but in the movies, as in literature, everything was done according to standardized, preconceived notions. This was by no means only because of injunctions passed down from above. If this had been the case, we could have expected a few genuine things to have survived in manuscript – at least some odds and ends hidden away at the time in their authors' desk drawers. But very little has in fact come down to us, and even that was already known. Nor do I believe there is much hope of any great new works still unexpectedly coming to light. No one has even seriously pondered the reasons for this. Akhmatova has told us of all the things she was deprived of when 'the cruel age deflected' her, 'like a river from its course', but she omitted to say anything about our intellectual deprivations. All of us, M. and Pasternak included, were never able to develop some of our ideas, or rather, certain ideas never even occurred to us and were thus never embodied in words. The earth really did cost us ten heavens – though our share was no greater than that of the deported kulaks, or of those who 'liquidated' them for that matter. The horizon narrowed to a point at which we could no longer recognize it. Even the few who had kept their inner freedom were forced to think only of the immediate concerns foisted on them by the age we lived in. The mind was captive. To some extent the mind is always captive to the times, but these can either enlarge or limit its horizon; in ours it was reduced to the most beggarly dimensions. We were so weighed down by the cruel realities of our epoch and the prevailing philosophy of life that we were incapable of real thought – only of idle talk. The times favoured those who really had nothing to say, except to praise the era they lived in, or to complain of its cruelty. In either case they were only responding to the dictates of the era itself. Three poets who had something to say also had to pay their price: for a time they were stricken dumb.* This was by no means the highest price one could pay. Prose writers, whose work by its nature depends vitally on ideas, paid even more dearly.

* *Hope Against Hope*, page 194.

We were surrounded by swarms of prose writers. Though we met them only in editorial offices, we knew how their minds worked. Tynianov declared that poetry had had its day and we were now in an era of prose. M. put it another way: jailers, he said, have more need of novels than anyone. Prose writers were hence on the crest of a wave, and after the initial boom in stories about the Civil War and Revolution, they began to cast around for new ideas in their efforts to come up in the world and make a better living. Money proved to be an excellent stimulus to their inventiveness, and they all dreamed of writing long novels or plays. Writing for the stage was particularly attractive: anyone receiving royalties from performances prospered before one's eyes. Katayev was always telling tall stories about successful playwrights. One, for instance, had supposedly hired a chauffeur-driven car which followed along behind him at a snail's pace everywhere he went, just in case he suddenly wanted to go somewhere in it. This would have been the very height of distinction; until the end of the thirties nobody could even dream of owning his personal motor-car. Any lucky fellow who had a play put on at the Arts Theatre always got himself a new wife immediately afterwards: he would find himself besieged by beautiful little gold diggers who had not learned how to earn their daily bread the hard way. They were generally film actresses who got a part in crowd scenes once a year and were always on the lookout for 'temporary husbands' to keep them in food and buy them a new pair of shoes. Playwrights were as much sought after as members of the ruling elite. The next best were writers who had already published a novel, and right at the bottom of the scale came verse translators – even the busiest who worked like machines and turned out a hundred lines a day. (Shengeli managed a hundred and fifty, and was very proud of the fact). They were thought of as quite shopworn, the poor drudges.

These dreams of writing a play or a novel were not explained solely by a healthy desire for material well-being and money; they were also due to a general trend towards the so-called major forms. People repeated the Russian saying that big ships should sail in big seas. The word 'big' was defined in purely quantitative terms. For a prose writer this meant the number of pages, and for a poet the number of lines. There was a peculiar 'gigantomania' in the air, and even Pasternak, among others, was affected by it. He began to talk about writing a novel as early as the mid-twenties, and before very long he was thinking of a play as well. Gladkov is neither lying nor boasting when he refers in his memoirs to the extraordinary interest that Pasternak showed in him. In the account he gives I recognize straightaway the Boris Leonidovich who was desperately anxious to write a play and made a keen study of successful play-wrights. He revealed his thoughts about writing a novel in a letter to M.: now that *Noise of Time* had come out, he urged, all was set fair for a novel, and it was the moment to get started on one . . . In Moscow, when we lived in Furmanov Street, Pasternak quite often looked in, particularly if Akhmatova was staying with us. On these occasions he frequently talked about a novel, moving M. to remark that 'to write a novel you need either the country estate of a Tolstoi or the prison experience of a Dostoyevski . . .' Akhma-tova is wrong when she says this was said about Kolia Chukovski – M. would never have wasted such a splendid quip on him. To write a novel like one of Kolia Chukovski's one needed nothing more than a typewriter or a fountain pen. What else was there for him to do except write lengthy novels? While M. was still alive Chukovski had not in any case shown any sign of going in for them and was still making his living out of children's books and translations. Actually, I know very little about him. He came to see us only once and later invented a story that I lay hidden in a trunk during his visit. Why do people always tell such lies the moment they speak about M.?

I was quite staggered by all Pasternak's talk of writing a novel. For me the word 'novel' has always been associated with light reading, and I have never used it of *War and Peace* or *The Idiot*, and never shall. Nowadays I use the word 'novel' only of *Zhivago*. I still firmly believe that someone is moved to write by his ideas, his view of the world, and that the form in which he expresses them does not have to be sought – it comes by itself. But when Pasternak now spoke of first choosing a particular genre, I had the impression that the process was reversed: the desired form, instead of being dictated by the idea, was actually the prime mover. It seemed as though he was not satisfied with the best that nature could have given him: his lyrical gift, his 'wet and trembling hands'. He wanted to conquer his 'beautiful incoherence' as a poet and speak in the universal language of concepts. Later he was to refer to this as 'simplicity' ... I understand Pasternak better now – he was drawn by the need to 'externalize', to look at things from the outside, 'objectively'. As a poet he was wholly dominated by his feelings, and his lyrics are essentially part and parcel of his ordinary, workaday life – this indeed is their charm. In the everyday life around him he only rarely glimpsed 'objective' factors beyond, such as history and the country as a whole, and even then he saw them chiefly in the perspective of the immediate present. But he was prey to a nagging urge to analyse, to look at things from a distance, to see them in larger perspective. This was because he felt that for someone like himself who lived by inner feeling there was an unfortunate cleavage between subject and object. Pasternak's novel is a remembrance of times past, an attempt to determine his own place in the swift-flowing movement of days, and to seek understanding of this movement itself.

Dostoyevski also wrote at a time of crisis, but the fabric of society had not yet collapsed. This meant that social, philosophical, and religious ideas could still crystallize in various sections of the community, or in the minds of individual members of it. But Pasternak began to think about writing a novel at a time when all movement of ideas had ceased and instead we had only the question of how best to achieve the final aim already decided on for us. Our vaunted 'unanimity' meant that the links connecting molecule to molecule had dissolved; society is a complex structure and can be reduced to a bipartite formula – the crowd, a seething mass of humanity on the one side, and leaders, giants, and geniuses on the other – only by purely artificial means involving the deliberate destruction of all cross-connections binding people together. The basic principle of our life has always been the systematic displacement of people, and by this I mean not only the deportation of whole nations* and social classes (like the 'kulaks' during collectivization), or the mass transfer of entire sections of the population to labour camps or enforced residence

*See note, page 201.

in remote areas, but the normal way in which people's lives were ordered without any particular use of force. On completing their education or training, for instance, they would always be sent to work – whether in the Party apparatus or in their chosen profession – to places as far away from their homes as possible, where they knew nobody and dared not open their mouths because they were alone among strangers. Everyone was constantly being recruited for work in distant parts; in the case of workers and peasants the lure was a little more to eat. By such mechanical jumbling up, people were constantly uprooted, and the process of atomization and loss of personality went even faster. Pasternak lived in the midst of this disintegration and like everybody else – in one form or another – was affected by all the sicknesses of the age. It was hence extremely hard for him to collect his thoughts and actually embark on a study of the times.

For a brief moment the war brought people together again, and it was this momentarily restored sense of community which prepared the ground for the events of the fifties and the ferment in the minds of the younger generation that followed. For this reason Pasternak was able to complete his novel only after the war. I find it significant that the hero of the novel is a poet with a biography parallel to the author's, but much more disastrous. Pasternak was trying to see what his own life would have been like if the river had been deflected into a different course. When Akhmatova looked back at the life she might have lived, she always imagined how much better it could have been. Pasternak saw himself as the tragic wanderer and outcast he would have been if he had immediately expressed the same view of the new era as he did a few years after the war. For M. there could be no question of a hypothetical alternative: he paid the price of living in his day and age as he went along, and he saw himself at the very outset as one who must fight the general breakdown by standing against it. The 'cruel age' did not deflect him into another course – he went his own way, but the going was so hard that much of what he might have done was never accomplished.

M. did not write stories, novels, or any other kind of fiction, only prose and poetry. These were the only two words he ever used to define his work. He was firmly convinced that any literary form is

in constant need of renewal, and that anybody who launches out
into a new one must begin by totally remaking it. He regarded
War and Peace not as a novel but as an amalgam of epic and
chronicle, while Dostoyevski, in his view, had used the form as a
vehicle for something resembling tragedy. How is it that in our
literature tragedy was expressed only in narrative prose, never in
plays written for the stage? M. often spoke of tragedy, but rather
in terms of its essence than as a literary form. He realized very early
that tragedy was impossible in the theatre here. 'I shall never see
famed Phaedra,' he says. He was destined never to hear how
'smelted by suffering the voice grows stronger, / and speech in the
furnace of indignation / attains to sorrowing incandescence'. The
reason for the end of tragedy is to be found in the antipathy of the
audience to whom it was addressed: the 'jackal-spectators' always
ready to 'hound the Muse to death'. In an article he wrote in 1922
M. tried to explain why there could be no tragedy in our days. He
made the point in connection with Annenski, of whom he says
that he 'bore his lot of renunciation and resignation with great
dignity'. In Annenski's poetry, he continued, 'the spirit of
renunciation feeds on his awareness that tragedy is impossible in
modern Russian art because of the lack of one essential pre-
requisite: an integrated national consciousness which is absolute
and ungainsayable; a poet born to be a Russian Euripides is
throwing a doll into a waterfall, and "his heart grieves more at the
doll's hurt than at his own".'

An integrated national consciousness can exist only during eras
when a people preserves 'the torch bequeathed by its forbears',
that is, when it lives by established values whose desecration or
upholding is then the concern of tragedy. What is catharsis but a
cleansing or illumination of the spirit, following the triumph of
values, the affirmation of their inexorable power? The European
world was based on the supreme catharsis, accessible only to the
religious mind: the conquest of death by atonement.

In the whole of the European-Christian world the basic values
have been under attack for many decades, if not for centuries, but
they have never anywhere been trampled and mocked to such a
degree as in this country. If, however, one were to gather all our
'jackal-spectators' together and re-enact this defilement of our

values before their eyes, they would howl with joy at the sight. For decades now this is how they have been trained to respond to any spectacle of desecration, whether it be of altars, private homes, or the hallowed rights of a whole nation. Some aided and abetted the desecrators, and all that can be said of the very best is that they turned away indifferently and attended to the business of keeping themselves alive. Unworthy of tragedy, we were capable only of melodrama staged with all the trappings of expressionism and pseudo-realism, and – more importantly – a topsy-turvy plot in which the desecrator of values and the unrighteous judge is held up to us as a hero defending his claim to power over the human masses under his control. In other words, the theatre was commandeered by that literature which 'everywhere ... helps the rulers to keep their minions in order and the judges to visit punishment on the doomed'.

In Voronezh, in 1935, M. approached the idea of the tragic from a different angle. The local newspaper had asked him for an article about Serafimovich, but after he had written the first few pages he realized he could not possibly show it to anybody. Serafimovich was officially regarded as something in the nature of a little god, and it was inadvisable to say a word against him. 'We are ruined,' said M. – as he always did whenever he wrote something – and threw the pages into a suitcase (the trunk in which we kept his manuscripts had been left behind in Moscow). These handwritten pages – knowing how hopeless it was, I refused to take them down by dictation – happen to have survived, and they contain the sentence: 'The tragic, however small the scene of its enactment, inevitably amounts to a general picture of the world.'

In my view, a 'general picture of the world' can be given only by something connected in one way or another with the values of the 'open', as opposed to the 'closed', society, in the precise Bergsonian meaning of these terms – that is, with the Spirit that dwells where it will. The very fact of death, for instance, insofar as man is mortal, inevitably enters into the general picture of the world, but a general picture of the world can be given by no other death except the one with which our era began, laying the foundations of the 'open' society. M. was astonished by the naïvely self-centred attitude to death of nice old ladies who had grown up in the nineteenth century – the one, for example, who once said to me in his presence: 'Your uncle Misha died *tragically* on the operating table' . . . I noticed a somewhat different attitude to the tragic in Akhmatova, but found it no less unsatisfactory. Once I brought Vasilisa Shklovski's pretty three-year-old grandnephew (whose name was Perepelkin) to see her. She liked the boy very much, and when we met the next time she said to me: 'Now that will be a tragedy if a little boy like Perepelkin dies.' 'It will be sad,' I replied, 'but not a *tragedy*; one is very sorry when children are ill or die.' Akhmatova insisted that the death of a very young person was tragedy in the fullest sense. I recalled the lines 'so terrible is the sight of early death / that I can look at God's world no more,' but this is an expression of sadness and grief, not a statement about the nature of tragedy. It is easier for me to share M.'s sense of death as a triumph, rather than to think of it as a tragedy.

M.'s words about the tragic always giving a picture of the world as a whole raises another question in my mind: Why is it that in this country the individual, the particular, is never seen as a token or symbol of the world as a whole? The reason, it seems to me – a purely psychological one – can be found only in the kind of quantitative approach so characteristic of the positivists. In its original form, the problem was posed in these terms: May one do away with one man who bars the road to happiness for millions? And if you can do away with one, then why not several? In 1937, Shaginian, lovesick for her fellow men and for Goethe, was indignant at our intellectuals: 'Just because a few people have been arrested, they make all this fuss . . .' (Why am I always harping on this woman, of whom nothing but a handful of dust will remain? The point is that she was a typical figure of our times, and furthermore she blurted out things on which others were silent.) As soon as one starts dealing with the indefinite plural 'several' or 'a few', then it is all plain sailing: after that one can speak of 'several' million, a quite negligible fraction of the sum total of humanity – especially if one takes into account all those future generations of happy, carefree people. The first mass operation, the liquidation of the peasants ('kulaks') who had got on their feet during NEP, was not even noticed at the time: people would say that one kulak had been got rid of in such-and-such a village, and 'a few' house-holds in another. It was not thought proper to add up all these minor items to make an actual total. We always preferred to deal in percentages and indefinite numbers – what was a million, after all, but a certain number of groups each numbering only 'a few' people? There was, in fact, no mention of people at all; one always spoke about a 'dekulakicized' farm or homestead – which was likewise a unit of indeterminate size.

In all factories, offices, and every other kind of institution throughout the country there were people (themselves counted as 'units') whose sole function was to add up and keep track of the number of man-hours spent on each particular job or operation, and then to calculate their value in relation to other incommensur-able factors. This infinite mulling over of numbers large and small resulted in total indifference to all the tiny drops that made up the boundless ocean. The whole country had learned its dialectical materialism very well and took good care that quantity should never become quality. This law of the dialectic was never applied in cases in which it might have given food for thought – neither 'a few' nor some percentage or other was even felt as a quantity, so the question of quality did not arise. We were too dazzled by statistics expressed in percentages to realize that every insignificant unit (but how can anything be insignificant if it is an entity in itself?) spelled disaster for some individual, and that each such individual stood for millions. Alexander Gladkov keeps saying he intends to write about the indifference with which the news of M.'s arrest and death was received in literary and theatrical circles in 1938. The death of single 'units' is smothered in statistics about the rise of the birthrate and the constant upsurge in production – as those in charge of us during this great epoch have always been well aware.

In 1937 M. returned to the question of tragedy, this time in verse. He already understood that tragedy was now played out not on the stage but in ordinary, workaday life. As he put it:

> It cannot be: tragedy is gone,
> but these trespassing lips,
> these lips lead straight to the core
> of Aeschylus the stevedore, of Sophocles the lumberjack.

The European world based its culture on the symbol of the Cross, to remind us of the One crucified on it. At the centre of this culture, hence, was the notion of the personality as the highest value. We have to learn to understand all over again that every individual human life is a symbol of a certain day in history – only then will the 'particular', however small the scene of its enactment, appear to our minds as a general picture of the world. But will this ever come about? Have we left it until too late? Has the moment passed by, perhaps, when we might still have come to our senses and stopped the process of endlessly churning over indeterminate quantities and percentages? I do not and cannot know. In all likelihood things have gone too far and the process of disintegration is irreversible.

II: PROLOGUE

Pasternak had always wanted to write a play as well, and he has left some strange fragments of one;* Tsvetayeva was continuously turning out elaborate dramatic episodes (so much for her girlish infatuation with Rostand!). Akhmatova had never had any such ideas, until out of the blue, in Tashkent, she wrote her *Prologue*, which she burned at the end of the forties, the night after her son Lev was arrested and taken away. It was thrown into the stove together with some notebooks containing verse. She had not forgotten how they came to us in Furmanov Street to pick up what they had not confiscated on the first visit.† Known as 'the second search', this kind of thing was a standard concept in our life. Everything could be repeated without any warning whatsoever: house searches, deportations, arrests. Lev, who in effect had been seized as a hostage for his mother, would have been dealt with even more harshly if *Prologue* and the verse in those notebooks had found their way to his interrogator's desk. Indeed, on reading the play, the authorities concerned would scarcely have been able to resist the temptation of picking up Akhmatova herself. She had

* 'The Blind Beauty'. See Pasternak, Appendix A.
† *Hope Against Hope*, pages 16 ff.

been permitted, as a favour bestowed from the highest quarter, to remain at liberty – in the two capital cities, what is more.* It was inadvisable to presume on such gracious favours by scribbling plays . . . The best policy was always to sit tight and say nothing. The logic of this was clear and unquestionable. Akhmatova was very conscious of the fact that, thanks to the favour shown her, she was living on borrowed time: 'And, leading me to the very edge, they left me there / – a madwoman walking the city's every silent square.' We all knew we were at liberty only on sufferance, for just as long as we were allowed to continue going to our daily work and buying salted herring in the shops to eat in our own homes. As infinitesimal units subsumed in the concept 'a few million', we were grateful for small mercies and were as mute as though we had swallowed our tongues.

If it had not been for the accident of the special favour shown to her, Akhmatova would also have found herself in one of those rooms with false doors.† I can just imagine how she would have stood before her interrogator and said no. It was the custom of police interrogators in Leningrad to spit in the faces of their victims – a small thing, perhaps, compared with real torture, but not for nothing was it said: 'This place shall be empty . . .'‡

Akhmatova read *Prologue* to me in Tashkent in the summer of 1942, the year in which epaulets suddenly appeared on the shoulders of cadets graduating from the military schools.§ 'They look like Decembrists‖ now,' Akhmatova commented as we caught sight of a whole covey of them walking home one day from the Botanical Garden. They really did look like Decembrists; any of these earnest youths could have been the ideal young man at the station of Krechetovka, and at that very moment, in some

---

* 'Suspect' persons were often banned from residence in Moscow and Leningrad as a minimum sanction.
† *Hope Against Hope*, page 99.
‡ See note, page 121.
§ Stalin reintroduced officers' epaulets, together with the pre-revolutionary names of military ranks, as part of his appeal to Russian national sentiment during the war. (These symbols of the old regime had all been abolished immediately after the Revolution.)
‖ Young officers who attempted an uprising against the autocracy in December 1825.

different town or village, another young man, an artillery officer, was thinking about Russia (though God knows what went through his mind in those days), already fated to become a convict and a writer.* Our paths never crossed in Tashkent: we had already left by the time he came to the hospital there. Even if we had not gone by then, he would hardly have found us for the simple reason that he had never heard of us, either in school, his two universities, on his training course for the artillery, in exile, or in the hospital. Even if he had come to see us, we should have been suspicious of him as a stranger and would have given him no help in the further development of his ideas. I do not know what was going on in his head in those years, but he did indeed share the fate of enormous numbers of other Russian youths with epaulets on their shoulders: the Decembrists, the Petrashevtsi,† all those who perished after the First World War and were sent to camps after the second . . .

In *Prologue* I could hear the authentic voice of Akhmatova. She did not herself, of course, make any claim to have written a tragedy of nationwide significance, but as far as I am concerned, the particular case with which the play deals does nevertheless amount to a 'picture of the world' – on the simple grounds that any era should be judged by the degree to which it is possible to exercise the basic human right of professing one's faith and speaking one's mind. I do not know whether this has always been a valid criterion for past ages in history, but I have read somewhere that when the teachings of the Church were taking shape the men and women trading in the market-places of Byzantium argued about them with such passion that their business declined considerably. That, to my mind, is true freedom of thought. A man deprived of this freedom gradually loses his human qualities and begins to howl like a

---

* Solzhenitsyn served as an artillery officer until his arrest at the front in 1945. His story 'Incident at Krechetovka Station' is about the arrest of a young officer during the war. After his release from the forced labour camp in Kazakhstan in 1953, Solzhenitsyn went to Tashkent in 1955 to be treated at the hospital there (as described in *Cancer Ward*). Akhmatova had left Tashkent in 1944, Mrs Mandelstam in 1946. Solzhenitsyn's 'two universities' were Rostov-on-Don and the Moscow Institute for Philosophy and Literature (Mifli).

† Revolutionary group led by Mikhail Petrashevski. Its members – who included Dostoyevski – were arrested in 1849.

jackal. Speech and ideas wither away. Society sinks into a hypnotic slumber. In a manner of speaking, Akhmatova's *Prologue* was a dream within a dream.

The people who first heard it were reminded of Gogol, Kafka, Sukhovo-Kobylin, and Lord knows who else besides. There certainly were elements of Sukhovo-Kobylin, if only in that Akhmatova was dealing with officialdom in the play, and the very idea of officials engenders a certain tendency towards the abstract, to action on the stage reminiscent of ballet in its almost mechanical precision of movement. Akhmatova was concerned not with government officials as such but with those of the literary organizations. The theme of the play is the trial before a writers' tribunal of a woman poet who is then sentenced to prison. There was nothing more to it. Since they *consciously* betray freedom of thought, Akhmatova's literary bureaucrats are far more terrifying than the government officials portrayed by Sukhovo-Kobylin.

Prologue, as produced by Akhmatova herself in Tashkent, was a biting and very tightly constructed whole. The only 'stage prop' was a ladder which Akhmatova dragged over from the *balakhana*** where we later went to live. There was no other concession to stage craft or theatrical inventiveness. The heroine descended from this rickety ladder after being awakened at an unearthly hour, and she appeared before her judges in a nightgown. Night was always a time of terror for us. The hours of sleep and love were only too often interrupted by the ringing of the doorbell, though M.'s second arrest was heralded not by the bell but by a hideous knocking on the door in the middle of the night; in either case the sound was like nothing else, and there was something inhuman about it. One's ears never rested, straining to catch the slightest night sound: if a car drove past we listened intently ('Will it stop here or go on?'). If someone walked up the stairs we cocked our ears for the tread of soldiers' boots. Then there was the sound of the elevator: even now my heart thumps painfully whenever I hear the creak of an old-fashioned elevator, a ringing or knocking at the door. Yet, we always got undressed to sleep. I am surprised we did not form the habit of going to bed with our clothes on – it would have made much more sense – and the heroine of *Prologue* (played by

* Uzbek-style house.

Akhmatova herself) would not have had to stand trial in her nightgown.

Below, on the 'stage', there was a large table covered by official-looking baize. The 'judges' sat behind it, and writers congregated around it to lend their support. Two of the writers had packages in their hands, one with a fish head and the other with a fish tail sticking out of it. During periods when we were rationed (and there were several), nothing ever caused greater excitement in literary circles than the news that the stores (similar to the government ones) which served the most favoured writers were about to 'issue' something. Zhdanov himself (!) had telephoned Tashkent on a special government line to say that Akhmatova must be taken care of. He had probably explained who she was ('our best', or 'our oldest poet', or words to that effect), and thanks to this, one decent writer who had also been evacuated to Tashkent managed to wangle two rations for her from different stores. His wife, who had once served in the militia, used to bring the extra one to her. When this couple left Tashkent, the second ration petered out, since every three months the writer had been obliged to go down on bended knees to get it renewed. Everybody else managed to get an extra ration like this, but we were hopeless at fending for ourselves and couldn't do it on our own. Once, we were delighted to hear from a very unassuming academic lady by the name of Miklukha-Maklai that she had the same problem. She told us sorrowfully that she was unable to do what everybody did – draw a ration of *boubliks*,* for example, exchange them for bread and a little cash, then barter the bread for something else and buy a handful of rice with the cash. Such deals, with all their permutations – child's play for everybody else – simply made our heads spin, and we had no luck at all, often missing our chance to snap up the most obvious things for use in barter. During the last winter in Tashkent, when we lived together, it was I who went to the store to collect the ration. Once I came away with a quantity of salted herring wrapped in newspaper from which heads and tails were sticking out. A gang of urchins raced past me along the pavement one after another, with a few yards' distance between them. They were all a little taller than I, and as each one went past he slapped my parcel with his hand, so

* Ring-shaped bread rolls.

that one or two fish heads and tails fell out and dropped on the pavement to be snatched up by the boy behind. By the time I got home, I only had about half a dozen left. Akhmatova was in utter despair and told me off for not being more wide awake. She was not at all amused by this virtuoso technique of the local boys, which they had brought to a fine art by raiding writers carrying fish ends wrapped in newspaper. There was something invincible about them, and in my heart of hearts I liked them better than their victims. There were no girls among them. Girls were accepted as equals only by criminal gangs. One such gang of young bandits which was tried for murder and robbery – they put out their victims' eyes to prevent subsequent identification of themselves – was led by an angelic-looking girl in a starched dress. Her parents were highly placed members of the *apparat*, privileged to use the most select of the 'closed' stores, where the goods were wrapped in proper paper, or delivered to them at home: no fish heads and tails sticking out of newspaper for them! At the beginning of our new era pigs' heads were used to make up the so-called academic ration. Tashkent kept literature alive with fish heads and tails. The parts in between were reserved for higher purposes.

Writers holding manuscripts and their rations wrapped in newspaper scurried all over the 'stage', inquiring about the trial. They waved their rolled-up manuscripts ('I do not liked rolled-up manuscripts. Some are as heavy and tarnished by time as an archangel's trumpet') and asked where the trial would be, who was going to be tried, and who had been appointed 'public accuser'.* They addressed these questions to each other and to a 'secretary of inhuman beauty' who sat at a small table right in front with dozens of telephones. The writers fell over themselves telling her of their eagerness to attend the trial and acclaim the undoubtedly just verdict which the court would pass. Decisions concerning the distribution of material goods – apartments, rations, dachas, fish heads and tails – always reached people through a secretary, and she was consequently a person of great importance. The 'secretary of inhuman beauty' brushes off all the ration-carrying writers, answering their questions with the standard and by now famous phrase: 'Not all at once – there are many of you and only one of

* See Vasiliev, Appendix A.

me' . . . Akhmatova had a wonderful ear for phrases of this kind heard on the street or in offices. She always picked them up and then used them herself with gusto (for example: 'Here you are, pay at the cash desk!').*

The trial begins, and the main point to emerge from the proceedings is that the heroine has not the faintest idea what she is being accused of. Her judges and fellow writers are indignant because her answers bear no relation to the questions she is asked. The trial is an encounter between two different worlds in which the two sides are talking at cross purposes, although they seem to speak a common language. *Prologue* was written in prose, and every line cut to the quick. All the commonplaces of official literature and ideology were reproduced in fantastically concentrated form and with deadly accuracy. They are rained down on the heroine's head when she starts muttering her verse – some pitiful, disconnected lines about a world in which there is air and water, earth and sky, leaves and grass (in other words: Akhmatova's 'blissful somewhere'). As soon as she begins to speak she is interrupted by a great hubbub: nobody, she is reminded, has given her the right to mumble verse like this, and she should pause to consider whose mill she is providing grist for by writing such stuff; what is more, she must remember she is on trial and will answer to the People for everything going through her mind – the People with its fish heads and grubby manuscripts is right there in front of her. (At this point spotlights were to pick out her head, sweeping back and forth over her hair.)

The heroine is not frightened. She is simply aware that there is no longer any place on earth for a human being, among all this rabble of writers and officials. At such a trial all one can feel is dismay and bewilderment. Since the trial takes place in a dead world, the ghouls who stand in judgement over her cannot deprive her of life. She is sent to prison, and here, for the first time, she feels free. Her voice is heard on the stage as she reads poetry in her cell. The writers, meanwhile, wander around and clamber up and down

---

* The cry of the harassed woman cashier in a Soviet shop – customers have to line up to get receipts showing they have paid before going back to the counter to pick up their goods. Since there is no alternative but to pay at the cash desk, the phrase illustrates the divorce between cliché and reality.

the ladder, grumbling about the fact that 'writers do not read each other' – the words are a kind of refrain. They demand that a decree should be issued requiring writers to read everything written by their colleagues . . . The voice of the heroine grows louder, and a strange dialogue begins between her and them. The gist of what she says is the same as something Akhmatova later wrote down in verse form:

> From beneath what ruins do I speak?
> What weight of debris smothers my cries
> here in the quicklime of my stinking crypt?
> They will say it is the hush of winter
> and lock me away behind eternal doors.
> But my voice will still be heard,
> and people will believe it once again . . .

But there is more than this to her words. They also convey the acute sense of delirium, of hallucination, which was everybody's experience in those years. The heroine in her nightgown was like all the many women who woke up at night in a cold sweat, unable to believe what had happened to them. Akhmatova once had a horribly lifelike dream: suddenly she hears the tramp of jackboots in the wide corridor of Punin's apartment (where there was a table and at the end, behind a curtain, a bed in which her son Lev sometimes stayed the night, as did M. and I). She rushes out into the corridor and learns they have come for Gumilev. She knows that Nikolai Stepanovich is hiding in her room – the last door (on the left, like all the other doors) at the end of the corridor. Lev is asleep behind the curtain; she brings him out and hands him over to the soldiers: 'Here is Gumilev' . . . Only a woman tormented by such dreams could have written *Prologue*.

III: THE DECREE

Prologue was written a long time before the Decree on Akhmatova and Zoshchenko (it also mentioned Khazin, but this is not a relative of my brother's and mine, only a namesake). Many people who had read, or rather heard, *Prologue* were now staggered at how prophetic it had been. It seemed as though she had foretold it all: the special sessions, newspaper articles, speeches by writers, the meetings at universities and schools on each anniversary of the Decree when black masses (or rather just drearily grey ones) were celebrated, during which everybody spat in the faces of two of the accused and at the grave – wherever it may be – of a third.* 'Why do they talk as if I were some old soothsayer?' Akhmatova asked in astonishment. 'Things were *always* like that; they were never any different.' She instanced the articles of Lelevich, all the speeches, articles, and talk that had emanated from RAPP, LEF, and everybody else; they had been determined to bury her and M. alive and drive a stake through them to lay their ghosts, making sure they would not pop out of their graves and walk the forbidden earth again, as ghosts will. Akhmatova had borne with the anathema on herself over the years, and she took the Decree as one would have expected, that is, without any emotion except natural fear of the consequences. She was frightened for herself and for those near and dear to her: it is impossible not to tremble when this dead brutish force draws near to you, ready to drag you from your bed and haul you off to limbo.

Poor Zoshchenko was completely unprepared for the blow. This was clear from his conversation with some Oxford students who had come to try to help the victims.† It is said that they were sent

---

* In his 'report' accompanying the Party Decree on Zoshchenko and Akhmatova, Zhdanov also scurrilously denounced Mandelstam as having been an apologist for the Middle Ages. (It is noteworthy that there is no indication in this mention of him by Zhdanov that Mandelstam was already dead.)

† This 'conversation' took place a little over a year after Stalin's death, in the first week of May 1954. The occasion was the visit to Leningrad of a group of twenty British students, one of whom was Russian-speaking. None of the students was from Oxford, nor was any of them sent by Isaiah Berlin who knew nothing of the visit. Akhmatova and Zoshchenko were 'produced' for the group – who had not asked to see them – on the premises of the Leningrad branch of the Union of Writers. It should be remembered that at this time Akhmatova's son was still in a camp. For another, more circumstantial, account of this affair, see Lidia Chukovskaya, 'Notes on Anna Akhmatova', in *To the Memory of A. A. Akhmatova*, YMCA Press, Paris, 1974, pp. 99–102. It is quite evident from a conversation with Akhmatova recorded in her diary by Chukovskaya at the time that

by Berlin, the Oxford 'visitor from the future' who had been to see Akhmatova shortly before this whole drama. Did those Oxford students ever realize what danger they put Zoshchenko in? He was subjected to a second wave of persecution from which he never recovered. A wonderful, pure man, he had always tried to find points of contact with the time he lived in. He believed in all the high-sounding schemes for universal happiness and thought that eventually everything would settle down – all the cruelty and savagery were only incidental, a temporary ruffling of the surface, not the essence, as we were always being told at political lectures. (In these, needless to say, there was never any actual mention of cruelty, only of things that still 'ruffled the surface'.) Many people failed to notice the transition from the popular upheaval of the Revolution, with all its spontaneous barbarity, to the carefully planned, machine-like callousness that followed. People who had tended to find excuses for the first of these phases also reconciled themselves to the second. This was true of Zoshchenko, one of the subalterns of the Revolution (in 1917 his actual rank was higher, but psychologically he belonged to this category).

Zoshchenko was a moralist by nature; his aim in his stories was to bring his contemporaries to their senses, to help them become more human, but his readers saw only the funny side and neighed like horses when they read him. Zoshchenko kept his illusions and was completely without cynicism – he always used to think everything over carefully with his head slightly on one side – and he paid a terrible price. With his artist's eye he sometimes got to the heart of things, but he could not really make sense of them because he believed implicitly in progress and all the wonderful things it would bring. During the First World War he was poisoned by gas and after it by the pseudo-philosophical brew of materialism concocted for weaker spirits. Somewhere in the background there had been a

---

Akhmatova could have had no valid reason for supposing (if indeed she did suppose any such thing) that any of the English students present was an emissary of some kind. It is clear, however, that she was forced by an innocent question into a position of seeming to aquiesce, even after Stalin's death, in the judgement passed on her by Zhdanov eight years previously.

Isaiah Berlin saw Akhmatova twice in Leningrad; the second visit took place in the first week of January 1946. Their meeting is referred to in her *Poem Without a Hero*, where he is described as a 'visitor from the future'.

pre-Revolutionary high school with its radicalism and lack of restraints – the rest followed naturally. The crisis in people's thinking went hand in hand with the crisis in their schooling.

What did those Oxford students make of Akhmatova's behaviour? She told us how she had sat like a graven image with unseeing eyes and reeled off the required official phrases with total indifference and a magnificently impassive manner. The nice English boys, brought up always to speak the truth and stand by their convictions, were doubtless quite dumbfounded when Akhmatova told them how greatly she had benefited from the Decree. Taken together with her verse in *Ogoniok*,* this must have convinced them that all Russians are absolutely venal and can be bought for a farthing. Or they may have felt they had been afforded a fleeting glimpse of the Russian soul, mysterious and Asiatic, with its predilection for Decrees, poverty, forced labour camps, and the firing squad . . . They see us rather as we do the Chinese. The farther east you look the more everything merges into one dun-coloured blur. Akhmatova must have struck them as sheeplike in her docility, and Zoshchenko as a wild rebel by comparison. In fact, we *are* sheep in a way . . .

The Tashkent *Prologue* was burned together with a notebook full of verse. Akhmatova alluded to the fact in her poem 'The Burned Notebook'.† When her volume of poetry was being put together, Surkov winced at this article: what did she mean by hinting that people had to burn their verse? . . . For propriety's sake he suggested she change it to 'Notebook Lost in a Fire'. Akhmatova duly made the change in her own hand, saying: 'Very well, let people think I had a fire . . .' Some future born idiot of a pedantic editor is bound to accept this as the final title when he sees her handwritten alteration to the text. He will take it as an expression of the author's will.

After the Twentieth Congress Akhmatova tried to put down on paper again the poems she had burned. But her memory was no

---

* In 1950 Akhmatova published a series of poems praising Stalin and his works in *Ogoniok*. They have nothing of Akhmatova in them and read like a parody of the standard doggerel of the time. She wrote them for the sake of her son, already in a camp for the second time after his arrest in 1949.

† Written in 1951, but first published only in 1963.

longer so good, and there was a lot she had forgotten. Some things had been remembered by her friends, who were thus able to make her a present, so to speak, of her own poetry. As a result relatively little has been lost: the first verse of 'Boyarinia Morozova' (the manuscript was given to the literary scholar Makogonenko for safe-keeping, but he now blankly denies it); a passage in *Poem Without a Hero*, in which, after flying back to Moscow, she has some harsh words to say about the dowager capital;* the exact test of 'I Am What I Am, I Wish You Another' (in the surviving text there is a mix-up with the rhymes – goodness knows how it happened); one verse of her poem about the 'businesslike Parisian'. This is probably not a complete list, but we could not think of any others.

It is easier to reconstruct verse than prose. While M. was still alive I destroyed the first chapter of *Fourth Prose*, without having the good sense to learn it by heart beforehand (as I had the whole of 'Conversation About Dante'). Now I shall never be able to write it down again. I remember only two phrases: 'Who needs this kind of socialism: shopworn . . .' (after this came other epithets), and: 'If the citizenry decided to have a new Renaissance, what would come of it? Something called "Café Renaissance" at the best.' It was a pity to destroy this chapter, but for such skylarking as this we should have been wiped out together with anybody who had ever so much as nodded a greeting to us. M. was upset, but he agreed it was much too risky to keep.

Neither M. nor Akhmatova bothered much about looking after their manuscripts, but for different reasons. In his case it was because he believed people would preserve whatever they needed, but with her it was because she disliked any reminder of death: 'What's the hurry,' she would ask, 'when I am still alive?' She was essentially a pagan, and her splendid pagan nature revolted against the idea of death. At our very last meeting, two or three days before she died, she said to me with a sigh: 'Some people live to be ninety, but it doesn't look as though I shall . . .' It was not that she had any premonition of being so close to death at that moment, but having recently survived a dangerous illness she was now loath to

* Pushkin's epithet for Moscow in *The Bronze Horseman* (because it had been replaced as the capital by Petersburg).

part with life. If Olshevskaya, Ardov's wife, had not insisted on taking her to an out-of-the-way sanatorium (for people who had suffered strokes – and hence of use only to Olshevskaya herself, not to Akhmatova), she would certainly have lived on a little longer. They had a terrible time getting there: the taxi broke down and they had to stand around by the roadside for a long time trying to beg a lift. The previous day had also been very trying for Akhmatova. Ania Kaminskaya – Irina Punina's daughter – had made her go to the savings bank to draw out some money 'for mama'. She had refused to let her mother have a hundred rubles previously given to her by Akhmatova – the grasping little harpy was out for everything she could get. On the last evening she would not let me see Akhmatova: 'They are talking about Lev, and Akuma is very upset' (Punin had brought the word *akuma* back from Japan; he said it meant 'witch', and it had been adopted as Akhmatova's nickname in the family). Ania also had a hand, together with her mother, in the purloining of Akhmatova's papers. 'Akuma used to eat our bread,' was the favourite saying of both of them. By this they meant that when Akhmatova lived with Punin she had taken her meals together with them at the same table. The moral of this is clear: such grotesque arrangements make no sense, and if you go to live with somebody else's husband, then do not set up house in the same apartment with both him and the wife he has thrown over. Not that I have anything against going off with other people's husbands – it happens all the time and seems, therefore, to be in the nature of things. Akhmatova was speaking of herself in the splendid lines: 'Most faithful mate of other women's husbands / and of many the sorrowing widow.' The only bad thing was living all together 'under the roof of the House on the Fontanka'. This idyllic setup was devised by Punin to spare Akhmatova the need to keep house, and himself the strain of earning enough to support two different establishments. Apart from this the desperate housing shortage inevitably complicated any divorce or love affair. It is always vital to separate completely, and the idyll did not work out. Her relations with Punin would probably have been much easier and simpler if they had not all shared the same apartment. The most important thing in life for any Soviet citizen is his tiny bit of 'living space'. No wonder so many crimes have been committed for the sake of it. I only hope I die in my own precious little cooperative apartment. This is my one remaining wish, but I fear it may not be granted . . .

IV: THE DREAM WITHIN A DREAM

Akhmatova was not able to reconstruct *Prologue*. She started trying to as soon as Lev came back from the camp, but there was nobody who could help her. The people who had heard it in Tashkent could no longer remember the general plan, let alone the individual lines which had given it so much bite at the time. In vain she begged them to jog her memory by recalling some little part of it. Although nothing came of this, she could not let it rest there and decided to write something similar in its place. But by this time she had entered her final phase of resigned old age and no longer saw tragedy in such ordinary day-to-day matters as the persecution of people for what they thought and said, their use of two different languages, the mutual estrangement and lack of understanding between them. What she now found tragic was the 'flight of time', the natural course of things, our progress from cradle to grave. This was when she wrote the four-line stanza:

> What are wars? What is the plague?
> Their end is foreseen, their sentence is almost passed.
> But what about the horror
> Which once was called the flight of time?

I would be glad to die believing that wars are a thing of the past, but I cannot share such optimism. I did not like the new *Prologue*. Any distortion of life is for me much more terrible than death. Clearly, together with M., I must have got used to the idea of death, and I smile as I repeat the line from a poem he wrote when he was still almost a child: 'If it were not for death I should never know I am alive' . . . Death is a structural element ('The tissues of our world are renewed by death'). Life, like history, is not an eternal merry-go-round, but a path. The very theme of the second *Prologue* or *Dream Within A Dream* is unacceptable to me.

Perhaps I was being unfair, but from the start I shook my head whenever Akhmatova tried to persuade me to reconsider and have another look at it. *Dream Within a Dream* was never finished, and all that remains of the whole enterprise are a few verse fragments and an elaborate design for the staging of it. Just as Pasternak in his old age – not to be outdone by anybody else – took it into his head to write a melodrama of a traditional kind, so Akhmatova too succumbed to the fashionable mania for playwriting, with a small dash of primitive mysticism thrown in. Both of them had never before had anything to do with the theatre, and I can only explain this sudden attraction to the footlights as a foible of old age. I am certain that neither Pasternak nor Akhmatova had any idea of that 'little box with the funny little men walking up and down it' (to my mind, the story about the little box is the best thing ever done by Bulgakov). To be able to visualize the stage and hear the voice of the actors is the first essential for anyone writing any kind of drama. The brief Tashkent *Prologue* was rather like an intermezzo in form, and it contained no detail that Akhmatova had not seen with her own eyes: the writers, the judges, the secretary, the fish tails and heads, the official telephones of various types. She played in *Prologue* herself, keeping her costume, a nightgown made of sackcloth, in her trunk. I am not sure it is a good thing for an author to act in his own play, but for someone of Akhmatova's temperament it was irresistible.

Too many things would have been needed to resurrect the old *Prologue*: the isolation and poverty of the prewar era, the hungry wartime rations, and the ladder from the *balakhana*. The second *Prologue*, on the other hand, was written during that brief moment when life smiled on Akhmatova and when, in recollecting the past, she began to add up all the things she had missed or been deprived of during her life because the 'cruel age' had deflected it, 'like a river from its course'. The recurring theme of the second *Prologue* is '. . . how many friends / I never had the chance to meet'. Such a totting up of the account and its presentation to the era is in itself quite justified, but here it is shrouded in nebulous talk and soulfulness quite out of this world. Only one short dialogue between 'He' and 'She' ever got into print, and this she then eked out by several other poems written independently of it: 'Third

Voice.' 'Heard from a Distance,' and 'The Blind Man's Song.' (These titles were added only when she tacked them on to the 'tragedy'.)

Akhmatova first introduced the theme of the 'meeting that was not to be' in some verse about her chance encounter and abruptly terminated friendship with a foreigner. In 'Cinque', the five poems which she wrote about this meeting almost immediately after they had parted, there is a sharp sense of both triumph and catastrophe. It had been given to her to meet someone whom fate had not decreed she should see. While it was thus a forbidden joy, it was also 'that bitterest of days when we met'. It is said that the foreigner asked people beforehand whether his visit might not harm her. He was told there could be no harm – she was not an engineer after all, and could not therefore betray any secrets. (They forgot that *everything* is secret here: even the way we breathe.) It appears that this meeting with the foreigner was one of the trump cards for those who argued in favour of the Decree. More indirectly it led to the re-arrest of her son and his imprisonment in a camp. Akhmatova was hence quite entitled to claim: 'They'll visit enough on you and me / to shame the twentieth century.' A few years later Akhmatova refused a further meeting (the proposal came through Pasternak), and this came out in verse as 'the meeting that never was': 'In this world you and I are not to meet,' and: 'The triumphs are empty, the words mute and unspoken / of our mysterious meeting that never was.' Towards the end of her life they did in fact meet again, but it was too late – a few months before her death when she was already very tired, and in another country.

The reason for this 'non-meeting' was all too real and tangible: the artificial barrier, the blank wall, the impassable moat dividing the two worlds . . . People who might have had something to say to each other were absolutely cut off in space. Words were left hanging in the air. In the second *Prologue*, however, the reason for the failure to meet is different; here it is *time* that separates the souls of the two potential lovers; it is because of a gulf in time that they cannot come together or find each other. This is not the heavy-hearted reaching out for a loved one we find in Zhukovski, whose belief in life everlasting is accompanied by inability to imagine it:

'and borne on wings of hope, flying through their realms of bliss, he calls out there: Isolina! And receives back the whispering echo: Isolina, Isolina – there in those mute realms of bliss.' These are marvellous lines, and the feeling they convey is one deeply rooted in the human soul. But the passion of Akhmatova's 'visitor from the future' (who was unable to fall on his knees before her), though romanticized, is completely of this world. To judge by the published fragment 'he' and 'she' might seem never to have met in this life: 'he' appears in her dream, and 'she' keeps him on tenterhooks, arousing his passion from the other side of life's threshold. From this he can escape only by killing her. There were several other fragments in which 'he' had managed, in some other existence, to give her a goblet of poison, and for this reason they are both condemned always to live on earth at different times, never meeting, but eternally longing and pining for each other. The goblet of poison and his vow that 'I will kill you with my song, without spilling your blood on the ground' are all part of a Romantic rigmarole about a suspect kind of eternity where people wander around in circles, or keep aimlessly returning to earth to fret away in passion and longing.

Akhmatova's strength is in precision of detail and economy of words. A single line of hers often has the bleak terseness of an epigram, as one sees in such a late poem as 'Native Soil'. In the 'Midnight Verses' and the second version of *Prologue* this quality abandoned Akhmatova, and to my mind the task she set herself was in any case an unreal one. After living our terribles lives, how could we console ourselves with a 'non-meeting' in time, yearn for lovers we had never lived with, or look for a loved one among our descendants and ancestors when our own contemporaries had been wiped out before our very eyes? A 'non-meeting' in space is so much more painful than a 'non-meeting' in time or any other imagined tragedy caused by the 'flight of time' that I was saddened to hear this verse. I reminded Akhmatova how in her middle years she had always been very sceptical of late-blossoming passions and laughed at women who could not bring themselves to call a halt. I am sorry, however, about the 'yellow star' in the published fragment; this could have been developed into a theme with a real basis in her own life instead of serving as the mere ornament of a heroine who inspires passion not in a reader of a later generation, but in a lover pining for a woman once of this world. M. took a very poor view of invention and fantasy, regarding them as the bane of poetry. In this I follow him.

Nevertheless, I believe that Akhmatova did have some real grounds for all this. In our old age we suddenly found ourselves surrounded not by our children, but by our grandchildren. These 'friends of the final levy' came too late – not in our years of horror when, like outcasts with yellow armbands, we needed 'a friendly handclasp in the hour of danger'. Akhmatova thought this was unconscionably bad timing on the part of our new friends who had simply left their entry into the world too late. She felt that if they had been born fifty years earlier, then we would not have endured all the loneliness and lack of understanding which dogged us all our lives. I was sceptical about this theory of 'bad timing', and it gave rise to violent arguments between us. It was my view that if the people who gathered around Akhmatova in her old age had been adults in the twenties, thirties, or forties, it would never have entered their heads to go anywhere near a banned poet. At best they would simply have taken refuge in their work as humble engineers or the like, but even so the chances are that we should have heard them making speeches calling for the eradication of pernicious tendencies in Soviet literature. It would have been a toss-up whether they died in camps or decayed in the august chancelleries of the Union of Writers or one of the state publishing houses. We knew people among our own generation of tougher fibre than any 'friends of the final levy', but they were ground down by the times and turned traitor, or were shipped off to Kolyma. Are our young contemporaries any better than those of our own age? Once Akhmatova had written: 'You will not have to answer for me / – you can sleep in peace, my friends. / Might is right, and it is your children / who will curse you on my account.' But the children were in league with their fathers and would never have thought of reproaching them for anything. Now times have changed, and the grandchildren do seem to have it in for their daddies and grand-daddies. In my view, however, the main change is that the era has mellowed a little and no longer destroys everybody who 'wakens prematurely'. At the same time, these grandchildren belong to the 'unfrightened' generation, and I have no great faith in them. Who knows how they will behave if really put to the test?

Of even greater significance now, I think, is the fact that it has become harder to recruit people to do the dirty work. This was suggested to me by an almost chance encounter. Some friends of mine with a dacha in the country employed a cleaning woman who was not quite right in the head. She had living with her a son, a semi-moron with a terrible, fixed expression on his face. The woman complained that her house in the village was falling apart and asked our advice about where she should go to live. She refused all offers of work in the nearby town, even though some were very good – with a free room and the prospect of good pickings on the side. But she decided that for the sake of her son she must go to Moscow. In our naïvety we laughed at the idea: who would give a job to this idiot youth when the only thing that produced any flicker of life in him was a shot of vodka? But we were quite wrong: the son enrolled in the paramilitary security forces, and both he and his mother were given an apartment and a permit to reside in the world's most forbidden city. There must obviously be a great shortage of people willing to shoot at their fellow men if they had to give such work to a cretin. But it is a big country, and there will be enough cretins to do whatever shooting and executing may be needed. The only question is whether the lust for blood has been sated, or whether it will come back again.

Akhmatova and I found that our roles had been reversed. In the second half of the fifties I was the optimist ('Now that things have gone this far, there is no going back'). But Akhmatova kept talking about there always being both good and bad Caesars. This is a very important point: in a disintegrating society life is so unstable that nothing is predictable. During a slow process of decomposition it is sometimes shakier elements that come to the fore, and sometimes firmer ones. When the shakier ones are on top there is more persecution: the clampdown is characteristic of a society in decline, when delirium and the throes of death have set in. Lovers of strong-man regimes fail to realize that the stability and efficiency of a society stands not in direct but in inverse proportion to the increase in the use of dictatorial powers, and that 'unanimity' is a sign of decay, not of vitality. Tikhonov, it is said, now talks sadly about how much more order there was under Stalin, and our latter-day nationalists dream of a return to the recent past (everybody marching in step, Party decrees, unanimity) with an infusion of their own catchpenny ideas. This is clear proof that they are ignorant of Khomiakov and the other Slavophiles who all knew very well that society is the prime motive force, and that in keeping order the state should be careful not to stifle it. In Khomiakov's view the state should be like the rim of the barrel, not an iron hoop (of the kind used to smash the skull of Titsian Tabidze). I am frightened by these *Rusity** who are bent on bringing out the iron hoop again to clamp as tightly as they can around the heads of our grandchildren.

Living out her last few years under a good Caesar, Akhmatova recovered her spirits. She was overjoyed by the great surge of interest in poetry and thought it a special characteristic of the 'grandchildren'. This was why she was so sorry they had not been born earlier, to bring her solace in all her years of trial. Hence also the new *Prologue* with its lamentations about a 'non-meeting' in time. She took pleasure in naïvely formal things and spent a lot of time designing a stage set for her lost souls to wander around upon – it had a second level, an orchestra above that, and plat-forms at various heights, including some out in the auditorium. But she soon stopped hovering in this theatrical empyrean. Sharp-eyed even in old age, she glanced through one or two Western plays and was quick to see that her flights of fancy had been thought of by others long ago. I knew they had been old hat since the twenties. After this she told me she had given up the play altogether and destroyed the fragments already written. But I put little credence in this. Her papers were in such disorder that much of the play certainly survives. Some interesting bits of verse may still emerge, but I have no great hopes of the rest.

The first *Prologue* is an irreparable loss, but the second is a self-indulgence of her complacent old age, when she tried to invent

* 'Rusites': term currently in unofficial use for the extreme Russian nationalists in the Soviet Union, who want a return to strong government (unlike the nineteenth-century Slavophiles who, as the author points out, believed in an organically developing society).

torments and passions outside space – as though the ones on this side of the fence were not enough for us! I have had much more than my fill, and I would rather not witness the spectacle of our 'grandchildren' going frantic with terror the next time the screws are put on.

V: THE SEAMY SIDE OF LIFE

I read the Decree on *Zvezda* and *Leningrad* in Moscow just after a week's visit to Akhmatova in Leningrad. In other words while we had been together, happy in each other's company, the Decree was being put into final shape. Its anonymous authors had done their work well . . . During those days we had glimpsed outward signs of disfavour, but, being so used to them, we had paid no attention, though we could not help feeling a slight chill running down our spines. This and the accompanying attacks of nausea were something we always concealed. Shrugging our shoulders or swiftly exchanging glances, we would pretend that 'all was sweetness and light', and go on talking as though nothing untoward had happened. (Akhmatova had once been to visit a paralysed old actor with a word of introduction from somebody, but he just nodded, wrinkled up his nose, and said: 'Not a bit interested in knowing you . . .' When Akhmatova complained to M. about this reception, his comment was: 'And then all was sweetness and light . . .' This mot had stuck in our minds, and we were always using it on the most unsuitable occasions. How could such a graceful expression ever apply to the gorgeous realities of our daily existence?)

The first sign of disfavour was the sudden appearance near the gate of the Sheremetiev house on the Fontanka* of two young men with ugly mugs (or one young man and a girl with an ugly mug). On the Fontanka side there is a broad forecourt protected by magnificent railings, and the old mansion itself stands at the back

---

* Canal in Leningrad on which the former Sheremetiev palace was situated. Akhmatova lived here after leaving Shileiko for Punin.

of this, its front also facing the Fontanka and with a garden behind. The garden is enclosed on all sides by three-storey buildings, and the only way into it is through the back door of the house – in a direct line with the front entrance. The building in which Akhmatova lived was on the right side of the garden. In this inner garden Akhmatova had once used to walk with Tapka, a huge Saint Bernard passed on to her by Shileiko.* At the beginning of the Revolution Petersburg had been full of stray dogs of the most extraordinary breeds. On fleeing abroad, their owners had left them in the care of faithful servants, who then abandoned them during the famine. Shileiko had found the dog in a starving and wretched state but did not want to take it to Moscow with him, so Tapka, a noble dog of impeccable upbringing, stayed behind as part of the complicated Punin household, where he probably lived better than any other of its members. When he died – which was not long after, since he was already old – Akhmatova never walked in the garden again. She preferred the street. The garden is associated in my mind with one delightful little scene which has nothing to do with the present story. M. and I were once standing there together with her and Tapka when suddenly M. was overcome with delight at the spectacle of some little girls running past us one after another in single file – they were pretending to be horses. The first 'horse' stopped in her tracks and asked angrily: 'Where is the front horse?' The pigtailed 'front horse', tired of kicking up her hoofs, had bolted. I grabbed M. by the arm to prevent his taking her place as the leader. Akhmatova also saw the danger and said to him: 'Don't run away: you are *our* front horse.' We went inside to drink tea with the Punins. This was a thousand years ago, a long, long time before we lost our 'front horse . . .'

In 1946 Akhmatova and I were still vigorous and energetic and walked around the city a good deal, now without either Tapka or our 'front horse'. At the beginning of every walk, as the couple loitering at the gate saw us come out, they began to say good-bye to each other. If they were of the same sex they only shook hands, and if of the opposite sex, they kissed each other on their ugly

* Akhmatova's second husband.

mugs as we crossed the forecourt from the front entrance of the mansion. Their long handshake or kiss ended the moment we stepped through the gate on to the Fontanka, and one of them, detaching himself from his male or female partner, tagged along after us. These people did not have faces, but mugs as blank and featureless as pancakes which it was quite impossible to memorize, however much we tried. We wondered what the system was: did we always get any pair that happened to be available, on a purely impersonal basis, or had they attached the same ones to us permanently – specialists, as it were, in us and the itineraries we took on our walks, just as engineers and chauffeurs might be assigned to particular locomotives or cars? Our view was that every 'tail' should have his own special assignment. We did not call them 'tails' but referred to them as 'Berties' – though it was a shame to waste such a nice name on them. They were dressed quite decently in identical overcoats, which were neither pea green* nor of covert cloth (such as those of the operatives who come by night), but of a coarser-textured material like the ones worn by young workers. I was always dying to speak to one of our 'Berties', but Akhmatova would never let me. Her theory was that it was better to pretend you had not noticed them if you did not want the august institution which had sent them to destroy you – we were not supposed to try to fathom its secrets, or rather, its techniques of blatantly open surveillance . . .

We never made any attempt to shake off our escort and just went our way at a leisurely pace while he sauntered along behind. For someone battened on state-supplied victuals it would probably have been easier to serve as one of those footmen who used to run beside the master's carriage instead of having to adapt his pace to ours, but our 'Berties' were forbidden by their instructions ever to overtake us. If we went into a shop, our man came right in behind us, but while we queued to buy something, he never went near the counters or cashiers. The escorts were all issued with rations of a quality greatly superior to anything found in the ordinary shops. A friend of mine was recently in hospital and got into a ward next to a lady who also got her supplies from a privileged special store. This

* The traditional colour of the overcoats worn by police spies in tsarist times.

lady was in the ward by right, together with others of similar status, but my friend had wangled her way in. She told my friend that she had fallen ill through eating some 'shop sausage'. Not wishing to get stomach trouble, our tails were equally chary of 'shop sausage' and waited for us by the door or even on the street – they knew it was not our habit to slip out by the service entrance. If we happened to call on somebody, our tail would wait outside on the street, sometimes handing over to another one quite indistinguishable from himself and not a whit less devoted to duty. They never abandoned us on the way, and we were always seen safely home. 'We are well protected,' Akhmatova used to say. 'We shall never be pestered by hooligans: of that you can be absolutely sure.' Towards the end of her life she sometimes thought she was being followed again, but then it stopped. Somebody – probably Ardov or one of his circle – tried to persuade her that she was just seeing things, or if she wasn't, then it must mean they were shadowing her for her own protection, to prevent her, with all her precious gifts, from being kidnapped by one of those sinister foreign intelligence services. This was a flattering idea, of course, but she was not taken in: 'You wouldn't believe what they say . . .' was her comment.

We got so used to our ill-favoured watchdogs that we successfully mastered the art of ignoring their dedicated attentions. I stayed with Akhmatova for more than two weeks, and we went out walking often – two or three times a day. This was sufficient to grow quite used to your escort. Akhmatova had been familiar with them somewhat longer: this time they had been in constant attendance for about a month and a half before my arrival. (In earlier years they had always appeared only intermittently.) It was something of a promotion if they escorted you everywhere, as they did now; previously they had only stood at the gate, noting Akhmatova's comings and goings, and you cannot even be sure this type of surveillance is directed at you rather than at someone else in the same building . . .

On returning home one evening we had a little trouble in the lobby of the mansion: the door through into the back garden turned out to be locked. This door had never been locked before, either at night or during the day; only the gate on to the street was locked at night. The whole of the property belonged to

Sevmorput* and for that reason it had a doorman who always sat at a small desk by the door leading into the rear garden and court-yard. When we asked him what the matter was, he eventually came out with some utterly preposterous cock-and-bull story about the key being lost. After a few moments of argument he went off to 'look for it'. We stood there and waited, fuming with rage. Even now I remember the flush of anger at this meaningless delay: it was the kind of cold fury when you turn pale and your throat goes dry. With Akhmatova it also produced a change in her voice. When this happens to weak people, their voices become high-pitched, but in the case of strong ones like Akhmatova the voice drops to a lower register, becoming quite magnificent.

The doorman returned. 'They're looking for it,' he said, and disappeared again. At last, having kept us there seething for a good fifteen minutes, he took the key out of his pocket and flung open the door. We went along a narrow paved path to the right (what fools we were not to turn left and make things a little harder for the wretched bunglers!). A bright white light suddenly flashed in a window of the first floor ahead of us, and I involuntarily closed my eyes. 'Magnesium,' Akhmatova said calmly. I am by nature slow on the uptake, and on this occasion too my mind worked with shameful lack of speed. 'Why?' I asked, hearing the familiar word 'magnesium', and for a long time afterwards Akhmatova made fun of me for it. The numskulls had evidently been ordered to photograph me with Akhmatova – this capital offender about-to-be – for purposes of identification: literature is a matter of state. The people with the camera must have given orders to hold us up and then muffed their preparations to take the shot. Perhaps this was a boy-and-girl combination who had been practising their parting kisses in the line of duty? Such, then, was the explanation of the 'lost' key and our absurd wait in the lobby. They never sent us any prints, and I must say that their technique was pretty antediluvian: did they really have to use magnesium in the second half of the forties?

In the period before the Decree came out, Akhmatova had

*'Northern Seaway' – the organization responsible for navigation between the Atlantic and Pacific over the Arctic route. Oddly enough, it is the subject of one of Akhmatova's *Ogoniok* poems. (See note, page 406.)

learned to keep her mouth shut in her room. Here too the technique was antiquated: the holes they had bored in the walls and ceiling were all too obvious. It is said that the listening devices were all war loot from Germany, but instead of the neat holes drilled nowadays they made very clumsy ones and left little heaps of plaster on the floor. Akhmatova kept one of these little heaps intact and used to point it out to all her visitors. Wasn't it a complete waste of effort? Why did the state need to know what one lonely old woman said and thought, or where she went? Despite all intimidation and threats, despite surveillance by the well-fed oafs ordered to follow her (and long since unaccustomed, no doubt, to any other kind of work), she still managed to write her poems. All the expense involved was thrown down the drain – but, of course, we are so rich that we can always afford to overdo things . . . One might well ask who needs it, and how it jibes with all the frantic appeals for economy which are constantly being dinned into our ears.

In Moscow the Decree on the Leningrad literary journals made quite an impact – more than any clampdown in previous years. People were a little different after the war: not very much, but at least to some extent . . . I was living at the time in my brother's room (he and my sister-in-law were living out in their dacha) together with friends, a man and wife who had no place of their own. The wife was from the Moscow Jewish intelligentsia and belonged to the same circles as Pasternak. Her reaction to the Decree was the same as mine, though without the personal element since she did not know Akhmatova. Her husband was of a very different breed, a village youth who had managed to get through secondary school in tsarist times and, finishing the First World War as a subaltern, had at once joined the Reds. This was a very typical case during the Revolution. He had spent the twenties in the Caucasus and rapidly moved up the ladder of promotion, soon becoming a People's Commissar in one of the republics. He had met his wife at a resort when she was married to some very academic type, from whom he had snatched her away. This match was also typical of the times: it was said about women then that they were all avid to 'go to the people'.* But almost immediately after their marriage my friend's career had come to an abrupt end – he

* Term originally used of populist intellectuals in the 1870s.

was arrested and expelled from the Party and his government office. These were still 'vegetarian' times, to use Akhmatova's expression, and after six months in prison he was allowed out again. He was accused of crimes which are not considered as such anywhere else: ignorant of economic management, like everybody else, he had simply made a mess of things. The most probable reason for his downfall was that he had stood in the way of various swindlers and smart operators. People with his background were being thrown out of their jobs all over the place in those days. Naïve as children and scrupulously honest, they spouted their incredible nonsense and stood out very conspicuously among all the sharp-witted and rapacious bureaucrats of the new type. My friend had been lucky: his wife stayed with him, and he changed his profession and moved to Moscow. As for many people who fell from favour at the dawn of our era, life had not been easy, but at least he had been spared the worst.

We read the Decree on *Zvezda* and *Leningrad* together, and he just did not know what to say or think. His six months in jail had taught him prudence, but his wife and I were so enraged by this latest display of vileness that he began to waver despite himself and for the first time had a slight doubt about the infallibility of our supreme authorities; however, he still could not bring himself to come out on our side. It was impossible for him to disavow the authorities which had made him what he was since those early days. (He probably put his arrest down to 'local mistakes', or to the fact that he really had messed up the plan.) All he could do was try to be flippant about it: 'As a bureaucrat I believe in order – she has been breaking the rules'; or: 'Everybody in this country is replaceable – except for one person.' In other words, if you destroyed one poet, another would take his place; an empty 'slot' could always be filled. He saw everything in terms of his own life: after a brief moment of power he had become a nobody, but things had gone on just as before. I kept my temper with him only because I had always felt sorry for these subalterns of the Revolution turned bureaucrats. Carried away by propaganda just about on their own intellectual level, they had landed themselves in something quite beyond their comprehension. This was the tragedy of the semi-educated, and my friend, the former subaltern and one-time

People's Commissar, had all the gullibility of a callow youth – he was a twentieth-century Kolia Krasotkin.* Afterwards I learned how he had come to lose his religious faith as a child. He had prayed God to cure his toothache, but God had failed him . . . He harboured no grudge against the lords and masters who failed him in later life because he had at least learned that happiness must be won by one's own unaided efforts, but as he had found by long experience, his own efforts had been unskilled and fumbling. It never occurred to him that there had been a real miracle in his life – namely, that he had not become involved in the events of the end of the twenties and the thirties. God saved him.

I was desperately worried about what might happen to Akhmatova – whether she would be arrested or not. The only slight comfort was that a few people were visibly very upset and gloomy about it all. The drunken Olesha telephoned me and bewailed the whole business at great length, saying he was sick to death of everything. On my way to the Shklovskis I ran into Pasternak. Not to be recognized by passers-by, we ducked into a doorway – it was not safe for him to be seen talking with me at such a moment, and the vicinity† was hazardous because of all the writers constantly walking around there either singly or in groups. We stood talking for a long time in the wind. Pasternak wondered whether we could go on living if they killed Akhmatova. His next question was what we could do for her. I suggested he go to Leningrad and see her: 'They probably won't do anything to you. She is completely alone now, and it would be good if you could see her – only do not call her on the phone.' He said he would go but didn't in fact manage to. When she came to Moscow, however, he went to see her and put a thousand rubles (a hundred in today's money) under her pillow. Psychologically this sum was worth much more than that – there was very little money in those days, prices were high, and people managed on even less than nowadays.

Zoshchenko told us that the Decree had come out after a report by Zhdanov to the Boss himself, who had been particularly con-

---

*Impressionable boy in Dostoyevski's *Brothers Karamazov* who precociously picked up all the half-baked radical ideas of the times.

†i.e. of the apartment building for writers, on Lavrushenski Street (the same one referred to on page 174).

cerned over the evening at the Polytechnic Museum when the whole audience had stood up at the appearance of Akhmatova.* He had supposedly asked: 'Who organized this standing ovation?' The remark, as Pasternak said, was so much in character that it could not have been invented. It was quite beyond the Boss to imagine that anybody might have achieved popularity without the aid of the *apparatchiks* who specialized in 'promoting' the idols of the day among the masses. As he was being eliminated, his main rival† was reminded that he owed his popularity only to the *apparat*, and that he was not therefore allowed to exploit it for his own ends. Zhdanov was now using the case of Akhmatova to get rid of his rival,‡ who had given the go-ahead for the publication of her book. It was all part of a struggle between the heirs to the throne, and people were sacrificed to it, as was Akhmatova's book – which was pulped. Of the whole edition, which had already been packed for distribution, the only copies to survive were a few stolen by workers at the printing press. One can regard it as having appeared in an edition of twenty copies. We live in a country where editions can be fabulously large or fabulously small.

A rumour was spread about Akhmatova's foreign visitor that he was the biggest spy of them all, and she was accused of having failed to realize this and let her tongue wag.

Akhmatova told me how she had gone cold all over with horrible forebodings when people had started to stand up and acclaim her that time. When the applause died down, she had spent a long time trying to find her glasses and putting them on her nose. Eventually she began to read from a piece of paper in a low, faltering voice and, to prevent a new outburst of applause, avoided looking at the

---

* On her way back to Leningrad from Tashkent in May 1944, Akhmatova stopped briefly in Moscow, where she read a poem at this gathering. The Polytechnic Museum is one of the largest auditoriums in Moscow. (There is another account of this occasion, as told by Ehrenburg on a visit to Paris after the war, in Yuri Annenkov's *Diary of My Meetings*, Vol. I [New York, 1966], pages 127–8. According to this, the meeting was in the House of Columns and was attended by 3,000 people.)

† In 1926, in a last desperate throw, Trotski tried to appeal to the rank and file, by-passing the Party machine.

‡ Presumably Malenkov, who staged a comeback after Zhdanov's death in July 1948.

audience. She could not afford to curry favour with a crowd which had forgotten what sort of a world we lived in. My brother was present at the occasion. According to him, Akhmatova seemed completely calm and after quickly reading her verse made her exit without a backward glance. She looked as though she were not the mother superior, but just one of the rank-and-file nuns, strictly observing the rules of the convent. In reality, however, she was the stern and overbearing abbess of a convent in which the rules were strict to a fault and all sins had to be atoned for – even though now and again, for old times' sake, she permitted wild bouts of revelry. We founded a convent on these lines for both of us when we shared a *balakhana* in Tashkent. One of the rooms we referred to as the refectory. There was nothing in it except my bunk, an unpainted table with two benches, and an earthenware washbasin perched on a triangular shelf which had been fixed to the wall in one corner. During the day, like any mother superior, Akhmatova attended to secular matters, but the nights were devoted to poetry, melancholy and – when we recalled the jokes of our departed one – laughter. He lived with us always and never left us.

VI: TRIALS AND WITCH HUNTS

All our lives we knew nothing but trials. The heroine of *Prologue*, as she stands in her nightgown before her judges and mutters her incomprehensible words, could serve as the emblem of our age. Trials, 'open' or secret, were the alpha and omega of our existence. Behind any open trial there always loomed a secret one, casting an ominous shadow on it. Shall we never be rid of such things, or are we fated to endure them forever?

Is it any wonder that at secret trials people went out of their minds if even the open ones (regarded as 'democratic' after our exalted fashion) had such an effect on the accused that for weeks they behaved like sleepwalkers, unable to give relevant replies to any questions? In open trials there was crowd participation: the 'masses' were called upon to make what contribution they could to the process of destroying the accused, who were always condemned beforehand and for whom it only remained to guess at the punishment already prepared, agreed, and tucked away in the chief judge's pocket. The sentence is devised in secret recesses off stage, but it is pronounced at the table covered in green cloth where the judges sit, after the 'voice of the people' has been heard – as though it were a gathering of the old *veche*** and they were simply giving formal expression to the 'popular will'. The sentence is then sent to the typists for copying and exhibited on the court's notice board. The accused (or rather, the condemned) frantically tries to get a copy for himself, but all he can do for the moment is stand by the board and write down all the menacing words into his notebook.

In previous years the defendant was barely able to stammer a few pitiful words, interrupted by the shouts of the 'indignant People', but now he is allowed to make a final plea, during which he sometimes manages to show up his accusers and judges – but a fat lot of good it does him when everything has been decided beforehand. Oksman, for instance, countered all the charges against him with his usual brilliance, but it made no difference to the outcome. Frida Vigdorova opened a new era by writing down the proceedings at Brodski's trial, and this first genuine record of its kind had a shattering impact. Even the unspeakable woman judge at the trial realized this could not be permitted, and she forbade Vigdorova to take notes, but only towards the end, when it was already too late. She can scarcely be blamed for not having acted more quickly. It must never have entered her head that a Soviet journalist, a staunch upholder of the powers-that-be and the courts, would dare to hawk her notes, uncensored by herself or anyone else, around the editorial offices of the newspapers; here somebody – despite the care in selecting such people – purloined and circulated them in *samizdat*, whence they speedily found their way across the frontier to be published in the pages of the enemy press. Nothing like this had happened in decades.

Frida, a grey-haired old girl with large eyes and an earnest gaze, believed in truth and justice and went to see various minions in their offices, trying to make it plain to them, crafty and cynical though they are, that it made no sense to run wild like this and

* Popular assembly in medieval Novgorod.

mount such courtroom farces. The Brodski case had not been heard in the capital, and he was charged not with a political offence but with 'parasitism'. For this reason, after being kept a couple of years in a distant swamp, he was allowed to return home. This was the first and almost only case in which public opinion triumphed over the authorities. The second was the release of Zhores Medvedev from a mental hospital after protests by academicians. Brodski has no idea how lucky he was. A spoiled darling of fate, he fails to appreciate it and sometimes mopes. It is time he understood that a man who walks the streets, the key to his own door in his pocket, has been well and truly let at liberty. This is something I know from my own case: instead of being killed, I drew a lottery ticket granting me a further span of life. It is important to take full advantage of one's good fortune. Even if they eventually do me in, I shall still be one up on them through having enjoyed my 'extra day'. This is the only kind of luck we ever have. I could not have hoped for it, but it chanced to come my way.

Although I went out to work for almost twenty years altogether, I managed by extreme ingenuity, as well as by pretending, after forty, to be an old woman, never to get roped in for attendance at any trial. Nor did I once go to the yearly meetings in honour of the Decree on Zoshchenko and Akhmatova, or to any other gathering called to denounce heretics and Judaizers.* In 1938, when I first took up a job, things were comparatively quiet, and then came the war with its emphasis on national unity. I did not witness what happened at the end of the forties in Moscow (and at the beginning of the fifties in the provinces) for the simple reason that I was the first to be 'tried' and expelled from the Teachers' Training College where I then worked. All I ever saw myself were purges of girl students for sexual indiscretions. I was present at two such cases. One was an outright prostitute who occasionally gave birth to a child and then neglected to feed it until it died (this was during a period when abortion was forbidden). The other was just an ordinary girl who had slept with a student and got herself pregnant; after a little moaning and groaning, her parents had given the

---

* Fifteenth-century Muscovite heretics influenced by Judaism, probably through contact with Jews from Lithuania. The author is here alluding to the campaign against 'cosmopolitanism' in the late Stalin years.

young couple a curtained-off corner of their room to live in. Both girls were vilified in the same language, but the prostitute got off rather lightly because she was held to be a mother in distress. In another college where I worked the teachers were always being dressed down on the subject of their morals, and the main speaker on such occasions was an old maid of forty-five who taught English grammar. She would end with the words: 'This I can only describe as immorality.' In Cheboksary we once had special meetings in all departments about a student who had refused to marry a girl supposedly made pregnant by him. He doubted whether he was responsible, but she insisted he was and threatened suicide. On this occasion various girls got up and denounced their friends, reminding them how important it was to go to the Register Office before indulging in sexual relations. They threw dirt at each other with gay abandon. In their speeches they quoted the Komsomol official who had briefed each of them beforehand. I also used to hear rumours about formal hearings of complaints made by wives against their husbands for refusing to sleep with them. It was said that one husband, summoned before the Party committee, gave as his excuse a complete loss of potency. Sometimes there were dramas because the courts would not allow a man to divorce, and he was ordered by the Party committee to give up his illicit relations with another woman and return to the wife he could no longer stand the sight of. As long as the major concern was with such lurid storms in a teacup, I knew I could sleep peacefully in my bed. Minor tempests always raged in the intervals between political witch hunts, and hence marked a breathing space of a kind. Such interludes were succeeded by an ominous lull during which the Party organization prepared some new campaign, putting the finishing touches not only to the speeches that would be made from every platform, but to contributions 'from the floor' as well. The production of the show and the participation of the 'People' were worked out beforehand down to the last detail. The 'People' neither dared nor would have wanted to be silent, and they flocked eagerly to such performances, which took place behind closed doors – sometimes before large audiences, but more often before small ones. Large meetings were generally held as the grand finale to the lesser rituals enacted at the departmental or faculty level. The representatives of the security organs might take part, but not necessarily. At the end of the forties and beginning of the fifties, these affairs always proceeded in 'democratic' fashion – that is, supposedly on initiative 'from below'. I would like here to tell the story of how the 'People' rose up in its wrath against me, tore the mask from my face, and sent me to blazes. The whole operation went off very smoothly under the direction of a philosopher, a specialist in Spinoza, who wore on his chest a medal awarded for his part in the liquidation of the kulaks.

The time of which I speak was the very end of February or the beginning of March 1953. In all provincial towns the signal had been given for a roundup. It was to have been the ultimate purge. By April all institutions were supposed to be 'cleaned up' in such a way that it would never again be necessary. Talk about the country's having made its 'last sacrifice' was a constant refrain, but life never became easier as a result. This was the first time we had heard our rulers speak of a 'final purge'. It was intended to be on a colossal scale, sweeping over the whole country. This was just business as usual for us: night searches and arrests, the tracking down of people who had been in prison before, and other such joys. Everybody got on with his work, scarcely daring to breathe, as silent as fish. You never knew where the next blow would fall. Every night I undressed and went to bed as though all was right with the world – until before long it was my turn to be rudely awakened and summoned forth at the usual ungodly hour. What happened to me was fairly trifling in the upshot and not worth complaining about. My purpose in mentioning it here is not to complain, but only to record a piece of folklore.

It was very late, and I had already gone to bed when the knock came on the door. I was not frightened because it was a quite ordinary knock, not the kind that sounded ominous. It was the woman caretaker on night duty in the student hostel where I lived who had come to tell me that I was wanted at a special faculty meeting – they had just phoned, and two students had been sent over to take me there. I said I would manage without an escort – the main college building was only a stone's throw away. The students were waiting for me, however, when – resisting the temptation to plead illness – I got dressed and went outside. The evening classes had long since come to an end, and the cloakrooms were shut. I entered the room to which my guides took me in my fur coat. It was the language study room, full of teaching aids, charts, and phonograph records, but quite bare of books, except for the very primitive textbooks we now used – after the discovery of ideological errors in them, earlier ones had been withdrawn or sometimes even burned. The members of all three departments were already gathered there in full strength. They were all dolled up to the nines, with my female colleagues wearing crepe de Chine dresses, as was then the custom for Soviet women from the lowliest milkmaid to the lady professor. They must all have been given advance notice of the meeting, otherwise they would not have had the time to change into their best clothes. I was astonished that the meeting had not yet begun, as though they were waiting for me before they could start. But before I had a chance to ask what was afoot, the director, who never came to faculty meetings but was now for some reason sitting here with everybody else, proposed we should begin. When I heard him say that the meeting had been called to discuss my case, I felt my legs give way under me. I slumped down in a chair obligingly held ready by someone, and forgot all about taking off my fur coat. The chair had been placed somewhat apart, facing the serried ranks of my colleagues sitting on chairs or benches.

The meeting was presided over by Glukhov, the secretary of the Party organization, alias Spinoza. I suddenly remembered the nightgown in *Prologue*, but at once decided a fur coat would do just as well. Thrown over my shoulders, it marked me off from the crepe de Chine crowd in front of me. Such rituals always give one the shivers, and nothing could have been more suitable.

Spinoza – wearing his medal on this solemn occasion – opened the meeting. The first person he called on was a young woman member of the Komsomol with very white teeth who had only recently been appointed to the faculty. I had thrown her out of my exams, but voiced no objection when Spinoza had proposed her appointment to a teaching post in the spring of that year: we were not supposed to try to protect ourselves from informers. The white-toothed young lady spoke with great feeling. To begin with, she accused me of inventing Grimm's and Rask's law* and forcing it down the students' throats. The other teachers confirmed that they had never heard of any such thing, even though they had taken their degrees in Moscow and Leningrad (it was in the curriculum, but was not in fact taught after being rejected by the Marrists).† 'This law wasn't even taught in the Sorbonne,' the woman chairman of the faculty declared. She had been to a secondary school for upper-class girls before the Revolution and attended a foreign language course at the Sorbonne. Her relations with our college authorities and the security organs were of the best.

The second accusation levelled at me by the white-toothed Komsomol was that I was hostile to youth. In my lectures on the theory of grammar I had said that the young English gerund was ousting the old infinitive. This statement of mine was seen as a hint of some kind of struggle between fathers and sons – an inconceivable thing in the land of socialism. Here the young lady smiled shyly and cast a demure look at her audience. The rude language and sheer loutishness of the twenties were a thing of the past and had given way by now to diffidence and coy glances. Word must have been passed down that young ladies should be modest and feminine.

People now began to speak from the floor, some having been briefed beforehand and others off their own bat. A woman laboratory assistant with a six-month 'perm' revealed that she had once seen me sitting on a windowsill – though everybody knew from going to the films that the proper thing is to sit on a chair. (Their ideas of 'etiquette', as well as their notions of love and honour, all came from the movies. The way they laughed, on the other hand, showed the influence of radio – they imitated the peculiar modulated peals affected by our women announcers. Several generations have learned to ape not only this odious titter, but also the speaking voices they hear coming over the air: nothing in the world rings more false. Even the women announcers on

---

*Basic law in Indo-European comparative linguistics, usually referred to in the West as 'Grimm's law'.

† See Marr, Appendix A.

foreign radio stations have adopted the same intonation, evidently imagining that this is how Russian should be spoken. There was once a discussion about the best way of speaking on the radio: in Yakhontov's manner or 'with expression', as in the theatre. The second view prevailed, and the voices of our women announcers register every kind of emotion as the need arises – tears, indignation, or joy. So did that of our laboratory assistant with the 'perm' – she had learned how to do it from them.)

One of the faculty ladies, a graduate of our college, tried to put in a good word for me, saying I had given her some grounding in a few things. The rest at once accused her of being 'out of touch with the masses', and she had to beat a retreat. She too had picked up a few ideas from motion pictures and wore a silver fox stole over one shoulder, in the manner of our film actresses. She had once told me that everybody was awaiting the appearance of a book on etiquette which had already been accepted for publication.

The college director wore a pince-nez on a black string and looked astonishingly like Chekhov. He stroked his little beard and nodded sagely whenever anybody delivered a telling thrust. The combined forces of Spinoza and Chekhov were evidently required to encompass my expulsion. Both of them translated what the women said into the language of the State: lack of attention to Stalin's brilliant teachings on language, the dragging in of Marrist doctrine (Grimm's and Rask's law!), the persecution of progressive younger elements among the staff, and the setting of excessively high standards in the award of examination marks. The meeting then ruled that I should be dismissed from my post after being given one or two weeks in which to 'round off' my work, that is, quickly finish my lecture courses (in particular those I gave on the history of language, which everybody else hated being saddled with).

The whole of this operation took several hours, during which those present kept absolutely straight faces. Nobody smiled, and I never once saw anyone give me a look of sympathy. All faces had turned to stone and wore morose and sullen expressions. The only person, it seemed, to appreciate the sickening humour of the whole affair was myself, sitting there in my fur coat like Menshikov in exile.* I was expelled exactly in the way and on the charges – I swear it – described above. This is the kind of utter barbarism that terror brings in its train, and scenes like these were enacted throughout the length and breadth of the country.

All's well that ends well. My expulsion could have been only the first stage, to be followed by a series of further measures concerted at the highest level. I was spared this only because of the death of one man. They say he might have been saved if people had been quicker to force the door of the room in which he had locked himself. He inspired such terror that no one dared enter until it was too late. There are many stories about his end, but nobody is interested except the faithful upholders of his methods. I never see such people, and I pray God to send deliverance before they break into *my* room.

I was packing my belongings in the hostel when suddenly a woman from the same department as I burst in to see me. She had been going out of her mind for fear they were about to hold a similar meeting to denounce her as well. At the time of my expulsion she had been in the hospital. She had grown up in Galicia,† where she eagerly read Soviet writers and believed every word they said. After her arrival in Ulianovsk she had continued to spout the Komsomol balderdash for foreign consumption she had soaked up at home, even though she had already had a slight taste of persecution: in the first college where she worked she had been dismissed because of Point Five.‡ She had put this down as a 'local mistake', but when Point Five proved to be a major issue and the idylls of socialist realism had worn thin, the scales suddenly fell from her eyes. 'Stalin is dead!' she shouted now, from my doorway. I went cold all over and pulled her into the room. As long as a dictator lives he is immortal. I decided my colleague must finally have taken leave of her senses: for such words you could easily be accused of plotting to kill the Leader and be packed off to rot in a

---

*Peter the Great's favourite, and victor over the Swedes at Poltava, eventually exiled to Siberia. The painting of him there by Vasili Surikov ('Menshikov in Beriozov') hangs in the Tretiakov Gallery, Moscow.

†The western Ukraine, part of Poland until annexed by the Soviet Union in 1939.

‡Entry in Soviet identity papers giving a person's ethnic origin. It has become notorious in connection with discrimination against Jews.

camp to the end of your days. I switched on the radio and was overcome by a joy such as I had never known before in the whole of my
life. It was true: the Immortal One was dead. I now rejoiced as I
went on packing my wretched rags and tatters, and for the first
time in many years I looked at the world with new eyes. The next
day, as I was 'rounding off' one of my courses with the students
(that is, just going through some rigmarole to fill the prescribed
time), we were all called out of the classrooms to the main auditorium, which was already packed with an enormous crowd of
sobbing people. The lady with the silver fox stole informed me she
was in such a state that she might have lost her own father. Spinoza
kept a stiff upper lip and declared that, although Stalin had died,
his work would live after him forever. He himself soon had a stroke,
went blind, and died, leaving two daughters who undoubtedly
carry on their father's good work. Is it conceivable that the whole
of this vast country, which wept in 1953, might likewise be ready
one day to carry on the work of its dead master? The old guard and
the *Rusity* would be glad at any time, I believe, to restore the camps,
shipping people there wholesale in freight cars to be worked to
death. The younger generation crave only for the good life and are
utterly indifferent to anything which does not affect their material
well-being. Faculty meetings of the kind I have described continued
right up to the removal of Beria. The last to be arraigned and
expelled in my college was Professor Liubishchev, a biologist who
had taken refuge there from the Lysenkoites. They threw out not
only people who aroused suspicion under Point Five, but anyone
else they just wanted to get rid of. Anybody with real education and
knowledge was anathema to them and would be hounded by the
whole pack. Liubishchev and I happened to find ourselves in the
same college together after knowing of each other's existence for a
long time previously, but until Stalin's death we never dared openly
converse on forbidden topics, risking nothing more than a few
words about the place of Ivan the Terrible in Russian history. In
March 1953 we suddenly started talking for all we were worth, and
Liubishchev's wife exclaimed in astonishment: 'To think that for
so long you two said nothing.' The only other person I shared my
feelings with was a cheap dressmaker who used to make my ghastly
clothes for me. 'What are you howling for?' I asked her. 'What did

he mean to you?' She explained that people had somehow learned to live with him, but who knew what would come now? Things might even get worse . . . She had a point.

In the few days immediately before this I had taken note of who still greeted me, and who went by pretending not to see me. One of those who still recognized me – on the street, right in front of the college, furthermore – was that same poor gadabout who had been forced by the Party organization to resume his conjugal duties. (Under Khrushchev, when there was a let-up in the campaign to 'strengthen the family', he managed to get away from his bitch of a wife by fleeing to another city.) A woman colleague who had done her graduate work in Leningrad came to see me. Her husband had fallen foul of Point Five and could not even get a job teaching in school. Women who had married Jews were hard hit by this whole business, though sometimes they could behave just as badly as the rest. Almost on the eve of the rehabilitation of the doctors* this same woman with a higher degree from Leningrad had raised a great hue and cry over a woman doctor in a local clinic, and got her dismissed on the accusation of having tried to kill her son. Things like this were happening all over the place. Everybody was obsessed by saboteurs and 'killer doctors'.

On the day of my departure, as my belongings were being loaded into a car, I noticed a little group of people standing in the court-yard. It turned out to be a short-legged Jewish couple, who worked in the mathematics department, and their numerous children. Only recently they had wept bitterly at the news of the Leader's death, and now, the previous night, they had been dismissed from their posts at a special faculty meeting. Both of them, taking on trust everything they had always been taught, had decided to have a large family in the confident expectation of a happy future. Unable to stand the blow that had now fallen, they had gone off their heads and were dancing hand in hand around the courtyard, yelling at

---

*Nine Kremlin doctors (seven of them Jews) were arrested in January 1953 and accused of having conspired to kill Soviet leaders at the behest of Zionist organizations and the American intelligence service. The survivors (two died under interrogation) were released in April 1953, almost exactly a month after Stalin's death, when it was officially admitted that the charges had been fabricated.

the top of their voices – to the genuine amusement of their student onlookers. They were taken away to the mental hospital, as Liubishchev told me later, where they recovered. In the autumn they were reinstated in their jobs. They had both been given teaching posts immediately after graduating, and this was their first brush with the facts of life. She was said to be a good mathematician, but he taught methodology and, like all people in this field, was an ignoramus.

In Moscow I learned that two learned ladies, Akhmanova and Levkovskaya, had blocked my dissertation at the Institute of Linguistics. They had spoken at a specially convened session of the Institute's Party organization, accusing me of both 'Marrism' and 'Potebnism'.* It was the Spinoza and Chekhov act all over again. Akhmanova produced another weighty argument against me: she informed her listeners that I had been married to a scoundrel. Both these ladies had taken an active part in every political witch hunt. Zhirmunski complained that they were constantly writing denunciations, but academician Vinogradov had shown special favour to them, in particular to Akhmanova. She had been awarded her doctor's degree for a dissertation done in the department of Russian language, where Vinogradov was king – no one would have wanted her anywhere else. I am not sure what was wrong with Vinogradov: whether it was fear that turned him into the person he became, or whether there was something rotten in him to begin with. It is rumoured that he gave expert evidence in the Siniavski case on condition that his name not be mentioned.

Moscow was in a state of fever. I have never seen such sombre, demented faces as that spring which was marked by the 'Khodynka'† at the Leader's funeral. People were constantly snarling at one another: in queues, in buses, and in offices. In the Institute of Linguistics, where I went to pick up my rejected dissertation, the director's secretary, who looked like a decent enough woman, had a fit of hysterics. She started screaming, for everybody to hear right down the corridor, that saboteurs had poisoned all the drinking water in the building and anybody who touched it got sick. On

---

* Linguistic theories of Alexander Potebnia (1835–91) that were, in fact, incompatible with 'Marrism'.

† See note, page 238.

another occasion I was detained at the post office when I wanted to send a dozen registered letters to colleges which had advertised vacancies in my field. The vigilant woman at the counter suspected me of trying to circulate anti-Soviet materials, and hauled me off to the director. They agreed to accept the letters only after I had opened them and the director had convinced himself that the contents were innocent. I sent off altogether about a hundred applications, but every one was turned down.

By the end of the summer – after the fall of Beria – the corridors of the Ministry of Education were thronged with teachers who had been dismissed and were now seeking reinstatement. There were not enough chairs or benches, and the crowd had to stand, shifting constantly from one foot to another. Every now and then somebody would be summoned into an office and emerge with a new appointment – mostly to eastern Siberia or Sakhalin. I was one of the last to be dealt with – only after a woman inspector had returned from my former college, where she had ordered the dismissal of 'Chekhov'. She told me there were more denunciations than it was possible to cope with, but that she would try to speed up the process of getting me a new job. Later, Liubishchev and Amusin, a specialist on the Dead Sea Scrolls, came to put in a word for me at the Ministry. They had been to my lectures, and were now doing a report for the Trade Union* on the department I had worked in. Their statements, together with the woman inspector's efforts on my behalf, earned me an appointment to Chita.† There I was given money to cover my travel expenses, but later I had to return it: the Ministry feared financial ruin if it paid the travel expenses of everybody who had been reinstated. We were just like 'displaced persons'.

In the corridors of the Ministry I got to know a young woman by the name of Blagonadiozhnaya.‡ She looked a little like the Komsomol girl with the white teeth who had denounced me, but

---

* Soviet trade unions are state controlled, but they have nominal powers to investigate abuses, etc.

† City not far from the border with China, in the Buriat-Mongol area beyond Lake Baikal.

‡ An unusual surname whose literal meaning ('loyal') is ironical in the context.

Blagonadiozhnaya was now one of those who had come to ask the Ministry for a new job. She kept showing everybody her 'work-book',* which was full of commendations – but then all of a sudden she had been sacked on the grounds that she was 'totally unsuit-able'. In her distress she had smashed her glasses, and a splinter of glass had hit her in the eye, removing the cataract from which she suffered and enabling her to see properly again. She told me she would never forget this crowd in the Ministry. How will she behave during the next campaign – against readers of *samizdat*, for ex-ample? It is impossible to tell, since the actions of a Blagonadiozh-naya, like our politics, are completely unpredictable.

VII: THE UNBROKEN FLOW

M. used to say people had destroyed Yesenin by telling him to write a long poem, a 'major' work, thereby causing him to feel strain and frustration: as a lyric poet, he was incapable of turning out a full-length epic. M. was himself totally immune to the modern cult of bigness in all its forms. I put this down to the fact that he had arrived at his own conception of a 'major' work in lyric poetry, namely a book of verse all composed during the same period and having a certain unity. Verse arranged in a volume like this – as an interlocking whole, covering a broad range, yet bound together by a single lyric concept and way of looking at the world – constitutes a special kind of literary form with its own type of subject matter and governed by its own rules. The arrangement of the material is sometimes worked out in accordance with a conscious plan, as was done by Annenski and Akhmatova. Akhmatova even joined to-gether and published under one title groups of poems written at various periods, but on the same general theme. Here, however, I am concerned not with this kind of externally imposed structure, only with the organic unity which comes from a single poetic impulse, one particular unbroken flow of verse.

A real book, like life, unfolds in time. It is the manifestation of

* Containing a person's work record, essential in seeking new employment (which may be hard to get if there are adverse entries).

a man's growth, of his deepening sense of contact with the world – but only as these appear at the stage concerned, and always provided the threads binding the author to the world are the same throughout. Each individual poem reveals a new aspect or marks a new element in the poet's growth, and there can be nothing haphazard about their sequence – growth is an organic thing and cannot be ordered at will. As they follow one after another, books of verse reflect the consecutive phases in a poet's life and thought, displaying the structure that underlies them; in some poets the inner dynamic thus revealed is supplied by the external events of their biographies, but in others – Baratynski, for example – by their spiritual growth alone. Some themes may be present throughout the poet's life, but they will assume different aspects at different stages, or in different books: an integrated personality of unified structure undergoes a number of changes in the course of time. Although we all go through the same stages as we move from childhood to old age, each one of us nevertheless experiences them in his own way. It is a kind of victory over death to preserve the unity of one's personality from beginning to end; but, with all that, it is a good thing to give each time of life its due – youth and old age should be simply what they are.

Every moment of growth has its spiritual meaning, and a man's personality attains fullness of being only if it continues to unfold, exhausting the possibilities of each successive time of life. It is a matter of great good fortune if an artist can pass through all stages without losing the unity of his personality or capacity to go on growing, but this is given to very few, or rather, almost to nobody. He may sometimes be prevented by external circumstances (M. used to say this was the excuse of the faint-hearted, but 'external circumstances' could include violent death); more commonly, however, he comes to the end of his inner resources because he has played fast and loose with them on the way. It is a good thing if a poet manages to give expression to his true self both in his younger years and in his later ones – but this is by no means within everybody's power.

In an almost entirely unknown newspaper article written in 1922 (he used bits of it in other articles) M. compares the Symbolists' attitude to the West with youthful infatuation and in this con-

nection has a few words to say about the growth of the poetic
personality:

Instead of calmly possessing themselves of the treasures of Western
thought . . . they fell head over heels in love with them, like adolescents,
and, as always when someone gives way to infatuation, the worst
effect was on the personality: the artist's self became so inflated that
there was a blurring of the boundary lines between it and the captivating
new world just discovered by him; having no firm outlines any more, as
though swollen by dropsy, it was swamped by the great world outside
and could no longer feel that any single cell was its own. This state of
affairs led to an interruption of a most interesting process – the growth
of the poetic personality; by straining to sing the very highest note right
at the beginning, they succeeded only in deafening themselves, instead
of using their voices as a potential for organic development. (In 1922 M.
was evidently not yet entirely consistent in his distinction between
'growth' and 'development'.)

The same idea appears in the lines: 'Not to hurry. Impatience is a
luxury, / I shall gradually pick up speed . . .'

In *Stone* M. published by no means all of the poems from his first
flow of inspiration. Some of the unpublished ones were preserved
among his papers. *Stone* is a book of his youthful days, a time of
wonderment at the world, of first endeavours to make sense of it
('Can I be real, and will death truly come?') and discover a firm
core of life and culture. It used to be commonly said – this was the
judgement of people debauched by the self-indulgence and wanton
outpourings of the first decade and a half of the century – that M.
was lacking in emotion, cold and 'classical' (whatever this absurd
word may mean). I believe they simply failed to read him properly –
whom *did* they read properly? – and never noticed the youthful
anguish of the early verse and the particular tone of the last third
of the *Stone* poems, beginning with the one that mentions 'Joseph
sold into Egypt'. In *Stone* life is still an accident, a mesh of pain in
which M., a stranger among strangers, is searching for meaning,
first discovering it in death. His interest in historiosophy already
makes its appearance in *Stone* as a quest for the mainspring of life
in society. At that period he saw its basis in the church – the
Catholic one, moreover. This explains why he constantly harks
back to Rome, right to the end of his life (one of his very last poems
is about it). In his mature years he saw the central core of our

society in Christianity and the European culture based on it – the culture whose desperate crisis we have witnessed in our lifetime. The architectural theme running through all his books is linked with his belief that man's task on earth is to build, to leave tangible traces of his existence – that is, to defeat time and death.

All M.'s books, except the first two editions of *Stone*, were put together in my presence, and I saw how he took out of the 'store-house of memory' poems which for one reason or another had not gone into the early volumes. In the case of the two editions of *Tristia*, M. had no say in their publication, and a number of poems from various periods appear there in an arbitrary order; these should be given their proper place in the books to which they belong, together with items banned by the censors. In the third edition of *Stone* M. included a few poems he had left out in the previous editions: two poems from the Roman cycle, for example – 'Nature Is the Same as Rome', and 'Let the Names of Thriving Cities . . .' Under the first one he put a date, and the time of writing of the second can be inferred from the internal evidence of the line: 'Wars are justified by priests', which could have been written only at the beginning of the First World War. There was probably a brief interval between the writing of these two poems. They were begun together, but finished at a different time, when M. had already begun to move away from his ideas about Roman Catholicism, inclining instead towards Russian Orthodoxy. This shift took place under the influence of Kablukov, but even before M.'s meeting with him, there were already some signs of it. Later on he begins to talk about Christianity in general: 'I drink the cold mountain air of Christianity.'

I do not know whether these two poems, which for a long time were preserved only in M.'s memory, were modified in any way before he published them. In Voronezh, recalling poems written earlier in the thirties, he sometimes changed things deliberately, but sometimes unwittingly – his memory was no longer as good, having lost its erstwhile retentiveness and precision. A poet's memory is always unbelievably overloaded, even if he is the kind who writes down his verse straight away and keeps the drafts. But before the draft stage, that is, even before the poem has taken shape – or is only in the process of doing so – there is a lengthy period of preparation which goes on only in the mind, and none of this gets on to paper. During this period words and combinations of words are marshalled in the poet's head, together with lines or even whole stanzas that have still not fallen into place, or in which no idea has formed or – as is more frequently the case – exists only in embryo. Such lines and stanzas sometimes go into a later poem, or prompt the appearance of a new one. In themselves they are mere raw material and may linger in the mind for years before suddenly surfacing to be allied with new material. Even in periods of apparent silence or rest, a poet is still at work mentally preparing his stocks of raw material.

These stocks of material are used only when they can be endowed with meaning – that is, when they are exposed to a poetic idea. Until this beam of light, as I call it, illuminates them, they cannot be transmuted into poetry and must remain submerged in darkness. It occasionally happens by accident that such items of raw material get written down on paper, and then one may later have a chance of actually seeing how they are plucked from the darkness by a poetic idea and stirred into life. In 1932, when I was lying ill in the Botkin hospital in Moscow, M. came to visit me there and was struck by the smell of carbolic acid. This momentary quickening of his olfactory sense led him to jot down some lines about smells in a notebook. The notebook then lay in Moscow in our trunk together with rough drafts of 'Journey to Armenia', but it was only in Voronezh, in 1936, that M. used this item about the smell of carbolic acid – in a stanza beginning 'The tiny adjunct of sixth sense...', which refers to a poem about his own death in 'sexless space'. 'Sexless' for M. meant passionless, indifferent, incapable of moral judgements or choices, knowing neither life nor death, but existing only by inertia, and self-annihilating. In the world of human beings – of 'men' faithful in friendship and ready 'with a handclasp in a moment of danger' and of 'wives' who are soothsayers, mourners, and gatherers of the 'light ashes' when their husbands perish – everything good and creative is endowed with sex, while everything dead or destructive is sexless (as in the line: 'Sexless malice possesses you'). M. was convinced that the basis of life, the source of goodness, and the higher illumination of love are to be found in the intimacy between two people, in the friendship of 'men' (after the death of Gumilev he had no real friend). I believe his faith in the church as the foundation of society flagged in the twenties, and he never returned to the subject – though not before he had written his poem on St Isaac's (1921), where he refers to cathedrals as 'ecumenical granaries of good / and the gospel's threshing floors', up whose 'broad and sombre steps / the pariah trail of suffering shambles'. His loss of faith in the church, it seems to me, can be explained not only by the general deafness of those years, but also by developments within the church itself – the debates between Lunacharski and Vvedenski, and the propaganda of the so-called Living Church. We saw many painful things, and although M. knew that a priest is not elected, any more than a father is elected, and that what happens within its precincts does not detract from the significance of the church as such – not to mention the rumours we heard about the martyrdom and heroism of priests in the camps – all the same he could not help noticing how the church, which was going through the same crisis at the country at large, had lost much of its power to bind people together. All the forces of social cohesion had collapsed, and people, 'falling apart like spray', joined hands to form tiny associations of not more than two or three – just enough to have company in the last moments of life. But a man dying in a camp – already a so-called goner, no longer able to drag himself along any more – found himself hopelessly alone at his last moment. The only person who might be there to catch his last look before reason was extinguished would be a doctor from among his fellow prisoners. I am told that doctors sometimes remained human beings even in that hell.

In M.'s scheme of things the world of human beings had as its antipode the blind, indifferent sky: 'Blood – the Builder spurts from the neck of earthly things . . . and from that high bird's cage, from dank blue masses, indifference rains down on your deathly hurt.' Indifference is the mark of dead, and therefore sexless, nature.

The impulse for this poem about death in 'sexless space' (the one beginning: 'No, this is not migraine . . .', in which M.'s note on carbolic acid – the smell of sickness and death – appears in a context that illuminates it with meaning) was the funeral of some airmen. The two poems on the funeral were a prelude to 'Verse on the Unknown Soldier', in which M., rather than sharing, as it were, the death of others – that is, preparing for death, 'practising' at dying – talks instead about killing on a mass scale, wholesale slaughter of people, 'herded with the herd' in the concentration camps and wars of the twentieth century.

The 'coexperiencing' of death precedes the phase of writing about mass holocausts and is characteristic of M. in his mature years. It underlies the whole cycle in memory of Andrei Bely, in which the central poem is 'January 10, 1934' – here there are elements of a lament for St Alexis which he had long since forgotten and lost. But even forgotten, these lines had been stored somewhere in the darker recesses of the mind and came to the surface once the rays of a poetic idea picked them out. Work on the cycle about Bely continued until the summer of 1935, when he wrote the poems about the airmen and 'No, this is not migraine. . .' It was only then that M. became fully aware that this theme of 'sharing' another's death, of 'feeling with' it, was preparation for his own end. When I said to him, 'Why are you holding your own funeral?' he replied that he must hold it while there was still time – who knew what was now in store for us?

In the 'January 10' poem, the ending stubbornly refused to work out. At first it triggered off another short poem (the one with the line 'It seems he fought shy of dying . . .') and three eight-line stanzas, one of which ('Overcoming Nature's Familiarity') was immediately transferred to the cycle entitled 'Octets'. This is the only group of poems in which the chronological principle is violated – not so much through the inclusion of the fragment about Bely, which was written at the same time as 'Octets' (editors never suspect, in their folly, how many pieces of work may be simultaneously in progress without actually being put down on paper) as by the reference to Lamarck.[*] In Voronezh M. settled on a final version of the ending of 'January 10' with a stanza in which he speaks of his sense of *sharing* in the death of Bely:

> I seem to hang by my own eyelashes,
> And, ripening there, all inertia,
> Waiting to drop, I act out
> the only part we know today.

[*]The French botanist and zoologist (for Mandelstam's interest in biology see *Hope Against Hope*, page 272).

Before this he had toyed with the idea of ending on a merely decorative note with something about the craftsman, the artist, and the engraver. After this the question was what to do with the eight-line and other stanzas which had come into being as by-products of the main poem. Even though they had some lines in common with it, they were by no means mere variants. They should more properly be thought of as 'variations': it is just as legitimate in poetry, as in music, to have 'themes and variations' – not for nothing was this the title given by Pasternak to one of his books of poetry. By the mere fact of using such a title he said a great deal about the nature of the poet's work, but nobody took the trouble to ponder his meaning. The composers made the same point much earlier, but everything is easier in music, which has theory and counterpoint.

Still wondering what to do with his 'theme and variations', M. asked me to start copying them all out as one poem (a page of it has survived in this form), but he soon told me to stop because the various parts failed to form a coherent whole. He then spread out all the poems, each written on a separate sheet, and suddenly said: 'Look – it's just like "Armenia" again' – by which he meant that the seven poems made a cycle, like the twelve poems in 'Armenia'. The last of the seven ('Where Have They Brought Him From?') has the end missing. After the search of our apartment I had given the page with this poem to Emma Gerstein. It had lain on the floor, unnoticed by the men conducting the search. While we were on our way to Cherdyn,* Emma Gerstein burned it. For some reason I am repelled by the fact that instead of throwing it into the stove, she held it in the flame of a candle. Some years later she wrote a book in which she sermonizes Lermontov's contemporaries on the way they should have treated him, but she makes no mention of her exploit with the candle. Neither I nor M. was later able to remember the full text of this poem burned by our Lermontov scholar. All the same, M. assigned it a place – the last in the cycle – and said: 'I'll finish it off if we publish it.' He lived neither to finish nor to publish it.

I copied out the poems to Bely in their right order – all seven of them – in the 'Codex Vaticanus', as we jokingly called the note-

* First place to which Mandelstam was deported in 1934 (*Hope Against Hope*, pages 69 ff.).

book in which I recorded the poems written between 1930 and 1934. It took some effort to reconstruct them, since after all our ordeals (house searches, arrest, exile, and illnesses) we had forgotten much of them. I had brought from Moscow the manuscripts we managed to save – those hidden during the search in a saucepan in the kitchen and in a pair of grey overshoes. The way people had always laughed at me for hiding things, or giving them to others for safekeeping! Not everybody entrusted with manuscripts proved to be a dirty coward or a scoundrel; the majority behaved honourably and preserved what I had asked them to save for me.

The 'Codex Vaticanus' included the 'First Voronezh Notebook'. When I copied out the cycle in memory of Bely, I asked M. what should be done about the two poems which have identical second halves. He told me to write down both: these were variations, and since the beginnings were different they were separate poems. He felt exactly the same about the 'Kama' cycle: here he wanted to have the third variant, written with an eye to the censors, published in third place, though it differed from the other two only in the final lines; a little later, and perhaps with better reason, he applied the same principle to two poems with an identical first line ('I have lost my way in the sky . . .'): 'They must be printed side by side,' he said, 'as two developments of the same theme' . . . In the Bely cycle, however, the two variants are too close to each other; I fear that he kept them both only because of his fondness for his favourite number: seven. I do not know what he would have done if it had actually come to publishing them, but since they were not published in his lifetime, and will not be in mine, this is a matter for the textologists to decide.

Future editors please note: the cycle to Bely is no longer to be found in the 'Codex Vaticanus' manuscript because it was ripped out and destroyed by Khardzhiev, the first 'well-wisher' to work on M.'s poetry. I had to let him have all the manuscripts at the time when he was preparing the Poet's Library edition – which has never appeared – and I was still not allowed to live in Moscow. He took advantage of the fact that, being more or less in the same situation as an exile, I had no rights – exiles are always robbed (and I wonder whether only in Russia?) of the things they leave behind, and cheated of their inheritances. Scholarly and scientific work done by camp prisoners was appropriated by others; this happened very often, particularly with dissertations when it became both lucrative and stylish to have an academic degree. Political persecution corrupts everybody who breathes its poisoned air. Quite apart from this, Khardzhiev is a sick man with grave physical and psychological disabilities. I had thought that his love for M. and his friendship with me – as well as the tragic nature of these papers which had so miraculously survived – would have restrained him from such an action, but it was not so. He did nevertheless return the bulk of the manuscripts, keeping a few items for his 'collection' and destroying things on which he wished to change the date or replace with some other text not considered the final one by M. – as in the case of 'January 10'. He even tried to explain to me that a poet is not always the best judge of what is good and what is bad, and that in any case he would have to 'tidy up' the archives by removing the drafts of variants he rejected, so that it would 'always be the same as I have made it' . . .

I am myself to blame, of course, for entrusting the papers to someone who is mentally ill, but who except madmen ever did anything about the work of forbidden poets? I must say, too, that I have suffered less from Khardzhiev than from Rudakov, whose widow returned nothing at all.* But my greatest sufferings I owe to those who killed M. and kept his very name under a ban for more than thirty years, forcing me to wander all that time from place to place, and still today preventing the publication of his work. It has been only four years since – by an oversight, needless to say – they allowed me to settle in Moscow and acquire a place to live here. These are the people who must really be held to account. If it were not for them, both Khardzhiev and Rudakov would have been pure and honourable, and M.'s papers would be lying in my cupboard, together with his books, photographs, proofs, drafts, recordings of his voice, and everything else regarded as the poet's due in any normal country where the government does not exercise tutelage over literature.

Just as M. carefully put his cycles of poems in order, so he always attended himself to the arrangement of his books, giving each poem its precise place. Even if he was not sure of the year –

* *Hope Against Hope*, pages 325 ff.

which happened particularly often in the case of poems written during the winter, when he could not remember whether it was before or after January – he always knew the sequence in which they had come to him. There is a logic and consistency in this sequence which may be hard to put into words, but which is none the less real for that. I was only an observer during the creation of his poems, but I have an exact memory of the order in which they arose and I understand their relationships to one another. This cannot be forgotten by even a mere onlooker like myself, never mind by the poet himself – and it would be just as unthinkable to change the order of the movements in a symphony or sonata. Sometimes a poem matures slowly in the mind without being committed to paper, and when I was numbering the items for a book, M. would occasionally ask me to leave out a number somewhere, saying: 'We'll put one there, but I'll read it to you later . . .' In other cases, without telling me beforehand, he simply put some newly 'matured' poem in the place where it belonged, and I had to change all the numbers throughout. This is what happened in the case of the poem about the 'beggar woman', which for some reason he hid from me a long time – perhaps he was ashamed at the idea of my being a 'beggar woman'? But it is more natural to be a beggar woman than a rich woman, particularly in this country, where to be well off has always smacked of blood or treachery. Besides, everybody here is a beggar, apart from our rulers and their lackeys, and I prefer to be with the majority, rather than pick up crumbs from the master's table.

I remember only one case in which a poem was switched from its old sequence and included in a completely new one, after it had been reworked and given a different meaning. If Akhmatova had not pointed it out, I should never have suspected that the poem with the first stanza: 'Oh, how we love our make-believe / And easily forget / that in childhood death is nearer than in later years' actually grew out of an old poem which had been eliminated from the final selection of verse for *Stone*. Akhmatova's memory for M.'s verse was as good as for her own, and she had immediately reminded him of the origins of this one; it had never been written down, but had been stored in his memory for a quarter of a century, to emerge just at the right moment. I do not know what the first version was like, but it is self-evident that the notion of death being kept at bay by maturity is a theme which came to him in the thirties. These lines express defiance of those who were already digging his grave: he knew by now that he was in mortal danger and that his end was not far away. Death could come at any moment, and I remember the friendly warning we were given by someone who worked for *Izvestia* in Leningrad.* M. had read out to him 'I Have Returned to My Native City', and the man's comment was: 'Be careful, or they'll be coming to see you one night, stamping their boots.' The point made in the poem about death in childhood and one's years of maturity was that M. knew he must live in defiance of the murderers and carry on with his work to the end; but, alas, he was unable to do this because of the very nature of his position – he was 'alone on every road', as he says in the poem. It is the opening one in his second notebook of 'New Verse' where the political theme appears in a veiled form (as in 'Lamarck', for example). This was to break through undisguised only after our journey to the Crimea when we saw the starving fugitives from the Ukraine and the Kuban.

Each work – *Stone*, *Tristia*, *Poems* (1921–5), 'New Verse', 'Voronezh Notebooks' – has its leading idea, its poetic beam of light. In the early verse of *Stone* it is youthful anguish and his search for a place in life; in *Tristia*, coming to maturity, forebodings of catastrophe, the doom of a culture (Petersburg), and the search for salvation (St Isaac's); the truncated, strangled book of verse 1921–5 shows the poet as a 'drying crust' in an alien world; 'New Verse' is an assertion of the value of life for its own sake, and also the sense of being an outsider among people who had turned their backs on values accumulated over the ages, a new awareness that his isolation was a form of opposition to the forces of evil; in the 'Voronezh Notebooks' there is resigned acceptance of life for what it is, in all its vanity and with all its horrors, an awareness that this was the brink, the end, the era of wholesale slaughter, the 'beginning of grim deeds'. Here he names the 'Judas of peoples to come'. In the last year of his life there were two further bursts of

* *Hope Against Hope*, page 324.

poetry, but this has all been lost. These final poems expressed a new view of Russia as a country which, despite everything, still lived on, though dormant and oblivious of itself. In this lost verse the country stands up to the forces of destruction by its hushed silence, its passive resistance, its traditions, its self-sacrificing readiness for any ordeals. M. was impressed by the 'fan-shaped lathwork of invincible sloping roofs'. This was only the beginning of a new book, and there is no point in guessing what it would have grown into if it had not been abruptly cut short. It is almost unbelievable that M. managed to do anything at all in the conditions of the last dreadful year. 'We can always find time to die,' he used to tell me consolingly. This was the period when I lived through death and extinction, entering into a posthumous existence here on earth.

His notion of a 'book', or a cycle, as a complete whole relating to a given period preserved M. from the sickness of the age – to which people succumbed as children do to measles or dogs to distemper; it took the form of a craving to write 'major' works – novels, or if one was a poet, then at least a long narrative in verse, ideally an epic. 'Major' works were demanded by the State, but the State was only responding to what was being urged in literary circles. I remember one protégé of the Futurists, a fat brute of dubious personal proclivities who is now always making pronouncements in the higher councils of the Mayakovski Museum. He still maintains that Khlebnikov is superior to Pushkin because he wrote an epic – something quite beyond Pushkin's reach. Lord knows what is actually meant by an 'epic' in this context, but it is clear that such woebegone theoreticians as this man have no understanding of ideas and fail to realize that the whole value of poetry is in the quality of the poetic thought behind it, in the poet's view of the world, not in the externals of poetic form. The harmony of verse is only, after all, the concentrated essence of the poet's thought, and what is really new in his work is not the serrated arrangement of his lines,* the originality of his rhymes, Futurism, or a return to 'classicism', but his exploration of life and death,

---

* Typographical arrangement favoured by Mayakovski that was much imitated: by its distinctive visual effect on the printed page it is intended to convey the staccato beat of the poem's rhythm.

the fusion of his life story with his poetry, the play of the children with their Father, and the endeavour to link the passing moment with the flow of historical time. The poet's work is but the mirror of his personality. Who made the marvellous remark that the creator is always better than his creations?

Another active figure in the Futurist camp, the naïve and innocent Sergei Bobrov, always used to curse and swear, demanding a new Pushkin – nothing else was good enough, and the tears came into his eyes as he spoke of his longing for one. What could Pushkin have done in our age? What room was there for Pushkin after the end of the Petersburg period of Russian history? How would Pushkin have fared in the Muscovite Kingdom of the Soviet rulers? All the same, it was better to call for a new Pushkin, however impractical the vision, than to issue decrees abolishing all forms of art, as LEF did, or to place orders for novels on predetermined topics, in the manner of RAPP and the Union of Writers.

In the twenties everybody tried to reason with M., but in the thirties they were already pointing their fingers at him; not concealing his distaste, he went on living among the barbarians and did what he had to do. He was not tempted by the idea of a 'major' work and never even gave it a moment's consideration, since he thought in terms of 'books' and 'cycles' of verse. There were sometimes also interconnected series larger than 'cycles' and on a common theme; of these, using a precise musical term in preference to a vague literary one, he said that they were 'like oratorios'. It was thus that he referred to his 'Verse on the Unknown Soldier' and the group of poems on the death of Andrei Bely. If he did not put the group of poems about Armenia into this category, it was, I believe, because he thought of an oratorio as having for its subject matter the crowning moment in the life of man and humankind as a whole: death. Dying, death, mass slaughter, and the general doom – such is the theme of M.'s two oratorios.

VIII: 'ORCHESTRAS AND THYMELES'

At the very beginning of the twenties M. noticed that everybody was trying to teach the poets, demanding a thousand things from them. 'Poor poetry,' he wrote, 'chafes under the revolver barrels of imperious demands. What does poetry owe to anyone? It may be that it owes nothing and that all its creditors are bogus.' At that time it was a question not of official demands but of what the public wanted, and M. attributed this profusion of demands to a readership debauched by the rapid turnover of new poetic schools. In the twenties readers were indeed exceptionally spoiled and immoderate, but they only parroted one or other of the many rival claimants to the position of supreme arbiter in literature. Each of these had his own proposals about the quickest way to impose order, to introduce uniformity and make sure everybody thought alike. Something similar was going on in all fields, but in poetry, the most personal of literary forms, it proved in fact impossible to impose order, and the poets did the best they could to remain true to themselves to the end of their lives. Most died before their time, but two lived until old age. Considering that the very first blows fell on her,* one could scarcely have imagined that Akhmatova would have been allowed to survive. Fortunately she was spared the *coup de grâce* – by sheer luck she drew a winning lottery ticket which gave her the right to live out her days to the end.

By now, looking back, one may well ask: How could it happen that 'unanimity' was introduced in accordance with proposals coming 'from below' – that is, on the initiative of the public, not of the State? It was the public which advanced the claims of various people to be dictators in art at a time when the future victors still gave no thought to such matters – they were too busy first with their preparations to seize power, and later with the Civil War. 'Unanimity' came about not as a consequence of bribery or intimidation. Terror works only when people are impressed by the very idea of it; bribes can be placed only in outstretched palms, and 'unanimity', by the same token, is possible only when people

* She was banned in a special Party instruction in 1925 from publishing original work. (It was lifted only temporarily in 1940.)

are ready to abandon independence of thought in order to enjoy the feeling of being surrounded by the like-minded. Such types do not appear en masse in a single day. A long period of preparation is needed.

We are speaking here only of the intelligentsia – not, however, of the revolutionary intelligentsia that made the Revolution, but of the one which subsequently supported the dictatorship and strove mightily to impose 'unanimity' on itself. The most vivid example was Meyerhold, of whose sincerity there cannot be the slightest doubt. Zealots of this type (who, unlike the spiritual advisers to secular rulers in days of old, had not been appointed to the task) energetically promoted those forms of art they had decided to back and vigorously campaigned for 'unanimity', issuing their 'orders of the day to the army of the arts'.* Mayakovski himself was a mere instrument, not a prime mover, and his 'order' is only a rhymed version of hundreds of more matter-of-fact instructions produced in all spheres by the champions of unanimity who had immediately rushed to take up posts as commissars of art. I am sure that a little research would turn up excellent examples of such orders drafted by Punin or, say, Sternberg, who were later so upset when they fell foul of other people's counterorders. In later years, alas, these orders of the day were backed up by the State and its punitive organs. According to my information, Punin's downfall was brought about by mediocre artists who looked askance not so much at his understanding of contemporary art as at his views on the history of painting.

M. worked in Lunacharski's Commissariat of Education, but with his customary improvidence, he issued no orders of the day to the army of the arts, and was chiefly concerned to keep out of the way of his secretary, an ardent supporter of the dictatorship, who despised him. This episode cannot be held against M., since he took no part in the struggle to achieve unanimity; he only frankly told other poets what he thought of them . . .

For so many supporters of the new regime to appear at once, the ideas making for unanimity and dictatorship must have arisen before the Revolution. The process went on in all spheres, but I am dealing here with only one aspect – art, and poetry in particular. In

* Allusion to Mayakovski's poem of 1918.

the pre-revolutionary years a lot of attention was attracted by Viacheslav Ivanov's article 'Merry Craft and Mental Practice'. The influence of Viacheslav Ivanov in those years was very great. He was one of the lawgivers, and I shall never forget the hush that fell on the audience when he ascended the rostrum (this I once witnessed as a young girl when my father took me to hear him lecture on Scriabin, or Medtner).

In his article (the 'mental practice'* of the title is a term borrowed from Christian philosophy – with which the article has nothing in common) Ivanov outlines his vision of the future of Symbolism and proposes a way of overcoming the schism between the people and the intelligentsia, which had always been so agonizing to the latter. Even now there are those who regard Viacheslav Ivanov as a thinker without peer. One very clever woman, a student of literature in the tradition of OPOYAZ, once said to me with a sigh that after the appearance of Viacheslav Ivanov's articles, the general intellectual level had fallen off sharply. (I wonder whether she had bothered to re-read these articles, or whether her judgement was based on the reverence she had felt at the time.) Our modern nationalists, the *Rusity*, are drawn to Viacheslav Ivanov and occasionally peddle his ideas in a grossly cheapened form – at bargain prices, so to speak – adapting them for present-day consumption and giving them a nationalist flavour. In the West they like to speak of our 'Silver Age'. Pushkin's time was the 'Golden Age', and the 'Silver Age' was that of Viacheslav Ivanov with his Tower – the apartment where poets and philosophers gathered to hear him preach his 'realist symbolism', an abortive movement of which miracles were expected.

Like all the other Symbolists, Viacheslav Ivanov had an exaggerated view of the artist. For him a poet was theurgist, prophet, and source of revealed truth – or at least such he would have become after mastering the tenets of 'realist symbolism', according to which 'the artist's spiritual receptiveness makes him the vehicle of divine revelation' (a little overstated this, perhaps?). The aim of the Symbolists was to create myths, and their usual

---

* Term used by the Hesychasts on Mount Athos in the fourteenth century to describe the art of prayer advocated by them.

triad, metaphor-symbol-myth, suffers from the very serious fault of not bringing out the meaning of the word 'myth'. (Even now the heirs of the Symbolists stretch this term to mean whatever they will. Isn't it time to define its limits?) Viacheslav Ivanov wrote: 'The symbol naturally unfolds as myth *in posse* or in embryo,' and: 'In the organic course of its development, symbolism turns into mythopoeia.' This sounds very grandiloquent, but it flies in the face of history. Man has always used symbols, and there have been many great artists during the course of human history, but can their work really be called the creation of myths? Are Beatrice and Laura myths? Is Rembrandt's *Prodigal Son* a myth, rather than the artist's depiction of his longing for the Father? Rembrandt, who lived in an age when Christian teaching had still not lost its hold, would scarcely have regarded the idea of his painting as a 'revelation'. In those days men were conscious of being fallen, sinful creatures, and the misuse of words was frowned on. The meaning of even the most crucial words is eroded by misuse.

Viacheslav Ivanov calls on us to achieve knowledge of reality, but the prophecies with which he was so open-handed can be described only as flights of fantasy, wishful thinking, and dreams – luckily impractical ones! He dreamed, for instance, of reuniting the people with the intelligentsia and worked out a number of schemes to bring this about. The artist, in his view, was always an individualist and ought to go on to become a 'superindividualist' (an echo of Superman evidently). However, the myths elaborated by the 'superindividualist' would not be individual but universal in their significance: 'When the makings of new myths burst forth from symbols,' he says, then the ordinary people, 'the natural creators of myths,' will take them up at once and, by virtue of this encounter with myths in the poetry of individualists, will regain awareness of their mythopoeic power and once more begin to create new ones of their own. 'The growth of myths from symbols,' he continues, 'leads back to the free play of elemental power embodied in the people,' and elsewhere: 'We put our hopes in the elementally creative powers of the people's barbarian soul.' When and where did the term 'barbarian' ever apply to the so-called people? Only the dregs of the cities may have earned this description. There was no end to such fantasies about the people: one moment it was supposed to be 'God-bearing',* and the next it was being credited with a special kind of 'barbarian soul' . . .

Ivanov hoped that the 'Dionysius of a barbarian renaissance will restore myths to us'. The Russian and German peoples, according to him, were endowed with this barbarian, Dionysiac quality (both were later to show a high degree of discipline – surely not also Dionysaic? – as storm troopers, or members of equivalent organizations) It is only fair to mention that Ivanov was nevertheless apprehensive about the unleashing of the elemental forces of Dionysius: 'In Russia Dionysius is dangerous – he could only too easily become a death-dealing force, taking on an aspect of purely destructive frenzy.' (But I am not myself convinced that the 'people' which went on the rampage at the beginning of the Revolution, demanding land on which to sow their crops, was simply the embodiment of a destructive 'elemental force'.) When all was said and done, however, Ivanov was less put off by the chance of an outburst of destructive frenzy than he was by the progress of education, and he called for the preservation of the people's 'all-seeing blindness'. Why was everybody so afraid of education? Most unfortunately our present school system serves anything but the cause of education – its main effect, evidently, is to reinforce Ivanov's celebrated 'all-seeing blindness' and 'barbaric Dionysian soul', which are demonstrated every time a foul-mouthed slanging match breaks out in a queue, bus, or communal apartment.

When the union of artists and people took place, the whole country would be covered 'with orchestras and thymeles for the dancing of choruses'. (Why do such dreamers always think of unity among people in terms of a *chorus*? Were they incapable of visualizing fellowship of a profounder kind?) After this, tragedy and 'mysteries' would be reborn and 'true mythmaking will revive'. It is difficult to see what Ivanov means by 'mysteries', and even less clear how he proposed to revive tragedy. Did he really believe it was so simple? As for 'Dionysianism', he thought of it as a certain psychological state, a 'sphere of inner experience' which was independent of religious faith – by such sophistry he was able

* As in Dostoyevski.

to convince himself that it was possible to combine Dionysian ecstasy with Christianity. While, in his view, artistic creation was necessarily religious, as an 'aesthete' he felt entitled to make use of what he called the 'religious-psychological phenomenon of Dionysianism'. The Symbolists were all Nietzscheans (it was Nietzsche, according to Ivanov, who had first awakened the contemporary spirit), hence their search for a synthesis between Christianity and the pagan religions. Dionysius, moreover, proved very handy, since in Greek eyes, as a suffering god, he was a 'hypostasis of the Son' – no more, no less! This mixing up of concepts was a game typical of the nineteenth century, when people were always trying to find external similarities between the religions without regard to differences of substance. What did they hope to gain by combining religions of nature with the religion of Atonement and the Spirit? Ivanov even went so far (in his 'Premonitions and Presages') as to see in Christianity elements of a 'peculiar pantheism modified by contact with it'. He was engaged in a search for 'religious syncretism', and the so-called elite of the pre-revolutionary years listened to his every word.

Being individualists, or – as Ivanov suggested – superindividualists, the Symbolists always opposed the principle that the work of an artist must be integrated with his personality. They were also responsible for the hankering after 'major works'. I see an echo of this vogue in Gumilev's advice to the young Akhmatova to write ballads. Gumilev himself paid dearly for it, particularly in his early books with the rudimentary thread of narrative running through them. The retreat from Christianity had undermined people's view of the personality – which, in turn, sharply affected their idea of the artist's role in society – and the Symbolists were no longer content with the notion of the artist as a private person whose work could be either accepted or rejected by society. They sought new ways of strengthening the position of the artist, of assuring his place in a country soon to be covered with 'orchestras and thymeles'. Here, in fact, we have the origin of the idea of artists receiving orders from society which was so eagerly taken up in the twenties by various 'activists' in the arts, whatever movement they belonged to – in particular by the Symbolists and their direct successors, the Futurists of LEF. All of them were in sympathy with Viacheslav

Ivanov's ideas on the role of the artist and his propaganda in favour of art being commissioned. The artist – who is 'theurgist, prophet, vehicle of revelation' to boot – 'needs to receive orders', so Ivanov tells us, 'not only for material reasons, but for moral ones as well, and he is proud to receive them; if he occasionally proclaims himself a "monarch" who thus "stands alone", this is only because he is angry at the failure of people to come to him with their orders'. Though Ivanov believed the age he lived in was a critical one, an age of Cain, he expected it to be succeeded by an 'organic era' in which the creation of myths would flourish. In the years before the Revolution 'organic' was a highly fashionable catchword, and it implies links with the ordinary people, the sharing of common roots with them, the ability to reach down to them. The concept was cheapened in Soviet times into what was at first described as 'art for the people' and then as 'People's art' – in other words, since the Party stands for the People, 'Party art'. The twenties were spent in the search for a style appropriate to the People – from LEF's poster art to RAPP's 'call-up of shock workers to literature', but all this ended with the establishment of 'socialist realism'. Thus Ivanov's prophecy came true: the artist was turned into the practitioner of a 'merry craft', the executor of 'creative orders from the community'. Since the 'community' had no money, the orders actually came from the State – acting, needless to say, in the name of the People.

In his vision of the idyllic times to come, Ivanov dreamed of 'like-mindedness'. In the era of rampant Dionysianism, the individual spectator at tragedies and mysteries was to 'merge with the like-minded multitude'. Like-mindedness was indeed achieved; it was not, however, the work of the elite with its grand dreams, but of the revolutionary intelligentsia which, after its victory, knew very well how to curb freedom of thought and person. Instead of 'orchestras and thymeles' we got *samodeyatelnost*,* which flourished particularly in the concentration camps, where it could earn one an exemption from hard labour. From Marchenko's testimony it appears that the situation has changed: nowadays only wartime collabora-

---

* A Soviet-coined word (literally 'self-activity') referring to any kind of 'spontaneous' (though generally organized) amateur cultural activities in factories, labour camps, etc.

tors with the Nazis go in for amateur theatricals and choir singing, while everybody else prefers hard labour.* For a long time we used to boast of the number of copies of a book which were published, treating this as the criterion for the degree of their closeness to the People, but it appears that lately books have somehow ceased to sell as they did. Only Kochetov still causes a stir – much like a good thriller in the West. Perhaps the clever sleuth from a detective novel *is* our modern myth?

When M. took me to see Viacheslav Ivanov in his humble room in Baku, where his son was sitting doing his lessons and a charming daughter served us something resembling tea, we heard our host's complaints about his failure to come to an arrangement with the victors. He had tried to do it through Kamenev's wife, but nothing had come of it. 'I was always in favour of *sobornost*,† you know,' he told us, trying to explain why he had offered his collaboration. On our way home – that is, to the sidings in which our railway carriage stood – M. recalled these words and expressed his astonishment at them: where did Ivanov see *sobornost*? In the army? The mob? Public meetings? In his articles Ivanov made no distinction between *sobornost* and collectivism. In actual fact, however, *sobornost* is a term relating to religion and the church which not only has nothing in common with collectivism, but is even used in a contrary meaning. *Sobornost* is the brotherhood of people who are part of the *sobor* and see themselves as children of the same Father. A 'collective', on the other hand, is a mechanical association of individuals who have banded together for self-defence, or to define their position in an alien and terrifying world. People are driven into a 'collective' by fear, bewilderment, the need of a ration card. Here there is not a trace of brotherhood, and the most one can hope for is an occasional exception to the rule *homo homini lupus*. The collective, while demanding subordination, at the same time rids a man of any sense of responsibility. The modern state, given the way it organizes its economy and such things as scientific research, lends itself to the formation of 'collectives'. This is true of all advanced states, by no means only of totalitarian ones, although these have been particularly adept at the subjugation of

* See Marchenko, Appendix A.
† See note, page 131.

man – they simply do it in a more open way than states still preserving a democratic structure. But the essence is the same.

A man enslaved by the collective inevitably becomes an individualist; *sobornost*, on the contrary, is unthinkable without full freedom of the personality. Ivanov believed that *sobornost* assumes 'the principle of mutual responsibility', 'the responsibility of all for all'. But this is the principle of collectivism, not of *sobornost*, which is the responsibility of each individual for his neighbour as well as for the world at large. For Ivanov the concepts of *sobornost* and collectivism, of personality and individualism, are inseparable. Was anybody able to distinguish them in the pre-revolutionary years? I believe the difference was always clear to the religious philosophers, but the Symbolists – as individualists striving to become superindividualists and being under the enormous influence of Nietzsche and Schopenhauer – inculcated into the Russian elite (I use this term of Berdiayev's to define the circles close to Symbolism) ideas and the theories which prompted them to change their values, reject the notion of free personality, and seek to combine Christianity with paganism. This kind of mixture only hastened the process of decay.

One characteristic detail is that in the pre-revolutionary writings of the Symbolists, including Viacheslav Ivanov, one always finds an apologia for cruelty. In Ivanov, for example, I came across the following: 'Cruelty is distinguished by a serene expression', while the victim 'drinks in . . . the radiant energy of the tormentor'. The elite preached indulgence for the cruelty of superindividualists. In this way, it might well be thought, the Russian intelligentsia was conditioned to accept the notion of terror.

In many of M.'s articles there is a hidden polemic with Viacheslav Ivanov, whose only service to Acmeism at its birth was hence the impetus provided by repulsion from his doctrines. Neither the Symbolists nor the other adepts of collectivism ever recognized M. In this they were right: he was not on their side.

IX: THE FUNCTIONARY

Viacheslav Ivanov's dreams and prophecies, his suggestions to the new regime, were, to borrow his own expression from *Sporades*, nothing more than 'lightning forks of imagination'. Rejected by the victors, he sat in the last refuge he was to find in his own country and presided over a university department, leaving with his colleagues an abiding memory of the 'poisonous prettiness' of his words. By giving his imagination its head he made his contribution to the spirit of the times and paid cruelly for it. In his loneliness this imperious man was almost tragic, but the tragedy stemmed from the 'flight of time' and its death sentence on a generation addicted to licence. In his Vatican exile he was probably homesick for Russia and the Tower where he once laid down the law, but it was very lucky for him that he got away in time. If he had stayed, his fate would have been much worse. He would not have had the strength to endure the isolation to which he would have been prey in his own country, and neither his learning nor his cunning would have saved him. Nothing was of any avail here: the new rulers knew perfectly well what they wanted, and they were very good at getting their way, quick to dispose of all who did not cooperate in the aims they adopted on the way.

Nobody was interested in the 'natural creator of myths' or in what it might have to say: the People was henceforth an object of indoctrination and received its myths ready-made from above – after careful editing at the centre, they were passed down to the 'masses' through the appropriate channels. Literature was perhaps the sole field in which this mechanism worked very well from the start. The orders fulfilled by writers did not come to them from the community, which had been all but done away with; they were passed down from unimaginable heights in the form of suggestions and recommendations of a most general nature, eventually reaching those for whom they were intended via an army of editors. The second stage was the editorial processing of the completed order, the organization of a low-level debate about the published work, followed by new recommendations, this time more specific and taking account of 'errors' and 'achievements'.

The main intermediary between literature and its patrons at the

highest level was the editorial apparatus. This, with its grossly
inflated functions, had come into being after the normal role of an
editor – to define the identity and viewpoint of his publishing
house, newspaper, or magazine – had been totally abolished. From
now on, everything fed into the machinery of printing and publishing was done in fulfilment of the same general instructions, and in
pursuance of the same aim: to proclaim the myth of the kingdom
destined to last a thousand years. For this it was necessary to dismiss and denigrate the past, to show the present as the path to
happiness, and to give some vague picture of this promised future
bliss. The basic idea to be propagated was that there was only one
possible way to one possible future. Faith in the completely predetermined nature of events, in their being a simple matter of cause
and effect, became very widespread and captured people's minds.
The only concession was an admission that 'mistakes' were
possible – and subject to punishment, though only in the middle
and lower reaches of the administration. The men at the top, as the
possessors of scientific truth, were infallible – until the moment
they fell from grace. The man at the very top never made mistakes.

Although they belonged to the lower ranks of the apparatus,
editors were extremely important, since without them it would
have been impossible to pass down and give shape to the ideas and
moods of the 'top'. Where they came from was always obscure, but
it certainly was not from the world of literature itself. Occasionally
you saw one of them wearing a decent suit: this meant he had been
transferred to editorial work after slipping up in a diplomatic
career. The rest just appeared out of some mysterious backwoods
or, as Akhmatova put it, 'curdled out of nothing'. On first seeing
these new-style editors, M. opened his eyes in amazement: where
on earth had they come from? He called them 'the beautiful
strangers', or 'the mummers'. Editors were strictly distinguished
according to function and rank, and there was an elaborate grada-
tion into junior, senior, and chief editors, with the directors of
publishing houses as supereditors at the top. The higher their rank,
the more mysterious they became. In relation to a writer, his editor,
though only the humble channel by which instructions were
handed down, served rather as mentor, judge, and final authority.
In the twenties they cultivated a bluff, aggressive style, but they

gradually acquired good manners to such a point that their politeness became unbearably brazen and openly patronizing. Almost
straightaway they assumed powers of censorship, deciding on their
own initiative what should be forbidden or allowed through; in this
way they guarded against getting into hot water themselves for any
'ideological errors' which might be picked up after the book's
publication. Since there were constant changes in the 'line', and it
took time to publish a book, editors learned to anticipate future
twists and turns, and constantly erred on the side of caution. After
a book had been thoroughly worked over by one editor after
another, little remained for the censor to do except to pick a few
minor holes here and there in order to justify the butter he got with
his daily bread.

At the end of the twenties and beginning of the thirties there
were still a few editors who tried to 'get away with things'. Caesar
Volpe, for example, not only published 'Journey to Armenia' in
Zvezda, but even included the passage, after it had been forbidden
by the censorship, about King Arshak, imprisoned by the Assyrian
in a dungeon without a ray of light and from which there was no
escape: 'The Assyrian holds my heart in his hand . . .' Volpe was
dismissed from his job but not arrested. He was lucky. He died
during the war – nobody knows how – as he was making his way
out of Leningrad across Lake Ladoga during the siege. Editors like
this were completely exceptional, and even in the present free and
easy times there are precious few of them. The difference nowadays
is that many more would gladly take liberties if only their own
complete immunity were guaranteed: that is, if there were no
danger of losing their jobs and the favour of their superiors. This
is in contrast to earlier years when every editor believed in his
mission and the absolute rightness of what he did. He then regarded
his work as important and progressive, as a fight against alien
ideology and hostile tendencies. 'Unanimity' did not fall from the
skies – it was eagerly created by crowds of active, energetic supporters of the new order who made a fetish of 'science' and the
tangible products of their own activities. Fingering the bindings of
their books, they knew none of the doubts against which no real
thinker or scientist is immune. The 'science' in question was a very
convenient one for the unscientific: absolutely proof against doubt

and abstruse beyond belief, the whole of it could nevertheless be carried in one small briefcase and was thus astonishingly portable. To all questions and misgivings it offered a ready answer, giving the representatives of the new order a permanent feeling of easy superiority from the height of which they looked down on poor fools unable to master its truths. The devotees of these 'truths' included some out-and-out crooks, who were indeed the most fulsome of all in their hallelujahs – it came easily to them, since they really believed in nothing except the fees they collected from the publishing houses, or in plain, sealed envelopes containing surreptitious payments for good behaviour and service to the People.

Not to get bored with the purely preventive aspect of their work, editors liked to think of themselves as connoisseurs of style, guardians of the language, and sponsors of new literary forms. One of the first to fancy himself in such a role was Marshak. In his hoarsely rhapsodic voice he lectured his *authors* (as he liked to call them) on the art of writing, on how best to develop and embellish their subject matter, becoming masters of style in the process. As treated by Marshak, poetry could be understood by anyone at all: everything seemed poetic when he spoke of it in a quivering voice. Oleinikov sheltered behind his back, and Kharms composed nursery rhymes under his aegis but this was not what counted most for Marshak. He set far greater store by his efforts to make a writer of almost anybody who wished to become one, as long as he had the slightest experience in any walk of life. Engineers, sailors, hunters, meteorologists – all qualified, since practical experience was the very stuff of literature and needed only recounting in the right language. To this end he created a special staff of junior editors, gradually promoting them to senior status, who polished, filed, and honed every sentence, every word and turn of phrase, until all manuscripts were reduced to the same presentably average level. The thought that they were creating literature with their own hands fairly made their heads spin, and no editor who worked under Marshak will ever forget the heroic days when he made works of art out of nothing, converting what would otherwise have been mere propaganda pieces into smooth-flowing tales. The work of people turning out detective fiction, one imagines, is very much the same, though they have the advantage of knowing their market and writing for it in everyday language, without reference to Shakespeare or Milton, and having no grand literary pretensions. When literature becomes an industry the production of such cheap reading matter is the inevitable consequence. A vile age is served by vile books, but the worst is when they are dressed up in decent-seeming garb. I prefer the hacks who make money out of thrillers to the Marshaks.

Some of the writers with whom Marshak worked are still with us and fondly recall the advice he gave: know your hero down to the last detail, the way he walks, the things he likes, the suit he wears, and the size of his apartment . . . watch the newspapers for likely subjects for a story so you can re-create the life of our great era in all its immediacy . . . Marshak was exceptionally clever at avoiding ideas or aspects of real life that were taboo, always talking instead about the 'poetic'. In addition to this kind of twaddle, he produced Shakespeare's sonnets in a commonplace Russian translation and wrote nasty political doggerel for the newspapers. For the good of his own soul he had devised a glib philosophy which he could spout endlessly, plucking at the heartstrings even of his masters. One of his ideas was the creation of a literary university for schoolchildren (M., who could not stand the thought of incubators, was highly indignant about this). Marshak was very much a man of his times in his determination to sweeten the pill of writing under orders, to create an illusion of literary life when it had been destroyed, and to smooth over all the rough edges. He would have done great harm if there had been any budding new ideas still to be stifled, but such things had disappeared already, so there was nothing left for him to spoil or corrupt – not even the children in his 'university'. These children belonged to the doomed generation and died during the war or after.

While Marshak put on his maudlin act and a hard-nosed teacher in his 'university' inspired schoolchildren with a lifelong distate for Pushkin, the censor wielded his vulgar red pencil and hordes of editors laboured at raw manuscripts, trimming, polishing, and making them uniform. This was how books were turned out, one after the other, winning their authors a place in school and university curricula, both here and abroad – while all the time those chiefly responsible, the editors, remained hidden from view in the background. Yet their power was enormous. They had their special rules for 'developing the subject matter' and a peculiar style all their own. Every book bears the insipid imprint of its editor. Since the dictatorship over literature was actually implemented through the Soviet editor, he could ignore the consumer with impunity: his main task, after all, was to 'educate' both author and reader. In so doing he erected barriers through which no manuscript could pass without losing its individuality and being refurbished according to the standard pattern. The readers to whom this swill was fed may now be old-age pensioners already, but the Soviet editor hatched out in those days continues just as before, astonished that his books no longer sell and lie piled up in the warehouses. There is an anecdote about a mother who copies out *War and Peace* on her typewriter because her son reads only *samizdat*!

Ever since the twenties the entire apparatus in charge of our 'literature to order' has been waging war on any manifestation of the free personality. It was this apparatus which glorified the idea of 'major works' and fought so hard for all those musty productions described as 'novels'. The new generation of prose writers has renounced the novel,* but they are in a quandary because no new ideas have crystallized, and they therefore imagine that the only solution is to chase after 'originality' – but this cannot and will not save them. When Tynianov proclaimed the end of the age of poetry and the coming triumph of prose, he completely forgot that prose is impossible without *ideas*. Can he really have mistaken the minor stirrings of the twenties for a new intellectual awakening? There was in fact no age of prose. We had only the age of literature-to-order, which has now come to an end.

It transpires that very little of value was preserved in anybody's desk drawer, only trifling deviations from the stuff written to order. The exceptions were Platonov and Zoshchenko, and a few poets who had preserved their personalities intact. The rest, having lost it, were happy enough to go and learn their trade from Marshak and his like.

A beggar's greatest windfall is to pick up something that has been lost, but to regain one's own 'self' is harder than finding a needle in a haystack. For the moment *samizdat* thrives on the opposite of

---

* In favour of the short story or novella (*povest*).

'literature-to-order' – which means that it is only a variant of the same thing. The value of our main *samizdat* writer, Solzhenitsyn, is that he restores our memory of time past. This is the first step towards the recovery of one's sense of being human. Only after passing through this stage will people understand that the individual, the distinctive, stands for the whole or the general, and is a symbol of it. Literature can exist only where there is pain, and pain can be felt only by a human being, a personality. Where there is pain, people do not talk about 'major' or 'minor' works, about 'style' or 'subject matter', but only about pain – which itself knows how best to express itself. Pain warns a man of illness and thus gives him the chance of healing himself. But there are illnesses that end in death. Only the future can show what ails us and what is in store: extinction or survival.

X: 'COMPLETELY PERVERSE VIEWS'

One of the editors of the State Publishing House (Gosizdat), Chechanovski, with whom I once worked on the newspaper *For a Communist Education*, used to visit us from time to time. He was a believing Marxist, but not a very aggressive one. M. rather enjoyed getting into arguments with him, although they always ended in complete deadlock. The authorities apparently never received any information about these arguments – at least they never came up during M.'s interrogation later on. This speaks in Chechanovski's favour. I was irritated by the debate between them. To Chechanovski it was self-evident that M.'s view of the world was quite outmoded, and that he was unable to reform, poor fellow. M., on the other hand, was just wasting his breath by disputing Chechanovski's not very sophisticated dialectical constructions, which were food neither for the mind nor for the heart. If Marxism had not been the official ideology, binding on everybody who wanted to earn his daily bread, M. would scarcely have allowed himself to get seriously involved in a discussion of the 'basis' and the 'superstructure', or the theory of 'leaps' in the historical process, let alone the problem of matter – such as how, in the course of its development, it eventually gave rise to that original contraption called the brain. In arguing against Marxism, its opponents were forced to use the same language, and by the very nature of the subject, any discussion of it inevitably led to a drop in the intellectual level. But M. was so desperate to have someone to talk with that he was only too glad of these conversations even with such an ill-matched (but on the whole innocuous) companion as Chechanovski. There really was no one to talk with, and the level was being systematically lowered all the time. Marxists and non-Marxists were becoming equally dreary.

The latest collection of M.'s work, which had been sold to the State Publishing House, was being edited by Chechanovski. M. was quite indifferent as to who exactly curtailed, mutilated, and destroyed his books, and in any case we had no great faith that this edition would actually come out. Bukharin had arranged the contract and the payment of an advance, simply to give us something to tide us over. On this money – it was not very much – we had been able to go to the Crimea, and we still had the last part of the advance to look forward to in the late autumn of that year. The edition was planned in two volumes, but payments to authors were niggardly and there was no question of living on them. (Favoured authors were looked after in some obscure way – by means of the mysterious 'packets', or in like fashion.) We had got used to the lack of a steady income and were glad of this momentary relief, particularly as it gave us the chance of a trip to the Crimea, where we stayed two months.

We returned to Moscow at the beginning of July and at once moved into our new apartment there – the one from which M. was taken to the Lubianka the following May. Here we were able to enjoy our new-found home life in all its confusion: arguments with Chechanovski, the gossip of Narbut and Zenkevich, callers who had still not mastered the art of telephoning instead of just dropping in, the usual contingent of police spies (whose profession barred them from giving advance notice of their arrival), and frequent visits from Akhmatova, whom M. had learned how to lure down from Leningrad by summoning her on the telephone (it took five calls). Her son Lev stayed with us after he had been told to leave Leningrad, where things were getting difficult for him.

Not long before he came to us in Moscow he had been arrested for the first time and then released a few days later. This was, so to speak, his baptism of fire. When his mother met him at our place, they found it hard to tear themselves from each other's embraces. Punin could not stand Lev and at the mere sight of him always began a 'Punic war' against him. But we liked him just as much as his mother, and they were able to enjoy their meetings in our apartment without anyone disturbing them. We put Akhmatova up in the kitchen (where the gas had not yet been installed), and she received her visitors there: Chulkov, people from the Arts Theatre, Yesenin's widow,* and various other women unknown to me . . . Early in 1934 Petrovykh turned up. We had no money. The rest of the fee for the collected works was brought to us in a briefcase by Bublik, a drunken ex-criminal who had once attended the same grammar school as M.'s brother Alexander.† M.'s father ('Grand-dad') was staying with us and complained that nobody paid any attention to his 'little philosophy'. This was the most chaotic period of my life, a real bedlam, during which we somehow managed to overlook one sinister portent of the much more serious ordeal to come. Perhaps, though, it was as well we failed to notice it – otherwise we should have been overcome with utter gloom and brooded all the time on the future. In our conditions it is inadvisable to let one's mind dwell on the future. The future spells only disaster and casts its shadow on the present; it poisons your life, grips you by the throat in paroxysms of terror, drains away your strength and your very life's blood. It is fatal to start feeling afraid beforehand. The clever people who, seeing the shape of things to come all too clearly, began to worry in advance, found themselves incapable of anything else – of thinking, loving, writing, or of breathing almost, but they still did not escape their lot. Even now, if I were to start thinking about the future, I would sink into total lethargy – despite the fact that the present is like paradise compared with the past. But, of course, on this large planet of ours 'paradise' is a relative concept. Some pampered people might take our paradise for nothing less than hell on earth. It all depends what you compare it with and what you take as your base of comparison.

* Yesenin's last wife, Sofia Tolstaya (a grand-daughter of Leo Tolstoy).
† *Hope Against Hope*, pages 264 ff.

Optimists like me start off from the period before the Boss's death until the Twentieth Congress.

We moved into our new apartment at the beginning of August and gradually settled down, getting used to the ceaseless gurgling of the toilet and to the view from the fifth floor over the vast expanse of Moscow, whose skyline was still low. On one occasion during this period I visited the State Publishing House by myself on M.'s behalf. How this happened I do not remember. Normally we went together, or M. went alone. It may be that he was not feeling well and had sent me to collect some money from them; or perhaps Chechanovski had called and asked to see me personally . . . Whatever the reason, however, I remember being there alone with Chechanovski, who took me out to a quiet corner in the corridor for a confidential chat, out of earshot of the younger colleagues who shared his office. Though a senior editor, he probably did not have a room of his own. On the other hand, he had the sort of desk used by the most exalted of officials or by real Soviet writers engaged in the composition of novels. Desks such as these were not provided without reason.

A person sitting behind a desk always inspired great respect. This was once vividly demonstrated by a small incident involving Pasternak. His former wife, Zhenia, had asked him to get her a pass for a place on the reviewing stand during some parade or other (there was a fad for this at one time). To humour her fancy, he raced to the Union of Writers and begged for a pass. On the eve of the parade he was given the precious piece of paper, but it turned out to have been issued in his name. A woman secretary said how sorry she was for the muddle, but told him not to worry: his wife should nevertheless take the pass as it was, since nobody would bother to check such a detail on the spot. Zhenia duly went along with it, but she was not admitted and there was a frightful fuss about this illegal transfer of the pass. 'Why did you take the secretary's word for it?' I asked Pasternak, when he told me his tale of woe. 'How could I doubt her word,' he replied, 'when she was sitting at a *desk*!' We stood in mortal awe of anybody who sat at a desk. For ever after, if we wanted an idea of somebody's importance, we always asked: 'Does he have a desk?' Chechanovski had a desk with drawers – a sure sign that our conversation in the corridor would be one of moment.

It turned out that he wanted me to tell M. it would be advisable for him to disavow 'Journey to Armenia' without a moment's delay. It did not occur to me to ask what form his 'disavowal' should take, since I thought Chechanovski was talking about the forthcoming collected works and simply meant that M. should throw 'Journey to Armenia' out of the second volume. Later he told me that what he had had in mind was a repentant letter in the newspapers. The era of 'letters of repentance' was by no means over, and they were all the rage during the period I worked with Chechanovski at *For a Communist Education*. There was always a queue of people at his door imploring him to publish their 'letters of repentance' – a lot of them written by psychologists and writers on education, since certain trends in these fields had recently been condemned by the Party. There was something else I did not ask Chechanovski: Why was he telling me this instead of M. directly? He was always coming to see us, and nothing would have been easier then to mention it to M. himself. This question I deliberately refrained from putting because I was aware by then of the special technique by which husbands were 'got at' through their wives. At the first hint of trouble, being concerned first and foremost to preserve their home life, wives took their husbands to task so severely that, after a slight show of resistance within their own four walls, the men went off as meek as lambs to the authorities and dutifully signed anything put before them, renounced their previous views, or crossed whole pages out of their novels. The husband's conscience would be eased by the reflection that he was sacrificing himself for the sake of his family. His wife would walk around with a distraught, tear-stained look, secretly rejoicing, however, at the thought of having saved him. The days were not far off when nothing would save one except chance. But in August 1933, a timely public confession could still avert, or at least postpone, disaster.

I would have been quite ready to work on M. in order to save him, but nothing would have come of it. Far from getting him to repent, I would only have brought a flood of mockery down on my head. I told Chechanovski I would pass on his words to M. and asked who had been so displeased by 'Journey to Armenia'. Ignoring my question, he asked whether I would undertake to bring M. to his senses and what chance I had of success. When I replied that M. was unlikely to disavow anything, a complete change came over Chechanovski: his usual courtesy vanished and he began to talk like a real 'man at a desk'. Why, he demanded to know, was M. meddling in things he knew nothing of? Why all these strange passages about Goethe, Lamarck, and God knows what else besides? 'We will not allow him,' he continued, 'to make derogatory remarks about development and progress – let him remember that . . .' He then referred to 'veiled hints' (about what, he refused to say) and 'completely perverse views'. It was a powerful onslaught, and he ended with the words: 'I have warned you, do as you think fit – only let's hope you don't live to regret it . . .'

How much did Chechanovski know? It may be that he put this pressure on me under instructions, but it also is quite possible that he had overheard some talk or other and decided to warn M. on his own initiative. He was not a bad colleague, as I had reason to learn from experience when somebody once denounced me to the editor of the newspaper (on the grounds that I had not read the most important philosophical work of our age,* and confused empiricism with imperialism – it was true that I had not read the great work, and had put one thing instead of another somewhere). Chechanovski stood up for me like a lion. He made mincemeat of the person who had denounced me, and declared that I was a comrade with a good philosophical education who could not but have read the complete works of all four founding fathers . . . It would thus have been quite in character if he had become frightened on M.'s behalf and decided to help him. He certainly seemed to be talking for himself, but there was a lurking suggestion that others might be involved in his occasional use of phrases like '*we* will not allow . . .' How far up did Chechanovski's contacts go? I do not and cannot know.

It was either, therefore, a case of Chechanovski's having got wind of something and trying to help, or of a 'warning' to M. being passed down via the director or Party authorities of the State Pub-

*Lenin's *Materialism and Empirio-criticism* (1909).

lishing House, with Chechanovski serving only as the final link in the chain. 'Journey to Armenia' would be known to the authorities 'at the top' without a manuscript having to be brought to their attention: it had already been published, and Volpe had been duly punished as a result. It is quite out of the question that Chechanovski should have suddenly got worried about it entirely of his own accord, or that his warning was not prompted in some way. He was at that time still sweating over the first volume of M.'s collected works, throwing out everything that aroused his misgivings in the early verse. An editor reads only what he happens to be dealing with at the moment. To tell the truth, however, it must be said that everything of M.'s, not just 'Journey to Armenia', was 'out of harmony' with our doleful times and equally subject to proscription. This indeed is what happened: the collection never saw the light of day. Some young men who went through the archives of the State Publishing House in recent years could find no trace of the manuscript. It may have got lost, but it was more likely destroyed or handed to the security organs eight months or so later. M.'s arrest was only eight and a half months away. But we did not think of the future.

On 30 August 1933 an article appeared in *Pravda*. I would swear I saw a copy of the newspaper in which the article was published unsigned, as in the case of editorials. In other copies, however – like those preserved in the Lenin Library, as well as in the version reprinted in *Zvezda* – it appeared as a signed article. This was something that occasionally happened: part of the edition would appear in one form, and part in another. After reading the article, M. wrote to Gusev in the Central Committee. Gusev received him at once, imagining he had come as a penitent, but M. simply wanted to tell him outright that he thought it impermissible of the country's leading newspaper to print 'yellow-press articles'. 'Mandelstam, you are talking of *Pravda*,' Gusev expostulated. 'It's not my fault if the article was published in *Pravda*,' M. replied. I think M.'s other conversation with Gusev must have taken place earlier (when Gusev said everybody except M. – Pavlenko and others, for example – were 'evolving', and made threatening remarks about certain 'innuendos' in M.'s poem 'The Piano'). At any event, the conversation I am describing now was the last, and we never again saw Gusev, or tried to contact him. I do not know whether he survived 1937 – in style he seemed like one of the generation who came up with Stalin, a rambunctious fellow in an embroidered Ukrainian shirt, but among these there were many who had made 'mistakes' in the past, and they paid for them with their lives.

Throughout his exchange with Gusev, M. was calm and restrained. I noticed that he had exactly the same expression as during his argument with Ivanov-Razumnik about terror. On such occasions he was always sparing with words and as firm as a rock. It was quite clear that he was utterly unafraid. The article in *Pravda* had left him largely unmoved. He just, as it were, spat it out and forgot it. The fact is, however, that it was the first really ominous warning. It was a long article, and most of it referred to M. Here are some extracts:

> The Petersburg of cocottes, government officials, priests, decadents, mystics, intellectuals 'seeking God' and a warm place under the wing of the old Russian aristocracy and bourgeoisie, is dead and buried. But leftovers from the Petersburg period of literature, of the old classes and literary movements, are still alive: V. Shklovski, O. Mandelstam, Vaginov, Zabolotski. It makes no difference that some of them have come down directly from the past, while others simply continue its traditions.

> Osip Mandelstam went on a journey to Armenia, and in 1933 he told us about it in the pages of *Zvezda*. One could pick out enough stylistic posies to fill a flowerbed: the 'nasturtium leaf is halberd-shaped'; 'the lighthouse turned its Tate diamond'; a beam of light 'the colour of the cloth on a billiard table'; tea roses resembling 'whorls of ice cream'; books have 'the taste of the flesh of pink pheasants.'

What a poverty-stricken world! A world in which the most brilliant object is the false Tate diamond, where a beam of light looks like the cloth on a billiard table, and tea roses are like ice cream. 'I stretch my sight like a kid glove,' is another of Mandelstam's mannered phrases. One can well understand that a poet with such a tawdry inner world should go to Armenia and live there a month 'revelling in the stillness of water at a height of four thousand feet and growing accustomed to the contemplation of two or three dozen tombs.' The whole of this 'opus' of Mandelstam's is filled with reflections which suffer from intellectual poverty, decked out in a high-flown but none the less anaemic declamatory style.

Here are some of his observations about Armenia as such: 'The Armenians are people with large mouths and eyes drilled directly in their skulls'; 'the language of the Abkhasians . . . breaks forth from a gullet overgrown with hair.' Mandestam's images are redolent of an old, musty great-power chauvinism which, seeming to shower praise on Armenia, actually extols only its exotic side, its slavish past. Not one word does Mandelstam write about the present. In this way one could 'travel' just sitting at home surrounded by old prints, ancient tomes, and Armenian curios . . .

Mandelstam's jibes at Bezymenski one can only pass over in disgust: this is the boundless malice of a man who has no understanding of proletarian literature.

This is a style of speaking, writing, and travelling cultivated before the Revolution by the poets from the dive on Morskaya Street known as 'The Vienna,' the poets of stuffy salons, the heroes of all those literary 'Fridays' and 'Wednesdays.' The old Petersburg Acmeist poet O. Mandelstam failed to see the thriving, bustling Armenia which is joyfully building socialism . . .

An article of some vigour and originality, I must say. Akhmatova was right to comment: 'They have never written any differently about us.' It was picked up in Armenia, where M. was described in print as a *dashnak*.* This meant he would never be able to go back there; but he knew in any case that he was not fated ever to make a return journey. He had already said his farewell to the 'Sabbath land which is called Armenia'. Human nature is indeed peculiar: nowadays M. is read and loved in Armenia, and the fact that some of his work has been published there is no accident . . . In the thirties, however, the *Pravda* article would have been endorsed not only by every jack-in-office with a desk, but also by the general run of our intelligentsia. I would love to know what causes these changes in mentality from one generation to another. How is it that fathers manage to inspire such loathing in their sons (and grandfathers in grandsons) that they reject the opinions, tastes, and ideas of the older generation *in toto*? The case of M. is only a minor example, but it is very typical of this phenomenon. I have witnessed two such abrupt changeovers in my life, and both were as unexpected as they were inexplicable.

Even today there are people of fifty or older who are nostalgic

* Member of anti-Soviet Armenian nationalist movement.

for the sort of article I have quoted above. Their sons go in for every conceivable thing from drunkenness to the reading of religious philosophers, but none of them – apart from some who sit at highly privileged desks – want any truck whatsoever with their fathers and grandfathers. They have, in fact, got quite out of hand. But it is too early to say what fresh misfortunes coming generations will bring on this unhappy country. The sort of gentlemen who read Leontiev and refer to M. as a 'Jewish abscess on the pure body of Tiutchev's poetry' can be expected to write articles about his work which will put even the *Pravda* article in the shade. This could happen in the not too distant future.

XI: POETIC MOMENTUM

It was in those primordial times on the Dnieper, in the days of our Kiev carnival, that, talking about Akhmatova, M. once told me she never published her poems in chronological order but always deliberately jumbled them up, so people should not know whom they were addressed to.

M. himself was against taking such liberties with one's verse. He never did anything of this kind, feeling to a large extent under its power – his poems themselves defined their place in a book, being linked with those that went before and came after by invisible but nonetheless discernible threads. In the case of Akhmatova, however, the interconnection between poems is much weaker, and they can always be switched around, each being an independent whole, rather like an extraordinarily condensed novella confined within rigidly defined limits. It was this 'novelistic' quality of Akhmatova's verse which prompted M. to suggest that its genesis must be sought not in poetry at all, but in Russian psychological prose fiction. Nowadays some clever people have arrived at the brilliant conclusion that Akhmatova is descended directly from Pushkin, but they give us no proof for such statements. It sounds like a compliment to her, but is based, when you get down to it, on the following very uncomplicated logic: I understand Akhmatova and I understand Pushkin; therefore she is descended from Pushkin.

She belongs to the twentieth century, he to the nineteenth; hence she is his heir and successor. If there were a way of subjecting poetry to precise analysis, we should discover that the only link between her and Pushkin is her completely disinterested love and admiration for him. Otherwise they have nothing at all in common: their approach to their subject matter and the way they handle it, their metaphors, images, metres, vocabulary, and attitude to language are utterly different. But in general, is there any poet of whom one can say that he is 'of the Pushkin school', or 'carries on the Pushkin tradition'? It could be said that all Russian poets have a starting point in Pushkin in the sense of having fastened on some particular thread in his poetry, or even just one line, intonation, or other detail among all the vast riches of his work. But it is easier to say a poet derives from Pushkin – or from King Solomon for that matter – than to demonstrate the existence of a specific connection, however modest, with Pushkin or anyone else. Such a connection is something quite different from all the myriad little threads binding a poet to his heritage, without which he would float up beyond the clouds where no one would hear him.

Akhmatova's closeness to the Russian prose tradition made it likely that she would attempt a long narrative poem – once defined as a 'big story poem' by Vadik, the young son of the dressmaker at the theatre in Voronezh with whom we lodged during our last winter there. The boy had run off with a one-volume Pushkin I had brought from Moscow, and we overheard him giving this explanation to a playmate (we lived in cramped but friendly proximity to our hosts and could always hear every word spoken in the next room). M. was struck by the neatness of the definition. He was always more impressed by readers of poetry than by scholars who theorized about it.

Akhmatova had indeed always been attracted by the idea of writing a long poem, but only her first approach to one, the fragment called 'By the Sea', is actually conceived as a 'big story poem'. In her subsequent longer works the typically 'novelistic' vein in her manner disappears, and in both 'Woman of Kitezh' and *Poem Without a Hero* we suddenly hear a markedly lyrical voice. Both these works are essentially lyrical in concept ('Woman of Kitezh', if not strictly speaking a long poem in our definition, lies somewhere between the lyrical and the narrative). Long poetic works of the kind we are speaking about always have a special momentum of their own which carries the reader along – as it has previously carried along the author – in an irresistible poetic surge, snatching him up like a wave, and setting him down again only at the very end, at the final pause. In his 'Conversation About Dante' M. speaks of the uninterrupted, 'form-creating impetus' which is at work in *The Divine Comedy*. In the wake of the author himself, the reader allows himself to be borne along by this impetus, following it through to the end in the manner which M. referred to as a 'sympathetic rendering'. The word 'momentum', one would imagine, is valid for any genuine long poem, which by its nature always possesses a driving force that sweeps one along with it. I first noticed this as a child when I read Lermontov's *Mtsyri* and was carried away by the flow of verse. While feeling the same about other long poetic works, I had no sense of an irresistible flow in reading Pushkin's *Eugene Onegin* – perhaps this is connected with the fact that it is called a 'novel in verse', not a 'poem'. Even from *The Bronze Horseman* – despite the flood described in it! – I do not get the sensation of being at the mercy of a poetic current carrying me where it will.

I believe that this 'momentum' constitutes the basic structural feature of a long work, giving it the quality of an uninterrupted river of verse with whirlpools, rapids, and cross-currents, like any swift-flowing and not unduly shallow mountain stream. But there is no comparison between the 'momentum' of *Mtsyri*, or other long poems of the nineteenth century, and the 'form-creating impetus' M. noted in *The Divine Comedy*, particularly in its second and third parts. In the case of the former it is a question of the reader's being intoxicated and swept along willy-nilly, but in *The Divine Comedy*, the power that carries us with it is a cleansing one. Rather than intoxicate, it illuminates (is this catharsis?).

In talking of poetry one inevitably introduces concepts which cannot be properly defined, but this does not mean they are merely subjective. Something not capable of being explained – or rather, of being *rationally* explained – is still not necessarily subjective, even though some yahoos (like the author of a certain article on Mandelstam) might regard the word 'momentum', and indeed poetry in general, including *The Divine Comedy*, as something suspect to be dismissed by the word 'subjective' (if not by an even stronger term of abuse – our old-fashioned rationalist yahoos, after all, would have nothing to do with *Purgatory* and *Paradise*, agreeing only at a pinch to thumb through the *Inferno*). Our modern yahoo will not say anything against *The Divine Comedy* – overlooking its 'medieval prejudices' for the sake of the first glimmer it offers of the Renaissance outlook – or against Pushkin and Lermontov either (he can understand them!), because he will have been told, during a six months' course on 'culture', that there are writers who have been labelled as 'classics', to whom homage must hence be paid. But it is not so much the yahoos we are concerned with here as the average person who often fails to distinguish the 'subjective' – that is, the expression of the personal peculiarities, tastes, and feelings of the individual – from the 'objective', namely, things that have a real existence outside the mind of the individual, however indefinable they may be. These are two very different categories, and the poetic 'momentum' of which I speak is not 'subjective', even though it manifests itself as a 'subjective' sensation on the part of anyone who falls under the spell of a long poem's prosodic flow. The difference between the 'momentum' experienced in the reading of *Mtsyri*, on the one hand, and of *The Divine Comedy*, on the other, is also completely 'objective' – though anybody who has read the second in some painstaking but plodding translation might well find it hard to believe. The reader is affected by the poem's 'momentum', albeit to a lesser extent, in the same way as the author – provided, of course, that he is susceptible in the first place. Many people are immune, being as insensitive to poetry as others are to music. It is regarded as quite legitimate not to appreciate music – one is allowed not to understand it, or not to like 'serious' music, or to have 'no ear' for it (the commonest excuse). But there is no such indulgence for poetry. Poetry is always suspect because everybody believes he is bound to understand anything expressed in *words*. There is only one country in the world where music too has come under suspicion and been subject to violent denunciation. Only here was it possible for 'Nonsense Instead of Music' to appear in print, and for a certain person to explain the composers' mistakes to them by picking out tunes on the piano. It is said that Shostakovich has been carrying this article around with him in his pocket ever since.*

Akhmatova complains about the way in which *Poem Without a Hero* totally swallowed her up from the very beginning and never let go of her. She threw herself into her housework – scouring saucepans, washing clothes, sweeping, cleaning up, and all the other things she normally neglected – in a desperate attempt to gain some respite and struggle free of this current carrying her off into the unknown. She remained in the grip of the poem for a number of years.

Akhmatova had always been interested in the idea of the long poem as a form in its own right, and often spoke about it – but never with M. She was afraid to with him, except on one occasion when there was some conversation about *Spektorski*† – we thought we detected in it a certain resemblance to the long 'story-poems' of Sluchevski and Polonski. 'Sure enough . . . ', said M., when we mentioned this. Later, alone with me, Akhmatova remarked that *Eugene Onegin* had held up the development – this word came easily to her lips, and she had no objection to it in principle – of the long poem because everybody who had subsequently tried his hand at it could not help imitating the ready-made model before his eyes. 'A great poet,' she observed, 'holds up the flow of poetry like a dam.' The first to break free of the influence of *Eugene Onegin* had been Nekrasov in *Who Lives Well in Russia?* Of Mayakovski she said that he would always have his place in Russian poetry because he had created a new form of long poem. She read Keats and Browning, not making very much of the second (this was later, when she had already written the first draft of *Poem Without a Hero*), but finding him very disturbing nevertheless. All she could think of to say was something about the dramatic character of Browning's talent. She quoted the obvious example of this: several people describe the same event (the murder of a woman who has run away from a cruel husband), each account resembling some soliloquy from a tragedy that might have been written. Akhmatova has another special reason for being interested in Browning: Gumilev had once said to her that he and she would be just like

---

* See Shostakovich, Appendix A.

† By Pasternak.

the Brownings in the sense that all the glory would go to the wife while they were still alive, but the husband would suddenly become famous after his death, and the wife's stature would dwindle almost to nothing. Why were they all so eager for fame? Surely nothing was ever less worth thinking about.

M. never said anything about the specific features of the long poem as a form in itself. He remembered a few bits and pieces from *Who Lives Well in Russia?* and occasionally referred to *The Bronze Horseman.* At the very beginning our Soviet era might well have seemed somewhat analogous to the age of Peter the Great, but after only a short lapse of time the dissimilarity became all too obvious: each of these ages had a totally different starting point and led to quite different results. I do not believe our age will go down in Russian history as anything remotely like the 'Petersburg period'. Though who knows how things will look a few hundred years hence? There may even be connoisseurs of ancient literature with a fancy for books written by the method of 'socialist realism' . . . The only thing is: Will there be any future centuries of human history, or people capable of reading?

The best definition of 'socialist realism' I have ever heard was given me by a brash young photographer in 1938. I was expecting to be arrested at any moment, and I wanted to leave behind a photograph of myself, as a memento for my family and friends. The photographer kept telling me to raise my head, lower it, or lean it over to one side. I got tired of this and at last said rather crossly: 'Don't try to be too clever – just take me as I am.' 'You must be against socialist realism,' the photographer replied. I asked what he meant: 'Socialist realism,' he explained, 'is when something looks a little better than it really is . . .' This is absolutely true except for the adverb of quality – not 'a little' but 'a lot'. Actually, I never read the products of 'socialist realism' – there is certainly no 'momentum' here, nor are they a source of illumination. They smell of privileged rations and writers' dachas.

Personally, I am indifferent to the whole question of literary forms, and am sure of only one thing: real lyric poetry never clouds the mind. Exposure to it, however tragic, illuminates and purifies the mind – which, in other words, goes through something akin to catharsis (another concept not easily defined, but nonetheless real for that). In the long poem, on the other hand, there always lurks something obscure and dangerous born not of the depth and integrity of the poetic impulse, but of 'momentum' for its own sake, the outward brilliance and fluency of the rhythm, the temptation to cast spells and engage in sorcery of a kind that beckons alluringly without, however, bringing emotional release or purification. Lidia Ginzburg told Akhmatova that in the *Poem Without a Hero* she was using 'forbidden techniques', though who had forbidden them was not clear. The words Akhmatova once spoke about herself apply to *Poem* as well: 'I am as I am, and wish you another.' I am far from believing that everything that exists is rational (particularly since existence can be real or false), but the *Poem* has to be seen for what it is, as it has taken shape in actual fact, with its sweeping flow, its faint aura of individualism, its occasional quirkishness, and the unfailing air of mystery that lies over it like a slight haze. Its momentum carries you with it, like a river, from source to mouth – yet, looking back over the way he has travelled, the reader may well feel that because of the speed with which he has been swept along, he never got a proper view of the banks of the river itself. A long poem is in some ways similar to time passing so swiftly that in retrospect everything appears to run together in a blur. (M. must have experienced this, since he talks about how *The Divine Comedy* 'accelerates time'.) The only thing I remember of many long poems is the 'story' and a few odd lines here and there. But Akhmatova took a quite different view of the form – a view I found as hard to share as her cult of 'beauties'. She called her *Poem* a 'century-old enchantress', decking it out with all kinds of feminine paraphernalia, such as 'a shoulder painted by Briullov', 'a lace handkerchief': 'And the century-old enchantress / Suddenly comes to life, deciding / To amuse herself. (This is out of my control) / She drops her lace handkerchief, / peeps out languorously from behind my lines / And summons with a shoulder painted by Briullov' . . . Akhmatova herself refers to the 'magic power' of her *Poem* and evidently regarded it as something spawned by Romanticism. Is this the reason for its surface glamour and allurement?

In a review of Huysmans, M. once wrote that the Romantics did not know life, while the Decadents – such as Huysmans – did.

Insofar as it is derived from Romanticism, the long poem skims over the surface of life and thus possesses no quality that might be called life-affirming – something ever present in lyric poetry, whose main theme is always the growth of the poet's personality. In the process of attaining self-awareness, the personality discovers itself and its place in life. For a Romantic, death is an undeserved outrage against his person. But for someone who has found his place in life – a life replete with meaning – death is simply his last creative act. I believe that the cleansing power of lyric verse flows from the poet's acceptance of life with its sorrows and misfortunes, from his certainty that through ordinary everyday existence one achieves awareness of another life, thus coming to know the Creator through what He has created. For me, therefore, lyrical poetry is the greater form, compared with narrative or epic verse, which is greater only in the quantitative sense: a long poem has many more lines.

XII: THE ROUGH DRAFT

Poem Without a Hero is comparable with *Noise of Time*. Both owed their appearance to a mental impulse of the same kind. Both are concerned with the remembrance of things past – seen as providing a key to the present. In Akhmatova's case it was also a last, backward glance at the 'red towers' of her 'native Sodom' * – a temptation very hard to resist, even knowing the price one pays for not doing so. M. claimed he had employed memory in an attempt not to 'summon up the past, but to exorcize it'. To a certain extent Akhmatova could say the same of herself, but in banishing the past, one tends to see it with unbearable clarity and sharpness of outline. *Noise of Time* is a story about a past which no longer exists. But as this past comes to life again in memory, it is so full of concrete detail, so sharp in its glimpses of people and things symbolic of the age, that it almost hurts: the concert-going craze, the 'crammer', the Jewish apartment with its smell of leather and armchair with the motto 'More haste less speed', the parades on the

* From Akhmatova's poem 'Lot's Wife' (1924).

Field of Mars, and the members of the Sinani household – all good Socialist Revolutionaries . . . In *Noise of Time* M. sought an answer to questions which tormented him, in particular to the most important one: Why was he so alienated from the present? The book came between the two poems 'The Age' and 'January 1, 1924', and was written for the most part in 1923 during our stay in Gaspra, when our isolation was still only self-imposed. The theme of the prose work, though it lurks out of view just under the surface, is the same as in the two poems. M.'s phrase about his memory being hostile to everything personal explains the veiled, heavily disguised character of the book's main theme.

When you recall the past with affection, it may look quite idyllic, but M. had no time for idylls of any kind. Nor was he prone to the irony which so often serves to mask the idyllic approach. His hard and sober look at the past creates the illusion that he is writing quite dispassionately, but in actual fact *Noise of Time* is a deeply personal work, much as M. manages to conceal his own involvement in all the things he touches on.

M. was moulded by the dual world of the Jewish family apartment he grew up in, and St Petersburg, the doomed city he describes as 'familiar to the point of tears'. In the Tenishev school he had his first literary encounter and his initiation into poetry. Here too he was first exposed to the revolutionary ferment of the times, and began to prepare himself for the future. The main things in his childhood were his mother, music, and the architecture of the city. The wealth of early impressions was offset by the domestic chaos in which he grew up. Unlike Akhmatova, he was not afraid to describe this. Akhmatova never said much about her childhood years. There was nothing in the least idyllic about them – indeed, they were every bit as unsettled as M.'s – and she simply ignored them, as though they had never been. Once, in Tashkent, we talked about the insecurity of her early life, and I said: so you had the same feeling of belonging to the rootless intelligentsia as M.? She was terribly offended by the suggestion. Nothing would have induced her to admit that she was a *raznochinets*;* she liked to

*The term used, particularly in the 1860s, for Russian intellectuals who were not of noble origin and constituted the archetypal intelligentsia with its rootlessness and social heterogeneity.

think of herself as coming from a somewhat more exalted background in which social insecurity was cloaked in outward respectability. She apparently thought of her life as having begun only with her return to Tsarskoye Selo as Gumilev's wife, or rather, perhaps, with her separation from him. She tended to gloss over separations and all such untidy events in her past, while M. preferred to rise above them by bringing them out into the open. (I sometimes think that Akhmatova maintained her relations with Punin's daughter only because of this need to smooth over the past – in this case by a touching show of attachment to a stepdaughter as if she were her own flesh and blood. The result was quite monstrous, as was already painfully obvious while Akhmatova was still alive; indeed we often talked about it.)

Noise of Time is a backward glance at something that has vanished forever, with M. retracing his steps as a child on the streets or at concerts, in a life destined to fall apart. He sums up the events which overtook it in the short chapter on the dream of Colonel Tsygalski, who, his jet-black eyes 'glowing with feminine tenderness', is contrasted with his Cossack subalterns 'smelling of dog and wolf', a breed 'with child-like, dangerously vacant eyes', on whom the opportunity of killing with impunity offered by the Civil War had the bracing effect of a 'fresh Narzan* bath'. It is significant that in the Colonel's somnambulist vision of a new landscape what he calls 'the Regalia of the Law' are engulfed by the deep, together with the whole of Russia – the waters of the Black Sea rush into the void thus formed, surging right up as far as the Neva.

This Colonel Tsygalski is the same who saved M. from one of Wrangel's jails, where they could hang a man as soon as look at him. The savagery always unleashed by a civil war leaves its mark on people for many generations afterwards.

In *Noise of Time* M. also deals with literature's recent Symbolist past, which reminded him of Pushkin's *Banquet During the Plague*.† During the Symbolist interlude, literature had become conscious

---

* Mineral water from the Caucasian spa of Kislovodsk.

† One of Pushkin's 'little tragedies', an adaptation of a scene from John Wilson's *City of the Plague*. Pushkin supplies a toastmaster not in the original. Mandelstam paraphrased it in *Noise of Time* to describe the atmosphere of the Russian 'Silver Age', before the Revolution.

of its noble rank and was inclined to be very lordly: 'At the broad table Walsingham sat with his guests, and the call went around – uttered, as it always seemed, for the last time, a doleful entreaty at the final banquet: "Sing us a song, Mary"' . . . From the beginning of the thirties, or rather, right from the first days of the Revolution, with a brief interval in the second half of the twenties up to collectivization, we were always convinced that anything we did was for the last time and would never be repeated. Every trip we made to the south was felt to be the last, as was every makeshift feast, every new dress, and every embrace. This sensation was particularly strong with regard to the verse that M. wrote in those years. An artist is always haunted by the feeling that each new work he produces is destined to be his last, never to be followed by anything else, and it was made ten times worse by our awareness of permanently standing on the edge of an abyss, our constant expectation of a sudden end. At the beginning of the thirties, M. once woke me late at night and told me that every poem was now written as though death were coming tomorrow. Later on he sometimes reminded me of his words that night about what it meant to write poems in those days . . . Did we both find such contentment in our life together precisely because it was always on the verge of being cut short by death? The death of the individual only foreshadows the general end of everything: 'As the end of History approaches, the domes of the Holy Church are touched by the new, rose-tinted, hitherto almost invisible rays of the coming Day that shall never grow dark.' These words I once read in a splendid book about the man who spoke them – he perished in the early days after the Revolution. In the same book I discovered the text of a prayer to be said by two people together, which, alas, we did not know when M. was still alive:

Lord my God, Jesus Christ. With thy most pure lips Thou didst say: 'If two of you shall agree on earth as touching anything that they shall ask, it shall be done for them of my Father which is in heaven. For where two or three are gathered together in my name, there am I in the midst of them.' Thy words, O Lord, cannot be gainsaid, Thy mercy is without equal, and Thy love of man without end. We beseech Thee, O Lord, grant to us, Osip and Nadazhda, who have agreed to ask Thee for our meeting. Yet not as we wish it, but as Thou wishest it, O Lord. Let Thy will be in everything. Amen.

This is now my prayer, because I am not alone, but together with M. It is true, as he wrote to me: 'No one shall take your loved one from you.'

In 1924, when M. wrote: 'A little more and they'll cut short / my simple song of earthen hurts / and seal my lips with lead', he still thought he had some time to live – 'a little more', not very much perhaps, but all the same a breathing space, a brief span in which to go on voicing his grievances and sorrows for a while. Death was not yet upon him. He still had fifteen years in which to complete his work, though about two of them would be spent in dying. But from the beginning of the thirties he began to feel pressed for time, as though the end might come any moment – that very night, or first thing in the morning. Even now, as I write these lines, I always feel a little queasy or feverish as night comes on, though not in expectation of death – it is no longer far away and will come unsummoned when the time is ready – but for fear that young men 'smelling of dog and wolf' might ring the doorbell and take away all these pages I have written, and with them my memory; or even worse: all the books with M.'s poetry, the three volumes for which I waited so many years. This gives me an even keener sense than before of what M. went through: how unthinkable it was for him to disengage from the poetry that came to him in cycles, one after another, when all the time he knew that a violent death was approaching, that it was already standing at the threshold like the three visitors – there are always three – with their smell of wolves. Even at the time I understood and shared this feeling, but now it has returned with renewed force and again clutches me by the throat.

This sense of a last 'banquet during the plague' never deserted M. until the very end of his days. In reading his verse and prose one can always see the thread from Pushkin's 'little tragedy' running through everything. He loved the image of the toastmaster with his hoarse voice, occasionally feeling identified with him. But in the line: 'This is the toastmaster of the plague lost with his horses', he is referring not to himself or to Walsingham, but to the celebrated *tamada** who spoke for the whole of the Soviet Union, hiding his

* Georgian word for toastmaster – a standard figure at social gatherings in Stalin's homeland.

'terrible features' behind a 'leather mask'. In 1937–8 we sometimes visited the now-luxurious apartment buildings for writers,
where many a banquet, cheerless and obscene, took place before
the hosts were plucked, one after another, from the bosoms of their
families. M. and I also banqueted – just as we had in the past – but
with us it was not obscene, even though the plague raged all
around. And the host at our feast also disappeared – having been
snatched, however, not from his apartment, but from the cage into
which he had been lured* by the Union of Writers, the last and
meanest of its 'rest homes'. Nobody escaped the common fate.
Colonel Tsygalski was right about the 'Regalia of the Law' being
swallowed up by the deep. What are 'regalia'? Something just as
indefinable as Law.

XIII: *POEM WITHOUT A HERO* AND MY GRIEVANCE

The date under the 'First Dedication' of *Poem Without a Hero* is
27 December.† This is the date of M.'s death – at least according
to the 'official' information, which is all we have. Official information cannot be trusted, but in the absence of any other we are bound
to accept this date. At first Akhmatova put a different one: 28
December. This is what someone had told her, and she accepted it
without question. She did not believe what I told her because she
was convinced that – unlike herself – I always got things wrong. I
had to bring her the slip of paper issued by the Register Office, and
even then she put up a little show of resistance ('But perhaps they
have another piece of paper with a different date – how can you be

---

* Samatikha, where Mandelstam was arrested in 1938.

† 'First Dedication' is 'To the Memory of Vs. K.' The initials are those
of Vsevolod Kniazev, a young poet and Guards officer ('cornet of Dragoons')
whose suicide in 1913 is a central theme of the *Poem*. Apart from the date at
the bottom, there are other indications of a deliberate blurring of Kniazev's
image with that of Mandelstam, evidently on the grounds that both, though
in different ways, were sacrificial victims of the age.

sure?'). In the upshot, however, she capitulated and changed the date. In the same way she used to say that M. had never travelled anywhere, had never set foot in Italy, or taken any examination – just as she believed that I was quite ignorant of foreign languages, knowing neither Latin nor English, and had never read a book in my life . . . Worse still, she insisted that the sanatorium in Samatikha had been a special one for nervous complaints, not an ordinary rest home with the usual kind of non-specialist doctor in charge. It was absolutely impossible to persuade her of the contrary. She was as prone to error as the rest of us, but her 'incomparable rightness' made it hard for her ever to admit the fact. I regard it as a great triumph, therefore, to have got her to change the date of her 'First Dedication', but I should mention here, by way of a caution, that there are some copies in circulation with the date 'December 28'. She complained that nobody paid any attention to the date at the foot of the 'First Dedication' and for this reason she had transferred it to the top and thereby given it the greatest possible prominence. A few copies with this change are also liable to turn up.

The 'First Dedication' has a mention of eyelashes.* M.'s eyelashes were extraordinarily long. In Kiev, during those first days after our meeting, a certain (rather nice) operetta star, having gazed at M. for a time, said: 'He doesn't look a bit like a poet – except for the eyelashes.' Her husband was also a poet who composed turns in verse for the variety stage, and she thought him a much better one of course, but she was nevertheless very envious of M.'s eyelashes. M. himself was rather put out by them and often referred to them in his verse. I used to tease him by saying that he must belong to the *Ciliata*, which was why they cropped up so much (for example, in the line: 'the patter of flickering eyelashes'). Akhmatova once came into possession of some poems by Olga Vaksel (M. never knew that she had written any) and took a particular fancy to one which mentioned 'eyelashes': 'This is to Osia, of course,' she commented. I expressed my astonishment: 'Was Osia the only person to have eyelashes? And then, the year is wrong . . .' Olga's poem about eyelashes had been written after her

* 'The dark eyelashes of Antinous . . .'

visit to us at Tsarskoye. We had then immediately left on our trip
to the south and never again returned either to Tsarskoye or to
Leningrad. Akhmatova dismissed the question of the date as
unimportant: love poems, she pointed out, often appear many
years after the end of an affair. As to M.'s eyelashes: 'Where have
you ever seen their like?' she demanded. I must admit that I have
seen similar specimens only among the children of the Caucasus;
they lose them when they grow up. But to come back to the 'First
Dedication', whose are the eyelashes mentioned here?

After hearing Akhmatova recite her *Poem* for the first time in
Tashkent, I asked to whom the 'First Dedication' was addressed.
'Whose first draft do you think I can write on?' she replied with
some irritation.* Vilenkin and a few others were actually told by
her in so many words that the 'Dedication' was to M. (Vilenkin
wrote me a letter to this effect which I have among my papers).
The 'Dedication' mentions a snowflake melting on the hand, and
at first I thought this might be an allusion to some lines by her or M.
'Osia would know . . . ,' she assured me. This conversation we had
almost in the sixties, already at a time when she was making extraordinary efforts to keep her 'treasured notes' from me. As if this
were not enough, the voice of M. himself and his own authentic
words are heard for one brief moment in the *Poem*: 'I am ready
for death.'† Akhmatova quotes these words in her *Pages from a
Diary*. (There was, by the way, no diary as such, nothing but these
'pages'. Catch us keeping diaries!)

I have two copies of the *Poem*. In one of them Kniazev's initials
stand just above the 'First Dedication', but have been crossed out
by Akhmatova – she did this in my presence, saying it was a typing
error. The other copy does not have his initials at all. The *Poem* has
appeared in print with Kniazev's name on it. Whose 'first draft',

---

*The 'First Dedication' begins: '. . . and since I have run out of paper / I
am writing on your first draft'.

†The phrase is spoken by Kniazev, just before he shoots himself, in Part I
of the *Poem*. In her *Pages from a Diary*, Akhmatova wrote: 'We were
walking along the Prechistenka [February 1934], talking about what I do
not remember. We turned into Gogol Boulevard and Osip said: "I am ready
for death." It is now 28 years ago, but I still remember this phrase every time
I pass the spot.'

then, was she writing on, and whose 'eyelashes' is she referring to?
If the *Poem Without a Hero* is supposed to be about two people,
one of whom took his own life before the beginning of our new
era, while the other accepted his lot unflinchingly, then the meaning
of the work takes on a somewhat wider sense. His inner freedom
led M. to meet death 'herded with the herd', but the 'cornet of
Dragoons with his verse / and a meaningless death in his breast'
evaded his fate by committing the greatest act of licence: suicide.

> (So many ways of dying lay in store
> Yet he chose this one, silly boy;
> unable to bear life's hurts,
> he did not know on what threshold
> he stood or what road would open up ahead . . .)*

In view of such an attitude to Kniazev's death, it is scarcely surprising that Akhmatova alludes later to the suicide of Kirillov, that
supreme exponent of licence, in *The Possessed*: 'Again someone
stands between stove and cupboard.'†

In *Poem Without a Hero* Akhmatova is throughout evasive and
equivocal – quite the opposite of her usual manner, whose strength
lay in forthrightness, the head-on attack. In her article about *The
Stone Guest*‡ she attempts to justify herself by suggesting that any
facts about a writer's life that may be buried in his work always
undergo a peculiar kind of 'processing' – thus, Pushkin put something of himself in both Don Juan and the Commander. Both
heroes are, as it were, embodiments of the author. In a narrative
poem of a nineteenth-century type this procedure was perfectly
justified, but *Poem Without a Hero* is an extended *lyrical* statement, a dirge for times past, for a bygone age which concealed
within itself the seeds of a terrible future. In such a work, any
attempt at a 'literary' treatment of the theme results not in
'externalization', but in evasiveness of a deceptive kind. A 'casket
with a triple bottom'§ makes sense only if one can really hide

---

Poem Without a Hero, Part I, lines 440–45.

†*Poem Without a Hero*, Part I, lines 169–70. (For the description of
Kirillov's suicide see *The Possessed*, Part III, Chapter 6.)

‡Another of Pushkin's 'little tragedies'.

§*Poem Without a Hero*, Part II, line 96.

something in it – but, alas, during a house search, or after your death, false compartments are broken open in a trice, and then what do you find in them?

In the end, Akhmatova evidently decided to 'blend' Kniazev and M., after passing them through a literary meat grinder. This is how she came to write her *Poem* on Kniazev's 'first draft', even though the 'cornet of Dragoons' may well not have had any first drafts to speak of. You have to earn the right to such esteem for your first drafts. Time will show whether M. has done so – in 1919 he still doubted it, and later he never raised the subject again.

It would be even sadder if Akhmatova's intention was to make Kniazev and M. into 'doubles', two aspects of the same person, one of whom departed the scene early, while the other stayed to the end. The two simply cannot be combined like this: the right to say 'I am ready for death' also has to be earned. My grievance, therefore, is that, for the sake of a literary game, Akhmatova misappropriated both M.'s words and the date of his death.

This preoccupation with 'doubles', however, was not a mere literary game with Akhmatova; it was something rooted in her psychology, a result of her attitude to people – in whom, as in mirrors, she always sought her own reflection. She looked at people as one might look into a mirror, hoping to find her own likeness and seeing her 'double' in everybody. She described Olga Sudeikina as 'one of my doubles' and Marina Tsvetayeva as a 'mocking double, out of sight'; and she once dedicated a book to me with the words: 'To my second self.' But how many 'second selves' can a person have, and how can they be so unlike each other? When she first got to know Petrovykh, Akhmatova asked M. and me whether we recognized her in this new acquaintance. In her old age she suddenly 'recognized' herself in Ania Kaminskaya, Irina Punin's daughter, and even got her to grow a fringe like her own. Ania looked to me quite ridiculous with her hair done in this way, and when I said so, Akhmatova was absolutely furious with me. In her final years Akhmatova also began to see 'doubles' in the men she knew – not of herself, of course, but of each other. All of them, dead or alive, had one thing in common: namely, that they were, or had been, in love with her and had written poems to her. In her middle years there was nothing of this in Akhmatova, and it was only a feature of old age – though I suspect, from what M. told me, that she may have been the same in the early, still-unclouded days of her youth. The self-centredness typical of both youth and old age finds an outlet in this game of 'doubles'. In fairness to Akhmatova, however, I must say that, apart from the element of self-centredness, it was due as well to another quality which she displayed in high degree: a capacity to become so passionately involved in others that she had the need to tie them to herself as closely as possible, to merge herself in them. This was particularly so in the case of those many women on whom she conferred the status of 'beauties'.

This cult of the beautiful woman, of the reigning belle, was something peculiar to the pre-revolutionary years and had started in Petersburg rather than Moscow. When I was a young woman, these belles were past forty already. They had been through the hungry years and lost a good deal of their lustre by then. M. used to point them out to me, and I could only gasp with astonishment: Why all the fuss? My generation was more notable for the concept of the woman as girl friend and companion. Even the most good-looking of these – such as Liuba Ehrenburg and Susanna Mar – had no pretensions to playing the role of belles. In *The Egyptian Stamp* M. inveighed against this absurd cult: 'What wretched Trianons they have set up . . . some slut, harridan, or bedraggled strumpet' . . . In fairness to them, it must be said that they scrubbed floors, did the washing, and stood in queues as well as anybody else when the new era dawned. Akhmatova remained true to the cult of the beauties she had been friendly with, praising them to the skies, but she was merciless in her denunciation of those who belonged to other clans. I loved to hear Akhmatova when she let herself go and spoke in her most earthy manner about the 'beautiful ladies' of the Symbolists. The raciness of her verbal portraits was breathtaking. Such power of language sometimes broke through in her poetry, but not as often as it should have.

Akhmatova had ambivalent feelings about the pre-revolutionary years. On the one hand, 'to a wild flowering there remained but the space of a sigh', but on the other, there was the carnival, the breaking loose from all bonds, the bacchanalia of mummers and masqueraders revelling in their sheer irresponsibility: 'And he is guilty of nothing. / Neither of this, that or the other. / In general sin is not for poets.'* In her *Poem*, Akhmatova treats the pre-revolutionary years as a threshold, the gateway to a future in which retribution would be exacted from all. Like many of her contemporaries she heard the 'boom' of future events: 'And always in the frostbound stifled years, / debauched and ominous, of pre-war times / a mysterious boom lurked in the air.' She could clearly see the connection between the two eras: 'As the future ripens in the past, so the past rots in the future – a terrible festival of dead leaves.'† This is her answer to those who still look back on the pre-revolutionary years as a blissful 'Silver Age', and regard everything that came after as an unfortunate accident, a dislocation caused by the age's stumbling. This theory of a 'dislocation' ('The time is out of joint') is wishful thinking based on the comforting knowledge that a bone which has been merely dislocated can be set. The émigrés clung to the 'dislocation' theory for half a century and waited hopefully with their bags packed ready to return. Akhmatova had no illusions of this kind and showed what the real upshot had been: the barbed wire of concentration camps and the Second World War (and, I would add, let's hope not a third – but in the complacency of old age she did not think of this). The carnival revelry I witnessed in Kiev was just a last flicker from the pre-war years – as were a few other things in the twenties. Even now there are feather-brained old men who still crow about those great days, which had their roots in the pre-revolutionary era.

The 'wild flowering' and the carnival of vacant masks – harbingers of death and decomposition – are perhaps not as incompatible as might seem at first sight. Trees, after all, may blossom before they are cut down, and in the same way, a human society, with its power to express its collective thoughts and feelings, may explode during its time of anguished forebodings in a luxuriant, though false, flowering. The whole of our society and every member of it inherited from the pre-revolutionary years a little touch of licence, a tiny canker which stained his personal life and his public behaviour. I detected it in myself, in Akhmatova, and

---

* *Poem Without a Hero*, Part I, lines 122–5. The implication is that guilt and a sense of sin were disclaimed.

† *Poem Without a Hero*, Part I, lines 79–81.

even in M. – he possessed an antidote, but he was by no means always able to use it in time. The legacy of the pre-revolutionary years was self-indulgence, a loss of criteria, and an incessant craving for happiness. I do not believe any preceding age has been marked by such a passion for self-advancement as ours. This is the disease of the times, still as rampant as ever today.

The question arises: Was Akhmatova right to put all the onus on the elite? The 'goat-legged bacchante',* the 'cornet of Dragoons', the crowd of false teachers of whom she says: 'Hammurabi, Lycurgus, Solon, should learn from you'† – all this was just the thin upper crust, one might think, which had no real influence on the course of events. The chief misfortune, it seems to me, was the fact that this thin upper crust *thought* of itself as an elite. It was in the nature of the times that whenever a few people gathered together, they constituted themselves into an elite – the ambitious clique at the top which in any group always arises, by a process of self-assertion, as the 'chosen vessel'. Such elites were everywhere, and were able to arrogate power to themselves because true authority had been trampled underfoot, shattered, or destroyed. Art, like every other field, was in a constant state of noisy upheaval, with new authorities springing up all the time. Some lasted five minutes, some an hour, and some for fifty years, but none have left anything but dust behind. In the pre-revolutionary years a few healthy seedlings began to sprout as well, but they passed almost unnoticed in the uproarious free-for-all of the various contending groups, schools, individual demagogues and seducers, each shrieking forth his own claims and promising to lead people heaven alone knew where. In the Moscow of the twenties we saw the fragments of the old intellectual elite eagerly vying to put themselves at the service of the victors, while different groups within the victorious elite settled accounts with each other.

In the face of the Revolutionary *fait accompli*, the people who had made their mark in the previous decade or so began to wonder how it had come about. The poets, each after his own fashion, tried to figure out what the role of poetry and poets had been. By now they knew that the poet was no theurgist, prophet, or bearer of a

* See Glebova-Sudeikina, Appendix A.
† *Poem Without a Hero*, Part I, lines 114–15.

new revelation. Marina Tsvetayeva decided 'in the light of conscience' that the poet is less useful to his fellow men than a doctor
or member of any other profession. Economists judge a man by the
amount of his output, moralists by the number of commandments
he has broken. Tsvetayeva was also applying utilitarian standards –
a basically incorrect approach. M. said in 1922 that Acmeism had
introduced an ethical principle into poetry and that 'man must be
harder than anything'. It is not for me to judge whether or not this
hope was justified, but that was how M. understood the role of
poetry. In some notes he made towards the end of his life he also
has this to say about his attitude to people and their work: 'Attention to detail is the virtue of the lyric poet. Carelessness and
sloppiness are the devices of lyrical sloth.' And finally, in a note
hastily jotted down during the period when he was working on
'Journey to Armenia', he expressed his doubts as to the utility
of art: 'By his nature, the artist is a doctor, a healer. But if he heals
no one, then who needs him and what is he good for?'

Art has done more than enough to confuse, befuddle, and mes-
merize people – not only in our days. Perhaps one of the first
questions to ask about any work of art is the extent to which
it has a real power to heal, rather than merely to cast a spell. I am
convinced that true poetry has a healing power, derived from the
sense an artist has of his own inner 'rightness' and freedom. A
poet, painter, composer, or any other kind of artist cannot belong
to an elite because he knows that men are created equal. He is therefore a deeply social being, not setting himself against the crowd –
though he refuses to accept the 'orders' of the society he lives in.
He cannot be an instrument of evil because an ordinary person,
anyone who is just part of the crowd, embarks on evil only under
the influence of some seducer or spellbinder, and the place of the
true artist is with the crowd, right in its midst, sharing its sins, joys
and sorrows. The failings of the artist – and he is bound to have
some – are the failings of the crowd, but a true artist can scarcely
be capable of taking part in the crimes so often committed by his
fellowmen. If the artist has his own guiding light, however faintly
it flickers, he will turn away in despair from a crowd which others
are inciting to iniquity.

The only things utterly unbecoming to a poet are power and the role of preacher. How can he preach to people, unless he regards himself as part of an elite, as a lawgiver and leader? In the first article he ever wrote – it was a polemic against Viacheslav Ivanov, or rather an attempt to define his own differences with the Symbolists – M. spoke of the falsity of setting oneself up as a teacher. He ascribed Pushkin's quarrel with the mob to his fear of the listener close at hand who could always fasten on him with a cry of: 'Let's hear what you have to say.' He showed that Pushkin was quite fair to the mob, not picturing it as violent and unruly, but that he was concerned less with the mob as such – even an enlightened and reasonable one – than with his belief that a poet may not be a teacher and a fisher of men. For this reason Pushkin was free of any temptation to write 'to order' – which implies accepting the role of teacher to the mob, particularly when it is not entirely uncivilized and hence prepared to listen. The poet frees himself of this temptation by addressing himself not to the listener at hand, but to the listener far away, whom he cannot seduce, lecture, or even merely entertain. This listener, removed in time and space, will remember the poet only if he wants to, or rather, if he feels the need, but the poet cannot solicit his attention, either by his poetry or by preaching to him.

Akhmatova shared M.'s views on the ethical nature of poetry. This is perhaps why, in her notes on Pushkin, she tried to bring out the ethical problems confronting him, and even naïvely described him as a 'moralist'. A poet cannot, of course, be any such thing ('moralists' are always so eager to preach!), since he is far too conscious of his own sinfulness – as witness Pushkin's marvellous poems of repentance – and though Akhmatova uses the wrong word, this is what actually emerges from her study. In *Poem Without a Hero* she talks about sin in those years when the awareness of it had been lost by everybody, particularly by those who regarded themselves as the elite. It took courage to look back on her youth and judge it by the standards of the 'valley of Jehoshaphat',* when everybody else is so lenient on the pre-revolutionary years and the twenties. Akhmatova could find it in herself to say to the 'goat-legged bacchante': 'I blame not you, but

* Prophesied as the site of the Day of Judgement (referred to in *Poem Without a Hero*, Part I, line 73).

myself.' This indeed is the hidden theme of the *Poem*, which she tried to conceal in the 'casket with a triple bottom'. ('And what if it suddenly breaks loose, this theme / And bangs on the window with its fist?') Overlaid by a frenetic rhythm, the *Poem* tells of retribution for a heedless youth spent among people who reckoned themselves part of the elite, and speaks volumes on the 'Silver Age'. This is the strength of *Poem Without a Hero*.

The cult of 'beauties', the evasiveness, the triple bottom, the 'mirror writing', even the musical allusions and many of the adornments are borrowed from the legacy of the Symbolists. This is the weakness of the *Poem*. In the parts where the 'century-old enchantress' coyly displays her 'Briullov shoulder', Akhmatova ceases to be true to herself, to her poetry of renunciation, to the pitiless austerity and terseness of the best of her mature writing. Zhirmunski even told Akhmatova that the *Poem* was a work such as the Symbolists would have loved to write, if they had been able to – and for some reason she was tremendously pleased by this remark. Renouncing, as she did, the false flowering of the pre-revolutionary years she should not have allowed herself to be dazzled by its illusory riches.

Akhmatova was haunted by anxiety about the *Poem* to the end of her days. She believed it was justified only if it was better than anything else she had ever written. Quite apart from my personal grievance (occasioned by the initials added above the 'First Dedication'), I believe that the *Poem* in many ways reflects the delusions and licence of the pre-revolutionary era, the borrowed rhythms and ideas which opened the way for the astral flights of Akhmatova's later years.

The 'Visitor from the Future' in the *Poem* is not the mysterious being pictured in the imagination of those who fancy themselves able to unlock the secrets of the 'casket with a triple bottom'. It is a compound image of which the first element is an abstract 'reader of the future', and the second a real person whose visit to the 'House on the Fontanka' was one of the reasons for the Decree against Akhmatova and Zoshchenko. He did indeed pre-figure the 'future reader'; in that accursed year there was nobody in this country who had yet learned to read.

Can one say that now, in 1970, we have more people who have

learned to read? I doubt it. I do not know, see, or hear them. I fear the things brewing in people's minds at present may be quite grisly, even more horrible than anything during the era of barbed wire and the mass extermination of people 'herded with the herd'. When such processes are taking place in the minds of their fellow citizens, only a few individuals, sad and lonely souls, try to learn to read, seeking salvation as the world around them crumbles. There may be a few like that even nowadays. How many? There is no way of telling: people are too isolated from one another.

32   First Meeting

I am now going to tell the story of another disagreement I had with Akhmatova, this time about something completely trivial, of no importance whatsoever. In her old age she was impervious to argument and would simply take refuge in her own authority, brooking no challenge to it: 'What are you trying to tell me? I *know*.' The slightest attempt to contradict provoked a storm of furious indignation. 'Annush, you're like an angry cat,' I used to say to her, whereupon she would erupt in resounding fury, and there was nothing to do but give in. She once confided to me in Tashkent that as a girl she had been quick-tempered, moody, and quite unrestrained, stopping at nothing in her impatience to make the most of life. At the time I found this incredible, even when she explained that she had later learned to control herself. But in her old age, when the basic features of her character broke to the surface again, I could see how hard it was for her to keep herself in check. People who knew her when she was young were well aware of the trouble she had in imposing restraint on herself – it was indeed a difficult task.

On one occasion when she stayed with us at Furmanov Street, M. tried to persuade her to put off her departure. The scene is still printed in my mind, like a snapshot. I can see them now, standing in the long, narrow room, she with her back to the window, and M. uneasily standing next to her, lighting a cigarette. Akhmatova said she must go, or else Punin ('Nikolasha') would 'walk out' on her.

'I can just see him doing that to you,' M. said, laughing at her . . .
She bent her neck meekly and said: 'I am so retiring . . .' M. burst
out into loud laughter, repeating the word 'retiring' and rolling the
r's so that it sounded like the neighing of a young filly not yet
broken in. Suddenly Akhmatova began to implore him. 'Don't
give me away! You knew me before, but I'm a changed woman
now . . .' M. told her not to worry, but said: 'You're just the same
all right, except that you've hidden it well away . . .' A quarter of a
century later, I saw that 'it' had indeed been extremely well
hidden in previous years, and I asked her what had become of her
celebrated reticence and reserve. There was no sign of them now.
'They have vanished, sunk without trace,' she confirmed.

I took Akhmatova's 'meekness' in her middle years at its face
value, but in her best poems of that time, even the most 'reserved'
of them, you can detect the voice of the boyar's wife wailing over
the dead, fasting, praying, cursing her enemies or extolling her
friends and allies in a way that would have given Nikon himself
pause.* Akhmatova once described Tsvetayeva as a 'poet of
strength'. Strength must be a specially feminine quality – it is the
striking thing about both the open turbulence of Tsvetayeva and
the tightly controlled passion of Akhmatova. Akhmatova's
strength at first showed itself in renunciation, and later in her
refusal to accept the untruth of the times in which she lived. The
manner in which she uttered her 'No' was a real feat of non-
acceptance.

My difference with Akhmatova was about something not worth
wasting breath on, and I never properly had it out with her, but
it still rankles in my old age. I too have suddenly discovered I have
a streak of innate belief in my own infallibility. For this reason I
cannot refrain from setting down here my side in the argument,
which at the time she refused to listen to, muzzling me with an
appeal to her own 'incomparable rightness'. Akhmatova writes†

* Allusion to Morozova, who, together with the Archpriest Avvakum,
fiercely opposed the church reforms of Patriarch Nikon in the seventeenth
century. In Surikov's famous painting of her she is shown shouting defiance
as she is hauled off on a sleigh to be imprisoned in a nunnery, where she
died.

† In *Pages from a Diary*.

that in 1924 M. brought his young wife to see her. But I believe that we went to see her twice before we ourselves went to live in Leningrad – the first time in 1923, and the second in 1924, when we called on her in two different apartments: the one on the Neva, and the other, if I remember rightly, on Kazanskaya (both of which she shared with Olga Sudeikina, who later left for France). I cannot now be sure in which of these two apartments we had our first meeting. Akhmatova tried to confuse me as to which she lived in earlier and in which later, though she may possibly not have remembered herself. My recollection is that on the first visit we saw her on Kazanskaya (or near the Kazan Cathedral), where there was a rather dark lobby in which she came out to meet us. The next time – a year later – we went to see her in the apartment on the Neva. M. recognized the apartment as the one we had looked at on our previous visit to Leningrad, when we were preparing to move there ourselves, but had decided against because it would have cost too much to do up. M. now thought Olga must have paid for the repairs: 'Where would Anna Andreyevna have got the money from?' . . . Akhmatova later told me it was her own money; she had sold a book to Petropolis, a private publishing firm in Leningrad (though even ten books would not have been enough to pay for what was needed). According to Akhmatova, Olga had no money and was being kept by her. Whether this was true in the case of Olga I do not know, but I was certainly kept by Akhmatova in Tashkent. During the time we lived separately there, she always put aside a little bread or macaroni for me from every meal, and later, when we set up house together, we both lived on her rations. I had the salary from my job, but on this alone I would have died of starvation. Money was no good by itself – one had to be entitled to draw proper rations at fixed state prices, not market ones.

Anyway, whoever paid for the repairs, both Akhmatova and Olga moved into the apartment on the Neva. According to Akhmatova we first went to see her only in the spring and summer of 1924 when she was between apartments, and on moving to Leningrad ourselves that autumn found she had meantime gone to live in the empty rooms belonging to Shileiko in the Marble Palace. It was no easy matter, even in Leningrad, to find a suitable apartment. I believe that Olga may have sold the one on the Neva

to raise money for her departure to France, but this is only guess-
work on my part. All I can be absolutely certain of is that if
Akhmatova had been moving back and forth between apartments
at the time of our first meeting, we would surely have remembered
this . . .

The second meeting is easily dated. We moved to Leningrad in
the autumn or late summer of 1924, and I was visited by Akhmatova at our new apartment on Morskaya in the very first few days
after that. Olga Glebova-Sudeikina had already left for France,
and Akhmatova had gone to live in the Marble Palace. She
explained that she did not want to stay in the Neva apartment all
by herself now that Olga had left. She was afraid, as I know, of
servants, but her women friends had all gone, and she was quite
incapable herself even of lighting a stove. (It is very hard to
imagine how Akhmatova and Shileiko had managed together
during the hungry years – both of them were absolutely helpless.)
In the Marble Palace there was a C E K U B U hostel from which it
was always possible to get a cleaning woman to come to tidy up
and light the stoves. Unfortunately Akhmatova was no good at
keeping in with these women and always needed some intermediary or other – a female friend or admirer of her poetry who,
sharing her apartment, would look after all the domestic chores.
Her inability to cope with servants was a sure indication of what a
disorderly household she had grown up in. Andrei Andreyevich
Gorenko* used to say that nothing could have been more untidy
and cheerless. Akhmatova put it down to her mother's good nature
and bewilderment. Her own sterner character she had probably
inherited from her father. He kept aloof from his children and
referred to Anna with horror as a 'decadent poetess' when she was
still only a girl and had not even begun to think of writing verse.
He hated disorder and occasionally came out with remarks
that Akhmatova never forgot for the rest of her life. His favourite
saying was: 'With your sins that's the best we can hope for.'
Once, failing to find her at home in Tsarskoye – she was spending
the night at Valia Sreznevskaya's – he phoned her the next morning and said: 'Always getting caught out like this, you women.'
The woman he himself went to live with after he had left his family

* Akhmatova's brother. See note, p. 257.

seemed an incomprehensible choice to Akhmatova, who said she was 'practically a hunchback'. (This story I put down to bias.) His children treated her with studied courtesy – as Akhmatova was always recalling in connection with Irina Punin's rudeness towards her. Her own peculiar explanation for her father's choice of this woman was that 'she must have been a good listener'. The impetuous young Akhmatova obviously did not get on well either with her mother or with her father and brothers, though it must have been from her mother that she inherited her inability to run the domestic side of her life. She was always dependent either on whatever woman friend happened to be living with her, or on the household in which she had pitched her tent. While she was staying with us in Tsarskoye, Punin transferred her things from the Marble Palace to the Fontanka. I was in the Marble Palace twice – not to see her, however, but Shileiko, after she had left him.

We spent two months of 1924 in Aprelevka* in a State Publishing House rest home situated on what had once been a country estate. It was easy to date these months, since it was the season for gathering wild strawberries – something I was able to do better than any village girl. Our first journey to Leningrad that year was made before our stay in Aprelevka and it can also be dated by my memory of various minor details after our arrival. Setting off to see Shileiko in the Marble Palace, we met him on the way. We were lightly dressed, almost certainly without coats, since the only summer coat I ever possessed was acquired much later, in Voronezh; I had it made from material bought in Torgsin (the foreign currency stores of those times, which gave me a hundred roubles for an old insurance policy of my father's). Shileiko, tall and thin, and rather forbidding in appearance, was walking along in a fur coat. M. asked why he was so warmly dressed, and Shileiko explained that because of his wretched tuberculosis he constantly felt shivery. He had two rooms next to each other in the Palace. We were met by Tapka, his Saint Bernard, and he said he would always take in any stray dog: 'That's how it was with Anichka† too,' he added. We said nothing.

Shileiko spent a long time teasing the dog with a bun he had

* Near Moscow.
† Akhmatova.

bought for it. The poor creature was driven nearly frantic, rearing up on its hind legs to the whole of its enormous height and putting its front paws on Shileiko's shoulders, as he just dangled the bun in front of it, refusing to let go. M. was indignant: Why are you making him suffer? he asked – give him the bun, he's earned it by now . . . Is this how you treated Anichka too? . . . Shileiko said he would not give up the bun yet: the longer the dog had to wait, the sweeter it would seem to him. This, he went on, is well known to our rulers: they force us (or did he say 'you'?) to whimper and beg for a long time before they throw us a titbit. (I noticed the bun was a so-called French one and quite tiny – just as ludicrously small for a Saint Bernard as the pittances thrown to our whining people) . . . After giving us this opinion on the best way to educate both dogs and citizens, Shileiko suddenly asked M., without any further preliminaries: 'I hear you have written some verse saying "I bow low". Is this true?' From a few vague details added by Shileiko it became apparent that this was the construction being put on 'January 1, 1924' by 'well-wishers'.

Tapka, at last allowed to take the bun, swallowed it, stretched out on the floor, and bared his teeth in a contented smile. We sat down at the table and M. recited 'January 1', asking when he had finished: 'Well, now, is this bowing low?' 'No,' Shileiko replied, 'but perhaps you do it somewhere else?' M. then read out all the poems he had written since *Tristia*, asking the same question after every one: 'Is this bowing low?' and every time Shileiko answered, 'No.' Since M. read 'January 1', the meeting must obviously have been in 1924 – in the spring. By the autumn we were already living in Leningrad and Shileiko had moved to Moscow. The fact that Shileiko was wearing a fur coat, in contrast to our light clothes, also points to its having been spring.

Shileiko complained that 'Anichka' had thrown him over altogether and did not even want to bear his name. 'If she doesn't want to call herself Shileiko, what can she call herself? She can hardly use the name Gumilev!' To this M. replied that Akhmatova would always simply be Akhmatova. But Shileiko would not take this for an answer: what sort of a name is Akhmatova? . . . Later I learned that Akhmatova was indeed unhappy about her pen name (it was 'Tartar, backwoods, coming from nowhere, cleaving to every disaster, itself a disaster'), and she would have kept the name Shileiko if their marriage had been properly registered. But Shileiko's first marriage had been a church one, and he could not bring himself to get a divorce, so he had taken 'Anichka' to the house manager's office and registered her there. Nobody was quite certain in those days about the procedure for getting married, and Akhmatova thought this had been sufficient. It was only when she separated from Shileiko that she understood the difference between the Register Office and the house manager's office. Rather comically, she bore a grudge over this with her timid companion and even complained to me many years later in Tashkent that she was stuck with her pen name because of his deceit. It was while we were living together in Tashkent that Garshin became a widower and wrote her a letter with a formal proposal of marriage. He made it conditional on her taking his name. I burst out laughing when I saw the letter, but she took it very seriously. She was attracted by the idea of a real, 'legal' surname: 'You have Osia's name, after all!' I would in fact have been glad enough to use my maiden name, but nobody could ever remember it – I was no Akhmatova . . . She was tired of her pen name, and wanted to escape from it. She was weary of 'figuring' as Akhmatova. M. had suffered from a similar weariness with his own 'image'. But it was not to be: she became neither Gumilev, nor Shileiko, nor Garshin. It never entered her head to try to become Punin – this was the exclusive prerogative of Anna Yevgenievna, née Arens. When we were living in the boarding-house in Tsarskoye Selo, incidentally, it was Punin who went to register her papers as Akhmatova. How could the poor woman possibly get away from the name? It had stuck to her so fast that there was no getting rid of it anymore.

In the days of Khrushchev something rather comic happened to her in connection with her 'pen name'. She had come to Moscow for the Writers' Congress* (why did she do this? To convince herself of her own reality at this most unreal of gatherings? It still baffles me). She was given a room in the Metropole Hotel, and every evening a crowd of her friends congregated there. On one occasion, when I happened to be there as well, she was visited by

*In 1959.

an unassuming woman from the Caucasus who was also attending the Congress and whose name also happened to be Akhmatova. She had come with the express purpose of apologizing; she was embarrassed at being called Akhmatova, and of writing verse (in Ossetian, I believe) into the bargain, but could not bring herself to renounce her own name. Akhmatova chatted happily with her namesake and did her best to 'render first-aid' (her private expression for offering consolation). The two Akhmatovas got on very well, and when her namesake had left Anna Andreyevna said sadly: 'She's a genuine Akhmatova, and I am not.' Who is the real one? Perhaps both are ... I am almost certain that Anna Andreyevna invented her Tartar grandmother of this name to justify having adopted it as a nom de plume. There was once a woman translator called Akhmatova – no relation at all – and the name was most likely borrowed from her by the young Gorenko-Gumilev, rather than from a fictitious Tartar grandmother. It is noteworthy that Akhmatova never for a moment considered reverting to her maiden name. Another curious point is that though so sensitive about the pen name which had stuck to her, she felt it a pity that M. had not taken a pseudonym, since she thought his Jewish name was a great hindrance to him. This is something I would rather leave to the judgement of the *Rusity* with their hatred of 'Jewish abscesses on the pure body of Russian poetry', but I can testify that M. himself never for one moment entertained the idea of taking another name. He was amazed that Sologub should have changed his real name Teternikov (which was 'so much like him') for a ludicrously pretentious pen name – the Sologubs were counts, it seems, apart from anything else. With Akhmatova, on the other hand, he felt it was somehow different: she had merged with her name and it was inseparable from her. I believe this was indeed so, and if he had lived on, he would probably have joined me in laughing at her in Tashkent when she was suddenly fired with the ambition of becoming a respectable professor's wife with a name hallowed in Russian literature and much loved by middle-brow intellectuals. Anna Andreyevna Garshin of 'Red Flower' fame* . . . God preserve us!

M. finished reading his poems, and Shileiko started showing us

* See Garshin, Appendix A.

some plaster of Paris casts – copies of archaeological finds with Egyptian bas-reliefs, if I remember rightly. Just at this moment Akhmatova arrived. She was no longer Gumilev or Shileiko, and was not destined to become Garshin, but by now there was nothing left of Aniuta Gorenko either . . . She was extremely slim and tall with a rather frightened expression on her very winsome face. She did not so much sit as perch on the edge of a chair, as though ready to leap up and flee at any moment. We had already met, and she asked whether we had come for long. I think we then agreed on a date to go and see her, and she gave us her new address. But I cannot vouch for this: in one's anxiety to prove a case it is all too easy to invent false recollections. All I can say for certain is that after we had been to see her in her apartment on the Neva, M. got a cab and took me for a drive along the embankments to show me what his native city looked like during the White Nights. This must have been the end of May, or June (but what Style?). Our first visit to her had been in summer or autumn the previous year at her other apartment – with no view of the Neva through the windows. This was when we also went to inspect the still-vacant apartment on the Neva. It had been empty for a long time – the whole city was still deserted and derelict. We were shown dozens of grand apartments, empty and needing repairs. We kept thinking about them during our last days on the Yakimanka in Moscow, and I longed for a decent place to live with a bathroom of our own. We had been discussing the idea of moving to Leningrad ever since the spring of 1923, before our trip to Gaspra. At first M. just shook his head: he did not want to go back to Leningrad. But later he broached the idea himself – how much longer, he asked, could we go on wandering from pillar to post in dirty, alien, and overcrowded Moscow? The notion of returning to the dead city of Leningrad grew on him little by little. We finally made up our minds on that white night, as the cabbie drove us along the embankments and over the bridges. The first of the bridges had been drawn up, and we had to cross over to Vasiliev Island by the next one. We gave the cabbie a huge fare, but our first small payments were beginning to trickle through from Book House.* Moscow, the bastion of progressive ideology, was no longer willing to feed us.

*Headquarters of the State Publishing House in Leningrad.

33 Olga Glebova-Sudeikina

In the apartment where I first saw Akhmatova there was a large number of porcelain statuettes. My earthenware soul cannot stand such things – I always think they go together with a pederastic notion of home comfort. These figurines later disappeared: Olga Glebova-Sudeikina must have sold them to get the money for her departure. Akhmatova was left with only a few broken earthenware pieces, which she kept to the end of her life in a glass case. In her apartment on the Neva one whole wall was hung with icons from Sudeikin's collection. Later she put them in a trunk, and after her death Irina Punin took possession of them.

Visiting Akhmatova the first time, we had gone on foot. M. was very much on edge. Just as I continue to harbour a grudge over the tangled affair of the 'First Dedication', M. still resented the suggestion Akhmatova had made years previously that he should visit her less frequently – what he had called 'Akhmatova's quirkishness'. Her defensiveness both with women and, in particular, with men, all of whom she regarded as liable to fall in love with her, and therefore to be held at bay, really was a rather ludicrous game, and it meant that her warm-heartedness and friendship – something at which she was unrivalled – could suddenly be withdrawn. But M. was also apprehensive about the meeting because of the two articles he had published (in *Russian Art*) in which there were incidental references to Akhmatova. What he had said there about her 'stylitism on a block of parquetry' was quite simply a nasty dig of which he was later very ashamed. Yet a third reason for his apprehension was anxiety about the reception I might get from her. Not long before, he had taken me to see Tsvetayeva and was very upset when she went for me as only she could. 'With these wild women you never know what to expect,' he had said afterward . . .

All his fears proved groundless. Akhmatova came running out into the hallway, genuinely delighted to see us. I remember her saying: 'Show me your Nadia, I've been hearing about her for so long.' We drank tea, and M. finally thawed out. They spoke about Gumilev, and she told him that the place where he had been buried (or rather, put in a hole in the ground) had supposedly been located. Then they talked about Otsup, Gorki, and the note received from Gumilev by his wife.* They referred to Gumilev as Kolia, and spoke about his death in a way which showed it was a personal sorrow shared by both of them. Even though they had first met when they were very young, they addressed each other rather formally by name and patronymic, never using first names alone except out of each other's presence. Even among my contemporaries it was still customary to start addressing people by the patronymic at an early age, and it sounded well in the ears. Nowadays, it seems, the patronymic is dying out. Next Akhmatova asked M. what he had been writing, saying: 'You read first – I like your verse better than you like mine.' Here it was, one of the sly 'pinpricks' for which Akhmatova was famous: almost imperceptible, but just enough to make her point. This was her only allusion to M.'s articles. He read his new poems for a long time, and I could see how well she thought of them. One thing I can say to my credit is that I was always able to sit and listen quietly, not trying to assert myself or constantly butting into the conversation, like so many wives. I must say that I regard this as a great virtue. Why was I never given a prize for it?

On our second visit to Akhmatova – this time in the apartment on the Neva – M. again read to her, 'presenting his accounts for the period under review', as they liked to put it. He recited 'January 1' and told her the story about 'bowing low'. This had upset him more than he had shown to Shileiko. He had nothing else to offer her for this particular 'period under review', since his poem about not being anyone's contemporary was still to be written. They never had to read new poems to each other more than once – everything was memorized at first hearing.

It was more interesting for me to see Akhmatova than it was for her to have a look at 'your Nadia', and this alone is reason enough for thinking that my memory of our first meetings is better than hers. She often told me that her friendship with M. had been renewed because of me. I would be happy to believe it, but I think it was due only to her: she clearly showed how much it meant to

*Gumilev's second wife, Anna Nikolayevna Engelhardt, whom he married a year after his divorce from Akhmatova.

her, and how anxious she was to avoid any new breach. She did everything to make it possible, first and foremost by striking up a friendship with me. This was largely a matter of her initiative, and I am grateful to her for it. Olga Sudeikina also played a part in the renewal of good relations. Of all Akhmatova's 'doubles' (one can hardly say 'doublesses' as a feminine form of the word!) Olga was the most friendly and good-natured – a nice, light-headed, flighty creature who had suffered from hunger and other ordeals during the terrible years of Revolution.

I only ever saw Olga twice indoors – both times with Akhmatova – but was always running across her in the street. As M. used to say, she had a 'high coefficient of encounterability'. She chased all over town, obtaining the papers and raising the money needed for her departure, complaining about officials, 'house managers', and the reform of the Russian alphabet. In her opinion the abolition of the letter *yat* meant that her name Glebova now had to be pronounced *Gliobova*. She was much nicer at home than in the street. She had countless playful little mannerisms calculated to bring solace to any weary Petersburger, taking his mind off serious matters and putting him in a good humour. These mannerisms had a sharply defined Petersburg character which made them quite distinct from those of her Moscow contemporaries. The 'dolls' of the two cities had brought the tricks of their trade to a fine art. Both put on fancy airs, but the Moscow ones added a racy, down-to-earth touch, while those of Petersburg preferred the 'kittenish' style. Olga was never still for a moment. Heels clicking, she pranced and pirouetted about the room, setting the table for tea, flicking away imaginary dust with a cambric or muslin duster which she would then flourish like a handkerchief before sticking it behind the top of her tiny apron. I always had the impression that she was all frills and flounces, but in reality they had disappeared, together with her youth and 'admirers'. Olga was older than Akhmatova, and even though she moved around like a whirligig she had a faded, tired look about her. Cold and hunger had taken their toll, but she still had the smooth, pale skin and ageless appearance – she was then forty or more – characteristic of women who wash with the water of the Neva – though they are always a trifle wan, both in the bloom of youth and long after they have passed their prime. Like all the 'dolls' of Petersburg, Olga dressed elaborately but without any flair at all. Everything about her was old-fashioned – like the frills and ruches which I perhaps only imagined because they were so much in her style.

When she had served us tea, Olga vanished, leaving us to talk in peace. She knew the ways of her friend very well: if Akhmatova had visitors she always threw out the person living with her, practically slamming the door as she did so. When we lived together in Tashkent most visitors came to see both of us, but on two occasions she threw me out of the room when I lingered for a moment after the arrival of visitors only she knew. In her restless old age, when she spent the winter in Moscow, moving from one woman friend to another and never staying longer than two weeks with any of them, she used to throw out whoever had given her refuge, until they themselves learned to withdraw the moment someone came. In her last years Akhmatova 'put on her phonograph record' for each visitor, that is, told him or her the story of Acmeism and her own life, hoping they would commit it to memory and pass it on in the only permissible version – her own. In Moscow these 'records' were soon erased from people's minds, but it is said that in Leningrad they were carefully noted down by Naiman. I wonder whether M. figures in the list of men who were in love with her. She added him to it thirty years after his death. During her brief visits abroad, she managed to deposit some of her 'records' there, as she had dreamed of doing. If any of this is written up by Emma Gerstein, it will be distorted out of all recognition. She has a genius for getting everything wrong. She has sometimes told me stories from my own life at which I could only gape in astonishment. Akhmatova was terrified of what Emma might write in her memoirs and therefore did everything possible to propitiate her beforehand. Akhmatova's account of Acmeism is more or less the same as the one I got from M., though he was reluctant to talk about it. Everybody who knew her in her young days – and Andrei Gorenko – confirms that Gumilev really was very much in love with her, but nobody knows the real reason for the breakup of their marriage, and I doubt whether it will ever be known. Such things are a mystery which even the couple directly concerned do not always fully understand. Akhmatova herself used to say that if there had been no Revolution, she would probably not have divorced Gumilev, but just gone on living in a wing of his house, gathering her friends there and actively engaging in literary politics. For me, as a friend of the tempestuous, un-settled Akhmatova of later years, this idea of her as a hostess presiding over her salon in a wing of Gumilev's house is quite inconceivable. I fear that the leading light in her salon would have been Nedobrovo, who would have taught her not to make the terribly unladylike gesture of putting her hand on her knee. Who could ever imitate this gesture?

In 1923 Akhmatova was not yet putting on 'records', and her one desire was to talk in private with a friend – despite the presence of his wife. This was why Olga fled, though she reappeared from time to time, clicking her heels on the floor and causing us some amusement. She came back into the room while M. was reading, and stood a little way off, playing the part of the female admirer breathless with excitement; then she went out again. M. was nice to her in a playful way, but Akhmatova he treated very much as an equal, in an open, direct, and serious fashion. She reciprocated.

Somebody has invented a story that Olga was an outstanding dancer. This is nonsense: 'flower of the drama schools' and 'actress slender as a pin' indeed! She was rather mincing, and there was a hint of Kuzmin about her, as there was also about the hero of *Poem Without a Hero*. I have read, by the way, that in the West they think Kuzmin was Akhmatova's only friend. Stuff and nonsense! They were like cat and dog, and it was quite natural that Kuzmin should have plumped for the other Anna – Anna Radlova. Otherwise, however, Akhmatova had a million friends and maintained deeply personal relations with all of them. Hordes of woman and bat-talions of men of the most widely differing ages can testify to her great gift for friendship, to a love of mischief which never deserted her even in her declining years, to the way in which, sitting at table with vodka and *zakuski*, she could be so funny that everybody fell off their chairs from laughter. Why should she have wanted to be a great lady of the kind – if they exist – before whom people go down on their knees, when she was such a wonderful, madcap woman, poet, and friend?

Akhmatova regarded Olga as the embodiment of all the feminine qualities and was always giving me some tip or other about how to manage various domestic problems, or to look my best in the way recommended by the goat-legged heroine of the *Poem* which has no hero . . . Dusters and dishcloths, for instance, should be made of muslin. Tea must be strong and served in cups of thin china . . .

One of the secrets for preserving one's good looks and youth was: dark hair must be worn smooth and plain, while light hair was to be fluffed up or curled. Then there was the secret (à la Kseshinskaya) about how to be a success with men: never take your eyes off them, always look straight at their mouths – that's how 'they' like it . . . These were typical Petersburg fads of the beginning of the century. I told Akhmatova that it was all old hat, but she wouldn't listen to me – though her own way of charming people was quite different.

I also heard a lot about the dolls and other things Olga made out of rags in the style of the 'World of Art'. By that time I was already tired of the 'Knave of Diamonds', the 'Ass's Tail',* and such-like, let alone the 'World of Art'. But it was through talk about these things that Olga continued to live alongside us in the new life, even though, to her great good fortune, she had a much smaller dose of it than we. She had several times played a rather fateful part in Akhmatova's existence by taking her friends away from her – notably the one in the *Poem* who killed himself. But the friendship between these two 'doubles', who were so remarkably dissimilar, was all the more touching for their refusal to allow anything or anyone to come between them. It may be that I was less impressed than I should have been with Olga's beauty. Perhaps she really was a 'fair-haired marvel'.† But one should not forget that tastes change and the ideal of womanhood for my generation was similar to the one still in fashion. We had no time for dolling ourselves up like mannequins and inventing rules about how to treat our hair, depending on whether it was light or dark – or, at least, if we had any rules they were quite different. Actually, I am already behind the times, and our type of woman – the girl friend and partner combined – is no longer so fashionable. Nowadays, they say, there

---

* Group started in 1912 (Goncharova, Larionov, Malevich, and others) stressing national Russian motifs.

† Description in *Poem Without a Hero*.

is a new breed of energetic, pushing women who marry weak-willed milksops and run their lives for them, Perish the thought . . .

And now a word about a woman we once saw crossing the Red Square. She walked with mincing steps and was clutching a tiny handbag. Her elaborate, light-coloured costume was richly decorated with various oddments, and the hat on her head looked like a toadstool with a spray of tiny flowers on top. It was this spectacle which moved M. to write his lines – as a later addition to the poem on Feodosia – about women who invent outlandish things to wear. 'She's mad,' I said. 'Look how stiffly she moves her limbs.' 'She's like Olga,' M. replied. The sight of such 'Olgas' reminded me of the original one, as I had seen her in the streets of Moscow, always conspicuous by her way of walking, the knick-knacks that adorned her person – and the manifestly unfair disadvantage of not having a carriage at her disposal. But perhaps a carriage would not have been much good to her: unable to sit still for a moment, she would always have been leaping out to walk clickety-clack along the pavement in her high heels. In Paris she probably adapted to the thick rubber soles just coming into fashion when she arrived there. Rubber is even better: you do not slip.

34   Old Friends

In our very early days, still in Kiev, M. and I had once gone into Ogloblin's bookstore, where I asked him: 'Who is this Radlova?' He replied that she was Zelinski's disciple, a poetess who tried to compete with Akhmatova and spoke badly of her – with the result that Akhmatova's friends no longer visited her. M. recited a comic rhymed parody about an archangel taking his place in an iconostasis. It ended with the suggestive line: 'And has a smell of Valerian' – an allusion to Radlova's affair with Valerian Chudovski. He was the sort of person who shook hands without taking off his glove. In 1930 or thereabouts I saw him in a CEKUBU rest home with his wife. They had a wonderful small son who was brought out to see them there, and I remember feeling horrified at the thought of children being brought into the world at such a time: what would become of them? Chudovski's wife said that members of the intelligentsia should have children to offset all the little proletarians. I am not at all sure, however, that intellectual parents necessarily have intellectual children: the qualities involved are not hereditary. What has happened to them all? The Chudovski family already looked as though they would not last long – particularly his wife's brother, who skied like an archangel.

As we stood looking at the books in Ogloblin's window, I there and then decided that Akhmatova was first among the women poets. M. and Ehrenburg had told me about Tsvetayeva, but I would have none of her. I admitted the possibility that there might be more than one male poet, but for the women I adopted a much stricter standard: there could be only one at the top, and no more! I have stuck to this ever since – the rest come nowhere as far as I am concerned. In my young days, everybody had his 'first' poet, and I was only following the general custom of the times. Roman Jakobson – just as I picked my woman poet – has spent a lifetime doing battle for the poet he chose as his 'number one' at the beginning: Mayakovski. He was ready to countenance all kinds of misinformation about other poets as long as it was to the greater glory of his 'favourite' (though it is said that his real favourite was Khlebnikov).

I first came across this business of 'promoting' a favourite poet while I was still at high school. My Latin teacher and friend Volodia Otrokovski persuaded me to 'give up' Blok and switch my allegiance to Annenski instead. He thus taught me to appreciate Annenski, but at the same time spoiled my first innocent reading of Blok. The same sort of thing can still happen nowadays. At the end of the fifties when M. suddenly re-emerged from the void to which he had been consigned, readers of Pasternak – not all, of course, but a great many – reconciled themselves to the fact that there were henceforth two great poets, but the glorious traditions of the past were brought back by an admirer of Shengeli who went so far as to strike a 'Jew-loving Mandelstamite', drawing blood. I explained to the victim that whenever any great poet comes on the scene, there is always a revival of poetry and many other poets make their appearance as well, so that it was time to give up this ridiculous game. The 'Mandelstamite' just covered his face with his hands and groaned.

How can one explain to such people that a poet cannot exist in isolation and that Pasternak's line about two nightingales responding to each other in song is not an idle one? The fight over the 'first' woman poet lasted longer, and the violent arguments between Akhmatova's and Tsvetayeva's 'fans' are only just beginning to die down. The *Rusity*, however, are still looking for a male candidate without suspect blood in his veins. For some reason, digging around in the past for one, they have overlooked Kluyev. I fear their choice may eventually stagger us all by its originality and brilliance. There is more than a hint of Leader worship about these efforts to put one poet at the top . . .

The poets themselves have had no part in this sordid tug of war. Yesenin's antics do not count: he knew himself that it was mischief, a game, anything but a serious bid for first place. It was the hangers-on who went in for this kind of thing, not the poets themselves, since they were much more inclined to be drawn to each other in a spirit of fellow feeling. When Mayakovski came to Petersburg in 1912 or so, he struck up a friendship with M., but they were quickly separated and dragged off in opposite directions. However, before this happened, Mayakovski managed to give M. one piece of practical advice: 'I eat only one meal a day, but a good one.' In the hungry years, M. often advised me to do likewise, but the trouble was that in such times you just cannot get enough for even one good meal a day. In telling the story of Mayakovski and M. meeting at Yeliseyev's Katayev has of course – being a typical senile buffoon – confused and distorted things. Mayakovski shouted to M. across the narrow counter where sausages were displayed: 'I am like an Attic soldier – in love with the enemy!' Already then it had been brought home to him that he had enemies, 'class' and other kinds. Luckily, however, he did not lose his capacity to love poets on the wrong side of the 'class' barrier. As for M., he fell in love with poets, with their books, with one poem, or just a single line . . .

One thing that M. admired about Tsvetayeva was her enthusiasm not only for poetry other than her own but for the poets themselves as well. There was an astonishing selflessness about this. I have been told that Tsvetayeva's enthusiasms were short-lived, but tempestuous while they lasted, like a hurricane. The most durable of them was for Pasternak, after the appearance of *My Sister Life*. For many years Pasternak held undisputed sway over all other poets, and none of them was immune to his influence. Akhmatova used to say that only Tsvetayeva came through this trial with honour: Pasternak enriched her and perhaps thanks to him she not only kept her true voice, but even found it in the first place. I believe that her long poems ('Mountains', 'The Staircase', etc.) are the strongest things she ever wrote.

Though I met Tsvetayeva several times, we never really became friends. To a certain extent this was because I had decided on Akhmatova as 'top' woman poet, but the initiative for our 'non-friendship' came largely from her. It is possible that she was just totally intolerant of the wives of her friends (though she accused *me* of being jealous of *her*!), but the main thing was that in those days, and probably to the end of her life, she was completely indifferent to M.'s poetry. I have read the letters of Tsvetayeva circulating in *samizdat*, in which she says that she too could write like M., that she knew his secret, so to speak. Shortly after our meeting Pasternak became the chief source of wonder for her. Such clever people they all were, yet their view of things or, rather, of their own craft was often so naïve: a real poet can never write like some other real poet. Each poetic manner, like someone's personality, is inimitable. Even a very minor genuine poet has his own unique voice. The only people capable of writing in somebody else's manner are the parodists and verifiers – the kind who turn out 'magazine poetry . . .'

Out of indifference, prejudice, or sheer cantankerousness Tsvetayeva and I were unable to say a human word to each other or – as they used to say in the old days – break the ice. Instead we stood on our pride and were much the poorer as a result. It was in Moscow in the summer of 1922 that M. took me to see her in one of the side streets off Povarskaya, not far from Trubnikovski, where I used to go to see Ostroukhov's famous collection of icons. We knocked on the door – bells had not survived the Revolution – and it was opened by Marina. At the sight of M. she gasped with pleasure, but it was all she could do – not taking her eyes off him for a moment – to offer me her hand. She made it quite plain that

she had no time at all for wives. 'Let's go and see Alia,' she said to
M. 'You remember Alia, don't you?' And then she added, speaking to me, but still not looking at me: 'You wait here. Alia doesn't
like strangers.'

M. turned green from fury, but went with her all the same to see
Alia. A large double door slammed behind them and I was left
alone in what looked like an entrance hall, a completely dark room
piled with junk. As M. told me later, it had previously been a dining
room, with a light in the ceiling, but the bulb had not been washed
since the Revolution and let through no proper light at all, only a
dim glow. Like all former upper-class apartments, it was now given
over to dust, dirt, and decay, but here there was also an atmosphere
of witchcraft into the bargain. The walls were hung with stuffed
animals of all kinds, and the place was cluttered with old-fashioned
toys which the Tsvetayeva sisters – all three of them in their turn –
had no doubt played with as children. There was also a large bed
with a bare mattress, and a wooden rocking horse. I thought of all
the giant spiders that might be lurking unseen in the darkness, the
mice frisking about, and Lord knows what other vermin besides;
all this was supplied by my spiteful imagination.

The visit to Alia could not have been briefer. After a couple of
minutes, M. hurried out from the next room (another living room,
as it now appeared, to which Marina had not seen fit to admit me)
and talked for a while in the entrance hall with our hostess, who at
last had the sense to switch on the light. He refused her offer of a
chair and they both remained standing while I sat on a rickety,
creaking chair in the middle of the room, unceremoniously looking
her up and down. She was evidently conscious of having gone too
far, and tried to make conversation, but M. answered coldly and in
monosyllables, with his most Petersburg accent. (He should have
given her a piece of his mind, the fool, in the recklessly open way he
would have done in the early thirties, when he became young and
cheerful again, and all would immediately have blown over.)
Marina managed to tell him about the death of her second daughter, whom she had put in an orphanage because she was unable to
feed two children. There were some terrible details better not mentioned here. Next she took a stuffed cat or monkey down from the
wall and said to M.: 'Do you remember?' This was the 'secret

token', now covered in dust. M. looked at it with horror, hastened to assure her he remembered everything, and signalled me with his eyes to get up. But I made no move.

The conversation never got going, the whole visit was a washout, and M. availed himself of the first pause to take me away. One of the most absurd experiences in 'married life' is this one of being taken away. M. used to indicate it was time to go by rolling his eyes, but I always stubbornly ignored his signals, until finally he said, 'Let's go,' or came over without a word and started helping me to my feet. I always felt I was being carried out by the scruff of the neck, like a kitten. I suppose I used to scratch, but there was nothing to do but go when he decided the time had come. This happened most frequently during visits to old friends of his when the meeting, for one reason or another, was not a success. Once we were invited by Pronin, who had opened a new version of the Stray Dog in Moscow. There were two girls lounging on a divan. They started making a fuss of M., but no sooner had I settled down next to them than I was forcibly taken away. One whiff of this Bohemian atmosphere was enough for M., and he fled – Pronin ran alongside, begging him to stay and saying there would be coffee if we waited just a minute. I would have loved to stay, drink coffee, and gossip with the girls, but a kitten is helpless when it is grabbed by the scruff of the neck and taken away.

Tsvetayeva was getting ready to leave the country. Shengeli had moved into her big room, next to the one where she had taken M. to see her daughter. Going to visit Shengeli, we now always bumped into her, and each time she made a point of talking to me as well as to M. He was icily polite, and I, still smarting from our first meeting, simply played the fool and made serious conversation difficult. On one of these occasions she told us how she had gone to Nikitina, the publisher, to ask for money and, failing to get anything out of her, had had a great row with the wretched woman. Alia, outraged by this treatment of her mother, took a book of Tsvetayeva's lying on Nikitina's table and ran out into the street with it; she thought a house where her mother had been so shabbily dealt with was no place for her books. In this instance my sympathies are entirely with Tsvetayeva and Alia, particularly since Nikitina's capacity for survival seems odd to me. To this very day she has managed to keep her archives, despite the fact that so many people have spent years in the camps just for one entry in a diary or the mere suspicion of keeping notes for posterity. Has she just been lucky, or was there some other reason? It is certainly better if children do not grow up in this kind of atmosphere. I wonder whether there is any possibility at all of protecting them in such disastrous conditions. I would not have been able to do it. What a good thing we realized in time that the age we lived in was not propitious to raising a family.

My impression of Marina Tsvetayeva was that she was absolutely natural and fantastically self-willed. I have a vivid recollection of her cropped hair, loose-limbed gait – like a boy's – and speech remarkably like her verse. Her wilfulness was not just a matter of temperament but a way of life. She could never have reined herself in, as Akhmatova did. Reading Tsvetayeva's verse and letters nowadays I realize that what she always needed was to experience every emotion to the very utmost, seeking ecstasy not only in love, but also in abandonment, loneliness, and disaster. I can see there is a rare nobility of mind about this attitude, but I am disturbed by the accompanying indifference to people who at any given moment were not needed at her 'feast of feelings', or in some way impeded it. I noticed something similar in her sister Asia, with whom I formed a much more human relationship than with Marina, It was not only in the Tsvetayeva sisters, however, that I observed this extraordinary combination of uninhibited feeling and indifference. It was very much the fashion of the times – a peculiar form of petty self-indulgence, of licence based on the principle 'I do as I please'. It was first cultivated in the pre-revolutionary years and took on ludicrous forms among the less talented female representatives of the twenties, in whom there was no emotional depth at all, only a tremendous ability to snub people they thought 'of little interest' at any particular moment. The kind of feeling which erupted from the Tsvetayeva sisters (particularly the elder one) with almost elemental force took on the appearance of mere bad manners in other Moscow women of the twenties – I refer, of course, only to such of them as were connected with the arts. I might well have been the same myself if it had not been for M., who would not tolerate such antics in anyone: you had to choose between him and indulgence in these stylish modern tricks. I knew one unsuccessful woman painter who used to *lie down* with her back to people when they came to see her husband, a man of outstanding worth, just to show that she had her own life and was indifferent to anything unconnected with her art. This kind of prank was typical for the twenties. Such women, shallow adherents of the I-do-as-I-please principle, were totally devoid of the manners which, when all is said and done, add grace to our lives. In women this self-will took the form of private nastiness in the home. In men it was less conspicuous, but their public behaviour – something of much greater consequence – boiled down to the same I-do-as-I-please principle translated into terms of 'What's in it for me?' In such degenerate forms, the brilliant and gifted art of self-indulgence as practised in the decade before the Revolution showed its true quality. We have no right to complain that we were the victims of circumstances. We got what we deserved. The little inner world in each of us reflected the greater world outside and helped to prepare the way for all that happened in it. I am saying this about the past, but it is just as true of the present: isn't it time for every person now active, however slight his connection with those spheres where the future is made, to give thought to the influence his attitude, his ideas, and his aspirations may have on this future as it takes shape – even though it seems so predetermined at first sight? It is in fact shaped not only by the spirit of the times, but also by the attitude of every individual, his tastes, ideas, and desires.

Tsvetayeva went abroad, and we did not see her again. When she returned to Moscow, I was already living in the provinces, and no one even dreamed of telling me she was back – in the Stalin period it became a matter of second nature to ignore people who had returned from the West, not to mention any chance surviving relatives of victims of the terror at home. Akhmatova was soon told by either Khardzhiev or Gerstein that I had turned into a 'provincial' and become a teacher – as could have been expected of me all along. (Provincial teachers, as a matter of fact, were very much more human than any of our dazzling Muscovites.) Akhmatova refused to tell me which of them had 'denounced' me in these terms, and I did not insist on knowing. This sort of thing was all too typical. It was a little awkward to disavow the family of a victim outright, and the best of us always tried to offer a decent excuse for doing so, most often by explaining that the person in question had become a bore, or gone to seed. Every day was a red letter day in our bountiful new-fangled Empire and brought new marvels to talk about: the latest play by Svetlov, new poetry by Selvinski, the basis and the superstructure, an Eisenstein film complete with Prussian Knights in armour, or grand schemes to make Siberian rivers flow backwards. Who had any time for the widow of a nobody like Mandelstam, or for some woman by the name of Tsvetayeva? They had both turned into 'back numbers' – one in Paris and the other beyond the 'hundred-and-five-kilometre limit'.

I soon learned never to call people on the telephone, or to visit then unless repeatedly invited. (Before the war nobody at all invited me, and after the war only very few – two or three. The one person who stood firm in her friendship was Akhmatova.) Tsvetayeva could not stand the new isolation in which she found herself in the little town on the Kama.* Aseyev and Trenev lectured her on the need for patience: in time of war, they pointed out, nobody was concerned with the fate of mere individuals, or former poets. The same was true not only in time of war, but also during all the years of our 'achievements', great and small. To this we have always held firm – not a difficult thing to hold firm to – and the techniques involved have been brought to a fine art.

I felt a pang of regret at not having seen Tsvetayeva when Akhmatova, in Tashkent, told me of their meeting – the first and only one. Tsvetayeva complained to her about all the lies told by Georgi Ivanov, who had said that M.'s poems to herself were really addressed to some unknown woman doctor, the mistress of a rich Armenian. (What an imagination he had, this lickspittle!) I knew very well that the poems in question ('On a Broad Sleigh Covered with Straw', 'Among the Many Voices of the Girlish Chorus', 'Not Believing in the Miracle of Resurrection') were addressed to Tsvetayeva. Perhaps it is just as well we didn't meet after all. The author of 'Attempt at Jealousy' evidently despised all the wives and mistresses of her former friends, and suspected me of not having permitted M. to 'dedicate' the poems to her. Where had she ever seen dedications at the head of love poems? She was well

* Yelabuga, where she committed suicide.

aware of the difference between 'dedicating' and 'addressing' a poem to someone. M.'s poems are addressed to her and are about her, but a dedication is a quite different thing, a much more neutral affair, so it made no sense to blame a 'new-found, jealous wife', that is, me, for the lack of one. Both Akhmatova and Tsvetayeva, women in every sense of the word and persons of great brilliance, were very prone to jealousy, and I was not fit to hold a candle to either of them. Akhmatova rightly regarded lack of jealousy as a mark of feminine ineptitude and delighted in repeating the words of G.K. that if ever she had any rival, she would throttle her with her own two hands. Akhmatova warned one of her lovers that 'from behind the shoulder of your bride / My half-closed eyes will peer' and: 'Mind you do not tell your sweetheart / of my inimitable ravings'. Yet she could remain on friendly terms with her rivals and even feel pity for them: 'But tell me, will you dare condemn / another woman to this Calvary?' Her anger was reserved for the real villains. Tsvetayeva, on the other hand, went for her rivals tooth and nail: 'How can you live with a simple woman? . . . Without divinities? Paying the tax of undying commonplaceness? . . . How can you live with such a piece of merchandise? / How can you live with your hundred-thousandth, / After trampling Lilith underfoot!' She would soon have shown a 'piece of merchandise' like me what for, if I had tried to trespass on her territory. I am struck by the demoniac strength and abandon of Tsvetayeva. Such women are prodigies. She was right, of course, to trample on all who could not share in her 'feast of feelings'. These two, Akhmatova and Tsvetayeva, knew how to extract the maximum of joy and pain from love, and one can only envy them for it. I really did not know pain in love, and set no store by it. It is not for ordinary mortals. (The pain bestowed on me was of a different order, and I wouldn't wish it on anyone.)

In the poem in which M. describes how he walked through a cemetery with Tsvetayeva and suddenly realized that 'to stay with such a mist-wreathed nun means to court disaster' (Tsvetayeva made out that 'nun' here stood for 'nurse' and something else besides), two lines in the version as first published in *Apollon* were later replaced by ellipses. Khardzhiev at first asked me to confirm his supposition that these two lines were written by Lozinski, but then decided it was safer to refer to a conversation he once had with M. himself: 'In 1932 Mandelstam informed the editor of the present edition that these lines were written by M. L. Lozinski . . .' It is true that Khardzhiev came to see us in 1932 together with Trenin, and M. read them some new poems while I went out into the corridor because I was cooking something there. But I swear that M. could not possibly have told him what never was. The poem originally consisted of five stanzas. M. never read the whole of the omitted stanza to anyone at all. In the abbreviated form as published he kept just two lines of it, 'the wide horizons of the steppes', but this led to a distortion of the syntax. The word *ovid* (horizon), furthermore, was not part of his vocabulary – he had heard it from Tsvetayeva. I have seen the manuscript of the original five-stanza version. M. had put it in a wicker basket which had belonged to his mother, where he kept her letters to him and all his manuscripts. While M. was away once, his brother Shura played cards with some soldiers who broke the lock off the basket and used all the paper inside to roll cigarettes.* M. remembered the stanza left out of the published version, but preferred to leave it to turn up one day in Tsvetayeva's archives. He had faith in archives and in poetry lovers. In this case he believed the ellipses in the published version would be a sufficient clue to lead them to the missing lines. Tsvetayeva must have forgotten them, however, and lost the manuscript. In our age archives and poetry lovers have proved to be equally unreliable. All the same, several things have turned up and come into my hands. In his story 'Sukharevka' M. quotes a line from a poem: 'All is foreign to us in the unseemly capital' and adds: 'Let people look for it after my death.' I made no attempt to find it, but suddenly, out of the blue, it was sent to me by Gabrichevski. Perhaps the missing stanza from the poem addressed to Tsvetayeva will also turn up one of these days.

His friendship with Tsvetayeva played an enormous role, I believe, in M.'s work (which in his case was synonymous with his life). She was the bridge over which he crossed from one period to another. His *Second Book* (or *Tristia*) opens with a poem to Tsvetayeva. Kablukov, who regarded M. as his protégé at that time, at once sensed the new tone of voice and was upset by it.

* *Hope Against Hope*, page 322.

People never like a youthful prodigy to grow up. Kablukov would have wished M. to return to the reserved, thoughtful manner of *Stone*, his first volume, written while he was still very young. But growth cannot simply be halted. Bestowing on him the gift of her friendship, and of Moscow, Tsvetayeva somehow broke the spell which Petersburg had cast on him. It was a magic gift because with only Petersburg, without Moscow, it would have been impossible to breathe freely, to acquire the true feeling for Russia and the inner freedom of which M. speaks in his article on Chaadayev. In *Stone*, M. takes a staff in his hand ('My staff, my freedom, the core of being') to set out for Rome ('I took my staff and in good cheer set off for Rome'), but in *Tristia*, having come to know Russia, he renounces Rome: 'Rome is far away, and he never loved her.' Kablukov had not succeeded in getting him to give up Rome and failed to notice that Tsvetayeva had managed it by presenting him with Moscow.

I am sure my relationship with M. would not have been formed so easily and simply if he had not previously encountered Marina with her verve and her wild passions. She released his zest for life and his capacity for spontaneous and unstinting love which so much struck me at the very beginning. I did not at first realize that I owed this to her, and I am sorry I was not able to become friends with her. Perhaps she would have taught me how to surrender totally to my feelings, in the way she did herself, with such utter abandon. Akhmatova talks of the 'hidden line' in the relations between two people which love, passion, and other higher human feelings cannot cross. I now know very well that failure to achieve a full union with someone comes much less from a person's being bottled up in himself than from petty individualism, paltry love of self, and the need to assert oneself. These are the vulgar qualities not of a woman great even in her jealousy, but of the narrow-minded, self-centred, empty-headed kind of hussy branded by Tsvetayeva as a 'piece of merchandise'. I curse myself for having spoken too few wild words, for having been neither very generous nor completely free – as Tsvetayeva, M., and Akhmatova were.

When she met Akhmatova, Tsvetayeva complained bitterly about her fate, and then, suddenly, leaning closer, she said she had been to see the house where she had spent her childhood and found her favourite lime tree growing there just as before. She begged Akhmatova not to tell anyone lest 'they find out and cut it down'. This lime tree was all she had left: 'The abyss has swallowed my loved ones, and my parents' home has been pillaged.' I know of no fate more terrible than Marina Tsvetayeva's.

35   The Prodigal Son

I: BEGINNING AND END

All his life M. felt drawn to the south, to the shores of the Black Sea, to the Mediterranean. He first got to know the Crimea and came to love its eastern coast; then, in 1921, he spent six months in Georgia with me, and in 1930 we lived from May to November in Armenia and in Tiflis, where after a long silence he began to write poetry again. I mention here only real journeys, not short holidays, of which there were many more.

For M. the Mediterranean, the Crimea, the Caucasus, constituted the historical world, the book 'by which the first people learned to read'. This 'historical world', in his eyes, was limited to the people who together made up Christendom, and he regarded Armenia as an outpost 'at the world's edge' ('The whole morning of your days at the world's edge / you stood, swallowing your tears. / And with shame and pain turned away / From the bearded cities of the East') . . . In those years the traces of the Musavatist* pogroms were still visible everywhere – one had only to see Shusha! – and this deepened the feeling of the country as a borderland, surrounded by alien peoples. In M.'s poetry on Armenia the theme of doom, the end, finality, unexpectedly slips in: 'And the death mask of your face is taken.'

As he was leaving, M. said good-bye to Armenia forever: 'I shall never see you again, / Myopic Armenian sky, / And shall not look up, squinting, / At Ararat's nomad tent,' but in Moscow he con-

* Musavat: Azerbaidzhani nationalist movement, in power from 1918 to 1920. Shusha: Town in a predominantly Armenian area of Azerbaidzhan.

stantly thought back to it and dreamed of making another journey there. Armenia now completely displaced the Crimea and figured as the symbol of his yearning for the south in the poems of the Moscow period (1930–34). The Crimea is mentioned in 'Conversation About Dante' in the passage where he says that, reflecting on the structure of *The Divine Comedy*, he had consulted the pebbles of Koktebel. Not long before this, in Old Crimea* he had written the poem 'Cold Spring, Hungry Old Crimea', which was on a topical political, rather than historiosophical, theme. The Crimea we now saw prompted thoughts not on the genesis of our culture, but on the destruction and end of everything.

The small town was crowded with people who had fled from the Ukraine, where the famine among the peasants caused by collectivization and the liquidation of the kulaks in the early thirties was equal in horror and scale only to what happened in the Volga region at the end of the Civil War. I cannot believe that even Tamerlane and the Tartar invasions had an aftermath anything like that of collectivization. Fleeing from the Tartars, people at least kept together for mutual protection or the settling of new lands, but collectivization really scattered its victims in a literal sense – everybody made off on his own, or at the most with his wife and children. The old were just left to die. Uprooted peasants took refuge in *zemliankas* that sprang up around the cities, where they, or rather their children, were gradually absorbed – the parents were generally too exhausted to start a new life. It so happens that I later visited some of these *zemliankas* when, as a teacher in Ulianovsk, I was sent to register voters for the elections. I was struck by how clean they were, despite the overcrowding. The parents, who were usually over forty, had still not lost their traditional peasant friendliness. I never once saw any old people among them. The young ones, who had gone through collectivization and then the war, were by no means the worst of the adolescents growing up in the towns. Life in the *zemliankas* was very poor, but there was no drunkenness, and with their suspicion of strangers they kept away from bad company, doing their utmost to better themselves and escape their holes in the ground. I used to drink thin tea with them, or an infusion of wild strawberry leaves. We

* Name of a town in eastern Crimea, near Feodosia.

always sounded each other out very cautiously. Most of them had left their villages during the war, some in the thirties. Asking too many questions was not done. Both I and they had learned to hold our tongues. All the same, we felt an unspoken sympathy for each other – which they showed by coming to vote very early in the morning so I was not kept hanging around too long at the polling booth. Each 'canvasser'* is responsible for his voters and must stay until everyone of them has voted. As they left the booth, 'my' voters often asked: 'Will you be able to go soon now? Who is there still to come?' and when they got back to their *zemliankas* they rounded up the stragglers for me. Playing our respective parts in the compulsory ritual, we tried to make it a little easier for each other, but all the same we never dared exchange a single frank word. Nobody in the polling booth could understand how a citizen of my dubious background, and most likely a very poor canvasser besides, had managed things so quickly and smoothly, while the leading lights of the Teachers' Training College – where we were all responsible for the same electoral area under the college's 'patronage' – had to stay until late at night, combing the town in search of voters out on a spree. None of my voters ever once asked me whom they were supposed to be electing, or to what. Such questions were put only to the 'leading lights' in the hope of tripping them up and landing them in trouble. We went on the simple principle that we had to do it because 'they' demanded it and would not leave us alone until we had. This was towards the end of Stalin's life, when M. had been dead for more than ten years.

We were always coming across people who lived in *zemliankas* or similar makeshift dwellings. In 1933, in Koktebel, M. brought back to our room a small boy who was going around begging at all the boarding-houses and rest homes. M. gave him some milk to drink, and the next day he brought his brother and sister, who were even smaller than he was. M. had gone out in the morning to buy milk, knowing the children would come to be fed. A few days later we were visited by their father, a young Ukrainian who had fled from his native village because of the famine. We were living in a

*There is no choice of candidates in Soviet elections and the role of 'canvassers' is simply to make sure everyone records his 'vote'.

writers' rest home, but it was out of season and no writers were yet in residence (by 'writers' I mean *real*, Soviet ones, not the likes of M. and Andrei Bely, who did not count).

That spring the only people there were minor employees of the Leningrad publishing houses, and the daughter of Rimski-Korsakov, with her son. The rest home for Moscow writers was the former house of Voloshin, which was similarly occupied by employees of the Moscow publishing houses in the period before the summer season began. We would never have dreamed of going to Koktebel when all the writers were there – it was a terrifying thought. The employees of the publishing houses – accountants and other office workers – were good-hearted, simple folk. They began to put aside scraps from their meals to give to the hungry children, and a little later collected some money among themselves to pay for the whole family to go back where they came from: the famine there had begun to abate.

This particular family were not even victims of the campaign against the kulaks. They had simply joined in the headlong flight with everybody else. In the Ukraine and the Kuban the famine had raged unchecked and whole villages had died. Many of those who fled fared no better and simply perished by the roadside. There was no escape, nor ever can be in such conditions. Nowadays people realize this and do not try to flee. In any case, life has become easier and the age of panic flight is over. The only people to run away from the villages now are youths who have finished their military service: they marry the first girl they meet just to be able to live in the nearest small town.* Actually, however, my knowledge of such matters goes back ten years, to the beginning of the sixties, and things could already have changed again – people say that at the present day the villages have enough to eat.

During M.'s last visit to the Crimea, it was overrun with fugitives – 'terrible wraiths from the Ukraine, Kuban . . .' Every morning we heard stories about how a hole had been knocked in the *saman*† wall of some local storehouse or other and a bag of rationed flour or buckwheat stolen. In Old Crimea we had to live for a month on rusks we made by drying bread brought with us

* Marriage to a town-dweller entitles one to a residence permit.
† Kind of adobe brick.

from Moscow – though meat and butter were on sale in the market. Shops no longer existed, and our ration cards were scarcely honoured at all. For refugees the only thing left, unless they were to die of hunger, was to roam the streets and beg – not that the townspeople had anything to give – or to steal. The most amazing thing is that some managed to survive and settle down to live in *zemliankas*. Nowadays one can buy buckwheat, butter, and sugar in the shops of small towns. This blissful state of affairs has existed for the last ten years.

In Koktebel everybody used to collect pebbles on the beach. The most prized of all were pieces of carnelian. People showed their finds to each other over dinner, and I used to go in for the same kind as everybody else. M. always walked along the beach with me in silence and picked up odd ones, ignoring the precious carnelian and suchlike treasures. 'Throw them away,' I would say. 'What do you need those for?' But he paid no attention to me. Soon after this we got hold of some paper: the manageress of the rest home and the director of a 'closed' store* gave us a pile of grey-coloured forms – we have never had proper paper, nor ever shall – and M. began to dictate 'Conversation About Dante'. When he came to the part about how he had consulted the pebbles on the beach at Koktebel in order to make sense of *The Divine Comedy*'s structure, he said reproachfully: 'And you told me to throw them away . . . Now you see why I needed them . . .' In the summer of 1935, when we went to Voronezh, I took a handful of the pebbles from my collection, with a few of M.'s peculiar ones among them. They immediately stirred memories of the Crimea – which now suddenly appeared for the first time as a theme, with strong overtones of Koktebel, in M.'s permanent nostalgia for the sea. Voronezh is located on the boundary line between forest and steppe. Peter the Great built his flotilla there for the Azov campaign.† M. was keenly affected by this landscape, and even grew fond of it, but after touching our Crimean pebbles with his fingers, he wrote a poem in which,

* i.e. one serving only some category of privileged persons entitled to use it.

† Voronezh is situated on a tributary of the Don, which flows into the Azov Sea. With his flotilla built in Voronezh, Peter defeated the Turks and thereby gained access to the sea of Azov in 1696.

for the first time, he took his leave of the seashore he loved so much: 'The wild strawberries of a different summer lie here before me in banishment / doubly sincere carnelian and jet, brother to the ant.' The poem echoes our old argument about whether there was any point in picking up ordinary pebbles: 'But I prefer the simple soldier of the deep, uncouth, grey, loved by none . . .'

By now M. was preparing for his departure from this life, and he was saying farewell to people and things he loved: Armenia, the Crimea. Only to me he did not say good-bye. He was absolutely convinced that I would follow him almost at once. Will he understand that I lingered on for his sake? After his death I never returned to the Crimea or the Caucasus; once he had said good-bye to them, there could be no way back there for me. Nor have I see the sea since, because this too he took leave of (in 'Gaps in Round Bays') – the word can scarcely be used of the light-grey, fresh waters of the inlet near Komarovo in Soviet Finland where I once stayed very briefly with Akhmatova. She also took her leave of the sea ('my last link with the sea has long been broken'*). Artificially – or rather, forcibly and unnaturally – torn away from everything dear to us, we were forever mourning things or saying farewell to them. Everything proved to be forbidden, even bread (as in the variant line: 'And forbidden bread is blameless'). Yet all the same we still belonged to the privileged section of the community, since we did have enough to buy bread, and received ration cards which were not of the lowest category. We were not reduced to breaking into storehouses, nor were we sent away to do the work of lumberjacks or loggers. When M. was cast down to the lowest depths, he fortunately died at once. Poor health, in particular a bad heart, is a trump card which ensures that a man dies in good time.

The summer of 1935 was very eventful. Shortly after my return from a trip to Moscow, we looked out the window of our room (a rented one – our landlord had taken part in the liquidation of the kulaks, and his wife was from a kulak family) to see a funeral procession going by with the bodies of some airforce men killed in a flying accident and now being buried with military honours. This was something quite exceptional: natural disasters and other catastrophes were usually hushed up. As part of the same cycle as

* From *Requiem*.

his verse about the funeral of the dead airmen, M. produced a small poem in two variants, 'No, This Is Not Migraine, / But Give Me a Menthol Stick'. In one variant he asks me to place under his head a spray of Koktebel *chobr*, an aromatic steppe grass, which is the thread connecting this group of poems with the Koktebel pebbles. In the second variant – which should be considered the final one – M. 'coexperiences' the death of the airmen, is killed in the same way, and at the moment of the disaster sees the beginning of his life, his infancy and childhood, and the 'colours of carefree space' before they are abruptly blotted out by the plunge from the sky with its 'cold of sexless space' (by 'sexless' he means inhuman and empty), and the earth below looks like an enormous rust-coloured bald pate, as though seen through tinted glass. This description of the earth seen from a great height owes something to his travels in mountain country, as well as to the stories he heard from Boris Lapin about flying. The tinted glass goes back to a childhood memory: among M.'s papers there is a description, more detailed than the one in *The Egyptian Stamp*, of the hexagonal coronation lamps with glass of various colours in them. As a child M. dismantled one of them and was very much struck by the appearance of the world when viewed through glass of different colours – red, dark blue, or yellow. (How many of us are capable of looking at the world as it is, not through the tinted glasses of the conventions and preconceptions peculiar to our culture, society, and times? Is it possible to view the world directly, as it really is – and if so, what would we see? Certainly not the product of blind chance which our twentieth-century pundits love to go on about.) To enter into M.'s world, one has to appreciate – as I shall never tire of repeating – the keenness of all his perceptions: his sight, his sense of hearing, smell, taste, and even touch. Furthermore, the memory of particular experiences remained with him for years; a man of his intense capacity for feeling never forgot anything that made a strong impact on his senses. He saw and heard things I could only barely make out, if at all, and was affected by smells and tastes which made no impression on me. He served me as a kind of additional organ of sense, so used I became to seeing with his eyes and hearing with his ears. When I was left without him, my own eyes and ears were not enough. In any case, I no longer wanted to look at the world, and I blocked my ears against its sounds. Why should I look at what he could see no more, or rather already perceived in a way quite different from someone still alive, like myself? One must beware of the kind of closeness that existed between us – the surviving partner in such a relationship always loses the ability to feel and use his senses like other human beings, virtually becoming a corpse as well and continuing to live only by inertia. This kind of existence has no point; it is a mere semblance of life . . .

Both versions of the poem about the 'menthol stick' refer to strong sensations of smell. When he went out walking, M. often looked for fragrant grasses – particularly *chobr* – and would rub them between his fingers. We found we had this in common already in Kiev, where we walked in the parks, picking leaves and blades of our favourite plants and grasses to give to each other. What artificial scent could ever compare with the smell of walnut, which everybody loves and knows? I felt sorry for Berdiayev, who adored perfumes, about which there is always something crude, adulterated, and vulgar. In Sukhumi there was a small factory where they pressed the oil out of geraniums to make perfume and over which there always hung a strong smell of ammonia. This made us realize what we disliked about perfume: some essence used in its manufacture inevitably has this rank ammonia quality, overpowering in large doses and still perceptible in the tiny ones that go into perfumes. It goes without saying that the chemicals used in perfumes nowadays are even more intolerable.

In the second, final, version of the poem M. refers to the smell of rancid blubber – that is, a smell of decay – and of the hospital ('the throb of the carbolic guitar' – the smell of carbolic acid always seems to come in waves, ebbing and flowing). His nostrils had first been assaulted by the smell of carbolic much earlier, in the late autumn of 1931, when he came to see me in the Botkin hospital, and some 'stray lines' he wrote down about carbolic acid are to be found among his rough drafts for 'Journey to Armenia'. There were various reasons why he was unable to write a whole poem about smells at that time. For one thing it needed the illumination of a poetic idea. M. never wrote poems based solely on sensory perceptions, without an idea. (Indeed, does anybody? Pasternak is

very much a poet of the senses, but even with him, ideas are paramount and sensory perceptions merely serve as the medium for
them.) There was no possibility of a poetic idea coming to him at
that period, if only because he was then busy writing prose. The
two distinct processes of writing prose and poetry never occurred
simultaneously. Some poets may interrupt the writing of verse and
switch to prose, or vice versa, but with M. it never happened –
except in the case of 'Goethe's Youth', but this was not something
he wrote of his own inner prompting: it was simply an honest piece
of work done to order, in which his own voice comes through only
incidentally.

In his poem about sudden death M. describes how the whole of
his past life flashes before his mind's eye at the final moment. I
know that he got this idea from a translation of a Spanish story
which he read, I believe, in the days when we first went to live
on Tverskoi Boulevard (1922–3). As he recounted it to me at the
time, the story told how a man falling from a bridge recalled and
relived the whole of his life. The story cannot have been anything
out of the ordinary, otherwise I should have remembered the
author's name, but it either happened to accord with M.'s own
ideas about dying or they took shape as a result of his reading it –
namely, that at the moment of death, the whole of a person's life
flashes through the mind, bringing home to him why he has lived
and the nature of his experience. While we were still together I was
unaware of the extent to which death and dying were ever present
in our lives. As long as M. himself lived, I did not understand death,
but once I was on my own, it became the main theme in my life.
Brooding on it, the question I thought of first was: if a man is dying
on the bunk of a camp infirmary – dying of exhaustion and the
sheer impossibility of continuing to live – how on earth can he
remember anything at all? That kind of death, I believe, must be
like a slow extinction, a gradual fading away of all links with the
past and with life – in other words, you are cheated not only of life
but of death too . . . The present is so unreal and incredible that
you lose contact with yourself, with life, with the past, with other
people, with the normal rules of social conduct, with ordinary
notions of good and evil. Dying the same death as M. in my own
mind, I found myself forgetting everything else in the world –

including all hope for the future. Under the inhuman conditions of life in the era we have lived through, I often felt I had forgotten everything. All that was left to me was one burning focal point and a tangible, physical sense of the camp: mounds of bodies in stinking padded jackets, a jumble of human forms, some still alive and moving, others already frozen and stiff, and the burial pit into which, 'herded with the herd', they were thrown.

I was able to summon up the strength to bear these thoughts only because I had abandoned all reflection on the meaning of life and devoted myself exclusively to a single purpose. In ages of calamity, when monstrous, inhuman torments are prolonged beyond all reason, one must put aside thoughts of meaning – which cannot be fathomed anyway – and live only for a single purpose. This is the lesson I learned from my experience, and I would not advise anyone to ignore it: it might still prove useful, in this country and elsewhere. School yourself to disregard meaning and to pursue only aims.

II: A LITTLE TEXTOLOGY

The poem 'No, This Is Not Migraine' was the first approach to the 'Verse on the Unknown Soldier', an oratorio on the coming war (perhaps on the one still to come today), mass extermination, and M.'s own death. A future researcher, going through M.'s papers, will find the first version (the one mentioning *chobr*) on the reverse side of a sheet of paper on which a poem from the 'Wolf' cycle had been copied out, but this should not lead him to assign a different date to it: the fact that a poem has been copied out on the same piece of paper as another is reason for redating only in the eyes of editors of the Khardzhiev type who are unable to analyse the content. Khardzhiev has changed the dating of a number of poems on these grounds and prides himself on the fact, but these changes should be disregarded. He redated some poems in *Stone* because he discovered copies written out on the same sheet of paper as later ones. Poems of different periods may be written on the same piece of paper for no end of reasons. The author might, for instance, copy out a selection of items to send to a magazine, or to give to a friend who has asked for certain things he particularly likes. I know very well why 'Migraine' appears on the back of a sheet of paper with a 'Wolf' poem. In the same trunk as the Koktebel pebbles I had brought from Moscow to Voronezh were all the pages with verse written on them that had survived the ransacking of our room during the first search. (Some had been hidden in a saucepan – which I still have on the shelf in my kitchen – and others in a pair of overshoes; a few things were simply overlooked by the men carrying out the search.) I spread all these papers out on the only table we had in our room in Voronezh to list them in the 'Codex Vaticanus'. M. would pace the room, composing verse in his head, and occasionally come up to the table and stand there for a moment to jot down a few lines. At some point – obviously while I was away – he must have used one of the pages that happened to be lying on the table in front of him. If I had been at home he would have dictated to me, or I would have given him a blank sheet of paper.

Poets least of all resemble office workers or teachers of calligraphy, and their manuscripts are never models of tidiness. Akhmatova started using notebooks only in her old age, and M. even boasted that he never wrote at all, working only with his voice ('While round about double-dyed scoundrels scribble away'). If ever he made a fair copy of a poem, it was usually not to keep but to give to someone who had asked for an autograph. This quite often happened when he was still at work on the poem, before it had taken final shape, so that these neat, autograph copies do not represent the end product. The final versions were generally taken down by me to his dictation. As he dictated, he always grumbled because I could not at once memorize the whole poem at first hearing. He was a hard and ungrateful taskmaster. The number of times he made fun of me for my bad spelling and eternal doubts about when to put one or two *n*'s in a word – I grew up in Kiev, and in the south Russian dialects the double *n* is never pronounced. (Nowadays, incidentally, one hears it only in the speech of snobs, or very old people – and they, needless to say, are dying out.)

M. just failed to understand why I could not remember a poem he already had in his head, or why I did not automatically know what he knew. Because of this we had umpteen rows a day. With Akhmatova it was the other way around: she could not bear me to know things she did not know. She was particularly incensed by my knowledge of English. She had discussed English pronunciation a couple of times with Marshak and was always trying to put me right, saying how musical he was and that he had lived in England. She also pricked up her ears if I used certain French idioms: she wondered how M. and I could possibly know them, though in fact they were of the kind we all learned as children in the old days. But what really infuriated her was my knowledge of Latin. I had attended a classical grammar school where the teachers had managed to din some Latin even into the laziest of us, but Akhmatova flared up whenever anybody – as happened several times – asked me in her presence to translate something. 'How can they know?' she would ask sternly. 'They know nothing at all!' Whom she meant by 'they' I cannot imagine – presumably people who had been to grammar schools where the classics were taught. Both M. and Akhmatova, the one as temperamental as the other, were thus constantly taunting poor me, though alone with either of them I gave as good as I got. When they were together, on the other hand, I was careful not to offer provocation, in case they joined forces to attack me. On these occasions I had to take avoiding action. This is a difficult art. If I had been allowed to go on living with M., I should have mastered it. I am not without talent – as M. recognized.

When a poem contains the germ of future work within itself, it becomes incrusted with variants and produces numerous offshoots in different directions. In such cases the author often has the feeling that the parent poem has no independent existence of its own, and has failed to 'work out'. This happened with the 'Wolf' poem, and also with 'Migraine'; for this reason he never included it in the main body of his work, but kept it with other drafts. In normal conditions it would have lain dormant until he found a place for it in some new book. Unfortunately, however, there was nothing normal about our life. I gave the drafts in question to Rudakov and have not been able to recover them from his widow.

The first variant of 'Migraine' came to light among the papers

I kept myself, and for a long time it looked as though the second and final variant had been lost, but then it turned up in a notebook of M.'s verse given me by Ehrenburg. M. had copied it out in his difficult handwriting, though he had typed the other poems. I took this notebook to Khardzhiev, and he did one of his lunatic things: unbinding the pages, he took out the one with 'Migraine' and destroyed it because the date underneath conflicted with the one he had decided on! 'What's the point of keeping a bad copy?' he asked when I reproached him. The only excuse for the behaviour of Soviet people, whether in big or small matters, is that they are mentally sick. Everybody is sick – some more so, because, like Khardzhiev, they were born that way, and others to a lesser degree because their psychosis is only acquired. But that anybody could be normal is quite out of the question. Fifty years of this life could produce no other result. Even today's young, 'unfrightened' people seem mad to me. Some just walk around as though they don't give a damn for anything, while others make ready for a new wave of terror – they will take to killing just as easily as their grand-fathers did. They have learned nothing from past slaughter, and since the smell of blood from those days is now only very faint in the nostrils, there is nothing to prevent the whole thing from beginning all over again, in a somewhat modernized form. It can happen not only here, but throughout the whole vast expanse of the world which once called itself Christian.

I asked Ehrenburg where he had got the missing poem, but of course he could not remember (defective memory is one of the symptoms of our psychosis). He had got some of the other poems from Tarasenkov, the 'fallen angel', a well-known collector of verse, the author of some vile articles on poetry. I can only hazard some guesses. Ehrenburg came to Voronezh in the spring of 1936, and it could be that M. dictated a few poems to him at that time, including 'Migraine' – before his work had been completely black-listed. The notebook could then have been kept by Ehrenburg in Paris, or left with his daughter in Moscow. The trouble about this hypothesis is that before the war Ehrenburg showed very little interest in Mandelstam and thought of him as a figure from the past. It was only later that he changed his mind. After the fall of France Ehrenburg took refuge in the Soviet embassy in Paris, but our pact with Hitler still being in force, he was later allowed by the Germans to leave for the Soviet Union. Shortly after his return I ran into him on the Kamenny Bridge* – during all the years when my papers were not valid for residence in Moscow, I nevertheless contrived to come back on short visits. He was out walking his dog. We got into conversation, and I was struck by the change that had come over him; there was no trace of his former ironical and jocular self. He was in despair: Europe had collapsed, the world had gone mad, the Nazis had begun a reign of terror in Paris. The fall of Paris was like a personal tragedy for him and made him quite oblivious to the reign of terror also raging in Moscow. In this mad and unfamiliar world Ehrenburg was a changed person, utterly unlike the one I had known for many years. And his tone in talking about M. was also quite different. 'There is only poetry left,' he said. '"Wasps," and everything else by Osia.' I remember how dejected he looked, but when I next saw him, this mood had passed; the war with Hitler restored his spirits, and he came into his own again. All that remained from his despair was his feeling about M., who had come to stand, against the background of universal insanity and destruction, for poetry and life. This proved to be a permanent change, but in all other respects Ehrenburg tried to revive the illusions which made life easier for him. This no doubt explains why he was able to combine M. with Éluard and Neruda, and in earlier years even with Aragon. He believed, for example, that life in this country had begun to develop along rational lines after the Civil War, and that catastrophe struck only in 1937, a point of view characteristic of the 'victors'. 'But what about Mandelstam?' people would ask him. They did not mention the names of others among all the countless victims because it was known that Ehrenburg was indifferent to the rest, suffering agony only on M.'s account. To still his conscience, he tried to make out that M. had brought it all on himself: his behaviour had been foolish, his verse on Stalin was not much good and went against the whole poetic tradition. If he had just gone on writing about wasps, nothing would have happened to him ... This kind of argument was also typical of the 'victors' – and it was with just such people that Ehrenburg associated during his years in

*One of the main bridges over the Moscow River.

Paris. The Soviet embassies were staffed by them, and it was they who travelled abroad as members of delegations. From their point of view, it was not the fate of someone like M. that must have seemed an unfortunate accident, but rather the whole episode of 1937, which robbed them of the fruits of victory. Everything prior to that they regarded as a legitimate and reasonable expression of 'class warfare', directed to the crushing not of their own kind, but of 'alien' elements.

In the years when he was on close terms with the 'victors', Ehrenburg used to return to Russia on visits to look at the exciting new pioneering developments there, and he did not concern himself with M. He then believed he had no more to learn from M.'s work – this was evidently a rather general view if such a very different person as Tsvetayeva also failed to appreciate M.'s later poetry. An era of passionate devotion to novelty had no need of a Mandelstam, with his failure to 'respond to the demands of the times'. The crestfallen Ehrenburg I met walking his dog on the Kamenny Bridge was capable of preserving the verse by M. in his possession, but I would not have vouched for the man I knew in the prewar years, the one always on the lookout for the 'new', who had been so captivated by the *Thing*,* and by other eye-catching innovations. The prewar Ehrenburg might have kept, but could equally well have lost, M.'s verse. It is a moot point. (All the rest of the writers could only have destroyed it, as indeed most of them did.)

As of May 1938, only two copies of the 'Migraine' poem were known to exist: the one I had given to Rudakov and the one which had been in my trunk at the time when all the papers were removed from it, put in a sack, and taken off to the Lubianka. One of them has now turned up in the possession of Zenkevich, and the question arises: Which is it, the copy I gave to Rudakov or the one taken to the Lubianka? Is it possible that both Zenkevich and Ehrenburg got their copies from Tarasenkov? This is the crux of the matter. Since Tarasenkov had no links at all with Rudakov, it may be assumed that the manuscript produced by him is the Lubianka one. I noticed that Tarasenkov's copy of 'The Apartment' is two stanzas short – exactly as M. gave it to his interrogator in the

* See Ehrenburg, Appendix A.

Lubianka in 1934. (We had been chary about making copies of it.) If one thing has re-emerged from the abyss like this, the other missing poems – all ten of them – might still turn up as well, but why are they taking so long to surface after all these long and hideous years? I am tired of waiting, but still go on hoping. A peculiar feature of hope is that it tends to be fulfilled if you cling to it long enough. Odd, but true.

In 1919 or 1920, in Koktebel, M. wrote the poem 'You Have No Offspring, Alas, Sexless Malice Governs You', which he would not let me commit to memory. With the sort of regimes we live under in the modern age, it is indeed a wise precautionary measure not to store too much in the memory; anybody can wind up in the Lubianka, so better remain in childlike ignorance. From the very first M. was worried that I had such a good memory. He lived in constant awareness of our proximity to the 'Big House'* and was concerned to protect me. He was always saying things like: 'You must be a perfect fool there and know nothing' or: 'Don't remember this – it will give them something to go on. You must understand where we live.' (These precautions were valid only until 1937. After that facts were of no interest to them in any shape or form; they sought only to 'prove' what had been decided on beforehand: that you were guilty of 'terrorism', an attempt on the life of the 'Boss', or whatever else they fancied.) M. himself had forgotten his 'dangerous' poem, but a copy of it was preserved in Rostov by Lenia Landsberg, a diminutive hunchbacked lawyer. We learned this when Lenia came to Moscow in 1922. I do not know what happened to him later. He must almost certainly have perished either under the Germans or at the hands of our own people. Everybody was likely to end in a concentration camp or torture chamber. I thought the poem must surely have perished with him.

A few years ago a woman friend with whom I had lived in Kalinin after M.'s death told me that a young poet from Rostov was dying to see me. I was not anxious for a meeting, but she brought him all the same. All three of us sat gossiping and drinking wine, when suddenly she said: 'Look how they publish Mandel-

---

* Usual nickname for the secret-police headquarters in Soviet cities, specifically the Lubianka in Moscow and the Kresty prison in Leningrad.

stam in Rostov.' I have seen countless such bound, typescript volumes, and I opened this latest one with no great interest. It looked like all the others, but leafing through, what should I find but the full text of the lost poem – slightly garbled, it was true, in one place, but I was easily able to correct this from memory. It turned out to have been transcribed from a version written into a copy of *Poems** which had turned up in a secondhand bookstore. The book had probably belonged to Lenia Landsberg. The poem had thus proved more enduring than either its author or its custodian.

These typescript collections often contain verse which has nothing to do with M. In one of them I came across a poem with a reference to Brigitte Bardot, but the owner would not believe me when I told him it should be thrown out. I have to remind people that no poet continues to write after his death.

Russia is the country of *samizdat*. Already in Pushkin's day books used to circulate in manuscript, and the authorities, when copies came into their hands, called the authors to account. If I don't watch out, I'll be in trouble myself for producing a *samizdat* prose work . . .

III: 'VERSE ON THE UNKNOWN SOLDIER'

Natasha Shtempel has written a letter to say that M. read the 'Migraine' poem and 'Not as a Floury White Butterfly' to her, and told her that these were the first approaches to 'The Unknown Soldier'. I thus have a witness to confirm my own testimony on this score. There are very few people left who knew M. – and only one or two casual acquaintances such as Nikolai Chukovski (now he has died too), or Mindlin. Some of them (Mindlin and Borisov, for instance) are highly inventive and fashion M. in their own image, or describe meetings which never happened, often in Voronezh, where one of them claims to have seen M. together with Narbut in 1919 and talked with him about poetry. Then there are

*The edition of Mandelstam's work published in 1928.

scoundrels like Khardzhiev and Rozhdestvenski who pretend to have been able to read M.'s mind and managed to discuss every point with him before writing their commentaries and memoirs. The only reliable witness who was really close to us is Natasha Shtempel. Unfortunately she is in no hurry to write down her memories – which are invaluable, and more trustworthy than anyone else's. If, as I believe will be the case, a living interest in M. is maintained, then it should be borne in mind that a great deal is stored up in Natasha Shtempel's memory about the last two years in the terrible life of this doomed and wonderful man who continued to write poetry – now widely circulated in *samizdat* – almost until his death.

In the 'Verse on the Unknown Soldier' he speaks not of his own death, but of the coming of an entire era of wholesale annihilation, in which everyone dies 'herded with the herd' (do people realize that *gurt* in this phrase means 'herd'?)* and becomes an 'unknown soldier', the author himself among them. (What price your 'lyrical persona',† when the theme is life and death? Just tell me that, all you connoisseurs of literature.) It is an oratorio in honour of the 'real twentieth century', in which we have seen a complete revision of the traditional European attitude to the personality. As we know, the individual has become nothing more than manure for a beautiful future as conceived in the chancelleries of socialism. The future has one marvellous advantage: it always elusively recedes – particularly when it promises happiness. For half a century our people believed in the future. Nowadays there seems to be greater interest in the imperfect past – which is closely connected with the present. Taxi drivers and courtyard domino players‡ recall the days gone by with respect and fondness. The poet Tikhonov has said in no uncertain terms that there was more order in Stalin's time. As for the people as a whole, they believe in nothing and are interested in nothing. When they get home from work, some simply

*The word is a less usual one, derived from Ukrainian *hurt*, which in its turn comes through Polish from the Middle High German *hurt* (modern German *Hürde*), and is thus ultimately of the same etymology as the English 'herd'.

† Discussed in the section 'Literary Theory', pages 368 ff.

‡ Standard figures on the Soviet urban scene, often pensioners. A byword for conservative nostalgia.

sleep, while others go and stand in line at the beer kiosks. Wonderful people they are – there will be no trouble about calling them out for a pogrom, in case of need. Whom they will beat up, I cannot say. The Jews and the intellectuals, probably. How should I know? The authorities do all our thinking and worrying for us.

The subject of the poem on the unknown soldier is death in the air, but here it is not simply an accident, of the kind that happened earlier, but a result of the death wish in people ravaged by inner emptiness, for whom an 'air pocket' is an irresistible attraction ('And in lieu of Lermontov I will describe exactly, / how the grave cures hunchbacks and air pockets beckon.') What M. foresaw could not have come to pass without the urge to kill, but equally necessary was the urge to die, a longing for the end, an 'air pocket', self-destruction, emptiness, nonbeing . . . This longing is a very real thing, for the self-destructive forces of evil, as well as for all those who have lost their faith in life after death. In the second half of the nineteenth century people arrived at the profound and subtle notion that the spirit is but a product of matter in its most highly organized form, and subject, hence, to extinction together with it. Oddly enough, this idea aroused a quite unprecedented feeling of pride in people, though it is very hard to see why. Such pride assumed myriad forms: there was he who stood 'between the stove and the cupboard', and those who modelled themselves on birds of prey; others preached the ideas of Superman, lorded it over whole nations, and unleashed their military might against neighbouring ones. In all his doings, the proud man grew enormously in stature – but he invariably shrank again, until he looked for all the world like a wizened little toadstool. It was rather like the curious visual trick played by that mosaic at one of the Metro stations.* I always used to go out of my mind on my way past it because the full-length portrait of Stalin on the ceiling looked gigantic when seen from one vantage point, but when I walked to another place and glanced up from there, he was reduced to a small egg-shaped homuncule in which the neck was indistinguishable from the waist. I stopped looking when I noticed people were beginning to

---

*The station on Arbat Square, not far from the Kremlin. The mosaic, made of multicoloured semi-precious stones, was removed some years after Stalin's death.

turn around and stare at me. If I had lingered an instant too long, I could very well have been hauled off to the Lubianka and accused of something or other – this was how such things were done in those days. Since they would not have dared put into words a charge based on the fact that I experienced a momentary upsurge of hope whenever I saw the Father of the Peoples thus cut down to size on his mosaic, they would most probably have accused me instead of contemplating an attempt on his life. M. always said that, as a general rule, they were usually right in their choice of victims – instinctively picking on all who had retained a little sanity but, reluctant to admit the naked use of terror, always inventing a case based on some grotesque accusation. Pride drove people to denounce each other and themselves, to kill each other and to destroy themselves – this is the most essential feature of the 'real twentieth century'. Only seen in proper perspective do killers and suicides dwindle to the size of pinheads – which does not prevent many from looking on them as giants.

At the time when M. wrote 'Verse on the Unknown Soldier', the Second World War was already not far away, though all the newspaper hacks, despite their incessant clarion calls about a decisive encounter between the old world and the new, were the last to believe in the reality of it. It began to look like a certainty only after the pact with Hitler, which M. foresaw, though I disbelieved him ('What funny ideas you get!' I said). He did not live to see the pact with Hitler – or at least it happened after he had disappeared for ever – but even while he was still alive everyday events were already becoming so fantastic and implausible that people longed for the future merely to escape the present. This applied to us as much as to anyone, yet even so when M.'s verse was suddenly invaded by forebodings of a future war, we could not help feeling alarmed. At the same time we were sure there was no future for us and knew that every extra day we lived was a miracle, so I tried to make light of it: what was the point of worrying about a future we would never see? Enough of your 'Soldier'! But the poem had taken such a hold over M. that, with the best will in the world, he could no longer give it up. It assumed its final shape only in Savelovo – outside the 'hundred-and-five kilometre zone' around Moscow. I do not remember whether it was there or later on, in Kalinin, that M. suddenly said, as he was glancing through the newspapers in his usual fashion: 'We shall end up making an alliance with Hitler, and then everything will be just as in the "Soldier".' How could anybody have believed it?

I believe M. sensed the approach not merely of one war but of a whole series of them. The lines: 'Do you hear, night, step-mother of the stars' gypsy camp, what comes now and later?' clearly refer to two stages: 'now,' that is, soon, imminently; and 'later,' after some interval of time, when people would have to fight for 'air to live on', for every gulp of it, for the mere possibility of breathing. The foreboding about a coming lack of air may well have been provoked by his own shortness of breath, which could frequently be *heard* in his verse. 'I am I, life is life,' is a line that could have been uttered only by a man gasping for breath. This line even makes it possible to diagnose his trouble: cardiac asthma. (I was pleased to see that this has been noted by a distant friend.) In 'Verse on the Unknown Soldier', however, the concern about a shortage of air is dictated not by his own condition but by appre-hension about the more distant future, denoted in the poem by the word 'later'.

The air, the earth's atmosphere, and the sky in particular – the 'lower level of the darkened heavens' and what we can see of the stars – turn into an element full of menace. The air and the sky appear in two connections: first there is the 'all-devouring and dynamic' air of the trenches and dugouts, depicted as a feature of the World War (and of the Second one, still to come), together with the 'implacable sky above the trenches, the sky of vast, wholesale deaths'. This is the sky which hangs over a man when he sticks his head out of the trench – huge and indifferent, as it looks down on the mass slaughter of the creatures crawling over the face of our planet. Man is a tiny creature, but 'millions killed on the cheap / (What is cheaper than a human life?) / have trodden out a path in the void,' leaving behind the faint trace of an existence hardly yet brought to fruition. The sky makes its second appearance in connection with the stage referred to as 'later'. Here, things taking place in the sky foreshadow something new: 'we are menaced by these worlds / astir like grapes on the vine,' and there is a pre-sentiment about an explosion of unknown origin which will be brighter than light itself: 'These tidings speed along a path of lightdust, / while all is still bright from yesterday's battle: / "I am not Leipzig, nor Waterloo / nor the War of the Nations. / I am the New – / light shall be made lighter yet by me."'

This poem was a real agony to M., and he felt sure it was more than a bad dream only after the appearance in it of a paean to man, his intellect and special structure. I refer to the stanza in which the human skull is called 'chalice of chalices' and 'homeland of home-lands'. 'Just look how my skull is chirping away,' M. said, showing me the sheet of paper with what he had written. 'Now we shall have a poem.' (What a curse it is to have such a good visual memory: I can still see him standing there by the table and writing down the final words.) Man, as the possessor of a skull, is the true miracle, and every man is unique and irreplaceable. By virtue of living, thinking, and feeling, he is a Shakespeare. And Shakespeare is Shakespeare by virtue of being a man, of possessing a skull ('the bonnet of bliss, the father of Shakespeare') . . . Man is the best that exists on earth and in the world – until, thanks to his suicidal urge, he ceases to do so.

M. was tormented by the idea of a world without people. It first came to him in the doomed city of Petersburg, and occurs again in the verse, written in Voronezh, about the death of the airmen: 'Marching past in broken ranks were people, people, people, / But who will carry on in place of them?'

I have noticed that the key line, the one in which the whole meaning of a poem is concentrated, was always the last to come to M. – not, of course, that it was necessarily the final line of the poem – as though he was trying to ward off the outright expression of it, struggling to do without it, to evade or pass it over in silence, but eventually giving in. The theme was always stated in the first line (or sometimes stanza) to come to him, and was resolved in the last. In the poem about the airmen the key line is the one at the very end, where he poses the question of what will happen to man's handiwork if the human race ceases to exist.

The idea running through the whole of M.'s poetry is that of man as the hub and embodiment of existence (each man is a sun drawing others into his field of gravitation), and of mankind as the summation of life's meaning. The end of man, the disappearance of the human race – this is the threat hanging over the world. The fear he voiced in his essay 'The Word and Culture' when he had understood that the rot could no longer be stopped, gradually came to be expressed in ways that were more and more specific. This apocalyptic theme unfolded through several successive phases: the end of Petersburg and the Petersburg period of Russian history; the premonition of a world without people in the desolate Petersburg of 1921 (still, however, a refuge to which 'the spirit drags itself' during 'times of grievous woes'); death bereft of meaning 'in sexless space' and the grim question about who will carry on mankind's work for it; and, finally, the oratorio on future wars as a last suicidal act of the whole human race. The idea of the threat from the air had cropped up already in a poem of 1922 where in the last stanza he says: 'And battling through in face of odds, / In the scaly armour of his mutilated wings, / Azrail takes the vanquished earth / under his high hand.' There are two further poems about death, but now it is his own: 'And when I die, my service done, / a lifelong friend of all who live' (a precise definition of his attitude to other people), and the one in which he apostrophizes someone coming in the form of a cloud. These two poems are not variants, but simply the two parts of a complete whole.

The last poems of the Voronezh period are the one about me, the woman of Kiev looking for her husband ('A wife, whose I do not know, seeks her husband'), and the one addressed to Natasha Shtempel, where he says her 'vocation' is to 'greet the resurrected'.

In the days when all these poems were being written, the weapon capable of totally annihilating life on earth had still not been invented. M. himself described them as prophetic in their 'poetic substance'. More by intuition rather than by any conscious thought process he had come to feel that the end would be brought about by some new weapon of war. Since there had been a beginning, there must also be an end – which, however, he envisaged as the death of the world, rather than as the suicide actually threatening us. Kirillov decided on suicide as a way of self-assertion, hestitating a little before actually doing away with himself. The peoples of the earth, similarly bent on self-assertion, also hover on the brink while the brilliant executors of their will, the guardians of their national dignity, sovereignty, and other such chimeras, renouncing freedom and the idea of the personality in favour of individualism (personal as well as national), devise a weapon so advanced and progressive that it will destroy not only man but all other forms of life on earth. We shall be lucky if even the vegetation or anything else at all is left of this beautiful, insane world where we have become so gloriously skilled at murdering each other in the name of universal or national happiness, exterminating all who are not themselves killers by nature.

IV: CULTURE WORSHIP

M. never talked about Mediterranean or any other kind of 'culture'. I have introduced the word in a way he would not have approved solely because my vocabulary is so poor, but he was always extremely cautious in his handling of it. In his article 'The Word and Culture' he uses it in speaking about wisdom, inherited values, and the people who embody them. In olden times the centres of enlightenment, the storehouses of spiritual treasure, were the monasteries, which temporal rulers turned to for their counsel and whose part in the political life of the country, in matters of state, was thus only indirect. In our age of secularization, the educated section of the community has become separate from the keepers of the religious spirit, and M. hoped that those who now embody 'culture' would remain outside the state – just as the monasteries did in their time.

M. felt compelled to use the word 'culture' in this context because the only alternative was to speak of the intelligentsia as its modern embodiment. But he was too mindful of how badly our intellectuals had served the Word, as in the passage where he writes of the 'half-educated mass of the intelligentsia, infected by snobbery, bereft of an inborn sense of language – already, in fact, without a language, or linguistically amorphous, capable of titillating their jaded linguistic nerve centres only by the use of cheap and empty stimulants, dubious lyrical devices, and neologisms, often alien to the spirit of the Russian language . . .' Elsewhere he spoke of 'half-education and the snobbery that goes with it, the loss of a feeling for language and the consequent creation of a poetry obligatorily experimental and presumptuous – these are merely the symptoms of illness, not the illness itself; one might think that only the outer form were going through travail, whereas, in fact, it is the spirit which is decaying and decomposing . . .' I believe that such a decline of feeling for language is closely connected with secularization and the belief in half-education as a matter of principle – this was something M. constantly dwelled on, both in conversation and in his articles. Half-education is the worst form of ignorance, and we have been reaping its fruits for quite a few decades now.

If M. did not speak about the 'culture' of the Mediterranean, it was because the area aroused thoughts and feelings of a different order in him, and was associated with another quite different set of notions: 'Here is that immovable land, and with it / I drink the cold mountain air of Christianity.' In the Crimea and in Armenia he sought 'the keys and rough apparel of the Apostolic churches'. For M., Christianity was always associated with mountain country – hence the 'cold mountain air of Christianity', and also the line 'the mountains of Siena intercede for us'. When he wrote, 'And bright nostalgia does not let me leave the still-young Voronezh hills for those of all mankind so bright in Tuscany', he was referring not to Tuscany's geological age, but to the fact that its intimate ties with the Judaic and Hellenic-Christian world went so far back. (And now, indeed, they were killing Abel in Tuscany and crucifying Christ once more!) . . . Rome was 'man's place in the universe' because it is the centre of historical Christianity, of the Church. I cannot say exactly what caused his aversion to Byzantium, but it can be demonstrated from both his poetry and his prose. He once said to me (in connection with Akhmatova's line: 'And the stern Byzantine spirit / abandoned our Russian church') that Orthodoxy derived not from Byzantium, but from Athos. I do not know whether this is true or where he got the idea, but it is what he thought. This prejudice against Byzantium could quite possibly have come from Viacheslav Ivanov, in whose mind it was inextricably linked with Dionysianism. M. placed the highest value on what he called 'teaching by word of mouth', and there was certainly a period during which he paid some attention to Viacheslav Ivanov.

In the early articles ('The Morning of Acmeism' and the one on Scriabin's death) he several times refers to Dionysianism, which he learned about not from Nietzsche, but from Ivanov. But he was not a faithful disciple, since in the article on Scriabin he is obviously taking issue with Ivanov when he writes: 'Smiling, the Christian world said to Dionysius: "Well, then, just try it on, order your maenads to tear me to pieces – I am wholeness, personality, a welded unity"'; in other words, the strength which art derives from Christianity is certitude of personal salvation. The second source from which M. might have got his ideas about Byzantium was Leontiev, whom he regarded as a writer of significance, even while numbering him among the false teachers. After Tsvetayeva had 'presented' Moscow to him, M. looked for features linking it with Italy, rather than Byzantium, and found them in the Kremlin churches: '... the five-headed Moscow cathedrals with their Italian and Russian soul'. The Cathedral of the Dormition he called 'Florence in Moscow'. We often looked at Rublev together, and he always tried to find signs of acquaintance with Italian painting. The poem 'Hagia Sophia' does not belie M.'s aversion to Byzantium – in the cathedral of Holy Sophia he saw a reflection not so much of the specifically Byzantine world as a synthesis of Hellenism and Christianity. We were also very impressed by pictures we once saw of the mosaics in a small church near Constantinople. I refrain from giving the name because it has probably been distorted in my mind by the passage of time, but I remember that the ceiling depicted the miracle of the turning of water into wine, and I was particularly impressed by the superbly dynamic way in which the vessels were arranged. M.'s dislike of Byzantium was, in a word, not very consistent. The truth is that his dislike was directed more against the Byzantium of Viacheslav Ivanov and Leontiev than against the real one, which he did not know well at all. Apart from that, he felt that Byzantium stood for a canonical rigidity which barred any living sense of the world, of ordinary things, of warmth and light. In the Russian icon, on the other hand – particularly in that of Novgorod and Pskov – he felt the presence not of a restrictive canon, but only the joy and freedom of the artist. M. respected not canons, but tradition and the freedom granted to the artist by Christianity, a freedom which always enables him to surmount and refashion the heritage handed down by his predecessors: 'And our forbears no longer awe us – / they are dissolved in our blood'.

The Crimea and Armenia – which had turned away 'with fear and shame' from the 'bearded cities of the East' – were seen by M. as outposts not of 'culture' but of Christianity, of the Hellenistic and Judaic world. Of 'culture' as such he spoke very little, and then chiefly about its static nature, its tendency to 'stand still' at any given moment in the onward flow of time. People who make a fetish of culture always try to reduce it to a canon, insisting that it requires the repetition of what has gone before. But in fact the contribution of the individual personality to culture, or rather to history, is always an infringement of the canon, a disruption of what has congealed or solidified in the course of time. M. says in his article: 'Egyptian culture means in effect the accepted conventions of Ancient Egypt, and "medieval culture" those of the Middle Ages. Champions of the idea of "culture", though not actually themselves worshippers of Ammon or upholders of the theses of the Council of Trent, find themselves committed willy-nilly to the maintenance of conventions which are, as it were, no longer decently tenable. This indeed is the essence of the culture worship which in the last century swept over the universities and schools of Europe, poisoning the existence of every true creator of new historical forms and – saddest of all – lending an air of consummate shallowness to knowledge that might otherwise have been living and tangible, capable of transporting us back to the past in order to carry us into the future.'

M. regarded poetry as being 'outside both culture and convention', for the simple reason that, as he put it, 'poetic speech is infinitely more raw, infinitely more unpolished, than so-called conversational speech'. This is indeed so. Our ordinary everyday speech consists to a very large extent of set phrases, hackneyed combinations of words which stand in the way of any new thought struggling to burst forth. In poetry words have to penetrate the fog of ready-made, congealed speech in order to convey poetic ideas as effectively as possible. Such words gain strength in the very process of overcoming the obstacles, as they thrust up through the mounds of debris under which they are buried, emerging in fresh combinations to bring out whatever ideas are seeking expression.

This does not mean that there are *no* ready-made elements in poetry. Words themselves have been shaped by centuries of use before coming down to us. All the world's poetry and folklore are there for the poet to draw on. The ideas expressed in poetry are rooted in the history of ideas in general, in what has been handed down by everybody who has ever breathed and thought. For some reason impossible to explain or understand, the flash point in art comes through contact between what has been accumulated (or concentrated in the bloodstream) over the ages and something occurring at a single passing moment which, as a particle in the flow of time, is unique and never to be repeated, yet also eternal by virtue of having been stopped in its tracks. (Stravinski made a similar observation about music.) The passing moment is eternal for him who halts it, and his reward for this brush with eternity is a sense of poetic rightness: 'How to describe this roundedness and joy?' ... The passing moment is embodied in a combination of words uttered for the first time, though each by itself has long been in existence. What it amounts to is that the sudden contact between time past and the present moment, between the individual personality and the inherited world of other people, sparks off new ideas and words never before spoken. The falsity of experimentalism is that it always skims over the surface in pursuit of some startling novelty or other. (For some reason, innovators always favour form at the expense of thought. Even Andrei Bely, in *The Silver Dove* and *The Moscow Eccentric*, was quite happy to borrow his plot and ideas from elsewhere, offering novelty only in a sentence structure which became standard practice with astonishing rapidity.) Novelty of this kind has a very brief life, since it lacks the unique and inimitable qualities obtained through the conjunction of time past with the present moment, of the personal with the universal, of one's own ideas and experiences with those of all humanity.

To experience 'roundedness and joy' is its own reward for the poet. If his words reach other people, so much the better, but this does not depend on him – hence, he cannot go out and solicit readers, but only hope that one day people will commune with him at a distance ('In posterity I shall find my reader'). If he does find a reader, the moment of 'contact', of embodiment in words, is re-lived, though in a weakened form. In his article on Villon, M.

wrote: 'The passing moment has all the pressure of the age bearing down on it and yet remains precisely what it is. But you must know how to pluck it from the time in which it is embedded without damaging the roots – otherwise it will wither.'

'Culture' understood as a set of conventions seeks to create a school and requires the use of words with the 'right' stylistic colouring. It permits and even values novelty of form, as long as this means nothing more than putting new life into components of the accepted style. It is striking to see how rapidly such a kind of formal innovation establishes itself as the dictatorship of a school.

If M. stressed the static and stultifying side of 'culture' in this sense, perhaps he was influenced by the spectacle of a frantic culture worship that was particularly frightening at a time when 'culture' understood in the wider sense of a way of life – the tending of the fields, the building of homes, a means by which people lived together in amity – was becoming extinct; he saw it, in other words, against a background of the utter degradation of our daily life. For me this incongruity was typified by the books put out by Academia (the successor to World Literature),* which specialized in fancy editions of the 'classics' produced by the most 'cultured' of hands. The members of the victorious class eagerly snapped up these works, placing them in rows on their shelves and imbibing 'culture' from them. Such lack of discrimination always has a smell of death about it. Despite all this, however, I believe that there is nevertheless a positive side to the inhibiting effect 'culture' tends to exercise on any movement – not only in periods of general breakdown but at all other times as well. Movement itself can only benefit and gain strength if, in the initial stages, at any rate, it is compelled to overcome the inertia of stable measured and rigid forms. The birth of a new movement is indeed much more hampered by the chaos and frantic helter-skelter of general upheaval,

---

* See note, page 381. Academia (written thus, in Latin characters) began as a private concern in Petrograd in 1922, until it was taken over by the State Institute for the History of Art in Leningrad and then transferred to Moscow. At one time Maxim Gorki was the chairman of its editorial board. At the end of the twenties it began to put out a vast and comprehensive series under the title 'Treasures of World Literature'. In 1938 it was virtually liquidated, and merged with the State Publishing House for Literature (Goslitizdat).

when culture worship becomes for many the sole pursuit, the hope of salvation. This was clearly so in our earlier past and is apparent again today, when we are witnessing not dissolution but something incomparably more fundamental – what exactly is not within our power to understand.

Watching this process of disintegration (or rather, perhaps, its consequences already), one cannot help feeling it is bound to end with the destruction of everything, and the question naturally arises whether there might not be a direct correlation between the decay of our culture and an approaching end to life itself. There is no logical necessity about this. Unless we have a war – a total one – children will go on being born as before. (Nowadays they are even taller than they were, as is very obvious to anyone who saw how previous generations became progressively more stunted from undernourishment.) They will grow up, and life may go on in the same old way. Frightened by the madness of our times, many a false prophet has been led to expect the end of the world before now. I have already quoted the great omniscient sage* who once opined that eschatological moods are typical of dying classes. ('Great stuff, I must say,' would have been Akhmatova's comment.) The sage's pronouncement contains more unknowns than it does words, but when he began to wipe out whole classes in actual practice, he certainly proceeded from the theoretical premises contained in this remark. Since, however, his actions did not produce the results he expected, there are no good grounds for taking what he said on trust. We have already paid a high enough price for listening to sages and geniuses. Not everybody did, of course, but there were always vast hordes of people eager to swallow it all, infecting each other with their enthusiasm and heedless of the price they would have to pay . . . In our days feelings of doom are too widespread to be ascribed to this or that social class – that is, to some particular section of the community whose very precarious sense of solidarity is actually never greater than that of a line of people waiting to receive their wage packets.

Our era is witness to the dissolution of any deep-rooted sense of community and to the creation instead of mechanical agglomerations based on arbitrarily chosen features of little significance. Yet

* Probably Lenin.

at the same time there are slight signs, just beginning to appear, which point to a yearning for the only thing that can possibly bring about true unity. Which will prove stronger: the rivalries and selfishness of nations equipped with modern weapons, or the invisible church armed with the torch received from our forbears? Only time will show, and I shall not live to learn the answer. I believe that M., in seeking for the link between Rublev and the Italians, was trying to find something which united the European world, as opposed to all the things dividing it. Not for nothing did he define Acmeism as 'nostalgia for world culture'.

I do not know whether M. was right to regard Byzantium (though not Athos) as a symbol of division. All that matters is what comes next, and whether forces will emerge to prevent ultimate destruction, the complete extinction of people, things, grass, animals, and trees. When I look at the faces of people on the escalators in the Metro or in queues to buy food, they seem to me already drained of life. But every once in a while you hear a human word even from them, utterly weary as they are, and then hope flickers once more. Even knowing how illusory it is, a man does not lose hope until his dying day. But there is another kind of hope which does not deceive. It is beyond the reach of any fears about the end of the world. It is outside space and time.

V: UNDERSTATEMENT AND OVERSTATEMENT

'Culture', a word with more than one meaning, is an indefinable concept. Thousands of volumes have been written on the subject, but for all the study of such things as the rites and customs of so-called primitive peoples, we come no nearer to understanding the secret of human society or the nature of man. We do not even understand very well why ancient cultures died out – except in cases in which they were overrun by barbarian invasions – or how a flourishing land could turn into a dreary province, barren of ideas and reduced to silence. But one thing is clear to those of us who have witnessed the breakdown of a society: the construction of a

Tower of Babel does not unite people, but divides them. People can be united only by something that has *meaning* for them, not by a *goal* that somebody sets them (as T. S. Eliot has pointed out: 'Enthusiasm and goals are transitory'), and culture is an aspect of communal life, that is, it implies unity, not division. In saying this I am not trying to define or describe culture, but simply pointing out a very elementary fact which Bergson would have classified as a biological feature of man.

If much thought is now being given to the idea of culture as a unifying factor, it is because everywhere, both here and in the West, people are beset by the same anxiety and fears. It was with hope and curiosity, therefore, that I opened T. S. Eliot's little book *Notes Towards the Definition of Culture*, but I soon saw that he actually makes no attempt at a definition. What is more, he does not even try to get to the core of the problem. His approach is conservative in the literal sense: he would like to see the preservation of certain features of European society which, so he believes, have contributed to the blossoming of its culture: the class structure, the regional diversity and so forth . . . He is more than cautious in his handling of certain questions, and, trying at all cost to avoid controversy, he sometimes makes play with 'facts' he has taken on trust. One of his main points, for example, is to insist on the connection between culture and religion, but to anticipate objections from his student audience (the *Notes* consist of a series of lectures he gave at Oxford), he grants that culture nevertheless flourishes in Russia, a country which has abandoned religion. Both Eliot and the students he was addressing have thus swallowed our propaganda whole and do not doubt in the least that culture thrives amain in our mysterious Eastern world. This misapprehension must be at the root of one of Eliot's principal assumptions, namely that England, if she finally 'consummates her apostasy', will then 'reform' herself according to the prescriptions of some 'inferior or materialistic religion'. In such a case, Eliot believes, England might produce a culture even more brilliant than her present one, since, as he puts it: 'any religion, while it lasts, provides the framework for a culture, and protects the mass of humanity from boredom and despair' . . .

Eliot was a Christian, a Catholic, it seems, but instead of consistently applying Christian standards of judgement, he goes off here on a tangent of what he fancies to be 'objectivity'. As a result, he falls into the pit always waiting for those who stray from their central idea and base their opinions on something else. To begin with, the expression 'materialistic religion' makes no sense whatsoever. It must be based on all the silly talk to the effect that here in Russia we have a 'religion' too, only a 'materialist' one. Would he also apply the term 'materialistic religion' to the various forms of paganism? And since when has religion been expected to fulfil the purely social function of protecting people from 'boredom and despair'? These two words should not in any case be linked together in the same phrase like this. The masses sometimes relieve their boredom in utterly hideous ways: we have seen how, in their dementia, they all too often fill the emptiness of life by rallies, parades, pogroms, lynchings, and denunciations – until they come to their senses in their ruined homes, sated by self-destruction. As regards despair: is this something a Christian should protect himself from, lulling himself with consoling thoughts, when he is surrounded by people who have deliberately repudiated good and think only of pandering to the most fiendish instincts in themselves and their fellow countrymen? (It is quite a different matter that the despair of the Christian, since he believes in the ultimate triumph of good, is utterly different from the atheist's.) Only faith, hope, and charity, not 'any religion', as Eliot claims, can protect one from despair. There are religions which require human sacrifice. Surely Eliot would not be saved from despair by that kind? At this point the awful suspicion crosses my mind that he may regard himself as someone apart from the ordinary mass of people. What manner of man is he? Can it be that he considers himself a member of some elite? I know that such an attitude has nothing to do with Christianity.

There remains the question: Why does Eliot suppose that English culture might suddenly flourish anew by virtue of some mysterious new religion, as conceived by him? He wrote these notes on culture after the Second World War, by which time the consequences of two great countries renouncing Christianity were plain for all to see. Had Eliot so cut himself off from the world that he failed to notice them?

He makes no mention at all of Germany, though the two countries with which he has ties, England and the United States, expended much effort and made great sacrifices in the struggle again the Nazis. His silence on this point, whether one likes it or not, gives food for thought. When it comes to Russia, on the other hand, he is rather too ready with his judgements. He regards Russia as a primitive semi-Asiatic country so backward at the time of the Revolution (it looks as though he might never have heard of Russian literature) that it was able to profit from things which, in the West, would have done nothing but harm. Russia, for example, 'eliminated' her upper classes and was much better off for it (how does he know? Or rather, why does he allow himself to say things he does not in fact know?), but this was possible only because of her exceedingly low level of development. Real European countries, he suggests, would not have fared so well. It is not clear what Eliot means by 'elimination', whether he thinks it happened through emigration or terror, but before talking about Russia he ought to take heed of the fact that the use of brute force is the very foundation of our state system. How terrifying to think that even he, a Christian and a poet, sees value in transformations brought about by violence and cruelty, the trampling underfoot of human rights and everything holy. It is clear to me that Eliot, confronted by a student audience sympathetic to Russia after the victory over Nazi Germany, hoped to placate them with the idea that what would be unthinkable in civilized England was perfectly all right in barbaric Russia. It scarcely, I fear, redounds to the credit of England that a major poet felt compelled to curry favour with the students of its ancient university by putting forward such a proposition. Can it be that even if Eliot took the trouble to consider the meaning of terror, he would still not judge the results of it in the light of his conscience and religion? I forget why the venerable bishop loses his life in one of Eliot's plays, but after reading his essay on culture I cannot bring myself to look at it, now I know his distaste for barbarism is so great that he no doubt saw nothing wrong in the 'elimination' of all the bishops in Russia.

Even where Eliot speaks of the need for sparing enemies, his argument jars on my ears: enemies must be preserved, he says, because the clash between various opposing forces and views is useful for society. The only difference between this attitude and the Soviet one is that what he regards as useful we regard as harmful. His criterion, therefore, is just as inhuman as ours, since human life should not be spared or destroyed merely on the basis of whether it is useful or harmful. In this country, too, people have sometimes been spared on account of their 'usefulness'.

Eliot believes, incidentally, that we are able to distinguish between progress and retrogression. In actual fact, however, nobody has ever been able to do any such thing, and the very concept of progress is a highly doubtful one. Talk about it fools no one in the atomic age. History is not like a road on which we can move in either direction, forward or backward. By destroying our own culture we move back neither to the age of enlightenment nor to the Middle Ages. We are not even granted the chance of reverting to the society of primitive man. Like time itself, the historical process is irreversible, and we cannot save ourselves by retrogressing.

Eliot frequently confuses cause and effect even in simple cases. He says, for example, that society needs a normal, rather than an excessive degree of 'cohesiveness', because 'an excess of unity' comes from barbarism and may lead to tyranny. Experience shows the opposite: that excessive unity – complained of by Eliot with obvious reference to Russia – comes from tyranny and may lead to barbarism. By avoiding any mention of Germany in this connection, Eliot puts himself in an awkward position. It is, after all, quite obvious in the case of Germany, as appeared strikingly after the defeat of Nazism, that the 'excessive unity' of the country was artificial, that it stemmed from tyranny (the cause) and resulted in barbarism (the effect). Eliot is thus ill-served by his contempt for one country and his incomprehensible silence about another. How can anyone discuss modern society if he ignores the tragic experience of the twentieth century?

Eliot several times says that culture is organic and cannot therefore be created artificially. For this reason I should hope that the translator (I have seen the book only, alas, in a Russian version) rather than the author is responsible for the following sentence: 'Modern culture must be grown from old roots.' To describe something as 'organic' means to say it has arisen spontaneously in the course of history, and one is bound to be confused by the combination of words '*must* be grown'. Any reader familiar with Leontiev and Danilevski knows how fond they were of likening the various national cultures to trees with different roots, trunks, and foliage. Which of the two, then – the author or the translator – found himself unable to resist putting in this figure of speech from the vegetable kingdom? Perhaps the translator is quite innocent, and Eliot, having studied what used to be called 'social biology', has taken it a step further by comparing society to plants which, sprouting afresh from old roots, can be tended in gardens and nurseries.

In reading these notes of Eliot, one certainly catches a whiff of Leontiev with his thirst for picturesque variety in our dreary, colourless world. Isn't it so much nicer to live in a world of country gentlemen, landed estates, good cooks, horse-racing and other trappings of the elegant life – not forgetting a typewriter at which the poet can sit down whenever the urge comes over him? . . . Leontiev, as a citizen of our barbaric country, of course overstated his case, while the cautious Eliot understates it, but the essence is the same. In our age, everything has become so serious that any view not rooted in values sets the teeth on edge like a knife drawn over glass. Culture worship has never saved us, and it never will. Without a firm set of standards, all judgements are very dubious.

History does not repeat itself. Judgements made by analogy always lead to false conclusions, particularly when they are buttressed by garbled facts. The drama of history can be revealing only if we look at it in the light of higher criteria. It is worth recalling here how Berdiayev, reflecting on the destiny of the Jews in the days when he was still a Marxist, suddenly understood that neither Marxism nor any other materialist theory is applicable to the history of this people. Conservative, aesthetic theories like those of Eliot or Leontiev are even more irrelevant, just as the end of Europe would be quite other than the fall of Babylon, playing a role in the history of mankind very different from the fall of an ancient culture (indeed the very concept of history could scarcely survive such a disaster). We must always bear in mind that it would be something totally dissimilar, with much more serious issues at stake than Derby Day or nice things to eat.

At the beginning of the twenties a great stir was caused by

Spengler's book on the decline of Europe (it was conceived in much the same way as Danilevski's work, of which it is reminiscent). When M. and I read it, he did not agree with Spengler's conclusions, thinking them inapplicable to the Christian world. He was much more pessimistic than Spengler, who threatened us with no worse a prospect than a transition from 'culture' to 'civilization', as a result of which everybody would be bored. Events have shown that neither civilization nor boredom will be our lot. I adore 'civilization' and good plumbing, but I have lived my life without the benefit of either.

VI: THE WANDERING JEW

M. used to tell me that the yearning to travel south was in his blood. He felt he was really a southerner who had been thrown by fate into the cold and gloom of the northern latitudes. To me it seemed ridiculous of him to talk like this of his links with the Mediterranean. The ancestors of today's Russian Jews, after all, have had no connection with its shores from time immemorial and came to settle among alien peoples on the western fringes of the Russian empire not even from the lands of the first Exodus, but via the minor German principalities and other countries of the Diaspora. This was how it was in biblical times as well: the first patriarchs settled on alien lands, near alien cities, purchasing from alien peoples the right to bury their dead in alien caves among alien pastures. Does the blood keep its memory of wanderings such as these?

The favourite sons of the biblical patriarchs broke away from the tribe and went off to become part of an alien culture, but always remaining Jews. They were absorbed by their new surroundings and 'with quicklime in their blood gathered night grasses for an alien tribe . . .' I have read somewhere in S. Trubetskoi that at the beginning of our era these Jewish Josephs were recruited among the Sadducees. The Russified, or Europeanized, Jews of our times are also a little like Sadducees who have long forgotten their original homeland. How has it managed to survive, this people without land or roots which for so many centuries has been letting its favourite sons go away to serve the Pharaohs, the Hellenes, the Romans, the Spaniards, the culture, science, poetry, and music of all Europe? The biblical Joseph grew up in the midst of his tribe and spoke its language, but the ancient Sadducees went over to Greek. The Jews came to Russia speaking a dialect of German, the language of the land of their exile, and later they switched to Russian, but they still remained Jews, partaking of all the misfortunes visited on their tribe. They were burned in gas chambers and denounced as 'killer doctors'.* There are still barracks waiting for them in some infinitely remote swamp, to which they were not deported thanks only to an unbelievable stroke of luck.† It is still too early to write off those barracks. Their timbers may have rotted by now, but they could easily be repaired by the labour of new inmates. There would be no trouble about shaking the money for such repairs out of the pockets of the modern egalitarian jacket which has replaced the old *lapserdak*.‡ In this country we have some experience of turning out people's pockets.

M., who was *Osip*, not *Joseph*,§ in his birth certificate, never forgot he was a Jew, but his 'blood memory' was of a peculiar kind. It went right back to his biblical ancestors, to Spain, and to the Mediterranean, retaining nothing from the wanderings through central Europe. In other words, he felt his affinity with the shepherds and kings of the Bible, with the Jewish poets and philosophers of Alexandria and Spain, and had even decided that one of them was his direct ancestor: a Spanish poet who was kept on a chain in a dungeon during the Inquisition. 'I must have just a drop of his blood,' he said in Voronezh, reading the life of this Spanish Jew, who composed sonnets during his confinement ('You could not take away his moving lips') and wrote them down after he had been released for a brief period. Later he was chained up in the dungeon again (a second arrest!), and once more composed a great number of sonnets in his head. I think he must have chosen the

---

*See note, page 435.

†In his final months Stalin decided to deport all Jews to remote areas of the Soviet Union, but died before the plan was put into effect.

‡Long coat formerly worn by Jews in the Pale of Settlement.

§The first is a popular Russian form of the second.

sonnet because the stricter the form of a poem, the easier it is to memorize it. The Spanish poet must have had an even better memory than M., since he seems to have remembered his verse for years, probably without even writing it down. M., on the other hand, began to forget his own verse towards the end of his life. But perhaps one was better off in the dungeons of the Inquisition than in our concentration camps? I have never heard of anybody composing real poetry in the camps, only rhymes – fondly remembered by survivors because turning such stuff round in the mind helped them to go on living.

I often wonder whether I have in me a single gene or drop of blood inherited from my biblical ancestors, or even from the ghettos of the old Spanish and German cities. Who knows, perhaps I have? Where else could I have got the staying power that enabled me to survive and preserve M.'s poetry? For this one needs a maniacal obstinacy bred only by centuries of disaster, persecution, pogroms, and gas chambers. Things like this temper the spirit and toughen the fibre. One way or another I expect I shall now live out my life to the end, spurred on by the memory of Akhmatova's Russian powers of endurance: it was her boast to have so exasperated the accusers who had denounced her and her poetry that they all died before her of heart attacks. ('I go deaf from the raucous curses, / I have worn my padded coat down to the thread.')

In the first half of our century, which has such a curse on it, many Jews conceived a feeling about their ancient homeland somewhat different from M.'s. G., a doctor descended from a medical family which in its day had tasted the horrors of the Inquisition, with its dungeons and burnings at the stake, once told me of a meeting he had with some people of this different cast of mind. Right after the surrender of Nazi Germany, G., then a military doctor in captain's uniform, had to travel from one small town to another in an area annexed to Poland in order to get his demobilization papers. He managed to elbow his way into a train already so crammed with people that he thought he would have to stand the whole way. But suddenly he was hailed by a strapping fellow in civilian clothes, which were as ragged as everybody else's at that time just after the war. He invited the 'comrade captain' of the Medical Corps to take a place by the window from which he at once ejected another man in civilian clothes, equally ragged. The two strangers exchanged a few words with the doctor – they spoke Russian, but with a peculiar accent. They asked him when he expected to return to the station at which he had got on the train. He said he didn't know how long he would have to be away, but the strangers assured him they would meet him without fail any time he came back there . . .

At one of the stations on the way the doctor got out, followed by the one who had given him the seat by the window. The station building was crowded with people, but they managed to get a place at the buffet. The stranger ordered four mugs of beer (the luxuries you could get in those parts!), took two for himself, and offered the other two to the doctor. 'You'll soon understand who we are,' he said. Another man came up, whom he introduced as his brother, and only then did the doctor understand that the stranger was a Jew. Merely from his accent and the look of him he could have been anything at all, but there was no mistaking the brother's origins.

When G. eventually travelled back to the small town he had come from and got out at the station, he found that there was indeed a little group of people waiting for him. They knew the doctor had no friends in this town, and invited him to stay with them: 'Come and see how we live, spend the night with us. We don't want anything from you – we will part just as we have met, but perhaps you will remember us one day.' The doctor went with them. The small town was plastered with posters calling on the Jews to return to their original homeland. The strangers brought the doctor to an almost empty barracks and invited him to have supper with them. Everybody ate together at a common table, and the meal consisted of pork. His hosts pointed out to the doctor that there was not a single woman among them. Under the Germans, they had been constantly on the move with partisan detachments in the forests, and their families – parents, wives, and children – had all been killed by the Nazis. Strangers to one another, they had first met in these barracks, having come from all parts of Poland. Here they were waiting to be sent off to Palestine. All they had in common was the experience they had been through: the forests, partisan units, the killing of their families. They showed the doctor a copy of the local newspaper; in the town where they were now living there had been an attempt to start a pogrom, but it had ended only in the death of three of the ringleaders.

These Jews, who had been through the crucible of underground resistance, said to the doctor: 'We know the attitude of you Soviet Jews. You believe you have equality. You haven't been through what we Polish Jews have been through – but there's no escaping it in the end. The same thing will happen to you. All well and good if it doesn't, but there's not a hope. It will be fine if you don't have to remember our words, but most likely you'll have to . . .'

The military doctor indeed thought of himself as enjoying equal rights, but the day came when he was compelled to recall this conversation. The 'Doctors' Plot' – fortunately called off in the spring of 1953 – dispelled all his illusions. In this instance too a personal confrontation with the facts of life was required; people cease to turn a blind eye to what is going on around them only when they are hit over the head themselves, when their own blood is shed. If a neighbour is having the dear life squeezed out of him, this is none of one's business. Blindness is a feature of our times – people take refuge in it from the horrors of life. Indignant as I am at the blind, I also have a sneaking sympathy for them: unless you spare yourself, after all, you will simply fall to pieces and never put yourself together again. Having myself now opted out of the life around me, I am completely blind to the things – all utterly trivial compared with what fell to the lot of the older generation – that so much concern people younger than myself. In the building where I now live there are a hundred apartments, and the occupants are all right there inside them. So what is there to worry about? Until I am myself dragged from my home, I shall refuse to give way to panic. Fear only makes it harder to live and concentrate the mind.

I should emphasize, however, that my present blindness is quite deliberate. At the moment I simply do not *want* to see what goes on. If anybody starts telling me, I ask him to shut up: I'm sick to death of what I've seen already, and my eyes are now closed. This is the great difference between me and those who were blind in a previous generation – they did not suspect their disability and even boasted constantly about how keen-sighted they were. In those days the people who really had eyes to see were denounced and mocked because of their supposed blindness. Reading my first book, survivors of those older generations accuse me of not having shared in the life of my contemporaries, saying I ignore the Cheliuskin expedition, the Stakhanovites, Meyerhold's productions, those brilliant films with shots of baby carriages, Ukrainian dumplings, and the end of St Petersburg, not to mention the country's great industrial upsurge, the dazzling performance of our literary critics, and the immortal novels written during the years of our great Achievements. It is a matter of taste, but personally I cannot bear to look back at all those carnival years. I am too acutely aware of the other side of the picture: the concentration camps, the prison cells, the gas chambers, and all that vile drivel turned out by people who knew exactly what to see and what not to see. Not for nothing am I the widow of Mandelstam – whom they continue to hate just as much as if he were still alive and walking the streets.

A remarkable thing about the Jews is that, apart from suffering the lot of their own people, they also have to share the misfortunes of those in whose country they have put up their tents. Even a Jew who publicly renounces his Jewishness still goes to the gas chambers with the others, or is sent to Kolyma, like any member of the alien tribe whose language he speaks. M., a Jew and a Russian poet, paid – and still pays – a double or treble price for everything. Even worse, he was a European and a Russian intellectual brought up to believe that words were not to be treated lightly. All these crimes, taken together or separately, were punishable with all the severity of which our laws were capable. The fight against 'idealism' was and will continue to be regarded as the prime task of our times. The military doctor – a Jew, a Russian intellectual, and a humanist – who told me the story of his encounter in Poland is consequently liable on three counts. In these days, when we all borrow aspects of our destiny from one another, I often think that any real intellectual is also bound to be a little bit of a Jew, equally condemned to pay a triple price.

The young Jews in that small Polish town with its traditions of pogroms had chosen to defend themselves. They had decided there was no point in just waiting for their enlightened European neighbours to herd them into the gas chambers or slaughter them indiscriminately on the streets. My own chance has been a different one, and I have no thought of trying to defend myself. I am ready to answer on all the counts under which I am liable: for belonging to a mysterious tribe which survives despite all the laws of history and logic, for not losing my memory and for preserving M.'s verse, for putting my trust in a higher law and a higher truth, for believing that the spirit does not decay in the ground together with the perishable flesh – not to speak of all the other sins and crimes for which I could be called to account under the laws and customs of this cruel age.

Though myself categorically renouncing any attempt to save myself, I do not suggest that others should follow my example. Let people take every precaution and lead as quiet a life as they can, taking good care not to see, understand, or know anything, and not signing any futile letters of protest. There is nothing in the least bit enviable about having eyes to see. Blindness is much more agreeable and conducive to peace of mind. To others, therefore, I can only recommend caution and self-protection.

VII: THE FAMILY TREE

Everybody has relatives, and to my astonishment I found that M. was no exception – even though he had always seemed someone quite unique and apart (if one did not count his charming, feckless brother Shura). But he turned out to have relatives on his father's side. His father was a fantastic old man with his own 'little philosophy', as he called it. He was always saying with a sigh that he had distinguished ancestors and offspring but was himself merely an intermediate link between them with nothing at all to show for his life. He had covered reams of paper with his spidery German handwriting and was peeved at his sons for never having the patience to listen to even a single page when he read it out to them. Hearing about these literary efforts, Shklovski kept urging M. to insert something from the old man's memoirs or philosophy into his own prose and threatened to do so himself if M. refused. But nothing came of it because no one at all could make any sense of the old man's flowery turns of phrases, or decipher his Gothic handwriting.

The old man was friendly towards me, though he thought it a pity Osia had not consulted him about me. He would have taken him to Riga and found a wife for him there, a real Jewish girl. I failed to understand why I did not qualify as a real Jewish girl, but the old man was unable to make himself clear on this point. He also thought M. had married below himself, but after meeting my father he had second thoughts. It turned out that Shura had made some indiscreet remarks to him about the hasty and ill-considered way M. and I had taken up with each other, and the old man had been very shocked.

He tried to outline his philosophy to my father. One of his points was that one should eat eggs boiled, not scrambled or fried, since this was 'closer to nature'. My father was so dumbfounded by this particular aspect of the 'little philosophy' that M. hastened to his rescue. M. and my father shared a common interest in music. Whenever my father came to Moscow he stayed at my brother's, and on our journeys down to Kiev to see my parents, he and M. went to concerts together. Once, my father went to hear M. read at a poetry evening in Kiev, and afterwards he said to me: 'You know, he reads well, your Osia.' He avoided making a judgement about the verse itself because he did not feel competent to do so. Most of all he loved the Greek tragedies, which he used to read in the original for relaxation. He was a man with a very orderly mind – an expert on law and government, and a mathematician. In him I had a standard of comparison by which to gauge the gradual fall in the level of education after the Revolution – it did not happen all at once. There was nothing to match the training in law and the classics received by my father and brothers. All my friends were struck by this and took good care not to try to show off their learning in my father's presence. Ehrenburg used to make fun of me by saying: 'A pity you don't take after your father . . .' He was particularly respected by Makkaveiski, who felt there was something about him of his own father, a professor at the Theological Academy.

M.'s father, who was the same age as mine, represented no particular generation. He was something completely unique,

utterly unlike a *stetl** philosopher, a Jewish craftsman or merchant, or anybody else under the sun. As a manufacturer of suede
leather, he apparently knew his job very well, but felt frustrated by
an inner restlessness and craving to express himself. He used to
quote Spinoza, Rousseau, and Schiller, but in such incredible
combinations that people could only gasp. Not just a dreamer, but
a spinner of fantasies – or, rather, phantasmagorias – he was the
sort of person of whom one could not say whether he was good or
bad, mean or generous, because the main thing about him was his
quality of being totally abstract. It was beyond belief. Between
preaching his own peculiar brand of deism, he would complain
about his late wife for having taken his sons away from him, but it
was hard to imagine what else besides his 'philosophy' he would
ever have wanted to discuss with them. As far as I could make out,
their mother had tried to protect them from him. She took them
out to dachas in the country, or to holiday resorts, arranged for
them to go to high school (choosing very shrewdly – she got M.
into the Tenishev school), hired governesses for them, and in
general did her best to provide a normal intellectual background
in their home life. She had also tried, it seems, to straighten out her
husband's business affairs, but all her efforts came to nothing. M.
remembers how once, going home with her in a cab, he suddenly
saw she was crying – no doubt after making an unsuccessful
attempt to persuade a creditor not to press an account. The stable
family life she was trying to create kept slipping out of reach. This
struggle for a secure existence affected her three sons in different
ways. M., the eldest, was led to the firm conviction that security
should not be an aim in life; the middle one was very proud of his
ability to manage on next to nothing; and the youngest thought
only of living well – which he did by applying his commercial
talents to the literary field. Not lacking in such talents, he always
managed to get by pretty well. From the day he gave up his medical
career – apart from the twenty years or so (1934–53) during which
he forgot M. altogether – he exploited M.'s name with astonishing
ingenuity. To this very day he never speaks of me except in terms
appropriate to a secret denunciation. He is quite unlike his father,
or his brothers.

* Jewish village or small town in the Pale of Settlement.

M. loved his mother and was the only one to inherit her feeling for music. He was attached to the second brother, Shura, because of his facial resemblance to her. He always got Shura to follow him everywhere he went and looked after him, bringing him down to Moscow from Leningrad and wangling him a job in the State Publishing House, where he spent his whole life working as a minor clerk in the sales department. M. gave him material and moral support, laughing at his constant dread of losing his job or making a mistake in handling some book. Neither of M.'s brothers had any feeling for language, and Shura suffered from a peculiar kind of aphasia which affected his use of the written word. He was literally quite incapable of putting a sentence together because he agonized too much over every detail – the word order, the prepositions, the verb forms and phraseology. His speech, on the other hand, was quite normal – not at all tongue-tied. He had evidently somehow managed to inherit this incoherence from his father, in whose case it was also not particularly evident when he spoke about ordinary everyday matters. Every time Shura had to write a note on some new book he would come running to M., who passed him on to me. M. always asked me to spare his feelings ('He's so much like mother'). There was something touchingly helpless and bewildered about him. (How unobservant people can be: where did Ehrenburg get the idea that Shura was a practical, businesslike, and efficient person – this after living with him at very close quarters in Koktebel?) His temperament went with the moral idea which he was intent on cultivating and believed he had achieved. This ideal was to merge completely with the crowd, to be totally self-effacing. He never stopped going on about it, like his father about his 'little philosophy', and found it just as hard to get anyone to listen.

The three brothers, so extraordinarily different, each owed some feature or other to their father, but none of them was really like him. Shura, abandoned by his wife, sad and lonely, died in the Urals, where he was evacuated during the war. Yevgeni is still alive; he has his father's good strong heart, while the two older brothers had weak ones like their mother. Yevgeni recently bought two volumes of M.'s collected works from Joseph Brodski (which Joseph foolishly let him have at half price). He will soon see the third volume, which includes the letter in which M. forbids him to refer to him as his brother. Knowing that Yevgeni always threw his letters out with the garbage, M. made a particular point of keeping copies, and these, written in his own hand, have survived. This will be an unpleasant surprise for the old man who still uses his brother's name to get access to members of the academic world when he needs advice or opinions on his documentary science films.

Old Mandelstam, like two of his sons, Osip and Shura, died completely alone and abandoned. Shura reached his deathbed too late to say good-bye to him, though he arrived in time to bury him. Osip was thrown into a common burial pit; the old man's grave and Shura's are untended. The graves of my parents, as well as those of my brother and sister, are also abandoned. I would like my grave to be untended too, like everybody else's.

The Revolution scattered families and countless people of several generations lost their roots, knowing nothing of their relatives or where they were buried. It deformed the lives of my grandparents' generation and still casts a baleful shadow on the existence of people young enough to be my grandchildren or great-grandchildren. With the Revolution family ties were abruptly sundered. M.'s father had a brother in Riga who made a good living out of his business. The old man was invited to go and stay with him, but he never actually went because the problem of getting an exit visa was just as much of a trial then as it is today. Sometimes the Riga brother sent the old man gifts, of which he was very proud. In 1932, when we were living on the Tverskoi Boulevard, M.'s cousin came to visit us. He had heard people were living very well in the Soviet Union, while abroad they were going into an economic crisis. His family back in Riga had started wondering whether it might not be a good idea to move to the Soviet Union, and they had sent him, the most alert and level-headed of them, to sound out the prospects. He had come with a tourist group – these existed then already, but we avoided them like the plague because any contact with a foreigner was construed as espionage. One could easily get ten years for it.

M.'s cousin had brought a pair of warm underpants as a present for the old man. He inquired how matters stood in the Soviet Union with regard to commerce and law practice. M. told him there was no such thing as commerce, but he was not in a position to say anything about practising law. He could only advise his cousin to take a careful look around before making any hasty decisions. The cousin was no fool. A couple of days later he came to see us again and told us we had an economic crisis like every-body else, only didn't realize it because we were kept on in our jobs for next to no pay. People thus had the illusion of employ-ment, but were so unaccustomed by now to earning a proper living that they failed to notice they were simply working for nothing. He wanted to know why everybody was so badly dressed: didn't people have enough money to buy themselves decent suits? M. was amused by his cousin's notions about our economy and decided he must 'put him right' in the approved fashion, as Soviet citizens were supposed to if they suddenly got involved with a foreign visitor. He assured his cousin that our white-collar workers bought two suits a year, but the trouble was that the trouser seats wore through in a month, and the jackets were so badly tailored that they looked like the drapes on a public monument. This was the best M. could do by way of proving how well we lived. The cousin was forced to admit that no minor clerk in Riga could afford two suits a year. Then, chuckling to himself for no apparent reason, he left. We never saw him again. Not for him the practice of law in the Soviet Union, and it was the last time anybody ever gave M.'s father a pair of underpants.

Apart from relatives, we occasionally came across people who just happened to be namesakes. The first time M. himself had such an encounter was in Terioki in 1910 or so. (It was then, in the same boarding-house, that he met Kablukov for the first time.) This Mandelstam was an ophthalmologist from Kiev and a prominent figure in Jewish public life. I was once taken to him at the age of ten when I suddenly felt a desperate longing to wear glasses and began to complain about my eyesight. An astute old doctor like him would normally have seen through such deceit, but it is not so easy if there is no obvious motive. How could he have known that this little girl with pigtails had simply got it into her head, for no reason at all, that she would like to wear glasses? The poor namesake of my future husband racked his brains over me for a whole hour until he finally came up with the idea that I must be suffering from 'weakness of the optic nerve' and prescribed glasses. I wore them for a week, never to acquire another pair until half a century later.

I thus had no difficulty in fooling the first Mandelstam I met. The second was much more perspicacious – though no oculist – and could never be taken in. He told me so himself in the very early days of our friendship, as we were standing on a square just opposite the house, it so happened, of his eye-specialist namesake. It was a spot where in springtime you could feel the breeze blowing in from the Dnieper – which always made me nostalgic for the sea. All the city's gardens and parks, as well as Vladimir Hill, came out at this square. I do not know what it looks like now, but in the days of my youth Kiev was a remarkably beautiful city of a European type. Down by the river was the Podol, the Jewish quarter, where all the pogroms took place, and up on the hill Pechersk, noted for its priests and soldiers. We were living there when the Arsenal blew up,* smashing all the windows in the district, and when members of the military were hunted down and slaughtered wholesale. In the Lavra† all the valuables were looted and the monks killed. People were taken into the gardens and parks to be shot. The town was already soaked in blood well before the Second World War.

When the two Mandelstams met in Terioki, someone asked the senior one whether M. was a relative. Probably not, he replied – otherwise he would surely have come and introduced himself. To my mind, however, this reply sounded so much like something said by M.'s father that it seemed to me a sure sign of some relationship. The Mandelstams we met later: the Leningrad doctors of this name; the physicist to whom M. was introduced by the translator Isai Benediktovich Mandelstam during their efforts to save the five men condemned to be shot (as described in *Fourth Prose*); the typist in Leningrad who took dictation with a speed and accuracy almost unheard of in those illiterate days – none of these had ever heard of Benjamin Mandelstam of Riga, nor of his son Emil (M.'s father). But they all knew about one another and were able to

* In January 1918, after it had been temporarily occupied by Red Guards and workers.
† Monastery founded in 1051.

figure out precisely how they were related, either through the Kiev ophthalmologist or the Mandelstam mentioned in the Brockhaus encyclopedia as the translator of the Bible. At the same time all the Mandelstams – including Emil's three sons – had a very marked physical resemblance. It was a family likeness with the same recurring features: a head of identical shape, a slightly irregular nose, narrow face, and prominent brows. The same first names seemed to run in the family: Osip (or Joseph), Benjamin, Emilian or Emil, Alexander, Isaiah. M.'s father evidently belonged to a minor branch of this large and clearly talented clan. The women, according to M., besides having large legs, were distinguished by great earnestness and remarkable honesty – like Tatka, the daughter of Yevgeni Emilievich, who unexpectedly inherited these specific qualities of the female Mandelstams, even though she had not the slightest resemblance to her father or grandfather. M. was very fond of the girl; she was the only member of the whole family who missed him and knew his poetry.*

We should never have known that all the Mandelstams belonged to the same clan if it had not been for a chance encounter in Yalta. My mother had given me an enamelled watch which was considered to be a very good timepiece and could always fetch a good price in the pawnshops. M. had his own peculiar way of measuring time, and he boasted of always knowing what hour of day it was. But in Yalta, staying in a boarding-house run by a Greek called Lalanov, we had trouble. The food, a cross between that of a cheap Greek eating house and a Soviet cafeteria, was completely inedible when cold, and we kept arriving late for dinner. We decided we must have my watch fixed so as to be more punctual at meal-times. On the seafront at Yalta there were still a few private tradesmen – watch-menders, photographers, people selling fancy goods. NEP was wound up in the course of the next two years. For us these were the last few months before M.'s break with Soviet literature. In other words: a hundred flowers were still in bloom, but the scythe was already being sharpened. M. was a month late getting to Yalta, having been held up in Moscow over the affair of the old men condemned to death. He brought with him a copy of his *Poems*, which had just been published. Collectiviza-

* *Hope Against Hope*, pages 369 ff.

tion was almost upon us. The NEP men were complaining about the fantastic taxes they had to pay. The writers had by now managed to have themselves freed of the taxation imposed on them in 1925, and were agitating for the creation of *Literary Gazette*.* It was still not certain which way things would go, though a year before, in Sukhumi, we had read Bukharin's speeches against the Trotskiists, and M. had wondered why he was trying so hard.

The Jewish watchmender to whom we took my watch praised the movement and the enamel. On hearing our name as he wrote the receipt, he gasped with surprise and ran to fetch his wife. She also happened to be a Mandelstam, and she told us that the family was counted as an *Yiches*, that is, one coming from a noble rabbinical line. M. was unable to give the old woman any details of his branch of the family – he did not even know the patronymic of his grandfather. The old couple took us into the back room behind their shop, where they opened up a trunk and produced a large sheet of paper with a carefully drawn genealogical tree on it. Everybody was there: the translator of the Bible, the Kiev ophthalmologist, the physicist, the Leningrad doctors, the watch-mender's wife, even M.'s father and grandfather. There turned out to be a terrific number of Mandelstams, far more than we would ever have imagined. The old couple now drew in the three male offshoots from M.'s father, but we forgot to mention Tatka, the poor little tendril whose life was to be cut short.

The beginning of the family tree went back to just before the time when the founding patriarch, a watchmaker and jeweller, moved from Germany to Kurland at the invitation of Biron, the duke of this Baltic province, who was eager to attract craftsmen to his newly acquired domain. We later read somewhere that the Armenian kings of the Tigran and Arshak dynasties had similarly imported Jewish craftsmen, but these later assimilated to the local population. At the time he moved to Kurland, the ancestor of the Mandelstams still had an ancient Hebrew name, a sure sign that he came from a venerable rabbinical line. I did not bother to note the name because I could not understand why M. felt it necessary to

*The weekly paper of the Union of Soviet Writers. The first number appeared in April 1929.

study the family tree with such curiosity, questioning the old watchmender and his wife about every branch and offshoot. *The Egyptian Stamp* had already been written, and there M. had stated bluntly that our only ancestor was Goliadkin.* Goliadkin certainly appealed to me more as an ancestor than M.'s father or his brother from Riga, let alone the Kurland watchmaker or the Kiev eye doctor. The old couple invited us to drink tea with them, and M. behaved just like a respectful relative from a minor, impoverished branch of a distinguished line. I had the impression that he was envious of the watchmender and his good, kindly, old wife for having kept this feeling of a bond with their ancestors. The old woman also mentioned that in her family, which was clearly marked on the family tree, it was customary to marry off all the daughters to jewellers and watchmakers – in memory of her forbears at the court of the Duke of Kurland.

The story of this court jeweller was probably common knowledge in the family of M.'s fantastic father. This would explain some of the details in M.'s description of his aunt Johanna in *The Egyptian Stamp*: 'A dwarf. The spitting image of Empress Anna Leopoldovna. Talks Russian atrociously. Biron could have been her brother . . .' Whenever M.'s father tried to talk about his family, nobody would listen. The watchmender and his wife made it all sound much more plausible, and M. was delighted to hear what they had to say. All the same, he still preferred to think of himself as a Russian *raznochinets*† by descent, rather than as a scion of rabbis. This was how he saw his own lineage: 'Did those *raznochintsi* wear out the dried leather of their boots that I should now betray them? / We shall die like infantrymen, / But never glorify greed, jobbery, or lies . . .'

* Hero of Dostoyevski's *Double* (1846).
† See note, page 484.

VIII: THE OUTSIDER

The feeling that he was an outsider first came to M. in the twenties. This is something quite different from the anguish and loneliness of youth, and there is no sign of it in his early verse. He took the upsets of adolescence in his stride and did not feel at odds with the world. The most he complains of in his early verse is 'the light cross of lonely walks', not of any feeling of alienation. He had his own inborn cure for the pains of growing up – his sense of poetic rightness (as he said at the age of twenty: 'poetry is a sense of rightness'), a trusting attitude towards his fellowmen, respect for everybody except 'enemies of the word', and a capacity to take life as it came. Even hunger – as long as it did not kill – could whet the appetite for life and make bread taste like the food of the gods. Indeed, bread *was* the food of the gods.

The years of revolution – from 1918 to 1922 – were as overwhelming as a natural disaster, and their first effect was to heighten one's sense of the present. Knowing that death might come at any moment, everybody learned to make the utmost of each passing moment. Nobody gave much thought to the actual shape of the future, longing only for stability, peace, a let-up in the fantastic pace of events set off by the Revolution. Blood flowed in every street, outside every home. Bullet-riddled corpses lying in the roads and on the pavements were a familiar sight to us all, but more than bullets we feared the indignities and tortures that could be inflicted before death. So incredible were the things perpetrated that they suggested an obsession with killing and destruction for its own sake, rather than purposeful action. I remember, for instance, the 'shooting up' of a house in Kiev. It was a peaceful, four-storey house with large windows on Institutskaya Street (which led from the Duma to Lipki). Once, while an armed detachment was passing in front, somebody thought they heard a shot fired from it. People constantly imagined they could hear shots or were about to be ambushed, particularly if they were doing any shooting themselves. Such people would jump out of bed at night and seize their revolvers, shrieking so loudly that they woke their neighbours – who also broke into shrieks from sheer terror. It was lucky when such things ended without bullets flying. In their waking hours people often acted as though they were asleep; the newly acquired right to shoot and kill had an overpowering effect on anybody who thought he had emancipated himself by hitching a gun round his waist. The armed detachment of forty men lined up on the pavement in front of the four-storey house and began to blaze away at the 'bourgeoisie', shooting indiscriminately at all the windows until not a single pane of glass was left. Having thus 'executed' the house, the detachment marched on its way, after which the terrified inhabitants gradually began to re-emerge from the back rooms, which faced on to the courtyard, and ran off to find glaziers. It is easier for a house to heal its wounds than for a human being; forces of destruction operating within a limited space are also incomparably less deadly than a systematically functioning state machine which shoots not windows (these might be needed and must be spared), but people.

The 'Russian revolt, purposeless and cruel' did not last long. All such armed detachments were merged into an army under central control; eventually demobilized, the soldiers returned to their villages and towns where, after letting off steam for a while, they were formed into the militarized shock brigades of the central government. The dream of stabilization, that is, of a strong regime, was thus fulfilled. Society willingly put itself at the service of the new state because it offered salvation from the elemental forces of popular upheaval. In the first half of the twentieth century (God knows what the last decades of the second half have in store) it was a case of having to choose between two equally desperate alternatives: anarchy, or a rule of iron which demanded the sacrifice of all values, material and spiritual, as well as personal freedom and the most elementary principles of law. People of the new outlook – and they were in the overwhelming majority – opted for a rule of iron. Not content with condoning the regime's crimes, they even exalted them and sincerely believed that this was how things should be run: 'It's time for all the fools to go.' Today, all the cruelties have been much scaled down and some members of the old generation, skulking in their corners, can be heard to mutter about the people getting out of hand, now that the reins have been loosened. They continue to prize 'unanimity', whatever the cost,

above all else and like nothing better than to see the citizenry march
in disciplined ranks, oblivious to the straits this had landed them in.
Most of all they would like to gag everybody again, so that people
will line up in silence for their salted cucumbers and not grumble.
These champions of order talk as they do because of the fear and
horror once inspired in them by the elemental fury of popular
revolution – though most of them were still at a tender age when
it happened. They were suckled on fear of it at their mothers'
breasts.

By the time we had stability again, M. was only thirty years old
but everybody – even I – thought of him as belonging to an older
generation that had had its day. He himself felt he belonged not
among his contemporaries (Katayev, for example, only four years
his junior, he regarded as a mere puppy) but among those he called
the 'loaves long since taken out'. I now understand that in eras of
great upheaval generations are classed not by age, but by outlook.
When M. speaks of 'my beautiful woebegone century', he is thinking not of the nineteenth century or the pre-revolutionary years in
the calendar sense, but of a community of those who were like-
minded in not wanting to kill, or be associated with killers. Whether
they thought of themselves as humanists or Christians, the majority
of our intelligentsia believed that moral and aesthetic (how I hate
this word!) values are a real achievement of mankind, the essential
product of history. This is what Soloviev says in his *Justification of
the Good*, and Bergson arrives at the same idea in his speculation on
the origin of religion and ethics. In Bergson's view, the biological
species endowed with intellect called 'man' forms 'closed societies'
with the aim of preserving the species. Religion and a moral code
evolve as a means of consolidating such societies. The next stage is
that certain individuals, the guiding lights of humanity, create new
religious and moral doctrines addressed to the whole world ('the
open society'). The laws and religion of the 'closed society' are
derived from man's biological nature, but the religion and high
moral code of the 'open society' arise only when man surmounts,
or even triumphs over, his biological nature; in any case, they are
not mere derivatives of it. For Bergson, the highest manifestation
of the 'open society' is Christianity. The triumph over the laws and
institutions of the 'closed society' and the breakthrough into the

'open society' is essentially the result of historical evolution, in which an enormous role is played by outstanding personalities. I believe that Teilhard de Chardin's theory of the 'noosphere' betrays the influence of Bergson. Both take their starting point in biology, and the historical process is thus seen not so much as something specific to the human race, but as a product of biological evolution.

Vladimir Soloviev started off from an entirely different premise – namely, that a sense of good is inherent in man, a sign of his being the son of God. In his highest activity, in love, man stands out quite distinctly from the rest of the animal kingdom. With man, love and his social life in general are not directed to the preservation of the species, as in the case of animals, but have a completely different meaning and function: to give a glimmering of higher love – in other words, knowledge of God. Soloviev understands the religions peculiar to human society as different stages of revelation and the achievement of a knowledge of God. The notion of good – the essential feature marking man off from the animals – gradually manifests itself in human society, in the course of its history. The humanist ideas of the nineteenth century were welcomed by Soloviev as a sign that good was striking deeper roots and beginning to conquer. As an illustration he mentioned the campaign against the death penalty that had gained more and more supporters during his lifetime. Soloviev's optimism was essentially based on the absolute faith of his age in progress. Though not the vulgar idea of progress preached by the 'men of the sixties', this was nevertheless an optimistic view of history as forward movement. Soloviev was indeed very much a man of the last century – *The Justification of the Good*, as well as *The Meaning of Love*, was written in the nineties. It is hard for people in our century to share Soloviev's optimism, but even I still cling to a very faint hope (it gets fainter by the second, and will soon be extinguished altogether) that all the trials endured by mankind will not prove to have been in vain. Every day hope diminishes as one sees how the younger people in the West have no faith in anything and are blind to what has happened elsewhere. Their blindness, indifference, and idiotic egotism will lead to what we have already experienced; but now it is infinitely more dangerous, if only because it will no longer be localized in one area but will spread over the whole world, until there will be no corner of the earth without its armed bands ready to obey any command their leaders give them: to shoot at windows, people, the human soul itself, to crush the thinking human skull in a Chinese helmet of stone, to break the wrists of pianists.*

With all his acumen, even Bergson, who despite his rationalism saw and knew more than many of his contemporaries, frequently failed to see what was going on in the world. He knew that 'closed societies' are always ready to spring at each other's throats, but he still believed that man enjoyed protection and security within the 'closed society' he happened to live in. But Bergson should surely have seen how the super 'closed societies' of a new type all around him were destroying, crushing, and intimidating the individual with the sole aim of satisfying their craving for grandeur. What a vile grandeur, that has to be measured by the blood shed and the corpses piled up in its name!

It is clear that 'closed societies' of an earlier kind were by no means as hermetically sealed off from each other as the modern ones, in which self-destructiveness has been elevated to a fundamental principle. The world's last optimist, Teilhard de Chardin, putting his trust in chiliasm (a thousand years of happiness on earth!), mapped out his 'noosphere' with due regard to the experience of the totalitarian states. Who was it said everything that exists is rational? The person who uttered these words completely left out of account the use that can be made of the freedom given to man, a creature capable of any degree of madness and evil. There is always an army of propagandists (or, as they were called in my childhood, 'hired hacks') to present the most monstrous evil as the height of goodness and sanity.

While a man is absorbed in his day-to-day activities, the meaning of the historical process is obscured for him by the concerns of the moment, by his striving to achieve transient purposes – everything he does becomes an urgent task to be fulfilled there and then. This is certainly true of those who lay the foundations of new social structures: they construct one purpose after another, caring very little how it is achieved (though, fortunately, not always overstep-

---

* Such incidents were reported by the Soviet press to have happened during the 'Cultural Revolution' in China.

ping the bounds of the permissible). They are never at a loss to justify their actions – mostly by pointing to the achievement of their aims – and are blind to the overall significance of what is happening, perhaps coming to their senses only at the very last moment, when it is too late.

A person looking back at past events may also fail to see their significance. What can it mean to us, this jumble of facts into which a historian can read any sense he likes? The future historian, striving for 'objectivity' and quite insensitive to the agonies of people at the time, will look at all points of view expressed in contemporary documents and try to find 'middle ground' between them. If the world survives, there are bound to be scholars who will study the activities of my contemporaries, shake their heads over them, yet still manage, in their wisdom, to discover some positive sides to our bloody era. The positive sides will indeed outweigh the negative ones, since there are already huge quantities of documents specially prepared with an eye to future historians. Such materials will ease the task of finding good things to say about it all. Some of the evidence for the prosecution will, it is true, also survive, and many of the documents intended for the defence have been concocted in such haste and with such monstrous clumsiness that they are more likely to support the other side of the case. But this will make little difference: facts pale after a certain passage of time, and blood shed in the past loses its red hue. (A fat lot we care nowadays about the way Peter the First crushed and mangled people – we will call him 'the Great'.) The particularities of an era are soon forgotten, and those that are remembered tend to be dismissed as 'incidental', or simply as a reflection of the customs or manners of a bygone and none-too-enlightened age. Since there is more than enough material to choose from in support of any interpretation, it is quite possible to ignore even events or phenomena that, as it were, epitomize the age. In the 'impartial' branch of learning known as 'history', everything depends on the particular point of view of the researcher – he will always find the documents to back up what he wants to say. There is a very good chance that the historian of the future will be a believer in the creation of universal bliss on earth and may decide, after a careful reading of André Gide, Barbusse, Fedin and Fadeyev that he is dealing with what was a genuine endeavour to establish a reign of happiness for everybody, even if the means employed were occasionally a little on the harsh side.

In fact, the only possible moment at which to make proper sense of events is immediately afterwards, while they are still fresh, before the blood has congealed and the special pleading of the 'hired hacks' can still be seen for what it is worth. Just as in looking back on one's life, this is the only possible vantage point – all later ones give a distorted perspective. In a period of ferment and disintegration, the significance of the recent past all of a sudden becomes clear. The indifference of the future is still to set in, but the specious reasoning of yesterday has collapsed, and truth can be sharply distinguished from falsehood. The time to hold an inquest is at the moment of transition, when an old era is completely played out and the new one has not yet begun. But the chance is almost always missed, and people enter into their new future without having properly digested the meaning of their past. This was always the case, and will be again now.

M. was neither a historian nor a philosopher. He did not need to seek support for the values he believed in because he never for one moment doubted them. He probably felt that they simply followed logically from Christianity, together with humanist ideas in general. Hence in his poem 'Dry Leaves of October', he says that people possessed by 'sexless malice' know nothing of Bethlehem and the Nativity ('the manger'). It is also quite plain from this poem that M. regarded 'the new' not as the beginning of an era, but only as the culmination of something which was already past and had no future: 'You will go down childless into your whited sepulchres . . .' In those years, the champions of 'the new' maintained that they alone were the defenders of man, human rights, and the humanist heritage. They claimed to be proposing not new aims, only new and potent means to achieve the old ones. Most of them believed in their humane mission and were absolutely sincere when they developed the famous argument that violence and killing were now needed only to eradicate them once and for all, that the war being fought at the moment was necessary to put an end to all wars in the future. In practice, everything turned out differently and the first to perish were the very people who had advocated killing, terror, and war in the name of abolishing them for ever more.

The really important and tragic stages of secularization were not the separation of church from state, or theology from science, since these were only a consequence of the more crucial moment when humanism was divorced from the Christianity which gave it birth. As a result of this process, which was completed in the first half of the twentieth century, we have witnessed an unparalleled dehumanization of people – individuals as well as whole societies and nations. This dehumanization has taken place in two different ways: either under cover of the sweetest words in the humanist's lexicon and promises of a social idyll which would vouchsafe a hitherto-undreamed-of flowering of the personality, or through an open appeal to a cannibal creed in whose name the strong enslave the weak and batten on the fruits of victory. The camouflage of humanist vocabulary needed to disguise the first of these approaches was so flimsy that open expressions of murderous intent were constantly showing through. This was something that could be overlooked only by the wilfully blind – of whom there is never any lack in the world. At present people have run out of fine words, and this is the only thing that offers the faintest glimmer of hope.

At the beginning of the twenties, when M. was first tormented by doubts and it was borne in on him that he was now living among 'an alien tribe', he nevertheless still considered it possible for this alien world to absorb humanist ideas, even if not all at once. He had faith in people, believing that good was inborn in them as a gift from on high and that evil is self-destroying. In effect he shared Vladimir Soloviev's view that once they have reached a certain stage in achieving knowledge of good, people can no longer turn back, and, despite the fact that he burst into tears when he first heard the word as a child, he thus came to hold a belief in 'progress' of some peculiar kind. (Can people live without it?) Though I know the world lies in evil, even I sometimes feel there must be just a little to be said for optimism. Perhaps it is justified by the real existence in our world of a tiny sprinkling of people who in childhood heard about the campaign against the death penalty – just as they knew about the Nativity and the gospel – and were so horrified by the bloodbaths of the twentieth century that the notion of it being wrong to destroy one's own kind was firmly implanted in their minds? (The same people also knew that the end does not justify the means.) Those people, on the other hand, who were employed in the carrying out of mass murder had never heard of anything at all. Trusting blindly in their superiors, they soon developed a taste for killing and torture. It is a well-known fact that particular cruelty was often displayed by adolescents and people of abnormally small stature. The Nazi air force used sixteen-year-old pilots on strafing missions against peaceful civilians. A boy of that age is capable of anything – he sets no value on his own or anybody else's life. For all the relative fewness of their numbers, those who corrupted the young succeeded in isolating them at the right time and instilling the ways of wild animals into them. This is quite apart from the hordes of people corrupted by war – the First World War, and after that the Civil War, during which everybody came to know the smell of blood. I have noticed that one of the chief ways of corrupting people is by playing on feelings of envy. Envy is generally the characteristic of a man who is conscious of his own weakness. He finds an outlet for his envy in atrocities and crimes – they give him the illusion of strength. He will always try to excuse the foulest of deeds by saying they are done in the name of justice for the whole world. Little though he needs them, he is never at a loss for a few phrases in defence of himself.

There may well have been individuals among the frenzied mobs of the Civil War period, or among the servants of the new regime in the subsequent years of peaceful reconstruction, who might just have heard of the commandment 'Thou shalt not kill', but it had already been dinned into their heads that murder for the good of the cause is both permissible and necessary. Cowardly and self-indulgent, themselves capable only of writing denunciations and poison-pen letters, such people egged others on to do the dirty work and were thrilled by the insolence and strength of the real killers. These were the people who flocked to chorus their approval of executions at public meetings; or who looked on as red-haired women, mistaken for 'Rosa of the Cheka', were torn limb from limb by the mob; or howled their encouragement to Jew-baiters or liquidators of kulaks. But this omnipresent claque was nevertheless only a very small percentage of the population. The vast majority of the glum rank and file wanted nothing to do with the killers, even though not daring to breathe a word against them. In any case, there was nothing they could say – they did not 'know the manger' and the only language they were familiar with, the language they heard constantly on every side, was that of hollow propaganda claims and calls for blood. Both the howling mob and the passive mob can be manipulated at will, and in any society you can always recruit 'cadres' – all those people with vacant eyes – to do the work of destroying their fellow men. It depends only on whether there are forces ready to seduce and make use of them. It is as simple as that. I am curious nowadays about the long-haired youth of the West. Whom do they envy, I wonder, and what undersized creatures are manipulating them? Why do Sartre and his like fawn on them, and what allurements do they hold out to them? Do they know the technique of the Chinese stone helmet? On whose heads will they clamp it?

The twenties was a time in which seducers and killers were carefully selected and recruited. First they were tried out in small operations, taking part in 'light cavalry charges' (the lame girl in *Fourth Prose*, for example), in newspaper campaigns, in the setting up of the *kolkhozes*, at public meetings, and as functionaries in millions of institutions. This was the preparatory stage – they were still only being trained for their real unleashing in the thirties. Some of the seducers operating among the intelligentsia still mouthed humanist phraseology, but for the most part they were cynics and careerists skilled in the art of making life a misery for the 'waverers', whom they accused chiefly of being outmoded in their thinking, and thus fit only to be 'cast overboard from the steamship of modernity'.* Among these cynics there were relatively inoffensive types who did what was expected of them simply to be able to maintain expensive girl friends in food and clothes. Some, like Olesha, shed a tear as they sold themselves; others, like Katayev, smacked their lips. Everybody, for some reason, was anxious to keep abreast of the times. Never have people harped so much on the need to be 'up-to-date', to be in tune with the 'present day'. Everybody wanted to keep up to the minute and was mortally afraid of lagging behind.

*See note, page 300.

M. knew very well that he belonged to 'another age' and was nobody's contemporary. But conscious as he was of being an outsider, some of the pseudo-humanist rhetoric in which the call for mutual destruction was dressed up had stuck in his mind, and for a time he was not sure of himself. If it was all in the name of a future happy life for mankind, then why was he 'alone on every road' and so hagridden? How was it possible for him alone to be right while all others were sunk in iniquity? Wasn't it a little overweening of him to set himself in opposition to everybody else? This is why he called himself 'a dried crust of a loaf long since taken out', and felt like someone dwelling among an 'alien tribe', forced to gather 'night grasses' for it. Hence, also, his early 'lime in the blood', a feeling of belonging to a totally different generation, already living in the past, and bankrupt. (Why was it bankrupt? I should like to know. Because it was unable to produce any answer to the advocacy of violence and bruality? How come the church was unable to keep its flock, such as that boy with a toothache?* What were the fatal mistakes we made in the past, and what fatal mistakes is the West making now? People should try to answer such questions – it might help them to come to their senses. Is it possible that the work of corruption is done not only by the Sartres and the Aragons but also by the defenders of the status quo – those whose main concern is with their own safety, peace, and comfort, who are bent exclusively on assuring happiness for themselves and the proper functioning of their own digestive systems?)

In the years before the Revolution M. was regarded as an outsider in various circles and walks of life. At the Merezhkovskis' he was referred to as 'Zinaida's Jewboy'; the Symbolist maenads turned their backs on him,and would gladly have torn him to pieces at a sign from their leader.† It was in Gertsyk's memoirs – if I remember rightly – that Akhmatova came across a passage about their nasty treatment of M. when he was young. She describes how he was once expected to come and read his verse at the Tower, and everybody was looking forward to having a good laugh at the expense of him and 'Grandma'. ('Grandma' was evidently their nickname for some elderly woman who loved M.'s verse, but

* See page 423.
† Viacheslav Ivanov.

otherwise played no role in his life. I don't know who it was.) All this, however, was the natural rivalry between generations, feuding among different sets – what M. called 'literary malice' – and the 'Jewboy' did not feel estranged from his surroundings, because he was aware of living in a society made up of many different circles, each with its particular attitude to people. He already had his own group of friends, his 'we', and even in circles where he was not accepted there were always one or two people who stood up for the 'Jewboy', recognizing that he was endowed with a sense of his own 'poetic rightness'. In every era one may be rejected by some circles and accepted by others. In this the pre-revolutionary years were no exception. As late as 1919 M. was still trusting, cheerful, and light of heart. But in the twenties the structure of the new society, now well on its way to becoming a monolithic state, began to work against us. At first M. tried to project this new feeling of being an outcast back into the pre-revolutionary years, recalling how already at that time he had had his ill-wishers, people who looked right through him, ladies who had created their own 'Trianons', much preferring 'the officer class' to a penniless youth like himself. This is the point of *The Egyptian Stamp*, where he suggests that the feeling of alienation experienced only in the twenties was already there in the Petersburg of 1910. He was thus attempting to trace the roots of his isolation back to that time. (The problem of why some people are at home in any society while others are estranged and isolated still interested him in later years, when he compared the attitudes of Tasso and Ariosto to the world around them: one went in morbid fear of it, and the other felt completely in his element.) But there is one detail in *The Egyptian Stamp* that nobody has noticed: Captain Krizhanovski goes around with a red stripe in his shirt during the days of the Provisional Government, and right at the end of the book he travels to Moscow and puts up at the Hotel Select – a hotel that, so we were told, was requisitioned for the use of Lubianka officials in the very first days after the Revolution. Not bankers or guards' officers were alien to M., but that biological type which, under any regime, represents power or money. Nor is it simply a matter of the particular political system. Every system has done enough to inspire eternal disgust, even if its crimes were not on the unprecedented scale we have seen in this country, but it is mainly a question of the conditions which enabled such as Captain Krizhanovski to make the most of his natural qualities – and one must bear in mind the qualities needed for self-advancement in the twenties and thirties. Each of these baleful decades produced its own type. The forties gave birth to yet another, to a large extent still with us today. (It was not the war but the years after that gave us this one.)

I am fortunate to have lingered on till the seventies, when the people who made their careers in the 'heroic years' are already disappearing from the scene. The new criminal stock of more recent times has not so far managed to climb to the top. They are still awaiting their hour. But there is just a chance that their hour will never come. I do not believe the older generation now at the helm wants to see a new orgy of terror and killing. Knowing so well what this means, they are cautious. There are young people with no memory of the terrible years who would be capable of anything, but so far they have not succeeded in getting their hands on the levers of power ... In our present transitional stage everything depends on the turn events take next. The forces of good show faint signs of life and the forces of evil from the past are enfeebled. The new, emergent evil is still only gathering strength. Which will win in the coming contest nobody can say. The fact that the old forces of evil are enfeebled gives no grounds for optimism: even so they can create havoc beyond repair. We used to talk of an actor making his final gesture 'as the curtain comes down'. It will require tremendous good management if something fatal is not to happen 'as the curtain comes down' this time, if a new kind of evil, with new blandishments and new watchwords, is not to sweep into power.

Evil has great momentum, but the forces of good are inert and passive. The masses, for all their conservatism, have no fight in them and will acquiesce in whatever happens. This is the reason for the present anxiety among so many people, including me. But I shall not live to see the outcome. This is my only consolation.

IX: THE GLASS CAGE

M. went to work for the newspaper *Moscow Komsomol* in the autumn of 1929. He lasted there till February of the following year. In December 1929, or thereabouts, he began to dictate *Fourth Prose*. We were then living in a room rented from a Nepman who traded in the market, selling haberdashery made by other Nepmen. Our landlord had to pay quite fantastic taxes – this was the method by which NEP was now being brought to a close – and after sadly making some calculations on his abacus, he decided he would be better off going to prison and Siberia than getting hopelessly into debt by paying his taxes. Like this he would at least be able to leave his family some money he had salted away, as well as the apartment, which was in his wife's name. He reckoned that by letting a room they would be able to hold out till he returned from his Siberian exile, where he counted on learning some new trade, thus being able once more to support his wife and children. In those days poor devils like him still thought they must look after their families. They were the last of the Mohicans, a kind now long since forgotten ... Anyway, our Nepman decided to sacrifice himself for his family, though he did not think of it like this – it was a simple calculation worked out on his abacus and scribbled on a piece of paper which he later tore up and flushed down the toilet.

When the usual three young toughs came for him, we could hear them ransacking his room – it was separated from ours by a thin partition, as was generally the case in this kind of two-room apartment – and they took all night to do it. We said good-bye to him as they led him away, and his sad parting words were: 'We shall need some repairs now.' During the search of his room the floor had been torn up and in making his rigorous calculations he had not reckoned with the expense of re-laying it. (Nor could he know, poor fellow, that in a year's time there would be a new famine and a sharp drop in the value of money.) The searchers had found a pile of *chervontsi** hidden in a crack in the floor, but we knew they had been put there deliberately in a fairly obvious place as a decoy. The Nepman had agreed beforehand with his wife that she would break into desperate wails as soon as the money

*Ten-ruble notes.

was discovered – we heard her talented performance, as well as the quite unfeigned howls of her children, who had not been initiated into the secret. The Nepman had calculated that the money would be found at once and that the searchers, thinking their work was done, would then take him away. But they were so bad at their job that they discovered the hiding place only in the early hours of the morning, after making a dreadful mess of the floor.

After the arrest of its breadwinner, the family ceased to be a happy, united one – something he had also not foreseen. The only right – indeed it was a duty – left to the family of a Nepman who had been forced out of business (and arrested by the security organs into the bargain) was to continue sending the children to school. There were three of them: two small girls and a boy somewhat older. The girls got used to the new situation – females are always more adaptable than their tender male counterparts! The boy, it soon appeared, could not stand up to the difficulties now being made for him in school by his fellow pupils and the teachers. Day after day we heard him weeping, while his mother shouted at him to pull himself together and not be such a milksop. She kept telling him to remember his father had gone to jail for his sake, so he should behave like anybody else in their position and start looking after his sisters . . . The boy howled his head off. Then the girls would return from their evening shift at school, eagerly telling their mother all about it as she gave them their supper of beet, cabbage, and *kasha*. Prices were already beginning to rise and the mother, sighing all the time, told them how much she had spent that day. The mornings began with breakfast of *kasha* and a special kind of 'tea'. Since ordinary tea is without nutritive value, no money was spent on it in this household, and instead they bought milk which the mother diluted with water in the kitchen, making a slightly cloudy mixture. The boy kept asking for tea, and the mother bemoaned her lot. He howled from morning to night, but fortunately he went to bed early – his wailing ceased after eleven – and then M., drinking his tea (which I tried to brew just once a day,* but he was always asking for it to be freshly made and grumbled when it wasn't), lay down on the bed and stretched out

---

*The Russian system of making tea is to brew a strong concoction that, with boiling water added, can last the whole day.

quietly, enjoying the peace. I gradually dozed off, but as soon as I was really asleep, he would wake me: 'Nadia, don't sleep – you can get up as late as you like, but I can't manage without you . . .'

I wrote on pieces of paper brought home with me from the office, in large, childish letters – because I was so sleepy – and with spelling mistakes, but always legibly. The work went on like this till the early hours every night, and was only interrupted in February, when I had to go down to Kiev for my father's funeral. On my return, I went the rounds of various offices with him to make the arrangements for our journey to Armenia. Bukharin found the right 'transmission belt' and fixed it for us through Molotov – as, later on, M.'s pension. The arrangements were not exactly in the brilliant style reserved for 'real writers', but 'considering our sins' we could count ourselves lucky. It was still possible at this time for such things to be done for M., but it became harder each year. Constantly relegated to a lower and lower category, he found himself forced down the human ladder, rung by rung.

I do not know what eventually happened to the Nepman's family. When we got back from Armenia, they were no longer living in the apartment. Whether they had left of their own accord or been evicted – as was more likely – I was unable to gather. All the people in the building were new, and there was nobody to tell us. It was a co-operative building in which all the apartments were privately owned by their tenants. Many houses had been built under this system during NEP, but now the owners were being evicted, or allowed to stay on as rent-payers only after being forced to give up their 'superfluous space'. The hopes placed by the Nepman in his apartment were thus disappointed, since the State must surely have covered the arrears of taxes he owed by confiscating it. What is the point of making such calculations in our kind of life, whose basic law is insecurity? What is one Nepman and his family, what is one howling brat when you are building a new world? Who has time for such trifles when the aim is universal happiness and, as our theorists put it, 'the flowering of the personality'? The first chapter of *Fourth Prose* is about the kind of socialism which required the sacrifice of the Nepman and his dimwitted son. There was one way, incidentally, in which the son could easily have assured a radiantly happy future for himself: he only had to denounce his father, promise to start a new life, and render a service to the authorities by looking through our papers. To be on the safe side, I always carried *Fourth Prose* around in my handbag, even though I knew the authorities took scarcely any interest in us in those years. If they did try to use the son, it was more probably against the father (where had he hidden the rest of his *chervontsi*?) or his friends and acquaintances (in whose back gardens had he buried the cashboxes with his paper rubles?). I do not remember when *chervontsi* were taken out of circulation, but I imagine that many people did not have time to dig up their holdings and exchange them for the new notes. It is possible that by this time they simply had no value at all and were now only kept hidden away in trunks by lonely old recluses, together with piles of worthless paper money issued by Kerenski's Provisional Government and, later, by the various authorities in the Civil War period. The fall in the value of money usually took place gradually – you found you could no longer make ends meet on your wages, and your pension turned into a meaningless fiction. It was either a question of money losing its value or of prices rising. There was only one occasion – at the beginning of the Second World War – when it was done openly, by a sudden increase in prices (of sugar, for instance) all on the same day. I generally do not notice gradual processes and I have no head for figures, but I do know that my wages were always insufficient, even when they were nominally high, as during the last years of my working life. That is what one expects of wages.

On the *Moscow Komsomol* M. was paid so little that his month's salary went in a few days. In this country, the privileged have always been rewarded not through their pay envelopes, but by means of unofficial handouts – cash in sealed envelopes, special rations, the privilege of using 'closed' stores, etc. There were times when even M. received favoured treatment. From 1930 until his arrest in May 1934 we were able to buy our supplies in a luxurious 'closed' store which had a notice by the cashier's desk saying: 'Members of People's Will served out of turn.' During our *Moscow Komsomol* days, we had to live on our salaries. The editorial offices were in an arcade on Tverskaya Street (now Gorki Street) and bore the general name of 'The Combine'. They were run by a 'daredevil manager' (as M. describes him in *Fourth Prose*) called Giber. In his notes, Struve writes that he has not been able to find out who Giber was. Giber was simply Giber, a manager or commercial director with an exuberant imagination. The structure of 'The Combine' was really something of a mystery. It seemed to have managed to spread in some way to the whole of the arcade and, besides the editorial offices, it included a miniature theatre, a restaurant, and perhaps a few other things, of no interest to us. Employees of the newspaper were welcome to eat in the restaurant on credit and the money was later deducted from their wages. I used to go there to eat as well, and once the waiter (they still had proper waiters) astonished me by saying, 'That old man of yours has already eaten.' The 'old man' was only thirty-eight, but he already found it harder and harder to breathe.

The attitude to M. in the editorial offices, and later on at the theatre in Voronezh, was trustful and friendly. They wanted him to be a purveyor of 'culture' to them, and they were always suggesting various topics (in the man-eating spirit of the times) on which he might write. He used to tell me about them with horror over lunch in the restaurant, or at home in the evening. All his colleagues sincerely believed in the radiant future to come and were doing their best to speed its approach. To this end they all threw themselves into the 'fight against inertia', 'raised their qualifications' in study groups, and went to evening school. The newspaper was put out by a huge staff. Every employee doing real work was supervised by a horde of idlers. The whole lot of them lunched in the restaurant on credit and went to the theatre to relax in the evening. We once saw a funny show about a butcher, a terrible moustachioed Caucasian who cracked jokes in the style of the times as he chopped up meat. He vaguely reminded us of someone whose name was already on everybody's lips . . .

On leaving for Armenia, M. resigned his job with the newspaper and was given a favourable reference. It said he was one of those members of the intelligentsia who could be allowed to work, provided it was under the guidance of Party supervisors. He was somehow upset by this, but I made fun of him for taking offence at his 'hooved' friends: long before he got his reference from them, he had decided they had hooves instead of feet, so what could be expect? I treasured this charming piece of paper, and I forget now when it disappeared; it was either confiscated during a search, or just got lost in the ordinary way. There was very much a flavour of the Komsomol at the end of the twenties about it – the Komsomol as it was just before the era of Great Deeds. At that time its members still thought themselves the salt of the earth, though they recognized the need to pick up a smattering of 'culture'. They were born under an unlucky star and later perished at the front, or in the concentration camps, accused of Trotskiism, open or secret, real or invented. This whole generation went to the slaughter, but it must be said that before being arrested, or dying in the war, they were themselves very busy conducting purges and sending people to jail. A few of them were lucky and survived the camps. You can now hear them playing dominoes in the courtyards, praising the old Boss for his firmness and willpower, and denouncing Nikita [Khrushchev] for his crudity – they forget that it was he who let them out of the camps and set them up in splendid apartments in Cheriomushki,* though they are no longer of any use to the State. How odd they should run down Nikita, who gave us all pensions, apartments, and telephones. I, for one, am very grateful to him, despite the fact that he did not know what he was doing.

At that distant time when M. worked on the newspaper with such men as these, who used to wonder how they might pick up some 'culture' from him, they were still, in their way, kind, and good-natured young fellows. I sometimes saw them giving lunch in the restaurant to friends who had been disgraced. In later years nobody would have dared so much as say hello to a fallen colleague, let alone give him a meal. Those were innocent, halcyon days, which the older generation nostalgically recalls even now. If they were given back their youth, they would repeat everything all over again.

M.'s sense of slight over that ridiculous reference I can only explain by the fact that he could not bear the thought of anybody trying to influence him. This was no doubt an aspect of his difficult character – something of which his contemporaries still complain. Even I never attempted to 'get at' him in any way, despite the genius Jewish wives are supposed to have for taking their husbands

* Vast housing project in Moscow.

in hand. As an example of his impatience with people who tried it, I can mention a trivial but characteristic incident that happened during the strange interlude of stability in our lives when he was working for the newspaper. He suddenly received a visit in the editorial office from the critic Selivanovski who had been asked by RAPP to seek M. out and tell him how they viewed him at that moment. It appeared that their attitude was cautiously optimistic: at last M. had become a real 'Soviet man' (i.e. by the mere fact of working on a newspaper), though for some reason he had written not a single new poem, nothing to demonstrate any shift in his outlook. (Why are people nowadays so staggered by the Chinese? We invented all this kind of thing, not they.) I had never seen M. in such a rage. He turned to stone, pressed his lips very tight and glared at Selivanovski. Then he asked why RAPP did not inquire about his sex life, what technique they and the Central Committee recommended in this sphere, and whether the 'class approach' was applicable here also . . . Selivanovski, as I saw from his face, was quite terrified. He tried to say something in reply, but M. would not let him speak. For several minutes he had to stand and listen to a torrent of furious words, at the end of which M. turned his back on him. Selivanovski, who was one of the mildest of the RAPP fraternity, must have thought he was dealing with a dangerous lunatic, particularly since the message he had been asked to deliver was regarded as a mark of special favour, normally received respectfully and with joy by any Soviet writer. In the peculiar idiom of Averbakh and Fadeyev, such an approach amounted to an offer of collaboration.

M. went on to say that his work only became public property when it was printed, after which 'the whole pack of you can go for me if you like'. ('Osip Emilievich,' Selivanovski managed to get in, 'how can you call us a pack!') Until that time, M. continued, it was just as outrageous to probe into a poet's 'outlook', as it would be to poke around in his bed linen and check whether he was sleeping with his wife or not: 'You wouldn't ask whether I sleep with my wife, and how many times a week, would you? Or perhaps you would . . .' Selivanovski tried to counter with something about this being the bourgeois concept of so-called creative freedom, but that a writer always worked for one class or another

... M. ignored these faint bleats of protest, but hearing the word 'creative', swore obscenely and stormed off to the restaurant, whisking me along with him. I was furious at having been dragged in like that, but he just hissed at me: 'You don't understand ... Shut up.' It was because of my fury that I remember his actual words so well. But I don't remember how long my anger lasted. He probably said something to amuse me over lunch and we made it up ...

We never saw Selivanovski again. I imagine he reported on his exchange of pleasantries with M. to the proper quarter. He was not a malicious person, but reporting on such things was regarded as a duty – all the more so in this case, since M. had mentioned certain august institutions in such an unseemly context. Selivanovski ended up in the same place as nearly everybody else: a man's fate was not determined by what he thought and said.

The writing of *Fourth Prose* did not bring complete inner emancipation, but it did clear the ground for new verse. It was important for M. not only to name the 'alien tribe', but also to dissociate himself from it, to stop gathering 'night grasses' for it. He needed to conceive of himself not as an outsider, but as a Joseph among barbarians (although this was not what the original Joseph felt about the Egyptians), a stranger among strangers with whom, in the absence of a common tongue, there was no point in trying to speak.

He was divided from the 'alien tribe' by language in the deepest sense, since all our ideas and concepts turned out to be totally different. Everybody was alien, not only the 'victors', but also the 'vanquished', who had surrendered and thrown themselves on their mercy. People were so shattered by the defeat that the older generation never recovered from the blow. Some fell silent and tried to keep out of sight, others learned to speak commonplaces that would earn them an approving smile from the 'victors'. They were followed by a generation who embraced defeatism as a way of life. People whose fathers had been executed told themselves and others how glorious and important it was to write to order. They insisted on the need not simply to adapt, but to join the 'victors' wholeheartedly, serving them in all sincerity, not out of fear, thus becoming at last really Soviet. An example was poor

Rudakov,* the son of a general, who almost foamed at the mouth as he tried to persuade M. to fall in step with the times. During the Second World War he was terribly upset at being only a lieutenant, not a general, as his father and brothers (also killed in the Revolution) had been. This was his only grievance, since in all other respects he had simply stopped thinking. The only thing wrong with the poor fellow was his taste in poetry: he liked Tsvetayeva, and also M. a little bit. But he made up for it by considering it his role in life to explain everything to those who had strayed – there were many more than might have appeared at first sight – and set them on the right path.

During the time when M. still made efforts to reach an understanding with the strangers he lived amongst, explaining how in the pre-revolutionary world he had not been a privileged person, the darling of society ladies and fashionable tailors, he got nowhere at all. (Why, actually, did they think he must have been a society favourite, as Gorodetski was?) He found his true voice only when he deliberately set himself against them. It returned the moment it dawned on him he must smash the glass cage in which he was imprisoned and regain his freedom. You cannot write poetry in a glass cage – there is no air.

Poetry had deserted him in the middle twenties and would not come back. In those years, whether his mood was good or bad, and despite the fact that he really had no one to talk with, M. kept all his old brilliance in conversation. But there was something missing, something broken inside him. It was not easy to define this something, but it was very crucial, a vital, crystallizing particle, without which it was impossible to live. I could call it his 'inner rhythm' or the 'spirit of music', but this would be to oversimplify. For the most part the 'spirit of music', indeed music as such, had already run out in the decade before the Revolution. M. had, if anything, kept his inner music, together with his fondness for real music and his capacity for love – as one can see from his letters to me, most of which were written in this period. People speak of a man's 'inner freedom', and, for want of a better expression, that is how I shall define the 'something' he had lost – which is not to say, however, that he had not kept his independence of judgement.

* *Hope Against Hope*, page 325.

In this sense he was as free as ever. But he needed to emancipate himself from the *times* in which we now lived: they weighed heavily on him. Although he claimed to have no contemporaries, the fact of the matter was that he had still not struggled free of the new age.

There was nothing in itself unusual about a lengthy period of poetic silence. His verse always came to him in spurts, after which his inner voice died away, sometimes for a year, sometimes for longer. I believe he describes the state between the end of one cycle and the beginning of another in a poem, 'God's name, like a large bird, / flew out of my breast. / Ahead of me thick mist swirls, / And behind there is an empty cage.' This state is well known to every artist (and perhaps to the scientist as well) when he has come to the end of some phase in his work and feels he has now dried up for a long time, if not for ever – such is the normal interlude between poetic cycles, phases of work, or books. But M. speaks of his silence in the second half of the twenties in a quite different vein, as the time 'when I slept without countenance or form'. It is quite clear that silence of this kind has nothing to do with an ordinary period of quiescence during which the poet gathers strength, grows, and matures. M.'s reawakening came only after his meeting with the young biologist Kuzin, which took place in Erivan, in the courtyard of a mosque to which we went constantly to drink delicious Persian tea (drunk with a small piece of sugar held in the mouth). About this meeting M. wrote the line: 'I was wakened by friendship as though by a shot.'

In our life any encounter with a person able to talk about something other than his own achievements and success in carrying out official orders seemed like a real miracle. This 'conversation' with Kuzin was short-lived, since his range was fairly limited and he was unable to extend it, but the encounter with him nevertheless played its part. Furthermore, it showed that there were still people with whom a feeling of tribal kinship was possible. Shortly after meeting Kuzin, we went on to Tiflis and it was here that poetry returned to M., never to desert him again, though there were lengthy intervals of 'rest' between cycles. I am sure this would have happened even if he had not met Kuzin, but it might have been harder. And it was not only this meeting that brought about his emancipation, but also the very sense of his splendid isolation in an alien land. This too was quite essential. Once he had recovered the vital particle he had momentarily lost, M. blossomed out again and became as carefree as ever. He was henceforth as though possessed, and now there was only one way to stop the flow of verse: by killing him. But before that he still had seven years of life and work ahead of him. He used them to the very best advantage he could. Despite all the monstrous external pressures, these seven years were the best in our whole life together. There were other wonderful times when we were happy and light of heart. We really got on quite famously with one another . . .

X: POWER OF VISION

The poem overleaf, written by Mandelstam in Moscow in 1931, not long after his return from Armenia, is frequently quoted in this section and the next, which together form an extended comment on it. TRANSLATOR'S NOTE

We returned from Armenia in the late autumn of 1930. With hindsight I know, of course, that disaster was only two and a half years away, but fortunately the future is hidden from the present, so although we lived in constant readiness for it we had no inkling of the actual form in which it would strike: the tramp of boots and sound of voices outside, the ringing of the doorbell, the house search, the arrest. We even imagined, before it happened, that the screws had already been tightened to the utmost, and that there must be some relaxation. Indeed, the screws could scarcely have been tightened any further, and what came later was simply beyond the wit of man to comprehend. But we gave little thought to it all and lived a full, if very hand-to-mouth, existence. For the first year and a half we had a very thin time of it, living in other people's apartments, sometimes even separately. The 'Wolf' cycle was written while M. was staying with his brother Shura, and I was staying with mine.

There was always a lot of noise in Shura's room. Long and

narrow, it was wedged between two of the same kind, equally overcrowded; in one Alexander Gertsovich* constantly plunked away on the piano, and in the other an old Jewish woman could always be heard busily attending to all the wants of her children, grandchildren, and neighbours. In these conditions M.'s verse came to him only at night, with the onset of 'forbidden peace'. (Otherwise he was not at all the sort of poet who composed best by night, even though he might sometimes continue working until very late. It was simply that he needed freedom from noise, and solitude denied him during the day, so at this period he was forced to work at night.) Fearing he might forget everything by morning – as always happened to verse which flitted through his mind while he was asleep – he wrote it down on pieces of paper by the light of a night lamp. Almost every morning he brought me a pile of these notes written in pencil. Some of them have survived – despite all the depredations of the security organs, the Rudakov couple, and Khardzhiev.

CANZONE

> *Tomorrow, heart pounding, praise flowing,*
> *I'll see you – can it be? –*
> *you bankers of mountain ranges,*
> *holders of prodigious shares in gneiss,*
>
> *with the eagle eye of professors,*
> *Egyptologists and numismatists,*
> *or of sombre-crested birds*
> *lean in flesh, wide-breasted,*
>
> *and, like Zeus, with the golden fingers*
> *of a cabinetmaker, expertly adjust*
> *those astounding onion-lenses,*
> *the Psalmist's legacy to a seer,*
>
> *then peer through exquisite Zeiss*
> *binoculars, King David's precious gift,*
> *spying out wrinkles in the gneiss,*
> *a pine, or tiny village-nit.*

*The hero of one of Mandelstam's poems.

Thus I'll quit these Hyperborean parts
to steep in vision destiny's finale
and say selah[1] *to the Chief of the Jews*
for his crimson caress.

The land of unshaven peaks still looms unclear.
Stubble of low forest pricks the eyes
and, fresh as a laundered fable,
a green valley sets the teeth on edge.

Military binoculars rejoice my heart
with their usurer's power of vision;
the world has only two unfaded colours left:
bilious yellow and impetuous red.

May 26, 1931

'Forbidden peace' comes only after midnight ... People generally fear insomnia, but in our overcrowded communal apartments, with the incessant hullabaloo and the extra bunks crammed into every room – all our life was lived like this – it was possible to commune with oneself only late at night. Later on, during all my years in various provincial teaching establishments, when I would be given a miserable room in a hostel for students or staff (which was even worse), I could really appreciate the lines: 'After midnight you take the silvery mouse between the teeth / and the heart can feast . . .' (Someone – Voloshin, I believe – once told M. that in Greek mythology the symbol for time was a white mouse, but I suspect the idea is more likely to have been suggested by Pushkin's 'life's scampering of mice'). Worn out by all their carryings-on during the day, people sleep blissfully in the airless stench, their mouths wide open because it is so difficult to breathe. (Something even I find impossible to imagine, despite my almost physical awareness of the camps all these years, is the combination of a suffocating stench with *cold* in the prisoners' barracks . . .) Apart from snoring and wheezing, there is nothing to disturb the peace, and then the homeless wanderer tastes the joy of solitude, his heart feasts. (All you nice long-haired boys in the West, is this

---

[1] Hebrew word which frequently appears in Psalms and is generally explained as a musical direction meaning 'pause' or 'rest'.

what you want, too? Or do you hope to seize the mansions of the rich for yourselves and cram all the rest of the mangy citizenry into communal apartments? What a pity you can't do a ten-year stretch in China, or here, back in our 'heroic' epoch!) I was upset that M. did not sleep at night, indulging in these wild feasts of poetry instead. But he calmed me by saying that the more difficulties you had to contend with, the better it was for your poetry – you would write nothing superfluous. I believe he was right.

At the beginning of the summer Shura and his wife went down south for one and a half or two months, and I was able to move in with M. in their wretched little room on Starosadski Street. The feast of poetry now went on not only at night but during the day as well, and his poems grew in length – they were no longer so compressed by the nocturnal vigil. This was a hungry time. It was the beginning of the dreadful famine in the Ukraine, the rise in prices as well as all the other joys which came in the wake of the liquidation of the kulaks and the First Five Year Plan. We had noticed already in Tiflis that something odd was going on: goods disappeared from the shops, particularly cigarettes, and we used to go round with Charents hunting for them. We were saved by street urchins who proffered us their quite outlandish wares with dirty but congenial hands. 'Vigilance,' as always during times of famine, was stepped up; there was a direct relationship between the two – the worse the one, the keener the other. If people could not be fed, it was important to increase the number of arrests, to stop them grumbling. Such is the policy of our wise rulers as they prepare to save the world. Monsieur Sartre will not, of course, read my book, but I hope someone will pass this on to him: he should at least be told . . .

We arrived in Moscow from Tiflis and when, in the evening, we began to feel hungry and tried to buy something, we found there was nothing to be had in any of the shops. I remember how we scoured the Petrovka* but could find nothing except some coffee. (Then, as now, I would have been prepared to put up with any amount of hunger and live in the worst poverty if only our rights had been respected, and we had been subject to human law, not the

* Street in central Moscow with shopping arcades.

law of wild animals.) We were soon given ration cards again –
though you could get precious little in the shops for them – and
the privileged, among whom we were at that time counted, received
special handouts of food. But meanwhile street hawkers appeared
all over the place offering for sale only what they could hold in their
hands – an egg, a turnip, a couple of potatoes. There was one of
these hawkers just two steps from where we lived and I used to go
out and buy the wherewithal for a princely meal – generally a
handful of flour and a little vegetable oil. The fussy old Jewish
woman from the next room told me off for being too sparing with
the oil, so that my fritters were not the real thing and had the consistency of bread rolls. But M., finicky as he was about his food,
was not bothered by my cooking and counted himself very lucky
indeed if I fed him on my unorthodox fritters twice a day. At the
end of the war I made them in exactly the same way for Akhmatova, and she gulped them down like a baby elephant. The kind of
food people eat to save themselves from starvation also makes
them fat – they bolt down heavy, indigestible things improvised
from their rations and become all distended as a result. Over the
years I have stored up many observations on the psychology and
physiology of hunger – but, of course, in this country we are only
interested when people starve in the 'capitalist countries'.

Our idyllic life on Starosadski Street was unclouded by anything, least of all by thoughts of the future. We had no particular
work to do. 'Old man' Margulis, a refugee from hunger and
unemployment in Leningrad, often came to see us. He was full of
hope about getting translating work or a job of some kind. In the
meantime he dug holes in the ground (to earn his daily bread), and
copied out M.'s poetry. Each time he did so, everybody we met the
next day was able to quote it. Boris Lapin used to call on us with
his typewriter and tap out some new poem on it. Once, I remember,
he brought along with him a strip of film that we held up to the
light and studied. Kuzin was rather lost when it came to new
poetry. He preferred to read it in books, where he felt he could take
it on trust, but anything fresh put him in something of a tizzy. He
was quite genuinely upset by any new verse read out to him, and M.
actually destroyed one poem he had written in his honour. Later
he realized that Kuzin, not the poem, was to blame, and he simply

stopped paying attention to anything he said. Kuzin was the kind of person who longed above all for stability, who recognized only what had firmly established itself, and could not bear anything in process of coming into being. He gradually became more and more set in his ways and, I am told, is now completely hidebound. Emma Gerstein also often looked in on us. She was the kind who begins every sentence with a little sermon: 'I told you so . . .' She was friendly with Akhmatova for many years, but when Akhmatova died, Emma turned out not to have a single poem by her. I had to give her a few of the ones I had kept myself; otherwise she would have looked very silly in the eyes of anybody who loves poetry. Too many people take an interest in poets without really knowing a damn thing about poetry. It's ridiculous but true.

We had other visitors as well, not too many and not too few – just about the right number for us. We got around a good deal ourselves and often went out for walks. Everything we saw found a place in M.'s verse: the Chinese laundry to which we took our washing; the bazaar with all the goods laid out on the ground, where we looked at books we could not buy because we had no money and no home to take them to; a street photographer who took a snapshot of me, M., and Shura's wife; a Turkish kettle-drum; a jet of water playing from a barrel over the street. His return to writing poetry had brought back his feeling of oneness with the world, with people, with the crowds on the street . . . It was a wonderful feeling and we had the time of our lives, but I still don't understand how we managed on money that was hardly enough to keep a dog alive. Bukharin must already have obtained an advance for us on the two-volume edition of M.'s work, and it was being paid in tiny monthly instalments. At least we had enough to buy tea and make fritters – though we did not grow fat since there was never very much flour. What we missed most was sugar. We were able to buy a little on our ration cards and drank our tea in Russian fashion – straining it through a lump of sugar held in the mouth. As a connoisseur of tea I am always being laughed at by other experienced drinkers of it because nowadays I put my sugar in the tea. I shut up the chief of these critics by telling him that for forty-five years I never had enough sugar and thought it a miracle every time I laid my hands on some. Before long

Khalatov managed to get M. registered for special rations at the shop where old members of the People's Will were served out of turn, and he bullied the writers' organization into renewing our right to this privilege every three months. This meant that we got three extra kilos a month, apart from the kilo to which our ration cards entitled us. This was luxury indeed. Bread we always had enough of: a writer's ration card entitled you to draw as much as a worker – about eight hundred grams. You are really starving when you can think only of bread, but this came only later, when M. was no longer with me, in the war.

During those days in Starosadski Street M. wrote a poem – the one where he envies the long-range eyesight of the eagle – whose meaning at first escaped me. He was always saying how glad he was to have such good eyes. Akhmatova also liked to claim that nobody could see as far as she. 'I have the eye of a sailor,' she declared proudly, giving one to understand that she came from a seafaring family. I always reminded her that the sailors in her family never put out to sea. Her father worked for the Admiralty, where you scarcely needed the eye of a sailor, and, like most officials there, he probably had nothing to do with the sea. 'Isn't that just like you, Nadia,' Akhmatova said reprovingly. This was the phrase she used when she was hurt, and M. hastened to supprt her: 'She's always like that. That's just how she is . . .' He leapt at any opportunity to 'tease', as horrid little boys and girls do. Akhmatova and I were the easiest targets because we always appreciated the performance. How hard it was for me, so used to being teased, when I was left all alone, without the mocking, laughing, frolicsome and quick-tempered companion of walks that were never lonely . . .

Boasting to each other about the keenness of their vision, Akhmatova and M. invented a game possible only in Petersburg, with its straight streets and avenues stretching into infinity: Who would be the first to make out the number of an approaching streetcar? Failure was penalized and success rewarded under a complicated system of scorekeeping that they took very seriously. With my indifferent eyesight I could not compete, but they insisted I act as umpire and settle the constant disputes between them. They kept getting confused about their own rules, and each tried to cheat by claiming to have seen a number when it was really only a lucky guess. Akhmatova, much to M.'s envy, always came out on top. Like any woman, she was very good at passing off her own wishful thinking as the truth, cheating with much greater skill and doggedness than M. As umpire, I naturally took his side, unless Akhmatova managed to win me over beforehand. In an early article, M. described Akhmatova as a 'thin-waisted wasp'. After playing this streetcar game with her he readily accepted that her eyesight was quite exceptional. Is that why he credits the wasp with special powers of vision in one of the Voronezh poems? . . . Kuzin could not understand why M. was always visiting him in the Zoological Museum to consult books about the visual apparatus of birds, insects, lizards, and quadrupeds. Why should M. be interested in the sincipital arrangement of the eyes in lizards? A rigorous specialist himself, Kuzin just shook his head in wonder: every creature had the eyes suited to it, but this was not something for M. to bother his head about – it should be left to the biologists. Much as he grumbled, however, he let M. see the books he wanted.

For M. the five senses were a window on the world, an incomparable gift of knowledge and joy. A good sense of touch appears to be rare in modern man, but with M. it was highly developed, and I always took this to be a sign that he was uncommonly well endowed in a physiological sense. Whenever we met after any separation, however brief, he always closed his eyes and passed his hand over my face, like a blind man, lightly brushing it with his fingertips. 'So you don't trust your eyes then?' I would tease him. He said nothing, but the next time he would do the same thing again. I should have known better than to make fun of him over this: in his poetry and prose he constantly refers to the sense of touch. A jug, for instance, is described as manifesting its true form only to the hand that touches and feels its warmth. Just as a blind man has 'seeing fingers', so the poet 'feels' the inner form of a poem when it is still only a sound in his head, before any words have come. The flautist's 'recalling tread of lips' also involves the sense of touch – of the lips this time, not the fingers. The act of recalling (as opposed to passive recollection) and of recognition is the primary impulse of poetry, and it comes through 'feel'. In his poem about the word he has lost, M. seeks it with his fingers, described as 'seeing'. In one of the variants of the poem he talks of words being 'rounded' ('how to express this roundedness and joy / when a word smiles at us through tears'). In the final text this became 'the rounded joy of recognition' – just what he experienced when he passed his hand over my face. This was the essence of the sense of touch – 'rounded joy', the skin's capacity to perceive, see, and feel. On my first meeting with M. I was very struck – as was Tsvetayeva – by a tenderness and delicacy of feeling which I have never encountered in anyone else.

But for all the refinement of his senses, M. never forgot that their role was only ancillary. In his 'notebooks' (or rather, the scraps of paper and a couple of memo pads that are all that remain of them) he remarks that '. . . the five senses are only vassals, the liegemen of a self endowed with reason and conscious of its superiority'. In his article about the twentieth century, M. condemns our era of rationalism because it has spurned the 'source of light', the historical legacy of our ancestors, and turned into a 'huge Cyclopean eye'. The sole property left to this eye is 'vision, empty and rapacious, devouring any object, or any era, with equal greed'. The strength of the thinking self is in its capacity to discriminate, and whether it does so correctly depends on the criterion, that is, on the degree of success in turning to the 'source of light', even at times when it only gleams dimly through the surrounding murk, the dense clouds of exhaust fumes. This is the light in the darkness of which Semion Frank wrote.

His poem entitled 'Canzone', written at a time when M. was tied to Moscow, unable to travel, confined to one small area, is about ways and means of escaping into the open spaces. Later on, in Voronezh, he used to say that the change of seasons was equivalent to travel, but during those Moscow days in Starosadski Street, he thought of another way: to increase the power of one's vision a thousandfold and thus enable the eyes to see enormous distances. The range of vision can be vastly extended either by possessing the optic apparatus of a bird of prey, or by using a pair of ordinary field glasses. On the island on Lake Sevan,* where we had stayed for a while before returning to Moscow and going to live on Starosadski Street, we had noticed that lenses heighten the

* In Armenia.

intensity of colours, making them, I would say, somehow simple and naïve. Old Khachaturian, one of the Armenian scholars we met on the island, praised the unsurpassed quality of his Zeiss binoculars, which were like a new toy to him.

The 'Egyptologists and numismatists' of the poem also refer to the Armenian scholars we met on Lake Sevan. They had travelled here to their home country from every corner of the earth. Real Europeans, they seemed much more like scholars than the kind we encountered in Moscow, mainly in the hostels and rest homes of CEKUBU. This very type of scholar was destroyed here – if he wasn't always a rare phenomenon everywhere. M. told me that Turayev's seminar was attended by no more than two or three students. Nowadays scholars of that kind in the humanities have simply disappeared without trace. Instead we have a horde of rabid females showing off their degrees and titles and the amount of undigested information stored in their craniums. Once a woman gets something in her head, it stays there for good. In the exact sciences they are a little more modest – and so are the men; at least they are incomparably more human than they were in the twenties. In the academic world the broom has swept mercilessly throughout the last fifty years, and it began with the humanities. The institutions of higher learning have been devastated by purges over and over again. Nowadays M. would not find any numismatists; after attempting a comeback, they were polished off altogether: ancient coins are like hard currency and must be rationally exploited for their value . . .

The learned old Armenians we met on Sevan possessed formidable powers of *historical* vision which enabled them to see far back in time. All colours had already faded in our world, but had still not lost their lustre in the ancient land of Armenia, justly proud of its learned men. The 'Canzone' was followed by blank verse, in which M. again talked of Moscow as 'Buddhist', that is, static and outside history. He firmly believed that 'Egyptologists and numismatists', by scrutinizing the past, were able to see into the future as well. The same idea later occurs in 'Conversation About Dante': the dead in the *Divine Comedy* are not very good at distinguishing nearby objects, but their eyes can see into the future – just as birds of prey, though barely able to see things close to them, can pick out the slightest detail from a great height over the vast expanse of their hunting territory. M. was always returning to the question of historical vision: a very important question in an era which has distorted our perspective on the past, while claiming to predict the future on the basis of this very same false perspective. M.'s refusal to consider himself a contemporary of his fellow citizens stemmed to a very large extent from the fact that, though our neighbours in time had completely lost the most elementary sense of the past, they constantly boasted of their supposed ability to forecast the future. But in M.'s view true contemporaries were joint 'tenants of time' (as he calls them in 'Conversation About Dante'), who see events from the same perspective and – by virtue of not having renounced the past – share the same general standards. Not only M., but I too, was deeply aware of the total gulf between us and the active elements among our chance neighbours in time, not to mention the great horde of passive half-wits chasing head over heels after the 'victors'. Even nowadays I always feel ill at ease with members of the older generations who once dwelled in their orderly 'super-structure' above the 'basis', holding forth about 'leaps', the liquidation of enemies, socialist realism, and the other fancy notions at which our leaders merely laughed up their sleeves. But to hell with them, all these damned old fools. There is no point in even being angry with them – they are just too insignificant – but the smell of decay that comes from them is insufferable; it stinks in the nostrils and makes one feel sick. I must say that the liquidation of the kulaks made a much greater impression on me than the 'list of blessings'.* Furthermore, all these people who are now old men were active enemies of language and ideas – they had no appreciation of the first and no understanding for the second. Some of these unclean spirits were not without talent and knew how to manipulate language, people, and the devil alone knows what else besides. They were absolutely without conscience.

Just to relieve my feelings I would like to mention here one very insignificant specimen of the 'unclean', an unhappy, downtrodden creature of revolting cowardice. Akhmatova had declared him to be a 'major poet' and at her funeral he broke down in real sobs –

---

* See Olesha, Appendix A.

almost like poor Brodski. When the students of the Mathematics faculty decided to hold a meeting in her memory, they asked the 'major poet' to make all the arrangements. (He is, incidentally, a very handsome man and it would have been a pleasure to watch him presiding over the meeting if he had not trembled all the time like an aspen leaf.) One of the people present, – K.I., I believe it was – recited Akhmatova's poem with the lines, 'But here, in the murk of conflagration, / where scarcely a friend is left to know, / we, the survivors, do not flinch / from anything, not from a single blow,' and commented on the remarkable way in which poets have a sense of the future and their own destiny. They must, he concluded, have the gift of premonition. No sooner had he finished than the chairman, shaking all over, hastened to say the following: 'The gift of premonition has just been mentioned. That should not be understood in some kind of mystical sense, but as scientific prediction'. The audience – consisting of mathematicians, who cannot get through their studies without some brains – burst out laughing. I later learned that the university authorities, in the person of the Dean, had instructed the poet to see that the evening went off in as seemly a fashion as possible. He was so used to cringing before Authority that he obeyed the Dean's orders as though they had come from his own superior. So much for the handsome 'major poet' on whom Akhmatova expended a 'token'.

M. described poetry as prophetic by its nature, as something that penetrates the veil of the future. In 'Canzone' the seer receives his gift of second sight from the Psalmist. Our times have shown how right M. was: it is only poets who do not succumb to the hypnosis of the age, inevitably finding themselves in one way or another at odds with it. (I mean, of course, real poets, not those who have had the title conferred on them by token.)

To fathom the meaning of events you need a heightened sensitivity. The world has been given to us, and so have the organs by which we perceive it. The whole question is how a man uses them, whether he carries a thinking self within and sees the light shining from the darkness.

XI: THE CHIEF OF THE JEWS

'To steep in vision life's finale' – this was why M., not yet forty, but already nearing his end, irked by his immobility and confinement to Moscow, was desperate to get back to the south, and dreamed of annihilating distance by sheer 'power of vision'. (He hated all restriction on movement – cells with locked doors, residence permits, whether for Moscow or Voronezh. I hope to die at least without ever learning how I would stand up to being locked in a prison cell.) It is scarcely surprising there should be so many references to colour in a poem based on this visual impulse: 'crimson caress', 'a green valley sets the teeth on edge', red and yellow, the only two colours still unfaded in a world forcibly brought to a halt and rendered immobile. I had always taken these colour references for granted and never given them much thought until Irina Semenko pointed out the allusion to Krylov's fable in the line about the 'green valley'. The fox affects to scorn the green grapes because they are sour and will set his teeth on edge. In his poem M. escapes into the open spaces and, seeing this inaccessible green valley in his mind's eye, self-mockingly remembers the fox's cry of 'sour grapes' – we knew only too well that there was no escaping anywhere. It would be interesting to count up all the times M. complains in his poetry about being tied to one spot – and not just with reference to his days in exile, which were only a logical extension of the general tendency to deprive people of their freedom of movement. Paradoxically, during this era marked by such vast shifts of population – through wholesale deportation and imprisonment in the camps, as well as all the voluntary wanderings in search of food – the materially more fortunate section of the community was very restricted in its choice of where to live: not just in a geographical sense, but also because accommodation was so hard to get that you never dared leave it. We used to tell an anecdote comparing our existence to life aboard ship: limitless ocean all around, but nowhere to go . . . I believe that all those locomotives in Platonov's stories must be symbols of man's yearning for movement when he is stricken with the paralysis of restriction on it. Enforced attachment of people to the land is a feature of Russian history and life – as is the accompanying vagrancy. Perhaps mutinies by the *kolodniki** were always particularly terrible because, having forgotten how to control the natural movement of their limbs, they went completely berserk and destroyed everything within reach . . .

Irina Semenko also asked me whether I knew the reason for the colour adjective in the line, 'And say *selah* to the Chief of the Jews / for his crimson caress.' In reading poetry we often overlook the sense of particular words or phrases, and just as often declare it to be meaningless because we expect everything to be pre-digested for us, and our ignorance of the images, or rather signs and symbols, of our culture is so abysmal. Worse still – what knowledge we do possess is general and imprecise, deficient as regards both concrete detail and appreciation of deeper meaning. Out of all the wealth of the cultural heritage our minds have retained little except a handful of names and anecdotes – and even so we are abominably vague about their connection with the times to which they relate and their inner significance. Apart from such vestiges, 'space has lost both colour and flavour' and we can never recover them now that we have given up our birthright. I have seen a learned comment by an erudite student of literature on the poem by Khlebnikov in which he imagines himself riding on an elephant formed of maidens, like some Indian god in a painting or bas-relief. The scholar tells us that Khlebnikov, like Mandelstam, only *appears* to be incomprehensible – if you think hard enough, you can always find the key to them. On meeting the scholar in question I told him that you do not need 'keys' to poems because they are not boxes waiting to be unlocked. The question you have to ask is not, 'What is it about?' but, 'Why was it written?' A poem has to be read as a whole in which words and meaning are inseparable; the minor details, which deepen your understanding of the basic sense of the poem, will become clear later. But if someone fails to grasp the overall meaning at first or second reading, then hadn't he better put poetry aside and turn to some more obvious form of writing? I speak of a second reading because it is easier to understand individual poems or lines in the light of the poet's entire

---

*Convicts whose movements were impeded by large wooden blocks clamped on the feet and arms and round the neck.

work, or the rest of the book in which they appear. Once the whole of the poet's work is clear in general outline, then it is possible to distinguish the different stages in it and finally to penetrate the meaning of individual words which at first eluded the reader, but now impinge on him in all their 'rounded' tangibility. Lazy readers will make do with poets of the type of Heine – from whom Tynianov derived his primitive conception of a book of poetry as a form in which the individual poems are equivalent to chapters in a novel. In that case, why not read novels to begin with?

As regards matters of detail, a really good reader will never pass them over. It was my father who once taught me to read by asking me a seemingly quite casual question: What kind of material was Chichikov's* frock coat made of? For my father, as for the author, this was a telling detail which put the stamp of the age on Chichikov and showed him up quite precisely, in an analytical way, for what he was: a semidandy who displayed his soul in his dress. The myth-maker Khlebnikov had always dreamed of being a pagan god, young and beautiful – as all gods were supposed to be in the eyes of an ignorant age – with bevies of abstractly divine maidens cavorting all around him. This theme crops up all the time in his poems, plays, and dramatic fragments – it is the voluptuous fantasy of a wandering ascetic. (There are people who foolishly confuse such fairy tales and fantasies with epic poetry!) Khlebnikov is 'incomprehensible' in a totally different way from M. – they are direct opposites of each other. They followed different guiding lights and their frock coats, if they had worn them, would have been cut from different material. Both had an equal right to exist – no poet can lay claim to more. Nor indeed does he need any more. It is not the poets themselves, but their hangers-on, who make invidious comparisons about who is greater. Poets may only be compared where they share commensurable features – anything else is the idle comment of lazy readers, whom I would advise to switch to novels (preferably thrillers). A poem is not a conundrum or a riddle to be puzzled out. Each poet has his own universe, his inner ideas or theme that has formed him as a human being. A poem is never a random thing, but an expression of the inner core of someone who has become a poet through his relationship to language.

* Hero of Gogol's *Dead Souls*.

Irina Semenko's question about 'crimson caress' set me thinking. As a result, almost by accident, I stumbled across several things that help to clarify not so much the final poem itself as the inner impulse behind it. I believe that glosses on a poem are an unnecessary extravagance, but inconsistency is part of human nature, and I have decided to put down here some of my discoveries.

At the time M. wrote the 'Canzone' Armenia, his 'Sabbath Land', as he called it, was still very much in his thoughts. Through Ararat alone it was connected with the Bible and with his ancient forbears – what country more worthy of the title 'younger sister to Judea'? M. complained that he had been 'returned by force' to 'Buddhist Moscow', and kept recalling the 'hundred days' he had spent in Armenia. (It was in fact nearly a hundred and fifty days, but a 'hundred days' is more suggestive of blighted hopes!) The setting of 'Canzone', the 'land of unshaven mountains' – that is of mountains covered by scrub – could be taken for Armenia if it were not for the 'green valley' that 'sets the teeth on edge'. Even Alpine meadows are not bright green: on high mountains they are rather grey, particularly in the dry air of Transcaucasia. Green valleys suggest a humid climate, but Armenia is 'a field of molehills sown, as though in mockery, with stone teeth'; it is the 'red dust of the valley of Ararat', a land where 'there is not enough salt for the eyes – you look for form and colour, but see only unleavened bread'. Curiously, although M. is here speaking of visual impressions, he uses 'salt' with reference to the sense of taste. This is not a transference of sense impressions, but rather something in the nature of a synthesis. In both prose and poetry one can probably find examples of how one of the senses activates all the others: if the inner hearing is aroused, it may produce tactile sensations, and visual impressions may sharpen awareness of smells. All the senses respond jointly, as it were, to the stimulation of any one of them.

The setting of 'Canzone', then, is not Armenian, but rather a generalized Mediterranean one – largely, in fact, a dream landscape. M. used to say that in folk tales people who have never seen the sea imagine it as the quintessence of blueness, and their idealized mountain is like Ararat – a pure cone with a well-defined base and a regular, snow-capped peak. (But for us even Ararat had terrible associations – during our days in Erivan there was a girdle of fire round it. The Turks were driving the Kurds up towards the snow-covered summit, setting fire to the scrub behind them so they could not fight their way down again. Noah had a better time of it when there were no people in the world and Ararat served as his refuge . . . The Kurds in Dzhulfa tried to get away by swimming across the river to the Soviet side, but our frontier guards opened fire on them. Everywhere they were met by fire. In the first quarter of the century the Kurds slaughtered the Armenians, but in the second quarter they were themselves slaughtered by their masters, who had sent them to kill Armenians. It's always the same old story . . .)

In the 'Canzone' M. virtually names the country to which he is so powerfully drawn – since he hopes for a meeting with the 'Chief of the Jews', this journey in the mind's eye is to the Promised Land. It can be reached only by way of the 'land of unshaven mountains', and the eruptions of colour begin only after the meeting with the 'Chief of the Jews', to whom he will say a Biblical *selah* in return for his 'crimson caress'. M., conscious of how ancient his lineage was, referred to the Jews as a tribe of shepherds, patriarchs, and kings. The colour of kings is purple and this is one of the explanations of the choice of adjective here. Of the deeper reds, 'crimson' has the best associations in Russian* and these provide a further justification for its use in 'Canzone'. I have asked experts whether there might be some red in the hems of Jewish ritual garments, but this proves not to be so. Even Joseph's coat was not red, but 'of many colours'. It was pure chance which eventually gave me the clue as to why, in M.'s mind, the endearments of the 'Chief of the Jews' should be tinged with a warm shade of red. What led me to it was a remark by E. S. (Zhenia) Laskina.

* In Russian *malinovy* derives from *malina* ('raspberry') and occurs in several expressions implying richness, mellowness, and warmth. The author mentions *malinovy zvon* for a rich chime of bells (though here the word is derived, by popular etymology, from Malines, in Belgium, where such bells were cast). *Malina* can also mean a feast or a treat, and is used in this sense in Mandelstam's poem about Stalin ('and every killing is a treat for the broad-chested Ossete' – quoted here in the text, where, as the author says, its use in a bitterly ironical sense does not contradict her point about the warm associations of the word).

Zhenia's father was a small, indeed, the smallest imaginable, tradesman, who brought up three daughters and dealt in salted herring. The Revolution made him blissfully happy: it proclaimed equal rights for the Jews and enabled him to realize his dream of giving his three clever daughters a good education. When NEP was launched, he took it at face value, and, to feed his daughters, started up his salted herring business again – only to have it confiscated when he was unable to pay the taxes. No doubt he too did sums on his abacus to see how he could save his family. He was shipped off to Narym,* or some such place. But he was broken neither by this nor by his previous stretch in prison – to which he went at a time when 'new methods', that is, tortures of a more refined kind than primitive beating, were being introduced in cases involving 'the confiscation of valuables'. From his first place of exile he sent a letter of such heartrending tenderness to his wife and three daughters that they decided to show it to no one outside the family. His whole life was spent in and out of exile, and later the same thing started with his daughters and their husbands, who also went into exile and camps. If it had not been for the father, who stood at the centre of it and never changed with the years, the fate of this family would have epitomized the typical Soviet life story. He was the quintessence of Jewish saintliness, possessing those qualities of mysterious spirituality and goodness which sanctified Job. (It might have been to old men like him that Goethe went in his youth to talk about the Bible.) Blessedly pure in heart, now an old man of eighty (though it would be more fitting to call him a *starets*,† rather than an old man), he has never in his whole life spoken ill of others or railed against fate. He is living out his days in a glow of beatific kindliness, surrounded by people who at one time or another have been touched by the grace that emanates from him. This patriarch, now living in a communal apartment on Kropotkin Street, formerly Prechistenka, once a dealer in salted herring (on which, to the end of his working life, he was employed as an expert by the State trade network!) is a Job whose children, though several times taken from him, happily survived, and who

* Traditional place of exile in western Siberia.

† Literally 'old man', but always used of someone with special spiritual qualities, like Father Zosima in *The Brothers Karamazov*.

greets all with loving kindness. 'He has kind hands,' his daughter said to me, and suddenly I remembered the circumstances in which M. had once spoken these very same words. When we lived in Leningrad, we were constantly visiting the Hermitage, and each time we always went to look first at Rembrandt's painting of the old man stretching out his hands to his kneeling son. On one of these occasions M. made exactly the same remark I was later to hear from Zhenia Laskina about her father: 'He has kind hands . . .' I have never myself met her father, but he had evidently assumed the likeness of the old man who greeted the Prodigal Son with compassion. In Rembrandt's days there were many more saintly old Jews than in our empty times. It must have been they who provided Rembrandt with the image of the father stretching out his kind hands to his son.

That seem evening, after Zhenia had used these words about her father, I phoned Irina Semenko and asked her to go and look how the warm colours are distributed in Rembrandt's painting. Here is the description she wrote down for me: 'The father is wearing a red cape. It seems to cast a red glow on his mouth and on the son – on his head, the folds in his clothes, even on parts of his body visible through the holes in them, on everything right down to his bare feet, which are also red. The red reflection also falls on the standing witness – his mantle is red not so much because it is made of red material as because the whole figure is illuminated by light from the inner source in the background. The witness looks almost like someone who is warming himself at a fire and is lit up by its flames . . .'

This warm red colouring of *The Prodigal Son* imprinted itself firmly on M.'s mind – he was far more keen-eyed than the ordinary run of apathetic visitors to art galleries. The compassion of the all-forgiving father and the fervour of the Prodigal Son's repentance were embodied for him in the red glow radiated like grace by the father. Thus, even though he is not mentioned, the Prodigal Son is quite clearly a theme in 'Canzone', and the manner of his treatment derived from Rembrandt. M. relied on his readers to see this, imagining that everybody must have been struck, as he was, by the warmth of colour in the painting. He was sure that everybody was endowed with the same powers of observation he had himself. But this is far from being so; by no means everybody is blessed with the same tenacity of memory and sharpness of vision. Very few people retain a lasting impression of things they have seen or taken pleasure in. With most people it all fades rapidly, but M. hoarded up his memories like treasure. As an example of how he used them, I can mention what happened to Kashchei's claws (*kleshni*) in Zhukovski's ballad.* M. had read this in his childhood and when he introduced Kashchei into a poem of his own, the claws become transformed into 'pincers' (in Russian almost the same word as 'claws': *kleshchi*) that Kashchei employs to move stones. This is a transposition of a kind usual in M., though in this case not of an adjective, but of the function of an object: pincers are for pulling out nails, not for moving stones. But in the next line the pincers also 'clutch the gold of nails', so that we have a visual image of the movement made with a pair of pincers just before a nail is pulled. When he was a boy M. loved to collect nails (which he refers to elsewhere as 'sharp-pointed bullion'), and Kashchei, another hoarder of treasure, is thus made to share his childhood passion . . .

The memory of any 'builder' is a storehouse of materials used by his predecessors: their discoveries, their signs and symbols. This is how poets carry on 'the conversation begun before us' – to use Pasternak's phrase for their response to each other that knows no bounds of time or space. As transformed in the mind of a new 'builder', such borrowed elements help to bring out his purely personal feelings, thoughts, and experiences. Words themselves, in fact, are nothing but distillations of the meaning put into them by all the generations who have ever spoken the language – besides what was already built into them during the pre-history of the language, before it split off from the group to which it belongs. With its warm colouring, Rembrandt's *Prodigal Son* was for M. the very emblem of return to the father's home. His poem belongs to the cycle on the 'outsider' theme, but it is clearly in a different key from the others .It is hard for a man to accept that his status as an outsider, an eternal wanderer rejected by the world, is something fated once and for all. If he thinks of himself as a prodigal son, it shows he has not lost faith in a reunion with his Father.

The question now arises: what are we to make of the 'Chief of

* See Zhukovski, Appendix A.

the Jews', at whose feet the Prodigal Son falls, after gathering 'night grasses' for an 'alien tribe'? Is he simply the father of the parable? Or was M. thinking rather of a return to his people, the longing of Joseph to see his father Jacob? The fact is that M. often thought of the exile after whom he was named: 'Joseph, sold into Egypt, could not be more sick at heart,' he said of himself. I believe that, given the concrete way in which M.'s mind worked, both the national and religious themes are here united in the same image: return to your own people from a world which has lost its guiding light is the same as returning to the God of the fathers who sent his Son into the world. It was a Christian parable which prompted this longing to return to the father's house. For M., who everywhere sought 'the keys and rough apparel of the Apostolic churches', the original unity of the Judaeo-Christian world was far more real than its subsequent division. He saw the Mediterranean, to which he was so drawn, as a blend of Christian-Judaic with Hellenic culture. In 'Canzone', therefore, he yearns with such intensity for Judaism and the 'Chief of the Jews' not in response to the call of his blood, but because they are the source of all the European ideas and concepts from which poetry drew its strength.

There are also a few pointers to a latent concern with the theme of death in the poem. (Poetry is ever close to philosophy!) Earthly powers of vision are limited and spatial divisions are insuperable – as are those of time. The only escape from time and space is through death, and M.'s thoughts on the subject are often linked with that of overcoming the limits they impose: 'So that outside time we wish with all our breath / for the meadowland where time stands still' . . . In church one prays that time should have an end – and also that we may be led into green pastures. (Though I am worried about what will happen to words, colours, and light in those pastures. Shall we lose them forever, together with the pronoun 'you'?)

While still alive, a prodigal son can throw himself at the feet of his father, who will kill the fatted calf for him, and then he need no longer say: 'I have been robbed of the cup at the feast of my fathers.' Dead, he will fall at the feet of his Father in those pastures spoken of in the funeral service and beg forgiveness for his sins. Someone who loved 'this poor earth' as M. did – because he had 'not seen another' – conceives of those pastures as the perfect embodiment of all the meadows and valleys of the earth, with grass of the brightest green that could ever be imagined by a city dweller pining in the springtime to see a land clothed in its finery, still not parched and covered with dust, nor destroyed by bombs, conventional or atomic. The more precise the image in the poet's mind, the greener the grass in the 'meadowland where time stands still', and where the passing moment, halted in its tracks, becomes eternity.

Such is the general conception underlying 'Canzone', the 'model', as my younger contemporaries would say, or the 'mould' – to use the word M. always applied to the overall sense in which he would cast a new poem. 'Canzone' is informed by the urge to overcome time and space, by a prodigal son's craving to return, while still alive, to his father's house, by the hope of fulfilling this dream – but also by the sober voice of reason which, at the sight of a green valley, recalls the fable of the fox and the sour grapes. A poem does not tell a story or deliver a message. The reader must always take it at the deepest level he is capable of. There is nothing to be said for leading him by the hand. Anybody who lives in a European world, absorbing its ideas and nurtured on their wealth, enters a treasure-house. (Not long ago the Chinese were being attacked here for still clinging to Confucius. I think it would not be half so bad if they really did remember him.) In this country you are rewarded for loss of memory, and can be killed for remembering too much. The ideas at the basis of European culture and the Christian world are a priceless inheritance, like the vocabulary of the language we speak. There are always attempts to limit us to a 'basic word stock'* and tawdry rationalist notions strained through the sieve of ideology. These notions were formed out of the detritus of humanism in the second half of the nineteenth century. As a result of secularization, humanism was debased and turned inside out during the twentieth century.

Without going back to basic sources it is impossible to understand what is meant by the pastures where time has become the contemplating of eternity. Even the details in 'Canzone' – the kind hands of Rembrandt's old man, the longing to return to the father's

---

* Phrase from Stalin's essay 'Marxism and Questions of Linguistics' (1950).

house, the use of the word 'crimson', Zeiss binoculars as a means of extending one's vision, the fable of the fox and the sour grapes – such things are the common currency of European, and consequently, Russian culture. Their introduction into poetry is like the use of gold as a means of payment, and equally natural, but people unacquainted with gold have to make do with whatever paper money happens to be in circulation, and they will simply fail to recognize items of genuine coinage, taking them for obscure 'associations', subconscious or otherwise. For some people who have written about them, M.'s poems are mysterious and highly condensed, decipherable only with the help of half a dozen keys or so. To most commentators of this type 'Bethlehem is strange and alien', and they fail to realize that 'keys' are no substitute for it. Not keys, but a feeling for the whole, is what is needed to understand a poem – the deeper sense will then gradually be borne in on you, and eventually the details will also become clear. The word 'crimson', perceived at first in a general way through the positive shades of meaning attaching to it in everyday language and in folklore, is later seen to refer more specifically to the warmth and reflected glow of the source of inner light in the Hermitage painting. All that really matters is the inner light. This, and only this, is important.

36   A Cautionary Tale

Travelling in a train a man feels as free as a bird on the wing and often talks to chance fellow passengers in a way he would never dare at home or at work, in his familiar, everyday surroundings. The authorities, needless to say, employ special agents to eavesdrop on conversations of this type. Ehrenburg was once approached by a woman who wanted his help because she had been sacked from her job on the railways without pension rights, after fifteen years' service, during which she had supplied the security organs with much valuable information. She assured Ehrenburg that she had given every satisfaction in her work, and that many cases had been investigated as a result of her reports. When Ehrenburg asked why she had come to him for help, she replied: 'Because you are for justice . . .' Now nearing forty, she was worried about her pension. Ehrenburg did not break a lance for justice on this occasion, but I am certain this police informer in a skirt must have got what she wanted – she will have been fixed up with a job to tide her over till she is needed for the next wave of terror; or perhaps she is employed as an instructress for new recruits. People with valuable experience do not go to waste in this country.

But since there are nevertheless more ordinary mortals than professional or amateur informers, intimate conversations took place in trains even at the most terrible periods. I myself have been party to some, but here I wish to put down a story once heard by the brother of Frida Vigdorova during what were for us the blissful few years following the mass rehabilitations.* Frida and her brother both died almost at the same time, and I fear they may not have managed themselves to record these confessions of this chance companion in a train. It would certainly be a pity if his evidence were lost to posterity. What distinguishes it from other confessions of the same type is the complete lack of embellishment or attempt at self-justification. I have heard thousands of stories on the same lines, but the speaker's object is always the same: to prove to himself and his listener that he emerged with honour from an impossible situation and managed to outwit the person putting pressure on him (or, alternatively, did and said only things he could not possibly get out of). One should not oversimplify the state of mind of these people – they are not lying or juggling with the facts, but dwelling obsessively on the events that have made their lives a misery, asking themselves all the time whether it would not have been better to put an abrupt end to their humiliation by choosing instead a lingering death in the camps and transit prisons. Many did just this, but they, of course, have not come back to tell their stories. Those who escaped this fate, on the other hand, try to vindicate themselves, painfully going over in their minds every word they said: Could they have avoided saying it? Was it perhaps a mistake? Could they be clear in their conscience about everything they had done? Not all of them, naturally, unburden themselves in this way – only those for whom their experience was a

* i.e. after the denunciation of Stalin at the Twentieth Congress (1956).

moral calamity. Needless to say, these are in a minority. Their misfortunes always began with a failure to realize that after their first meeting in a 'private apartment', they would never again escape the clutches of the infamous institution behind it. The said institution changed its name many times, its chiefs and personnel were constantly purged, but the name of anyone who had ever responded to its summons and yielded to its threats was preserved in the archives, and each successive new head of the relevant department, having acquainted himself with the files, had only to pick up his phone for any connection to be resumed. Some people have told me they were called in from time to time and then forgotten, but in most cases people were not left alone until their dying day.

The man whom Frida's brother met in the train was a so-called 'child of October', a representative of the new post-revolutionary breed whose attitude to such things was quite unlike that of the old intelligentsia. They were taught by kind-hearted schoolmistresses who had done two-year courses in the Ushinski method and shed tears over Katerina in *The Storm* ('the ray of light in the kingdom of darkness');* these educated their pupils in the spirit of Makarenko, conditioning them to believe that the best way to help a comrade was to inform the school authorities (and, in later life, 'the proper quarters') about any waverings, doubts or untoward actions. In 1938, when I suddenly became a school teacher myself, I saw how the older children, well disciplined, intelligent, earnest, and terrifyingly ignorant, watched each other like hawks – and me too – as they had been instructed. There was no concealment about this spying on me: the headmaster and director of studies were always repeating to my face something or other I had said in class, thus clearly giving me to understand that I was under constant surveillance. As I moved around in the classroom – from the blackboard to my desk and between the rows of my pupils – I could always feel them watching me, never moving their heads, out of the corner of their eyes. Some had picked up this way of looking at people from their parents, while others were imitating a mannerism

---

*Play (1859) by the nineteenth-century playwright Alexander Ostrovski that was seen by the radical critic Nikolai Dobroliubov in a famous essay, 'A Ray of Light in a Kingdom of Darkness', as a particularly effective exposure of the social evils of tsarist society.

they had observed in representatives of our foremost profession, the happy comrades of the iron legion. If, for one single moment, I had started speaking in my own language instead of in prescribed official jargon, none of them would have hesitated to ensure that I spend the rest of my life felling timber. I was not aware of such systematic surveillance only during the war, when it even began to look as though this hundred-percent uniformity was starting to give way to a normal kind of student behaviour – the first tiny breach in the system of mass indoctrination.

In their own way these boys with their habit of looking sideways at you were really quite kind and nice at heart. When I was being evacuated,* they all came to the landing stage to help me and my mother get on the steamer – there was a desperate free-for-all on the gang-plank and they got us on board by hoisting us over the side, together with our luggage. Taught to be 'always prepared for labour and defence',† they were prompt to come to the help of an 'older comrade'. This generation was practically wiped out during the war. At school they were all in the Air Training Corps, and later they became 'Stalin Falcons'.‡ How many of them survived? And what goes on in their poor heads nowadays? It is particularly hard for them to take in the events of the last few decades. They do not read *samizdat*, any more than the works once recommended to them by the good ladies responsible for their education.

It was a person of this type from whom Frida's brother heard a tale of how he had fallen into the pit dug for itself by his generation. He had first been summoned by the 'proper quarters' while he was serving at the front during the last year of the war. They had asked him a few questions about one of his comrades, and he had answered them without the least hesitation. Although he had only acted in response to a summons, he in fact belonged to the category of voluntary informants, since he spoke as candidly and freely as he would have done to his teacher about the peccadilloes of a school-mate. He willingly accepted a proposal to collaborate and signed a form undertaking not to divulge official secrets. In a sense he was even flattered by this display of confidence in him. He was asked to

---

* i.e. from Kalinin, as the Germans approached in 1941.
† Slogan of the Soviet physical culture organization.
‡ Epithet for Soviet airmen.

keep an eye on certain people and report what he observed. He obeyed his instructions to the letter. The authorities were concerned about signs of restiveness, and he was able to confirm that it really existed. After this one of the men he had been asked to watch disappeared. He was told he had been transferred to another company. At first he believed this story, but when other people disappeared as well, it gradually dawned on this model Soviet youth what was going on. Furthermore, he saw that a vacuum had formed around him – his comrades had also caught on, and they now gave him a wide berth. At the front loyalty to comrades was paramount – the first major breach in the solid monolith of 'unanimity'. Luckily for him, he was demobilized not long after all this and returned home to his native town.

He left the army with a deep sense of relief and happily embarked on his new life. After a few months' respite – which could be put down to the usual slowness of the bureaucratic machinery – he was suddenly invited to go to a certain address at a certain time. The summons was conveyed to him in a metallic tone of voice by one of his colleagues at work. His heart sank, even though it was a quite ordinary-sounding address, not the official one of the institution involved. He was kept waiting for several hours in an ante-room prior to a conversation in which he was asked to resume his previous activity. He no longer had any stomach for it at all, but the habit of obedience, instilled first at school and then in the army, was second nature. Now the whole story was repeated, this time in his native town: people who had talked too openly with him started to disappear, and he could no longer console himself with the thought that they had been transferred to another unit. His friends again learned to avoid him as far as possible, though, if they had to talk with him, their manner was very polite, even exaggeratedly so and, as a rule, they stuck to official platitudes, never indulging in confidences. He decided he just could not go on like this – to be isolated in your home town is much worse than in the army. He volunteered for work in some very remote area, packed his belongings, and left. For the first few weeks or months all was quiet, but then he once more received a summons to report to a 'private apartment'. Kafka describes how a man stands by the telephone and just listens to it ring, too terrified to lift the receiver. The feeling is a very familiar one to many Soviet people, and this man, who had never read Kafka but was sometimes called out to his rendezvous by phone, talked about it to Frida's brother, his chance travelling companion.

However often he moved to a different town or changed jobs, his 'file' always followed and, after a short breathing space, he would be given a new assignment, always on the same lines. Eventually, however, he was overtaken by the fate which so many others had met: he was arrested after being denounced by a colleague. But for him arrest and prison, which normally struck terror into people's hearts, brought only relief. He could now look forward to a clean break with his previous existence, and the prospect of becoming just one among innumerable prisoners in the labour camps. During the first year there he was a happy man, but in the second he suddenly got a shock: he was called in to the camp security officer and ordered to report on the other members of his work team and on those who lived with him in the same barracks.

He did not serve the whole of his term and was released during the period of mass rehabilitations. He could not return to the part of the country he came from, because people there knew about his double life. He chose a small provincial town, rented corners of rooms till he found work, and then, as a 'rehabilitated' person applied for a proper place to live. He firmly believed that a new age had dawned, so he got married – something he had never dared consider before. He told his tale of woe to his wife and she was sympathetic. He got a place to live in much sooner than he expected: half of a two-room apartment in a new building with all conveniences. A vast housing programme had started under Krushchev. As he was handed the papers entitling him to his room, he was told he must not change the lock on the outside door to the apartment. Some furniture of an official-looking type was installed in the second room and the door to it was kept unlocked. From time to time a man in civilian clothes appeared there and received one or two visitors – but always singly, and taking care they did not see each other. Most of these meetings took place while the man and his wife were out at work. They learned about the mysterious visits to the next room, which was never locked, only from such tell-tale signs as footmarks on the floor and cigarette butts in the ashtray. It turned out that this second room was in their name, and the man in civilian clothes asked them to keep it clean for him. They looked after it just as carefully as their own. The husband knew only too well from his own experience what went on in these 'private apartments' and suffered terribly at having such a neighbour inflicted on him. His wife took it all much more calmly. Both understood that moving to another town would not save them, but they started trying to get a room in a 'communal apartment' with a lot of tenants. The husband was summoned to a meeting at a 'private address' and told he must do no such thing. He felt he could not have children in these conditions, and his wife was very upset – what sort of a married life is it without children?

Thus, it all began with the young soldier feeling flattered when he was first approached – after which he was hooked for life. By no means everybody who gets into this fix is prepared to admit that his activities have done harm to people, or that he is unduly troubled in his mind by them. Most people's minds were poisoned by the age we have lived through and they continue to live by its laws. They would feel no aversion to cleaning the 'second room', or making the most of all the little privileges held out to them as a reward for obedience and docility. On returning from the war, many people of this generation were removed from the list of part-time informers when the whole network was overhauled and rejuvenated with younger recruits, but they continue to write secret denunciations on their own initiative, eating their hearts out when they see that such things are no longer acted upon. In Pskov I rented a room privately in a communal apartment and every pay-day my neighbour, a former partisan now working as a plasterer, got roaring drunk in the corridor and cursed Khrushchev. He blamed him for people 'getting out of hand', because nobody had paid any attention to his report on the 'accursed Vlasovites'* lying low in this very building. Ensconcing himself in the communal kitchen, the plasterer would offer his vodka to his ten-year-old son: 'Have a drink, my son, from your father's glass. Don't drink with strangers – they're all bandits . . .' He then told his son how, from his earliest days, he had fought against 'enemies of the people', and together,

---

* Members of the army formed under German auspices during the war and headed by the captured Soviet general A. Vlasov.

father and son, they drank a toast to the glorious past and the Leader, who after the war had given the partisan this sumptuous room of sixteen cubic metres* in a house built by prisoners of war . . . The other citizens with rooms there were equally select and are bound to have written reports about the unruly plasterer.

The plasterer's wife, who came from a peasant family liquidated during the campaign against the kulaks, had fled to a town where she managed to get a job as a servant in the family of a Party member. But her employer proved to be a 'harmful element', and she was asked to keep an eye on him. After the destruction of this 'harmful' family, she was rewarded for her services by a job as waitress in the town's most exclusive 'closed' restaurant, thus very much coming up in the world. During the occupation she had worked in a German officers' canteen – presumably acting also as a contact for the partisans, since it was then she got to know her husband. At the time when we lived in the same apartment, she was out of work because of ill-health and I gave her a little money for helping with my housework. She served me devotedly for a whole winter, but once spring was in the air, she became restive and reported to the police that I was living there without a residence permit in part of a room let to me in unauthorized fashion by a woman who was a 'former Vlasovite'. Her hope was that my landlady would be evicted, I would be given a permit to live there instead, and she would thus have a permanent source of income! When in the upshot it was I, not the 'former Vlasovite', who had to leave, there was no end to her tears of remorse – punctuated by complaints that she was no longer admitted to the institution where she had once served as a waitress, otherwise she would have got me a permit and seen to it that all these 'enemies' were destroyed . . .

My neighbours in Pskov were nothing out of the ordinary. The habit of denunciation is so ingrained that such people cannot help it, even though the only harm may be to themselves. The Pskov couple were about ten years older than the man who told his story to Frida's brother – he belonged to a generation which had second thoughts during the war, after coming to know the value of true

---

* 'Living space' is measured in cubic metres in the Soviet Union. This was about twice the usual allotment for those days.

comradeship. This seems to have been the first post-revolutionary generation among whom there were people with a feeling of concern and a conscience – not many, perhaps, but they do exist. In the case of the man with the two-room apartment, incidentally, it is quite possible that some part was played by a half-forgotten grandmother who once told him how wrong it was to harm people. Long since displaced in his mind by teachers and others in authority over him, perhaps she had returned in a dream to trouble his conscience? Since I have the story at second, or, rather, at third hand, I cannot throw light on the deeper motives for his need to confess. Perhaps one day, if we wait long enough, he may step forward and write it all down himself. The chances are infinitesimal, but miracles do happen . . . There is just no telling who may speak up and what they may say. In the last decade we have seen how 'nothing is hidden that shall not be known', and that even the dead sometimes give tongue. All that is needed is time – ten years, or fifty, or perhaps even a hundred. Nobody can know the number of those – but they are many – who are still biding their time and waiting patiently. I too am waiting, though I know it will be in vain. As far as I am concerned, what had to come out has already done so. It is too little, a mere drop in the bucket, but it was enough to break the silence forever. We lived most of our lives in the firm conviction that everything would always remain under seal and never come out. This at least is not entirely so.

Who in fact is left to tell their story? M.'s generation has died out, and of mine only a few demented specimens still survive, puffing and blowing as they go from doctor to doctor. The sort of people denounced by the plasterer are already living in retirement and spend their time peacefully playing dominoes. The man Frida's brother met in the train will by now be clutching at his chest and expecting a heart attack. The young neither know nor want to know anything. When the next round begins, they will be quite astonished at how it could have happened. Some of them are already learning how to stuff gags into the mouths of their fellow-men, and the rest will soon master the art of silence. And that will be that.

37 Complete Retirement

I once had an acquaintance who decided on total withdrawal before he would, in any case, have been weeded out during the complete overhaul of the informer network after the war. After thirty years of being summoned to a 'private apartment' for questioning and 'heart-to-heart' chats, he literally locked himself up in his room where, chainsmoking the strongest possible cigarettes, he sat at his desk, a heavy motionless hulk of a man, and did mechanical calculations just to occupy his mind and forget. The doctors warned him that he was asking for trouble, but this only made him laugh. His legs, gnarled with varicose veins, were like lead weights, but he was deliberately courting a slow death and never moved from his chair, throwing his cigarette butts into a huge ashtray which by evening was piled high with them.

He only left home once or twice a month when, unable to stand it any longer, he went out into the street at dead of night and greedily breathed in the city air. At such late hours he believed he could sally forth without risking an encounter with someone from the 'proper quarters' who might ask him to go and see them again. As long as he kept indoors he could pass for a sick man, and indeed he really was sick. On the phone he told people he was ill and could see no one. He lived on money he had saved and in order not to run through it too quickly, and leave something for his wife, he continued working at home on some designs that had been commissioned from him. He thought of his wife only as his future widow and was always carefully reckoning up – without an abacus! – how she might manage on a pension (which would, of course, be inadequate) eked out by his savings, taking into account that she might go on living for ten, fifteen, or even twenty years, since she came from a family with a tradition of longevity. She has indeed survived him by almost twenty years, but the money has so far lasted very well.

I once went to see him when his wife was out and he told me about his relations with the 'proper quarters'. He said that since I was the only person whose opinion of him he valued, he wanted me to know everything about himself. He had been 'hooked' at the very beginning of the twenties, after he had incautiously said a good word about one of the people who perished in the first wave of terror. He was threatened with execution, deportation to a labour camp (in those days that still meant Solovki), and the loss of his job. He was young and in love and not anxious to depart this life so soon and for no good reason. Fondly imagining he would be able to outsmart 'them' if he played for time, he also deluded himself into thinking that every meeting would be the last, that they would leave him alone after he had spun them one more yarn. But this they had no intention of doing. He was summoned not very frequently, at intervals of two or three months, and sometimes as much as six months, but there was no question of his being forgotten. After a few years he finally understood that they would never let go. At each meeting they demanded information of a concrete kind relating to the assignments they had given him previously. Every time there were new instructions, and requests for his opinion about one or other of his acquaintances. He tried to conceal his wretched position from his wife and allowed her only a glimpse of it. His main wish was to narrow the circle of his acquaintances to such a point that he could tell his persecutors he saw nobody, and knew nothing. But his wife, alas, liked company and was always inviting large numbers of people – among them some slippery customers who also reported to 'private apartments' on his other visitors and what exactly was said at table. It frequently happened that when my friend was summoned to a meeting, the 'man with a briefcase' would begin the conversation by telling him who his guests had been on such and such a day and then quote snippets from the conversation at him. Even at home he was thus always on his guard and firmly discouraged conversation on subjects that were in any way awkward. Any guest who uttered an incautious word was immediately suspected of being an informer.

At the end of the thirties he at last managed to frighten his wife out of inviting people. He avoided his professional colleagues and gradually went over to a system of working under contract at home. The only weakness he indulged was a fondness for women – he particularly valued his relations with them if they had escaped the attention of his persecutors, and quickly dropped those who had not. He soon learned to do without friends and felt no great need of them. During all those years, however, he did keep one friend, whom I believe he confided in completely, telling him about every meeting in the 'private apartment'. The friend may have been in a similar situation – which meant that they understood each other only too well. Curiously enough, the friend's name was never mentioned at the 'private apartment', as though nobody suspected his existence. I know nothing more about this person. As was quite natural, my friend gave me no details, except to say he was a prominent figure in the academic world; their fields of interest were different.

My friend swore that during all those years they got nothing out of him. He pleaded ignorance in answer to questions about people, saying he never met them. He claimed to have taken the initiative in some of the conversations and demanded to be left alone, telling the 'man with the briefcase' that he should use professionals instead of badgering private citizens. I cannot vouch that it was possible to talk like this at such meetings, but I could get no further details out of him. With his usual extreme caution, he talked to me only in the most general terms, so if ever I too fell into their clutches, I would not be able to give him away. Even without his telling me, it would have been easy enough to guess at the bare fact of his predicament. He was once summoned on the phone while I was in the room. He turned pale, looked very upset and began to act strangely, saying he must leave and could not say when he would be back. I immediately drew my own conclusions. There was, therefore, nothing to prevent me knowing this much, but it would have been a very different matter for him to reveal actual details of his conversations: after each of them he signed a slip undertaking not to give away official secrets, and woe betide him if he had – it would have meant being sent away to rot in a camp, as had happened to many of our mutual acquaintances. He knew how well they had learned to pry 'evidence' (even of the most grotesque kind) out of people and, although unable to resist telling me the gist of his situation, he never went so far as to impart any specific detail.

There is one thing I can say in defence of this man: he had many enemies because he was able to get lucrative work that others often tried to take away from him, but all these people are still alive and flourishing. In other words – unlike almost everybody in his position – he did not use his contact with the 'proper quarters' to his own advantage. Any material favours – such as his apartment and the contracts for the work he did at home – came to him from another source: a high placed personage to whom he had access through someone known to me. It is true that this other personage would have been able to do nothing for him against the veto of the 'man with the briefcase', and my friend must certainly have been compelled to play a very devious game, but even so he did not stoop to anything really despicable..

At the beginning of the war, when Moscow was being partially evacuated, my friend was ordered to stay behind and serve as a 'contact' in case the city should be captured. I know of a number of people in his situation who received identical instructions. Such networks were formed from people already so involved with the 'proper quarters' that they had no choice but to obey. My friend's wife, not realizing what she was saying, boasted of the trust which had thus been shown to her husband. Most people understood the implications very well but never had the heart to tell her. Even now, long after his death, she continues to prate and brag about it. She mentions by name her husband's protector in the institution for which he worked – it was he who obtained a pension for her and helped with all her other material problems when she became a widow. This protector walks around in civilian clothes, but everybody knows that he has a high military rank. She thus unwittingly gives her dead husband away – his own fault for hiding the painful realities of his life from her . . .

During all the war years in Moscow he was left in peace, but after the war they started calling him in again and he realized there would never be an end to it. It was then that he started keeping to his room – a way of life tantamount to slow suicide. He once told me about a strange attack during which he lost consciousness. He realized that his end would be exactly like that. Shortly afterwards he did in fact die.

I know that this friend of mine entered into relations of a kind it is absolutely wrong to enter into. However, I blame not him but his tormentors. I have known other people who went regularly to meetings in 'private apartments' and signed forms promising not to talk. Some of them were the purest souls imaginable, but they could not easily condemn themselves and their families to destruction. One cannot demand heroism from the ordinary run of people. A man who had been summoned knew that he, his wife and children, and his parents would immediately be packed off to rot in a camp if he refused outright. Afterwards he would pay dearly for his moment of indecision, agonizing for years over the question of whether it is better to die quickly in prison, or slowly at home. None of these people had a normal life span. Some deliberately courted death, and others were driven to their graves by insomnia, self-disgust, and horror. I am sure that an early death also awaits the man who, returning from work in the evening, clears away the cigarette butts and tidies up in his 'second room'.

One day a ten-millionth part of all those dead in the camps may be remembered, but nobody will spare a thought for the temporizers who avoided arrest and died at home. In theory, at least, I know it is wrong to compromise, but how can I tell people not to, when it means abandoning their children to the mercy of fate and plunging into an abyss? . . . All I can say to them is: do not bring children into this unspeakable world – an idiotic piece of advice, since children continue to be born, even though in much smaller numbers than before, and it is for their sake that compromises are made! Advice is pointless, the only thing is to weep, but I am incapable of tears, so not even this consolation is left to me.

If there were a way of reckoning it, the sum of all the lives cut short or wasted would amount to a fantastic indictment – an indictment that can be brought against no one, because everything was done not by human beings as such, but by a machine. People simply reacted to the instructions, signals, and rhythms of an autonomous mechanism into which a monstrous programme had been fed at some time out of mind.

Nobody can tell whether the impetus which first set the machine in motion has now exhausted itself. It may be that we are only living through a lull, a temporary slackening-off, and that tomorrow the whole thing will start up again. All I can be fairly certain of is that the machine will begin to operate in some new way: new words and arguments will be found to justify new crimes, thus taking the uncompleted process to its logical conclusion. The new arguments will offer salvation and people will clutch at them, oblivious to the fact that they lead in the same direction as the old ones. This is bound to happen for the simple reason that there are no criteria to judge theories, arguments, and actions. The right criteria cannot be inculcated artificially – they are always the fruit of an inner process in each individual, and preferably large numbers of them, not just a few lone and isolated ones.

I foresee the appearance of a new breed of impostors who will manage to give their slogans a veneer of conformity to higher values. But it will all be fake and crumble to dust. Whichever way one looks, there is nothing but the snare and the pit. We still have not paid for our millions of compromises and the loss of our standards. The reckoning is yet to come. I fear it cannot be avoided.

38 Surviving with Honour

For many years I worked as a teacher to earn my stale piece of daily bread, and every autumn, at the end of the vacations, I always uncomplainingly signed up for the study group in philosophy. I did not have to be asked twice. This was known as 'raising one's qualifications' and your livelihood depended on it. Year after year I had the Fourth Chapter of the 'Short Course'* dinned into me and since this kind of instruction for college and university teachers was regarded as belonging to the 'higher grade', the lecturer seconded from the Philosophy department always dealt in passing with the whole of world philosophy. Kant sometimes got twenty minutes. (Hegel was duly stood on his head, Plato was rarely referred to, but the Greek materialists received a favourable mention, and we were told about Zeno's flying arrow and Heraclitus with his 'all is in flux'.) Kant was always made fun of and demolished, together with his categorical imperative. In official ideology, the hapless categorical imperative was replaced, I believe, by the concept of class solidarity, though in actual practice

* See note, page 15.

the students of human nature who ruled over us put their faith in the instinct for self-preservation and the rational egotism preached in one offshoot of Russian literature.* (Of course I may be wrong about this, claiming priority for our literature by force of habit, a rational egotism may have originated in the West; but wherever it started, it gives little cause for joy.)

In the second half of the fifties, the Fourth Chapter lost its glamour and the attitude to Kant softened somewhat, but in the good old days it would never have occurred to anyone that man might have a soul and everybody was conscious of attending these study circles only out of an instinct for self-preservation. It was a very effective education. We all raised our hands and rattled off the required formulae with great proficiency. Many people still continue to parade the erudition acquired then, and cannot bring themselves to revise it: Why bother, when everything is so clear already?

In those woeful times the categorical imperative did indeed seem like the brainchild of an ivory tower thinker ignorant of real life. Everybody tried to save himself, avoiding trouble, and seeing a potential informer in every neighbour and colleague. In such conditions one is hard put to detect good in anyone, but it nevertheless continued to exist – nothing can destroy it altogether. Of all living creatures, only man is capable of crime, but then again, only man is able to set aside the instinct for self-preservation – this is what makes him human. However few in number, the mere existence of such people gives hope. It shows we are still capable of subordinating our primary urges to a higher voice that is part of our nature, however muffled it may be by the clangour of our daily life.

I particularly value those instances when people display the best side of themselves naturally, without any pose or high-sounding words. In our age man is a trembling creature, not the stuff heroes are made of. The highest concepts – valour, heroism, truth, honour – have been debased and turned into official commonplaces for the use of newspaper hacks and orators whose passionate speeches are previously cleared with the authorities down to the last word.

* i.e. utilitarian ethics, as expounded by such nineteenth-century radicals as Chernyshevski.

High-flown phrases have lost all value, and in the story I am about to tell – one which gives me hope – there is no place for them. This is the case of a stubborn girl who refused to bow to circumstances and obey her instinct for self-preservation. She evidently made a deep impression on those who met her in the camps. There is a brief mention of her in Yevgenia Ginzburg's book, in the passage about a scene in the common cell in Butyrka* when a German woman displayed the scar left by beatings at the hands of the Gestapo, and the more recent marks of her interrogation in the Lubianka. The other women in the cell, all members of the 'iron legion', immediately denounced the German woman as an 'agent of imperialism'. Ginzburg wanted to answer them, but she was stopped by another very young prisoner who said: 'Don't argue with them. You can see what fanatics they are.' Here was a person who had kept her reason, and something else besides, which predetermined her fate for many years to come.

N. N. was still a mere girl when she was put in the Lubianka. There were many reasons for her arrest – origins at once aristocratic and revolutionary, the fact that she had been born and brought up abroad among émigrés of the pre-revolutionary period, but most of all her open and independent character. Each of these factors was 'criminal' enough in itself to guarantee a person's downfall. If some people of this kind were spared, it was only because not everybody could be arrested – the general policy was to pick up those who came to hand, as a lesson to the rest. While some went to camps because of their 'bad character', others escaped. It was all a matter of luck. Astonishingly enough, many who did escape never realized just how lucky they were. The whole point of terror is that people are arrested at random in order to instil fear into everybody else. N. N. was unlucky and landed in prison through a nice young man whom she probably went dancing with, or some such thing. He was from a highly intellectual family which had been of the 'Legal Marxist'† persuasion. He had probably learned all about rational egotism as a child and when

* Jail in Moscow. The passage referred to here is on pages 155–6 of Yevgenia Ginzburg's book, where 'N. N.' is identified as Natasha Stoliarova, the secretary of Ilia Ehrenburg.

† i.e. who believed only in legal methods and were denounced by Lenin.

he was hauled off to the Lubianka he promptly put the theory into practice. To put it more plainly: in the face of threats and promises, he betrayed a young lady with whom he was only barely acquainted. He only had to give her name, address, and circle of friends, and quote a couple of sentences spoken by her. Sensitive soul that he no doubt was, he could console himself with the thought that since he was not aware of any crimes committed by the young lady, he could not in any real sense give her away. All he did was mention that N. N. had chatted at a party with so and so (a foreigner, perhaps), and had said such and such to him, this youth from a good family. To soothe his own conscience, the young man had every right to feel that such things did not amount to an actual denunciation. I know that after this he had a quiet life, was never arrested or persecuted and, when the new era dawned, showed not the slightest embarrassment on meeting N. N. again after her rehabilitation and return from exile. Easy going as ever, N. N. did not bring up the subject of the past with him, and only mentioned this charming meeting to a few friends.

I have no idea whether N. N. was the only victim of this youth from an intellectual family, but he can do no more harm, simply because the whole apparatus has been 'rejuvenated' and the heroes of those old dramas have now been pensioned off. N. N. has no desire for vengeance against this creature and he can live the rest of his days in peace, knowing that his 'rational egotism' has paid. Hosts of these rational egotists who once sent their friends and acquaintances to the labour camps are still at large – they receive visitors, buy furniture, and seem not to have a care in the world. Most of the people who returned from the camps just spat and then forgot their betrayers. There was a certain D. who dreamed throughout all his years in the camps of at least beating up the minor journalist responsible for sending him there. When he returned, D. went into the office where the man worked and beckoned him with a finger. They went out into the street and the man began to whine about his wife and family. D. then just gave up, invited the man to a café, drank a bottle of vodka with him, and let him go in peace. In another case, several people who had all been denounced by the same woman, a professional informer,

decided they would gatecrash a party she was giving on her birth-
day and expose her in front of her guests. When she opened the
door and saw these grim-faced people in whose lives she had
played such a part, she was quite aghast, clutched at her heart and
slumped down on a chair in the hallway. Seeing her turn so pale,
the people who had come to take their revenge got into a panic,
dashed to the kitchen for water, and, when she had calmed down,
went away without another word. The notorious Elsberg was really
very unlucky to have been so loudly condemned – there was even
an attempt to have him expelled from the Union of Writers. It is
said, however, that the campaign against Elsberg was started not
by someone he had sent to camp, but by a graduate whose thesis he
had rejected. The other graduates stood up for Elsberg because
they thought he would be useful to them in their careers. I am not
an advocate of vengeance. In this country, for the last half century,
not only individuals but whole categories and classes of people
have continually been the object of vengeance, and we have all
seen what a terrible thing it is. Yet, nevertheless, I believe there
would be nothing wrong in the country 'getting to know its
heroes',* just so it will be more difficult to recruit people for the
job in future. They need not be imprisoned or killed, but a finger
should be pointed at them, and they should be named. All the
killers and traitors, however, are under the highest protection
because they 'erred' together with those in authority over them.
They will now gradually die off and a new generation will have no
difficulty in finding its own murderers and informers, since neither
murder nor treason has been condemned and only a corner of the
veil has been raised on the secrets of the past. Rational egotism
has proved itself in practice.

N. N. was held in the Lubianka, and to complete his case the
interrogator needed only one small thing: a few names to be
supplied by her. A criminal was not a criminal without accomplices. For the sake of appearances – something very much valued
in this country – he had to uncover at least five other persons
involved with her, but the stubborn N. N. refused to play the game.

* Allusion to a phrase in Chapter 74 of Solzhenitsyn's *First Circle* about
the exposure of an informer.

The interrogator needed the names of accomplices for more than merely aesthetic reasons. There was also the serious consideration that even when the terror was at its height, some kind of nominal excuse was always found for a person's arrest: a denunciation, information from police spies, or best of all, the fact that your name was mentioned during the 'investigation' of someone else's case. I put the word 'investigation' in quotation marks because it scarcely applies to what went on at night in that house of mystery, even though the 'interrogator' (also in quotation marks!) observed all the 'legal forms', that is, kept a record, selected the relevant article of the criminal code and gathered all the necessary signatures under the sentence. Some prisoners were even taken to a formal hearing that lasted a few minutes and at which they received the death sentence, or anything from ten to twenty years' imprisonment, before they had time so much as to open their mouths. We always wondered why such trouble was taken to give an appearance of proper procedure to all these millions of cases that would then be buried forever in the archives. Surely nobody can have believed that a future historian going through all this stuff might take it at its face value? In the period of the 'rehabilitations',* the officials concerned had no illusions about the worth of all the records and 'confessions' in the files, and they hastened to issue the necessary documents to interested parties without showing them the details of the case. I thus never learned exactly what happened to M. in 1938. Shielding it from me, the woman prosecutor quickly glanced through the very thin file in front of her – it contained no more than a couple of sheets of paper – and told me that it was his 'second case' and was 'without basis'.† Later I received by mail a document certifying that the case had been discontinued 'for lack of evidence'. The court proceedings at which the case was 'closed' took placed on 29 August 1956, eighteen years after M. was sentenced or, to put it more exactly, after he was murdered. From this document (he was not judged worthy of formal re-

* After the Twentieth Party Congress in 1956. Surviving relatives were given certificates of 'rehabilitation' through the Prosecutor's Office.

† Mandelstam was formally cleared only of the charges brought against him after his second arrest, in 1938; the first case of 1934, based on his anti-Stalin poem, evidently remained on the record.

habilitation) I learned that the sentence was signed by a Special Tribunal on 2 August 1938. In those days even dates were treated as state secrets and nobody knew them. The case is thus officially regarded as closed, but no one should have any illusions, and it would be well to recall M.'s own words: 'The proceedings in the case are not yet over, and I assure you never will be. What happened earlier is only the overture.'* M.'s has been formally closed, but it now turns out that there was no case to begin with . . .

As I have said, the first reason for wanting 'accomplices' (that is, the names and addresses of acquaintances) was because it made the case look good. The second was that, given the scale of these operations and, since warrants could be issued for only one person at a time, there was always a shortage of names. The plan for the destruction of people was handed down from above with overall figures for guidance, and everyone involved was anxious to fulfil his quota and justify his salary increase. It was the duty of a patriot to fulfil his quota. Names given to an interrogator could either be used immediately or kept in reserve against a shortage. Names of 'accomplices' were the interrogator's stock in trade and, in case of need, he would dig into his reserves. Since it belonged not to him personally but to the desk he occupied, it would, in the case of his own liquidation (something that happened all the time), automatically pass to his equally faceless successor, who would use the lists he left behind. The machine went on working as smoothly as ever. At the moment it is idling, well oiled and in perfect condition. How long before it is started up at full speed again?

No interrogator has ever shared the secrets of his trade with me – except Furmanov's brother, who told me of the formula 'Give us a man and we'll make a case'.† On the other hand, I have heard accounts from hundreds of people about their treatment under interrogation. What emerges from them all is that the interrogator found it very easy to confuse a freshly arrested prisoner (after his psychological softening-up first through confinement in the

---

* Quoted from Mandelstam's *Fourth Prose*, written in 1930–31, in which he talks of a newspaper campaign against himself (see David Zaslavski, Appendix A), and a death sentence on five bank clerks. He took these signs of the times as the beginning of an unending witchhunt.

† *Hope Against Hope*, page 14.

'box',* and then the degrading body search) by mentioning the name of a friend or acquaintance already sentenced and sent to a camp. A person's arrest always aroused panic among his friends – for which they had very good reason, since it really was like having been in touch with someone suffering from a contagious disease. The interrogators could not, of course, mention the names of informants or agents – 'sources' had to be protected – and we could generally only guess at their identity through the results of their work, namely, the disappearance of people. The names of already convicted friends of a prisoner were hence a great boon to the interrogator and he knew how to use them to good effect. Most ordinary people sought comfort in the thought that if their neighbour had been arrested, it meant that he really was mixed up in something ('there is no smoke without fire'). Anyone reasoning like this was immediately confounded (as I would have been) after his own arrest to hear the interrogator say, 'You presumably know why you are here,' and then mention the name of some vanished friend. Before his arrest the poor devil may have thought himself purer than the driven snow, but at his first interrogation he would begin to quake in his shoes and feel hopelessly compromised by his contact with a criminal. The mere awareness of this deprived him of the will to defend himself and resist, and the interrogator could tie him in knots. I doubt whether even the subtlest self-defence could save anyone, but at least a man might hope to preserve his human dignity as he went under – this means a good deal. The only thing I fear myself nowadays is that they might use some new drug to paralyse my will and self-control. If ever I am hauled off to that accursed place and made to talk, it will only be through drugs. How has it come about that science is used against people like this?

There are thousands of stories one could tell about the terror caused by the arrest of an acquaintance. I am particularly haunted by the memory of a nine-year-old girl who, hearing that a friend of her parents had been arrested, went up to the bookcase and in a businesslike way took down a few books belonging to the man, tore

---

* Small boxlike cells (the word used is the English one) in which prisoners are held while awaiting their first search. The procedure is described in Chapter 82 of Solzhenitsyn's *First Circle*.

out the pages with his name on them, and burnt them in the stove. The girl had several times seen her parents destroy all evidence of their acquaintanceship with someone – letters, names, and telephone numbers in diaries. They say this girl later became an informer – if so, it could only have been out of abject terror. I never used to keep diaries with telephone numbers, and have acquired one only just recently. Perhaps the time has come to throw it down the toilet – we no longer have stoves in our apartments . . .

In those days when they were trying to extract five names from N. N., the whole country was numbed by fear – it affected everybody without exception. Anyone who did not succumb to fear could only have been an idiot in the literal sense. It was the year 1937, when the terror reached its climax. Even the people climbing up the ladder of promotion to take over from the victims trembled for their lives. One man's destruction made another man's career. This was the law of the times and clever people tried to exploit it for the benefit of themselves and their children. But knowing to what they owed their promotion, even such people went in constant fear and trembling. Trying to hide their terror, they postured and clowned and were ready to commit any crime to save their skins. There was no limit to what such people were capable of doing.

I have seen a photograph of N. N. taken not long before her arrest. It is a typical Russian face, very young, with pure, well-proportioned, oval features, stern eyes, and lips tightly pressed together. Such faces were found among both peasants and aristocrats, particularly in young women 'seekers after truth' or sectarians. There is something tragic and doomed about them, as though the future had already cast its shadow before. But N. N. was neither a 'seeker after truth' nor a sectarian. Very modern in her outlook and not given to thinking in abstractions, she had eagerly plunged into life, leading a hectic whirl of an existence. Even now she is much the same, living at such a pace that she never has enough time. Nobody is ever able to finish a conversation with her – she always breaks it off in midsentence and dashes away because she is expected somewhere else. You can never have your fill of her company, and like everybody else, I never see enough of her.

A foreign acquaintance of mine, still looking with curiosity at us mysterious Russians, asked N. N. whether she intended to write about her experiences. 'No,' she replied. He was astonished: 'Why not?' To this she replied that she was too busy. When he inquired what she was busy with, she said: 'With living.' It was literally true. In her youth she was probably no less full of a craving for life than she is today. She helped me to shake off the last vestiges of my fears and inhibitions. This was easier said than done. Akhmatova, for example, never rid herself of fear until her very last days. In the hospital, just before her death, she heard the news of the Siniavski-Daniel affair and was worried that the same thing could happen to her because of the publication of her *Requiem* abroad. But, thanks to N. N., I have been able to get over such fears altogether, even though anything could still happen. At the moment not much is demanded of us: we are left alone as long as we keep quiet about the crimes of the past and the present. All that is required of us is to put on a pretence of being as innocent as newborn babes and of firmly believing that our rulers are clothed in shining raiment. The only things forbidden are to act, speak, or – worst of all – to write. By comparison with the past, we are now living in a kind of paradise, but for some reason we are still unhappy. Like the dog in the anecdote, we long to bark now and then. It is time we understood that barking is 'against the rules'.

I remember a conversation with N. N. as we were walking along Herzen Street, away from the Conservatory. This happened at the end of the fifties. She told me that henceforth she was going to live just as she wanted and would not worry about 'them' any more. She would not try to adapt to 'their demands' ... At that time only very few people had already freed themselves from the general hypnosis, but this woman had such strength that contact with her restored the inner vitality of people deadened by fear. As she spoke, I realized she was trying to make good all the years wasted in the camps and exile, when even she did not dare raise her head. Involuntarily, listening to her, I came to the conclusion that I must do the same myself, that is, make up for all the years of silence and passivity. I suddenly felt liberated. I don't know why, but it happened right there on Herzen Street, after this conversation with N. N.

What is the source of N. N.'s independence and inner freedom? Being a true child of her times she believes in nothing, and talk about immutable values just makes her laugh. For her these are pure fictions, and good and evil are abstract categories to which she has never given a moment's thought – they simply have no place in her matter-of-fact mind. When I asked her: 'Why is it you behave well and not badly?' she replied without pausing to reflect: 'Because I want to.' By such licence I am quite disarmed. She hates the very idea of heroism, and self-sacrifice would seem false and supine to her, so she has no name in her language for the behaviour which her inner freedom makes her capable of.

During her interrogation, with an iron determination, she rejected proposals which would have saved her from the camp. Her sentence was already prepared beforehand, but because of her obstinate refusal to give him five names, the interrogator almost fell behind in his schedule – each case had its allotted time limit. He therefore decided on extreme measures, and handed the stubborn girl over to a colleague, an Azerbaidzhani who was noted for his skill in 'simplified methods of interrogation', or – to use a more old-fashioned term – torture. He was a legendary figure among prisoners. It was said that he tortured people with his own hands and could force them to confess anything he liked. In 'Conversation About Dante', M. describes how the powers-that-be are able to exploit terrifying stories about prison. This is the psychological equivalent of an artillery barrage in war, and a great help to the interrogator in his arduous (but well-paid) labours. Such stories were always encouraged here – though you could, on occasion, get a long stretch in prison, or even a death sentence, for the 'subversive activity' of spreading them.

N. N. had to wait standing up for quite a time in the office of the renowned Azerbaidzhani interrogator. Prisoners were often made to stand for very long periods, until their feet became terribly swollen. N. N. was not made to wait too long, however – only until the interrogator came to the end of a telephone conversation he was having with a lady. It was a Saturday, the only day of the week on which there were never any night interrogations. The Azerbaidzhani was discussing where he and his lady friend should spend the evening. They talked about theatres and movie houses, clubs and restaurants. Was this also intended as part of a psychological 'softening-up' process (how nice to be free to go dancing, spend the evening eating out or at the theatre!), or was the fat swine simply enjoying himself, relishing the thought of his evening's pleasures in the presence of his victim? It was hard for us to interpret the actions of these people of whom we knew very little apart from the nasty things they did to us. But there is no doubt that, like any other isolated, exclusive caste – the professional criminals, for example – they lived by their own laws, contemptuous of the interests of society as a whole. Closed societies of this kind respect only their *pakhan* and the 'parley',* cover up for each other (as long as it suits them), guard their secrets, avoid contact with outsiders, and sometimes, for obscure reasons, engage in mutual destruction. While we regarded them with horror and loathing, they looked down on us with mere disdain. The executioner always despises his victim. These people with whom he can do just what he likes – an exhausted man with his trousers slipping down, or a woman with a muddy, prison complexion, scarcely able to stand on her swollen feet – these are pitiful, comic figures to him. What to us seems fine or noble is merely ridiculous to them. I once knew a young philologist who was married to the daughter of a powerful secret-police boss in one of the republics.† In the Khrushchev days he lived in a rented room in Moscow – he had come here to work on his dissertation – and had put a picture of Akhmatova on the wall. His wife was visited by childhood friends, the sons of secret policemen recently dismissed for their brutality. But their offspring were now being sent to a special academy in Moscow for training in their fathers' profession. Every time they saw Akhmatova's portrait they could not resist poking fun at her. The very sight of her provoked guffaws. There were no such women in their exclusive circles. A *frau* of the Nazi type would have made much more sense to them. The tastes of these people are international. They say that there were special country villas for them where they could go to drink and have a good time with 'lady friends'. N. N., awaiting her fate in the office of the Azerbaidzhani, was a type of woman completely foreign to them.

* See note, page 315.
† i.e. one of the non-Russian areas of the Soviet Union.

Having finished his conversation, the interrogator at last turned to her. He explained that they needed five names from her – this was the minimum. If she refused, she would be sent to Lefortovo,* where he himself would 'attend' to her case ... Here, in the Lubianka, she was free to name anyone she herself wished, but in Lefortovo she would be glad to name her own father just to get a moment's respite. In either case, the sentence would be the same – eight years. If she was sent to the camp from the Lubianka, she would serve her term, come back, recuperate, and still be a young woman. If she went from Lefortovo, she would turn into an old woman, no good for anything ever again. It was true that people were totally destroyed by Lefortovo. I knew two sisters born only a year apart, one of whom went to Lefortovo and the other not. When they returned they looked like mother and daughter. I am told that in those days the Lubianka had the atmosphere of a front-line hospital – screams, groans, broken bodies, stretchers – and that the tortures practised in Lefortovo were of a much more refined quality (and there were reportedly even worse places). A common saying in the prisons then was: 'He's been sent to Lefortovo to sign ...' Very few people came out of Lefortovo without damage to their minds – at least, I have never met any. So there was N. N., faced with the prospect of Lefortovo and knowing very well what went on in that legendary place from stories she had already heard in the Lubianka. The interrogator came up to her, put his hand on her shoulder, looked her in the eyes and told her to be sensible and think it over very carefully. He gave her two hours to consider. She noticed that his hands were very hairy – when she told me this detail, I remembered the fear inspired in M. by the repulsive-looking hands of his all-powerful contemporaries.

N. N. was taken back to her cell. She sat down on her bunk and thought. Her first idea was to compromise. She went over all her friends in her mind, wondering whom she might name in order not to be sent to Lefortovo. She found there was nobody she could name, even to save her own life – one had children, another was in poor health, a third had a wife and the thought of parting them was unbearable to her. After two hours she was taken back to the same

* Interrogation jail in Moscow.

office. She said nothing and the interrogator waited for her to speak. At last he asked what she had decided. 'Send me to Lefortovo,' she replied. 'If I name my own father in Lefortovo, it will be because you make me. But name people here of my own free will – that I cannot do.' (As she recently emphasized to me again, she said not 'I do not wish,' but 'I cannot' – this seemed to make it sound much less exalted in her eyes . . .)

The interrogator bowed to her mockingly, and she was led back to her cell. She gathered her things into a bundle, sat on her bunk, and began waiting for her transfer to Lefortovo. A guard looked through the spy-hole and ordered her to lie down. She told him she was about to be taken off to Lefortovo. 'We'll wake you when we hear,' he replied. She stretched out and went to sleep.

N. N. spent another month in the Lubianka, expecting at any moment to be moved to Lefortovo, but in the upshot she was sent instead directly to the camp to begin serving her sentence. We have speculated about the reason. I suggested that the Azerbaidzhani must have taken a fancy to her, but she only laughed: why should he bother about a woman in prison when any number of glamorous creatures outside would think it an honour to let him do anything he liked with them? The strength and power of people like him were very attractive – as were their social position and privileged rations. He could take his pick of any number of beauties, but no woman's looks were improved by work and standing in queues, let alone by prison. (Have people noticed that a hare, running for its life, looks just as beautiful as ever? Isn't this because it is created to run? A human being, on the other hand, who goes in constant terror of his life is a pitiful sight because he is created to be free and to exercise freedom of choice.) With the best will in the world, N. N. could not bring herself to name five 'accomplices' It was an act of free choice, a truly human gesture, and this is why she remains so human and has such a zest for life.

She herself believes she escaped because it was Saturday. People like her interrogator are always so overwhelmed with work, particularly at peak periods of terror, that they rarely have a moment to pause for breath. The hairy Azerbaidzhani was perhaps so intent on seeing his lady-friend that evening that he forgot to sign the order for her transfer, before hurrying from his office. Even a specialist in 'simplified interrogation' may be prone to absent-mindedness and fatigue. In other words, was it simply that he was not exempt from ordinary human weakness? I am inclined to think this was not the reason either, but that the case was simply too minor – it was mere routine to pick up and crush a slip of a girl like her. M.'s case too had been a trifling affair, judged by their standards and given the scale on which they operated. The only cases regarded as really important were those connected with the struggle for power (potential rather than actual), and nothing else mattered. No time was wasted on the minor cases, though everybody was subjected to the same routine process of intimidation. Threats worked as well as actual torture.

Not everyone came into the clutches of the celebrated interrogator with the hairy hands or was threatened with Lefortovo, but it loomed large in all our minds – you knew you could land up in its dungeons at any moment. The mere existence of places like Lefortovo and the Lubianka is fantastically educational and the lessons will not be lost even on several generations to come. It deprives people of their will and their capacity for free choice – in fact, of their basic human qualities. We have all made small compromises and many, or rather the majority, have gone on to make major ones. In a primitive tribe man was bound by rituals and customs intended to strengthen its unity. People were set free by Christianity but, having tasted freedom, they abandoned it and turned to atheism with its sprinkling of sceptical phrases and the pseudo-rational formulae of a pitiful humanism. There is a glaringly obvious connection between the loss of inner freedom and the abandonment of Christianity, but it escapes the blind and those who deliberately close their eyes. Yet this is the basic feature of our times and could not have been demonstrated more dramatically. There has never been a worse spectacle. Shame and disgust are all that are left to us. The only mitigating human feeling was pity, but not many were capable of it. Did the specialist in 'simplified interrogation' know what pity was? Did he have a spark of it for anyone at all? In the end we became empty of all feeling except the will to go on living, a desire to survive the worst of the horror at any cost, if only to see what would happen afterwards. The present period is a temporary breathing space, and what will come later, I shall never know.

But we were offered a choice – of the simplest and most clear-cut kind. Nowhere indeed was it ever done with such brutal frankness: the camp straight from the Lubianka, or the torture chamber. Those who chose to go to their destruction were thereby condemned to silence, though not all of them perished. Paradoxically, the people who tried to put their own safety first also perished wholesale, even though seeming to have a greater chance of survival than someone like N. N., with her refusal to name five names. In this country the loyal were slaughtered on an even larger scale than the 'alien', that is, people like us. (I know who make up my 'we': those who would name 'accomplices' only under torture, never voluntarily, at the first invitation.) As long as there are people who try to overcome their instinct for self-preservation, hope is not lost and life may continue.

Even among those 'alien elements' mainly concerned to save their own skins and live well there were some who allowed themselves to be beaten almost to death rather than sign 'confessions' implicating people they respected. I have heard about a woman who died in jail for refusing to sign a statement incriminating ... Molotov. Many went before the firing squad because they could not be made to go into court and repeat their fantastic testimony. This means that among the 'victors' there were some people who sincerely believed in their cause. The trouble was that they had failed to realize what they were doing and where they were leading the masses.

The Azerbaidzhani specialist in 'simplified interrogation' is reportedly still alive and active in his profession. He will now be applying his energies and physical strength in accordance with the latest instructions on such matters. Even in the worst times he always acted strictly according to the rules and regulations: not even a simple beating was administered to some wretched prisoner without an authorization from his superior. He and his superiors arouse no hatred in me, but neither have I the moral strength to feel pity for them. When all is said and done, they too made a choice.

Cruelty was in their nature, and, far from trying to overcome it, they did everything to encourage and spur on their darkest and most terrible urges.

39 'They'

I have never met any real members of our ruling class – except Bukharin, who had already lost his power when our paths crossed, and various minor representatives of the apparatus which runs the country. Such minor officials have an essential role as intermediaries, passing down instructions from above and relaying upwards information about the moods and desires of the lower orders. I am thinking here particularly of the functionaries in the writers' organizations. Some of them once wrote verse, and even continue to do so. In fact it was because of their literary contribution that they were first promoted to 'administrative work'. They listen carefully to instructions 'from above' and send back reports 'from below', trying to keep people happy with promises – if they fail, they soon disappear or fade from the scene. Sitting in the next office and keeping a watch on him there is always a 'person in civilian clothes' – no ordinary functionary, but the 'vigilant eye' of the State. Each receives his instructions through different channels and their combined activities synthesize the power emanating from the two sources in question.* If the 'person in civilian clothes' is a man of few words, the functionary is honey-tongued – hence his common nickname of 'hyena in syrup'. The syrup is essential because he is dealing with the rank and file, and with each of them individually he must assume an ingratiating tone of bonhomie – he is expected to play the part of the human being in the whole comedy. In his moments of affability he must show how much he sympathizes with people and their problems. But the instant he is reined in by the 'person in civilian clothes', he becomes the bureaucrat incarnate and takes back all his honeyed words. The nickname 'hyena in syrup' suggests a combination of viciousness and hypocrisy, but actually he is neither good nor bad –

*The Party and the KGB (secret police).

his only qualities are those which once led to his being picked out to perform his function in the apparatus. He is not a human being, but merely plays the part of one. He is totally identified with his allotted role, and that is all there is to him.

In the summer of 1955 Akhmatova and I were walking along the Ordynka and noticed police agents standing in every doorway. Akhmatova said: 'There's something afoot. But don't worry, it's for us, not against.' It was, as we learned later, the plenum at which Khrushchev read out his letter.* We sat down on a bench in a churchyard and Akhmatova started urging me to go to the Union of Writers and talk with Surkov, who had moved up into top place there after the death of the Boss. But she warned me to be very careful: 'He's one of "them", though he does at least know who Mandelstam was. The others know nothing . . .'

So, pressed by Akhmatova, I went to see Surkov. At that moment I was without work—I had left Chita to take up a post which had been offered me by the Teachers' Training College in Cheboksary, but in Moscow I had received a telegram saying they had changed their minds and could not take me (somebody in the literature department, at the mere mention of my name, had probably advised against getting involved with me). I was again in the process of sending in applications for hundreds of vacancies, and getting one refusal after another. The 'rehabilitations' had already started on a large scale, and a thin trickle of people was beginning to return from the camps. We were no longer paralysed by fear, but there was still uncertainty about how things would go in the new era.

The 'thaw' was still several months away – it had started for the insiders, but came only later for the rest of us. At that moment, the insiders were already basking in the sunshine. It was a period of great expectations for them. I went to see Surkov when he too was full of hope, and maintained my relations with him till 1959, when he just evaporated, together with his syrup. I talked to him once again on the phone at the end of the sixties, but by now there was no trace at all of honeyed words or syrup, only the voice of officialdom. This was not a sign that the situation had become

*In which he denounced Stalin; this passage implies that he did so at a more restricted Party gathering, prior to the full Party Congress in 1956.

worse since 1959. On the contrary, it was incomparably better – even if still unbearable. Nor had Surkov's change of tone anything to do with M. In the intervening years new groups have appeared among whom M. is regarded as a 'Jewish abscess on the pure body of Russian poetry',* and at the same time he has become a *samizdat* author, circulating in copies made by madcap young people, but he remains absolutely irrelevant to present-day Soviet literature, and especially to the official literary organizations. I cannot believe that any except a tiny minority of the people in the poetry section of the Union of Writers copy out or read him. But this I regard as completely natural and as it should be. M. is not a poet for whom any room can be found in Soviet literature – he is as antipathetic to it as it was to him. By the same token. I have nothing further to say to Surkov, nor he to me. Our relations are past history, and it is quite natural that they have come to an end. All I retain from the brief period during which we met is the generalized image of a functionary, and I expect that all he remembers of me is the feeling of slight aversion I must have aroused in him. It could not be otherwise. We belong to different worlds – nothing could be plainer.

Once upon a time M. believed – as I did too – that a mysterious wad of three hundred rubles he found in his jacket pocket had been put there by Surkov. This was enough to pay for a privately rented room for a month. It happened in the winter of 1937/8. M. was standing in the corridor of the Union of Writers surrounded by people, among them Surkov. When we left, M. found the money in his pocket.† I now doubt that it was Surkov who put it there. Was this the action of a man destined to become the functionary of later times? Or did a change come over him during the years of terror, so that he lost his human qualities and turned into a frozen spectre of his former self? This I cannot tell, but I only went to see him in 1955 because I remembered that money.

I told the secretary my name and she went in to give it to Surkov. Some of the people waiting in his ante-room had returned from the

---

*Evidently something said or written by a representative of one of the extreme neo-nationalist (and anti-Semitic) groups that have emerged in the last few years, with their own *samizdat*.

†*Hope Against Hope*, page 362.

camps. Surkov was trying to find work for them. As soon as his secretary told him I was there, he shot out of his office, raced up to me and asked how I was related to M. When I told him, he said he would see me in a few days' time since he was terribly busy just then, simply overwhelmed with work . . . I knew very well what the real reason was. Before talking with me, he wanted to find out at a higher level (I do not know how far up he can go) what his line about M. should be and how he must talk to the widow.

I had to wait about two weeks. Every time I rang the Union of Writers they kept telling me not to go anywhere, but to be patient until the meeting was arranged. At last I was given an appointment – on a day on which people were not normally received. This meant that the conversation would be a long one. Surkov's first question was about M.'s papers and literary remains. He could hardly believe his ears when I said I had preserved it all – a small part he could have understood, but *all* of it! Then he wanted to know about Akhmatova, and I told him about Lev Gumilev, suggesting it was better to do something for the living before worrying about the dead. Surkov said he would discuss Lev's case with Ardov. Knowing how little Akhmatova trusted this writer of funny stories (I can imagine what he would have said about Lev, judging by the letter he later wrote to the court*), I suggested he should see Emma Gerstein instead. I had a second meeting with Surkov the next day. This time his ante-room was crowded with people waiting their turn – you always needed great patience to see a functionary. The children's writer Baro was entertaining the others with her complaints about the position of women: they had to wait their turn on the same basis as men – no privileges at all! . . . Surkov then rolled up in his car and strode into his office with a cry of 'Ladies first!' To my surprise, Emma and I, not Barto, were the 'ladies' to be served first. As I said to Emma: 'We represent good firms just now.' Akhmatova's and M.'s stock was indeed high at that moment. Surkov's parting words were: 'For Akhmatova, Mandelstam and Gumilev I will do anything I can.' He said he needed another two weeks, but it was clear enough already that there was nothing but good will at the 'higher level' – Surkov literally

* In the case involving Akhmatova's legacy, after her death in 1966 (see page 307).

danced in front of me. I was not used to such treatment and melted.

This first round ended in my applying for M.'s rehabilitation and with Surkov talking in my presence (so that I could hear how he did these things once it was allowed) with Kotov in Goslitizdat,* and with the Ministry of Education. The next day I was received by the Minister who repeated to me what I had heard Surkov saying to him the day before on the telephone: 'He (that is, Mandelstam) got caught in the meat-grinder. We are rehabilitating him. She is someone who can do translating work for us, and she is as pure as could be.' These words were heard not only by officials in the room, but also by some other visitors who had come to see the Minister. They spread round the building like wildfire and were seized on as the signal for a new policy. The heads of regional and district education departments undoubtedly took them as a model and began to use them in appropriate cases at their own more humble level. Thanks to this, a few unfortunate women were given work in the provinces and now, like myself, receive a pension in consequence.

During the dazzling first round of my negotiations with Surkov I learned one thing: a functionary of his exalted rank never commits anything to paper, thus leaving no material evidence of what he says. He prefers to waste any amount of time (the reason, no doubt, they are always short of it) as long as he can conduct all his business on the phone. The spoken word is no more than a momentary disturbance of the air, a sound wave which leaves no traces. Tape recorders have so far done nothing to alter this situation, and the spoken word remains as elusive as ever. It cannot be filed away for the record, like a letter, memo, or any other piece of paper. The length and breadth of the country, in every corner of it, the air is in a state of constant agitation from the flow of words spoken by officials who know very well that all instructions are subject to change, and that tomorrow they can be punished for what they are told to do today. Surkov preferred to wait an hour and a half while his phone call was put through to the Minister rather than write a note for him. He even explained: 'I can't put anything in writing – it'll be read by his secretary.' In fact, however, the Minister's secretary, like everybody else in the room, heard every word

* The State Publishing House for Literature.

spoken by Surkov on the phone and repeated to me by the Minister the next day. But this was not a document, only a slight air turbulence.

On the instructions of the Ministry, I was given the very same job in Cheboksary for which I had only just been turned down. I asked whether I couldn't be sent to some other place but I was told this would be 'against the teaching code'. I set off there with the feeling that a new era had begun, and with a promise from Surkov that he would get a room for me in Moscow in a year's time and make arrangements for the publication of Mandelstam. A little later he set up a committee on M.'s literary remains,* despite the fact that the authorities had refused to clear him formally of the charges on his first case and fully rehabilitate him. This was just after the Hungarian events† and a direct result of them: the panic caused by Hungary led to a tightening of the screws again. Surkov thus did take a first step towards carrying out his promise, but the brief era of great expectations was over, and I soon saw everything going into reverse. When this happens, nothing is ever said outright, in so many words, but only by means of formulae based on the experience of half a century. These well-tried formulae do not consist of words understood as ordinary units of meaning, but are crude signals indicating that the speaker is going back on what he said before. Devoid of precise significance, they are a perversion of language and have a bad smell. Many people have talked of such dead words ('Dead words smell badly,' says Gumilev) and in my dealings with Surkov I heard several dead formulae of the type in use nowadays. They are terrifying because they show the extent to which people have renounced the chief quality that makes us human: the gift of speech and thought.

The first thing Surkov went back on was his promise to help Lev Gumilev: 'The position with Gumilev is complicated – he was probably taking revenge for his father . . .' In the old days, as a matter of policy decided 'at the top', sons were always destroyed

---

* Such committees were set up in the early Khrushchev era to attend to the publication of the works of 'rehabilitated' writers. They usually consisted of three people: the nearest surviving relative, a writer who had known the dead man, and an official representing the authorities.

† November 1956.

together with their fathers, in case they tried to take vengeance. In refusing to do anything for a man whose father had been killed and whose mother had been persecuted, this formula about sons always seeking revenge was the simplest. I am absolutely certain that Surkov himself did not believe in it, but was only using it as an excuse to wash his hands of the whole affair. Lev was released after the Twentieth Congress, when special boards were set up and sent out to the camps to release the prisoners. Only people with very long sentences were still detained – though they too had probably committed no crimes but simply signed statements admitting monstrous charges against themselves under threat of torture.

Surkov got me a room and I even received the key to it, but then the necessary papers failed to arrive, and I believe that a 'person in civilian clothes' vetoed the idea. But Surkov's explanations was: 'They say you left Moscow of your own free will.' In other words, I was at fault for not having been arrested and deported myself. (In fact, I had been expelled from Moscow after M.'s arrest: I was summoned by the military and simply told to get out.) The formula about leaving 'of one's own free will' thus served to mask the continued refusal of a permit to reside in the capital. Surkov finally brushed me off with the words: 'I have no time to talk with the comrades about you.' This has been true ever since. The head of the committee on M.'s literary remains is now Simonov, but for a long time Surkov refused to take the necessary formal steps for his appointment, and I had to phone him in this connection. 'I have no time to talk with the comrades. You seem to think I have nothing to do but worry about Mandelstam,' was his reply this time. At least I did eventually get him ousted as head of the committee, such as it is – it exists only on paper.

At the beginning of our talks about getting me a place to live – the Union of Writers was theoretically obliged to help because it had taken away our Moscow apartment after M.'s second arrest – Surkov wanted me to share something with Akhmatova, who came down to Moscow to work. (She got her translating jobs here and in any case was always ejected from the Punin apartment in Leningrad for the winter, to keep her out of Irina's way.) This meant that she had to spend the winter months staying with the 'beauties' she knew in Moscow. She went from one to another, bringing noise, disorder, and life into their homes. Surkov got as far as allotting a two-roomed apartment to us, but then a 'person in civilian clothes' came to see him in his office, actually in my presence, and spoke against the whole proposal. I now saw how Surkov could suddenly wilt and lose his sparkle ... When we were alone again, I said: 'There is only one Akhmatova. You should have a word about her at the top.' (M. he didn't understand, the son of a bitch, but he knew and liked Akhmatova's work.) It was simply a question of getting her a kind of double permit, to reside in Leningrad and Moscow, so she would have a room of her own in both cities. Where else in the world is such a thing forbidden? In fact, even here there are writers with two apartments, one in their home town and another in Moscow – not to mention dachas in the country.

Surkov had a ready answer to my suggestion: 'Impossible,' he said, stammering slightly, 'we might be accused of lack of concern.' 'Concern' is the most highly rated quality in any functionary. Since nothing had been done for Akhmatova, 'concern' had patently not been shown in her case and to right the wrong now would have meant admitting the fact. This is typical of the way a functionary's mind works and any fool can see through it, but they always imagine people take their formulae at face value, evidently regarding everybody else as like themselves. They no longer have eyes or ears for the person they are talking to, believing we all think as they do and live by the same revolting formulae. (Perhaps this explains those fantastic statements the interrogators always tried to get prisoners to sign?)

Akhmatova had at first thought it was a good idea for us to share an apartment, but then she had doubts herself – the secret police she felt, always went out of their minds whenever we were together, putting every informer they could spare onto us. For this reason she was not grief-stricken by the news that our joint apartment had been vetoed, though she was upset at my not getting a place to live in Moscow. She felt she was entirely to blame, though she really had no reason to – the fact was they were not prepared to give me any kind of accommodation in Moscow, whether on my own or with her, as was shown later, when I was refused a single room.

(What brainless idiots they really are: if they had put me right away in a writers' apartment block with informers on all sides I should never have been able to write my first book, or the present one! If the committee on M.'s literary remains had done what it was supposed to, namely, bring out a collection of his poetry and reveal even a little of the truth, I would not have dreamed of writing all this – none of it calculated to bring them comfort!)

I had already left and was working in Pskov when Akhmatova, racked by feelings of guilt, invited Surkov to visit her and talk about me. Surkov arrived with a bouquet of unbelievably beautiful white roses. He needed no persuading at all and spoke of me in rhapsodic tones, doing a little dance in his excitement, and making a firm promise to get me a room and residence permit right away. Overjoyed, Akhmatova sent me a cable in Pskov, praising Surkov. That same day I got a second telegram – from the man I refer to here as the 'person in civilian clothes' – saying Litfond* was sending me two hundred rubles as a non-returnable loan. This was Surkov's way of demonstrating his 'concern' as a functionary: the promised room and residence permit had been converted into a small gift of cash. At first I thought of refusing the money, but then I remembered the words of Zhenia Levitin,† my 'first swallow,' who had once shouted at me in a similar connection: 'Take a tuft of wool even from a mangy sheep!' So I spent the money on a copy of Stone‡ which had once belonged to Kablukov – he had written other poems by M. in the margins and it was touching to see the interest he had displayed in his young friend. I think this was a good way to use money given me by such a sordid institution. Some time later I got my residence permit thanks to Frida Vigdorova, and also suddenly had the chance of buying an apartment in a cooperative housing project. Simonov asked Litfond to loan me a thousand rubles for the purchase, guaranteeing to return it out of his own pocket if need be. They refused point blank – not for fear of losing their money, since they would have received it back from Simonov, but clearly as a matter of principle.

* The Literary Fund of the Union of Writers.
† Probably the young man referred to anonymously in Chapter 71 of *Hope Against Hope*.
‡ Mandelstam's first volume of verse (1913).

Simonov then just loaned the money to me himself. I have already repaid half, and he will get the other half when I die – my heirs will raise it by selling back the apartment. I am very grateful to Simonov, and I should add that he was reluctant to accept repayment of the first half . . .

In the period of my dealings with Surkov we had a number of curious conversations which gave some insight into the mysterious stratum he belongs to. When all the fuss over *Doctor Zhivago* began, I happened to have an appointment with Surkov in his office right after Pasternak. Before this interview Pasternak had been very nervous, fearing he might be set upon and torn limb from limb by a whole pack of writers. The ritual on such occasions really is utterly disgusting and Oksman told me an interrogation in the Lubianka was less horrible than this. I waited my turn in the corridor, sick at the thought of how they might be baiting Pasternak inside. 'What do I want a room from them for?' I thought to myself. 'To hell with the whole lot of them.' Whenever I thought of functionaries or writers, only the crudest of language came into my mind. But Pasternak emerged looking happy enough. He had agreed with Surkov to cable the Italian publisher forbidding him to bring the book out.* Surkov was also happy because he had got his way. The Italian publisher must have been happy as well, since demand for the book was only increased by all the scandal – some people must have been praying for me to be put in clink as the very best publicity for my first book . . .

Surkov was in such a good mood that he forgot about the crowd of other visitors waiting outside and launched into a disquisition about the novel. He gave me his opinion of Pasternak's verse: he did not like his images because 'the comparisons never have anything in common with what they refer to'. He quoted as examples: 'beer flowing from the whiskers of a cliff,' and 'the tide turns them out like waffles' (the first line refers to foam and the second to waves). Surkov thought everybody should write comprehensibly, like Pushkin and Shakespeare. I translated from memory several Shakespearean images that occur in the speeches of my favourite, Mistress Quickly, but it was no good. His notions about literature were firmly fixed in his mind (or, as Akhmatova would have put it,

* See Pasternak, Appendix A.

his 'urine is normal' – that is, his views on poetry or Pasternak's breach of socialist propriety were those of the average Soviet writer). He then went on to talk about things of more immediate concern. Dr Zhivago, he said, had no right to make any pronouncements whatsoever on the Revolution. Surkov was here expressing his conviction that the Revolution could only be discussed by the 'victors' and that nobody else, particularly its victims, was entitled to hold an opinion. He was not open to argument on this point and my attempts to interject were brushed aside. His attitude is a matter of common ground between the 'victors' (whether dead or living) and functionaries like himself. Only those can have the floor who speak from notes prepared and approved in advance. The rest must keep their mouths shut – or go to jail. The following stage is that everybody is *obliged* to speak from the same crib on threat of being flung down into the pit. The necessary discipline was achieved in the writers' organizations with no difficulty at all at the very dawn of our new age, half a century ago. Surkov had been pleased by the Khrushchev speech,* but failed to realize that it signalled an end to the silence of the grave. He was so used to this silence and to the so-called 'unanimity' it entailed that he genuinely believed it to be the only possible and normal state of affairs in our society.

The crucial point in my negotiations for a room in Moscow coincided with the uproar over Pasternak's Nobel Prize.† I was in fact kicked out of Moscow again because of the new clampdown in the wake of the *Zhivago* affair. Before this, however, I did manage to say to Surkov during one of our meetings that it would have been better to publish the novel rather than kick up all this unholy fuss about it. Surkov thought for a moment and then said I might be right, but that 'for forty years now we have not let such novels come into the hands of our young people'. How old, one might ask, are these 'young people' who for forty (now already over fifty) years have never been given anything to read? Isn't it about time they were allowed to read something worthwhile, at least before they die?

Such is the mentality of the 'victors' and their faithful servants.

---

* i.e. denouncing Stalin at the Twentieth Congress in February 1956.
† October 1958.

They cannot bear the thought of giving up the achievements of their Revolution, of which the principal one is the carefully selected provender fed to the 'unanimous masses' through magazines, newspapers, and books – something dreamed of already in the pre-revolutionary decade.

Once, while I was sitting in Surkov's office, his secretary burst in, almost in tears. She was a very kind, nice woman, though, unfortunately, like anyone in her position, contaminated by the notions she got from her boss. She told him a message had just come in 'from them' about a slanderous attack on socialist realism, broadcast the previous night by one of those pernicious radio stations that disregard our censorship.* An 'answer' must be made at once. Surkov did not even inquire about the nature of the 'slander'. His 'answer' was already prepared. He there and then dictated a memo saying, in effect, that ninety-nine point nine per cent of the population (as at our 'elections') support socialist realism and read only works written by this method. The secretary scuttled off to type it, and I asked Surkov where he got this very precise figure from. 'Library statistics,' he replied, without batting an eyelid. Since all contemporary literature issued by our libraries, home-produced or translated, is exclusively 'socialist realist', Surkov was speaking the truth. One could, of course, ask what percentage of the population actually uses the libraries, but in a country with a hundred-per cent literacy, it is assumed that ninety-nine point nine per cent read library books. Surkov accepts such figures with the genuine faith of a functionary who knows exactly what his role in life is.

When I was told I could not stay in Moscow any longer, the secretary gave Surkov such a piece of her mind that he got me a two months' extension of my residence permit. Receiving a considerably smaller salary than her boss, she is still capable of human kindness. The further up the hierarchy you go, the more such qualities tend to disappear. At the lower reaches they still exist and always will. We should not allow ourselves to be too scared by the spectre of the 'man in the street'. He may not, it is true, be very independent in the way he thinks, but at least he remains basically good-natured – which is all that really matters. People

* See note, page 16.

are dehumanized by status, rank, and privilege. The secretary was called Zinaida Kapitonovna. She must have retired on her pension by now, if she's still alive. Even in such an exalted sanctuary as the Union of Socialist Realist Writers, the life of a secretary is pretty arduous.

In his conversations with me, Surkov always referred to a mysterious entity called 'they', saying such things as: 'I don't know what view they will take,' or 'I don't know whether they will publish Mandelstam.' 'They,' as I noticed, were always thinking this, that, or the other or giving it as their view. Once I asked him outright: 'Who are "they"? As far as I'm concerned, you are "they".' He was quite bowled over by such a question in the midst of this pleasant conversation between himself, a poet, and the widow of another poet – someone he had taken for a lady, even receiving her on one occasion out of turn! Later I realized that in a world horizontally divided, as it were, into floors, 'they' were always those on the next floor. Surkov went up to the only slightly higher level above him, where he was told he must wait until it was known what 'they' thought of it all – and so it went on, 'they' always receding higher and higher. I was right down at the bottom, of course – even lower than Zinaida Kapitonovna, and for me her boss was the embodiment of the mysterious 'they'. Surkov's 'they' are different from those of the 'person in civilian clothes'. The views filtered down through this channel are also relayed to Surkov. He thus spends his time racing frantically between 'them' (of more than one hierarchy) and his 'clients' – the writers, whom he must try to mollify with concessions wrung on bended knees from 'them', never forgetting the exigencies of the 'class struggle'. The most important thing in the 'class struggle' is to preserve one's allies. One writer, for instance, demands a four-room apartment for himself and his family of only two (wife and son). Surkov dare not refuse because otherwise the man might 'desert to the enemy camp'. In telling me of this distressing case, Surkov complained how ungrateful a task it was to be in charge of literature, standing at the helm as he did. Four-room apartments are allotted only to the upper crust, but unfortunately people were always counting themselves part of it before being picked out by 'them'. The trouble about turning down some rising star was that he might 'join the enemy' and later on there'd be hell to pay. He even had a sneaking suspicion that if Pasternak had been given a little more 'living space' in good time, it might have restrained him from writing that novel.

Surkov once had a phone call from Ardov, who told him Akhmatova had heard rumours that her book was again being held up (this was the volume with Surkov's preface – which Akhmatova took with good humour: 'At least it's all so clear, it doesn't need fools to explain it').* Hearing of these 'slanderous stories' – at some level or other 'they' were mulling the book over and throwing out everything not to their taste – Surkov was highly indignant: 'Why frighten her with tales like that? She might become an internal émigré again!'†

It is hard for Surkov, always having to be on the lookout to catch writers in time, before they 'join the enemy' or backslide into the 'internal emigration'. But even harder than all the shadow-boxing of the 'class struggle' is the actual business of allotting the material benefits at his disposal: the apartments, dachas, 'packets'‡ and other special favours (some paid in cash, others in kind). One can scarcely blame him for a manner in which syrup is mixed with treacle, or for lapsing into the same folksy brogue as Maxim Gorki. No wonder, either, that he sometimes snaps your head off or grovels and eats humble pie. I would hate to be in his shoes. It's no fun . . .

Surkov is no worse – and perhaps a little better – than other functionaries of this kind. During our brief acquaintanceship I came out with a number of things very hard for him to swallow (as we would have put it in previous years: I said enough to earn ten years), but the fact is he did not report on me. Not every functionary would have shown such self-restraint. Yet like all his kind he stultifies language, stifles thought and life. In so doing he also destroys himself, and none of his syrup will save him. Surkov and I are the same age. At our first meeting he looked at me in horror – that's what it meant to be past sixty! I saw him at Ehrenburg's funeral and was struck by his glazed, sclerotic eyes and the

---

* This volume appeared in 1958.
† The stock term for a writer who does not inwardly accept the regime.
‡ See note, page 70.

hanging lower lip with saliva dribbling from it. Now I am younger than he – nothing can save a functionary from premature senility.

The last pronouncement of Surkov to reach my ears is something he said about Solzhenitsyn: 'I understand of course that Solzhenitsyn is a major writer, but "if the enemy does not surrender, he must be destroyed".' In such a context this quotation from Maxim Gorki is tantamount to conveying the view held on the very highest floor of the house where 'they' have their abode. Such is the importance of literature in our country.

When I left the premises of the Union of Writers, after my last interview with Surkov, I wrote him a letter to say I would 'never again set foot in your filthy institution'. I may have broken my vow just once, and I have certainly been to their cinema a couple of times (to see *The Gospel According to St Matthew*,* which I hated, and *The Great Dictator* – Chaplin is good even in a mediocre film), and once I had a meal in the restaurant, after returning from Ehrenburg's funeral. Apart from this I have had no truck whatsoever with the 'socialist realists'. I have lived my life without them and they love me as much as I love them. And M., of course, they cannot stand at any price.

40   A Kind Person

Now and then you run into a kind person, someone who suddenly appears when you least expect it, like a messenger out of the blue telling you all is not lost, to hold your head high and never despair. But the important thing is not to let him pass you by and to say the right word so that he reveals himself: otherwise you will go your separate ways and the message will fail to reach you. Some of these kind persons I must have missed, simply going by without stopping, but others I recognized for what they were and the memory of them is still bright in my mind. I met one in Tashkent

---

* Directed by Pier Paolo Pasolini. Foreign films, rarely released for general showing, are sometimes shown to a restricted audience of writers, journalists, etc., on the premises of the Writers' Union or in 'Cinema House' (*Dom kino*), a meeting place for members of the Film Workers' Union.

in the last year of the war, when Akhmatova had already left for Leningrad and I was all by myself.

I had not been evacuated to Tashkent in organized fashion, but had made my own way there, getting rides as best I could in passing trains, hoisting myself and my things into the converted frieght cars of which they consisted. In all my fleeting encounters with chance companions on this journey I noticed one detail which has a direct bearing on the story I am about to tell, namely that in the space of two months after the beginning of the war, the entire fantastic horde surging east from the Ukraine, Byelorussia, the areas of Russia proper threatened by the German invaders, and everywhere else had completely worn out its footwear. I travelled an unbelievable distance – by train and steamer, several times making long detours, getting stranded on islands, passing now through deserts, now through parts lush with vegetation. Once I got stuck in a village near Dzhambul and spent a terrible winter there – I earned my living by carrying heavy loads, like a camel, and felling trees. After this, thanks to Akhmatova, I was able to get to Tashkent. It was not until I arrived there that I saw people with proper shoes again – and they were foreigners. In Kalinin (that is, Tver), already, I had noticed that the boots and shoes of all the refugees were in very poor shape: the soles were tied on with string, which chafed the skin terribly. The people I saw in the trains were not too badly dressed (by our standards) but their footwear had come apart – except, perhaps, in the case of refugees from Poland who still, oddly enough, had something decent on their feet. The Poles generally wore cheap sports shoes which stayed in one piece even on the feet of those who, after the partition of Poland, had been through the camps and were then released to join the Anders army, or at the request of Mrs Roosevelt. But for citizens of the Soviet Union, footwear proved to be a very weak point indeed. This had been so for all too long. As far as I was concerned the problem of what to put on my feet began when M. and I made our first trip to the Caucasus, and it ended only in the mid-fifties. True, it was not equally acute all the time, but I will never forget the pair of shoes I bought in 1938 when we were living on charity. The backs seemed to have been made of some kind of bark – something discovered by the Stakhanovites of our footwear industry to replace the leather not available for the manufacture of our wretched shoes. The skin on my feet was rubbed so raw by them that when I got back to Kalinin I lay in bed for several days with a temperature, and watched as my feet turned purple. Our footwear famine was at its worst during the years of the Civil War, and then again in the Second World War. I have a pleasant memory of the icy puddles in Tiflis and the splendid wooden sandals in which I waded through them. How lovely to be young – like the girl students in Tashkent, whose toes turned blue from cold in early spring, when they were already walking barefoot.

By the time I reached Tashkent I was barefoot too. Faina Ranevskaya, the actress, with whom Akhmatova was then friendly, presented me with a pair of slippers made from wads of raw cotton which had been twisted into rope. They disintegrated on the fifth day – evidently because I trod too deliberately. Faina sighed reproachfully at me for ruining something so delicate and handsome with my clumsy way of walking. By the mere inflexion of her voice she managed to convey her thoughts without words: how can we ever keep *you* in footwear . . . (They say she specialized in this sort of thing on the stage and was very good at it.) I was sorry I had accepted the gift – at least I should have been warned how flimsy it was. After my mother's death I was left a pair of tiny shoes and some galoshes. Somehow or other I managed, taking pains, to dry my shoes out with the electric coil – they were always getting wet. I learned how to steal electricity only towards the end of the war – it was generated in the defence factory next door to us on Zhukovski Street. I had to pay an enormous bribe to the fitters who installed it for me. Every day a sack of coal was thrown over the wall into our backyard and in the evening the worker who had stolen it came round to collect his money from tenants who had taken it. My stove was heated by this factory coal, and for each bucketful I paid a fair market price. The workers who carried on this business in coal and electricity referred to their earnings as 'surplus value' – they also attended courses in Marxism and were all ardent Stalinists.

As the last wartime winter approached, I began to shiver with cold in anticipation. Someone told me that in a neighbouring street, not far from the house where Gorki's daughter-in-law lived, there was a cobbler who did not turn up his nose at even the lowliest jobs. Most cobblers took on work only for people with assured access to 'surplus value'. This modest cobbler was a very rare bird, and I went to him with a pair of shoes in a state of total disintegration that had been left by some unknown person in the room where Akhmatova and I lived. The cobbler looked at my treasure in horror and asked whether I possessed nothing a little stronger. I said no, and never had. (As I later discovered, he was also tired of honest Soviet citizens wailing about how badly they lived now compared with previous years.) He asked a price that, though quite fantastic in relation to my salary, was perfectly normal for those times, and he knocked something together for me. Before long I had to take them back for repair and this time, I don't remember how, we got into intimate conversation. I told him something I would never have dared mention in front of my high-minded colleagues at the university, who never ceased denouncing me for my ignorance of English and for using expressions different from those they had been taught. As it was, the little they already knew about my background was enough to arouse their righteous indignation. But to the cobbler I poured out my woman's heart, telling him I had lost my husband not at the front, but in an East-Siberian camp, what a wonderful man he had been, and how I could not understand why I went on living this miserable life when there was nothing to hope for any more. This time the cobbler took my measurements and said I would never again have to walk around with wet feet.

He returned my confidence by talking about himself – something he never did with any of his other customers. In 1937 he had worked as a fitter at a building site near Tashkent. His family had lived in the same room where he was now carrying on his cobbling business. Luckily, he had not taken them out to live with him at the building site, despite a tempting offer of an apartment near by. One night he was picked up and taken to the Tashkent equivalent of the Lubianka, where he was held for over a year. In every city there is a large new building that serves as headquarters for this institution, commonly known as 'The Big House', the 'Lubianka', or something of the kind. He was beaten to within an inch of his life, but no marks were left on him. He clenched his teeth and said nothing, not even swearing to relieve his feelings. It was too dangerous to swear; not that he was trying to save himself – he no longer had any hope of this – but he just could not bring himself to tell lies about himself to these brutes. It was not even a case of not wanting to – he just could not. The trouble was that as soon as you told on yourself, or said anything at all, they would make you slander others as well. He had already, in his own mind, written himself off and said good-bye to his wife and young daughter, but then suddenly, with the fall of Yezhov, he found himself included among the lucky thousand or so who were released. They had tried to get him to confess to sabotage at the building site. He had vowed never to return to this kind of work – to hell with it, well paid and highly qualified as he was. He kept saying to himself: never again, this is enough for a lifetime, and on his release he bought a set of cobbler's tools – bench, lasts, and so forth – with help from his friends and neighbours (those of them who had not denounced him) and started up working on his own. The engineers and various Party officials at the building project (the very ones responsible for his arrest!) summoned him and tried to force him to return to his old job. They said he was letting down the Socialist motherland and the working class, but he would not budge. Luckily (or should one say unluckily?) he had developed all kinds of complaints, including angina pectoris, during his stretch in the cells and punishment block of 'The Big House'. In view of this even our well-drilled and subservient doctors were obliged to certify him unfit to resume his previous work. He had to go before a so-called M L B ('Medical Labour Board') – which in those years was harder than passing through the eye of a needle. When the war came he suddenly found himself in enormous demand – besieged by an ill-shod multitude with orders to repair, patch, vamp, and sole whatever they had on their feet. It was thus no hardship for him and his wife and daughter to do someone like me a good turn. I understood him very well, better than any of his other clients. I remember how, during our journey from Cherdyn to Voronezh, M. had sworn never again to involve himself in 'literary work' – editing or reading manuscripts for state publishing houses, the whole of this accursed, sickening traffic in 'culture': 'Enough!' he had said. It was easy to talk, but unfortunately we had never learned an honest trade, worthless pair that we were.

In my old age I have begun to forget street names, but I can always recollect very vividly conversations and their setting – where they took place and what was talked about. In my mind's eye I can conjure up scenes from the past with all the sharp relief of a good snapshot – this is the distinguishing feature of my memory. It is generally a static, rather than a moving, scene. Even if I remember someone I met walking down the street, it is only as a motionless figure, frozen as it were, at that particular moment in time. I also see myself, rather as I might have appeared to others, but the image is a blurred one. The background is always incomplete, in a way that would be unusual in a photograph – things that must have been there may be missing for some reason, and it is beyond my power to recall them. Sometimes, for instance, I see the entrance to a house, but not the house itself – as in a photograph taken from some peculiar angle. Every static situation so recollected has its own psychological aura and I always know what was going on just at that moment. I can still hear a sentence as it was spoken at the time with its unique intonation still sounding in my ears, and meaningful, in the majority of cases, only to me. This is particularly true of my life together with M. – as, for instance, those occasions in Yalta, still fixed in my mind, when we walked up a neighbouring hill 'to the dogs' (there were lots of them, all very friendly) and floated a model boat on the pond there. We had bought it from the former agent of an extinct shipping company. I continue to live in memory with M. because I know that when we meet I shall have to give him an account of everything I have done. He will forgive me many things – I only hope he is not angry with me for letting on about our little boat, and for writing all these pages when I should have found something better to do . . . But I know he will forgive me – he was easy-going and unresentful, surprised at me for being so unforgiving. Only I suppose I am not really angry at our Surkovs (with or without a Maxim Gorki accent), merely puzzled as to where they all come from, these people who distort everything that makes them human, including the ordinary words of our speech. It would hardly matter if they had only done this to themselves, but they ruin other people's lives, preaching iniquity to them, egging them on to despicable actions – all with quotations from their 'classics', which sanction the killing of enemies and friends alike.

It is nice for grandmothers to have children to dandle on their knees, but I did not want to have any, and am glad of it. At least in this respect I showed good sense. Instead I have the snapshots preserved in my mind. Going over them in whole sequences, I suddenly begin to understand their hidden meaning; the present (which was then the future) picks out the moments of 'documentary' value and unites them into a significant pattern. The mind's eye focuses only on those 'shots' which are charged with a certain significance in relation to the future or one's destiny. I find such meaning in that model boat, for example, and in the cobbler, who is also still there before my eyes. How does he fit into the picture, this man who made sure I should keep my feet warm and dry in the last year of the war and the hard winter that followed it? Needless to say, he remains in my mind because of something more important and elevated than the problem of my footwear, namely because he showed kindness and sympathy rarely met in life – particularly in mine. Only thanks to such encounters I did not lose my faith in people. As long as there are some like him, life still has a little warmth, the human qualities are not yet totally extinguished.

One 'still' preserved in my memory is of a bright street with small, squat houses and tall trees – a contrast peculiar to Tashkent, but probably lost now after the earthquake.* Steep and narrow alleys wound down from this street to the Alay Bazaar – a wonderful Eastern marketplace with enormous vegetables and fruit in great piles and, hanging high up, tantalizingly out of reach, whole sheep's carcasses. Flat white loaves were offered at a staggering price by hucksters, and sun-blackened women traded in all kinds of cloying oriental sweetmeats which stuck to the teeth. One end of this street led up to the sky and the other end down to a square which Akhmatova and I nicknamed 'The Star' ('in Paris there is a square which people call The Star') – we had conceived a fancy that General Kaufman, in laying out Tashkent, had indulged his nostalgia for Paris by making all the streets debouch into this square modelled on the Étoile. One day, walking away from the

* In 1966.

square, up towards the sky, I ran into my cobbler, Sergei Ivanovich, and he said: 'You still have no trouble getting about!' He breathed heavily as he walked, and was all bent, like a hunchback. His feet were evidently swollen and he shuffled along like an old man, though he was still not much over fifty. He was on his way to the Alay Bazaar, to the flea market, where even the meanest cast-off rags would have cost me more than a month's salary. I could only keep alive in those days by giving vast numbers of private lessons, receiving payment in cash or in rationed goods. For the recipients of privileged rations, rice and flour were a much-prized currency, and I remember one very important lady (who dispensed with my services after the decree on *The Star* – the magazine, not the square*) saying to me: 'You are very lucky to have the chance of sitting now and again in a nice warm place' – by which she meant her apartment.

About a week after this meeting on the street, Sergei Ivanovich knocked on my door to tell me he had made my shoes a little earlier because it was already cold and muddy in the streets. The long autumn was over and the suntan was fading from people's emaciated faces, leaving them a deathly, greenish hue. He feared I might get my feet wet – 'and then, God forbid, you'll catch cold and it really will be all over for you'. He handed me a pair of extra-ordinary clodhoppers that he had put together, like a patchwork or mosaic, out of four completely wrecked remnants of shoes he had bought in the flea market the week before, when I had met him on the way there. The vamps and the tops were of different colours, but they had been lovingly fitted together. The patches he had put on were all bright and shining, and he had fitted double soles – one tacked on to another. I paid him for the materials – which he had bought very cheaply – but he refused to take anything for his work: 'It's not a real cobbling job, just a mosaic,' he said. He must have seen the mosaics in Samarkand, and I had told him about those in the Cathedral of St Sophia in Kiev (and when his daughter had been little, he told me, he had bought her a game in a box called 'mosaics'). Now he had made a 'mosaic' of leather, fitting together odd bits and pieces. He apologized for the fact that all the pieces, particularly the patches and the toes, were of different colours, but

*See Zhdanov, Appendix A.

in order to reduce the motley effect he had evenly coated them with blacking, and bade me polish them often to preserve their appearance and keep the damp out. They were indeed waterproof, and from time to time Sergei Ivanovich came round in the evening and took them away over night, bringing them back in the morning after a thorough overhaul. It was a long time since I had known such kindness, not to mention the luxury of dry feet, and I was warmed and gladdened by it.

It did not escape his sharp eye when a new inhabitant took up residence in my room that winter. This was the minor Moscow poet Kazarnovski, who had arrived in Tashkent from Kolyma and happened to have been a witness of M.'s last days in the transit camp at Vtoraya Rechka near Vladivostok.* From him I got the first reliable information about M.'s death – which it was not easy to extract because of his endless prattle about the good old days in Moscow (where he had moved in the literary circles associated with Herzen House and the Press Club), and about poetry – French, Russian, and Muscovite. But in speaking of M. he was much less inclined to romanticize, if only because he saw nothing very glamorous about such a fate. In this respect his attitude suited me very well.

Kazarnovski had come to Tashkent in the late autumn. The militia had refused him a residence permit and he had been driven from pillar to post, going back and forth between the city and the surrounding district, completely destitute and in rags. I hid him from the militia in my room for several exceptionally long weeks until I managed to get him into a hospital through the good offices of a kindly woman doctor. The neighbours thought he was my lover but took a good-humoured view of my feminine frailty. They were pleased, furthermore, by the fact that I had not registered him with the militia. They hoped that, like all the evacuees, I would one day return home ('but where is my home and where my reason?') and they would then come in for a little extra 'living space'. An unregistered tenant could have no claims on it. There was hence no clash between my interests and theirs – no motive, that is, for them to inform the militia, though there was still some risk of my ending up behind barbed wire for breaking the rules on residence permits.

* *Hope Against Hope*, page 452.

In one respect, however, my neighbours were mistaken about Kazarnovski, that is, in thinking him capable of playing the part of a lover. He was a hopeless drunk who could no longer keep his feet after a single glass. I never saw him sober. Either he was sleeping it off or chasing round town trying to raise money for a shot of vodka. Sometimes he stole small sums – from me of course – or went off to the railway station to turn an honest kopeck by carrying people's luggage. How he coped with this I cannot imagine – he couldn't bring a bucket of water into the room without falling over half a dozen times. He had no strength for anything. Astonishingly, he lived another fifteen years and died in Moscow, having been allowed to return 'home' after the Twentieth Congress. There is a story by Leskov about an officer's widow who houses an old soldier in a shed in her backyard because he carried her husband's body from the battlefield. Drunken and rowdy, he does nothing but carry on like the devil right under her window, but she meekly puts up with him. I envied Leskov's widow – at least she had a shed and a backyard, but I had to bear with Kazarnovski in a corner of my tiny room. I just had not the heart to throw him out in mid-winter, and he had one way of disarming me completely whenever I got angry with him: I only had to see his feet, on which all the toes were missing. They had become frostbitten and his fellow-prisoners had chopped them off to stop the gangrene. That winter I gave him my padded coat and my mother's galoshes to wear – the galoshes were quite large enough for a man without toes. When Kazarnovski made the acquaintance of my cobbler he started going round to talk about literature and beg money for vodka. But Sergei Ivanovich, the brute, would give him nothing . . .

One day Sergei Ivanovich decided he must have a heart-to-heart chat with me about Kazarnovski and put me on my guard against him. Coming into my room, he seated himself with difficulty on my couch – covered with oilcloth, it looked like a piece of office furniture – and said to me point blank: 'What do you want with this fellow? Get rid of him . . .' If I needed a man all that badly, he went on, his wife, Marfa Ivanovna, would undertake to find me someone who could support himself and didn't drink. 'But my advice is to give up this kind of thing altogether – better be your own mistress,' Sergei Ivanovich concluded. I had no choice but to tell him the whole story: about this being my first news of Vtoraya Rechka and M.'s death there, and about Kazarnovski's troubles with the militia . . . It was now with the help of the cobbler, through a client whose only pair of shoes he had mended all during the war, that I got Kazarnovski into a hospital to be treated by the kind woman doctor. Sergei Ivanovich and his wife were both very pleased that I had so abruptly turned down their offer to find me a self-supporting and sober man friend. 'You'll manage somehow on your own,' he said, 'and anyway there'll soon be a bit more to eat . . .' (After leaving the hospital, Kazarnovski turned up again, evidently regarding my room as home. It was summer by now and I would not take him back in. He cursed, said M. would not have behaved like this, dug me in the stomach with his fist, and went away. I can well believe that M. would somehow have found a place for the drunkard instead of telling him to clear off. But I have no pangs of conscience.)

Sergei Ivanovich always came round on the eve of church holidays and in a rather formal way conveyed Marfa Ivanovna's invitation to visit them on these occasions. I went to see them at Christmas and Easter. Though not churchgoers, they kept the holy days. Marfa Ivanovna baked pies, and as often as not I was their only guest. They had little trust in people ever since they had learned how his fellow workmen and – worst of all! – some of his neighbours had slandered him. The daughter, who was a student, did not appear at these feasts. Apart from the pies, she regarded the whole thing as sheer superstition. She studied Chernyshevski and Belinski at the university and slightly despised me for being on such friendly terms with her parents. We really did get on very well, the three of us, because we had complete trust in each other.

In the summer Sergei Ivanovich made me an extraordinarily stout pair of sandals with heels from good leftover materials, and designed in the same way as another pair for his daughter (we belonged, of course, to the same institution – she as a student and I as a teacher). During those days I had been conducting examinations and scarcely saw him. Suddenly he came round to see me in the middle of the day, on a Sunday, but not on cobbling or match-making business. He simply lowered himself on to my sofa and just sat for a long time without saying a word. We both sat there quietly, and I saw he had something on his mind but couldn't bring himself to tell me what. He was somehow sad and solemn. Leaving, he kissed my hand – an unheard-of thing with him and totally out of character in someone so austere and grave. His parting words were: 'God grant we live to see better times.'

I wondered what on earth could have been troubling him. The next morning his wife came running to see me: 'Sergei Ivanovich died during the night.' I was invited to his funeral, which was very well attended. I noticed that in those days few people – and those only in their official capacity – attended the funerals of intellectuals. Among simple people it was still the custom to pay one's last respects to the dead by following the coffin to its burial place, holding a wake, and sometimes even wailing and lamenting in traditional peasant fashion. At the wake given by Marfa Ivanovna there was nothing of this kind; everything was very prim and proper, with no loud cries of grief. She kissed me and said she had sensed that he had come to see me not just for nothing, but to say good-bye. She had made no comment herself – not to hasten the coming of death.

After the death of her husband, Marfa Ivanovna went to work as a cloakroom attendant. Sergei Ivanovich left her and his daughter a supply of footwear to last them a very long time. On leaving Tashkent, I went to say good-bye to them. The daughter showed total indifference, but the mother wept a little. Old and young had quite different attitudes. The daughter laughed at her parents' oddities – among which she counted her late father's friendship with me. She was very proud of getting a higher education. In her childhood days, as an active Young Pioneer, she had taken her father's arrest very badly since she really believed in 'enemies of the people'. When he was released, however, her faith in their existence was somewhat undermined. Though not an activist at the university, she was nevertheless in good standing.

The thought of having been one of Sergei Ivanovich's 'oddities' still warms and gladdens me – as did the shoes which he pieced together like a mosaic from scraps of various colours and shades.

41 The Years of Silence

Though not actually taking a vow of silence, I always kept quiet about the past not only with strangers, but even with the very few people who had remained close to me – these were already tired of hearing anything I might have had to say. Even Shura, M.'s brother, was so wrapped up in his own problems, his wife and his work, that he scarcely listened to what I had to say, and I preferred not to waste my breath. To this very day, I prefer to say nothing to people of the older generation, for fear of hearing all those old tales, such as how puny M. was, and the way he once ate all the cakes at a party given by Kameneva. Fortunately, I scarcely ever see people of that generation: hidden away in their corners, they are now living out the last years of their joyless lives, still trying to justify themselves. For me, however, there can be no question of any living person justifying himself.

I too am coming to the end of my days, full of troubled thoughts about what will happen after us. We have muddied the waters for many generations to come and may never find our way back to their pure sources. I am haunted by the thought that what has happened to us is only the beginning. Until quite recently I still believed that our experience would make people stop for reflection, and perhaps cause them to turn aside from the paths we have trodden. Now I realize that nobody learns from other people's experience, especially when – as in our case – nothing is left of it but disjointed bits and pieces. For decades, indeed for more than half a century now, everything has been hidden and buried out of sight. Anyone who dares to reveal even the smallest crumbs of truth will find himself set upon by a whole pack of highly self-interested hounds. Some were simply blind and deaf in the past; others, for what they fancy to be shrewd political reasons, have always held the telling of the truth to be a disservice – not to themselves personally (God forbid!) but to the entire social class they represent; while others yet are simply paid to keep their mouths shut. Soon everything will be grown over with grass.

The most astonishing thing is that there are still a few people with just enough life in them to try making their voices heard, but only through an immense volume of water, from the bottom of the ocean, as it were. Among them I count myself – and I know, if anybody does, what superhuman efforts are needed just to preserve a handful of manuscripts. Yet I could not have departed this life without telling something about the blithe soul who once lived at my side, never letting me lose heart; about poetry and people, the living and the dead; about *stopiatnitsas* like myself, most of whom still go on carefully hiding their past. Formerly they kept quiet as a matter of deliberate choice, but now it is force of habit – they have lost the use of their tongues. What is more, they would have no listeners: enough, people would say, we're sick and tired of all that, why harp on it still? The young, they would add, are no longer interested – and we must always take the young into account, mustn't we? But I say there can be no limit: we must go on talking of these things, over and over again, until every injustice and every tear is accounted for, until the reasons for what happened (and still happens) are made plain for all to see. The Sartres cannot be allowed to go entirely unchallenged in their advocacy of false freedom and defence of brutality. Italian writers who go to China and return as champions of the Chinese way of 'fighting bureaucracy' should not be left unanswered. How can people drink like pigs to blot out reality, or collect Russian icons, or cultivate their cabbage patch until everything has been said down to the very last word, until we have remembered every woman who ever went to a camp because of her husband, or was left behind to sit at home in silence, as though she had swallowed her tongue? I wish I could convey all the bad dreams I have lived through in half a century – above all in those more than thirty years of utter loneliness. No one who could see all these would ever want to kill.

A woman whose husband has been arrested (unless she herself was responsible for it) chases around frantically selling off her possessions in order to raise enough money for food packages. I went the rounds desperately trying to sell books, not knowing where to turn, and at night I lay awake repeating M.'s poems to myself. While my packages were still accepted at the prison, I tried to live as close to Moscow as possible. I expected to be arrested myself at any moment: wives generally shared their husbands' fate at that time. Later we learned there was a special instruction laying down which wives were to be picked up and which left in peace. It depended on the number of years given to the husband, but the rule was not always observed. They came for me in Kalinin during the very first days after M.'s arrest, but this was after I had been there to pick up a basket with M.'s manuscripts. I thus escaped their clutches by a fluke, and was able to go and live in the village of Strunino, near Moscow. Here, too, I got away only by the skin of my teeth. If they did not find me, or did not look particularly hard, it was because I was like a needle in a haystack, an infinitely small particle – one of tens of millions of wives of men sent to the camps or killed in the prisons. In later years I often heard people from the outside world declare that they would do things differently, in a nice humanitarian, orderly fashion. But everywhere things were repeated in just the same way as here. Isn't it perhaps time to stop and consider why?

While waiting in lines outside the prison to hand over a package, or trying to get information in the prosecutor's office, I sometimes heard husbands just recently released from camp or prison (there were such cases, though only very few) inquiring about their wives, who had been deported after their arrest. The guard behind the window at which we asked for information would snarl something at them and slam down the wooden shutter. As though dazed, they would stand on one side, muttering to themselves, not daring to approach the window again. I was suddenly seized by the idea that I could be arrested and then M. might be released and start desperately going the rounds of these places with the guards and shuttered windows. During one of my sleepless nights I wrote him a letter just in case the incredible happened and he returned only to find me gone. I shall end my book with this letter.

Fortunately it was not too long before I heard of M.'s death and I started to think of the best place for me to go and live in. I decided on Kalinin. My things were already in the train and I was standing on the platform at the station in Moscow when someone told me how 'they' had come to look for me there with a warrant just after my previous trip. I could not be bothered to unload my stuff again and I got into the train, no longer caring what would happen. In any case, by this time 'legality' had been restored: Yezhov had been replaced by Beria. It is true that Beria put Babel, Meyerhold and hosts of others in jail, but for some reason he overlooked me, and I got away with my return to Kalinin. At first I worked there in a small cooperative that made toys, employing people who worked at home. Later I was given a job in a school. Then came the war and evacuation, or, rather, headlong flight from the Germans. I first moved to the Muynak peninsula in the Aral Sea. In the hospital there I remember seeing a 'lady with leprosy', as a woman doctor put it. Then I spent the winter in a village near Dzhambul. In the spring my brother discovered where I was and Akhmatova somehow by hook or by crook, obtained a permit for me to go to Tashkent. After the war I had to wander endlessly round the country in search of work. I can testify to one thing: the pain does not pass or lessen with the years. All that goes away is the utterly numbed feeling of the first days, weeks, and months – perhaps even years, when over and over again the same scene is re-enacted before your eyes – 'the only thing we know this day . . .' At that time, over thirty years ago, I was older than I am now that M. has come into his own, despite the fact that he is still under a ban in the country of his birth – which remains true to its old principles. The ban indeed confers a kind of legitimacy, and in a way I am even glad and proud of it.

Immediately after M.'s death I spent a few weeks in Maloyaroslavets with Galina Meck, who had just returned from a camp, proud that she had not allowed herself to die. 'Nadia,' she would say to me, 'I thought the people of your race were tougher . . .' In reply I would make some remark about German barons and go off to the shop for our wretched provisions. Galina mercilessly kept me on the move, shaking me out of my dazed state. There was always a long line in front of the shop. As I stood there waiting I would go through the scene of M.'s arrest, dwelling on the minutest detail. Sometimes I saw in my mind's eye, with all the clarity of an hallucination, a heap of bodies dressed in the grey rags of camp prisoners, and strained to make out the dying M. among them. Then suddenly I would hear curses from the line and start out of my bemused state on hearing the angry voice of the woman behind the counter demanding to know what I wanted. But I would have forgotten what I wanted and why I was there. Overcoming the inertia of silence with a great effort, my lips at first moving sound-lessly, I would ask her to weigh out some sugar, if there was any, or salt, or buckwheat. I often bought something quite different from what Galina wanted, and she then sent me right back to get it. She nagged me all the time, making me answer questions and chasing me out to the shop. 'Otherwise you'll fall asleep and never wake up again.'

I knew I had no right to fall asleep and not wake up again. For this reason I went to the shop and did everything Galina said. At night I would hear her talking deliriously in her sleep – her husband, whom she had met in the camp, had recently been re-arrested. He had been like a saviour for her – meeting him had given her a new lease on life. I spent most of my evenings sitting with Galina's mother, whose husband had been shot. She told me that when she had been allowed to see him in prison they had brought out a grey old man who wept and shouted: 'Do not believe them, do not believe anything!' He was dragged away again before they could even say good-bye. Galina's mother did not talk deliriously in her sleep because she had faith that she would be reunited with her husband in another life. She was waiting for her own death, and her only worry was how her daughter would cope with her small grandson when she was gone. It was she who forced me to get into the habit of reading: she was convinced it was the only thing for women without children. I schooled myself to read only books which make a great demand on you – such as grammars of ancient and modern languages, and a few books on linguistics. But I could never get through more than a few lines at a time because they would suddenly blur, and I saw instead a heap of bodies in the wadded jackets of camp prisoners.

Sometimes, all three of us read bits of Shakespeare together – particularly the speech of young Arthur's mother, who feared that in heaven she might not know her son, 'meagre as an ague's fit', tormented by the executioner, his 'pretty looks' lost because of all his terrible sufferings. I found it astonishing that the English, after reading about young Arthur and the way he softened the hearts of his executioners, had not given up killing their fellowmen forever. Galina said that people went on slaughtering in the same old way after Shakespeare because they had simply not seen this play: for a long time Shakespeare was not read or staged. (I have often met

Englishmen and Americans living in this country who laugh when they hear I am always reading Shakespeare: What do you need that old stuff for? they ask.) At nights I wept at the thought that executioners never read what might soften their hearts. It still makes me weep. But, at that moment, in Maloyaroslavets, and later in Kalinin, I read very little myself. (Kalinin, incidentally, is Tver, nothing else but Tver.*) It was only later, in Tashkent, that I really learned how to do it, when Akhmatova and I re-read Dostoyevski together.

By this time I had talked with many people who had returned from the camps (and most of whom were sent back to them in the second half of the forties). I first heard what it was like there – in a few words of great restraint – from a peasant who was making for home on foot. On the way he spent the night in an izba in a village near Dzhambul, where I was staying with my mother. The son of this man had received a high military decoration and managed to obtain his father's release. Until he got his award the son had probably never told a soul that his father had been deported as a kulak and put in a camp. Nobody could be expected to behave otherwise, but it was a rare son who would mention his imprisoned father while the Leader was pinning an order on his chest. It was a noble act. The father was an intelligent man, but for all my questioning of him I could not form a visual image of the camps – this only came when I read *Ivan Denisovich*. Shalamov was annoyed at me over this: the camp described here, he said, was one in which you could quite happily have spent a lifetime. It was an improved post-war camp, nothing like the hell of Kolyma. This was confirmed by other people who went into the camps and prisons at the end of the thirties, but none of them have been able to find adequate words to describe it. I am well aware, however, that what Solzhenitsyn shows was nothing like the horror that greeted M. in Vtoraya Rechka in 1938. But only people who went through the camps and survived can tell us about them. My concern here is with the women who, by some lucky chance, were spared this particular fate.

In Kalinin, I often had to cross a bridge over the Volga. I knew

*Like several ancient Russian towns, Tver has been renamed after a Soviet leader (see Kalinin, Appendix A).

the beauty of the steel-grey water below, but now that M. was gone it seemed like sacrilege to look – we had always walked over together and I could vividly remember the time we had done so on a night in late autumn in the last year of our life together (this accursed ability to conjure up scenes in my mind!). We had just travelled back from Moscow, where we had succeeded in getting a little money. We had enough to pay our landlady for a couple of weeks or so without having to go into Moscow again – in other words, about twenty-five rubles in today's money. The shops were selling dried peas which we boiled a handful at a time, eating them twice or three times a day with bread. This, together with tea and sugar, was our only sustenance. But the main thing for us was to have a break from our journeys into Moscow. We needed this as much as air to breathe. We just had no heart any more for the business of begging from people who were themselves quite poor – though by the standards of those times they seemed very well off. But even more to the point, we were almost dropping from fatigue. I do not remember who gave us this last sum, but as always, it had been a very wearing and humiliating process to get it. In those years nobody was yet accustomed to the idea of giving money to a proscribed person. People have only got used to it in recent times. We were desperately anxious for a respite before beginning a new round of self-abasement. At the station, on arriving back from Moscow that night, we had argued about whether to take a horse-cab. I was against it because they were so expensive. We lived right on the outskirts and the man would ask an outrageous price – there would be nothing left to buy peas, and our respite would be over before it began. M. complained about his heart and reminded me what a long way it was to walk. There are two possible ways of life for a beggar – one is to watch every penny and deny oneself all extras (which is what I do nowadays, except for taxis), and the other is to run through it as it comes and just go round again with outstretched hand whenever you need more. I always favoured the first way, but it was hard to refuse yourself a handful of dried peas.

Our argument lasted for no more than a minute, but by the time I had given in to M. and agreed to this infringement of our imaginary budget, the horse-cabs had all been taken. Only two or three, four at the most, came out to meet the trains. As private operators they were forced to pay such a huge tax that they had almost disappeared by then, and there were still no ordinary taxis to replace them. (Even now, arriving in a provincial town, you just stand with your suitcase, not knowing where to turn.) So thanks to this I had my way and we set off on foot. M. kept stopping for breath. It was particularly hard for him on the bridge where a keen wind was blowing. He said nothing, but I could sense how ill he felt and I had a moment of panic: Suppose he fell down, where could I go for help? It was night, the streets were empty and in darkness – there was nothing but the bridge and the river. But all was well. We got back, made some tea and our landlady brought us a little to eat with it. The next morning we went out to buy peas.

One might think that in our cruel age a pain in the chest and a bitter wind blowing over a bridge are nothing particularly worth recalling. But this happens to be the typical way for a *dokhodiaga** to die – both in the camps and outside. They just go on, dragging themselves along until they drop and give up the ghost (this is why I regard taxis as more important than food). When he drops, the *dokhodiaga* may still crawl a few more paces, probably just by inertia . . . I have seen many of them outside the camps, which is why I regard sudden death – even from a slug of lead – as a boon. There are various ideas of what constitutes a stroke of good luck, but some people will appreciate this one of the *dokhodiaga*.

Going over the bridge in Kalinin by myself, I now always recalled the night as M. stumbled along, gasping for breath. Better for us, I thought, if we had thrown ourselves into the icy waters below. The river had not yet frozen and we would have been able to drown. Or he could have died there and then of a coronary (a word we had not yet heard in those days). But if he had died like that, I should never have known it was deliverance from a much worse torment. The future is hidden from us. Evidently each of us must travel his own path to the very end, blessing death – not for nothing known as the deliverer – when it comes. I was always so buried in my thoughts going over this long bridge across the Volga that if a passing stranger or acquaintance hailed me, I looked at them with dazed, unseeing eyes. They sometimes even asked whether I was ill. I could scarcely tell them my illness was that of the times we lived

* See note, page 258.

in – a torpid state in which one could only converse with death. Seeing me in those days, some people said I must be not quite right in the head. They did not know that the same was true of them too.

This was not just I, but what the age had done to me. Millions of women walked the streets, crossed bridges, or stood in lines in exactly the same way, completely oblivious to their surroundings. They did not think of themselves as a special community, as a 'we', because they were simply a random collection of specks of dust who happened not to have been sucked up by the great vacuum cleaner. You hear it said that all this came about for inscrutable reasons of state, and there are still those who swear by the late Leader and his foresight in destroying a 'fifth column' – such people would be happy enough to begin the whole business all over again. That we have no reasons for hope I am now quite certain. And all the time I ask myself: What manner of people were they, those who first decreed and then carried out this mass destruction of their own kind? Can one indeed call them 'people'? Would it not be right, therefore, to regard them too as fit only to be destroyed? We saw the answer to both questions already then: anybody who begins to destroy his fellow men, even if they are themselves guilty of hideous crimes, inevitably turns into a wild beast. (Poor wild beasts – look who we compare them with!) Such a person cannot stop, because once you have embarked on this path, there is no stopping. Once a man has put himself above his fellows and arrogated the right to decide who shall die and who shall live, he is no longer responsible for his actions. Once the machine of destruction is in being, it is outside the power of man to control it. The machine will go on working until, glutted with human sacrifice, it runs down. Even when it is only idling, as today, it continues to function in essentially the same manner as before. At any moment, after lying dormant for a time, it could start up again at full speed. For the final stage, people say, it will work to the utmost extent of its awesome capacity. Programmed only to destroy, it will complete its task.

I had always understood this in a vague sort of way, but it was only borne in on me with total clarity, as a fact of life, during the first days of my loneliness, when I was persecuted by the general-

cum-writer called Kostyrev.* He had been put into our apartment
by Stavski, who had guaranteed that he would leave as soon as the
second room was needed, that is, as soon as M. came back from
exile. I was given a temporary residence permit (for one or two
months) enabling me to live with my mother in the *passageway* of
our apartment. On coming through to get to his room, Kostyrev
would say: 'These bitches should be sent to Birobidzhan.'† Then,
before my permit had expired, he had me thrown out on the street –
this was arranged through the special office in the militia station to
which I was summoned by a representative of the security organs.
In those years anti-Semitism was not yet officially encouraged, but
Kostyrev, connected as he was with two of our leading organizations – literature and the secret police – was 'ahead of his time'. He
was utterly vile – and even viler was his sullen wife. Can it be that
their daughter has taken after them and grown up to be equally
poisonous, with all the instincts of a killer? She seemed a most
ordinary kind of child and I am curious as to whether people are
born criminals, through their genes, or whether it is a question of
upbringing.

The Kostyrev couple rummaged through the whole apartment
in search of M.'s papers. They found a list of poems which I had
hidden behind the bath tub. But to use Akhmatova's expression,
'such strength entered into me', that I tore it from their hands, and
the general was too flabbergasted to say a word. I think this was
because I looked him straight in the eye. This is something they
cannot stand.

In the toilet, affixed to a nail in the wall, I once found some rough
drafts of letters he had addressed to the Leader. They were mostly
expressions of gratitude: I was nothing and now have become all
thanks to you. Each letter also contained a petty denunciation. The
Kostyrevs had funny eating habits, quite unlike other people's. She
used to boil macaroni, putting it first in cold water. She was quite
incapable of learning how to do anything properly, like some

---

* *Hope Against Hope*, page 156.

† The so-called autonomous Jewish region in the Soviet Far East. Jews
were encouraged to settle it as their own territory, but relatively few were
attracted there.

moron fit only to be employed as a night watchman. Where do they come from, this mysterious breed of people, whose only aptitude is for what creates havoc and brings destruction?

Like nearly all women in my situation, I had a vision one night that phantom protectors had come to avenge me, restoring order in my apartment and even taking away the man who had stolen it. But immediately, almost at the same second, I brushed it aside, deciding I did not want my own fascists. Better that all these monsters die of in their country villas, enjoying their retirement on pensions worthy of executioners. I would not want any band of killers to take vengeance on them for me. The last thing I wish is to resemble them, and even if, by some miracle, avengers were to present themselves, I should refuse their services. (I may say that I have never been, nor ever could be, in the position of having to resist such a temptation in real life. The avengers I am talking of here are purely hypothetical creatures of my imagination.) I fear that what I am saying may qualify as 'non-resistance to evil',* and if so, I must accept that I am a 'non-resister' – though I wish there were some other name for it . . .

But however one calls it, my attitude is based on the conviction that killers are impervious to any kind of argument or persuasion: debate with them is pointless and nothing whatsoever has any effect on them. Words and ideas do not penetrate to their minds, but fill them with repulsion and fear – this indeed is our only weapon. Yet the killers are only strong when they are supported and admired for their exploits by ordinary people, as we have seen in the first half of our century. Ordinary people, whether the inert and conservative masses, or the rampaging mobs of a popular revolution – brought to a white heat of fury by the brutishness of former rulers intent on preserving the status quo – are won over only initially by new modes of explaining the world. Beguiled by specious arguments, they learn to invert all our accepted notions in order to justify what previously was regarded as evil and begin to bow down to force as the only effective form of action. Not even pausing for thought, they find themselves supporting murderers, parroting their slogans and lauding their aims – aims that seem so

* Tolstoi's phrase.

practical on the surface, but are in reality hollow and deceitful. Never achieved, the aims in question gradually die away. People lose faith in them, but continue by inertia to hold to the cult of force. It was not a 'cult of personality' we had here, as the newspapers tell us, but a cult of force – even though, in the end, force itself is nothing but an absurdity, a farce, a ludicrous manifestation of impotence. Eventually we are left with only naked terror before the powers of evil. All that matters now is to overcome this terror, to fight for every human soul, to remind people what it means to be human, to show them that nobody has ever yet been saved by thirty pieces of silver.

Everything we have been through here was the result of succumbing to the temptations of our era – to which no one is immune who has still to be struck down by the disease of putting his faith in force and retribution. Vengeance and envy are the prime motives of human behaviour. No one should lightly dismiss our experience, as complacent foreigners do, cherishing the hope that with them – who are so clever and cultured – things will be different. As I never tire of repeating, I have heard such assurances a thousand times from many a simple soul who was reared in our hothouses, brought to ripeness, and transplanted at the right moment to his native fields with the task of scattering his poisonous seeds over them. A lot perished, only beginning to see the light as they did so. But others, even going to their doom, continued to reel off the vile tenets that had been hammered into their skulls. Those who survived go on just as they were supposed to, carrying out their programme to the end. Children brought up in such families generally carry within themselves the seeds of evil and crime, even if they are rarely killers – their sheltered upbringing is rather against this – but they talk the same language and are imbued by the same mentality as their parents. The experience we have had is the only thing that can give immunity – like a vaccine or inoculation . . .

The trouble is that we continue to hide our experience – it cannot be tapped without making a certain effort, but people have neither the patience nor the curiosity. Best of all would be if we could gradually accumulate powers of resistance to the use of brute force, until the machine ground to a halt and began to rust. But this would be a very long process for people like us with no language, no standards, no light to guide us. All we have is our craven fear.

To overcome our fears is the hardest of all – they are all too well founded. I only finally got over mine in a dream. For twenty or even thirty years I always listened intently as cars went by, straining my ears in case they stopped outside. At the beginning of the sixties, in Pskov, I dreamed I heard a truck come rattling into the courtyard, and then M.'s voice saying: 'Get up, they've come for you this time . . . I am no longer here.' And I answered him, still in my dream: 'You are no longer here, so I do not care.' After that I turned over and went into a deep sleep without dreams. In the morning I decided I would never open the door if they came for me, however loudly they hammered on it. Let them break it down (it was only made of cardboard anyway!), but I did not care any more. Let them have the satisfaction of bringing an extra charge against me – resisting arrest. I will never respond to their knock on the door, only to a human voice. But not every voice belongs to a human being – killers cannot be so described.

By the time I had that dream, M.'s poetry was already printed.* Now it is indestructible, and I therefore feel totally and absolutely free, and I can breathe easily (despite the lack of air). How many people will understand what joy it is to breathe freely just once before you die?

This book, which I have now nearly finished, may never see the light of day. There is nothing easier than to destroy a book, unless it already circulates in *samizdat* or has found its way into print (as used to happen to books in the Gutenberg period of Russian history). But even if it is destroyed, it may, perhaps, not have been entirely in vain. Before being consigned to the flames, it will be read by those whose expert task it is to destroy books, to eradicate words, to stamp out thought. They will understand none of it, but perhaps somewhere in the recesses of their strange minds the idea will stick that this crazy old woman fears nothing and despises force. It will be something if they understand that much. The thought of it will be like a little pinch of salt to sprinkle on their privileged rations, or a garnishing to whet their appetite for that other literature designed to edify and instruct people of their kind,

* i.e. in the United States.

functionaries to whom nothing matters, neither life, nor man, nor the earth, nor anything – dimmed by their very breath – that lights our way. Heaven help them. But will they really succeed in their task of universal destruction?

42 Last Letter

This letter was never read by the person it is addressed to. It is written on two sheets of very poor paper. Millions of women wrote such letters – to their husbands, sons, brothers, fathers, or simply to sweethearts. But next to none of them have been preserved. If such things ever survived here, it could only be owing to chance, or a miracle. My letter still exists by chance. I wrote it in October 1938, and in January I learned that M. was dead. It was thrown into a trunk with other papers and lay there for nearly thirty years. I came across it the last time I went through all my papers, gladdened by every scrap of something that had survived, and lamenting all the huge, irreparable losses. I read it not at once, but only several years later. When I did, I thought of all the other women who shared my fate. The vast majority of them thought as I, but many dared not admit it even to themselves. Nobody has yet told the story of what was done to us by other people – by those selfsame compatriots whom I do not wish to see destroyed, lest I thereby come to resemble them. Their present-day successors, the spiritual brothers of those who murdered M. and millions of others, will curse on reading this letter – why didn't they destroy the bitch (that is, me), they will ask, while they were about it? And they will also curse those who have so 'relaxed vigilance' that forbidden thoughts and feelings have been allowed to break to the surface. Now again we are not supposed to remember the past and think – let alone speak – about it. Since the sole survivors of all the myriad shattered families are now only the grandchildren, there is in fact nobody left to remember and speak of it. Life goes on, and few indeed are those who wish to stir up the past. Not many years ago it was admitted that some 'mistakes' had been made, but now it is denied again – nothing wrong is seen with the past. But neither can I speak of the past as a 'mistake'. How can one thus describe actions that were part of a system and flowed inexorably from its basic principles?

Instead of an epilogue, then, I end my book with this letter. I shall do what I can to see that both book and letter survive. There is not much hope, even though our present times are like honey and sugar compared with the past. Come what may, here is the letter:

22/10 (38)

Osia, my beloved, faraway sweetheart!
I have no words, my darling, to write this letter that you may never read, perhaps. I am writing it into empty space. Perhaps you will come back and not find me here. Then this will be all you have left to remember me by.

Osia, what a joy it was living together like children – all our squabbles and arguments, the games we played, and our love. Now I do not even look at the sky. If I see a cloud, who can I show it to?

Remember the way we brought back provisions to make our poor feasts in all the places where we pitched our tent like nomads? Remember the good taste of bread when we got it by a miracle and ate it together? And our last winter in Voronezh. Our happy poverty, and the poetry you wrote. I remember the time we were coming back once from the baths, when we bought some eggs or sausage, and a cart went by loaded with hay. It was still cold and I was freezing in my short jacket (but nothing like what we must suffer now: I know how cold you are). That day comes back to me now. I understand so clearly, and ache from the pain of it, that those winter days with all their troubles were the greatest and last happiness to be granted us in life.

My every thought is about you. My every tear and every smile is for you. I bless every day and every hour of our bitter life together, my sweetheart, my companion, my blind guide in life.

Like two blind puppies, we were, nuzzling each other and feeling so good together. And how fevered your poor head was, and how madly we frittered away the days of our life. What joy it was, and how we always knew what joy it was.

Life can last so long. How hard and long for each of us to die alone. Can this fate be for us who are inseparable? Puppies and children, did we deserve this? Did you deserve this, my angel?

Everything goes on as before. I know nothing. Yet I know everything – each day and hour of your life are plain and clear to me as in a delirium.

You came to me every night in my sleep, and I kept asking what had happened, but you did not reply.

In my last dream I was buying food for you in a filthy hotel restaurant. The people with me were total strangers. When I had bought it, I realized I did not know where to take it, because I do not know where you are.

When I woke up, I said to Shura: 'Osia is dead.' I do not know whether you are still alive, but from the time of that dream, I have lost track of you. I do not know where you are. Will you hear me? Do you know how much I love you? I could never tell you how much I love you. I cannot tell you even now. I speak only to you, only to you. You are with me always, and I who was such a wild and angry one and never learned to weep simple tears – now I weep and weep and weep.

It's me: Nadia. Where are you?

      Farewell.

         Nadia.

Chronology

1889	Anna Akhmatova born near Odessa.
1890	Boris Pasternak born in Moscow.
1891 Osip Emilievich Mandelstam born in Warsaw.	
1892	Marina Tsvetayeva born in Moscow.
1894	Alexander III dies and Nicholas II becomes tsar.
1899 Nadezhda Yakovlevna Mandelstam (née Khazin) born in Saratov.	
1904 M. attends Tenishev Commercial School in Petersburg, where he receives a classical education.	Outbreak of Russo-Japanese War; death of Chekhov; First Russian revolution and granting of a constitution by Nicholas II.
1907 M. makes his first trip to Paris where he becomes interested in the French Symbolists.	
1909 M.'s first appearance in print (two poems published in the Symbolist journal *Apollon*); makes acquaintance of Nikolai Gumilev.	
1910 M. studies Old French literature at Heidelberg University for two semesters, and also spends some time at the Sorbonne; makes two brief trips to Italy.	Akhmatova marries Gumilev; death of Tolstoi.
1911 M. studies in the Department of Romance and German philology at Petersburg University.	Gumilev founds 'Poets' Guild' and thus initiates Acmeism as a breakaway movement from the Symbolists.
1912 M. writes essay 'Morning of	Controversies between Symbolists,

Acmeism' (which is published only in 1919).

Acmeists, and Futurists; Akhmatova's first volume of verse (*Evening*) published and her son, Lev, is born.

1913 M. publishes first volume of verse, *Stone*, and essay on François Villon in *Apollon*.

Akhmatova's second volume, *Rosary*, appears.

1914

Outbreak of First World War.

1915 M. publishes essay on Chaadayev in *Apollon*.

1916 M. visits Crimea for the first time; second edition of *Stone* appears.

1917

February Revolution and Provisional Government under Kerenski; Lenin seizes power in October.

1918 M. briefly employed in the People's Commissariat of Education under Lunacharski; intervenes with Dzerzhinski, head of the Cheka, to save someone from execution at the hands of Bliumkin (the assassin of the German ambassador, Count Mirbach).

The Bolsheviks sign a separate peace with Germany; the Civil War begins; the Red Terror against the bourgeoisie and opponents of the new Soviet regime begins after the assassination of Uritski in Petrograd and an attempt on the life of Lenin.

1919 M. leaves Moscow for Kiev, where he works briefly on a journal with Ehrenburg; meets N.Y.M., but shortly afterwards leaves her (losing contact for a year and a half) to go to the Crimea, now under White occupation; stays briefly with Voloshin in Koktebel; arrested in Feodosia, but soon released.

1920 Leaves Crimea and goes by sea with his brother Alexander to Georgia, then an independent republic under Menshevik control; he and his brother jailed briefly in Batumi under suspicion of being Bolshevik agents; returns to Moscow from Tiflis with Ehrenburg (who is acting as a courier for the Soviet government), and from there to Petrograd – where Blok hears him recite verse at the Poets' club in October; takes up residence in the House of Arts.

1921 Leaves Petrograd at the end of January, distressed at the complete disappearance of the milieu he once knew there; hearing from Ehrenburg's wife that N.Y.M. is still in Kiev, he goes there and brings her to Moscow (March); they then travel together to the Caucasus in a train belonging to a relief organization and settle in Tiflis for six months, getting temporary employment with the embassy of the RSFSR there (by this time Georgia has been taken over by the Bolsheviks and the diplomatic relations with Moscow are only nominal); they leave at the end of the year by boat from Sukhumi on the Black Sea coast.

The Civil War ends, but there is widespread unrest, and several uprisings against the Bolsheviks; after the revolt of the Red sailors at the naval fortress of Kronstadt, near Petrograd (March), Lenin announces the New Economic Policy (NEP), which allows a small measure of private enterprise, including private publishing; in August Blok dies and Gumilev is executed for his alleged part in a conspiracy against the new regime – this casts a shadow on the Acmeists and there is discrimination against them even in the relatively relaxed conditions of NEP.

1922 M. and N.Y.M. arrive back in Moscow at the end of March via Novorossiisk, Rostov-on-Don (where M. publishes his 'Letter on Russian Poetry' in a local magazine), Kharkov, and Kiev; the commandant of the train from Kiev to Moscow refuses them a berth until they can prove they are married, so they get a certificate of marriage from the Register Office in Kiev; they are given a room in Herzen House, the headquarters of the Writers' Union on Tverskoi Boulevard in Moscow; M.'s second volume of verse, *Tristia*, is published in Berlin.

Pasternak publishes *My Sister Life*; Marina Tsvetayeva emigrates to Prague.

1923 M. makes his living by trans-

Mayakovski founds LEF.

lating; *Stone* reissued by the
State Publishing House and
Tristia republished in Moscow
with the new title *Second
Book,* but henceforth M. finds
it difficult to publish original
work in State-controlled Moscow
journals because of an official
instruction ordering the removal
of his name from the list of
people allowed to contribute to
them; in the summer goes to
Gaspra (Crimea) with N.Y.M.
for a two months' holiday and
writes his autobiographical story
The Noise of Time about his
childhood in Petersburg; hearing
of an intrigue against him in the
Writers' Union, sends a cable
from Gaspra giving up their
room, and, on arriving back in
Moscow, they find a private
room on the Yakimanka.

1924 M. and N.Y.M. make several
trips to Leningrad, where he
renews his friendship with
Akhmatova, and N.Y.M. meets
her for the first time; they
spend part of the summer in a
State Publishing House rest
home at Aprelevka, near
Moscow, where M. translates
Barbier; on the promise of
translating and editing work
from the Leningrad branch of
the State Publishing House,
they take an apartment and
move there in the autumn.

Lenin dies (January) – and the
struggle for the succession
begins, with Stalin assuming
complete control by the end of
the decade.

1925 Noise of Time published;
after a crisis in their marriage,
M. and N.Y.M. move to a
boarding-house in Tsarskoye
Selo, where Akhmatova also
stays (the close friendship
between her and N.Y.M. dates
from this time); M. ceases to

Party decree proclaiming a policy,
for the time being, of non-
intervention in the struggle
between various literary groups;
suicide of Yesenin.

write original poetry and only
resumes five years later; N.Y.M.
ill with TB and goes to spend
winter in Yalta (Crimea) while
M. remains behind and translates
in order to support her there.

1926 M. joins N.Y.M. in Yalta
(spring); they return (via Kiev
and Moscow) to Tsarskoye Selo,
where they spend the winter of
1926–7; M. entertains hope that
things may get better.

1927 M. continues to live in
Tsarskoye Selo with N.Y.M.;
writes second autobiographical
story, *The Egyptian Stamp*, in
the winter of 1927–8.

Trotski expelled from the Party.

1928 The high point of M.'s public
career as a writer (thanks largely
to the patronage of Bukharin):
The Egyptian Stamp appears,
along with the first collected
edition of his verse, *Poems*,
incorporating the first two books
(*Stone* and *Tristia*) as well as
new poems written between
1921–5; a volume of his
collected essays *On Poetry* is also
published; several not entirely
unfavourable reviews of his work
are printed in Soviet journals; he
spends the summer in Yalta with
N.Y.M. (he joins her a month
late, having been detained in
Moscow by his attempts to
intercede with Bukharin on
behalf of five old men condemned
to death); but at the end of the
year M. is accused of plagiarizing
a translation and becomes the
object of a virulent press
campaign led by David
Zaslavski.

Stalin defeats the 'right-wing'
opposition led by Bukharin (who
advocates a cautious policy in
agriculture); NEP comes to an
end and the First Five Year
Plan for the rapid industrializa-
tion of the country is launched;
Trotski is sent into exile; a
witch-hunting atmosphere
gradually spreads down to all
branches of Soviet life.

1929 M. defended against the
accusation of plagiarism in an
open letter to *Literary Gazette*

The beginning of the collectivization of agriculture – the peasants
slaughter their livestock, and

signed by a group of prominent Soviet writers (May); in the autumn M. is given a job on the newspaper *Moscow Komsomol* – his only regular employment under the Soviet regime, but he leaves it at the end of February of the following year; at the end of December he begins to write *Fourth Prose* (published only in 1966 in the United States), a pamphlet about the campaign against himself, the death sentence on the five old men saved by Bukharin thanks to his intervention, and the deteriorating atmosphere in Soviet literature ('sold to the pockmarked devil* for three generations ahead') from which he now dissociates himself.

food supplies fall catastrophically; the 'proletarian' writers (RAPP) begin a fierce campaign against the 'Fellow Travellers' and other 'uncommitted' writers.

1930 Again with the help of Bukharin, M. is able to arrange a journey to Armenia for himself and N.Y.M. (May to October); he is impressed by Armenia as an 'outpost of Christendom'; he regains his feeling of inner freedom and begins to write poetry once more.

After a brief retreat, collectivization continues; suicide of Mayakovski.

1931 M. writes 'Wolf' cycle of poems, in which there are presentiments of his coming exile and death.

1932 Three of M.'s poems published in *Literary Gazette* – the last to appear in print in his lifetime.

Collectivization reaches its height; mass deportation of kulaks (five million, according to later estimates); famine in the country's richest agricultural areas; severe rationing of foodstuffs, but privileges introduced for obedient writers and intellectuals (special rations, 'closed' stores, etc.).

Dissolution of RAPP and other

* i.e. Stalin.

literary groups, and the creation of a single Union of Soviet Writers under firm Party control.

1933 M. invited to speak at the beginning of the year at poetry evening in Leningrad – reads recent verse and passages from the description of his journey to Armenia, and answers a *provocateur*'s question about his attitude to other Russian poets of his generation by saying: 'What do you want of me? . . . I am the friend of my friends . . . I am a contemporary of Akhmatova . . .'; his 'Journey to Armenia' is published in the literary monthly *Zvezda* (May), including a final passage with veiled references to Stalin that had been forbidden by the censorship (the editor of *Zvezda* is dismissed as a result); M. spends two months (May–June) with N.Y.M. in Crimea – and is shocked on the way there by the sight of starving refugees from the Ukraine and the Kuban; on returning to Moscow in July they are given an apartment on Furmanov Street by the Union of Writers; M. is denounced in an article in *Pravda* (August) after failure of private attempts to persuade him to disavow 'Journey to Armenia'; in autumn he writes his poem denouncing Stalin as a murderer and 'peasant-slayer' – and reads it to a number of people.

1934 On a visit to Leningrad M. slaps the face of Alexei Tolstoi at a meeting in the Soviet Writers' Publishing House; he immediately returns to Moscow and is arrested a day or two

First Congress of Soviet Writers (August) – addressed by Bukharin on poetry; assassination of Kirov in Leningrad (December) and the beginning of political terror in earnest.

later (May 13th) during the night; interrogated by secret police about poem on Stalin; saved from death by the intervention of Bukharin, and exiled to Cherdyn in the Urals (N.Y.M. is permitted to accompany him); he attempts suicide; on the further intervention of Bukharin, allowed to choose Voronezh as his place of exile.

1935–6 M. lives in Voronezh with N.Y.M. (who is not technically in exile, and is hence allowed to make trips to Moscow); he is given employment at local theatre as 'literary adviser', and writes several scripts for the local radio station (till its closure in autumn, 1936); visited by Akhmatova (who writes a poem, 'Voronezh', about her visit) and other friends; writes 'Voronezh Notebooks', poems full of forebodings about the destruction of the world; attempts to write 'Ode to Stalin' (January, 1937) as a way of saving himself and N.Y.M., but cannot bring himself to do so.

1937 M. returns to Moscow at the end of his three-year term of exile (May); at first allowed to live in the apartment on Furmanov Street (now partly occupied by a police agent masquerading as a writer), but then ordered to live at least 105 kilometres from the city, in accordance with regulations for 'convicted persons', and moves with N.Y.M. to the small town of Savelovo (June); in autumn they move to Kalinin, a little further away, in

Popular Front. Congress of intellectuals in Paris attended by Pasternak, Babel, and Ehrenburg (June 1935); arrest of Nikolai Punin, Akhmatova's third husband, and of her son, Lev Gumilev, in the wave of terror after Kirov's assassination (1935, both released a year or so later); first of Moscow 'show trials' (Zinoviev, Kamenev and others, 1936); death of Maxim Gorki (June 1936); head of secret police, Yagoda, dismissed by Stalin for 'liberalism' and replaced by Yezhov (September 1936); promulgation of the new Stalin Constitution, 'the most democratic in the world'.

Beginning of the Great Terror: millions arrested and deported to concentration camps; unknown numbers executed; second 'show trial' (Piatakov, Radek, and others, January); Red Army leaders arrested and executed (June).

the same northwesterly direction from Moscow; with N.Y.M. he makes frequent trips to Moscow (sometimes staying overnight with friends) in search of work, but without success, and has to beg money from writers in Moscow and Leningrad (where he sees Akhmatova for the last time in the autumn); at the end of the year friends try to arrange for help from the Union of Writers.

1938 M. is received by Fadeyev, the secretary of the Union of Writers, and told there is no work for him, but at the same time he is promised a chance of staying in a rest home maintained by the Literary Fund at Samatikha, near Murom, about two hundred kilometres due east of Moscow (February or March); arrives at Samatikha with N.Y.M. (end of April); arrested there on the night of May 1st and is never seen again. N.Y.M. immediately returns to Moscow, makes a lightning trip to Kalinin to collect a basket with M.'s manuscripts (narrowly escaping arrest by police agents who come with a warrant to pick her up just after she leaves for Moscow again); she then goes to live for the time being in the small town of Strunino, northeast of Moscow, and in the autumn takes a job working night-shifts in the local textile factory, leaving her free to go into Moscow by day to line up at the jails to hand in food parcels and beg — in vain — for information as to M.'s whereabouts; leaves Strunino towards the end of the year, after

The Great Purge continues. The third 'show trial', at which Bukharin, accused of having plotted against Lenin's life in 1918, is sentenced to death, together with fifteen others (March); the terror begins to abate at the end of the year with the sudden removal of Yezhov and his replacement by Beria (December).

the 'personnel department' in the factory begins to show an interest in her; goes back to Moscow.

1939 N.Y.M. hears that at a Central Committee meeting the treatment of M. has been mentioned as an example of Yezhov's 'excesses' – from this she concludes that M. must be dead (January, or end of December 1938); this is confirmed a little later by the return of one of her food parcels with a note on it saying 'addressee dead'; she goes to stay for two weeks with Galina von Meck in Maly Yaroslavets, southwest of Moscow; after being allowed to live briefly in her Moscow apartment again, she is summoned to the NKVD (secret police) section of the local militia station and told she must leave the city; in the spring she returns to Kalinin, the last place in which she and M. had lived together; she obtains work, at first in a small cooperative and later as a teacher in a local school; remains here for two years, till the German invasion.

Mass arrests come to an end; many 'investigations' are dropped and some people released; a number of NKVD interrogators are arrested and at least one is executed; the blame for the 'excesses' of the previous two years is put on Trotskiists and other 'traitors', but there is no disavowal of the terror as such or official rehabilitation of the victims; at the Eighteenth Party Congress (March), Stalin says the purge has been accompanied by 'grave mistakes'; Ribbentrop and Molotov sign the pact between the Soviet Union and Germany (August); the Soviet Union and Germany invade and partition Poland, and England declares war on Germany (September); Marina Tsvetayeva returns from Paris to Moscow; Isaac Babel is arrested (May).

1940 M.'s brother, Alexander, is given a certificate by the Moscow Register Office, in which the date of M.'s death is stated to be December 27, 1938.

The pact with Germany is followed by a slight relaxation in the Soviet Union; Akhmatova is allowed to join the Union of Writers, and to publish original verse again for the first time since 1925 (but her poem *To the Londoners*, about the German threat to England, is of course not published – nor is *Requiem*, begun in 1935, after the arrest of Punin and Gumilev and completed in March 1940).

1941 N.Y.M. leaves Kalinin with her mother as the Germans approach.

Germany invades the Soviet Union (June); Moscow threatened (October); Marina Tsvetayeva

commits suicide (August);
Akhmatova is evacuated by air
from Leningrad to Tashkent in
Uzbekistan, Central Asia
(October).

1942 N.Y.M. and her mother
gradually make their way to
Central Asia via the sea of Aral,
eventually reaching Dzhambul
in Kazakhstan (here, for the
first time, she chances to meet
a man who was in the camp
where M. died); learning of
their presence in Dzhambul,
N.Y.M.'s brother arranges for
them to move to Tashkent,
and Akhmatova obtains permission for them to reside there.

1943–6 N.Y.M. lives in Tashkent,
sharing a *balakhana* (Uzbek-
style house) for part of the
time with Akhmatova, and
teaches English at the University of Central Asia; in 1944
she is visited by a former
journalist, Kazarnovski, who
was in the camp where M.
died and gives her an account
of his end; she leaves Tashkent
in 1946 and spends a week with
Akhmatova in Leningrad, just
before the Zhdanov Decree.

Battle of Stalingrad (February
1943); Akhmatova returns to
Leningrad via Moscow (May–
June 1944); victory over Germany (May 1945); Party Decree
and 'Zhdanov Report'
denouncing Akhmatova,
Zoshchenko, and others
(August 1946).

1946–53 N.Y.M. lives in Ulianovsk,
Lenin's birthplace, on the
Volga (from at least 1948, and
perhaps earlier); teaches in the
local Teachers' Training College.

Mounting post-war terror stifles all
cultural and intellectual life in
the country; mass arrests and
constant widespread purges in
almost all branches of life (e.g.
the Lysenko affair, 1948; the
campaign against 'homeless
cosmopolitans,' 1949) culminating in the so-called 'Doctors'
Plot', in which the Kremlin
doctors, mostly Jews, are
accused of poisoning Soviet
leaders at the behest of international Zionism and the CIA

(December 1952); Akhmatova's son arrested once more (1949) – as a result she is forced to publish verse in praise of Stalin (1950); Stalin dies in March 1953.

1953-5 N.Y.M. comes to Moscow immediately after Stalin's death, having been purged from the Ulianovsk Teachers' Training College just before; in the summer she is appointed by the Ministry of Education to a similar post in Chita, a city in Eastern Siberia not far from the Chinese frontier; she stays here till 1955 when, on a visit to Moscow, she is persuaded by Akhmatova to visit Surkov, Fadeyev's successor as secretary of the Union of Writers, in the hope of getting employment and a room in the capital.

End of the Stalinist terror; Jewish doctors released (April 1953); Beria removed and executed (June 1953), together with other high secret-police officials, during the course of a struggle for power in which the relatively 'liberal' Khrushchev is eventually victorious; Ehrenburg's novel *The Thaw* appears (March 1954) in the magazine *Znamia*, which the following month publishes ten poems by Pasternak with a note saying they are part of a novel, *Dr Zhivago*, to be completed that summer (but it is never published in the Soviet Union).

1956 N.Y.M. received a number of times by Surkov; she negotiates for a room in Moscow and the possibility of translation work, at first receiving considerable encouragement; Surkov arranges for her to receive a widow's pension and, since she is now out of work again, gets her a new teaching post, this time in Cheboksary, about 480 miles east of Moscow; there is talk about an edition of M.'s work in the prestigious Poet's Library series, and a committee on his literary remains is set up; N.Y.M. is informed by the Public Prosecutor that M. has been posthumously cleared of the charges brought against him in 1938, but a further application that he be cleared

The high point of post-Stalin liberalization comes with Khrushchev's 'secret speech' on Stalin at the Twentieth Party Congress (February); prisoners released en masse from the concentration camps (including Lev Gumilev, Akhmatova's son); many executed or disgraced intellectuals 'rehabilitated' (formally cleared of the false charges brought against them under Stalin) and, in some cases, committees are set up for the publication or re-publication of their work; Fadeyev commits suicide (May); Pasternak submits *Dr Zhivago* to the literary journal *Novy Mir*, simultaneously sending a copy to the Italian publisher Feltrinelli (January or February), but by the late summer pressure of the charges brought against him in 1934 is turned down after the Hungarian uprising; by the end of year N.Y.M.'s relations with Surkov have soured and all her hopes fade.

1957–64 N.Y.M.'s movements in these years are not entirely clear: in the late fifties or early sixties she apparently leaves Cheboksary (where she was reluctant to go) and obtains a post at a Teachers' Training College nearer to Moscow, in the ancient city of Pskov, about 430 miles north-west of the capital and within easy reach of Leningrad; she remains here till 1964, and during this period frequently visits friends in Moscow, Leningrad, and other places; her negotiations with Surkov for a room in Moscow finally break down in 1959 and she is refused a permit to reside in the capital. In 1961 she publishes two short stories under a pseudonym in the miscellany *Pages from Tarusa* (see Vigdorova, Appendix A); in the summer of 1964 through the efforts of her friend Frida Vigdorova, she is at last granted permission to reside in Moscow and, at the same time, thanks to a loan from Konstantin Simonov, is able to buy an apartment in a cooperative housing project in Cheriomushki, the new southwest suburb of Moscow; the literary monthly *Moskva* publishes nine of M.'s poems in August 1964, but there is no sign of the promised collected edition in the

is being put on him by Surkov to forbid its publication abroad; the Polish and Hungarian uprisings (October–November) cause panic in Soviet ruling circles, the 'conservatives' stage a comeback, and for the next two years 'liberalization' is effectively halted.

After two years of 'freeze' (1957–9) in the wake of Hungary, Khrushchev permits a new trend to 'liberalism' in his address to the Third Congress of Soviet Writers (May 1959) – this despite the furore over the publication of *Dr Zhivago* abroad and the award to Pasternak of the Nobel Prize (which he is forced to renounce) in October 1958; Pasternak dies in 1960; the renewed movement towards greater latitude in cultural matters reaches its climax with the publication of Solzhenitsyn's *One Day in the Life of Ivan Denisovich* in November 1962, and survives Khrushchev's outburst of anger at a Moscow art exhibition in December 1962; Khrushchev falls from power in October 1964 and is succeeded by Kosygin and Brezhnev.

Poet's Library; the first full collection of his work, in two volumes, appears in the United States in 1964 (expanded edition, in three volumes, 1965–71).

1965–70 N.Y.M. lives in Moscow and writes her memoirs; M.'s 'Conversation About Dante' is published in Moscow in 1967; the first book of N.Y.M.'s memoirs (*Hope Against Hope*) circulates in *samizdat* and is published abroad in Russian and foreign languages (1970); the second book (*Hope Abandoned*) is completed in 1970 and published in Russian in Paris (1972). The long-promised Poet's Library edition of M.'s work is at last announced for publication in Moscow 'in the second quarter of 1973'.

Cultural policy hardens; Siniavski and Daniel are tried and given long prison sentences for publishing works abroad under pen names (February 1966); Solzhenitsyn is unable to publish his two long novels *Cancer Ward* and *First Circle*, which then come out abroad (1968); from the second half of the sixties, tighter censorship controls are offset by the rapid growth of *samizdat* (circulation of unpublished work in typescript); Akhmatova dies in March 1966; Ehrenburg dies in 1967 and his funeral is attended by N.Y.M.

Appendixes

A. *Notes on Persons Mentioned in the Text*

Adalis (Efron), Adelina Yefimovna (1900–1969): Poetess and translator.

Admoni, Vladimir Grigorievich (1909–   ): Eminent linguist and literary scholar; professor of Leningrad University. He testified in defence of *Brodski* (q.v.) at the latter's trial.

Agranov, Yakov Savlovich (? –1939): Cheka investigator in the Kronstadt mutiny, the Tagantsev conspiracy (in which Gumilev perished), the Tambov uprising, the Kirov assassination, etc. Creator and chief of Litkontrol, a GPU department for the surveillance of writers. As deputy head of the NKVD under Yagoda and Yezhov, he was active in the preparation of the Moscow show trials of 1937–8. He was arrested and shot in 1939.

Akhmanova, Olga Sergeyevna: Linguist and lexicographer; professor of English language at Moscow University.

Akhmatova (Gorenko), Anna Andreyevna (1889–1966): Major Russian poet. Born in Odessa, she lived most of her life in St Petersburg (Leningrad). Her verse was first published in 1911 and won immediate acclaim. Together with Nikolai Gumilev (whom she married in 1910), she became a leading figure in the Acmeist movement, with which Mandelstam was also associated. Her marriage to Gumilev ended in divorce, as did her second marriage, to V. K. Shileiko, an Assyriologist. Her third husband, N. N. Punin, and her son, Lev Gumilev, were both arrested during the 1930s. She herself was never arrested, but for many years (1926–40) she published scarcely anything and, like Mandelstam, was virtually proscribed. In 1946 she was scurrilously attacked (as a 'half-nun, half-whore') by Stalin's chief lieutenant in cultural affairs, Andrei Zhdanov, and expelled from the Union of Soviet Writers. Subjected to intolerable pressures and threats of reprisals against her son, she wrote several poems in praise of Stalin in 1950. After the partial exposure of Stalin's crimes by Khrushchev in 1956 (when her son, like millions of others, was released from a forced-labour camp) she began to publish again, and swiftly won recognition from the younger generation. But her long poem *Requiem*, a dirge for her husband and son and all of Stalin's victims, has still not been published in the Soviet Union. Her *Poem Without a Hero*, a remarkable attempt to illuminate Russia's destiny in the last half century, was published with some cuts in the Soviet collection of her poetry, *Beg Vremeni* (*The Flight of Time*, Moscow, 1965). The most complete collection of her work has appeared only abroad in the two-volume edition edited by Gleb Struve and Boris Filippov (Washington, DC, 1968). In the last years of her life Akhmatova was allowed to travel abroad for the first time since the Revolution. In 1964, at the age of seventy-five, she went to Sicily, where she received the Taormina literary prize. In 1965 she was awarded an honorary doctorate by the University of Oxford. On her way home she visited France and Italy. As she makes clear in her short memoir on Mandelstam (*Pages from a Diary*, published in New York in 1965 in the literary almanac *Vozdushnye Puti* [*Aerial Ways*]), her close friendship with him was based on the natural affinity of two great poets.

Akopyan, Akop (1866–1937): Armenian 'proletarian' poet.

Aksionov, Ivan Alexandrovich (1884–1935): Poet, playwright, and critic, best known for his translations of the Elizabethans (Ben Jonson and others). Author of a book on Picasso. Husband of Susanna *Mar* (q.v.).

Alexandrov, Georgi Alexandrovich (1908–1961): Party philosopher criticized by *Zhdanov* (q.v.) for his *History of Western Philosophy* (1945); he was Minister of Culture (1954–5), but was dismissed from this post because of his involvement in a scandal concerning secret houses of ill fame for high Soviet functionaries.

Amusin, Joseph Davidovich: Biblical and Hebrew scholar. He has published articles in Soviet scholarly journals and a book on the Dead Sea Scrolls (Moscow, 1960).

Andronikova (Halpern), Princess Salomeya Nikolayevna (Salomé): Friend of Akhmatova and described by her in a poem as 'the beauty of the year '13'. Mandelstam addressed a poem to her ('Solominka', 1916). She now resides in London.

Annenski, Innokenti Fedorovich (1856–1909): Classical scholar and lyric poet.

Arbenina, Olga Nikolayevna (1900–   ): Actress of the Alexandrinski Theatre in St Petersburg, a well-known beauty and friend of Gumilev's second wife (Engelhardt). At one time she was reputedly married to Yuri *Yurkun* (q.v.).

Ardov, Victor Yefimovich (1900–   ): Writer of humorous stories, film scenarios, and satirical sketches for the variety stage.

Arens, Anna Yevgenievna: First wife of *Punin* (q.v.).

Aseyev, Nikolai Nikolayevich (1889–1963): Futurist poet influenced by

Khlebnikov and Mayakovski; a member of LEF. After Stalin's death, he helped some of the younger poets, but was very conformist in his public utterances.

Averbakh, Leopold Leopoldovich (1903– ?): Literary critic, militant proponent of the concept of 'proletarian' literature, and one of the leaders of RAPP. As such, he was virtually dictator of Soviet literary affairs from about 1927 until his downfall in 1932, when Stalin abruptly changed the policy in literature to one of support for all writers, whatever their background, who were willing to accept the Party line without question. Averbakh disappeared during the purges.

Avvakum, the Archpriest (c. 1620–81): Leader of the 'Old Believers' – schismatics who refused to accept the changes in Russian Orthodox ritual introduced by the Patriarch Nikon. Avvakum's *Life* (1672–3) is a remarkable account of his exile to Siberia with his wife.

Babel, Isaac Emmanuilovich (1894–1941?): Outstanding short-story writer, noted for his *Red Cavalry* (1923), and a series of *Odessan Tales*, in which one of the heroes is the Jewish gangster Benia Krik. Babel disappeared after his arrest in 1939 and the date of his death is uncertain.

Bagritski (*Dziubin*), *Eduard Georgievich* (1895–1934): Epic and lyric poet, translator of Burns, Rimbaud, and others. After serving in the Red Army, he organized the first 'proletarian' literary circle in Odessa, but moved to Moscow in 1925. He was a member of RAPP.

Balmont, Konstantin Dmitrievich (1867–1942): Poet who enjoyed a considerable vogue at the turn of the century. He emigrated after the Revolution and died in Paris.

Baratynski, Yevgeni Abramovich (1800–1844): Major poet, contemporary of Pushkin.

Barto, Agnia Lvovna (1906–   ): Poetess who writes edifying verse for children.

Batalov, Alexei Nikolayevich (1929–   ): Film actor.

Batiushkov, Konstantin Nikolayevich (1787–1855): Poet; served in Italy as a diplomat. Translated Tasso and wrote an elegy about him.

Bedny, Demian (*Yefin A. Pridvorov*) (1883–1945): a somewhat crude versifier of great vigour who enjoyed a vogue in the 1920s and was noted particularly for his anti-religious satires. In 1936 he incurred Stalin's displeasure by writing an opera libretto which made fun of Russia's past.

Belinski, Vissarion Grigorievich (1811–48): Radical publicist and literary critic.

Bely, Andrei (*Boris Nikolayevich Bugayev*) (1880–1934): Major Symbolist poet, novelist, and critic. Like other Symbolists, he was at first inclined to see the October Revolution as an event of mystical significance – indeed, as the second coming of Christ. He was the leading Russian disciple of Rudolf Steiner.

Benediktov, Vladimir Grigorievich (1807–73): Poet now little read because of his ornate and stilted manner.

Berberova, Nina Nikolayevna (1901–   ): Second wife of *Khodasevich* (q.v.); now resident in the United States. Author of memoirs.

Berdiayev, Nikolai Alexandrovich (1874–1948): Famous Russian philosopher and religious thinker. Berdiayev was a leading figure in the movement to revive philosophical and lay theological thinking in Russia (e.g. in the Free Philosophical Society). In 1922 he was expelled from Russian with other anti-Bolshevik intellectuals and settled in Paris.

Beria, Lavrenti Pavlovich (1899–1953): Head of Soviet secret police from 1938, in succession to *Yezhov* (q.v.). Executed after Stalin's death.

Bezymenski, Alexander Ilyich (1898–   ): Soviet poet noted for his political conformism. He was a leading member of RAPP.

Biron, Ernst Johann (1690–1772): Favourite and effective ruler of Russia under Empress Anna Ivanovna. Duke of Kurland.

Blagoi, Dmitri Dmitrievich (1893–   ): Soviet literary historian.

Blok, Alexander Alexandrovich (1880–1921): Leading Symbolist poet. His first volume of verse (1904) celebrated the semi-mystical 'Beautiful Lady', partly inspired by Vladimir Soloviev's vision of Holy Sophia. In later verse Blok bitterly mocked his own romantic delusions, but in his great poem about the Revolution, *The Twelve* (1918), he reverted to his visionary manner. He died broken and disillusioned.

Blok, Georgi Petrovich (1888–1962): Cousin of Alexander Blok. Editor and publisher.

Blok, Liubov Dmitrievna (1881–1939): Actress; daughter of the famous chemist Mendeleyev; wife of Alexander Blok.

Bobrov, Sergei Pavlovich (1889–   ): Mathematician, poet, novelist, and translator (of Voltaire, Stendhal, Hugo, G. B. Shaw, and others).

Borisov, Leonid Ilyich (1897–   ): Prose writer.

Bosio, Angelina (1824–1859): Italian singer who died in Russia (mentioned in Mandelstam's *Egyptian Stamp*).

Brik, Osip Maximovich (1888–1945): Friend and associate of Mayakovski. Originally associated with the Formalists, he later helped to create LEF. His wife, Lili (Lilia Yurievna), was the inspiration for many of Mayakovski's love poems. She is the sister of Elsa Triolet (died 1970), the wife of the French Communist poet Louis Aragon.

Briullov, Karl Pavlovich (1799–1852): Russian Romantic painter.

Briusov, Valeri Yakovlevich (1873–1924): Major poet, editor, and theoretician of the Symbolist movement. He joined the Communist Party in 1919.

Brodski, Joseph Alexandrovich (1940–   ): One of the finest poets of the young generation in Russia. A protégé of Akhmatova, he was exiled to the Archangel region in 1964 as 'a parasite', but was allowed to return to Leningrad the following year, after a world-wide outcry. Scarcely any of his work has yet been published in the Soviet Union, but much of it has appeared abroad in Russian and other languages. (In 1972 Brodski was allowed to emigrate from the Soviet Union and is now resident in the United States.)

Buchma, Amvrosi Maximilianovich (1891–1957): Leading Ukrainian actor.

Bukharin, Nikolai Ivanovich (1888–1938): Member of the Bolshevik Party from 1907, of the Central Committee from 1917 to 1934, and of the Politburo from 1919 to 1929. Editor of *Izvestia*, 1934–7. Expelled from the Party and arrested in 1937, he was the principal figure in the last great Moscow show trial in 1938, at which he was sentenced to be shot.

Bulgakov, Mikhail Afanasievich (1891–1940): Outstanding novelist, author of *The Master and Margarita*, which was not published till 1967, twenty-seven years after his death.

Bulgakov, Sergei Nikolayevich (1871–1944): Eminent thinker and theologian. Died in Paris.

Bulgarin, Faddei (1789–1859): Writer best remembered as a police informer during the reign of Nicholas I.

Burliuk, David Davidovich (1882–1967): Poet and artist; one of the founders of the Futurist movement and early associate of Mayakovski. Emigrated to the United States in 1922. (His brother Nikolai was also a poet and artist.)

Chaadayev, Piotr Yakovlevich (1794–1856): Author of *Philosophical Letters*, which condemned Russia's cultural backwardness and called for her integration into the European tradition. The publication of the first 'Letter' in 1836 led Nicholas I to declare him insane and to have him placed under house arrest for eighteen months. Mandelstam's essay on him appeared in the journal *Apollon* in 1915.

Chaplygin, Sergei Alexeyevich (1869–1942): Academician, leading authority on aerodynamics.

Charents (Sogononian), Egishe (1897–1937): Armenian poet who translated Pushkin, Mayakovski, and Gorki into Armenian.

Chechanovski, Mark Osipovich: Editor and translator.

Chekhov, Mikhail Alexandrovich (1891–1955): Nephew of Anton Chekhov, and outstanding actor associated with the Moscow Art

Theatre. In 1928 he emigrated and eventually settled in the United States where he started his own theatre and the 'Actors' Laboratory Group' in Hollywood.

Chernyshevski, Nikolai Gavrilovich (1828–89): Leading radical publicist.

Chudovski, Valeryan Adolfovich: Symbolist critic.

Chukovski, Kornei Ivanovich (1882–1969): Eminent Russian man of letters. His son, Nikolai ('Kolia') Korneyevich (1905–65), was a novelist.

Chulkov, Georgi Ivanovich (1879–1939): Poet and critic, associated with the journal *Apollon* (leading Symbolist, and later Acmeist, journal in St Petersburg, 1909–17). He and his wife kept a noted salon for writers and artists.

Dahl, Vladimir Ivanovich (1801–72): Ethnographer, story writer, and author of a great *Dictionary of the Russian Language* (1863–6), distinguished for its wealth of popular words and idioms.

Daniel, Yuli Markovich (1925–   ): Short-story writer who published abroad under the pseudonym 'Arzhak' and was tried together with *Siniavski* (q.v.) in 1966.

Danilevski, Nikolai Yakovlevich (1822–85): Exponent of Pan-Slavism and 'biological nationalism' in his influential book *Russia and Europe* (1869).

Derzhavin, Gavriil Romanovich (1743–1816): Poet, precursor of Pushkin.

Dobroliubov, Alexander Mikhailovich (1876–1944?): Early Symbolist poet and mystical anarchist. After publishing his first verse he disappeared and went to live among Russian sectarians. He apparently survived into the forties, living as a simple worker.

Dubrovin, Alexander Ivanovich (1855–1918): Notorious leader of an anti-Semitic organization before the Revolution. He was shot for 'anti-Soviet activity' in autumn 1918, which would seem to preclude his being the person mentioned on page 155.

Duvakin, V.: Literary scholar (specializing in Mayakovski) and colleague of *Siniavski* (q.v.) at the Gorki Literary Institute in Moscow. In 1966 he was subjected to reprisals for testifying in favour of Siniavski.

Efros, Abram Markovich (1888–1954): Noted art historian and translator.

Ehrenburg, Ilia Grigorievich (1891–1967): Famous Soviet novelist and journalist. After a youthful involvement with Bolshevik activities in 1906, he was imprisoned briefly. In 1908 he went abroad, and lived in Paris from 1909 to 1917. He returned to Russia as an anti-Bolshevik in 1917, went back to Paris in 1921, and after some wavering became increasingly pro-Soviet. In 1922 he was associated with a journal called *Veshch* (*The Thing*) that advocated a kind of Marxist utilitarianism in art. Until 1941, however, he managed to live mainly abroad (as European correspondent of *Izvestia*), making only brief visits to the Soviet Union. Notable among his vast output of novels, stories, essays, etc., are *The Extraordinary Adventures of Julio Jurenito* (1921), *The Fall of Paris* (1942), and *The Thaw* (1954). His memoirs were published in the mid-1960s and, despite the inevitable reticences, they give a fascinating picture of the fate of the Russian intelligentsia in Soviet times. His account of Mandelstam contains some inaccuracies (including the story, described as a legend by Mrs Mandelstam, that he read Petrarch by a campfire in the days before his death in Siberia). A sardonic, gifted, and basically ambivalent figure, Ehrenburg did much after Stalin's death to promote the cultural values all but destroyed by the regime to which he had long paid lip service as a novelist, journalist, and public figure. His novel *The Thaw* was of great importance as the first breach to be made in Stalinist mythology, and in his memoirs and essays after Stalin's death (such as those on Chekhov and Stendhal) he championed freedom of expression in literature and art.

Eikhenbaum, Boris Mikhailovich (1886–1959): Scholar and literary critic, once a leading member of the Formalist school. He was associated with LEF.

Eisenstein, Sergei Mikhailovich (1898–1948): Film producer best known for *The Battleship Potemkin* (1925) and *Alexander Nevski* (1938). The second half of his historical epic *Ivan the Terrible* was condemned by Party decree in 1946 for having represented Ivan's *oprichniki* (special troops) as a 'band of degenerates resembling the American Ku Klux Klan'.

Ekster (Grigorovich), Alexandra Alexandrovna (1884–1949): Artist and set designer. A pupil of Léger, she was active in Russian avant-garde circles, painting in a Cubist style, and illustrated books by the Futurists. After the Revolution she worked for the Kamerny Theatre in Moscow, but emigrated from Russia sometime in the 1920's.

Elsberg, Yakov Yefimovich (1901–   ): Soviet literary scholar, once secretary to Lev Kamenev, the Old Bolshevik purged by Stalin. In 1962 there was an attempt to have Elsberg expelled from the Union of Soviet Writers for his complicity as a secret police agent in the arrest and exile of fellow writers under Stalin, but apparently nothing came of this move (or he was speedily reinstated).

Engelhardt, B. M.: Literary scholar, author of an important article on Dostoyevski ('Dostoyevski's Ideological Novel', in a collection of essays edited by A. S. Dolinin, 1925).

Fadeyev (Bulyga), Alexander Alexandrovich (1901–56): Soviet novelist. Author of *The Rout* (1927) and *The Young Guard* (1945), both held up in the Stalin years as models of 'socialist realism' – though Stalin made him revise *The Young Guard* (revised version: 1951). From 1946 to 1953 he was secretary general of the Union of Soviet Writers. He committed suicide in 1956.

Fedin, Konstantin Alexandrovich (1892–): Leading Fellow Traveller novelist. Fedin has been secretary to the Union of Soviet Writers (in succession to Surkov) since 1959.

Fedorchenko, Sofia Zakharovna (1880–1959): Writer, best known for her children's stories.

Florenski, Father Pavel Alexandrovich (1882–1952): Originally a mathematician, appointed as a lecturer in philosophy at the Moscow Theological Academy in 1908, and ordained a priest in 1911. The publication in 1914 of *The Pillar and Foundation of Truth* was a landmark in the renaissance of Russian religious thinking. He was deported to Siberia after the Revolution.

Frank, Semion Ludvigovich (1877–1950): Russian religious thinker.

Fritsche, Vladimir Maximovich (1870–1929): Orthodox Marxist critic of the old school.

Gabrichevski, Alexander Georgievich (1891–1968): Art historian, specializing in Italian Renaissance architecture. Professor at Moscow University and corresponding member of the Academy of Sciences.

Garshin, Vladimir Georgievich: A Leningrad pathologist and nephew of Vsevolod *Garshin* (1855–88), a writer of short stories that had a great vogue in the 1880s. Apart from his harrowing descriptions of war, he is best known for *The Red Flower* (1883), a study in madness.

Gerstein, Emma: Literary scholar, acquaintance of the Mandelstams and Anna Akhmatova; author of *Sudba Lermontova* (*Lermontov's Fate*, Moscow, 1964).

Gertsyk, Adelaida: Sister of Viacheslav *Ivanov* (q.v.) and author of memoirs.

Ginzburg, Lidia Yakovlevna (1902–): Literary historian who has written on Pushkin, Lermontov, and others.

Ginzburg, Yevgenia Semionovna: The wife of a high Party official who was arrested in the purges in 1937. She has described her own prison and camp experiences in a book published only abroad (*Into the Whirlwind*, London, 1967).

Gippius, Vladimir Vasilievich (1876–1941): Poet and literary historian;

director of the Tenishev school, which Mandelstam attended before the Revolution.

Gippius, Zinaida Nikolayevna (1869–1945): Symbolist poetess, wife of *Merezhkovski* (q.v.), with whom she emigrated to Paris after the Revolution.

Gladkov, Alexander Konstantinovich (1912–   ): Playwright and author of memoirs on Meyerhold.

Glebova-Sudeikina, Olga Afanasievna (1885–1945): Actress, friend of Akhmatova and habituée of 'The Stray Dog' (which her husband, S. Sudeikin, had decorated). She figures in Akhmatova's *Poem Without a Hero* as the direct cause of the suicide of *Kniazev* (q.v.). In 1912 she danced in a ballet called *The Fauns* and a contemporary photograph shows her in the costume of a faun, with goat's horns.

Glinka, Mikhail Ivanovich (1804–57): His opera *A Life for the Tsar* was renamed *Ivan Susanin* after the Revolution, and the libretto was rewritten by *Gorodetski* (q.v.).

Gogol, Nikolai Vasilievich (1808–52): Before writing his great prose works, he tried his hand at poetry (*Hans Kuchelgarten*, 1827), but it was so badly received that he bought up all the copies himself and burned them.

Goldenweiser, Alexander Borisovich (1875–1961): Well-known pianist.

Gorki, Maxim (*Alexei Maximovich Peshkov*) (1868–1936): Major Russian writer, friend of Lenin (and, later, Stalin); author of the novel *Mother* (1906), which is regarded as a pioneering work of socialist realism. Gorki did much to help and give material aid to intellectuals during the Civil War. He emigrated in 1921, but returned in 1929 to become the chief exponent of 'socialist realism'. After his death in 1936, Yagoda and Professor D. Pletnev were charged by Stalin with his 'medical murder'.

Gorodetski, Sergei Mitrofanovich (1884–   ): Acmeist poet whose first volume of verse, *Yar* (1907), was notable for its use of pagan motifs from ancient Slav mythology. After the Revolution he successfully adapted to the new political requirements. In 1937 he began work on a new libretto for Glinka's *A Life for the Tsar* so that it could again be introduced into the Soviet opera repertoire – it was performed in the post-war years at the Bolshoi Theatre under the title *Ivan Susanin* (from the name of a Russian hero during the Polish invasion at the beginning of the 17th century).

Grech, Nikolai Ivanovich (1787–1867): Publicist and novelist hated by the liberals for his reactionary views and connections with the tsarist secret police. His name is generally linked with that of *Bulgarin* (q.v.).

Griboyedov, Alexander Sergeyevich (1795–1829): Playwright famous for his *Woe from Wit* (written in 1822–4), which contains elements of a liberal critique of contemporary society. Because of his association with the Decembrists, he was briefly arrested in 1826 and then cleared. In 1828 he was sent as Russian minister to Teheran, where he was killed by a Persian mob in the following year.

Grzhebin, Zinovi Isayevich (1869–1929): Publisher of a number of major Russian writers (Bely, Tsvetayeva, Gumilev, Zamiatin, etc.) in Berlin after the Revolution.

Gukovski, Grigori Alexandrovich (1902–50): Eminent literary scholar.

Gumilev, Lev Nikolayevich (1911–   ): Son of Nikolai Gumilev and Akhmatova; historian and Orientalist. He was arrested first in 1935 after the assassination of Kirov, and again in 1937. During the war he was released, and served at the front. In 1949 he was arrested again, and was released in 1956.

Gumilev, Nikolai ('*Kolia*') *Stepanovich* (1886–1921): Acmeist poet and co-founder of the Poets' Guild. Before the First World War he travelled to Abyssinia. His narrative and lyric poetry was influenced by his travels, his distinguished military service in the war, and his monarchist beliefs. After the Revolution he did translations for Gorki's World Literature Publishing House and taught poetry in the House of Arts. He was shot in August 1921, after he proudly confessed his involvement in the Tagantsev affair, a rather confused anti-Bolshevik conspiracy. His poetry is popular with Soviet youth, though he still has not been rehabilitated. He was the first husband of Akhmatova.

Gusev (*Drabkin*), *Sergei Ivanovich* (1874–1933): Prominent Party official. He was head of the Press Department of the Central Committee, 1925–33. (This appears to be the Gusev mentioned on page 473, but since he died in June 1933, M. cannot have met him in August of that year.)

Herzen, Alexander Ivanovich (1812–70): Famous Russian publicist and editor of *Kolokol* (the *Bell*), which he brought out in London after his emigration in 1847.

Ilf (*Fainzilberg*), *Ilia Arnoldovich* (1897–1937): Satirist and collaborator of *Petrov* (q.v.).

Ionov, Ilia Ionovich (1887–1942): 'Proletarian' poet. Head of the ZIF publishing house in succession to *Narbut* (q.v.).

Ivanov, Georgi Vladimirovich (1894–1958): Acmeist poet who emigrated to Paris after the Revolution. His book of memoirs, *Petersburg Winters*, was first published in Paris in 1928.

Ivanov, Viacheslav Ivanovich (1866–1949): Poet and leading figure in the Symbolist movement. His fifth-floor apartment in Petersburg, 'The Tower', was, until he moved to Moscow in 1913, the main gathering place for the Symbolists and the most renowned literary salon in the capital. It was Ivanov's cold reception of a poem by Gumilev on one of his 'Wednesdays' that led to the beginning of Acmeism as a dissident movement against the Symbolists. He was much influenced by Vladimir Soloviev and Nietzsche. He believed that a combination of Christianity and the cult of Dionysius could be fertile in new myths, which would be created by the whole of mankind. The language of his poetry was as eclectic as his philosophy, combining archaic Russian elements with Hellenisms and modern idiom. The result is rather cold and intellectual. His most famous collection of verse was *Cor Ardens* (1911). In 1921 he became professor of Greek in Baku (where the Mandelstams met him) and Deputy People's Commissar for Education (Narkompros) of the new Soviet republic of Azerbaidzhan. In 1924 he emigrated to Italy, where he became a Catholic.

Ivanov-Razumnik (*Ivanov, Razumnik Vasilievich*) (1878–1946): Influential thinker and historian of literature. He was much influenced by the Russian populist tradition (hence his ready acceptance of terror as a means of political struggle) and during the Revolution was associated with the Left Social Revolutionaries. In the thirties he was imprisoned, and left the Soviet Union for Germany during the war. He died in Munich. His memoirs have been published in the West.

Ivask, Yuri Pavlovich (1896–   ): Émigré critic and literary scholar now resident in the United States. He has written extensively on Mandelstam.

Jakobson, Roman Osipovich (1894–   ): Linguist and leading member of the Formalist school. Emigrated to Prague in the twenties and now resident in the United States.

Kablukov, Ivan Alexeyevich (1857–1942): Eminent physical chemist and academician.

Kablukov, Sergei Platonovich: Secretary of the Religious-Philosophical Society in St Petersburg.

Kachalov (*Shverubovich*), *Vasili Ivanovich* (1875–1948): Famous actor of the Moscow Art Theatre. Among his many notable roles was Hamlet.

Kalinin, Mikhail Ivanovich (1875–1946): Member of the Politburo from 1925; Chairman of the Presidium of the Supreme Soviet, 1922–46, and hence titular head of state.

Kamenev (*Rosenfeld*), *Lev Borisovich* (1883–1936): Old Bolshevik, member of the Central Committee from 1917, and one of the ruling Party triumvirate (with Stalin and Zinoviev) after Lenin's death. Arrested in 1934, he was executed after his confession at a show trial in 1936.

Kameneva, Olga Davyidovna: Wife of the above, and Trotski's sister. As head of the theatre section of Lunacharski's People's Commissariat of Education (Narkompros), an active figure in Soviet cultural life in the twenties.

Kandelaki: People's Commissar of Education in Soviet Georgia – probably *David V. Kandelaki*, sent by Stalin as commercial representative to Berlin in 1933. In 1936–7 he was asked by Stalin to put out feelers for an agreement with Hitler, but was rebuffed. (See Leonard Schapiro, *The Communist Party of the Soviet Union*, London, 1960, page 485). He was presumably liquidated during the purges, or later.

Kanegiesser, Leonid Ioakimovich (or *Akimovich*): Poet, executed in 1919 for the assassination of *Uritski* (q.v.). Some of his verse was published posthumously in Paris in 1928.

Karamzin, Nikolai Mikhailovich (1766–1826): Historian and prose writer who played an important part in creating the modern Russian literary language.

Kartashev, Anton Vladimirovich (1875–1960): President of the Religious-Philosophical Society; prime mover in the calling of the Church Council that, in November 1917, restored the Patriarchate (abolished by Peter the Great and replaced by the so-called Holy Synod).

Katayev, Valentin Petrovich (1897–   ): Prominent Soviet novelist. One of the leading 'Fellow Travellers' in the 1920s. His play *The Squaring of the Circle* was often produced in the West in the 1930s. After Stalin's death, as editor of the literary monthly *Yunost* (*Youth*), he encouraged new talent. His autobiographical story *Holy Well* and his memoir, *Grass of Oblivion* (both translated into English, 1967 and 1969), contain references to Mandelstam.

Katenin, Pavel Alexandrovich (1792–1853): Poet, contemporary of Pushkin.

Kaufman, Konstanin Petrovich (1818–82): Conqueror of Central Asia; planned the European part of the city of Tashkent.

Kerenski, Alexander Fedorovich (1881–1971): Head of the Provisional Government in 1917.

Khachaturian: Probably Professor *Astvadsatur Khachaturian* (1861–1937), historian and expert on cuneiform writing who returned to Soviet Armenia from Paris in 1921, was given a chair at Erivan University, but disappeared during the purges in 1937.

Khalatov, Victor Mikhailovich (1901–   ): Actor.

Khardzhiev, Nikolai Ivanovich (1902–   ): Literary scholar and editor.

Kharms, Daniil Ivanovich (1905–42?): Writer of 'absurd' stories, and of nursery rhymes, etc., for children. Together with Alexander Vvedenski, started a small modernist movement called OBERIU (standing for 'The Association for Real Art'; its members were known as *Oberiuty*) that issued a manifesto in 1928. Its members were soon forced to take refuge in writing for children, which they did under the patronage of *Marshak* (q.v.). (See George Gibian, *Russia's Lost Literature of the Absurd*, Cornell, 1971.) Both Kharms and Vvedenski were arrested shortly after the outbreak of the war, and apparently perished in 1942.

Khazin, A.: Author of a parody on Pushkin's *Eugene Onegin* in which the hero returns to Soviet Leningrad. Published in the journal *Leningrad*, it was angrily denounced by *Zhdanov* (q.v.) in his 'Report'.

Khlebnikov, Velimir (Victor Vladimirovich) (1885–1922): Futurist poet noted for his linguistic experimentation.

Khodasevich, Vladislav ('Vladek') Felitsianovich (1866–1939): Poet and critic. He emigrated in 1922 and died in Paris.

Khodasevich, Valentina Mikhailovna (1894–   ): Woman painter.

Khomiakov, Alexei Stepanovich (1804–60): Leading Slavophile writer.

Kibalchich, Nikolai Ivanovich (1854–81): Engineer and explosives expert for the People's Will terrorist organization. Executed for his part in the assassination of Alexander II. (While in prison he worked on a design for a flying machine.)

Kirsanov, Semion Isaakovich (1906–71): Poet, translator, and member of LEF, influenced in his early period by Mayakovski.

Kiukhelbeker, Wilhelm Karlovich (1797–1846): Poet, contemporary of Pushkin; subject of a study by *Tynianov* (q.v.). Took part in the Decembrist uprising of 1825 and died in exile.

Kliuchevski, Vasili Osipovich (1841–1911): Noted historian of Russia.

Kluyev, Nikolai Alexandrovich (1887–1937): Peasant poet. He was arrested in the 1930s and died in Siberia.

Klychkov (Leshenkov), Sergei Antonovich (1889–1937): Peasant poet and novelist, arrested in 1937.

Kniazev, Vsevolod (1883–1913): Poet and Guards officer whose suicide is a major theme in Akhmatova's *Poem Without a Hero*.

Kochetov, Vsevolod Anisimovich (1912–   ): Novelist who in recent years has become the spokesman of extreme anti-liberal forces in Soviet literature. Two of his novels, *The Brothers Yershov* (1957) and *What Do You Want?* (1969), are lampoons on the liberal intelligentsia. Kochetov is editor of the monthly *Oktiabr (October)*.

Kogan, Piotr Semionovich (1872–1932): Marxist critic and historian of literature.

Konevskoi, Ivan (I. I. Oreus) (1877–1901): Symbolist poet of Swedish origin.

Kotov, Anatoli Konstantinovich (1909–56): Literary scholar and editor. From 1948 to the end of his life he headed the State Publishing House for Literature.

Kozintsev, Grigori Mikhailovich (1905–73): Leading Soviet theatre and film director (he produced the Soviet screen version of *Hamlet*). Together with L. Trauberg, founded an avant-garde theatrical group in Leningrad in 1921 called FEKS ('Factory of the Eccentric Actor'). He began his career as a member of the 'herd' described in Chapter 2, and as such took part in the production of Lope de Vega's *Fuente Ovejuna* by *Mardzhanov* (q.v.).

Kozo-Polianski, B. M.: Botanist.

Krasnov, Piotr Nikolayevich (1869–1947): White General; author of memoirs, *From the Double Eagle to the Red Flag.*

Kruchenykh, Alexei Yeliseyevich (1886–1970): Futurist poet noted for extreme linguistic experimentation.

Krylov, Ivan Andreyevich (1768–1844): Famous writer of fables.

Ksheshinskaya, Adelaida Felixovna (1878–1971): Famous ballet dancer.

Kustodiev, Boris Mikhailovich (1878–1927): Well-known painter.

Kuzmin, Mikhail Alexeyevich (1875–1936): Poet whose work influenced the transition from Symbolism to Acmeism.

Kuzmin-Karavayev, Dmitri Vladimirovich: Acmeist poet.

Lapin, Boris Matveyevich (1905–41): Soviet writer and translator; son-in-law of Ilia Ehrenburg. He was killed at the front as a war correspondent.

Lavut, Pavel Ilyich (1893–   ): Painter and ex-actor. Arranged Mayakovski's poetry-reading tours, 1926–30, and is the author of a memoir on him (1963).

Lebedev, Vladimir Vasilievich (1891–   ?): Artist and illustrator. Husband of following.

Lebedeva (née Darmolatova), Sarra Dmitrievna (1892–1970): Famous sculptress; designed the bas-relief for Pasternak's grave.

Lebedev-Polianski, Pavel Ivanovich (1881–1948): Marxist critic and literary historian. Head of Soviet censorship (Glavlit) in the twenties.

Legran, Boris V. (1884–1936): A lawyer by training who was appointed People's Commissar for Military Affairs by Lenin in 1917. Following distinguished service in the Civil War, he played an active part in the Sovietization of the Caucasus – first Armenia and then Georgia. He was appointed Ambassador of the RSFSR to Tiflis in 1921. After further diplomatic service in Tashkent and Harbin (Soviet Consul-

General, 1926), he was made director of the Hermitage Museum in 1927 and later, in the thirties, of the Academy of Fine Arts.

Lelevich, Grigori (*Labori Gilelevich Kalmonson*) (1901–45): Soviet poet and critic. A member of RAPP until his expulsion in 1926 for opposing collaboration with the 'Fellow Travellers'. Arrested during the purges, he died in a camp.

Leontiev, Konstantin Nikolayevich (1831–91): Writer and publicist.

Lermontov, Mikhail Yurievich (1814–41): Great Russian poet and author of a famous novel, *A Hero of Our Times*. He was killed in a duel at the age of twenty-six.

Leskov, Nikolai Semionovich (1831–95): Writer of novels and tales full of colourful anecdote and notable for their intimate knowledge of popular life.

Levkovskaya, K. A.: Linguist, Moscow University.

Lezhnev (*Altshuler*), *Isai Grigorievich* (1891–1955): Editor and journalist.

Linde, Fedor F. (? –1917): Bolshevik philosopher, mathematician, and military commissar. He led the Finnish Guard Reserve regiment during the April crisis in 1917, and later that year was killed on the southwestern front by soldiers under his command. His death is described by Boris Pasternak in *Dr Zhivago*, where Linde appears as 'Gints'.

Lipskerov, Konstantin Abramovich (1889–1954): Poet and translator.

Liubarskaya, A. A.: Linguist and writer on fairy tales.

Liubishchev, Alexander Alexandrovich (1888–1972): Zoologist and entomologist who specialized in problems of evolution. Dismissed from his post and exiled to Ulianovsk in 1948 because of his stand against *Lysenko* (q.v.), on whom he has written an unpublished work.

Livshits, Benedikt Konstantinovich (1887–1939): Poet associated with the Futurists; translator of French prose and poetry. In his memoirs, *Polutoraglazy Strelets* (*The One-and-a-Half-Eyed Archer*, Moscow, 1933), he brilliantly describes the origins of the Futurist movement. He was arrested in the purges – apparently having been accused of complicity in the assassination of the head of the Cheka, Uritski, in 1919 – but has now been posthumously rehabilitated.

Lozinski, Mikhail Leonidovich (1886–1955): Poet and translator from Spanish, French, English, and Italian; one of the founders (with Nikolai Gumilev) of the Poets' Guild. He was awarded a Stalin Prize in 1946 for his translation of Dante's *Divine Comedy*.

Luknitski, Pavel Nikolayevich (1900–   ): Writer of novels and stories.

Lunacharski, Anatoli Vasilievich (1875–1933): Leading Bolshevik publicist and writer. As People's Commissar for Education, he was effectively in charge of Soviet cultural affairs during most of the twenties.

Lurye (also spelled *Lourié*), *Artur Sergeyevich* (1892–1966): Composer and musicologist. After the Revolution worked for a time under Lunacharski, but emigrated in 1922, and died in the United States. Author of articles on Mandelstam.

Lysenko, Trofim Denisovich (1898–   ): Biologist and member of the Soviet Academy of Sciences. With the support of Stalin, he tried to destroy all his opponents among the Soviet geneticists. He is now discredited.

Maikov, Apollon Nikolayevich (1821–97): Poet.

Makarenko, Anton Semionovich (1888–1939): Soviet educationalist who believed in educating children 'through the collective'.

Makogonenko, Georgi Panteleimonovich (1912–   ): Historian of Russian literature; professor at Leningrad University.

Makovski, Sergei Konstantinovich (1877–1962): Son of the painter Konstantin Makovski, he wrote poetry, organized exhibitions of avant-garde Russian art, founded the journal *Apollon* (in which Mandelstam published some of his early work) and edited it from 1909 to 1917. He emigrated to Prague and later to Paris.

Malenkov, Georgi Maximilianovich (1902–   ): Soviet leader. Disgraced and exiled by Khrushchev in 1957.

Malkin, Boris Fedorovich (1890–1942): Party official who headed the *Tsentropechat* (Central Press) agency.

Mandelstam, Alexander ('*Shura*') *Emilievich*: Mandelstam's younger brother.

Mandelstam, Emmanuil (1838– ?): Well-known ophthalmologist and lecturer at Kiev University.

Mandelstam, Yevgeni Emilievich (1898–   ): Mandelstam's brother; film editor and consultant who has written scripts for several successful popular scientific films.

Mandelstam, Isai Benediktovich: Well-known Leningrad translator (of Anatole France, among others); father-in-law of *Kanegiesser* (q.v.); perished during the purges of 1937–8.

Mandelstam, Lev Iosifovich (1811–89): Hebrew scholar and translator of the Old Testament into Russian; the first Russian Jew to graduate from a Russian university.

Mar (Chalkhushyan), Susanna Georgievna (1900–1965): Daughter of a prominent Armenian lawyer and public figure. In the twenties she belonged to the Nichevoki group (see note, page 168), but finding it increasingly difficult already in the twenties to publish her original verse, she became a translator (of A. E. Housman, Kipling, Yeats, among others, for an *Anthology of English Poetry*, 1937), and is particularly noted for her version of Mickiewicz's *Pan Tadeusz* (1956). In 1925 she married Ivan *Aksionov* (q.v.). Her four elder brothers disappeared during the purges of 1937–8. Her original verse still awaits publication. It includes a moving poem on the funeral of Pasternak.

Marchenko, Anatoli (1938–   ): Soviet worker who was sentenced to six years' hard labour in 1958 for wanting to leave the Soviet Union. His account of his experiences was smuggled out of the country and published in the West in 1969 under the title *My Testimony*.

Mardzhanov (Mardzhanishvili), Konstantin Alexandrovich (1872–1933): Director at the Moscow Art Theatre and many other theatres. Founder of the Georgian Theatre, now named after him. His production of Lope de Vega's *Fuente Ovejuna* in Kiev (described in Chapter 2) is still a famous event in the annals of Soviet theatrical history.

Marr, Nikolai Yakovlevich (1864–1934): Linguist of mixed Georgian and Scottish descent (his grandfather, Patrick Marr, went to the Caucasus to plant tobacco). His early work was in the field of Caucasian linguistics and archaeology, but he went on from this to a general theory of language based on the proposition that all languages are ultimately related, and will eventually merge again after millennia of differentiation due to social divisions. He claimed to be able to derive the vocabulary of the world's languages from four primordial roots. One of the few older scholars to accept the October Revolution, he claimed that his theories (which were scarcely taken seriously) were in accordance with Marxism. The militancy with which his disciples, such as *Meshchaninov* (q.v.), pressed this claim and the apparent willingness of the Party authorities to accept it led to a situation in linguistics rather like that created by *Lysenko* (q.v.) in biology. By the late forties, conventional linguistic theory and teaching were being persecuted in Soviet universities, and venerable scholars such as *Vinogradov* (q.v.), were forced to denounce their life's work and accept 'Marrism'. Soviet linguistics has only in recent years begun to recover from the enormous damage then inflicted on it. Ironically, and for reasons that are still obscure (he was no doubt repelled by the 'cosmopolitan' implications of Marr's theory when they were pointed out to him), the situation was saved by the intervention of Stalin, who denounced Marrism in his article *Marxism and Questions of Linguistics* (1950) and called for a return to more or less conventional ideas – thenceforth propagated with great fanfare as the 'ideas of genius of J. V. Stalin'. (There is a satirical account of Stalin writing his article in Solzhenitsyn's *First Circle*.)

Marshak, Samuil Yakovlevich (1887–1964): Translator (Shakespeare, Heine, Burns), poet, and children's writer. In 1924–5 he edited a magazine especially for children, *Novy Robinson* (*The New Robinson* [Crusoe]), in which some verse and translations by Mandelstam appeared. In 1925 and 1926, as head of the children's literature section of the State Publishing House, he published two books of verse for children by Mandelstam, *Balloons* and *Two Tramcars*. Though Marshak was noted for his political adaptability, he showed liberal tendencies after Stalin's death.

Mayakovski, Vladimir Vladimirovich (1893–1930): The leading figure in Russian Futurism. In addition to his vast output of poetry, he wrote two plays, *The Bedbug* and *The Bathhouse*, and edited the journal *LEF* (1923–5). Under attack by RAPP, involved in difficult love affairs and probably disillusioned by post-revolutionary reality (as one can judge from his two plays), he committed suicide in 1930. In 1935 Stalin said of him: 'Mayakovski was and remains the best and the most talented poet of our Soviet epoch.'

Meck, Galina von (1891–   ): The grandniece of Tchaikovsky; constantly in prison after the Revolution, she left the country after the German invasion and came to England in 1948. Her memoirs (*As I Remember Them*, London, 1973) mention Nadezhda Mandelstam's visit to her in Maly Yaroslavets in 1939.

Medtner, Nikolai Karlovich (1879–1951): Composer.

Medvedev, Zhores Alexandrovich (1924–   ): Eminent Soviet biologist. With his twin brother, Roy Medvedev, he has written an account of his incarceration in a psychiatric hospital and subsequent release thanks to protests from fellow intellectuals in the Soviet Union and abroad (*A Question of Madness*, London, 1971). He is also the author of a study of the Lysenko case, and of the position of scientists in the Soviet Union (*The Rise and Fall of T. D. Lysenko*, London, 1969, and *The Medvedev Papers*, 1971). Stripped of Soviet citizenship in 1973, while on a visit to London.

Mei, Lev Alexandrovich (1822–62): Poet.

Meletinski, Yeleazar Moiseyevich (1918–   ): Scholar specializing in the study of folklore.

Merezhkovski, Dmitri Sergeyevich (1866–1941): Influential writer and philosopher, husband of Zinaida *Gippius* (q.v.). Emigrated after the Revolution.

Meshchaninov, Ivan Ivanovich (1883– ?): Leading disciple of *Marr* (q.v.).

Meyerhold, Vsevolod Emilievich (1874–1940): Actor and producer. Prior to the Revolution he was associated with the Moscow Art Theatre and the Maryinski and Alexandrinski theatres in St Petersburg. Joined the Communist Party in 1918. He directed the Theatre of the Revolution until 1924, and then created his own theatre based on his 'bio-mechanical' system of acting. His theatre was closed in 1938. Arrested in 1939 (after a defiant public refusal to accept the doctrine of 'socialist realism' in art), he died in prison in 1940. Though he has now been rehabilitated as a person, there is still considerable opposition to his innovations in stagecraft.

Mikhoels (*Vovsi*), *Sólomon Mikhailovich* (1890–1948): Foremost Yiddish actor and director. Creator of the State Jewish Theatre in Moscow, which was closed down in 1949 during an officially inspired campaign of anti-Semitism. The previous year *Pravda* had published a fulsome obituary of Mikhoels after his 'sudden death'. At the time rumours were circulated that he had been run over by a drunken truck driver, but it is now known that he was killed by the secret police on Stalin's orders (see Svetlana Alliluyeva, *Only One Year*). Evidently Stalin needed to get him out of the way before proceeding to the destruction of all Yiddish cultural facilities. His brother, Vovsi, was one of the doctors accused in 1952 of trying to assassinate Soviet leaders by medical malpractice.

Miklashevski, Konstantin Mikhailovich: Artist.

Mindlin, Emili Lvovich (1900–   ): Writer, author of memoirs.

Miturich, Piotr Vasilievich (1887–1956): Artist, painted Mandelstam's portrait.

Morozov, Pavel (*'Pavlik'*) (1918–32): Village boy who during collectivization denounced his father as a person of 'kulak' sympathies. His father was shot and Pavel was then himself killed by a group of peasants led by his uncle. During the Stalin years Pavlik Morozov was held up to Soviet youth as a model who did not hesitate to denounce his father in the interests of the State. Books and poems were written about him, and there were many statues of him in public places.

Nabokov (*Sirin*), *Vladimir Vladimirovich* (1899–   ): Émigré novelist.

Naiman, Anatoli (1938–   ): Young Leningrad poet, protégé of Akhmatova.

Narbut, Vladimir Ivanovich (1888–1944): Minor Acmeist poet who joined the Bolsheviks but was expelled from the Party in 1928. He was editor-in-chief of the State publishing concern Land and Factory (ZIF). Arrested during the purges, he has now been posthumously rehabilitated.

Nedobrovo, Nikolai Vladimirovich (1882–1919): Critic. Author of important essay on Akhmatova (1915).

Nekrasov, Nikolai Alexeyevich (1821–78): Populist poet.

Neldikhen, Sergei Yevgenievich (1891–1942): Minor poet influenced by Acmeism.

Nemits, A. V., Admiral: Commander of the Black Sea Fleet under the Provisional Government.

Nikitina, Yevdokia Fedorovna (1895–   ): Soviet literary scholar, writer, and bibliographer. In 1914 she launched a literary association known as 'Nikitina's Saturdays' that also existed as a publishing house till 1931.

Nikulin, Lev Veniaminovich (1891–1967): Soviet novelist.

Odoyevtseva (Geineke), Irina Vladimirovna (1901–   ): Poetess associated with the Acmeists. Emigrated in 1922. In her memoirs, *On the Banks of the Neva* (1962), published in New York, she writes extensively of Gumilev and Mandelstam. She was at one time married to Georgi *Ivanov* (q.v.).

Oksman, Julian Grigorievich (1894–1970): Eminent literary scholar. In the last years of his life he fell foul of the Soviet authorities because of his uncompromising opposition to them.

Oleinikov, Nikolai Makarovich (1898–1942): Writer for children and parodist of considerable originality. Associated with the *Oberiuty* (see *Kharms*), he was arrested in 1937 and died in prison.

Olesha, Yuri Karlovich (1899–1960): Talented novelist and playwright, noted for his novel *Envy* (1927), one of the best 'Fellow Traveller' works of the period. Olesha's attitude to the Soviet regime was ambivalent and he was evidently much tormented by his eventual compromise with it. He portrayed his own indecisiveness, leading finally to acceptance of the status quo, in his play *The List of Blessings* (1929), in which the heroine, a Russian actress who goes to Paris on tours, draws up lists of points both in favour (the 'blessings') and against the Soviet regime. She eventually decides, not without an internal struggle, that the former outweigh the latter.

Olshevskaya, Nina: Wife of *Ardov* (q.v.).

Ostroukhov, Ilia Semionovich (1858–1929): Landscape painter and art collector, noted particularly for his collection of Russian icons.

Otsup, Nikolai Avdeyevich (1894–1958): Acmeist poet. In 1923 he emigrated to Paris.

Palei, Prince Vladimir Pavlovich (1895–1918): Son of Grand Duke Pavel Alexandrovich; wrote verse.

Papanin, Ivan Dmitrievich (1895–   ): Soviet explorer famous for his expeditions to the Arctic.

Parnok: A character in Mandelstam's *Egyptian Stamp* who personifies the *raznochinets* ('upstart intellectual') and is the author's 'double'. In real life the prototype of Parnok was a minor poet called Valentin Yakovlevich Parnakh who lived in Paris in the early1920's. From a portrait of him by Picasso it is clear that he bore a striking physical resemblance to Mandelstam. In 1926 Parnakh published an article in the American Jewish *Menorah Journal* in which he wrote about Mandelstam (as well as Pasternak and others).

Parnok, Sofia Yakovlevna (1885–1933): Poetess and translator. Belonged, with *Khodasevich*, *Lipskerov* (q.v.), and others to a 'neoclassical' group.

Pasternak, Boris Leonidovich (1890–1960): Poet and author of the novel *Dr Zhivago*. Though mainly a lyric poet, Pasternak attempted longer poems, in which he treated revolutionary themes in an epic manner: *The Year Nineteen Hundred and Five* (1925–6) about the first Russian revolution; and *Lieutenant Schmidt* (1926–7) – for the subject of this, see note on *Schmidt*. These were followed in 1931 by an ambitiously conceived 'novel in verse', *Spektorski*, about the whole era of war and revolution (thus, in conception at least, anticipating *Dr Zhivago*). Despite a certain ambivalence in his attitude to the Revolution, these works made it clear that Pasternak could never accept revolutionary violence, and that he believed in the absolute autonomy of art. Other prose works of Pasternak are *The Childhood of Luvers* (1922), the autobiographical *Safe Conduct* (1931), and the unfinished play, *The Blind Beauty*, which was intended as a nineteenth-century prologue to *Dr Zhivago*. *Dr Zhivago* was originally announced for publication in the Soviet Union in the monthly literary journal *Znamia* (where some of the verse from the novel was published) in April 1954. Pasternak finished work on it at the end of 1955 and submitted it to several Moscow publishing houses and journals that rejected it. At the same time – an unheard of thing for a Soviet writer – he gave a copy to an Italian Communist in Moscow for transmission to the Italian Communist publisher Feltrinelli. The 'fuss over *Dr Zhivago*' referred to on p. 662 began in the late summer of 1956, when this step of Pasternak and Feltrinelli's intention to publish the novel in Italian began to alarm the Soviet authorities. As mentioned by Mrs Mandelstam, Pasternak was asked to send a telegram to Feltrinelli demanding the manuscript back, pressure was put on Feltrinelli through Party channels, and later Surkov even flew to Milan to plead with him. There were probably two reasons for Pasternak's cheerfulness, noted by Mrs Mandelstam, when he left

Surkov's office after promising to cable Feltrinelli forbidding him to publish: (a) he had already sent a verbal message to Feltrinelli asking him to interpret any such cable as an instruction to proceed with publication, and (b) he had by now managed to send a second copy of the novel abroad with firm instructions to publish, should Feltrinelli fail him or yield to Party pressure. (For an account of the whole affair, see Robert Conquest, *The Courage of Genius*, London, 1961.)

Pavlenko, Piotr Andreyevich (1899–1951): Highly orthodox Soviet novelist who was awarded a Stalin Prize for his violently anti-Western *Happiness* (1947). He wrote the scenario for the film *Alexander Nevski*.

Pavlovich, Nadezhda Alexandrovna (1895–   ): Poetess much influenced by Blok, on whom she has published a memoir (1964). Another volume of her recollections of pre-revolutionary days came out in 1962 under the title *Thoughts and Memories*.

Petrov (Katayev), Yevgeni Petrovich (1903–42): Brother of Valentin Katayev; co-author with Ilf (Ilia Fainzilberg) of *The Twelve Chairs* and *The Golden Calf*, comic novels which still enjoy immsense popularity in the Soviety Union. The two novels are about a confidence trickster from Odessa, Ostap Bender, and contain many daring satirical sketches of life in the Soviet Union during NEP.

Petrovykh, Maria Sergeyevna (1908–   ): Poetess and translator.

Pilniak (Vogau), Boris Andreyevich (1894–1937): Prominent Soviet novelist. In his *Tale of the Extinguished Moon* (1927) he hinted that Stalin had killed the Red Army Commander Frunze by making him have an unnecessary operation. In 1929 he was chairman of the board of the Union of Writers, but was removed from this position after a violent campaign in the press because of the publication of his short novel *Mahogany* in Berlin. This attack on Pilniak signalled the beginning of Stalin's total subjugation of Soviet literature to his own political purposes. Pilniak was arrested in 1937, accused of spying for the Japanese, and either was shot immediately or died in a camp.

Pisarev, Dmitri Ivanovich (1840–68): Radical publicist noted for his extreme utilitarian approach to culture.

Platonov, Andrei Platonovich (1891–1951): Son of a railway worker, one of the most original prose writers of the Soviet period. In the later Stalin years he was virtually banned, but has now been partially republished and enjoys considerable posthumous renown. The story referred to on p. 287 is entitled *Dzhan*.

Polonski, Yakov Petrovich (1819–98): Poet.

Pronin, Boris Konstantinovich: Actor and stage director. He is best known as the owner of the famous literary 'cabaret', The Stray Dog

(Brodiachaya Sobaka), which before the Revolution was the favourite meeting place of the literary intelligentsia of St Petersburg. All the leading poets went there to recite their verse.

Punin, Nikolai Nikolayevich (1888–1953): Art historian and critic associated with Makovski's *Apollon*. After the Revolution he worked under Lunacharski in the Fine Arts section of the People's Commissariat of Education. He was the third husband of Anna Akhmatova. During the purges he was arrested and sent to a forced-labour camp.

Rabinovich, Isaac Moiseyevich (1894–1961): Leading Soviet set designer, graduate of the Kiev School of Fine Arts. After his design for the 'revolutionary' production of *Fuente Ovejuna* in Kiev in 1919, he went on to work for the leading Moscow theatres (Art Theatre, Kamerny, etc.).

Radek, Karl (1885–1939): Bolshevik leader who disappeared in the purges.

Radlov, Sergei Ernestovich (1892–1958): Leading Soviet producer who in the early twenties organized 'mass revolutionary spectacles' in Petrograd. After an association with Meyerhold, he became well known in the thirties for his original productions of Shakespeare.

Radlova (*née Darmolatova*), *Anna Dmitrievna* (1891–1949): Wife of above; poetess and translator, particularly noted for her versions of Shakespeare.

Raikin, Arkadi Isaakovich (1911–   ): Variety artist famous for his brilliant one-man sketches.

Rakovskaya: Sister of *Rakovski, Christian Georgievich* (1873–1941): An Old Bolshevik of Rumanian origin, sentenced to twenty years' imprisonment at the show trial of Bukharin in 1938.

Ranevskaya, Faina Grigorievna (1896–   ): Leading actress associated with several Moscow theatres.

Reisner, Larisa Mikhailovna (1897–1928): Bolshevik heroine of the Revolution.

Roginski, Y. Y.: Anthropologist. Co-author of a book on the origins of man (1951).

Rozanov, Vasili Vasilievich (1856–1919): Thinker and publicist of considerable originality.

Rozhdestvenski, Vsevolod Alexandrovich (1895–   ): Poet influenced by Acmeism.

Rublev, Andrei (1360–1430): The greatest of the Russian icon painters.

Ruderman, M.: Author of articles on Mandelstam in 1928 and 1932.

Sabashnikov, Mikhail Vasilievich (1871–1943), and his brother *Sergei* (1873–1909): Publishers famous for elegant and high-quality editions of Russian and foreign authors. Their publishing house was closed down in 1930.

Sannikov, Grigori Alexandrovich (1899–1969): Poet.

Schmidt, Piotr Petrovich (1867–1906): Lieutenant of the Black Sea Fleet, much revered in revolutionary legend, who helped lead the mutiny of soldiers and sailors in Sebastopol in 1905. Executed in 1906.

Scriabin, Alexander Nikolayevich (1871–1915): Composer.

Selivanovski, Alexei Pavlovich (1900–1938): Critic. Leading figure in RAPP. Arrested and evidently executed in the purges.

Selvinski, Ilia Lvovich (1899–1968): Poet.

Semenko, Irina Mikhailovna: Literary scholar and friend of Mrs Mandelstam.

Senkovski, Osip Ivanovich (1800–1858): Orientalist and critic whose stories, written under the psuedonym 'Baron Brambeus', were very popular but lacking in real literary worth.

Serafimovich (Popov), Alexander Serafimovich (1863–1949): Veteran Soviet writer, one-time associate of Gorki and regarded as a 'classic' in the Soviet Union.

Serov, Valentin Alexandrovich (1865–1911): Painter; some of his works (e.g. *Europa*) are on classical themes.

Severianin (Lotarev), Igor Vasilievich (1887–1941): Poet noted for his flamboyance and verbal extravagance; leader of the 'Ego-Futurists'. He emigrated to Estonia in 1919. After the Soviet occupation of Estonia in 1940, he managed to publish in some Soviet magazines. He died under German occupation.

Shaginian, Marietta Sergeyevna (1888–   ): Veteran Soviet novelist and (before the Revolution) a minor poet on the fringes of the Symbolist movement. During the 1920s she was known mainly for her attempt to write thrillers and detective fiction in Western style, decried at the time as 'Red Pinkertonism'.

Shalamov, Varlam Tikhonovich (1907–   ): Poet and prose writer who spent seventeen years in a forced-labour camp in Kolyma. His *Tales of Kolyma* have been published in the West in Russian and French.

Shcherbakov, Alexander Sergeyevich (1901–45): Veteran Communist official and associate of Zhdanov. He was appointed secretary of the Union of Soviet Writers in 1934, despite the fact that he had no connection with literature. Later he was in charge of purging provincial Party organizations, and during the war he was a secretary of the Central Committee (and candidate member of the Politburo) with special responsibility for political control of the army. His death in 1945 was later attributed to the Jewish doctors arrested on Stalin's orders in 1952.

Shengeli, Georgi Arkadievich (1894–1956): Poet, translator, and critic.

Shileiko, Vladimir Kazimirovich (1891–1930): Assyriologist. Akhmatova's second husband, from 1918 to 1924. Pupil of *Turayev* (q.v.).

Shishmarev, Vladimir Fedorovich (1872–1957): Eminent philologist, specialist in Romance languages. Member of Academy of Sciences.

Shklovski, Victor Borisovich (1893–   ): Eminent literary scholar and Formalist critic, a member of LEF. Shklovski's influence in the 1920s was immense, and he continued to write articles, books, and scenarios throughout the Stalinist era to the present day.

Sholokhov, Mikhail Alexandrovich (1895–   ): 'Classic' of socialist realism. Author of *Quiet Flows the Don*.

Shostakovich, Dmitri Dmitrievich (1906–75): Famous Soviet composer. In 1934 Stalin walked out of the premiere of his opera *A Lady Macbeth of the Mtsensk District*, which was then attacked in a *Pravda* article entitled 'Nonsense Instead of Music'. He and other leading composers were again condemned in a Party decree in 1948 for 'formalism'. *Zhdanov* (q.v.) is said to have picked out tunes on the piano for them to illustrate the kind of music the Party required them to compose.

Shtempel, N. E. (*Natasha*): Daughter of a schoolmistress in Voronezh who was friendly with Mandelstam during his exile there (see *Hope Against Hope*, pages 71 and 214). In 1966 Natasha Shtempel published some of Mandelstam's poems for the first time in a local Voronezh journal.

Simonov, Konstantin Mikhailovich (1915–   ): Popular Soviet author, best known for his wartime lyrics and novels on the war (such as *Days and Nights*, on the battle of Stalingrad, 1944). Since Stalin's death he has played a cautiously 'liberal' role in Soviet literary affairs. The writer Galakhov in Solzhenitsyn's *First Circle* appears to be at least partially based on him.

Sinani, Boris Naumovich: St. Petersburg doctor of Karaite extraction, a confidant of the leading Social Revolutionaries. He is described in Mandelstam's *Noise of Time*.

Siniavski, Andrei Donatovich (1925–   ): Russian scholar, critic, and novelist. Arrested in September 1965 for publishing stories abroad under the pseudonym Abram Tertz. In 1966 he was tried in Moscow together with *Daniel* (q.v.) and sentenced to seven years' hard labour. He was released in 1972 and emigrated to France in 1973.

Sluchevski, Konstantin Konstantinovich (1837–1904): Poet.

Sologub, Fedor (*Fedor Kuzmich Teternikov*) (1863–1927): Symbolist poet and novelist, famous for his novel *The Petty Demon* (1907).

Soloviev, Sergei Mikhailovich (1885–1942): Nephew of following. Poet and – after the Revolution – translator.

Soloviev, Vladimir Sergeyevich (1853–1900): Mystic, philosopher, and poet who greatly influenced the Symbolists. He saw visions of Holy Sophia (once in the reading room of the British Museum, at a time when Marx could well have been sitting at an adjacent table!) and his cult of her and of the 'Eternal Feminine' underlies, to some extent, Alexander Blok's early verse on 'The Beautiful Lady'.

Solzhenitsyn, Alexander Isayevich (1918–   ): Russian novelist who was in a forced-labour camp from 1945 to 1953. His *One Day in the Life of Ivan Denisovich* (1962) was the first account of the camps to appear in print in the Soviet Union. A larger novel on the same subject, *The First Circle*, has been published only in the West.

Spasski, Sergei Dmitrievich (1898–1956): Poet. Arrested in 1936 or 1937; despite the politically orthodox quality of his work, he was rehabilitated only after many years in prisons and camps.

Sreznevskaya (*née Tulpanova*), *Valeria*: Died in 1964. Lifelong friend of Akhmatova, and author of an unpublished memoir on her.

Stavski (*Kirpichnikov*), *Vladimir Petrovich* (1900–1943): Prose writer. Appointed secretary of the Board of the Union of Soviet Writers in 1936, he was active in the denunciation of writers for Trotskiism and other 'crimes'.

Steblin-Kamenski, Mikhail Ivanovich (1903–   ): Eminent literary scholar and linguist. Authority on Icelandic sagas.

Stenich (*Smetanich*), *Valentin* ('*Valia*') *Osipovich* (1898–1939): Poet and gifted translator (of James Joyce, John Dos Passos, Bertolt Brecht, William Faulkner, Joseph Conrad, among others). A friend of Mandelstam; arrested in 1938 and evidently died in prison the following year.

Stravinski, Igor Fedorovich (1882–1971): Composer.

Struve, Gleb Petrovich (1898–   ): Eminent émigré scholar, author of the standard *History of Soviet Russian Literature*. With Boris Filippov he has edited and published in the West the works of Pasternak, Akhmatova, Gumilev, and others. His three-volume edition of the poetry and prose of Mandelstam is the one frequently referred to in the text.

Struve, Nikita Alexeyevich (1931–   ): Nephew of above. Literary scholar and editor, resident in Paris. The article by him referred to on p. 151 is in Volume 3 of the edition of Mandelstam's work edited by his uncle.

Sudeikina: See *Glebova-Sudeikina*.

Sukhovo-Kobylin, Alexander Vasilievich (1817–1903): Playwright whose two plays *The Case* and *The Death of Tarelkin* (both 1869) present a macabre, almost surrealist picture of the world of officialdom. Meyerhold revived *The Death of Tarelkin* in a famous production in 1922.

Surkov, Alexei Alexandrovich (1899–   ): Poet; editor of *Literaturnaya Gazeta* (*Literary Gazette*), 1944–6; secretary of the Union of Soviet Writers, 1954–9.

Svetlov, Mikhail Arkadievich (1903–64): Poet, best known for his romantic ballads (such as *Grenada*, 1926). In the middle thirties he wrote several plays with a lyrical, romantic flavour.

Svirski, Alexei Ivanovich (1865–1942): Writer of stories about his early wanderings as a waif, rather in the style of Maxim Gorki. Also wrote stories on Jewish themes. His *History of My Life* appeared in 1947.

Tabidze, Titsian Yustinovich (1895–1937): Georgian poet. Friend of Boris Pasternak. Executed in 1937.

Tairov, Alexander Yakovlevich (1885–1950): Actor and, later, director of the Kamerny Theatre in Moscow. He was dismissed from this post in 1939.

Tarasenkov, Anatoli Kuzmich (1909–56): Literary scholar and critic; author of the article on Mandelstam in the Soviet Literary Encyclopedia (1932).

Terapiano, Yuri Konstantinovich (1892–   ): Émigré poet and critic. Author of memoirs, *Meetings* (*Vstrechi*, New York, 1953), in which he discusses the genesis of a poem by Mandelstam (referred to on pp. 133–4), and of articles on Mandelstam's work.

Tikhon, Patriarch (of the Russian Orthodox Church) (1865–1925): Courageously opposed the Bolshevik attack on the church, including the measures to confiscate its property (by decree of January 1918) mentioned on pp. 156–7. He was put under house arrest in 1922.

Tikhonov (*Serebrov*), *Alexander Nikolayevich* (1880–1956): Writer and editor. Headed Academia publishing house, 1930–36.

Tikhonov, Nikolai Semionovich (1896–   ): Soviet poet, influenced by Gumilev and Khlebnikov, who later adapted to the demands of 'socialist realism'. He was secretary of the Union of Soviet Writers, 1944–6, and from 1950 chairman of the Soviet Peace Committee.

Tiutchev, Fedor Ivanovich (1803–73): Major lyric poet.

Tolstoi, Count Alexei Nikolayevich (1882–1945): Poet, playwright, and journalist, famous for two historical novels: *The Road to Calvary* and *Peter I*. He was a prolific writer of novels and short stories and enjoyed a great vogue in the Soviet Union. In 1919 he emigrated, but soon returned to the Soviet Union. Known as the 'Red Count', he proceeded to adapt himself with unrivalled skill to the twists and turns of Party policy.

Tomashevski, Boris Victorovich (1890–1957): Leningrad literary scholar and editor.

Trenev, Konstantin Andreyevich (1876–1945): Story writer and dramatist, best known for his play about the Civil War *Liubov Yarovaya* (1926).

Trenin, Vladimir Vladimirovich (1904–41): Critic and literary scholar. Collaborated on studies of Mayakovski with *Khardzhiev* (q.v.).

Trubetskoi, Sergei Nikolayevich (1862–1905): Philosopher; disciple of Vladimir *Soloviev* (q.v.).

Tsvetayeva, Anastasia ('*Asia*') *Ivanovna* (1894–   ): Sister of Marina. Her memoirs about her sister were published in Moscow in 1971.

Tsvetayeva, Marina Ivanovna (1892–1941): Gifted Russian poet who was a friend of Pasternak, Mandelstam, and Akhmatova. All four dedicated verse to one another, and are regarded as having no equals in their generation. Tsvetayeva's fate was the most tragic of all. Her husband, Sergei Efron, whom she married in 1912, served during the Civil War as an officer in the White Army, but she was stranded in Moscow till 1922. From 1922 till 1925 she lived in Prague, and then in Paris till 1939. As a suspected GPU agent, Efron was forced to flee France and went back to Moscow. Tsvetayeva followed him there in 1939, only to find that he had been executed on his return, and that their daughter had been sent to a camp. When war broke out, she was evacuated to the town of Yelabuga on the river Kama, where in August 1941 she hanged herself. Volumes of her selected verse were finally published in the Soviet Union in 1961 and 1965. In addition to her poetry, she wrote plays and valuable critical essays. A memoir by her on her relations with Mandelstam was published in 1964 in the *Oxford Slavonic Papers*.

Turayev, Boris Alexandrovich (1868–1920): Eminent historian and Orientalist; specialist on Ancient Egypt and Ethiopia. Gave a course on the Ancient East at St Petersburg University from 1896, and was presumably teaching there during Mandelstam's days as a student (1911).

Tynianov, Yuri Nikolayevich (1895–1943): Eminent Formalist critic, noted also for his biographical novels (on Pushkin, Griboyedov, etc.).

Ulianova, Maria Ilyinichna (1878–1937): Lenin's sister. At one time in charge of the 'Complaints Bureau of the Commission of Soviet Control'.

Uritski, Mikhail Solomonovich (1873–1918): Menshevik who joined the Bolsheviks in 1917 and became head of the Petrograd Cheka. His assassination on August 30, 1919 (by the young poet Kanegiesser), and the wounding of Lenin the same day unleashed the first massive Red Terror: the Petrograd Cheka immediately shot 512 hostages.

Ushinski, Konstantin Dmitrievich (1824–70): Russian educationalist who laid much emphasis on education of children in love of the Motherland. His doctrines were given great prominence in the training of Soviet teachers in the later Stalin years.

Vaginov, Konstantin Konstantinovich (1900–1934): A little-known poet of considerable distinction.

Vasiliev, Arkadi Nikolayevich (1907–   ): Novelist. Achieved considerable notoriety in 1966 when he appeared as the so-called 'public accuser' at the trial of *Siniavski* (q.v.) and *Daniel* (q.v.). (In Soviet legal practice, the prosecutor may be assisted in presenting his case by a representative of the public organization to which the accused belonged – in this case the Union of Soviet Writers.)

Vazha-Pshavela (*Razikashvili, Luka Pavlovich*) (1861–1915): Leading Georgian writer and poet.

Vengerov, Semion Afanasievich (1855–1920) and *Zinaida Afanasievna* (1867–1941): Brother and sister; both literary scholars and critics, very influential in the years before the Revolution.

Vigdorova, Frida Abramovna (1915–70?): Prose writer concerned particularly with youth problems. Deputy of a Moscow district Soviet – it was probably in this capacity that she was able to obtain a permit for Mrs Mandelstam to reside in Moscow in 1964. Using her journalist's privilege, she made a record of the proceedings in the trial of Joseph *Brodski* (q.v.), the publication of which abroad led eventually to Brodski's release. In 1961 she contributed to a literary miscellany *Pages from Tarusa*, edited by Konstantin Paustovski. This created something of a furore because the editors managed to have it printed in the provincial town of Kaluga (Tarusa is nearby) without censorship. It is noteworthy that the contributor listed immediately under Vigdorova is 'N. Yakovleva', a pseudonym formed from Mrs Mandelstam's name and patronymic (Nadezhda Yakovlevna). This and another short prose piece by her in the same volume appears to be her only excursion into print in the Soviet Union.

Vilenkin, Vitali Yakovlevich (1911–   ): Art historian and writer on the theatre; author of books on Nemirovich-Danchenko and Amadeo Modigliani.

Vinogradov, Victor Vladimirovich (1895–1969): Eminent linguist, professor at Moscow University, and member of the Academy of Sciences. It appears that he was asked to give 'expert testimony' at the trial of *Siniavski* (q.v.) and *Daniel* (q.v.), but according to the indictment he did not actually appear at the trial.

Vishnevetskaya, Sofia Kasianovna (1899–   ): Theatre set designer who made her debut in Kiev in 1919, evidently as a member of the 'herd' described by Mrs Mandelstam in Chapter 2. Later associated with the Kamerny Theatre. Wife of the playwright Vsevolod Vishnevski.

Voloshin, Maximilian Alexandrovich (1878–1932): Poet associated with the Symbolists and artist (known for his watercolours of the Crimea, where he lived from 1917 until his death).

Volpe, Caesar, Samoilovich (1904–41): Critic and editor; was dismissed as editor of the literary journal *Zvezda* for publishing Mandelstam's *Journey to Armenia* in 1932.

Voronski, Alexander Konstantinovich (1884–1943): Old Bolshevik who edited the major Soviet literary journal *Krasnaya Nov* (*Red Virgin Soil*), which in the 1920s was the main outlet for the 'Fellow Travellers'. As an advocate of rapprochement between 'Fellow Travellers' and 'Proletarians', Voronski came under heavy fire from Averbakh's R A P P, and in 1927 he was expelled from the Party. Voronski finally disappeared during the purges in 1937 and probably died in a labour camp in 1943.

Vvedenski, Alexander: Priest; one of the leaders of the so-called 'Living Church', set up in 1922 after the arrest of the Patriarch and with the tacit approval of the Bolsheviks in the hope of provoking a schism. Vvedenski professed to believe in a form of Christian communism.

Vyshinski, Andrei Yanuarievich (1883–1954): a Menshevik until 1920, he was professor of law during the 1920s and later became Rector of Moscow University. From 1928 to 1931 he was head of the higher education department (Glavnauka) of the People's Commissariat of Education. He was appointed Procurator General in 1935, and as such was the chief accuser of all the Old Bolsheviks (whom he denounced as 'mad dogs') during the Moscow show trials. He replaced Molotov as Minister of Foreign Affairs in 1949 and died in New York while representing the Soviet Union at the United Nations. (On p. 221 there appears to be some confusion about Vyshinski's career. There is no record of his having publicly appeared as prosecutor at a trial until the so-called Shakhty trial of 1928. He interrogated two former Socialist Revolutionaries at the trial of Bukharin in 1938, but the record shows no exchange with them resembling the one mentioned by Mrs. Mandelstam. The trial of the Socialist Revolutionaries took place in November 1918 and two of the defendants, Kamkov and Karelin, were those interrogated by Vyshinski at the

Bukharin trial in 1938. The Yaroslavl rising of July 1918 was organized by the Socialist Revolutionaries, but a few Mensheviks took part as well. This means that Vyshinski could have been involved, perhaps as an *agent provocateur* – this would account for the extraordinary favour he enjoyed under Stalin, despite his Menshevik past. But there does not seem to be any published evidence regarding his role at that time.)

Wrangel, Baron Piotr Nikolayevich (1878–1928): Russian general who succeeded Denikin as commander-in-chief of the White Army in the south of Russia.

Yakhontov, Vladimir Nikolayevich (1899–1945): Prominent Soviet actor. Associated with the Moscow Art Theatre, he was also known for his readings of literary works, and his one-man sketches. He committed suicide in 1945.

Yakulov, Georgi Bogdanovich (1884–1928): Painter and set designer.

Yeliseyev (Grigori Grigorievich): Head of a Russian merchant dynasty famous for its wine and food shops in St Petersburg and Moscow before the Revolution. After the Revolution the main Yeliseyev building, a palace built by Rastrelli in St Petersburg, was converted into the celebrated House of Arts, a club and hostel for writers.

Yesenin, Sergei Alexandrovich (1895–1925): Popular lyric poet of peasant origin. He married Isadora Duncan in 1922 and travelled to Western Europe and America with her. After his initial acceptance of the October Revolution, he became disillusioned and came under increasing attack for his riotous behaviour. In 1925 he hanged himself in a Leningrad hotel.

Yezhov, Nikolai Ivanovich (1894–1939?): Member of the Central Committee from 1934 and chief of the NKVD, 1936–8. Stalin's Great Purge reached its height under his direction of the NKVD, and he was then made the scapegoat for its 'excesses'. He was succeeded by Beria in 1938, and was probably executed in 1939, although there has never been any official information about his fate.

Yurkun, Yuri Ivanovich (1895–1938): minor prose writer; a protégé and companion of *Kuzmin* (q.v.) from 1913 until the latter's death in 1936. He was shot in the purges.

Zabolotski, Nikolai Alexeyevich (1903–1958): One of the few outstanding poets who belongs wholly to the Soviet era. He was arrested and sent to a camp in 1938, but was allowed to return to Moscow after the war. The poetry he published in the late Stalin years shows the price he had to pay for this 'pardon'.

Zaslavski, David Iosifovich (1880–1965): Journalist. A notorious apologist for Stalinism, he made a vicious attack on Pasternak after he was awarded (and forced to renounce) the Nobel Prize in 1958. In 1928 Mandelstam was accused of plagiarism by a translator, A. G. Gornfield, because his name had been omitted from his translation of Charles de Coster's *La Légende d'Uhlenspiegel* after it had been revised by Mandelstam. The fault for this omission lay with the State Publishing House, which had commissioned Mandelstam to revise Gornfeld's translation. The whole affair was blown up into a scandal by the press, but a savage attack on Mandelstam by David Zaslavski provoked a strong defence of him by a group of leading Soviet writers, including Pasternak, Zoshchenko, Fadeyev, Katayev, Averbakh, and others, published as a collective letter to *Literary Gazette* in May 1929.

Zelinski, Korneli Lucianovich (1896–1970): Critic and historian of literature.

Zelmanova, Anna Mikhailovna: Painter. Famous St Petersburg beauty and wife of *Chudovski* (q.v.).

Zenkevich, Mikhail ('*Misha*') *Alexandrovich* (1891–1969): Acmeist poet.

Zharov, Alexander Alexeyevich (1904–   ): Popular Komsomol poet of the twenties.

Zhdanov, Andrei Alexandrovich (1896–1948): Close associate of Stalin who acted as his lieutenant in cultural matters. At the First Congress of Soviet Writers in 1934, he made a speech in which the doctrine of 'socialist realism' was first promulgated as the official Party line in literature. In 1946 he denounced Akhmatova, Zoshchenko, Pasternak, and others for attempting to 'poison the minds' of Soviet youth by their decadent, apolitical and 'vulgar' writings which had been published in the literary magazines *Zvezda* (*Star*) and *Leningrad*. By a special Party decree of August 14, 1946, *Leningrad* was closed and *Zvezda* was ordered to 'correct' its editorial policy and not open its pages again to Akhmatova, Zoshchenko, 'and their like'. The 'Zhdanov Decree' on literature was followed by similar ones on music and the cinema.

Zhirmunski, Victor Maximovich (1889–1970): Eminent literary scholar. Corresponding member of the Academy of Sciences.

Zhukovski, Vasili Andreyevich (1783–1852): Lyric poet, noted particularly for his translations of German Romantic poetry, and of Gray's 'Elegy'. One of his ballads is about Kashchei the Deathless, a wizard in Russian folklore.

Zinoviev. Grigori Yevseyevich (1883–1936): Bolshevik leader liquidated in the purges; at one time head of the Leningrad Party organization.

Zoshchenko, Mikhail Mikhailovich (1895–1958): Popular satirist He was attacked in 1946 by Zhdanov for his 'vulgar parody' of Soviet life and, together with Akhmatova, expelled from the Union of Soviet Writers.

Zvenigorodski, Andrei Vladimirovich: Poet.

B. *Note on Literary Movements and Organizations*

In the twenty years or so before the October Revolution, Russian literature, reacting against the nineteenth-century realist tradition, went through a period of ferment which is sometimes spoken of as the 'Silver Age'. Its main feature was a revival of poetry, which in the latter half of the nineteenth century had been almost completely overshadowed by prose.

The first and most influential of the new movements was that of the SYMBOLISTS (roughly 1894 to 1910), who transformed the aesthetic standards of the Russian public. Their precursor was the religious philosopher and poet Vladimir Soloviev, and among the leading figures were: Valeri Briusov, Viacheslav Ivanov, Alexander Blok, and Andrei Bely. There were different trends within Symbolism, but its hallmark was a certain otherworldliness: poetry was often a vehicle for mystical insights which could only be hinted at in 'symbolic' language.

The ACMEISTS were members of the so-called POETS' GUILD, which was founded in 1912 by Nikolai Gumilev and Sergei Gorodetski in opposition to the Symbolists. Their aim was to restore the autonomy of poetic language; they rejected 'mysticism' and strove for precision and clarity in the use of words. Akhmatova and Mandelstam were the most outstanding of the Acmeists, who existed as an organized group only until 1914.

Another important movement launched in 1912 was FUTURISM, which was also a reaction to the Symbolists. The Futurists (the most prominent of whom were Vladimir Mayakovski and Velemir Khlebnikov) espoused modern technology and urbanism, and in their poetry they were distinguished by their penchant for neologisms, slang, and words of their own invention. Temperamentally attracted to revolution, most of them were avant-garde in politics as well as in art. Largely for this reason, Futurism was the only literary movement to survive the October Revolution, constituting itself in 1923 as the so-called LEFT FRONT (LEF) and stridently claiming to be the only true voice of the new order.

This claim was successfully contested by the RUSSIAN ASSOCIA-

TION OF PROLETARIAN WRITERS (RAPP), founded in 1925. Though few were true proletarians by origin, the members of RAPP, such as Leopold Averbakh and Alexander Fadeyev, asserted that the chief role of literature must be to serve the interests of the proletariat, as the new ruling class, and to reflect its 'ideology'. From 1929 to 1932, RAPP was given its head by the Party and exercised dictatorial powers over literature. RAPP's leaders were convinced zealots who welcomed the rigours of the First Five Year Plan and collectivization – the relative 'liberalism' of NEP (New Economic Policy) had seemed to them a betrayal of the Revolution's promise.

In line with this 'liberalism', the Central Committee of the Party had in 1925 issued a famous resolution (supposedly drafted by Bukharin) proclaiming its neutrality, for the time being, as between the competing literary groups. In this atmosphere of relative tolerance, it was possible during the middle 1920s for most writers, whatever their 'class' background, to carry on as ' FELLOW TRAVELLERS ' (the name given them by Trotski). The Fellow Travellers, who formed the largest group of Soviet writers in the first post-revolutionary decade, were expected to give overall assent to the new regime, but were not yet forced to express positive commitment to it in their work.

Some of them, joining together in 1921 in a group known as the SERAPION BROTHERS (Mikhail Zoshchenko, Konstantin Fedin, Nikolai Tikhonov, and others), tried to establish the independence of literature from all political and social commitment, but this position became progressively more untenable in the latter half of the 1920s. The Serapion Brothers were allied with the FORMALISTS (Victor Shklovski, Victor Zhirmunski, and others), a new school of literary criticism (founded in 1916) which concentrated on problems of form in the artistic process. Towards the end of the 1920s the Formalists came under heavy attack, and 'formalism' became a standard term of abuse for any attempt to divorce literature from the political and 'educational' functions imposed on it by the Party.

In 1932 Stalin made such functions paramount by abruptly decreeing the disbandment of all separate literary groups, including RAPP, which had appeared to triumph over its rivals during its three-year 'dictatorship'. Stalin had no use for zealots of any kind, and wanted writers to be obedient instruments of his will, without convictions of their own. They were now all forced to join the UNION OF SOVIET WRITERS, a bureaucratic machine for the imposition of strict control over literature. The doctrine of socialist realism, promulgated at the same time, became binding on all writers who wanted to continue being published. In effect, it meant conveying the Party's 'message' in a humdrum realist style derived from the nineteenth-century Russian classics.

In the years since Stalin's death there has been some loosening of the controls imposed in 1932 (and reinforced after World War II in a series of Party decrees associated with the name of Zhdanov), but Soviet writers can still function legally only within the general administrative and ideological framework established under Stalin.

Index